Sociology in Our Times
The Essentials

Fifth Canadian Edition

Jane Lothian Murray
University of Winnipeg

Rick Linden
University of Manitoba

Diana Kendall
Baylor University

NELSON / EDUCATION

NELSON / EDUCATION

Sociology in Our Times: The Essentials, Fifth Canadian Edition

by Jane Lothian Murray, Rick Linden, and Diana Kendall

Associate Vice President, Editorial Director:
Evelyn Veitch

Editor-in-Chief, Higher Education:
Anne Williams

Acquisitions Editor:
Maya Castle

Senior Marketing Manager:
Amanda Henry

Developmental Editor:
Liisa Kelly

Permissions Coordinator:
Debbie Yea

Photo Researcher:
Kristiina Paul

Content Production Manager:
Jennifer Hare

Production Service:
KnowledgeWorks Global Limited

Copy Editor:
Karen Rolfe

Proofreader:
Jayaprakash

Indexer:
Kevin Broccoli

Manufacturing Coordinator:
Ferial Suleman

Design Director:
Ken Phipps

Managing Designer:
Franca Amore

Interior Design:
Dianna Little and Katherine Strain

Interior Design Modifications:
Peter Papayanakis

Cover Design:
Johanna Liburd

Cover Image:
Stockbyte/Getty Images

Compositor:
KnowledgeWorks Global Limited

Printer:
RR Donnelley

COPYRIGHT © 2012, 2008 by Nelson Education Ltd.

Adapted from *Sociology in Our Times: The Essentials*, Seventh Edition, by Diana Kendall, published by Thomson Wadsworth. Copyright ©2006 by Thomson Wadsworth.

Printed and bound in the United States
1 2 3 4 12 11

For more information contact Nelson, 1120 Birchmount Road, Toronto, Ontario, M1K 5G4. Or you can visit our Internet site at http://www.nelson.com

Statistics Canada information is used with the permission of Statistics Canada. Users are forbidden to copy this material and/or redisseminate the data, in an original or modified form, for commercial purposes, without the expressed permissions of Statistics Canada. Information on the availability of the wide range of data from Statistics Canada can be obtained from Statistics Canada's Regional Offices, its World Wide Web site at <http://www.statcan.ca>, and its toll-free access number 1-800-263-1136.

Library and Archives Canada Cataloguing in Publication Data

Main entry under title:

Lothian Murray, Jane, 1960-
   Sociology in our times : the essentials / Jane Lothian Murray, Rick Linden, Diana Kendall.
—5th Canadian ed.

Includes bibliographical references and index.
ISBN 13: 978-0-17-650257-7
ISBN 10: 0-17650257-2

   1. Sociology—Textbooks.
I. Linden, Rick II. Kendall, Diana Elizabeth III. Title.

HM586.L68 2011 301
C2010-906467-4

Rick Linden would like to dedicate this book to Catherine Jones and Lucy Cooke—two wonderful mothers who passed away in 2006.

To my amazing sons, Jonathon, Drew, and Mackenzie, with love and admiration.—Jane Lothian Murray

BRIEF CONTENTS

CONTENTS

BOXES

■ SOCIOLOGY AND THE MEDIA

■ SOCIOLOGY IN GLOBAL PERSPECTIVE

Welcome to the fifth Canadian edition of *Sociology in Our Times: The Essentials*. We are delighted to bring you this exciting new edition, which highlights the challenges and opportunities that come with living and studying social life in the 21st century.

More than ever before, people are interested in the workings not only of their own society, but also of the larger world. We are coming to understand how events in other countries directly affect life in Canada. We wrote *Sociology in Our Times: The Essentials* to capture the excitement of this new era and to help students understand how sociological theory and research can be applied to both everyday life and the pressing social issues we face in a rapidly changing world.

Sociology in Our Times: The Essentials is a cutting-edge book that highlights the relevance of sociology. It does so by including a diversity of classical and contemporary theory, interesting and relevant research, and lived experiences that accurately mirror the diversity in society itself, This text demonstrates to students that sociology involves important questions and issues that they confront both personally and vicariously (for example, through the media). It speaks to a wide variety of students, and captures their interest by taking into account their concerns and perspectives. The text applies the finest research of classical and established contemporary sociologists, and it weaves an inclusive treatment of all people into the examination of sociology throughout. Although a number of introductory sociology texts give the appearance of inclusion, many are written with class, race, and gender neatly compartmentalized into their "appropriate" chapters, with perhaps an occasional "diversity" box thrown in. That approach not only marginalizes an increasing proportion of the students in introductory sociology classes, as well as in the broader Canadian population, but also leads many students to view race, class, and gender as nothing more than variables in sociological research (as found, for example, in statistics on welfare, crime, and homelessness). That approach downplays the significance of the interlocking nature of class, race, and gender in all topics examined by sociologists.

We have also tried to ensure that all theoretical perspectives are represented throughout the book. Most chapters show how the functionalist, conflict, symbolic interactionist, feminist, and postmodern perspectives can each help us to understand our social world.

We have sought to make the research accessible and engaging for both students and instructors. Concepts and theories are presented in a straightforward and understandable way, and a wealth of concrete examples and lived experiences are woven throughout. For students, this approach serves to clarify both the relevance and the importance of sociological theory and research.

ORGANIZATION OF THE TEXT

Sociology in Our Times: The Essentials, Fifth Canadian Edition, is divided into 16 chapters and three parts.

- In Part 1, "Studying Society," Chapter 1, "The Sociological Perspectives: Theory and Methods," introduces students to the sociological imagination and the development of sociological thinking. The chapter sets forth the major theoretical perspectives used by sociologists in analyzing compelling social issues such as suicide, and it provides a thorough description of both quantitative and qualitative methods. Chapter 2, "Culture and Society in a Changing World," shows how culture can be either a stabilizing force or one that can generate discord and conflict in societies. Cultural diversity is discussed as an important contemporary issue.

- Part 2, "The Nature of Social Life," focuses on core sociological concepts. Chapter 3, "Socialization," looks at positive and negative aspects of socialization across the life course with a particular emphasis on the challenges of early childhood socialization. Chapter 4, "Social Structure, Social Interaction, and Collective Behaviour," examines social structure and social interaction in detail, using homelessness as an example of the dynamic interplay between these concepts. Unique to this chapter are discussions of the sociology of emotions and of personal space as viewed through the lenses of race, class, gender, and age. This chapter also explores the dynamics of collective behaviour as expressed in the formation of urban legends, protests, and social movements. Chapter 5, "Groups and Organizations," includes analysis of innovative forms of social organization and ways in which organizational structures may differentially affect people depending on their race, class, gender, and age. Chapter 6, "Deviance and Crime," examines diverse perspectives on deviance, crime, and the criminal justice system. Key issues are dramatized for students through an analysis of recent research on organized crime, gangs, and the experiences of biker gang members.

Part 3, "Social Differences and Social Inequality," looks at issues of class, race and ethnicity, and sex and gender. Chapter 7, "Social Stratification in Canada," addresses systems of stratification and surveys social inequality in Canada. Using child poverty as a recurring theme, the chapter analyzes the causes and consequences of inequality and poverty. Chapter 8, "Global Stratification," examines differences in wealth and poverty in rich and poor nations around the world and explores the causes and consequences of these differences. Chapter 9, "Ethnic Relations and Race," includes a thorough analysis of prejudice and discrimination, and presents the experiences of racial and ethnic groups, along with future global, racial, and ethnic issues. Chapter 10, "Sex and Gender," examines social constructions of masculinity and femininity and contemporary issues of gender inequality. Chapter 11, "Health, Health Care, and Disability," analyzes these issues from both national and global perspectives. Chapter 12, "Families and Intimate Relationships," focuses on the diversity found in families and current changes and challenges facing Canadian families. Chapter 13, "Politics," looks at the nature of power and at Canadian and foreign political systems. Chapter 14, "Education," is now a separate chapter, and explores many issues facing students today such as the costs and equality of access to education. Chapter 15, "Religion," examines religion in a global perspective, providing a survey of the world's major religions, and shows how religious beliefs affect other aspects of our social lives. Chapter 16, "Population and Urbanization," looks at demography, global population change, and the process and consequences of urbanization, with increased coverage of environmental issues.

UNIQUE FEATURES

The following special features are specifically designed to reflect the themes of relevance and diversity in *Sociology in Our Times: The Essentials,* as well as to support student learning.

Incorporating Interesting and Engaging Lived Experiences Throughout the Chapters

Authentic first-person accounts are used as opening vignettes and throughout each chapter to create interest and give concrete meaning to the topics being discussed. Lived experiences including racism, child abuse, political activism, social contraints of masculinity and feminity, poverty, disability, and homelessness provide opportunities for students to examine social life beyond their own experiences and to examine class, ethnicity, gender, and age from diverse perspectives. An unusually wide range of diverse experiences—both positive and negative—is systematically incorporated to expose students to a multiplicity of viewpoints. These lived experiences were selected for their ability to speak to students, to assist them in learning concepts and theories, and to determine how they can be applied to other situations.

Focusing on the Relationship between Sociology and Everyday Life

Each chapter has a brief "Sociology and Everyday Life" quiz that relates the sociological perspective to the pressing social issues presented in the opening vignette. (Answers are provided on subsequent pages.) Do official statistics accurately reflect crime rates in Canada? Does increasing cultural diversity lead to increasing incidences of hate crimes and racism? Do welfare benefits provide enough income for recipients to live comfortably? Topics such as these will pique the interest of students.

Using the Media to Encourage Critical Thinking

Like most people in our society, students get much of their information about the social world from the media. A significant benefit of a sociology course is the encouragement to think critically about such information. Focusing on various types of media depictions—including television shows, cartoons, movies, mainstream and alternative presses— "Sociology and the Media" boxes provide an overview of sociological topics as seen through the "eye" of the media. Topics range from racism in the media to cultural confusion in advertisements and news coverage of diverse topics such as immigration and people living with AIDS. New to this edition, Sociology in the Media boxes include a special focus on technology as a type of media that has changed how we communicate, how we learn, and how we conceive of ourselves in relationship to others. Technological topics now covered in this section include seniors in cyberspace, the Internet and urban legends, technology in the classroom, technology and crime, and cyberdating.

Emphasizing the Importance of a Global Perspective

In our interconnected world, the sociological imagination must extend beyond national borders. The global implications of all topics are examined throughout each chapter and in "Sociology in Global Perspective" boxes. Topics include the impact of AIDS, women's literacy, global advertising, wealth, and poverty.

Encouraging Students to Use Their Sociological Knowledge to Think Critically

From rights of the homeless to assisted suicide to reverse racism, "Critical Thinking" boxes encourage students to use their sociological knowledge to grapple with some of today's most hotly contested issues. This section now includes coverage of critical thinking as it pertains to the law, explored through topics such as racial profiling and crime rate statistics, AIDS, public health, and criminality, and Canada's historical immigration laws.

Looking Ahead to Sociology in the Future

In addition to highlighting the contemporary relevance of sociology, students are encouraged to consider the sociological perspective as it might be in the future. The concluding sections of Chapters 2 through 15 look into the future and suggest how our social lives may look in the years to come. Environmental issues, homelessness, technology, population, deviance and crime, and the economy and work are among the topics discussed.

In-Text Learning Aids

Sociology in Our Times: The Essentials. This includes a number of pedagogical aids to promote students' mastery of sociological concepts and terminology.

Chapter Outlines. A concise outline at the beginning of each chapter gives students an overview of major topics and a convenient aid for review.

Questions and Issues. After the opening lived experience in each chapter, a series of introductory questions invites students to think about the major topics discussed in the chapter.

Integrated Running Glossary. Major concepts and key terms are concisely defined and highlighted in bold print within the text flow to avoid disrupting students' reading. These concepts and terms are also listed at the end of each chapter and in the glossary at the back of the book.

End-of-Chapter Study Aids. The Chapter Review provides a concise summary of key points and theoretical perspectives, along with a list of Key Terms. Questions for Critical Thinking encourage students to assess their knowledge of the chapter and apply insights they have gained to other issues.

Web Links. Web Links, found at the end of every chapter, encourage students to explore the Internet. Included in the Web Links are links to research articles found on the Internet. These articles are indicated with an icon and can be used for further study or in-class discussion.

NEW FEATURES IN THE FIFTH CANADIAN EDITION

This edition of *Sociology in Our Times: The Essentials* provides us with the opportunity to continue improving a text that has been very well received by students and teachers. We have added dozens of new references that incorporate data from the most recent census as well as reflecting new developments in sociological research.

Chapter 1 introduces students to the main theoretical perspectives in sociology and includes a revised discussion of postmodernism. This chapter also includes a new example of survey research based on study of charitable giving.

Chapter 2 has the most recent data on language diversity, ethnicity, and Aboriginal peoples in Canada. It also features two new boxes, the first testing students' knowledge on global variations of food and culture and the other examining cultural diffusion and cultural imperialism in the context of shopping malls in China.

Chapter 3 examines the effects of positive socialization and interesting new issues relating to early childhood socialization. A new "Sociology in Global Perspective" box examines how Canada measures up internationally with respect to early childhood education programs. A second new "Sociology and the

Media" box examines how cell phones and text messaging have changed the way children and adolescents are socialized.

Chapter 4 has been streamlined and updated with new statistics and photos, especially in its coverage of homelessness in Canada. Additionally, Chapter 4 contains an updated "Sociology in Global Perspective" box, now called "Homelessness for Children is an International Problem." Revised coverage of nonverbal communication is also a highlight.

Chapter 5 now discusses how bureaucracies can perpetuate gender, race, and class inequalities. It also includes additional material on social networks including a section on the limitations of Milgram's "small world" research.

Chapter 6 The discussion of informal social control now includes the example of how magicians keep their tricks secret despite the fact that intellectual property laws do not apply to these illusions. The section on strain theory explores how this theory might explain Conrad Black's misconduct. Crime statistics have been updated to 2009.

Chapter 7 has been revised and now includes a section on systems of social stratification. It also includes the newest census data on wealth, income, and poverty in Canada.

Chapter 8 provides an expanded section on the relationship between consumption in high-income societies and global poverty as well as a new section on the "flying geese" theory of development.

Chapter 9 takes a closer look at ethnic diversity in Canada. It also includes the newest census data on ethnic origins, language diversity, and visible minorities.

Chapter 10 provides a more balanced discussion of gender by presenting more research on men and masculinity. Also highlighted in this chapter is progress made toward gender equity such as gains made in gender representation in colleges and university. This chapter also explores the outstanding disparities between men and women such as the wage gap and distribution of unpaid labour in the home.

Chapter 11 has new statistics showing the recent reductions in the incidence of HIV/AIDS cases around the world. The extensive revision of the box on AIDS and public health focuses on a case in which a man was found guilty of murder for transmitting HIV/AIDS to his sexual partners. New material has been added dealing with sociological perspectives on disability, with the impact of HIV/AIDS on the economies of low-income countries, and the impact of gender and class on health and health care.

Chapter 12 presents all of the new census data on families, including family types, same-sex families, and single-parent families. A new "Sociology in Global Perspective" box discusses the re-emergence of extended families as a response to financial hardship.

Chapter 13 now includes material on political economy. Some of the major issues related to Canada's political economy are highlighted and there are new sections on capitalism, socialism, and mixed economies. The chapter also discusses recent research on the social policy impact of women voting and on the political activity of young Canadians.

Chapter 14 is a new separate chapter on education. Included in this new chapter is an examination of changes in the education system, the rising costs of education and educational opportunities, and access for students with disabilities. A interesting new "Sociology and the Media" box proposes that educators need to adapt to a new era of "digital students."

Chapter 15 is now a separate chapter on religion. The chapter examines sociological perspectives on religion, religious trends in Canada, and the future of religion.

Chapter 16 deals with population issues, so there are extensive updates to population statistics for Canada and many other countries. The chapter also presents new material on public attitudes toward immigration and on the impact of these attitudes on immigrants. The role played by corporations and governments in encouraging suburbanization is also discussed.

Additional to the chapter-by-chapter changes listed above, *Sociology in Our Times: The Essentials,* Fifth Canadian Edition, also has a refreshing new design, including almost 30 new photos.

FULLY INTEGRATED SUPPORT PACKAGE FOR INSTRUCTORS AND STUDENTS

Ancillary materials that enhance teaching and learning are an important feature of a textbook. The supplements offered with *Sociology in Our Times: The Essentials,* Fifth Canadian Edition, ensure that the themes of diversity, inclusiveness, and contemporary issues are consistent with the text. These pieces work together as an effective and integrated teaching package.

Nelson Education Testing Advantage

tA Nelson Education
Testing Advantage

The **Nelson Education Teaching Advantage (NETA) program** delivers research-based resources that promote student engagement and higher-order thinking and enable the success of Canadian students and educators.

The primary NETA components are **NETA Engagement** and **NETA Assessment**.

NETA Engagement. The foundational principles underlying NETA Engagement are student-centred learning, deep learning, active learning, and creating positive classroom environments. The *NETA Instructor's Guide to Classroom Engagement (NETA IGCE)* provides an overview of the research underlying these principles. The structure of the Classroom Engagement Activities was created by Dr. Roger Fisher, and validated by an interdisciplinary editorial advisory board of scholars of teaching and learning.

Editorial Advisory Board:

Norman Althouse, Haskayne School of Business, University of Calgary

Brenda Chant-Smith, Department of Psychology, Trent University

Scott Follows, Manning School of Business Administration, Acadia University

Jon Houseman, Department of Biology, University of Ottawa

Glen Loppnow, Department of Chemistry, University of Alberta

Tanya Noel, Department of Biology, York University

Gary Poole, Director, Centre for Teaching and Academic Growth and School of Population and Public Health, University of British Columbia

Dan Pratt, Department of Educational Studies, University of British Columbia

Mercedes Rowinsky-Geurts, Department of Languages and Literatures, Wilfrid Laurier University

The Classroom Engagement Activities and traditional Instructor's Manual for *Sociology in Our Times: The Essentials*, Fifth Canadian Edition, were written by Professor Elizabeth Bishop at Confederation College in accordance with the principles of the *NETA IGCE*. Select the "NETA Engagement" button on the *Sociology in Our Times: The Essentials Instructor's Resource CD* to view the *NETA IGCE* with classroom engagement activities and the instructor's manual.

NETA Assessment. Recognizing the importance of multiple-choice testing in today's classroom and in response to instructors' concerns, Nelson Education has created the NETA Assessment program. NETA Assessment is a research-based program that improves the quality of our test banks by ensuring our test banks measure not only recall (as is typical with test banks) but also ***higher-level thinking*** skills.

The NETA Assessment program was created in partnership with David DiBattista, a 3M National Teaching Fellow, professor of psychology at Brock University, and researcher in the area of multiple-choice testing.

All NETA test banks include David DiBattista's guide for instructors, *Multiple Choice Tests: Getting Beyond Remembering*. This guide has been designed to assist you in using Nelson test banks to achieve the desired outcomes in your course. Select the "NETA Assessment" button on the *Sociology in Our Times: The Essentials Instructor's Resource CD* for this valuable resource. At the same location you will find the *Sociology in Our Times: The Essentials* test bank and computerized test bank (see "Ancillaries for Instructors" below for more information about the test bank.) The NETA Test Bank for *Sociology in Our Times: The Essentials*, Fifth Canadian Edition, was created by Vicki Nygaard of the University of British Columbia.

Instructor's Resource CD (IRCD)

This valuable *all-in-one* ancillary for the instructor includes the following, all on one easy-to-use-and-store CD-ROM (ISBN 0176606211):

■ Customized NETA Engagement package (Instructor's Guide to Classroom Engagement, NETA Classroom Engagement activities, and Instructor's Manual), written by Elizabeth Bishop, Confederation College

■ Customized NETA Assessment package (the computerized NETA Test Bank in Examview®, the NETA Test Bank in rich text format, and the guide *Multiple Choice Testing: Getting*

Beyond Remembering), written by Vicki Nygaard, University of British Columbia

■ PowerPoint® lecture slides, compiled by Anthony Iafrate, Lambton College

■ Image Library containing all photos, figures, and tables from the book

■ Day One presentation that describes the book and its assets

CengageNOW™ with CL eBook CENGAGENOW

CengageNOW™ is an **online learning and home-work assessment program** created in concert with *Sociology in Our Times: The Essentials*, Fifth Canadian Edition, to present a seamless, integrated learning tool.

With CengageNOW™, instructors can dramatically affect student success. Assigning text-specific tutorials requires no instructor set-up. Faculty can use the same system to **create tailored homework assignments, quizzes, and tests that auto-grade and flow directly into your gradebook!** This means you can assign marks to homework assignments, motivating students to study the material and come to class prepared.

Students can improve their grades and save study time with CengageNOW™. It isn't just reading—it provides a **customized study plan that lets students master what they need to know without wasting time on what they already know!** The study plan provides a roadmap to interactive exercises, videos, e-books, and other resources that help students master the subject. Pre-tests and post-tests allow students to monitor their progress and focus their studying via CengageNOW™.

The CengageNOW™ for *Sociology in Our Times: The Essentials*, Fifth Canadian Edition, written by Anthony Iafrate, Lambton College, includes a Cengage Learning eBook containing interactive media assets such as Web links, videos, and images, as well as highlighting, note taking, and bookmarking capabilities. To register and access this product and other multimedia tools please visit **www.NelsonBrain.com**.

Sociology on the Web

http://www.sociologyessentials5e .nelson.com

Sociology in Our Times: The Essentials, Fifth Canadian Edition, features a companion website designed for both students and instructors. Features of the website

include online material linked directly to the text, plus interactive quizzes, study resources, and a career centre. Instructors' resources include downloadable ancillaries.

INFOTRAC® College Edition

Ignite discussions or augment your lectures with the latest developments in sociology and societal change. Create your own course reader by selecting articles or by using the search keywords provided at the end of each chapter. InfoTrac® College Edition gives you and your students four months of free access to an easy-to-use online database of reliable, full-length articles (not abstracts) from hundreds of top academic journals and popular sources. Among the journals available 24 hours a day, 7 days a week are *Canadian Review of Sociology and Anthropology, Canadian Journal of Sociology, Canadian Ethnic Studies, Public Policy, American Journal of Sociology, Social Forces, Social Research,* and *Sociology.* Contact your Nelson representative for more information.

Society in Question, Sixth Edition

Society in Question, Sixth Edition, by Robert J. Brym, is the only introductory sociology reader that combines Canadian and international readings. This reader provides balanced coverage of the approaches and methods in current sociology as well as unique and surprising perspectives on many major sociological topics. All readings have been chosen for their ability to speak directly to contemporary Canadian students about how sociology can enable them to make sense of their lives in a rapidly changing world. (ISBN: 0-17-650193-2)

Wadsworth Classic Readings in Sociology, Fifth Edition

This series of classic articles written by key sociologists will complement any introductory sociology textbook, serving as a touchstone where students can read original works that teach the fundamental ideas of sociology. (ISBN: 0-49-560276-0)

Nelson Guide to Success in Social Science: Writing Papers and Exams

The *Nelson Guide to Success in Social Science: Writing Papers and Exams* by Diane Symbaluk is an indispensable resource for any social science student. The *Nelson Guide to Success in Social Science* is a roadmap to the often unfamiliar terrain of university or college academia. Leveraging best practices of master students, author Diane Symbaluk has created a book that will help students achieve their goals of excellence in writing and research. (ISBN: 0-17-625182-0)

Nelson Canadian Dictionary for the Social Sciences

The *Nelson Canadian Dictionary for the Social Sciences* by Gary Parkinson and Robert Drislane has over 1400 entries covering the fields of anthropology, sociology, and political science. This dictionary is designed for undergraduate students and covers the main concepts, names, and events in social sciences in Canada. Each entry is designed to provide sufficient information to grasp the basic content of a concept, how the term is used, and its connection to other concepts. (ISBN: 0-17-625237-1)

Nelson Videos for Introductory Sociology, Think Outside the Book

This seven-volume set of 54 video segments (each is 4 to 30 minutes in length) was created to stimulate discussion of topics raised in sociology. Produced in conjunction with Face to Face Media (Vancouver), the selections have been edited to optimize their impact in the classroom. Many of the selections are taken from films that have won national and international awards. Five of the selections are from the celebrated work of Gwynne Dyer, one of Canada's leading media intellectuals. Videos and an accompanying Video Guide and Instructor's Manual are available from your local Nelson sales and editorial representative. Visit **http://www.thinkoutsidethebook. nelson.com** for more information.

Opposing Viewpoints Resource Center

This online centre helps you expose your students to all sides of today's most compelling social and scientific issues, from genetic engineering to environmental policy, prejudice, abortion, violence as portrayed in the media, and much more. The Opposing Viewpoints Resource Center draws on Greenhaven Press's acclaimed social issues series, popular periodicals and newspapers, and core reference content from other Thomson Gale and Macmillan Reference USA sources. The result is a dynamic online library of current events topics—the facts as well as the arguments as articulated by the proponents and detractors of each position. Special sections focus on critical thinking (walking students through the critical evaluation of point-counterpoint arguments) and researching

and writing papers. To take a quick tour of the OVRC, visit **http://www.gale.com/OpposingViewpoints**. For college and university adopters only and is not sold separately. (ISBN: 0-534-12853-X)

ACKNOWLEDGEMENTS

This edition of *Sociology in Our Times: The Essentials* would not have been possible without the insightful critiques of these colleagues, who have reviewed some or all of this book or its previous editions. Our profound thanks to each reviewer for their candid and helpful comments:

Bill Adcock, Sheridan College; Gina Barber, Fanshawe College; Marilyn Bicher, Vanier College; Penny Biles, Sheridan College; Tom Callaghan, St. Clair College; Diane Clark, Lambton College; Larry R. Comeau, Sheridan College; David English, Durham College; Lindsay Harris, Algonquin College; Kelly Henley, St. Clair College; Shelly Kelly, Nova Scotia Community College; David Leland, Red River College; Raymond Liew, John Abbott College; Jock MacKay, Vanier College; Laurie Milne, Medicine Hat College; Parveen Nangia, Laurentian University; Michelle Owen, University of Winnipeg; Laura Pao-Mercier, Vanier College; John Patterson, Canadore College; John Pestana, John Abbott College; Tulsie Raghubir, Niagara College; Faith Richards, Georgian College; Robert Ritchie, Centennial College; Lance Roberts, University of Manitoba; Anna Lucy Robinson, Lambton College; Patricia Whaley, Durham College; Carolyn Willoughby, Durham College.

We would like to express our appreciation to the many individuals at Nelson involved in the development and production of *Sociology in Our Times: The Essentials*, Fifth Edition. Among them, Liisa Kelly has done an exceptional job of keeping the project on track and patiently "moving" us along on schedule despite many competing demands. Maya Castle (Acquisitions Editor), Jennifer Hare (Content Production Manager), Franca Amore (Managing Designer), Ferial Suleman (Manufacturing Coordinator) and Kristiina Paul (Permissions Researcher) have ensured the completion of a final manuscript we are proud of. We would also like to thank Amanda Henry, Terry Fedorkiw, Kelly Smyth, and other members of the Sales and Marketing staff for ensuring our book remains among the best selling in Canada. As always, it has been a pleasure working with such a professional and dedicated team.

Finally we would like to thank our families for their continued love, support, and encouragement throughout this project. Jane would like to thank her boys, Jonathon, Drew, MacKenzie, and Craig, for the endless supply of "lived experiences" reflected in her teaching and writing.

We would also like to thank our students for the wisdom, enthusiasm, and laughter they bring to our classrooms. We invite your comments and suggestions. Send them to us care of:

Nelson Education Ltd.
1120 Birchmount Road
Toronto, ON
M1K 5G4

Rick Linden   Jane Lothian Murray
University of Manitoba   University of Winnipeg

Sociology in Our Times
The Essentials

CHAPTER 1

The Sociological Perspective: Theory and Methods

Close to 50 years ago sociologist Peter Berger first introduced what he called "an invitation to sociology." In his classic work of the same name, he writes:

> *People who like to avoid shocking discoveries, who prefer to believe that society is just what they were taught in Sunday school, who like the safety of the rules and the maxims of what Alfred Schuetz called the "world-taken-for-granted," should stay away from sociology. People who feel no temptation before closed doors, who have no curiosity about human beings, who are content to admire scenery without wondering about the people who live in those houses on the other side of the river, should probably stay away from sociology. They will find it unpleasant or, at any rate, unrewarding. People who are interested in human beings only if they can change, convert, or reform them should also be warned, for they will find sociology much less useful than they had hoped. And people*

whose interest is mainly their own conceptual constructions will do just as well to turn to the study of little white mice. Sociology will be satisfying, in the long run, only to those who can think of nothing more entrancing than to watch men [and women] and to understand things human. (Berger, 1963:24)

Berger is writing about what may be described as a passion for sociology, a fascination with human social interaction. In my first year of university I discovered this passion sitting in the Arts building gazing out the window observing, watching, analyzing this new social world (campus life) around me. It was also during this first year that I learned another valuable lesson from reading Berger's works. As he explained, "The first wisdom of sociology is this—things are not what they seem. This too is a deceptively simple statement. It ceases to be simple after a while. Social reality turns out to have many layers of meaning. The discovery

of each new layer changes the perception of the whole" (1963:24).

Throughout this text, you will be invited to use a sociological perspective and to apply your sociological imagination to re-examine your social world and explore important social issues and problems you may not have considered before.

Can sociological theory and research help us understand the very individualistic act of taking one's own life? Do individuals (at least under some circumstances) have a right to end their own lives? Given who we are, what we know, and what we believe, our individual answers to these questions may vary. Along with others posed in this book, the questions may produce strong responses. In this chapter, suicide is used as an example of a problem that sociologists examine. We also will see how sociological research methods might be used to answer complex questions, and we will wrestle with some of the difficulties inherent in studying human behaviour. Before reading on, test your commonsense knowledge by answering the questions in Box 1.1 on page 5.

Chapter Focus Question: How do sociological theory and research add to our knowledge of human societies and social issues?

What is the sociological imagination?

Why were early thinkers concerned with social order and stability?

What are the assumptions behind each of the contemporary theoretical perspectives?

How do sociologists conduct their research?

PUTTING SOCIAL LIFE INTO PERSPECTIVE

Sociology **is the systematic study of human society and social interaction**. It is a systematic study because sociologists apply both theoretical perspectives and research methods to examinations of social behaviour. Sociologists study human societies and the social interactions within in order to develop theories of how human behaviour is shaped by group life and how, in turn, group life is affected by individuals. As sociologists examine these issues, they begin to use their sociological imagination.

The Sociological Imagination

Sociologist C. Wright Mills (1959b) described sociological reasoning as the *sociological imagination—* **the ability to see the relationship between individual experiences and the larger society**. This awareness enables us to understand the link between our personal experiences and the social contexts in which they occur.

The Promise

The first fruit of this imagination—and the first lesson of the social science that embodies it—is the idea that the individual can understand his own experience and gauge his own fate only by locating himself within his period, that he can know his own chances in life only by becoming aware of those of all individuals in his circumstances. In many ways it is a terrible lesson; in many ways a magnificent one. We do not know the limits of man's capacities for supreme effort or willing degradation, for agony or glee, for pleasurable brutality or the sweetness of reason. But we have come to know that the limits of

Events around the world affect us all. These anti-war demonstrators at the United States embassy in Ottawa are protesting the war in Iraq.

"human nature" are frightening broad. We have come to know that every individual lives, from one generation to the next, in some society; that he lives out a biography, and that he lives it within a historical sequence. By the fact of his living he contributes, however minutely, to the shaping of this society and the course of its history, even as he is made by society and by its historical push and shove (Mills, 1959:5).

The sociological imagination helps us distinguish between personal troubles and social (or public) issues. *Personal troubles* are the private problems of individuals and the networks of people with whom they associate regularly. As a result, those problems must be solved by individuals within their immediate social settings. For example, a person being unemployed may be a personal trouble. *Public issues* are matters beyond an individual's own control that are caused by problems at the societal level. Widespread unemployment because of economic changes, such as plant closings, is an example of a public issue. The sociological imagination helps us place seemingly personal troubles, such as contemplating suicide or losing one's job, into a larger social context, where we can distinguish whether and how personal troubles may be related to public issues.

SOCIOLOGY AND EVERYDAY LIFE

Test Your Commonsense Knowledge

JoinIn
on TurningPoint®

True	False	
T	**F**	1. One in two marriages end in divorce.
T	**F**	2. Women are more likely to be assaulted than men.
T	**F**	3. Individuals who are abused as children will most likely grow up to abuse their own children.
T	**F**	4. Rates of murder and other violent crimes have steadily increased over the past 20 years.
T	**F**	5. Most Canadians have a postsecondary education.
T	**F**	6. The majority of poor children in Canada come from single-mother households.
T	**F**	7. Children who grow up in a family with gay parents are more likely to be gay.
T	**F**	8. Today women who work full time make 90 cents for every dollar earned by their male counterparts.

Answers on page 7.

Suicide as a Personal Trouble Many of our individual experiences may be largely beyond our control. They are determined by society—by its historical development and its organization. In everyday life, however, we do not define personal experiences in these terms. If a person commits suicide, many people consider it the result of his or her own personal problems.

Suicide as a Public Issue We can use the sociological imagination to look at the problem of suicide as a public issue—as a societal problem. For example, we may use our sociological imagination to understand why suicide rates are so high in some Aboriginal communities in Canada. Early sociologist Émile Durkheim refused to accept commonsense explanations of suicide. In what was probably the first sociological study to use scientific research methods, he related suicide to the issue of cohesiveness (or lack of it) in society instead of viewing suicide as an isolated act that could be understood only by studying individual personalities or inherited tendencies. Contemporary societies often deal with suicide as a public issue by enacting legislation related to matters such as assisted suicide.

Why Study Sociology?

Sociology helps us gain a better understanding of ourselves and our social world. It enables us to see how behaviour is largely shaped by the groups to which we belong and the society in which we live. A **society is a large social grouping that shares the same geographical territory and is subject to the same political authority and dominant cultural expectations**, such as in Canada, the United States, or Mexico. Examining the world order helps us understand that each of us is affected by **global interdependence—a relationship in which the lives of all people are intertwined closely and any one nation's problems are part of a larger global problem**.

Individuals can make use of sociology on a more personal level. Sociology enables us to move beyond established ways of thinking, thus allowing us to gain new insights into ourselves and to develop a greater awareness of the connection between our own "world" and that of other people. According to sociologist Peter Berger, sociological inquiry helps us see that "things are not what they seem" (1963:23). Sociology provides new ways of approaching problems and making decisions in everyday life. It promotes understanding and tolerance by enabling each of us to look beyond intuition, commonsense, or our personal experiences.

Many of us rely on intuition or commonsense gained from personal experience to help us understand our daily lives and other people's behaviour. *Commonsense knowledge* guides ordinary conduct in everyday life. However, many commonsense notions are actually myths. A *myth* is a popular but false notion that may be used, either intentionally or unintentionally, to perpetuate certain beliefs or "theories" even in the light of conclusive evidence to the contrary.

By contrast, sociologists strive to use scientific standards, not popular myths or hearsay, in studying society and social interaction. They use systematic research techniques and are accountable to the scientific community for their methods and the presentation of their findings. Although some sociologists argue that sociology must be completely value free—free from distorting subjective (personal or emotional) bias—others do not think that total objectivity is an attainable or desirable goal when studying human behaviour. However, all sociologists attempt to discover patterns or commonalities in human behaviour. When they study suicide, for example, they look for recurring patterns of behaviour even though *individual* people usually commit the acts and *other individuals* suffer because of these actions. Consequently, sociologists seek out the multiple causes and effects of suicide or other social issues. They analyze the impact of the problem not only from the standpoint of the people directly involved but also from the standpoint of the effects of such behaviour on all people.

The Importance of a Global Sociological Imagination

Although existing sociological theory and research provide the foundation for sociological thinking, we must reach beyond past studies that have focused primarily on North America to develop a more comprehensive global approach for the future. In the 21st century, we face important challenges in a rapidly changing world.

The world's *developed* or *high-income countries* **are countries with highly industrialized economies; technologically advanced industrial, administrative, and service occupations**; and relatively high levels of national and per-person income. Examples include New Zealand, Japan, Canada, and the United States. As compared with other countries of the world, people in most high-income countries typically have a high standard of living and a lower death rate, due to advances in nutrition and medical technology. In contrast, *middle-income countries* **are nations with industrializing economies, particularly in urban areas, and moderate levels of national and personal income**. Examples of middle-income countries include Brazil and Mexico, which are experiencing rapid industrialization (see Chapter 8). *Low-income countries* **are primarily agrarian nations with little industrialization and low levels of national and personal income**. Examples of low-income countries include many of the nations of Africa and Asia, particularly the People's Republic of China and India, where people typically work the land and are among the poorest in the world. Generalizations, however, are difficult to make because there are wide differences in income and standards of living within many nations (see Chapter 7: Global Stratification).

Throughout this text, we will continue to develop our sociological imaginations by examining social life in Canada and other countries. The future of this country is deeply intertwined with the future of all nations of the world on economic, political, environmental, and humanitarian levels. We buy many goods and services that were produced in other nations, and we sell much of what we produce to the people of other nations. Peace in other nations is important if we are to ensure peace within our own borders. Famine, unrest, and brutality in other regions of the world must be of concern to people in Canada. Global problems such as these contribute to the large influx of immigrants who arrive in this country annually. These immigrants bring with them a rich diversity of language, customs, religions, and previous life experiences; they also contribute to dramatic population changes that will have long-term effects on this country. Developing a better understanding of diversity and tolerance for people who are different from us is important for our personal, social, and economic well-being.

Whatever your race or ethnicity, class, sex, or age, are you able to include in your thinking the perspectives of people who are quite different from you in terms of their experiences and points of view? (See Box 1.2 on page 8 for further discussion.) Before answering this question, a few definitions are in order. *Race* **is a term used by many people to specify groups of people distinguished by physical characteristics such as skin colour**; in fact, there are no "pure" racial types, and the concept of race is considered by most sociologists to be a social construction that people use to justify existing inequalities. *Ethnicity* **refers to the cultural heritage or identity of a group and is based on factors such as language or country of origin.** *Class* **is the relative location of a person or group within a larger society, based on wealth, power, prestige, or other valued resources.** *Sex* **refers to the biological and anatomical differences between females and males.** By contrast, *gender* **refers to the meanings, beliefs, and practices associated with sex differences**, referred to as *femininity* and *masculinity* (Scott, 1986:1054).

Answers to the Sociology Quiz on Commonsense Knowledge

The answers to all of the questions are false. See below for a more detailed explanation of each of the answers.

1. **False.** Current estimates are that one in three marriages will end in divorce (Statistics Canada, 2005d).

2. **False.** Rates of assault are similar for men and women. Men are more likely to be victims of physical assault whereas women are more likely to be sexually assaulted (Statistics Canada, 2005h).

3. **False.** This myth is an oversimplification of a statistic that indicates a large number of parents who abuse their children were abused by their parents as children. This does not mean that most individuals who are abused will themselves become abusers. The research that indicates a large number of child-abuse victims do not become abusers as adults (Department of Justice, 2002).

4. **False.** While violent-crime rates generally rose through the 1980s, they declined steadily throughout the 1990s and continue to decline. (Statistics Canada, 2009).

5. **False.** Although Canadians today are more educated than ever, the most recent Census indicates that 20 percent of adult Canadians have university credentials and another 16 percent have a college diploma (Statistics Canada, 2006a).

6. **False.** Just over half of the children in low-income families live in two-parent families (Statistics Canada, 2007g).

7. **False.** The research has consistently shown that children raised by same-sex parents are no more likely to be homosexual than are children raised by heterosexual parents (Ambert, 2005b).

8. **False.** Women working full-time year round make approximately 70 cents for every dollar earned by their male counterparts. This gap has not changed significantly in the past decade (Statistics Canada, 2006e)

THE DEVELOPMENT OF SOCIOLOGICAL THINKING

Throughout history, social philosophers and religious authorities have made countless observations about human behaviour. However, these early thinkers primarily stated what they thought society *ought* to be like, rather than describing how society actually *was.* The idea of observing how people lived to find out what they thought, and doing so in a systematic manner that could be verified, did not take hold until the 19th century, with the social upheaval brought about by industrialization and urbanization.

Industrialization **is the process by which societies are transformed from dependence on agriculture and handmade products to an emphasis on manufacturing and related industries.** This process occurred first during the Industrial Revolution in Britain between 1760 and 1850 and soon was repeated throughout Western Europe. By the mid-19th century, industrialization was well under way in North America. Massive economic, technological, and social changes occurred as machine technology and the factory system shifted the economic base of these nations from agriculture to manufacturing. A new social class of industrialists emerged in textiles, iron smelting, and related industries. Many people who had laboured on the land were forced to leave their tightly knit rural communities and sacrifice well-defined social relationships to seek employment as factory workers in the emerging cities, which became the centres of industrial work.

Urbanization **is the process by which an increasing proportion of a population lives in cities rather than in rural areas.** Although cities

BOX 1.2   CRITICAL THINKING

From Sociological Illiteracy to Sociological Imagination

Professor Judith Shapiro, an anthropologist and president of Barnard College in New York City, writes eloquently about the challenges of moving beyond the "personal" in our modern culture:

> At one point in the mid-1980s, when I was teaching I started paying attention to a common phrase, repeated like a mantra by students there and elsewhere: "racism, sexism, and classism." I had heard the phrase so often that I had become quite used to it, but it suddenly struck me as odd. The terms racism and sexism seemed unproblematic enough, referring to discrimination based on what we take to be physical differences of one kind of another. But what did "classism" really mean? Although my 1960s ears were expecting to hear students talk about class, instead I was hearing about classism. Had the students been talking about class, they would have discussed the structure of our society, and how socioeconomic inequalities were built into it. In fact, talk of that kind was relatively rare in students' political conversations. Rather, they seemed to be concerned about individuals—prejudice against individuals belonging to less-privileged socioeconomic groups.
>
> That discovery led me to wonder how the students saw race and gender. Were they also viewing racism and sexism exclusively in terms of individual identities and interpersonal relationships? If so, what did that say about the students' chances for improving the world? Had the goal of creating a more just society dwindled down into a matter of sensitivity training?
>
> Those students of the 1980s were missing something important, something we should have given them during their college years. Too many of them were deficient in the skills needed for analyzing society in economic, political, and structural terms. They seemed unable to move beyond their immediate experience to see how that experience was shaped by larger social and historical forces. They were suffering from a lack of what the eminent sociologist C. Wright Mills called "the sociological imagination"—which is in short supply among today's students as well. I have come to refer to that condition as sociological illiteracy. Just as a person may be illiterate in the most literal sense (unable to read or write), or scientifically illiterate, or innumerate (as we have come to call someone who lacks quantitative skills), so a person may be uneducated in the social sciences, and thus unable to make use of the insights and tools that those disciplines provide. . . .
>
> Many undergraduates today demonstrate impressive levels of civic engagement in the form of community service. They serve meals in soup kitchens, work in homeless shelters, and staff AIDS hotlines. They work as interns in a variety of social agencies. Too few of them, however, are able to raise their eyes to the level of policy and social structure. They need the sociological imagination to see how their on-the-ground activities fit into a bigger picture, so that more of them can cross the bridge from serious moral commitment to effective political participation.
>
> As teachers, we must admit our share of responsibility for that state of affairs. We need to adjust the focus between what we want to teach and what our students need to learn. Those of us who are faculty members in the social sciences must be sure that we are providing to all of our students, majors and non-majors alike, basic tools of social and cultural understanding, as they have evolved over time in our various disciplines.
>
> As faculty members, we must remember that our responsibilities extend beyond the academy. Sociologists such as Mills wrote with a force and grace that enabled them to reach a wide audience. We have not seen their like in years—too many years. More of us must follow their example and write for the general reader. And we should encourage our students—so full of energy, intelligence, and commitment—to move beyond the personal to the political.

Source: From Sociological Illiteracy to Sociological Imagination, by Judith Shapiro, *The Chronicle of Higher Education*, March 31, 2000, p. A68. Reprinted by permission of the author.

As Canada continues to become increasingly diverse, sociologists need to recognize the importance of considering all people's experiences as we confront public issues. In forming your own sociological imagination and in seeing the possibilities for sociology in this new century, it will be helpful to understand the development of the discipline.

existed long before the Industrial Revolution, the development of the factory system led to a rapid increase in both the number of cities and the size of their populations. People from very diverse backgrounds worked together in the same factory. At the same time, many people shifted from being *producers* to being *consumers*. For example, families living in the cities had to buy food with their wages because they could no longer grow their own crops to consume or to barter for other resources. Similarly, people had to pay rent for their lodging because they could no longer exchange their services for shelter.

These living and working conditions led to the development of new social problems: inadequate housing, crowding, unsanitary conditions, poverty, pollution, and crime. Wages were so low that entire families—including very young children—were forced to work, often under hazardous conditions and with no job security. As these conditions became more visible, a new breed of social thinkers turned its attention to trying to understand why and how society was changing.

Early Thinkers: A Concern with Social Order and Stability

At the same time as urban problems were growing worse, natural scientists had been using reason, or rational thinking, to discover the laws of physics and the movement of the planets. Social thinkers started to believe that, by applying the methods developed by the natural sciences, they might discover the laws of human behaviour and apply these laws to solve social problems.

Auguste Comte French philosopher Auguste Comte (1798–1857) coined the term *sociology* from the Latin *socius* (social, being with others) and the Greek *logos* (study of) to describe a new science that would engage in the study of society. Comte is considered by some to be the "founder of sociology." Comte's theory that societies contain *social statics* (forces for social order and stability) and *social dynamics* (forces for conflict and change) continues to be used, although not in these exact terms, in contemporary sociology.

Harriet Martineau

Harriet Martineau

Comte's works were made more accessible for a wide variety of scholars through the efforts of British sociologist Harriet Martineau (1802–76). Until recently, Martineau received no recognition in the field of sociology, partly because she was a woman in a male-dominated discipline and society. She not only translated and condensed Comte's work, but also was an active sociologist in her own right. Martineau studied the social customs of Britain and the United States and analyzed the consequences of industrialization and capitalism. In *Society in America* (1962/1837), she examined religion, politics, child rearing, slavery, and immigration in the United States, paying special attention to social distinctions based on class, race, and gender.

Herbert Spencer

British social theorist Herbert Spencer (1820–1903) used an evolutionary perspective to explain social order and social change. He believed that society, like a biological organism, has various interdependent parts (such as the family, the economy, and the government) that work to ensure the stability and survival of the entire society. According to Spencer, societies developed through a process of "struggle" (for existence) and "fitness" (for survival), which he referred to as the "survival of the fittest." Spencer equated this process of *natural selection* with progress, because only the "fittest" members of society would succeed. As a result of these ideas, he strongly opposed attempts at social reform that might interfere with the natural selection process and, thus, damage society by favouring its least worthy members.

Critics have suggested that many of Spencer's ideas had serious flaws. For one thing, societies are not the same as biological systems; people are able to create and transform their environment. Moreover, the notion of the survival of the fittest can easily be used to justify class, racial/ethnic, and gender inequalities, and to rationalize the lack of action to eliminate harmful practices that contribute to such inequalities.

Émile Durkheim

French sociologist Émile Durkheim (1858–1917) criticized some of Spencer's views while incorporating others into his own writing. Durkheim stressed that people are the product of their social environment and that behaviour cannot be understood fully in terms of *individual* biological and psychological traits. He believed that the limits of human potential are *socially*, not *biologically*, based.

In his work *The Rules of Sociological Method* (1964a/1895), Durkheim set forth one of his most important contributions to sociology: the idea that societies are built on social facts. **Social facts are patterned ways of acting, thinking, and feeling that exist** *outside* **any one individual but that exert social control over each person.** Durkheim believed that social facts must be explained by other social facts—by reference to the social structure rather than to individual attributes.

Durkheim observed that rapid social change and a more specialized division of labour produce *strains* in society. These strains lead to a breakdown in traditional organization, values, and authority, and to a dramatic increase in **anomie—a condition in which social control becomes ineffective as a result of the loss of shared values and of a sense of purpose in society.** According to Durkheim, anomie is most likely to occur during a period of rapid social change. In *Suicide* (1964b/1897), he explored the relationship between anomic social conditions and suicide.

Durkheim's contributions to sociology are so significant that he has been referred to as "the crucial figure in the development of sociology as an academic discipline [and as] one of the deepest roots of the sociological imagination" (Tiryakian, 1978:187). He has long been viewed as a proponent of the scientific approach to examining social facts that lie outside individuals. He is also described as the founding figure of the functionalist theoretical tradition.

© Bettmann/CORBIS

Émile Durkheim

Differing Views on the Status Quo: Stability versus Change

Karl Marx In sharp contrast with Durkheim's focus on the stability of society, German economist and philosopher Karl Marx (1818–83) stressed that history is a continuous clash between conflicting ideas and forces. He believed that conflict—especially class conflict—is necessary in order to produce social change and a better society. For Marx, the most important changes were economic. He concluded that the capitalist economic system was responsible for the overwhelming poverty that he observed in London at the beginning of the Industrial Revolution (Marx and Engels, 1967/1848).

In the Marxian framework, **class conflict is the struggle between the capitalist class and the working class**. The capitalist class, or ***bourgeoisie,*** **comprises those who own and control the means of production**. The ***means of production*** **refers to the tools, land, factories, and money for investment that form the economic basis of a society. The working class, or** *proletariat,* **comprises those who must sell their labour because they have no other means to earn a livelihood**. From Marx's viewpoint, the capitalist class controls and exploits the masses of struggling workers by paying less than the value of their labour. This exploitation results in workers' ***alienation—*** **a feeling of powerlessness and estrangement from other people and from oneself**. Marx predicted that the working class would become aware of its exploitation, overthrow the capitalists, and establish a free and classless society. Marx's social and economic analyses have inspired heated debates among generations of social scientists. Central to his view was the belief that societies should not only be studied but also be changed, because the *status quo* (the existing state of society) involved the oppression of most of the population by a small group of wealthy people. Those who believe that sociology should be value free are uncomfortable with Marx's advocacy of what some perceive to be radical social change. Scholars who examine society through the lens of race, gender, and class believe Marx's analysis places too much emphasis on class relations, often to the exclusion of issues regarding race/ethnicity and gender.

Max Weber German social scientist Max Weber (pronounced VAY-ber) (1864–1920) also was concerned about the changes brought about by the Industrial Revolution. Although he disagreed with Marx's idea that economics is *the* central force in social change, Weber acknowledged that economic interests are important in shaping human action. Even so, he thought that economic systems were heavily influenced by other factors in a society.

Unlike many early analysts, who believed that values could not be separated from the research process, Weber emphasized that sociology should be *value free*—research should be conducted in a scientific manner and should exclude the researcher's personal values and economic interests (Turner, Beeghley, and Powers, 1998). Weber realized, however, that social behaviour cannot be analyzed by the objective criteria that we use to measure such things as temperature and weight. Although he recognized that sociologists cannot be totally value free, Weber stressed that they should employ *ver stehen* (German for "understanding" or "insight") to gain the ability to see the world as others see it.

Weber was concerned that large-scale organizations (bureaucracies) were becoming increasingly oriented toward routine administration and a specialized division of labour, which he believed were destructive to human vitality and freedom. As we will see in Chapter 5, Weber's work on bureaucracy has had a far-reaching impact.

The Development of Sociology in North America

The first department of sociology in the United States was established at the University of Chicago, in 1892. Robert E. Park (1864–1944), an original member of the "Chicago School," assisted in the development of the sociology of urban life. George Herbert Mead (1863–1931), a sociologist and social psychologist, became one of the best-known members of the Chicago School and was the founder of the symbolic interaction perspective.

Jane Addams (1860–1935) is one of the best-known early female sociologists. She actively engaged in sociological endeavours throughout her career. Although Addams was awarded a Nobel Peace Prize for her contributions to the field of social work and her assistance to the underprivileged, her sociological work was not acknowledged until recently.

The second department of sociology in the United States was founded by W.E.B. Du Bois (1868–1963) at Atlanta University. Du Bois's classic work, *The Philadelphia Negro: A Social Study* (1967/1899), was based on his research into Philadelphia's African-American community and stressed the strengths and weaknesses of a community wrestling with overwhelming social problems.

The first sociology department in Canada was established in 1925, at McGill University in Montreal and remained the only sociology department until the early 1960s. Other Canadian universities offered sociology courses through other departments, particularly history and economics. The University of Toronto focused on how issues of political and economic history affected Canadian society. The works of Harold A. Innis and S.D. Clark laid the groundwork for the political-economy perspective, which is central to Canadian sociology today.

During the 1970s, pressure was put on Canadian universities to hire sociologists trained in Canada. As a result, graduate programs across Canada were developed and expanded, and a unique Canadian sociology was developed.

CONTEMPORARY THEORETICAL PERSPECTIVES

Given the many and varied ideas and trends that influenced the development of sociology, how do contemporary sociologists view society? Some see it as a stable and ongoing entity; others view it in terms of many groups competing for scarce resources; still others describe it as based on the everyday, routine interactions among individuals. Each of these views represents a method of examining the same phenomena. Each is based on general ideas as to how social life is organized and represents an effort to link specific observations in a meaningful way. Each utilizes *theory*—**a set of logically interrelated statements that attempts to describe, explain, and (occasionally) predict social events**. Each theory helps interpret reality in a distinct way by providing a framework in which observations may be logically ordered. Sociologists refer to this theoretical framework as a *perspective*—**an overall approach to or viewpoint on some subject**. The major theoretical

Many Canadians work in large-scale bureaucracies, which Max Weber famously analyzed nearly 100 years ago.

perspectives that have emerged in sociology are the functionalist, conflict, feminist, and symbolic interactionist perspectives. Other perspectives such as postmodernism, have emerged and gained acceptance among some social thinkers more recently. These perspectives will be used throughout this book to show you how sociologists try to understand many of the issues affecting Canadian society.

Functionalist Perspectives

Functionalist perspectives **are based on the assumption that society is a stable, orderly system**. This stable system is characterized by **societal consensus, whereby the majority of members share a common set of values, beliefs, and behavioural expectations**. According to this perspective, a society comprises interrelated parts, each of which serves a function and (ideally) contributes to the overall stability of the society. Societies develop social structures, or institutions, which persist because they play a part in helping society survive. These institutions include the family, education, government, religion, and the economy. If anything adverse happens to one of these institutions or parts, all other parts are affected and the system no longer functions properly. As Durkheim noted, rapid social change and a more specialized division of labour produce *strains* in society that lead to a breakdown in these traditional institutions.

Talcott Parsons (1902–79), perhaps the most influential contemporary advocate of the functionalist perspective, stressed that all societies must make provisions for meeting social needs in order to survive. Parsons (1955) suggested, for example, that a division of labour (distinct, specialized functions) between husband and wife is essential for family stability and social order. The husband/father performs the *instrumental tasks,* which involve leadership and decision-making responsibilities in the home and employment outside the home to support the family. The wife/mother is responsible for the *expressive tasks,* including housework, caring for the children, and providing emotional support for the entire family. Parsons believed that other institutions, including school, church, and government, must function to assist the family and that all institutions must work together to preserve the system over time (Parsons, 1955).

Functionalism was refined further by Robert K. Merton (b. 1910), who distinguished between manifest and latent functions of social institutions. *Manifest functions* **are intended or overtly recognized by the participants in a social unit**. In contrast, *latent functions* **are unintended functions that are hidden and remain unacknowledged by participants**. For example, a manifest function of education is the transmission of knowledge and skills from one generation to the next; a latent function is the establishment of social relations and networks. Merton noted that not all features of a social system might be functional at all times; *dysfunctions* **are the undesirable consequences of any element of a society**. A dysfunction of education can be the perpetuation of gender, racial, and class inequalities. Such dysfunctions may threaten the capacity of a society to adapt and survive (Merton, 1968).

Conflict Perspectives

According to *conflict perspectives,* **groups in society are engaged in a continuous power struggle for control of scarce resources**. Conflict may take the form of politics, litigation, negotiations, or family discussions about financial matters. Marx and Weber contributed significantly to this perspective by focusing on the inevitability of clashes between social groups. Today, advocates of the conflict perspective view social life as a continuous power struggle among competing social groups.

As previously discussed, Marx focused on the exploitation and oppression of the proletariat (the workers) by the bourgeoisie (the owners or capitalist class). Weber recognized the importance of economic conditions in producing inequality and conflict in society, but added *power* and *prestige* as other sources of inequality. He defined *power* as the ability of a person within a social relationship to carry out his or her own will despite resistance from others and *prestige* as a positive or negative social estimation of honour (Weber, 1968/1922).

C. Wright Mills (1916–62), a key figure in the development of contemporary conflict theory, encouraged sociologists to get involved in social reform. He contended that value-free sociology was impossible because social scientists must make value-related choices—including the topics they investigate and the theoretical approaches they adopt. Mills encouraged us to look beneath everyday events to observe the major resource and power inequalities that exist in society. He believed that the most important decisions are made largely behind the scenes by the ***power elite*—a small clique comprising top business, political, and military officials**. Mills's power-elite theory is discussed in Chapter 13.

Feminist Perspectives

In the past several decades, feminists have radically transformed the discipline of sociology. Feminist theory first emerged as a critique of traditional sociological theory and methodology. The primary criticism was that sociology did not acknowledge the experiences of women. Written by men, sociology involved the study of men and not humankind, much less women; sociology examined only half of social reality (Fox, 1989). Feminist scholar Dorothy Smith (1974) argued that sociological methods, concepts, and analyses were products of the "male social universe." If women appeared at all, it was as men saw them and not as women saw themselves. In this way, feminist sociologists argued, sociology actually contributed to the subordination and exploitation of women (Anderson, 1996). The first task of feminist sociology was to provide the missing half of social reality by generating research and theory "by, for, and about women" (Smith, 1987). In doing so, feminist sociology brought the personal problems of women, including violence against women, the poverty of women, and the invisibility of women's reproductive labour, into the public forum.

***Feminist perspectives* focus on the significance of gender in understanding and explaining inequalities that exist between men and women in the household, in the paid labour force, and in the realms of politics, law, and culture** (Armstrong and Armstrong, 1994; Luxton, 1995; Marshall, 1995). Feminism is not one single unified approach. Rather, there are different approaches among feminist writers, namely the liberal, radical, and socialist strains (discussed in Chapter 10). Feminist sociology incorporates both microlevel and macrolevel analyses in studying the experiences of women. For example, some feminist theorists, such as Margrit Eichler, have used a structural approach to explain how gender inequality is created and maintained in a society dominated by men (Armstrong and Armstrong, 1994; Eichler, 1988b). Other feminist research has focused on the interpersonal relationships between men and women in terms of verbal and nonverbal communication styles, attitudes, and values in explaining the dynamics of power and social control in the private sphere (Mackie, 1995). All of these approaches share the belief that "women and men are equal and should be equally valued as well as have equal rights" (Basow, 1992). According to feminists (including many men as well as women), we live in a *patriarchy,* a hierarchical system of power in which males possess greater

Margrit Eichler

economic and social privilege than females (Saunders, 1999). Feminist perspectives assume that gender roles are socially created rather than determined by one's biological inheritance, and that change is essential for people to achieve their human potential without limits based on gender. Feminism assumes that society reinforces social expectations through social learning: what we learn is a social product of the political and economic structure of the society in which we live (Renzetti and Curran, 1995). Feminists argue that women's subordination can end only after a patriarchal system of male dominance is replaced with a more egalitarian one.

Symbolic Interactionist Perspectives

Conflict and the functional perspectives have been criticized for focusing primarily on macrolevel analysis. A ***macrolevel analysis* examines whole societies, large-scale social structures, and social systems** instead of looking at important social dynamics in individuals' lives. Symbolic interactionism fills this void by examining people's day-to-day interactions and their behaviour in groups. Thus, symbolic interactionist approaches are based on a ***microlevel*** *analysis,* which focuses on small groups rather than large-scale social structures.

According to *symbolic interactionist perspectives,* society is the sum of the interactions of individuals and groups. Theorists using this perspective focus on the process of *interaction,* defined as immediate, reciprocally oriented communication between two or more people, and the part that *symbols* play in giving meaning to human communication. A *symbol* is anything that meaningfully represents something else. Examples of symbols include signs, gestures, written language, and shared values. Symbolic interaction occurs when people communicate through the use of symbols; for example, a gift of food—a cake or a casserole—to a newcomer in a neighbourhood is a symbol of welcome and friendship.

From this perspective, each person's interpretation or definition of a given situation becomes a *subjective reality* from that person's viewpoint. Individuals generally assume that their subjective reality is the same as that of others; however, this may be incorrect. Subjective reality is acquired and shared through agreed-on symbols, especially language. If a person shouts, "Fire!" in a crowded movie theatre, for example, that language produces the same response (alarm) in all of those who hear and understand it. When people in a group do not share the same meaning for a given symbol, however, confusion results; for example, people who did not know the meaning of the word *fire* would not know the reason for the commotion. How people interpret the messages they receive and the situations they encounter becomes their subjective reality and may strongly influence their behaviour.

Postmodern Perspectives

According to *postmodern perspectives,* existing theories have been unsuccessful in explaining social life in modern societies that are characterized by postindustrialization, consumerism, and global communications. Postmodern social theorists reject the theoretical perspectives we have previously discussed, as well as how the theories were created (Ritzer, 1996). These theorists oppose the grand narratives that characterize modern thinking and believe that boundaries should not be placed on academic disciplines—such as philosophy, literature, art, and the social sciences— where much could be learned by sharing ideas.

Just as functionalist, conflict, and symbolic interactionist perspectives emerged in the aftermath of the Industrial Revolution, postmodern theories emerged after World War II (in the late 1940s) and reflected the belief that some nations were entering a period of postindustrialization. Postmodern (or "postindustrial") societies are characterized by an *information explosion* and an economy in which large numbers of people either provide information or apply information, or are employed in service jobs (such as fast-food servers or health-care workers). There is a corresponding *rise of a consumer society* and the emergence of a *global village* in which people around the world communicate with one another by electronic technologies such as television, telephone, fax, e-mail, and the Internet.

Each of the sociological perspectives we have examined involves different assumptions. Consequently, each leads us to ask different questions and to view the world somewhat differently. Different aspects of reality are the focus of each approach. Although functionalism emphasizes social cohesion and order, conflict and feminist approaches focus primarily on social tension and change. In contrast, symbolic interactionism primarily examines people's interactions and shared meanings in everyday life. Concept Table 1.1 on page 16 reviews the major perspectives. Throughout this book, we will be using these perspectives as lenses through which to view our social world. You will see how sociologists use these perspectives to guide their research.

THE SOCIOLOGICAL RESEARCH PROCESS

Research is the process of systematically collecting information for the purposes of testing an existing theory or generating a new one. What is the relationship between sociological theory and research? The relationship between theory and research has been referred to as a continuous cycle, as shown in Figure 1.1 on page 16.

Not all sociologists conduct research in the same manner. Some primarily engage in quantitative research whereas others use qualitative research methods. With *quantitative research,* the goal is scientific objectivity, and the focus is on data that can be measured numerically. Quantitative research typically emphasizes complex statistical techniques. Most sociological studies on suicide have used quantitative research. They have compared rates of suicide with almost every conceivable variable, including age, sex, race/ethnicity, education, and even sports participation (see Lester, 1992) (Box 1.3 on page 17,

Concept Table 1.1	THE MAJOR THEORETICAL PERSPECTIVES	
PERSPECTIVE	**ANALYSIS LEVEL**	**NATURE OF SOCIETY**
Functionalist	Macrolevel	Society comprises interrelated parts that work together to maintain stability within society. This stability is threatened by dysfunctional acts and institutions.
Conflict	Macrolevel	Society is characterized by social inequality; social life is a struggle for scarce resources. Social arrangements benefit some groups at the expense of others.
Feminist	Macrolevel and microlevel	Society is based on patriarchy—a hierarchical system of power in which males possess greater economic and social privilege than females.
Symbolic Interactionist	Microlevel	Society is the sum of the interactions of people and groups. Behaviour is learned in interaction with other people; how people define a situation becomes the foundation for how they behave.
Postmodern	Macrolevel and microlevel	Societies characterized by postindustrialization, consumerism, and global communications bring into question existing assumptions about social life and the nature of reality.

explains how to read tables, how to interpret data, and how to draw conclusions.). One study examined the effects of church membership, divorce, and migration on suicide rates in the United States at various times between 1933 and 1980. It concluded that suicide rates were higher where divorce rates were higher, migration was higher, and church membership was lower (see Breault, 1986).

With *qualitative research,* interpretive description (words) rather than statistics (numbers) is

Figure 1.1	The Theory and Research Cycle

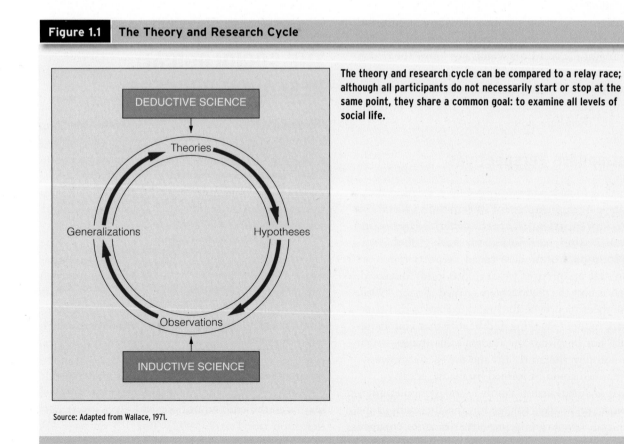

The theory and research cycle can be compared to a relay race; although all participants do not necessarily start or stop at the same point, they share a common goal: to examine all levels of social life.

Source: Adapted from Wallace, 1971.

BOX 1.3   CRITICAL THINKING

Understanding Statistical Data Presentations

Are men or women more likely to commit suicide? Are suicide rates increasing or decreasing? Such questions may be answered in numerical terms. Sociologists often use statistical tables as a concise way to present data because such tables convey a large amount of information in a relatively small space; the table below gives an example. To understand a table, follow these steps:

1. *Read the title.* The title indicates the topic. From the title, "Suicide Methods, by Sex, Population Aged 10 or Older, Canada, 1998," we learn that the table shows relationships between two variables: sex and method of suicide used. It also indicates that the table contains data for only individuals over the age of ten.

2. *Check the source and other explanatory notes.* In this case, the source is the *Canadian Vital Statistics Database.* Checking the source helps determine its reliability and timeliness. The first footnote provides additional statistical information. The asterisk footnote provides more information about exactly what is included in the "Other" category.

3. *Read the headings for each column and each row.* The column headings in the table are "Method," "Total," "Males," and "Females." These last three column headings are divided into two groups: number and percentage. The columns present information (usually numbers)

arranged vertically. The rows present information horizontally. Here, the row headings indicate suicide methods.

4. *Examine and compare the data.* To examine the data, determine what units of measurement have been used. In the table, the figures are numerical counts (e.g., the total number of reported female suicides by poisoning in 1998 was 319) and percentages (e.g., in 1998, poisoning accounted for 41.3 percent of all female suicides reported). A *percentage*, or proportion, shows how many of a given item there are in every 100. Percentages allow us to compare groups of different sizes. For example, percentages show the proportion of people who used each method, thus giving a more meaningful comparison.

5. *Draw conclusions.* By looking for patterns, some conclusions can be drawn from the table. Males complete suicide at much higher rates than do females. According to the table, males accounted for almost 80 percent of all suicides in 1998. Suffocation (which includes hanging or strangulation) is the most common means of suicide in Canada although, when broken down by sex, the most common method of suicide for females is poisoning (41 percent) and for males is suffocation (40 percent). We might also conclude from looking at the table that males tend to use more violent methods to commit suicide than do females.

SUICIDE METHODS, BY SEX, POPULATION AGED 10 OR OLDER, CANADA, 1998

METHOD (ICD-9 CODES)	TOTAL NUMBER	TOTAL %	MALES NUMBER	MALES %	FEMALES NUMBER	FEMALES %
Suffocation, total	1433	38.8	1171	40.0	262	33.9
Poisoning, total	965	26.1	646	22.1	319	41.3
Drugs and medication	487	13.2	246	8.4	241	31.2
Motor vehicle exhaust	269	7.3	229	7.8	40	5.2
Other carbon monoxide	164	4.4	135	4.6	29	3.8
Other/unspecified poisoning	45	1.2	36	1.2	9	1.2
Firearms	816	22.1	765	26.2	51	6.6
Jumping from high place	160	4.3	115	3.9	45	5.8
Drowning/submersion	122	3.3	79	2.7	43	5.6
Cutting/piercing instruments	59	1.6	48	1.6	11	1.4
Other/unspecified means*	143	3.9	101	3.5	42	5.4
Total suicide deaths	3698	100.0	2925	100.0	773	100.0

Data source: Canadian Vital Statistics Database

Note: Because of rounding, detail may not add to totals.

*Includes jumping or lying before moving objects, fires/burns, crashing of motor vehicle, other or unspecified means, late effects of self-inflicted injury, explosives.

used to analyze the underlying meanings and patterns of social relationships. An example of qualitative research is a study in which the researchers systematically analyzed the contents of suicide notes to determine recurring themes (such as feelings of despair or failure) and whether any patterns could be found that would help in understanding why people kill themselves (Leenaars, 1988).

The "Conventional" Research Model

Research models are tailored to the specific problem being investigated and to the focus of the researcher.

Both quantitative and qualitative research contribute to our knowledge of society and human social interaction, and involve a series of steps, as shown in Figure 1.2. We will now trace the steps in the "conventional" research model, which focuses on quantitative research. Then we will describe an alternative model that emphasizes qualitative research.

1. *Select and define the research problem.* Sometimes, a specific experience such as knowing someone who committed suicide can trigger your interest in a topic. Other times, you might select topics to fill gaps or challenge misconceptions in existing research or to test a specific theory (Babbie,

---

Figure 1.2 **Steps in Sociological Research**

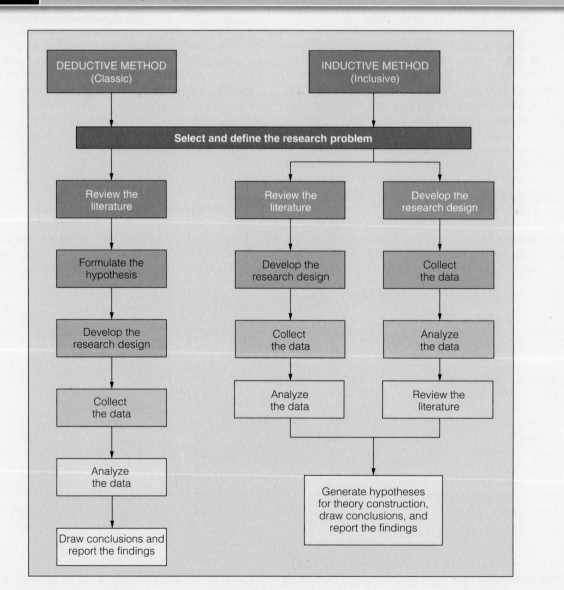

2004). Durkheim selected suicide because he wanted to demonstrate the importance of *society* with regard to what might appear to be arbitrary acts by individuals.

2. *Review previous research.* Before beginning the research, it is important to analyze what others have written about the topic. You should determine where gaps exist and note mistakes to avoid. When Durkheim began his study, very little sociological literature existed to review; however, he studied the works of several moral philosophers, including Henry Morselli (1975/1881).

3. *Formulate the hypothesis (if applicable).* You may formulate a *hypothesis*—a statement of the expected relationship between two or more variables. A **variable is any concept with measurable traits or characteristics that can change or vary from one person, time, situation, or society to another.** The most fundamental relationship in a hypothesis is between a dependent variable and one or more independent variables (see Figure 1.3). The *independent variable* is presumed to be the cause of the relationship; the *dependent variable* is assumed to be caused

| Figure 1.3 | Hypothesized Relationships Between Variables |

A. Causal relationship

PSYCHOLOGICAL

Depression → Suicide rate

"Depression causes suicide."

B. Inverse causal relationship (Durkheim)

SOCIOLOGICAL

Social integration → Suicide rate

"The lack of social integration causes suicide."

C. Multiple-cause explanation

Rate of social change

Poverty → Suicide rate

Religiosity

"Many factors interact to cause suicide."

A causal hypothesis connects one or more independent (causal) variables with a dependent (affected) variable. The diagram illustrates three hypotheses about the causes of suicide. To test these hypotheses, social scientists would need to operationalize the variables (define them in measurable terms) and then investigate whether the data support the proposed explanation.

by the independent variable(s) (Babbie, 2004). Durkheim's hypothesis stated that the rate of suicide varies *inversely* with the degree of social integration. In other words, a low degree of social integration (the independent variable) may "cause" or "be related to" a high rate of suicide (the dependent variable).

Not all social research uses hypotheses. If you plan to conduct an explanatory study (showing a cause-and-effect relationship), you likely will want to formulate one or more hypotheses to test theories. If you plan to conduct a descriptive study, however, you will be less likely to formulate hypotheses, since you may desire only to describe social reality or provide facts.

4. *Develop the research design.* You must determine the unit of analysis to be used in the study. A *unit of analysis is what* or *whom* is being studied (Babbie, 2004). In social science research, individuals, social groups (such as families, cities, or geographic regions), organizations (such as clubs, labour unions, or political parties), and social artifacts (such as books, paintings, or weddings) may be units of analysis. Durkheim's unit of analysis was social groups, not individuals, because he believed that the study of individual cases of suicide would not explain the rates of suicide in various European countries.

5. *Collect the data.* You must decide what population will be observed or questioned and then carefully select a sample. A *sample* is the people who are selected from the population to be studied; the sample should accurately represent the larger population. A *representative sample* is a selection from a larger population that has the essential characteristics of the total population. For example, if you interviewed five students selected haphazardly from your sociology class, they would not be representative of your school's total student body. By contrast, if you selected five students from the total student body by a random sample, they would be closer to being representative (although a random sample of five students would be too small to yield much useful data).

Validity and reliability may be problems in research. **Validity** **is the extent to which a study or research instrument accurately measures what it is supposed to measure**. A recurring issue in studies that analyze the relationship between religious beliefs and suicide is whether "church membership" is an accurate indicator of a person's religious beliefs. In fact, one person

may be very religious yet not belong to a specific church, whereas another person may be a member of a church yet not hold deep religious beliefs. **Reliability** **is the extent to which a study or research instrument yields consistent results** when applied to different individuals at one time or to the same individuals over time. Sociologists have found that different interviewers get different answers from the people being interviewed. For example, how might the interviewers themselves influence the interviews with university students who have contemplated suicide?

6. *Analyze the data.* Once you have collected your data, it must be analyzed. *Analysis* is the process through which data are organized so that comparisons can be made and conclusions drawn. Sociologists use many techniques to analyze data. After collecting data from vital statistics for approximately 26 000 suicides, Durkheim analyzed his data according to four distinctive categories of suicide. *Egoistic suicide* occurs among people who are isolated from any social group. By contrast, *altruistic suicide* occurs among individuals who are excessively integrated into society (e.g., military leaders who kill themselves after defeat in battle). *Anomic suicide* results from a lack of social regulation, whereas *fatalistic suicide* results from excessive regulation and oppressive discipline (e.g., in slaves).

7. *Draw conclusions and report the findings.* After analyzing the data, your first step in drawing conclusions is to return to your hypothesis or research objective to clarify how the data relate both to the hypothesis and to the larger issues being addressed. At this stage, you note the limitations of the study, such as problems with the sample, the influence of variables over which you had no control, or variables that your study was unable to measure.

Reporting the findings is the final stage. A report generally includes a review of each step taken in the research process in order to make the study available for *replication*—the repetition of the investigation in substantially the same way that it was originally conducted. Social scientists generally present their findings in papers at professional meetings and publish them in technical journals and books. In reporting his findings in *Suicide* (1964b/1897), Durkheim concluded that the suicide rate of a group is a social fact that cannot be explained in terms of the personality traits of individuals.

We have traced the steps in the "conventional" research process (based on deduction and quantitative research). But what steps might be taken in an alternative approach based on induction and qualitative research?

The Qualitative Research Model

Although the same underlying logic is involved in both quantitative and qualitative sociological research, the *styles* of these two models are very different (King, Keohane, and Verba, 1994). As previously stated, qualitative research is more likely to be used when the research question does not easily lend itself to numbers and statistical methods. As compared to a quantitative model, a qualitative approach often involves a different type of research question and a smaller number of cases.

How might qualitative research be used to study suicidal behaviour? In studying different rates of suicide between women and men, for example, Silvia Canetto (1992) questioned whether existing theories and quantitative research provided an adequate explanation for gender differences in suicidal behaviour and decided that she would explore alternative explanations. Analyzing previous research, Canetto learned that most studies linked suicidal behaviour in women to problems in their personal relationships, particularly with men. By contrast, most studies of men's suicides focused on their performance and found that men are more likely to be suicidal when

their self-esteem and independence are threatened. According to Canetto's analysis, gender differences in suicidal behaviour are more closely associated with beliefs about the cultural expectations for men and women rather than purely interpersonal crises.

As in Canetto's study, researchers using a qualitative approach may engage in *problem formulation* to clarify the research question and to formulate questions of concern and interest to people participating in the research (Reinharz, 1992). To create a research design for Canetto's study, we might start with the proposition that studies have attributed women's and men's suicidal behaviour to the wrong causes. Next, we might decide to interview individuals who have attempted suicide. Our research design might develop a collaborative approach in which the participants are brought into the research-design process, not just treated as passive objects to be studied (Reinharz, 1992).

Although Canetto did not gather data in her study, she re-evaluated existing research, concluding that alternative explanations of women's and men's suicidal behaviour are justified from existing data.

In a qualitative approach, the next step is collecting and analyzing data to assess the validity of the starting proposition. Data gathering is the foundation of the research. Researchers pursuing a qualitative approach tend to gather data in natural settings, such as where the person lives or works, rather than in a laboratory or other research setting. Data collection and analysis frequently occur concurrently, and the analysis draws heavily on the language of the persons studied, not the researcher.

Computer-assisted telephone interviewing is an easy and cost-efficient method of conducting research. The widespread use of cell phones, voice mail, and Caller ID is now making telephone surveys more difficult to conduct.

RESEARCH METHODS

How do sociologists know which research method to use? Which method is best for a particular problem? **Research methods are strategies or techniques for systematically conducting research.** We will look at four of these methods: surveys, analysis of existing statistical data, field studies, and experiments.

Surveys

A **survey is a poll in which the researcher gathers facts or attempts to determine the relationships among facts.** Survey research is the method of data collection most often associated with the discipline of sociology. Researchers frequently select a representative sample (a small group of respondents) from a larger population (the total group of people) to answer questions about their attitudes, opinions, or behaviour. The Gallup and Angus Reid polls are among the most widely known large-scale surveys. Government agencies such as Statistics Canada conduct a variety of surveys as well. Unlike many polls that use various methods of gaining a representative sample of the larger population, Statistics Canada censuses attempt to gain information from all persons in Canada. Surveys are an important research method in sociology because they make it possible to study things that are not directly observable—such as people's attitudes and beliefs—and to describe a population too large to observe directly (Babbie, 1995).

Survey data are collected by using questionnaires, and interviews. A **questionnaire is a printed research instrument containing a series of items to which subjects respond.** Items are often in the form of statements with which the respondent is asked to "agree" or "disagree." Questionnaires may be administered by interviewers in face-to-face encounters or by telephone, but the most commonly used technique is the *self-administered questionnaire.* The questionnaires typically are mailed or delivered to respondents' homes; however, they also may be administered to groups of respondents gathered at the same place at the same time.

Survey data may also be collected by interviews. An **interview is a data-collection encounter in which an interviewer asks the respondent questions and records the answers.** Survey research often uses *structured interviews,* in which the interviewer asks questions from a standardized questionnaire. Structured interviews tend to produce uniform or replicable data that can be elicited time after time by different interviews.

Survey research is useful in describing the characteristics of a large population without having to interview each person in that population. In recent years, computer technology has enhanced our ability to do *multivariate analysis*—research involving more than two independent variables. For example, to assess the influence on religion on attempted suicidal behaviour among Canadians a research might look at the effects of age, sex, income level, and other variables all at once to determine which of these independent variables influences suicide the most or least and how influential each variable is relative to the others. However, a weakness of survey research is the use of standardized questions; this approach tends to force respondents into categories in which they may or may not belong. Moreover, survey research relies on self-reported information, and some people may be less than truthful, particularly on emotionally charged issues such as suicide. Some scholars have also criticized the way survey data are used. For example, survey statistics may overestimate or underestimate a problem such as homelessness, as shown in Table 1.1.

Table 1.1	STATISTICS: WHAT WE KNOW (AND DON'T KNOW)	
TOPIC	**HOMELESSNESS IN CANADA**	**SUICIDE IN CANADA**
Research Finding	The number of homeless people in Canada is between 150 000 and 300 000 (Human Resources and Skills Development Canada, 2010).	In 1998 approximately 3 700 Canadians committed suicide, an average of ten per day.
Possible Problem	That estimate is very broad. Does it underestimate the total number of homeless people?	Are suicide rates recorded in the official death certificates?
Explanation	The homeless are difficult to count because they do not have any place to stay. They may avoid interviews with census takers.	Suicides for children under ten are not recorded in Canada. Some "accidental deaths" may in fact be suicides.

Secondary Analysis of Existing Data

In *secondary analysis,* **researchers use existing material and analyze data originally collected by others**. Existing data sources include public records, official reports of organizations or governmental agencies, and surveys conducted by researchers in universities and private corporations. For example, Durkheim used vital statistics (death records) that were originally collected for other purposes to examine the relationships among variables such as age, marital status, and the circumstances surrounding the person's suicide.

One strength of secondary analysis is that data are readily available and are often inexpensive to obtain. Another is that, because the researcher often does not collect the data personally, the chances of bias may be reduced. In addition, the use of existing sources makes it possible to analyze longitudinal data to provide a historical context within which to locate original research. However, secondary analysis has inherent problems. For one thing, the data may be incomplete, inauthentic, or inaccurate.

Secondary analysis includes *content analysis—* **the systematic examination of cultural artifacts or various forms of communication to extract thematic data and draw conclusions about social life**. Among the materials studied are written records (such as books, diaries, poems, graffiti), narratives and visual texts (such as movies, television shows, advertisements, greeting cards), and material culture (such as music, art, even garbage). In content analysis, researchers look for regular patterns, such as the frequency of suicide as a topic on talk shows.

Field Research

Field research **is the study of social life in its natural setting: observing and interviewing people where they live, work, and play**. Some kinds of behaviour can be studied best by "being there"; a fuller understanding can be developed through observations, face-to-face discussions, and participation in events. Researchers use these methods to generate *qualitative* data: observations that are best described verbally rather than numerically.

Sociologists who are interested in observing social interaction as it occurs may use *participant observation—* **the process of collecting systematic observations while being part of the activities of the group they are studying**. Participant observation generates more "inside" information than simply asking questions or observing from the outside. As William Whyte noted in his classic participant-observation study of a low-income Boston neighbourhood: "As I sat and listened, I learned the answers to questions I would not have had the sense to ask" (1988, 43).

Another approach to field research is *ethnography,* **a detailed study of the life and activities of a group of people by researchers who may live with that group over a period of years** (Feagin, Orum, and Sjoberg, 1991). Unlike participant observation, ethnographic studies typically take place over much longer periods. For example, researcher Daniel Wolf (1992) studied an outlaw biker gang in Edmonton, the Rebels, by hanging out and riding with them for more than a year. The results, published in a book titled *The Rebels: A Brotherhood of Outlaw Bikers,* provide some of the most comprehensive information on the inside workings of motorcycle gangs available to date.

Experiments

An *experiment* **is a carefully designed situation in which the researcher studies the impact of certain variables on subjects' attitudes or behaviour**. Experiments are designed to create "real life" situations, ideally under controlled circumstances, in which the influence of different variables can be modified and measured. Conventional experiments require that subjects be divided into two groups: an experimental group and a control group. The *experimental group* **contains the subjects who are exposed to an independent variable** (the experimental condition) to study its effect on them. The *control group* **contains the subjects who are not exposed to the independent variable**. For example, one experiment examined the effects of media violence and depictions of suicide on attitudes toward suicide by showing one group of subjects (an experimental group) a film about suicide.

Researchers may use experiments when they want to demonstrate that a cause-and-effect relationship exists between variables. To show that a change in one variable causes a change in another, these three conditions must be satisfied:

1. A correlation between the two variables must be shown to exist (**a** *correlation* **exists when two variables are associated more frequently than could be expected by chance**).
2. The independent variable must have occurred before the dependent variable.
3. Any change in the dependent variable must not have been due to an extraneous variable—that is, one outside the stated hypothesis.

The major advantage of the controlled experiment is the researcher's control over the environment and the ability to isolate the experimental variable. Since many experiments require relatively little time and money and can be conducted with limited numbers of subjects, it is possible for researchers to replicate an experiment several times by using different groups of subjects (Babbie, 1995). Replication strengthens claims about the validity and generalizability of the original research findings. Perhaps the greatest limitation of experiments is that they are artificial. Social processes that occur in a laboratory setting often do not occur in the same way in real-life settings.

ETHICAL ISSUES IN SOCIOLOGICAL RESEARCH

The study of people ("human subjects") raises vital questions about ethical concerns in sociological research. Because of past abuses, researchers are now bound by a professional code of ethics to weigh the societal benefits of research against potential physical and emotional costs to participants. Researchers are required to obtain written "informed consent" statements from the persons they study. However, these guidelines have produced many new questions, such as, What constitutes "informed consent"? What constitutes harm to a person? How do researchers protect the identity and confidentiality of their sources?

The Canadian Sociology and Anthropology Association has outlined the basic standards sociologists must follow in conducting research. Participation in research must be voluntary. No one should be enticed, coerced, or forced to participate. Researchers must not harm the research subjects in any way—physically, psychologically, or personally. Researchers must respect the rights of research subjects to anonymity and confidentiality. A respondent is *anonymous* when the researcher cannot identify a given response with a given respondent. Anonymity is often extremely important when obtaining information on "deviant" or illegal activities. For example, in a study on physician-assisted suicides conducted by the Manitoba Association of Rights and Liberties (Searles, 1995), ensuring the anonymity of the physicians responding to the survey was crucial because the doctors were being asked about their participation in illegal acts.

Maintaining *confidentiality* means that the researcher is able to identify a given person's responses with that person but promises to hold the information in confidence or keeps it secret from the public. Researchers may provide anonymity without confidentiality, and vice versa, although typically they go together (Neuman et al., 2004). Whether the researcher should reveal his or her identity is also a difficult issue. In some cases, it is useful to identify yourself as a researcher to obtain cooperation from respondents. However, there are other instances when revealing your identity can affect the content and quality of your research. Researchers also have an obligation to report all of their research findings in full, including unexpected or negative findings and limitations of the research.

Sociologists are committed to adhering to these ethical considerations and to protecting research participants; however, many ethical issues arise in

The social chaos of this scene of looting following the 2010 earthquakes in Haiti may be a "living laboratory" for sociologists. Field researchers would suggest that the situation could be best understood by being there and experiencing the situation with the people involved.

Lucas Oleniuk/GetStock.com

conducting research. For example, is it ethical to give students extra marks in a course if they participate in an experiment? Is it ethical to persuade institutionalized young offenders to be interviewed about their crimes by offering payment? Different researchers might make different judgments concerning these issues.

How honest do researchers have to be with potential participants? Where does the "right to know" end and the "right to privacy" begin? Let's look at a specific case.

The Humphreys Research   Laud Humphreys (1970) studied homosexuality for his doctoral dissertation. His research focused on homosexual acts between strangers meeting in "tearooms," public restrooms in parks. He did not ask permission of his subjects, nor did he inform them that they were being studied. Instead, he took advantage of the typical tearoom encounter, which involved three men: two who engaged in homosexual acts, and a third who kept a lookout for police and unwelcome strangers. To conduct his study, Humphreys showed up at public restrooms that were known to be tearooms and offered to be the lookout. Then he systematically recorded details of the encounters that took place.

Humphreys was interested in the fact that the tearoom participants seemed to live "normal" lives apart from these encounters, and he decided to learn more about their everyday lives. To determine who they were, he wrote down their car licence numbers and tracked down their names and addresses. Later, he arranged for these men to be included in a medical survey so that he could go out and personally interview them. He wore different disguises and drove a different car so that they would not recognize him.

Humphreys's award-winning study, *Tearoom Trade* (1970), dispelled many myths about homosexual behaviour; however, the controversy surrounding his study has never been resolved. Do you think Humphreys's research was ethical? Would these men willingly have agreed to participate in Humphreys's research if he had identified himself as a researcher? What psychological harm might have come to these men if people, outside those involved in the encounters, knew about their homosexual behaviour?

In this chapter, we have looked at the research process and the methods used to pursue sociological knowledge. We also have critiqued many of the existing approaches and suggested alternative ways of pursuing research. The important thing to realize is that research is the lifeblood of sociology. Without research, sociologists would be unable to test existing theories and develop new ones. Research takes us beyond commonsense and provides opportunities for us to use our sociological imagination to generate new knowledge.

Our challenge today is to understand how to determine what is useful for enhancing our knowledge, to find new ways to integrate knowledge and action, and to encourage the inclusion of all people in the research process. This inclusion would be on two levels: (1) as active participants in research, to give voice to previously excluded people's experiences, and (2) as researchers, to help fill some of the gaps in our existing knowledge of how the research process is shaped by the gender, race, class, and sexual orientation of the researcher and by the broader social and cultural context (Cancian, 1992).

CHAPTER REVIEW

What is the sociological imagination?

According to C. Wright Mills, the sociological imagination helps us understand how seemingly personal troubles, such as suicide, actually are related to larger social forces. It is the ability to see the relationship between individual experience and the larger society.

What is sociology and how can it help us to understand ourselves and others?

Sociology is the systematic study of human society and social interaction. We study sociology to understand how individual behaviour is largely shaped by the groups to which we belong and the society in which we live. Sociology also makes us aware of global interdependence.

What factors contributed to the emergence of sociology as a discipline?

Industrialization and urbanization increased rapidly in the late 18th century, and social thinkers began to examine the consequences of these powerful forces.

What are the major contributions of the early sociologists Durkheim, Marx, and Weber?

The ideas of Émile Durkheim, Karl Marx, and Max Weber helped lead the way to contemporary sociology. Durkheim argued that societies are built on social facts, that rapid social change produces strains in society, and that the loss of shared values and purpose can lead to a condition of anomie. Marx stressed that within society there is a continuous clash between the owners of the means of production and the workers who have no choice but to sell their labour to others. According to Weber, it is necessary to acknowledge the meanings that individuals attach to their own actions.

What are the major contemporary sociological perspectives?

Functionalist perspectives assume that society is a stable, orderly system characterized by societal consensus. Conflict perspectives argue that society is a continuous power struggle among competing groups, often based on class, race, ethnicity, or gender. Feminist perspectives focus on the significance of gender in understanding and explaining inequalities that exist between men and women in the household, in the paid labour force, and in politics, law, and culture. Symbolic interactionist perspectives focus on how people make sense of their everyday social interactions, which are made possible by the use of mutually understood symbols. Postmodern theorists believe that entirely new ways of examining social life are needed and that it is time to move beyond functionalist, conflict, and symbolic interactionist perspectives.

How does quantitative research differ from qualitative research?

Quantitative research focuses on data that can be measured numerically (comparing rates of suicide, for example). Qualitative research uses interpretive description rather than statistics to analyze underlying meanings and patterns of social relationships.

What are the key steps in a conventional research process?

A conventional research process based on deduction and the quantitative approach has these key steps: (1) selecting and defining the research problem, (2) reviewing previous research, (3) formulating the hypothesis, which involves constructing variables, (4) developing the research design, (5) collecting data, (6) analyzing the data, and (7) drawing conclusions and reporting the findings.

What steps are typically taken by researchers using the qualitative approach?

A researcher taking the qualitative approach might (1) formulate the problem to be studied instead of creating a hypothesis, (2) collect and analyze the data, and (3) report the results.

What are the major sociological research methods?

Research methods are systematic techniques for conducting research. Through experiments, researchers study the impact of certain variables on their subjects. Surveys are polls used to gather facts about people's attitudes, opinions, or behaviours; a representative sample of respondents provides data through questionnaires or interviews. In secondary analysis, researchers analyze existing data, such as a census, or cultural artifacts, such as a personal diary. In field research, sociologists study social life in its natural setting through participant and complete observation, case studies, unstructured interviews, and ethnography.

KEY TERMS

WEB LINKS

For more Web links related to the topic of this chapter, see the Nelson sociology website:
www.sociologyessentials5e.nelson.com

The website for Statistics Canada's Data Liberation Initiative gives you access to other Statistics Canada data as well as providing links to statistical agencies in many other parts of the world:
www.statcan.ca/english/Dli/dli.htm

The code of ethics that applies to all Canadian universities can be accessed at:
www.pre.ethics.gc.ca/english/ policystatement/context.cfm

One of Canada's leading social research organizations is the Institute for Social Research at York University:
www.isr.yorku.ca

QUESTIONS FOR CRITICAL THINKING

1. What does C. Wright Mills mean when he says the sociological imagination helps us "to grasp history and biography and the relations between the two within society" (Mills, 1959:6)?

2. As a sociologist, how would you remain objective and yet see the world as others see it? Would you make subjective decisions when trying to understand the perspectives of others?

3. Early social thinkers were concerned about stability in times of rapid change. In our more global world, is stability still a primary goal? Or is constant conflict important for the well-being of all humans? Use the conflict and functionalist perspectives to support your analysis.

4. The agency that funds the local suicide clinic has asked you to study the clinic's effectiveness in preventing suicide. What would you need to measure? What can you measure? What research method(s) would provide the best data for analysis?

ONLINE STUDY AND RESEARCH TOOLS

INFOTRAC®

InfoTrac College Edition is included free with every new copy of this text. Explore this online library for additional readings, review, and a handy resource for assignments. Visit **www.infotrac-college.com** to access this online database of full-text articles. Enter the key terms from this chapter to start your search.

CENGAGENOW™ CENGAGENOW

Use CengageNOW™ to help you formulate a customized study plan for this chapter. After you take the Diagnostic Quiz, CengageNOW™ will generate a customized study plan for you. It will identify sections of the chapter you should review.

Culture and Society in a Changing World

Crown attorney Rupert Ross describes the difficulties he had in learning to understand and accept the cultural traditions of the Ojibway. According to Ross, this story demonstrates how easy it is to misread people who have a "different understanding" of the world (1996:51):

My own cultural eyes have often tricked me into seeing things that Aboriginal people did not—or completely missing things they thought too obvious to point out. One of the most significant came one day when I was having coffee with an Ojibway friend. I asked her about something I often saw in the North: older couples walking along with the man twelve paces out in front, his wife bringing up the rear. I asked her how that behaviour fit with what I was being taught about equality between men and women in traditional times. She laughed, then said something like "Rupert, Rupert, that's only your eyes again! You have to look at it the way we do!"

She began by asking me to remember where those old people had spent their lives,

to imagine walking a narrow trail through the bush with my own family.

She asked me to think about who I would prefer to have out in front, my wife or myself, to be the first to face whatever dangers the bush presented. In one way, she said, it could be compared to wartime. "Where," she asked, "do you put your general? Are they out in front or are they in the rear, where they have time to see and plan and react?"

Viewed in that way, things appeared to be the opposite of what I had first supposed. Instead of occupying an inferior position, the woman was seen as the organizer and director, while the man out front was counted on for his capacity to take action under her direction. Instead of remembering the bush context in which they had lived their lives, I had put them in my own urban context where such a formation might indicate the opposite. "So," I said, "she's really the general and her husband is just the footsoldier!"

There was a pause then, and she chuckled again, shaking her head. "Not really," she said. "The problem is . . . you see everything in terms of hierarchies, don't you? Why do you do that?" . . . She tried to express her way then, the way she understood from the teaching of her people. In those teachings, all things have a purpose, and unless these are fulfilled, the strength of the whole is weakened. The jobs of the husband and of the wife were just that, their jobs, assumed on the basis of their having different skills and capacities—different *gifts*—none of which had to be compared with each other in terms of worth or importance. Comparison itself was seen as a strange thing to do.

As she spoke, I was flooded with recollections of other events that raised the issue of our Western dependence on hierarchies of worth and power. (Ross, 1996:52–53)

Source: Reprinted by permission of Corporate Administration, University of Saskatchewan.

To what extent does our own culture "blind" us—that is, keep us from understanding, accepting, or learning from other cultures? Is intolerance toward "outsiders"—people who are viewed as being different from one's own group or

Chapter Focus Question: What part does culture play in shaping people and the social relations in which they participate?

What are the essential components of culture?

How do subcultures and countercultures reflect diversity within a society?

How do the various sociological perspectives view culture?

way of life—accepted by some people in Canada? As our world appears to grow increasingly smaller because of rapid transportation, global communications, and international business transactions and political alliances—and sometimes because of hostility, terrorism, and warfare—learning about cultural diversity, within our own nation and globally, is extremely important for our individual and collective well-being. Although the world's population shares a common humanity, and perhaps some components of culture, cultural differences pose crucial barriers to our understanding of others. Sociology provides us with a framework for examining and developing a greater awareness of culture and cultural diversity, and how cultures change over time and place.

What is culture? Why is it so significant to our personal identities? What happens when others are intolerant of our culture? **Culture is the knowledge, language, values, customs, and material objects that are passed from person to person and from one generation to the next in a human group or society.** As previously defined, a society is a large social grouping that occupies the same geographic territory and is subject to the same political authority and dominant cultural expectations. While a society is made up of people, a culture is made up of ideas, behaviour, and material possessions. Society and culture are interdependent; neither could exist without the other.

If we look across the cultures of various nations, we may see opportunities for future cooperation based on our shared beliefs, values, and attitudes, or we may see potential for lack of understanding, discord, and conflict based on divergent ideas and worldviews. In this chapter, we examine society and culture, with special attention to the components of culture and the relationship between cultural change and diversity. We will also analyze culture from functionalist, conflict, symbolic interactionist, and postmodern perspectives. Before reading on, test your

knowledge about altruism by answering the questions in Box 2.1.

CULTURE AND SOCIETY IN A CHANGING WORLD

How important is culture in determining how people think and act on a daily basis? Simply stated, culture is essential for our individual survival and our communication with other people. We rely on culture because we are not born with the information we need to survive. We do not know how to take care of ourselves, how to behave, how to dress, what to eat, which gods to worship, or how to make or spend money. We must learn about culture through interaction, observation, and imitation to participate as members of the group. Sharing a common culture with others simplifies day-to-day interactions. However, we must also understand other cultures and the worldviews therein.

Just as culture is essential for individuals, it is also fundamental for the survival of societies. Culture has been described as "the common denominator that makes the actions of individuals intelligible to the group" (Haviland, 1993:30). Some system of rule making and enforcement necessarily exists in all societies. What would happen, for example, if *all* rules and laws in Canada suddenly disappeared? At a basic level, we need rules to navigate our bicycles and cars through traffic. At a more abstract level, we need laws to establish and protect our rights.

To survive, societies need rules about civility and tolerance toward others. We are not born knowing how to express kindness or hatred toward others, although some people may say, "Well, that's just human nature," when explaining someone's behaviour. Such a statement is built on the assumption that what we do as human beings is determined by

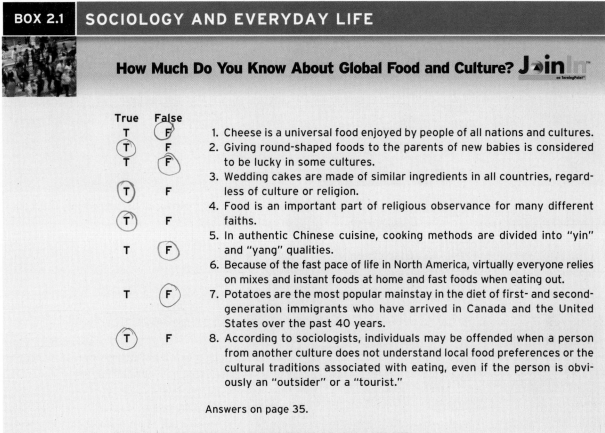

SOCIOLOGY AND EVERYDAY LIFE

How Much Do You Know About Global Food and Culture? Join In

True	False	
T	(F)	1. Cheese is a universal food enjoyed by people of all nations and cultures.
(T)	F	2. Giving round-shaped foods to the parents of new babies is considered to be lucky in some cultures.
T	(F)	3. Wedding cakes are made of similar ingredients in all countries, regardless of culture or religion.
(T)	F	4. Food is an important part of religious observance for many different faiths.
(T)	F	5. In authentic Chinese cuisine, cooking methods are divided into "yin" and "yang" qualities.
T	(F)	6. Because of the fast pace of life in North America, virtually everyone relies on mixes and instant foods at home and fast foods when eating out.
T	(F)	7. Potatoes are the most popular mainstay in the diet of first- and second-generation immigrants who have arrived in Canada and the United States over the past 40 years.
(T)	F	8. According to sociologists, individuals may be offended when a person from another culture does not understand local food preferences or the cultural traditions associated with eating, even if the person is obviously an "outsider" or a "tourist."

Answers on page 35.

Sources: Based on Better Health Channel, 2007; Ohio State University, 2007; and PBS, 2005a.

nature (our biological and genetic makeup) rather than *nurture* (our social environment)—that is, that our behaviour is instinctive. An *instinct* is a biologically determined behaviour pattern common to all members of a species that predictably occurs whenever certain environmental conditions exist. For example, spiders do not learn to build webs. They build webs because of instincts that are triggered by basic biological needs such as protection and reproduction.

Humans do not have instincts. What we most often think of as instinctive behaviour can be attributed to reflexes and drives. A *reflex* is a biologically determined involuntary response to some physical stimulus (such as a sneeze after breathing some pepper through the nose or the blinking of an eye when a speck of dust gets in it). *Drives* are biologically determined impulses common to all members of a species that satisfy needs such as sleep, food, water, or sexual gratification. Reflexes and drives do not determine how people will behave in human societies; even the expression of these biological characteristics is channelled by culture. For example, we may be taught that the "appropriate" way to sneeze (an involuntary

response) is to use a tissue or turn our head away from others (a learned response). Similarly, we may learn to sleep on mats or in beds. Most contemporary sociologists agree that culture and social learning, not nature, account for virtually all of our behaviour patterns.

Since humans cannot rely on instincts to survive, culture is a "tool kit" for survival. According to sociologist Ann Swidler (1986:273), culture is a "tool kit of symbols, stories, rituals, and world views, which people may use in varying configurations to solve different kinds of problems." The tools we choose will vary according to our own personality and the situations we face. We are not puppets on a string; we make choices from among the items in our own "tool box."

Material and Nonmaterial Culture

Our cultural tool box is divided into two major parts: *material* and *nonmaterial* culture (Ogburn, 1966/1922). **Material culture consists of the physical or tangible creations that members of a society make, use, and share**. Initially, items of material culture begin as raw materials or resources,

Food is a universal type of material culture, but what people eat and how they eat varies widely, as shown in these cross-cultural examples.

such as ore, trees, and oil. Through technology, these raw materials are transformed into usable goods (ranging from books and computers to guns and bombs). Sociologists define **technology as the knowledge, techniques, and tools that make it possible for people to transform resources into usable forms, and the knowledge and skills required to use them after they are developed**. From this standpoint, technology is both concrete and abstract.

At the most basic level, material culture is important because it is our buffer against the environment. For example, we create shelter to protect ourselves from the weather and to provide ourselves with privacy. Beyond the survival level, we make, use, and share objects that are interesting and important to us. Why are you wearing the particular clothes you have on today? Perhaps you're communicating something about yourself, such as where you attend school, what kind of music you like, or where you went on vacation. *Nonmaterial culture* **consists of the abstract or intangible human creations of society that influence people's behaviour**. Language, beliefs, values, rules of behaviour, and family patterns are examples of nonmaterial culture. A central component of nonmaterial culture is *beliefs*—the mental

acceptance or conviction that certain things are true or real. Beliefs may be based on tradition, faith, experience, scientific research, or some combination of these. Faith in a supreme being is an example of a belief. We may also have beliefs in items of material culture. For example, most students believe that computers are the key to technological advancement and progress.

Cultural Universals

Because all humans face the same basic needs (such as food, clothing, and shelter), we engage in similar activities that contribute to our survival. Anthropologist George Murdock (1945:124) compiled a list of more than 70 *cultural universals*—**customs and practices that occur across all societies**. His categories included appearance (such as bodily adornment and hairstyles), activities (such as sports, dancing, and games), social institutions (such as family, law, and religion), and customary practices (such as cooking, gift giving, and hospitality). These general customs and practices may be present in all cultures, but their specific forms vary from one group to another and from one time to another within the same group. For example, while telling jokes

BOX 2.1   SOCIOLOGY AND EVERYDAY LIFE

Answers to the Sociology Quiz on Global Food and Culture

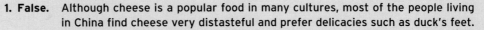

1. **False.** Although cheese is a popular food in many cultures, most of the people living in China find cheese very distasteful and prefer delicacies such as duck's feet.

2. **True.** Round foods such as pears, grapes, and moon cakes are given to celebrate the birth of babies because the shape of the food is believed to symbolize family unity.

3. **False.** Although wedding cakes are a tradition in virtually all nations and cultures, the ingredients of the cake—as well as other foods served at the celebration—vary widely at this important family celebration. The traditional wedding cake in Italy is made from biscuits, for example, whereas in Norway the wedding cake is made from bread topped with cream, cheese, and syrup.

4. **True.** Many faiths, including Christianity, Judaism, Islam, Hinduism, and Buddhism, have dietary rules and rituals that involve food; however, these practices and beliefs vary widely among individuals and communities. For some people, food forms an integral part of religion in their life; for others, food is less relevant.

5. **True.** Just as foods are divided into yin foods (e.g., bean sprouts, cabbage, and carrots) and yang foods (beef, chicken, eggs, and mushrooms), cooking methods are also referred to as having yin qualities (e.g., boiling, poaching, and steaming) or yang qualities (deep-frying, roasting, and stir-frying). Yin and yang are complementary pairs that should be incorporated into all aspects of social life, including the ingredients and preparation of foods.

6. **False.** Although more people now rely on fast foods, there is a "slow food" movement afoot to encourage people to prepare their food from scratch for a healthier lifestyle. Also, some cultural and religious communities encourage families to prepare their food from scratch and to preserve their own fruits, vegetables, and meats. Rural families are more likely to grow their own food or prepare it from scratch than are families residing in urban areas.

7. **False.** Rice is a popular mainstay in the diets of people from diverse cultural backgrounds who have arrived in North America over the past four decades. Groups ranging from the Hmong and Vietnamese to South Asians and Philipinos use rice as a central ingredient in their diets. Among some in the younger generations, however, food choices have become increasingly "North American" and items such as French fries and pizza have become very popular.

8. **True.** Cultural diversity is a major issue in eating, and people in some cultures, religions, and nations expect that even an "outsider" will have a basic familiarity with, and respect for, their traditions and practices. However, social analysts also suggest that we should not generalize or imply that certain characteristics apply to all people in a cultural group or nation.

Sources: Based on Better Health Channel, 2007; Ohio State University, 2007; and PBS, 2005a.

may be a universal practice, what is considered a joke in one society may be an insult in another.

How do sociologists view cultural universals? In terms of their functions, cultural universals are useful because they ensure the smooth and continuous operation of society (Radcliffe-Brown, 1952). A society must meet basic human needs by providing food, shelter, and some degree of safety for its members so that they will survive. Children and other new members (such as immigrants) must be taught the ways of the group. All the while, the self-interest of individuals must be balanced with the needs of society as a whole. Cultural universals help to fulfill these important functions of society.

From another perspective, however, cultural universals are not the result of functional necessity; these

The customs and rituals associated with weddings are one example of nonmaterial culture. What can you infer about beliefs and attitudes concerning marriage in the societies represented by these photographs?

practices may have been *imposed* by members of one society on members of another. For example, although religion is a cultural universal, traditional religious practices of indigenous peoples (those who first live in an area) have often been repressed and even stamped out by subsequent settlers or conquerors who hold political and economic power over them.

COMPONENTS OF CULTURE

Even though the specifics of individual cultures vary widely, all cultures have four common nonmaterial cultural components: symbols, language, values, and norms. These components contribute to both harmony and conflict in a society.

Symbols

A *symbol* is anything that meaningfully represents something else. Culture could not exist without symbols because there would be no shared meanings among people. Symbols can simultaneously produce loyalty and animosity, love and hate. They help us communicate ideas such as love or patriotism because they express abstract concepts with visible objects.

To complicate matters, however, the interpretation of various symbols varies in different cultural contexts. For example, for some Indo-Canadians, the colour green rather than white symbolizes purity or virginity. Flags can stand for patriotism, nationalism, school spirit, or religious beliefs held by members of a group or society. Symbols also can transmit other types of ideas. A siren is a symbol that denotes an emergency and sends the message to clear the way immediately. Gestures also are a symbolic form of communication—a movement of the head, body, or hands can express our ideas or feelings to others. For example, in Canada, pointing toward your chest with your thumb or finger is a symbol for "me." We are also all aware of how useful our middle finger can be in communicating messages to inconsiderate drivers. In our technology-oriented society, emoticons are a new form of symbols used to express emotions when people are communicating through e-mail or in chat rooms (see Figure 2.1).

Symbols affect our thoughts about social class. With regard to clothing, although many people wear casual clothes on a daily basis, where the clothing was purchased is sometimes used as a symbol of social

Figure 2.1   Emoticons

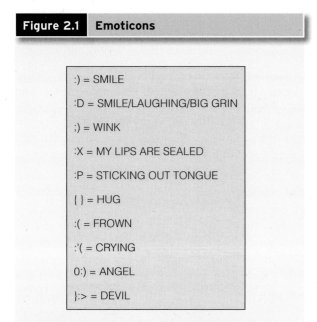

:) = SMILE

:D = SMILE/LAUGHING/BIG GRIN

;) = WINK

:X = MY LIPS ARE SEALED

:P = STICKING OUT TONGUE

{ } = HUG

:(= FROWN

:'(= CRYING

0:) = ANGEL

}:> = DEVIL

The symbols shown here are examples of "emoticons" or "smileys," a symbolic way to express moods in e-mail and text messages. Turn the page sideways and the meaning of each emotion will be clear.

status. Were the items purchased at Walmart, Old Navy, or Abercrombie & Fitch? What indicators are there on the items of clothing—such as the Lacoste alligator or the Nike swoosh, some other logo, or a brand name—that say something about the status of the product? Automobiles and their logos are also symbols that have cultural meaning beyond the shopping environment in which they originate.

Language

Language **is a set of symbols that express ideas and enable people to think and communicate with one another**. Verbal (spoken) and nonverbal (written or gestured) language help us describe reality. One of our most important human attributes is the ability to use language to share our experiences, feelings, and knowledge with others. Language can create visual images in our head, such as "the kittens look like little cotton balls" (Samovar and Porter, 1991a). Language also allows people to distinguish themselves from outsiders and maintain group boundaries and solidarity (Farb, 1973).

Language is not solely a human characteristic. Other animals use sounds, gestures, touch, and smell to communicate with one another, but they use signals with fixed meanings that are limited to the immediate situation (the present) and cannot encompass past or future situations. For example, chimpanzees can use elements

of standard American Sign Language and manipulate physical objects to make "sentences," but they are not physically endowed with the vocal apparatus needed to form the consonants required for verbal language. As a result, nonhuman animals cannot transmit the more complex aspects of culture to their offspring. Humans have a unique ability to manipulate symbols to express abstract concepts and rules and thus to create and transmit culture from one generation to the next.

Language and Social Reality   Does language *create* or simply *communicate* reality? Anthropological linguists Edward Sapir and Benjamin Whorf have suggested that language not only expresses our thoughts and perceptions but also influences our perceptions of reality. According to the **Sapir-Whorf hypothesis, language shapes the view of reality of its speakers** (Whorf, 1956; Sapir, 1961). If people are able to think only through language, then language must precede thought.

If language actually shapes the reality we perceive and experience, then some aspects of the world are viewed as important and others are virtually neglected because people know the world only in terms of the vocabulary and grammar of their own language. For example, most Aboriginal languages focus on describing relationships between things rather than using language to judge or evaluate. One Aboriginal author explains, "No, we don't have any gender. It's a relationship. . . . The woman who cares for your heart—that's your wife. Your daughters are the ones who enrich your heart. Your sons are the ones that test your heart!" (Ross, 1996:116). Consequently, many Aboriginal languages do not have any personal pronouns based on gender (such as words for *she* or *he*). As writer Rupert Ross explains:

> Because they don't exist there, searching for the correct ones often seems an artificial and unreasonable exercise. As a result, Aboriginal people are often as careless about getting them right as I am when speaking French and trying to remember whether a noun has "le" or "la" in front of it. . . . On the more humorous side, my Aboriginal friends appear heartily amused by the frenzied Western debate over whether God is a "He" or a "She." (1996:117)

If language does create reality, are we trapped by our language? Many social scientists agree that the Sapir-Whorf hypothesis overstates the relationship between language and our thoughts and behaviour patterns. While acknowledging that language has many subtle meanings and that words used by people reflect their central concerns, most sociologists contend that language may *influence* our behaviour and interpretation of social reality but it does not *determine* it.

AP/WIDE WORLD PHOTOS

Symbols are powerful sources of communication. What messages does this picture communicate to you?

Language and Gender

What is the relationship between language and gender? What cultural assumptions about women and men does language reflect? Scholars have suggested several ways in which language and gender are intertwined:

- The English language ignores women by using the masculine form to refer to human beings in general (Basow, 1992). For example, the word *man* is used generically in words like *chairman* and *mankind*, which purportedly include both men and women.

- Use of the pronouns *she* and *he* affects our thinking about gender. Pronouns show the gender of the person we *expect* to be in a particular occupation. For instance, nurses, secretaries, and schoolteachers usually are referred to as *she*, while doctors, engineers, electricians, and presidents are referred to as *he* (Baron, 1986).

- A language-based predisposition to think about women in sexual terms reinforces the notion that women are sexual objects. Women often are described by terms such as *fox, broad, bitch, babe,* or *doll,* which ascribe childlike or even pet-like characteristics to them. By contrast, men have

performance pressures placed on them by being defined in terms of their sexual prowess, such as *dude, stud,* and *hunk* (Baker, 1993).

Gender in language has been debated and studied extensively in recent years, and greater awareness and some changes have been the result. For example, the desire of many women to have *Ms* (rather than *Miss* or *Mrs.,* which indicate their marital status) precede their names has received a degree of acceptance in public life and the media (Tannen, 1995). Many organizations and publications have established guidelines for the use of nonsexist language and have changed titles such as *chairman* to *chair* or *chairperson.* Some occupations have been given "genderless" titles, such as *firefighter* and *flight attendant* (Maggio, 1988). Many scholars suggest that a more inclusive language is needed to develop a more inclusive and equitable society (see Basow, 1992).

Language, Race, and Ethnicity

Language may create and reinforce our perceptions about race and ethnicity by transmitting preconceived ideas about the superiority of one category of people over another. Let's look at a few images conveyed by words in the English language concerning race/ethnicity.

- Words may have more than one meaning, and create and reinforce negative images. Terms such as *black market, blackmail,* and *black magic* and expressions such as *black sheep of the family* and *a black mark* (a detrimental fact) give the word *black* negative associations and derogatory imagery. By contrast, the expression *That's white of you* and *white lie* reinforce positive associations with the colour white.

- Overtly derogatory terms such as *nigger, kike, gook, honky, chink, squaw, savage,* and other racial/ethnic slurs have been "popularized" in movies, music, comedy routines, and so on. Such derogatory terms often are used in conjunction with physical threats against persons.

- Words frequently are used to create or reinforce perceptions about a group. For example, Aboriginal peoples have been referred to as "savages" and described as "primitive," while black people have been described as "uncivilized," "cannibalistic," and "pagan."

In addition to these concerns about the English language, problems also arise when more than one language is involved.

Language Diversity in Canada

Canada is a linguistically diverse society. Language has been referred to as the keystone to culture because it is the chief vehicle for understanding and experiencing a culture (McVey and Kalbach, 1995).

The Québécois and Bilingualism

In 1969 the federal government passed the Official Languages Act, making both French and English official languages. In doing so, Canada officially became a bilingual society. However, this action by no means resolved the very complex issues regarding language in our society. According to the most recent census, 68 percent of Canadians speak English only, another 13 percent speak French only, and almost 17 percent are bilingual. Less than 2 percent of Canadians indicated they lacked the skills to converse in either French or English (Statistics Canada, 2006b). Although French-versus-English language issues have been a significant source of conflict, bilingualism remains a distinct component of Canadian culture.

Although it may be easy for members of the English-speaking majority to display such acceptance and tolerance of bilingualism, francophones are concerned that this policy is not enough to save their culture.

Canada's Aboriginal languages are many and diverse. These languages, tangible symbols of Aboriginal culture and group identity, are tremendously important to Canada's indigenous people. Aboriginal people's cultures are *oral cultures*, that is, cultures that are transmitted through speech rather than the written word. Many Aboriginal stories are passed on only in the Aboriginal language in which they originated. Language is not only a means of communication but also a link that connects people with their past and grounds their social, emotional, and spiritual vitality. For Aboriginal people, huge losses have already occurred as a result of the assimilationist strategies of residential schools. At these schools, Aboriginal children were forbidden to speak their language. An Ojibway woman from northwestern Ontario describes her experience:

> Boarding school was supposed to be a place where you forgot everything about being Anishinabe. And our language too. But I said, "I'm going to talk to myself"—and that's what I did, under my covers—talked to myself in Anishinabe. If we were caught, the nuns would make us stand in a corner and repeat over and over, "I won't speak my language." (Ross, 1996:122)

Despite the efforts of Canadian Aboriginal peoples to maintain their languages, these languages are among the most endangered in the world. Only three of the approximately 50 Aboriginal languages in Canada are in a healthy state. In the 2006 census, only 18 percent of Aboriginal persons reported an Aboriginal language as their first language and even fewer spoke it at home (Statistics Canada, 2007i). Steps to preserve indigenous languages include the introduction of Aboriginal-language courses in schools and universities, Aboriginal media programming, and the recording of elders' stories, songs, and accounts of history in Aboriginal languages (Ponting, 1997).

Values

Values **are collective ideas about what is right or wrong, good or bad, and desirable or undesirable in a particular culture** (Williams, 1970). Values do not dictate which behaviours are appropriate and which ones are not, but they provide us with the criteria by which we evaluate people, objects, and events. Values typically come in pairs of positive and negative values, such as being brave or cowardly, Since we use values to justify our behaviour, we tend to defend them staunchly (Kluckhohn, 1961).

Value Contradictions

All societies have value contradictions. *Value contradictions* **are values that conflict with one another or are mutually exclusive** (i.e., achieving one makes it difficult, if not impossible, to achieve another). For example, core values of morality and humanitarianism may conflict with values of individual achievement and success. Similarly, although the majority of Canadians feel that the poor have a right to social assistance, they have also shown strong support for governments that have dramatically cut budgets in order to reduce financial deficits.

Ideal versus Real Culture

What is the relationship between values and human behaviour? Sociologists stress that a gap always exists between ideal and real culture in a society. *Ideal culture* **refers to the values and standards of behaviour that people in a society profess to hold.** *Real culture* **refers to the values and standards of behaviour that people actually follow.** For example, we may claim to be law-abiding (an ideal cultural value) but smoke marijuana (a real cultural behaviour), or we may regularly drive over the speed limit but think of ourselves as "good citizens." The degree of discrepancy between ideal and real culture is relevant to sociologists investigating social change. Major discrepancies provide a foothold for demonstrating hypocrisy (pretending to be what one is not, or to claim to believe what one does not believe). These discrepancies are often a source of social problems; if the discrepancy is perceived, leaders of social movements may utilize them to point out peoples' contradictory behaviour. For example, preserving our natural environment may be a core value, but our behaviour (such as littering highways and polluting lakes) contributes to its environmental degradation.

Norms

Values provide ideals or beliefs about behaviour but do not state explicitly how we should behave. Norms, on the other hand, do have specific behavioural expectations. *Norms* **are established rules of behaviour or standards of conduct.** *Prescriptive norms* state what behaviour is appropriate or acceptable. For example, persons making a certain amount of money are expected to file a tax return and pay any taxes they owe. Norms based on custom direct us to open a door for a person carrying a heavy load. By contrast, *proscriptive norms* state what behaviour is inappropriate or unacceptable. Laws that prohibit us from driving over the speed limit and "good manners" that preclude reading a newspaper during class are examples. Prescriptive and proscriptive norms operate at all levels of society, from our everyday actions to the formulation of laws.

Formal and Informal Norms
Not all norms are of equal importance; those that are most crucial are formalized. *Formal norms* are written down and involve specific punishments for violators. Laws are the most common type of formal norms; they have been codified and may be enforced by sanctions.

Sanctions **are rewards for appropriate behaviour or penalties for inappropriate behaviour.** Examples of *positive sanctions* include praise, honours, or medals for conformity to specific norms. *Negative sanctions* range from mild disapproval to life imprisonment. In the case of law, formal sanctions are clearly defined and can be administered only by persons in certain official positions (such as police officers and judges) who are given the authority to impose the sanctions.

Norms considered to be less important are referred to as *informal norms*—unwritten standards of behaviour understood by people who share a common identity. When individuals violate informal norms, other people may apply informal sanctions. *Informal sanctions* are not clearly defined and can be applied by any member of a group (such as frowning at someone or making a negative comment or gesture).

Folkways
Norms are also classified according to their relative social importance. *Folkways* **are informal norms or everyday customs that may be violated without serious consequences within a particular culture** (Sumner, 1959/1906). They provide rules for conduct but are not considered to be essential to society's survival. In Canada, folkways include using underarm deodorant, brushing one's teeth, and wearing appropriate clothing for a specific occasion. Often, folkways are not enforced; when they are enforced, the resulting sanctions tend to be informal and relatively mild.

Mores
Other norms are considered highly essential to the stability of society. *Mores* **are strongly held norms with moral and ethical connotations that may not be violated without serious consequences in a particular culture.** Since mores (pronounced MOR-ays) are based on cultural values and are considered crucial for the well-being of the group, violators are subject to more severe negative sanctions (such as ridicule, loss of employment, or imprisonment) than are those who fail to adhere to folkways. The strongest mores are referred to as taboos. *Taboos* **are mores so strong that their violation is considered to be extremely offensive and even unmentionable.** Violation of taboos is punishable by the group or even, according to certain belief systems, by a supernatural force. The incest taboo, which prohibits sexual or marital relations between certain categories of kin, is an example of a nearly universal taboo.

Laws
Laws **are formal, standardized norms that have been enacted by legislatures and are enforced by formal sanctions.** Laws may be either civil or criminal. *Civil law* deals with disputes among persons or groups. Persons who lose civil suits may encounter negative sanctions such as having to pay compensation to the other party or being ordered to stop certain conduct. *Criminal law*, on the other hand, deals with public safety and well-being. When criminal laws are violated, fines and prison sentences are the most likely negative sanctions.

As with material objects, all of the nonmaterial components of culture—symbols, language, values, and norms—are reflected in the popular culture of contemporary society.

TECHNOLOGY, CULTURAL CHANGE, AND DIVERSITY

Cultures do not generally remain static. There are many forces working toward change and diversity Some suffer culture shock and succumb to

SOCIOLOGY AND THE MEDIA

Internet Cyberculture

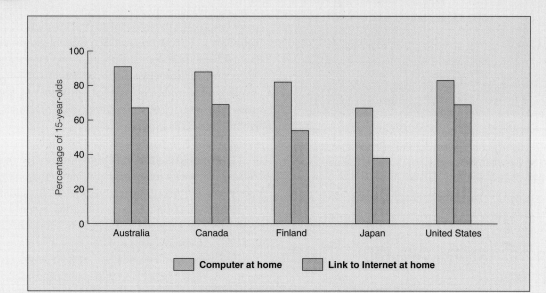

According to sociologist Michael Adams, "Thanks to virtual travel through the globalization of culture, teenagers in Toronto, Miami and Kiev often have more in common with each other than they do with their own parents" (1998:32).

Is there a new culture developing in cyberspace? Apparently so. The term *cyberculture* has been coined to describe this new form of popular culture. Cyberculture, which makes up a large portion of the World Wide Web, has been described as the melting pot of the world's diversity. The Internet links the world as never before, creating a global village where people from around the world can communicate with a simple click of the mouse. Through various Internet services such as chat rooms, newsgroups, and e-mail, people can connect with anyone, almost anywhere in the world. This allows for the sharing of ideas and the exchange of both material and nonmaterial cultural products.

Recent surveys report that Canada is at the leading edge of technology adoption. Among North American and European countries, Canada has the second-highest level of home PC use, and Canadians and Americans lead the pack for the rate of acquiring home Internet access. As a result of these advances in communication technologies, people can travel virtually in a cyberculture made up of networks, projects, and communities with people they have never met, in cultures they have never visited.

Is this universal cultural connection a good thing? What possible effects do you foresee for Canadian culture? On the positive side, this new Internet culture allows for the exchange of ideas and makes foreign cultures seem familiar. This can serve only to increase global cultural understanding and tolerance.

However, on the negative side, chances are we can expect the significant influence of U.S. culture on Canadian culture to become even more pronounced through this new form of popular culture. Furthermore, the Internet is a virtually uncensored forum for free speech. Anyone with Internet access can publish his or her own personal views—some of which may be racist, sexist, exploitative, or destructive. These ideas can be disseminated quickly and easily in cyberspace.

Does cyberculture open up the world? Experts on Internet culture remind us that although cyberculture may be an increasingly significant part of mainstream popular culture in Canada, we may be thinking in ethnocentric terms when assuming that this resource is readily available in all cultures. While industrialized countries are exploring sophisticated uses of the Internet, more than half of the world's population has never used a telephone.

Sources: Buckler, 1996; Hansen, 1995; Adams, 1998; Willms and Corbett, 2003.

Even as global travel and the media make us more aware of people around the world, the distinctiveness of the Yanomamö in South America remains apparent.

ethnocentrism, while other societies and individuals adapt to this change.

Ethnocentrism and Cultural Relativism

When observing people from other cultures, many of us use our own culture as the yardstick by which we judge their behaviour. Sociologists refer to this approach as *ethnocentrism*—**the practice of judging all other cultures by one's own culture** (Sumner, 1959/1906). Ethnocentrism is based on the assumption that one's own way of life is superior to all others. For example, most schoolchildren are taught that their own school and country are the best. The school song, the pledge to the flag, and the national anthem are forms of *positive ethnocentrism*. However, *negative ethnocentrism* can also result from constant emphasis on the superiority of one's own group or nation. Negative ethnocentrism is manifested in derogatory stereotypes that ridicule recent immigrants whose customs, dress, eating habits, or religious beliefs are markedly different from those of dominant group members. Long-term Canadian residents who are members of racial and ethnic minority groups have also been the targets of ethnocentric practices by other groups.

An alternative to ethnocentrism is *cultural relativism*—**the belief that the behaviours and customs of any culture must be viewed and analyzed by the culture's own standards**. For example, Marvin Harris (1974, 1985) uses cultural relativism to explain why cattle, which are viewed as sacred, are not killed and eaten in India, where widespread hunger and malnutrition exist. From

an ethnocentric viewpoint, we might conclude that cow worship is the cause of the hunger and poverty in India. However, according to Harris, the Hindu taboo against killing cattle is very important to their economic system. Live cows are more valuable than dead ones because they have more important uses than as a direct source of food. As part of the ecological system, cows consume grasses of little value to humans. Then they produce valuable resources— oxen (the neutered offspring of cows) to power the plows and manure (for fuel and fertilizer)—as well as milk and leather. As Harris's study reveals, culture must be viewed from the standpoint of those who live in a particular society.

Cultural relativism also has a downside. It may be used to excuse customs and behaviour (such as cannibalism) that may violate basic human rights. Cultural relativism is a part of the sociological imagination; researchers must be aware of the customs and norms of the society they are studying and then spell out their background assumptions so that others can spot possible biases in their studies. However, according to some social scientists, issues surrounding ethnocentrism and cultural relativism may become less distinct in the future as people around the globe increasingly share a common popular culture. Others, of course, disagree with this perspective.

Cultural Change

Changes in technology continue to shape the material culture of society. Although most technological changes are primarily modifications of existing technology, *new technologies* refers to changes that make a significant difference in many people's lives. Examples of new technologies include the introduction of the printing press more than 500 years ago and the advent of computers and electronic communications in the 20th century. The pace of technological change has increased rapidly in the past 150 years, as contrasted with the 4000 years before that, during which humans advanced from digging sticks and hoes to the plow.

Not all parts of culture change at the same pace. When a change occurs in the material culture of a society, nonmaterial culture must adapt to that change. Frequently, this rate of change is uneven, resulting in a gap between the two. Sociologist William F. Ogburn (1966/1922) referred to this disparity as *cultural lag*—**a gap between the technical development of a society and its moral and legal institutions** (Marshall, 1994). In other words, cultural lag occurs when material culture changes faster than nonmaterial culture, thus creating a lag between the two cultural components. For example, at the material cultural level, the personal computer and electronic coding have made it possible to create a unique health identifier for each person in Canada. Based on available technology, it would be possible to create a national data bank that includes everyone's individual medical records from birth to death. Using this identifier, health providers and insurance companies could rapidly transfer medical records around the globe, and researchers could access unlimited data on peoples' diseases, test results, and treatments. However, the availability of this technology does not mean that it will be accepted by people who believe (nonmaterial culture) that such a national data bank constitutes an invasion of privacy and could be abused by others. The failure of nonmaterial culture to keep pace with material cultural is linked to social conflict and societal problems. As in the above example, such issues often create change, set in motion by discovery, invention, and diffusion.

Discovery **is the process of learning about something previously unknown or unrecognized**. Historically, discovery involved unearthing natural elements or existing realities, such as "discovering" fire or the true shape of the earth. Today, discovery most often results from scientific research. For example, discovery of a polio vaccine virtually eliminated one of the major childhood diseases. A future discovery of a cure for cancer or the common cold could result in longer and more productive lives for many people.

As more discoveries have occurred, people have been able to reconfigure existing material and nonmaterial cultural items through invention. **Invention is the process of reshaping existing cultural items into a new form**. Guns, video games, airplanes, and the Charter of Rights and Freedoms are examples of inventions that positively or negatively affect our lives today.

When diverse groups of people come into contact, they begin to adapt one another's discoveries, inventions, and ideas for their own use. **Diffusion is the transmission of cultural items or social practices from one group or society to another** through means such as exploration, military endeavours, the media, tourism, and immigration. To illustrate, consider the comments of former Indian cabinet minister I.K. Gujral:

My granddaughter is 4, she is always talking about bubble gum, not Indian food, or she says, "I don't like Pepsi, I like Coke." She even speaks English more than Hindi. I asked her one day why she doesn't speak to me in Hindi, and then she went to her mother and asked: "Doesn't grandfather speak English?" The other day my granddaughter said she wanted pizza. So her grandmother said she would make her a pizza. My granddaughter said, "No, no, I want Pizza Hut." (Friedman, 1998:A10)

As this example demonstrates, in today's "shrinking globe," cultural diffusion moves at a very rapid pace as countries continually seek new markets for their products (Friedman, 1998:A10) (see Box 2.3 on page 44). However, critics believe that some contemporary forms of cultural diffusion actually amount to *cultural imperialism***—the extensive infusion of one nation's culture into other nations**.

Cultural Diversity

Cultural diversity refers to the wide range of cultural differences found between and within nations. Cultural diversity between countries may be the result of natural circumstances (such as climate and geography) or social circumstances (such as level of technology and composition of the population). Some countries, such as Sweden, are referred to as *homogeneous societies*, meaning they include people who share a common culture and are typically from similar social, religious, political, and economic backgrounds. By contrast, other countries—including Canada—are referred to as *heterogeneous societies*, meaning they include people who are dissimilar in regard to social characteristics such as nationality, race, ethnicity, class, occupation, or education (see the Census Profile on page 46).

Immigration contributes to cultural diversity in a society. Throughout its history, Canada has been a nation of immigrants. Over the past 150 years, more than 13 million immigrants have arrived here. Immigration can cause feelings of frustration and hostility, especially in people who feel threatened by the changes that large numbers of immigrants may produce. Often, people are intolerant of those who are different from themselves. When societal tensions rise, people may look for others on whom they can place blame—or single out persons because they are the "other," the "outsider," the one who does not "belong." Adrienne Shadd described her experience of being singled out as an "other":

Routinely I am asked, "Where are you from?" or "What nationality are you?" as if to be Black, you have to come from somewhere else. I respond

BOX 2.3   SOCIOLOGY IN GLOBAL PERSPECTIVE

The Malling of China: What Part Does Culture Play?

What is five stories tall and the length of six football fields? What has 230 escalators, more than 1 000 stores, 20 000 workers, and shops with names such as Ralph Lauren and Chanel?

Although many of us would think that the answer to this question is a shopping mall in Canada or the United States, the mall described here is the Golden Resources Shopping Mall, located in Beijing, China. Golden Resources is currently the world's largest shopping mall, at six million square feet (Marquand, 2004). Other giant shopping theme parks, or "temples of consumerism," are opening throughout China in an effort to lure consumers to settings that often resemble Las Vegas or Disneyland (Barboza, 2005).

Under communism, China had no shopping malls. Today, China is a hotbed for capitalist expansion, and shopping malls are viewed as "cash cows" by developers and entrepreneurs (Whiting, 2005). Many malls in China are being built by North American developers such as the Simon Property Group and Taubman Centers, Inc. In addition, many mall stores in China, such as Old Navy, Louis Vuitton, and Chanel, originated in the United States, Italy, France, or other nations of Western Europe. Although the first shopping malls were developed in North America (Kowinski, 2002), the "shop till you drop" spirit evoked by these shopping complexes has spread throughout the world as malls have sprung up in Western Europe, Mexico, South America, the former Soviet Union, and Japan.

Is the malling of China and other nations an example of *cultural imperialism*—the extensive infusion of one nation's culture into other nations? Or is "malling" nothing more than *cultural diffusion*—the transmission of cultural items or social practices from one group or society to another? Some analysts believe that "malling" and "branding" (the selling of a name-brand product for a higher price when a generic one would serve the same purpose) are not forms of cultural imperialism because people in nations such as China welcome the vast malls and see them as a source of cultural pride and as a sign of their own economic progress. However, other analysts disagree with this assessment because they believe that part of China's culture is disappearing forever. Open-air food markets and old department stores that traditionally sold Chinese clothing and other merchandise indigenous to the Chinese culture have been replaced by chain stores and big-box retailers such as Walmart, many of which are operated by giant U.S. corporations. From this perspective, culture is "for sale" in the giant shopping malls because malls are more than just a collection of stores that share a common geographic location. Theme-park shopping malls, for example, are carefully designed psychological selling machines that sell not only products and services but also cultural symbols of the good life and of social acceptance by one's peers. This is a powerful form of selling culture to people who desperately want to become players in the 21st-century global economy.

Is consumerism a cultural universal shared by people worldwide as they gain new opportunities to shop and have a vast array of merchandise set before them to choose from? Although "shop till you drop" consumerism may be possible for some middle- and upper-income families in China and other nations, many of the world's people cannot purchase the basic necessities of life, much less buy mall-hyped items such as the following, which are available at Beijing's Golden Resources Shopping Mall: "goat-leather motorcycle jackets, Italian bathroom sinks, hand-made violins, grandfather clocks, colonial-style desks, and Jaguars" (Marquand, 2004: 1). An ad for Golden Resources proudly proclaims that it is "the mall that will change your life" (Marquand, 2004: 1). If we think about this statement from a sociological perspective, it raises interesting questions for all of us: Will the malling of China change the way of life and culture of people in that nation? Has the malling of Canada changed our culture and influenced how we spend our time? What do you think?

Source: Marquand, 2004; Barboza, 2005; Whiting, 2005; Kowinski, 2002.

---

that I'm "Canadian." . . . I play along. The scenario usually unfolds as follows:

"But where are you *originally* from?"
Canada."

"Oh, *you* were born here. But where are your parents from?"
"Canada."
"But what about your grandparents?"

Is the proliferation of massive shopping malls in China—containing stores from the United States and Western Europe as well as local entities—an example of cultural diffusion? Or, is the malling of China an example of cultural imperialism? Can "culture" be sold?

As individuals delve further into my genealogy to find out where I'm "really" from, their frustration levels rise.

"No, uh, I mean . . . your *people*. Where do your people come from?"

At this point, questioners are totally annoyed and/or frustrated. After all, Black people in Canada are supposed to come from "the islands," aren't they? For those of us living in large urban centres, there are constant reminders that we are not regarded as truly "Canadian." (1994:11)

Have you ever been made to feel like an "outsider"? Each of us receives cultural messages that may make us feel good or bad about ourselves or may give us the perception that we "belong" or "do not belong." However, in heterogeneous societies such as Canada, cultural diversity is inevitable. In Canada, this diversity has created some unique problems in terms of defining and maintaining our distinct Canadian culture.

Subcultures

A *subculture* **is a group of people who share a distinctive set of cultural beliefs and behaviours that differ in some significant way from that of the larger society**. Emerging from the functionalist tradition, this concept has been applied to distinctions ranging from ethnic, religious, regional, and age-based categories to those categories presumed to be "deviant" or marginalized from the larger society. In the broadest use of the concept, thousands of categories of people residing in Canada might be classified as participants in one or more subcultures, including Muslims, Italian Canadians, Orthodox Jews, Generation Xers, and bikers. However, many sociological studies of subcultures have limited the scope of inquiry to more visible distinct subcultures, such as the Hutterites, to gain insight into how subcultural participants interact with the dominant Canadian culture.

The Hutterites As a subculture, the Hutterites have fought for many years to maintain their distinct identity. They are the largest family-type communal

Technology and tradition meet at the Fairholme Hutterite colony as these young women try out a new digital camera at school.

Census Profile   **Heterogeneity of Canadian Society**

Throughout history, Canada has been heterogeneous. Today, Canada is represented by a wide variety of social categories, including our ethnic origins and religious affiliations.[i]

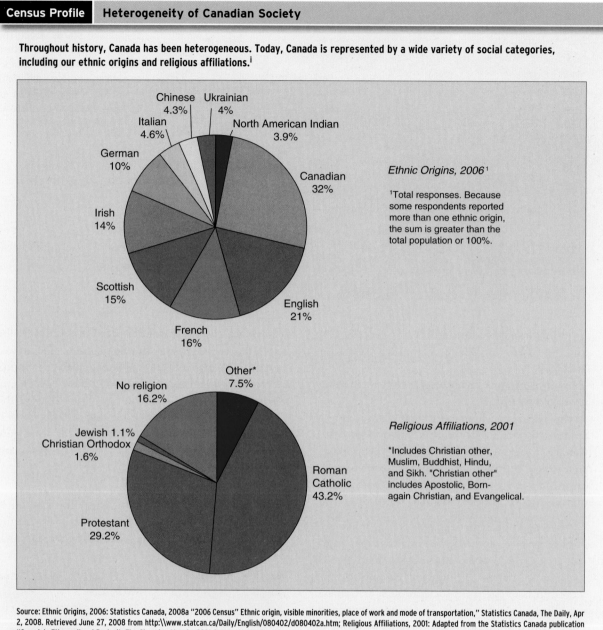

Chinese 4.3%
Ukrainian 4%
Italian 4.6%
North American Indian 3.9%
German 10%
Canadian 32%
Irish 14%
Scottish 15%
French 16%
English 21%

Ethnic Origins, 2006[1]

[1]Total responses. Because some respondents reported more than one ethnic origin, the sum is greater than the total population or 100%.

Other* 7.5%
No religion 16.2%
Jewish 1.1%
Christian Orthodox 1.6%
Roman Catholic 43.2%
Protestant 29.2%

Religious Affiliations, 2001

*Includes Christian other, Muslim, Buddhist, Hindu, and Sikh. "Christian other" includes Apostolic, Born-again Christian, and Evangelical.

Source: Ethnic Origins, 2006: Statistics Canada, 2008a "2006 Census" Ethnic origin, visible minorities, place of work and mode of transportation," Statistics Canada, The Daily, Apr 2, 2008. Retrieved June 27, 2008 from http:\\www.statcan.ca/Daily/English/080402/d080402a.htm; Religious Affiliations, 2001: Adapted from the Statistics Canada publication "Canada's Ethnocultural Portrait: The Changing Mosaic, 2001 Census (Analysis series)," Catalogue no. 96F0030, January 2003, available at <http://www.statcan.ca/English/IPS/Data/96F0030XIE2001008.htm>.

grouping in the Western world, with close to 30 000 members living in approximately 300 settlements. The Hutterites are considered a subculture because their values, norms, and appearance differ significantly from those of members of the dominant culture. They have a strong faith in God and reject worldly concerns. Their core values include the joy of work, the primacy of the home, faithfulness, thriftiness, and tradition. Hutterites hold conservative views of the family, believing that women are subordinate to men, birth control is unacceptable, and wives remain at home. Children are cherished and seen as an economic asset: they help with the farming and other work.

A key tenet of Hutterite faith is *non-assimilation;* that is, they do not want to be absorbed into the dominant culture. Their colonies are usually located far from towns, cities, and highways to emphasize this belief. However, the Hutterites do not attempt to achieve complete social isolation from the wider society. Although this subculture strictly adheres to centuries-old traditions, the Hutterites do not hesitate to take advantage of 21st-century advancements (Lyons, 1998).

Countercultures Some subcultures actively oppose the larger society. A ***counterculture* is a group that strongly rejects dominant societal values and norms and seeks alternative lifestyles** (Yinger, 1960, 1982). Young people are most likely to join countercultural groups, perhaps because younger persons generally have less invested in the existing culture. Examples of countercultures include the beatniks of the 1950s, the flower children of the 1960s, the drug enthusiasts of the 1970s, and members of nonmainstream religious sects, or cults.

Culture Shock

***Culture shock* is the disorientation that people feel when they encounter cultures radically different from their own** and believe they cannot depend on their own taken-for-granted assumptions about life. When people travel to another society, they may not know how to respond to that setting. For example, the American anthropologist Napoleon Chagnon (1992) described his initial shock at seeing the Yanomamö (pronounced yah-noh-MAH-mah) tribe of South America for the first time in 1964.

The Yanomamö (also referred as the "Yanomami") are a tribe of about 20 000 South American Indians who live in the rain forest. Although Chagnon travelled in a small aluminum motorboat for three days to reach these people, he was not prepared for the sight that met his eyes when he arrived:

> I looked up and gasped to see a dozen burly, naked, sweaty, hideous men staring at us down the shafts of their drawn arrows. Immense wads of green tobacco were stuck between their lower teeth and lips, making them look even more hideous, and strands of dark-green slime dripped from their nostrils—strands so long that they reached down to their pectoral muscles or drizzled down their chins and stuck to their chests and bellies. We arrived as the men were blowing *ebene*, a hallucinogenic drug, up their noses. As I soon learned, one side effect of the drug is a runny nose. The mucus becomes saturated with

the drug's green powder, and the Yanomamö usually just let it dangle freely from their nostrils to plop off when the strands become too heavy . . . I was horrified. What kind of welcome was this for someone who had come to live with these people and learn their way of life—to become friends with them? (Chagnon, 1992:12–14)

The Yanomamö have no written language, system of numbers, or calendar. They lead a nomadic lifestyle, carrying everything they own on their backs. They wear no clothes and paint their bodies; the women insert slender sticks through holes in the lower lip and through the pierced nasal septum. In other words, the Yanomamö—like the members of thousands of other cultures around the world—live in a culture very different from ours.

SOCIOLOGICAL ANALYSIS OF CULTURE

Sociologists regard culture as a central ingredient in human behaviour. Although all sociologists share a similar purpose, they typically see culture through somewhat different lenses as they are guided by different theoretical perspectives in their research (see Concept Table 2.1 on page 47). What do these perspectives tell us about culture?

Functionalist Perspectives

As previously discussed, functionalist perspectives are based on the assumption that society is a stable, orderly system with interrelated parts that serve specific functions. Anthropologist Bronislaw Malinowski (1922) suggested that culture helps people meet their *biological needs* (including food and procreation), *instrumental needs* (including law and education), and *integrative needs* (including religion and art). Societies in which people share a common language and core values are more likely to have consensus and harmony.

A strength of the functionalist perspective on culture is its focus on the needs of society and the fact that stability is essential for society's continued survival. A shortcoming is its overemphasis on harmony and cooperation and a lack of acknowledgment of societal factors that contribute to conflict and strife.

Concept Table 2.1	THEORETICAL ANALYSIS OF CULTURE	
Components of Culture	Symbol	Anything that meaningfully represents something else.
	Language	A set of symbols that expresses ideas and enables people to think and communicate with one another.
	Values	Collective ideas about what is right or wrong, good or bad, and desirable or undesirable in a particular culture.
	Norms	Established rules of behaviour or standards of conduct.
Sociological Analysis of Culture	Functionalist Perspectives	Culture helps people meet their biological, instrumental, and expressive needs.
	Conflict Perspectives	Ideas are a creation of society's most powerful members and can be used by the ruling class to affect the thoughts and actions of members of other classes.
	Symbolic Interactionist Perspectives	People create, maintain, and modify culture during their everyday activities; however, cultural creations can take on a life of their own and end up controlling people.
	Postmodern Perspectives	Much of culture today is based on simulation of reality (e.g., what we see on television) rather than reality itself.

Conflict Perspectives

Conflict perspectives are based on the assumption that social life is a continuous struggle in which members of powerful groups seek to control scarce resources. Values and norms help create and sustain the privileged position of the powerful in society while excluding others. As early conflict theorist Karl Marx stressed, ideas are *cultural creations* of a society's most powerful members. Thus, it is possible for political, economic, and social leaders to use **ideology—an integrated system of ideas that is external to, and coercive of, people**—to maintain their positions of dominance in a society. As Marx stated:

> The ideas of the ruling class are in every epoch the ruling ideas, i.e., the class which is the ruling material force in society, is at the same time, its ruling intellectual force. The class, which has the means of material production at its disposal, has control at the same time over the means of mental production. . . . The ruling ideas are nothing more than the ideal expression of the dominant material relationships, the dominant material relationships grasped as ideas. (Marx and Engels, 1970/1845–1846:64)

Many contemporary conflict theorists agree with Marx's assertion that ideas, a nonmaterial component

of culture, are used by agents of the ruling class to affect the thoughts and actions of members of other classes.

A strength of the conflict perspective is that it stresses how cultural values and norms may perpetuate social inequalities. It also highlights the inevitability of change and the constant tension between those who want to maintain the status quo and those who desire change. A limitation is its focus on societal discord and the divisiveness of culture.

Symbolic Interactionist Perspectives

Unlike functionalists and conflict theorists, who focus primarily on macrolevel concerns, symbolic interactionists engage in a microlevel analysis that views society as the sum of all people's interactions. From this perspective, people create, maintain, and modify culture as they go about their everyday activities. Symbols make communication with others possible because they provide us with shared meanings.

According to symbolic interactionist theory, people continually negotiate their social realities. Values and norms are not independent realities that automatically determine our behaviour; instead, we reinterpret them in each social situation we encounter. However, the classical sociologist Georg Simmel warned that the larger cultural world—including both material and nonmaterial culture—eventually takes on a life of its own apart from the actors who daily re-create social life. As a result, individuals may be more controlled by culture than they realize.

A symbolic interactionist approach highlights how people maintain and change culture through their interactions with others. However, interactionism does not provide a systematic framework for analyzing how we shape culture and how it, in turn, shapes us. It also does not provide insight into how shared meanings are developed among people, and it does not take into account the many situations in which there is disagreement on meanings. Whereas the functional and conflict approaches tend to overemphasize the macrolevel workings of society, the symbolic interactionist viewpoint often fails to take into account these larger social structures.

Postmodern Perspectives

Postmodern theories believe that much of what has been written about culture in the Western world is Eurocentric—that it is based on the uncritical assumption that European culture (including its dispersed versions in countries such as the United States, Canada, Australia, and South Africa) is the true, universal culture in which all the world's people ought to believe (Lemert, 1997). By contrast, postmodernists believe that we should speak of *cultures*, rather than *culture*.

However, Jean Baudrillard, one of the best-known contemporary French social theorists, believes that the world of culture today is based on *simulation*, not reality. According to Baudrillard, social life is much more a spectacle that simulates reality than reality itself. Many people gain "reality" from the media or cyberspace. For example, consider the many North American children who, on entering school for the first time, have already watched more hours of television than the total number of hours of classroom instruction they will encounter in their entire school careers. Add to this the number of hours that some will have spent playing computer games or surfing the Internet. Baudrillard refers to this social creation as *hyperreality*—a situation in which the simulation of reality is more real than the thing itself. For Baudrillard, everyday life has been captured by the signs and symbols generated to represent it, and we

ultimately relate to simulations and models as if they were reality. Baudrillard (1983) uses Disneyland as an example of a simulation that conceals the reality that exists outside rather than inside the boundaries of the artificial perimeter. According to Baudrillard, Disney-like theme parks constitute a form of seduction that substitutes symbolic (i.e., seductive) power for real power, particularly the ability to bring about social change. From this perspective, amusement park "guests" may feel like "survivors" after enduring the rapid speed and gravity-defying movements of the roller coaster rides or see themselves as "winners" after surviving fights with hideous cartoon villains on the "dark rides" when they have actually experienced the substitution of an *appearance* of power over their lives for the *absence* of real power. In their examination of culture, postmodern social theorists make us aware that no single perspective can grasp the complexity and diversity of the social world. They also make us aware that reality may not be what it seems. According to the postmodern view, no one authority can claim to know social reality, and we should deconstruct—take apart and subject to intense critical scrutiny—existing beliefs and theories about culture in hopes of gaining new insights (Ritzer, 1997).

Although postmodern theories of culture have been criticized on a number of grounds, we will examine only three. One criticism is postmodernism's lack of a clear conceptualization of ideas. Another is the tendency to critique other perspectives as being "grand narratives," whereas postmodernists offer their own varieties of such narratives. Finally, some analysts believe that postmodern analyses of culture lead to profound pessimism about the future.

CULTURE IN THE FUTURE

As we have discussed in this chapter, many changes are occurring in our Canadian culture. Increasing cultural diversity can either bring long-simmering racial and ethnic antagonisms closer to a boiling point or result in the creation of a truly multicultural society in which diversity is respected and encouraged. According to our ideal culture, Canada will "prosper in diversity." The Multicultural Act has legislated cultural freedom. However, it has been suggested that this freedom is more "symbolic" than real (Roberts and Clifton, 1999). In the real culture, anti-immigration

New technologies have made educational opportunities available to a greater diversity of students, including persons with disabilities.

Photos.com

sentiment has risen in response to the millions of newcomers who have arrived in Canada over the past decade. Cultural diversity and global immigration are affecting economic and employment perceptions. Many people accuse newcomers of stealing jobs and overutilizing the social service safety net at the Canadian taxpayer's expense.

In the future, the issue of cultural diversity will increase in importance, especially in schools. Multicultural education that focuses on the contributions of a wide variety of people from different backgrounds will continue to be an issue from kindergarten through university. Some public schools have incorporated a number of heritage languages into their curriculum. These schools will face the challenge of embracing widespread cultural diversity while conveying a sense of community and national identity to students.

Technology will continue to have a profound effect on culture. Television and radio, films and videos, and digital communications will continue to accelerate the flow of information and expand cultural diffusion throughout the world. Global communication devices will move images of people's lives, behaviour, and fashions instantaneously among almost all nations (Petersen, 1994). Increasingly, computers and cyberspace may become people's

window on the world and, in the process, promote greater integration or fragmentation among nations. Integration occurs when there is a widespread acceptance of ideas and items—such as democracy, rock music, blue jeans, and McDonald's hamburgers—among cultures. By contrast, fragmentation occurs when people in one culture disdain the beliefs and actions of other cultures. As a force for both cultural integration and fragmentation, technology will continue to revolutionize communications, but most of the world's population will not participate in this revolution (Petersen, 1994).

From a sociological perspective, the study of culture helps us not only understand our own tool kit of symbols, stories, rituals, and worldviews, but also expand our insights to include those of other people of the world who, like us, seek strategies for enhancing their lives. If we understand how culture is used by people, how cultural elements constrain or facilitate certain patterns of action, what aspects of our cultural heritage have enduring effects on our actions, and what specific historical changes undermine the validity of some cultural patterns and give rise to others, we can apply our sociological imagination not only to our own society but also to the entire world.

What is culture?

Culture encompasses the knowledge, language, values, and customs passed from one generation to the next in a human group or society. Culture may be either material or nonmaterial. Material culture consists of the physical creations of society. Nonmaterial culture is more abstract and reflects the ideas, values, and beliefs of a society.

What are cultural universals?

Cultural universals are customs and practices that exist in all societies and include activities and institutions such as storytelling, families, and laws. Specific forms of these universals vary from one cultural group to another, however.

What are the four nonmaterial components of culture that are common to all societies?

These components are common to all cultures: symbols, language, values, and norms. Symbols express shared meanings; through them, groups communicate cultural ideas and abstract concepts. Language is a set of symbols through which groups communicate. Values are a culture's collective ideas about what is or is not acceptable. Norms are the specific behavioural expectations within a culture.

What are culture shock, ethnocentrism, and cultural relativism?

Culture shock refers to the anxiety people experience when they encounter cultures radically different from their own. Ethnocentrism is the assumption that one's own culture is superior to others. Cultural relativism counters culture shock and ethnocentrism by viewing and analyzing another culture in terms of its own values and standards.

What causes culture change?

Culture change takes place in all societies. Change occurs through discovery and invention and through diffusion, which is the transmission of culture from one society or group to another.

How is cultural diversity reflected in society?

Cultural diversity is reflected through race, ethnicity, age, sexual orientation, religion, occupation, and so forth. A diverse culture also includes subcultures and countercultures. A subculture has distinctive ideas and behaviours that differ from the larger society to which it belongs. A counterculture rejects the dominant societal values and norms.

How do the major theoretical perspectives view culture?

A functional analysis of culture assumes that a common language and shared values help to produce consensus and harmony. According to some conflict theorists, culture may be used by certain groups to maintain their privilege and exclude others from society's benefits. Symbolic interactionists suggest that people create, maintain, and modify culture as they go about their everyday activities. Postmodern thinkers believe that there are many cultures within Canada. They suggest we need a new way of conceptualizing culture and society.

KEY TERMS

counterculture 47
cultural lag 42
cultural imperialism 43
cultural relativism 42
cultural universals 34
culture 32
culture shock 47
diffusion 43
discovery 43
ethnocentrism 42
folkways 40
ideology 48
ideal culture 39
invention 43
language 37
laws 40
material culture 33
mores 40
nonmaterial culture 34
norms 40
real culture 39
sanctions 40
Sapir-Whorf hypothesis 37
subculture 45
symbol 36
taboos 40
technology 33
values 39
value contradictions 39

WEB LINKS

For more Web links related to the topic of this chapter, see the Nelson sociology website: **www.sociologyessentials5e.nelson.com.**

The federal government has a website called "About Canada" that contains information related to society and culture, including multiculturalism, Aboriginal culture and heritage, and national cultural institutions: **http://canada.gc.ca/acanada/acPubHome. jsp?lang=eng**

The Department of Heritage has a site entitled "Multiculturalism" that includes current research on hate-motivated activities in Canada. To see it, go to: **www.pch.gc.ca/pc-ch/sujets-subjects/ divers-multi/multi/index_e.cfm**

QUESTIONS FOR CRITICAL THINKING

1. Would it be possible today to live in a totally separate culture in Canada? Could you avoid all influences from the mainstream popular culture or from the values and norms of other cultures? How would you be able to avoid any change in your culture?

2. What do you consider to be uniquely Canadian symbols? Generate a list of three or four. Can you identify examples of symbols that represent other countries?

3. How do we see cultural differences in our everyday life? What different cultural groups are you a part of and how do they intersect or interact?

ONLINE STUDY AND RESEARCH TOOLS

INFOTRAC®

InfoTrac College Edition is included free with every new copy of this text. Explore this online library for additional readings, review, and a handy resource for assignments. Visit **www.infotrac-college.com** to access this online database of full-text articles. Enter the key terms from this chapter to start your search.

CENGAGENOW™ CENGAGENOW

Use CengageNOW™ to help you formulate a customized study plan for this chapter. After you take the Diagnostic Quiz, CengageNOW™ will generate a customized study plan for you. It will identify sections of the chapter you should review.

Socialization

"Child care is a divisive issue—there's no question about it. To stay at home and care for your own children, or to do paid work and hire a caregiver? Either way it's a complex decision, with costs on both sides. I call it the Child Care Equation. Every parent has to determine for himself or herself the value of each variable in the equation. . . .

"When my first baby was born, I welcomed the opportunity to stay home, having been unhappy in my paid work position. Still, by the time my daughter was nine months old. I felt isolated—despite the baby 'playgroups' I had optimistically joined. So I accepted a temporary contract and arranged for daycare. Never have I wept so hard as I did on the second day—not when I dropped off my baby, but when I arrived at the caregiver's house at the end of the day only to learn we had effectively been "fired" because my daughter cried too much. Luckily I was able to find another caregiver. My daughter was treated with kindness and affection—yet, throughout the entire six months of my contract work, I was always concerned that she was in a less than ideal situation, although she seemed fairly content.

"When my contract expired, I seriously questioned the sense in leaving my child in a stranger's care so that I could work for other strangers for little reward, monetary or otherwise. . . . After a few months of unsuccessful job searching, I decided to stay at home and open a family daycare to help ends meet. Once again I cried, only this time it was from fear that the world would pass me by.

"Admittedly, there are days when I feel a little sad and out of the loop, when I long to restart my career, when I miss going to an office and ploughing through an in basket with no little voice whining 'Mommeeeeeeeee' in the background. But there are many more days when it is pure joy and privilege to be at home experiencing every single moment of my children's discovery of the world[.]

"Life is full of trade-offs, especially once you add children to the mix. I can't speak for all stay at home parents, and I know there are many who experience loneliness, frustration, boredom, and even depression. Yet, in spite of the toll it takes on their emotions and self-esteem, they choose to be at home with their children. Some mothers (yes, I'll come right out and identify the female sex here because in most cases when a parent stays at home it is the mother) delay returning to the outside workforce until their children enter school full-time. Others wait a little longer, while others never re-enter the outside workforce, happily complementing their mothering with equally valuable volunteer work.

"So, for the present, my Child Care Equation involves two parents, two kids, one moderate income household, a growing pile of bills, a healthy supply of fun, and an endless excitement about what the future may bring." (Sutin, 2002:14)

What this young mother is considering in her contemplation of what she refers to as the "childcare equation" is what is best for her children's healthy socialization. Today, more than ever before, parents are aware of the lasting impact of a child's early socialization. What is the formula to maximize a child's social, psychological, and intellectual potential? There are no easy answers, as parents are finding out. As sociologist Linda Quirke explains, "parents today are a formidable cohort" who are more educated, older, and with fewer children than previous generations (Ferguson, 2004:30). This may result in more effective parenting, with a more intensive focus on meeting the early socialization needs of individual children. However, there are potentially negative results as well—what has been referred to as "hyperparenting" (Rosenfeld and Wise, 2000). The choices are endless: home care, daycare, parent care, preschool, private school, home schooling, private tutoring, hockey, gymnastics, dance, music, Scouts, Girl Guides. Some of the results of these well-intentioned efforts present some disturbing outcomes in our "hyperparenting culture." Examples include a 60 percent increase in some provinces in private tutoring services in the past decade, two-hour homework sessions for Grade 1 students, flashcards for preschoolers, and crazed hockey parents expelled from games for attacking referees. Some experts

have suggested that children today are overprogrammed and overscheduled, and have lost the ability of unstructured play. What will be the effects of these early socialization efforts on this new generation of children?

Socialization is a lifelong process that includes socialization in childhood, adolescence, and adulthood. Each of these stages of life presents its own special challenges as we are socialized or "resocialized." In this chapter we examine why socialization is so crucial, and we discuss both sociological and social psychological theories of human development. We look at the dynamics of socialization—how it occurs and what shapes it. Throughout the chapter, we focus on positive and negative aspects of the socialization process. Before reading on, test your knowledge of early socialization and child care by taking the quiz in Box 3.1.

QUESTIONS AND ISSUES

Chapter Focus Question: What purpose does socialization serve?

What happens when children do not have an environment that supports positive socialization?

How do individuals develop a sense of self?

How does socialization occur?

WHY IS SOCIALIZATION IMPORTANT?

Socialization **is the lifelong process of social interaction through which individuals acquire a self-identity and the physical, mental, and social skills needed for survival in society.** It is the essential link between the individual and society. Socialization enables each of us to develop our human potential and learn the ways of thinking, talking, and acting that are essential for social living.

Socialization is essential for the individual's survival and for human development. The many people who met the early material and social needs of each of us were central to our establishing our own identity. During the first three years of our life, we begin to develop a unique identity and the ability to manipulate things and to walk. We acquire sophisticated cognitive tools for thinking and for analyzing a wide variety of situations, and we learn effective communication skills. In the process, we begin a relatively long socialization process that culminates in our integration into a complex social and cultural system (Garcia Coll, 1990).

Sociologists emphasize that social environment is a crucial part of an individual's socialization.

BOX 3.1   SOCIOLOGY AND EVERYDAY LIFE

How Much Do You Know About Early Socialization and Child Care?

True	False	
T	**F**	1. A child who experiences substantial amounts of child care, especially in the first year of life, is more likely to experience attachment problems with his or her mother.
T	**F**	2. Children cared for exclusively at home are better prepared for school.
T	F	3. There is considerable evidence that good-quality child care can play an important role in protecting young children from family-based risk.
T	**F**	4. Because of inadequate parental-leave programs, most Canadian mothers who work outside the home return to work when their children are less than a year old.
T	**F**	5. Social science confirms that children raised in daycare centres are often emotionally maladjusted.
T	F	6. Currently in Canada, more than half of preschool children spend time in some form of daycare.
T	F	7. In recent years there has been an increase in the number of stay-at-home dads.
T	**F**	8. The majority of children attend daycare in regulated daycare centres.

Answers on page 58.

Socialization is also essential for the survival and stability of society. Members of a society must be socialized to support and maintain the existing social structure. From a functionalist perspective, individual conformity to existing norms is not taken for granted; rather, basic individual needs and desires must be balanced against the needs of the social structure. The socialization process is most effective when people conform to the norms of society because they believe this is the best course of action. Socialization enables a society to "reproduce" itself by passing on this cultural content from one generation to the next.

While ways in which people learn beliefs, values, and rules of behaviour are somewhat similar in many countries, the content of socialization differs greatly from society to society. How people walk, talk, eat, make love, and wage war are all functions of the culture in which they are raised. At the same time, we also are influenced by our exposure to subcultures of class, ethnicity, religion, and gender. In addition, each of us has unique experiences in our families and friendship groupings. The kind of human being that we become depends greatly on the particular society and social groups that surround us at birth and during early childhood. What we believe about ourselves, our society, and the world is largely a product of our interactions with others.

Human Development: Biology and Society

What does it mean to be "human"? To be human includes being conscious of ourselves as individuals with unique identities, personalities, and relationships with others. As humans, we have ideas, emotions, and values. We have the capacity to think and to make rational decisions. But what is the source of "humanness"? Are we born with these human characteristics, or do we develop them through our interactions with others?

When we are born, we are dependent on others for our survival. We cannot turn ourselves over, speak, reason, plan, or do many of the things that are associated with being human. Although we can nurse, wet, and cry, most small mammals also can do those things. As discussed in Chapter 2, we humans differ from nonhuman animals because we lack some instincts and must rely on learning for our survival. Human infants have the potential for developing human characteristics if they are exposed to an adequate socialization process.

Every human being is a product of biology, society, and personal experiences—that is, of heredity and environment, or, in even more basic terms, "nature" and "nurture." How much of our development can be explained by socialization? How much by our genetic heritage?

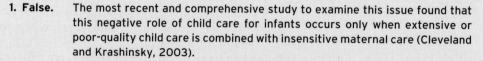

BOX 3.1 | SOCIOLOGY AND EVERYDAY LIFE

Answers to the Sociology Quiz on Early Socialization and Child Care

1. False. The most recent and comprehensive study to examine this issue found that this negative role of child care for infants occurs only when extensive or poor-quality child care is combined with insensitive maternal care (Cleveland and Krashinsky, 2003).

2. False. Results from analysis of data from the latest National Longitudinal Survey of Children and Youth suggest that children who are enrolled in early childhood programs and daycare centres appear to get a head start in school over youngsters who stay at home with a parent (Prochner and Howe, 2000).

3. True. For example, good-quality child care can reduce the negative effects of poverty and maternal depression on the development of infants and older preschoolers (Cleveland and Krashinsky, 2003).

4. False. In Canada, the Employment Insurance program provides one year of income-replacing maternity and parental benefits—15 weeks exclusively to the mother, and another 35 weeks that can be divided between the mother and father (Cleveland and Krashinsky, 2003).

5. False. Controlled studies of good child care for preschool children found that children were not, in general, harmed in their emotional development by daily short-term separations from their parents and indeed benefited in many ways from the experience (Cleveland and Krashinsky, 2003).

6. True. According to the National Longitudinal Survey of Children and Youth, the rate has increased from 42 percent in 1994/95 to more than 53 percent today. Of all children in child care, approximately 25 percent were enrolled in a daycare centre as their main care arrangement, up from about 20 percent six years earlier. The proportion of children who were looked after in their own home by a relative rose from 8 to 14 percent (Bushnik, 2006).

7. True. The proportion of families with stay-at-home fathers has increased from 1 percent in 1976 to approximately 6 percent (Marshall, 2009a).

8. False. While the number of regulated daycare spaces has increased dramatically, it is estimated that fewer than 20 percent of children whose mothers work can be accommodated. The majority of children in nonparental care continue to be cared for in unregulated homes or centres (Friendly and Prentice, 2009).

There is hardly a behaviour that is not influenced socially. Except for simple reflexes, such as dilation of the pupils and knee-jerk responses, most human actions are social, either in their causes or in their consequences. Even solitary actions such as crying or brushing our teeth are ultimately social. We cry because we are in pain or upset. We brush our teeth because our parents (or a dentist) told us it was important to do so. Social environment probably has a greater effect than heredity on the way we develop and the way we act. However, heredity does provide the basic material from which other people help to mould an individual's human characteristics.

Our biological and emotional needs are related in a complex equation. Children whose needs are met in settings characterized by affection, warmth, and closeness see the world as a safe and comfortable place and other people as trustworthy and helpful. By contrast, infants and children who receive less-than-adequate care or who are emotionally rejected or abused often view the world as hostile and have pervasive feelings of suspicion and fear.

Social Isolation and Maltreatment

Social environment, then, is a crucial part of an individual's socialization. Even nonhuman primates such as monkeys and chimpanzees need social contact with others of their species to develop properly. As we will see, appropriate social contact is even more important for humans.

Isolation and Nonhuman Primates Researchers have attempted to demonstrate the effects of social isolation on nonhuman primates raised without contact with others of their own species. In a series of laboratory experiments, Harry and Margaret Harlow (1962, 1977) took infant rhesus monkeys from their mothers and isolated them in separate cages. Each cage contained two nonliving "mother substitutes" made of wire, one with a feeding bottle attached and the other covered with soft terry cloth but without a bottle. The infant monkeys instinctively clung to the "cloth mother" and would not abandon it until hunger drove them to the bottle attached to the "wire mother." As soon as they were full, they would go back to the cloth mother, seeking warmth, affection, and physical comfort.

The Harlows' experiments show the detrimental effects of isolation on nonhuman primates. When the young monkeys later were introduced to other members of their species, they cringed in the corner. Having been deprived of social contact with other monkeys during their first six months of life, they never learned how to relate to other monkeys or to become well-adjusted adult monkeys—they were either fearful of or hostile toward other monkeys.

Because humans rely more heavily on social learning than do monkeys, the process of socialization is even more important for us.

Isolated Children Social scientists have documented cases of children who were deliberately raised in isolation. A look at the life of two children who suffered such emotional abuse provides important insights into the effect of social isolation on human beings.

Anna Born in 1932 to an unmarried woman with intellectual challenges, Anna was an unwanted child. She was kept in an attic-like room in her maternal grandfather's house. Her mother, who worked on the family farm all day and often went out at night, gave Anna just enough care to keep her alive; she received no other care. Kingsley Davis (1940) described her condition when she was found in 1938:

> [Anna] had no glimmering of speech, absolutely no ability to walk, no sense of gesture, not the least capacity to feed herself even when the food was put in front of her, and no comprehension of cleanliness. She was so apathetic that it was hard to tell whether or not she could hear. And all of this at the age of nearly six years.

When she was placed in a special school and given the necessary care, Anna slowly learned to walk, talk, and care for herself. Just before her death at the age of ten, Anna reportedly could follow directions, talk in phrases, wash her hands, brush her teeth, and try to help other children (Davis, 1940).

Genie Three decades after Anna was discovered, Genie was found in 1970, at the age of thirteen. She had been locked in a bedroom alone, alternately strapped down to a child's potty-chair or straitjacketed into a sleeping bag, since she was twenty months old. She had been fed only baby food and was beaten with a wooden paddle when she whimpered. She had not heard the sounds of human speech because no one talked to her and there was no television or radio in her home (Curtiss, 1977; Pines, 1981). Genie was placed in a pediatrics hospital, where one of the psychologists described her condition:

> At the time of her admission she was virtually unsocialized. She could not stand erect, salivated continuously, had never been toilet-trained and had no control over her urinary or bowel functions. She was unable to chew solid food and had the weight, height and appearance of a child half her age. (Rigler, 1993:35)

In addition to her physical condition, Genie showed psychological traits associated with neglect, as described by one of her psychiatrists:

> If you gave [Genie] a toy, she would reach out and touch it, hold it, caress it with her fingertips, as though she didn't trust her eyes. She would rub it against her cheek to feel it. So when I met her and she began to notice me standing beside her bed, I held my hand out and she reached out and took my hand and carefully felt my thumb and fingers individually, and then put my hand against her cheek. She was exactly like a blind child. (Rymer, 1993:45)

Extensive therapy was used in an attempt to socialize Genie and develop her language abilities (Curtiss, 1977; Pines, 1981). These efforts met with limited success: In the early 1990s, Genie was living in a board-and-care home for adults with mental challenges (see Angier, 1993; Rigler, 1993; Rymer, 1993).

Child Maltreatment

What do the terms *child maltreatment* and *child abuse* mean to you? When asked what constitutes child maltreatment, many people first think of cases that

BOX 3.2 SOCIOLOGY IN GLOBAL PERSPECTIVE

Early Childhood Education and Learning: How Does Canada Measure Up Internationally?

Since the early 1990s an extensive amount of comparative data has been generated which allows us to compare Canadian child care and early childhood education programs in an international context. According to the experts Canada does not measure up well when we step "beyond our borders" (Friendly and Prentice, 2009).

Canada's child care system is described as a "chronically underfunded patchwork of programs with no overarching goals." There is a shortage of regulated child care spaces—enough for less than 20 percent of children under six with working parents (CBC, 2006). Figure 1 provides international comparisons access to regulated child care.

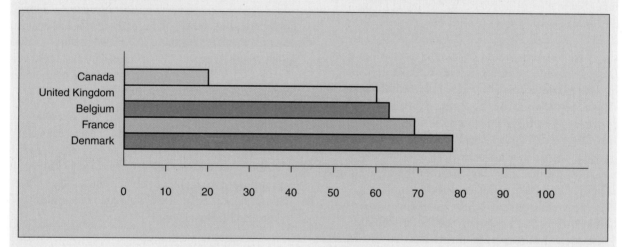

Source: Based on OECD (2006), *Starting Strong II: Early Childhood Education and Care*, p. 246.

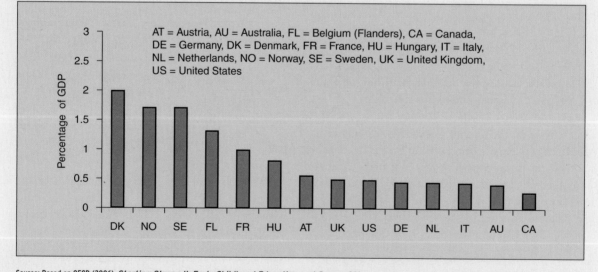

Source: Based on OECD (2006), *Starting Strong II: Early Childhood Education and Care*, p. 246.

In December 2008, a UNICEF report card on child care and early childhood education again indicated that Canada's early learning and child care situation ranked Canada last among 25 developed countries. For example, Figure 2 indicates Canada was ranked last of 14 countries on spending on early learning and child care programs, 14 of 20 countries for access to regulated child care for 0–3-year-olds,

BOX 3.2 SOCIOLOGY IN GLOBAL PERSPECTIVE

Early Childhood Education and Learning: How Does Canada Measure Up Internationally? (Continued)

last of 20 countries for 3-6-year-olds' access to regulated child care programs. These results are particularly disturbing given that Canada is one of the wealthiest countries in the world (Friendly, 2006b).

What are the implications of limited access and insufficient funding of early childhood education and child care? Canada is one of the most affluent industrialized countries but invests relatively little in the earliest years—a critical period of development that lays the foundation for each child's potential. Canada's poor showing represents a lost opportunity for economic growth at a time of economic uncertainly. Building a system of high-quality early-childhood care and education creates jobs and allows parents to work and pay taxes. (UNICEF, 2008). Early childhood education and child care has

huge potential to enhance children's well-being and development with significant long-term social and economic returns:

According to early childhood education expert Martha Friendly, Canada's poor showing should be a "head's up" to Canadians. What is needed is "Stronger pollicies to give all Canadian children the chance for the best start in life by guaranteeing quality child care and education for those who need it and want it according to cross-national min-mimum standards" (UNICEF, 2008b).

Child care experts have questioned how a country that leads the way internationally in terms of provision of universal health care can have such a poor standing in terms of provision of early child-hood education and daycare. Why do you think these services have not been given top priority?

Sources: UNICEF 2008a; UNICEF 2008c; CBC, 2006a; Friendly, 2006a; Friendly, 2006b;

---

involve severe injuries or sexual abuse. However, the terms *child abuse* and *child maltreatment* refer to the violence, mistreatment, or neglect that a child may experience while in the care of someone he or she trusts or depends on, such as a parent, other relative, caregiver, or guardian. There are many different forms of abuse including physical abuse, sexual abuse or exploitation, neglect, and emotional abuse. A child who is abused often experiences more than one form of abuse.

Child abuse is a complex problem that involves individual, familial, and social factors. Any child—regardless of age, gender, race, ethnicity, socioeconomic status, sexual orientation, physical or mental abilities, or personality—may be vulnerable to being abused. Sociologists argue that child abuse is linked to inequalities in our society and the power imbalance that exists between adults and children. A child is usually dependent on his or her abuser and has little power to control his or her abusive circumstances. There is increasing understanding that a child's vulnerability to being abused may be increased by other identifiable social factors, such as racism, sexism, homophobia, poverty, and social isolation. For example, historically, many children who were sent to institutions were abused. The majority of these children were from marginalized groups such as

Aboriginal children, children from racial and ethnic minorities, children with physical or mental disabilities, or children living in poverty.

AGENTS OF SOCIALIZATION

Agents of socialization **are the persons, groups, or institutions that teach us what we need to know to participate in society.** We are exposed to many agents of socialization throughout our lifetime. Here, we look at the most pervasive ones in childhood—the family, the school, peer groups, and the mass media.

The Family

The family is the most important agent of socialization in all societies. The love and nurturance we receive from our families are essential to normal cognitive, emotional, and physical development. From infancy, our families transmit cultural and social values to us. As discussed later in this book, families in Canada vary in size and structure. Some families consist of two parents and their biological children,

Daycare centres have become important agents of socialization for increasing numbers of children. Today, more than 50 percent of all Canadian preschool children are in daycare of one kind or another.

whereas others consist of a single parent and one or more children. Still other families reflect changing patterns of divorce and remarriage, and an increasing number are made up of same-sex partners and their children.

Theorists using a functionalist perspective emphasize that families serve important functions in society because they are the primary focus for the procreation and the socialization of children. Most of us form an emerging sense of self and acquire most of our beliefs and values within the family context. We also learn about the dominant culture (including language, attitudes, beliefs, values, and norms) and the primary subcultures to which our parents and other relatives belong.

Families also are the primary source of emotional support. Ideally, people receive love, understanding, security, acceptance, intimacy, and companionship within families. The role of the family is especially significant because young children have little social experience beyond its boundaries; they have no basis for comparison or for evaluating how they are treated by their own family.

Conflict theorists stress that socialization reproduces the class structure in the next generation. Conflict theorists stress that socialization contributes to a *false consciousness*—a lack of awareness and

a distorted perception of the reality of class as it affects all aspects of social life. As a result, socialization reaffirms and reproduces the class structure in the next generation, rather than challenging the conditions that currently exist. For example, children in low-income families may be unintentionally socialized to believe that acquiring an education and aspiring to lofty ambitions are pointless because of existing economic conditions in the family (Ballantine, 2001). By contrast, middle and upper-income families typically instill ideas of monetary and social success in children, as well as emphasize the necessity of thinking and behaving in "socially acceptable" ways.

The School

As the amount of specialized technical and scientific knowledge has expanded rapidly and the amount of time children are in educational settings has increased, schools have come to play an enormous role in the socialization of young people. For many people, the formal education process is an undertaking that lasts up to 20 years.

As the number of single-parent families and families in which both parents work outside the home has increased dramatically in the past two decades, the number of children in daycare and preschool programs has grown (Bushnik, 2006). Generally, studies have found that daycare and preschool programs may have a positive effect on the overall socialization of children. These programs are especially beneficial for children from less-advantaged backgrounds in that they provide these children with valuable learning experiences not available at home. Many researchers also have found that children from all social classes and family backgrounds may benefit from learning experiences in early childhood education programs outside their homes (see Box 3.2 on page 60).

Although schools teach specific knowledge and skills; they also have a profound effect on children's self-image, beliefs, and values. As children enter school for the first time, they are evaluated and systematically compared with one another by the teacher. A permanent, official record is kept of each child's personal behaviour and academic activities. From a functionalist perspective, schools are responsible for (1) socialization, or teaching students to be productive members of society; (2) transmission of culture; (3) social control and personal development; and (4) the selection, training, and placement of individuals on different rungs in the society (Ballantine, 2001).

© Gaetano/Corbis

© Roy Morsch/Corbis

The pleasure of participating in activities with friends is one of the many attractions of adolescent peer groups. What groups have contributed the most to your own sense of belonging and self-worth?

In contrast, conflict theorists assert that the educational system solidifies class inequalities in society and allows the elite to control the masses (Mooney et al., 2001). According to Stephen Richer (1988), much of what happens in school amounts to teaching a *hidden curriculum* in which children learn to value competition, materialism, work over play, obedience to authority, and attentiveness. Thus, schools do not socialize children for their own well-being but rather for their later roles in the workforce, where it is important to be punctual and show deference to supervisors. Students who are destined for leadership or elite positions acquire different skills and knowledge than those who will enter working- and middle-class occupations.

Peer Groups

As soon as we are old enough to have acquaintances outside the home, most of us begin to rely heavily on peer groups as a source of information and approval about social behaviour (Lips, 1989). A **peer group is a group of people who are linked by common interests, equal social position, and (usually) similar age**. In early childhood, peer groups often comprise classmates in daycare, preschool, and elementary school. In adolescence, peer groups are typically people with similar interests and include social activities. As adults, we continue to participate in peer groups of people with whom we share common interests and comparable occupations, income, or social position.

Peer groups function as agents of socialization by contributing to our sense of "belonging" and our feelings of self-worth. Unlike families and schools, peer

groups provide children and adolescents with some degree of freedom from parents and other authority figures (Corsaro, 1992). Peer groups also teach and reinforce cultural norms while providing important information about "acceptable" behaviour. As a result, the peer group is both a product of culture and one of its major transmitters (Elkin and Handel, 1989).

Is there such a thing as "peer pressure"? Individuals must *earn* their acceptance with their peers by conforming to a given group's *own* norms, attitudes, speech patterns, and dress codes. When we conform to our peer group's expectations, we are rewarded; if we do not conform, we may be ridiculed or even expelled from the group. Conforming to the demands of peers frequently places children and adolescents at cross-purposes with their parents. William A. Corsaro (1992) notes that children experience strong peer pressure even during their preschool years. For example, children frequently are under pressure to obtain certain valued material possessions (such as toys, clothing, or athletic shoes); they then pass this pressure onto their parents through emotional pleas to purchase the desired items. In this way, adult caregivers learn about the latest fads and fashions from children, and they may contribute to the peer culture by purchasing the items desired by the children (Corsaro, 1992).

Mass Media

An agent of socialization that has a profound impact on both children and adults is the *mass media,* which comprises large-scale organizations that use print or electronic means (such as radio, television, film, and the Internet) to communicate with large numbers of people. The media function as socializing agents in several ways: (1) they inform us about events, (2) they introduce us to a wide variety of people, (3) they provide an array of viewpoints on current issues, (4) they make us aware of products and services that, if we purchase them, supposedly will help us be accepted by others, and (5) they entertain us by providing the opportunity to live vicariously (through other people's experiences). Although most of us take for granted that the media play an important part in contemporary socialization, we frequently underestimate the enormous influence this agent of socialization may have on children's attitudes and behaviour.

According to media educator Arlene Moscovitch (2007), there is no doubt that media encounters are an inescapable part of everyday life.

One thing is certain: we are living through a technological revolution which infuses every level of our lives and there is no going back. It's not clear where we're going but the young are leading the charge . . . Unlike most of their parents, the media embrace feels entirely natural to them. In fact, when detached in some ways from their iPods or their cell phones or their laptops, they are likely to feel less than complete. (Moscovitch, 2007:23)

It is estimated that Canadian children spend just over two hours per day watching television and an additional two hours with computers, video games, or a VCR. Parents, educators, social scientists, and public officials have widely debated the consequences of young people watching that much television. Television has been praised for offering numerous positive experiences to children. Some scholars suggest that television (when used wisely) can enhance children's development by improving their language abilities, concept-formation skills, and reading skills and by encouraging prosocial development (Winn, 1985). However, other studies have shown that children and adolescents who spend a lot of time watching television often have lower grades in school, read fewer books, exercise less, and are overweight (Moscovitch, 2007).

Of special concern to many people is the issue of television violence. It is estimated that the typical young person who watches 28 hours of television a week will have seen 16 000 simulated murders and 200 000 acts of violence by the time he or she reaches age 18. A report by the American Psychological Association states that about 80 percent of all television programs contain acts of violence and that commercial television for children is 50 to 60 times more violent than prime-time television for adults. For example, some cartoons average more than 80 violent acts per hour (APA Online, 2000).

Undoubtedly, all mass media socialize us in many ways we may or may not realize. Cultural studies scholars and some postmodern theorists believe that "media culture" has in recent years dramatically changed the socialization process for very young children.

SOCIOLOGICAL THEORIES OF HUMAN DEVELOPMENT

Although social scientists acknowledge the contributions of psychoanalytical and psychologically based explanations of human development, sociologists believe that it is important to bring a sociological perspective to bear on how people develop an awareness of self and learn about the culture in which they live. According to a sociological perspective, we cannot form a sense of self or personal identity without intense social contact with others. The *self* represents the sum total of perceptions and feelings that an individual has of being a distinct, unique person—a sense of who and what one is. This sense of self (also referred to as *self-concept*) is not present at birth; it arises in the process of social experience. **Self-concept is the totality of our beliefs and feelings about ourselves** (Gecas, 1982). Four components make up our self concept: (1) the *physical* self ("I am tall"), (2) the *active* self ("I am good at soccer"), (3) the *social* self ("I am nice to others"), and (4) the *psychological* self ("I believe in world peace"). Between early and late childhood, a child's focus tends to shift from the physical and active dimensions of self toward the social and psychological aspects (Lippa, 1994). Self-concept is the foundation for communication with others; it continues to develop and change throughout our lives (Zurcher, 1983).

Our *self-identity* is our perception about what kind of person we are. As we have seen, socially isolated children do not have typical self-identities because they have had no experience of humanness. According to symbolic interactionists, we do not know who we are until we see ourselves as we believe others see us. We gain information about the self largely through language, symbols, and interaction with others. Our interpretation and evaluation of these messages is central to the social construction of our identity. However, we are not just passive reactors to situations, programmed by society to respond in fixed ways. Instead, we are active agents who develop plans out of the pieces supplied by culture and attempt to execute these plans in social encounters (McCall and Simmons, 1978).

Cooley, Mead, and Symbolic Interactionist Perspectives

Social constructionism is a term that is applied to theories that emphasize the socially created nature of social life. This perspective is linked to symbolic interactionist theory, and its roots can be traced to the Chicago school and early theorists, such as Charles Horton Cooley and George Herbert Mead.

Cooley and the Looking-glass Self

According to sociologist Charles Horton Cooley (1864–1929), the **looking-glass self** refers to the

Our self-concept continues to be influenced by our interactions with others throughout our lives.

way in which a person's sense of self is derived from the perceptions of others. Our looking-glass self is not who we actually are or what people actually think about us; it is based on our *perception* of how other people think of us (Cooley, 1922/1902). Cooley asserted that we base our perception of who we are on how we think other people see us and on whether this seems good or bad to us.

As Figure 3.1 shows, the looking-glass self is a self-concept derived from a three-step process:

1. We imagine how our personality and appearance will look to other people. We may imagine that we are attractive or unattractive, heavy or slim, friendly or unfriendly, and so on.

2. We imagine how other people judge the appearance and personality that we think we present. This step involves our perception of how we think they are judging us. We may be correct or incorrect.

3. We develop a self-concept. If we think the evaluation of others is favourable, our self-concept is enhanced. If we think the evaluation is unfavourable, our self-concept is diminished (Cooley, 1922/1902).

According to Cooley, we use our interactions with others as a mirror for our own thoughts and actions; our sense of self depends on how we interpret what they do and say. Consequently, our sense of self is not permanently fixed; it is always developing as we interact with others.

Mead and Role-Taking

George Herbert Mead (1863–1931) extended Cooley's insights by linking the idea of self-concept

Figure 3.1	How the Looking-Glass Self Works

We imagine how we appear to other people.

We imagine how other people judge the appearance that we think we present.

If we think the evaluation is favourable, our self-concept is enhanced.

If we think the evaluation is unfavourable, our self-concept is diminished.

to *role-taking*—**the process by which a person mentally assumes the role of another person to understand the world from that person's point of view**. Role-taking often occurs through play and games, as children try out different roles (such as being mommy, daddy, doctor, or teacher) and gain an appreciation of them.

According to Mead (1934), in the early months of life children do not realize that they are separate from others. They do, however, begin early on to see a mirrored image of themselves in others. Shortly after birth, infants start to notice the faces of those around them, especially the significant others whose faces start to have meaning because they are associated with experiences such as feeding and cuddling. ***Significant others*** **are those persons whose care, affection, and approval are especially desired and who are most important in the development of the self**. Gradually, we distinguish ourselves from our caregivers and begin to perceive ourselves in contrast to them. As we develop language skills and learn to understand symbols, we begin to develop a self-concept. When we can represent ourselves in our own minds as objects distinct from everything else, our self has been formed.

Mead divided the self into the "I" and the "me." The "I" is the subjective element of the self that represents the spontaneous and unique traits of each person. The "me" is the objective element of the self, which comprises the internalized attitudes and demands of other members of society and the individual's awareness of those demands. Both the "I" and the "me" are needed to form the social self. The unity of the two constitutes the full development of the individual. According to Mead, the "I" develops first, and the "me" takes form during the three stages of self development:

1. During the *preparatory stage,* up to about the age of 3, interactions lack meaning, and children largely imitate the people around them. At this stage, children are *preparing* for role-taking.
2. In the *play stage,* from about ages 3 to 5, children learn to use language and other symbols, thus enabling them to pretend to take the roles of specific people. At this stage, children begin to see themselves in relation to others, but they do not see role-taking as something they have to do.
3. During the *game stage,* which begins in the early school years, children understand not only their own social position but also the positions of others around them. In contrast to play, games are structured by rules, often are competitive, and involve a number of other "players." At this time, children become concerned about the demands and expectations of others and of the larger society. Mead used the example of a baseball game to describe this stage because children, like baseball players, must take into account the roles of all other players at the same time. Mead's concept of the ***generalized other*** **refers to the child's awareness of the demands and expectations of the society as a whole or of the child's subculture**.

According to sociologist George Herbert Mead, the self develops through three stages. In the preparatory stage, children imitate others; in the play stage, children pretend to take the roles of specific people; and, in the game stage, children become aware of the "rules of the game" and the expectations of others.

How useful are symbolic interactionist perspectives such as Cooley's and Mead's in enhancing our understanding of the socialization process? Certainly, this approach contributes to our understanding of how the self develops. Cooley's idea of the looking-glass self makes us aware that our perception of how we *think* others see us is not always correct. Mead extended Cooley's ideas by emphasizing the cognitive skills acquired through role-taking. He stressed the importance of play and games, as children try out different roles and gain an appreciation of them. His concept of the generalized other helps us see that the self is a social creation. According to Mead (1934:196), "Selves can only exist in definite relations to other selves. No hard-and-fast line can be drawn between our own selves and the selves of others."

However, the viewpoints of symbolic interactionists such as Cooley and Mead have certain limitations. Sociologist Anne Kaspar (1986) suggests that Mead's ideas about the social self may be more applicable to men than women, because women are more likely to experience inherent conflicts between the meanings they derive from their personal experiences and those they take from culture, particularly in regard to balancing the responsibilities of family life and paid employment.

SOCIAL PSYCHOLOGICAL THEORIES OF HUMAN DEVELOPMENT

Up to this point, we have discussed sociologically oriented theories; we now turn to social-psychological theories that have influenced contemporary views of human development.

Freud and the Psychoanalytic Perspective

Sigmund Freud (1856–1939) is known as the founder of psychoanalytic theory. He lived largely in the Victorian era, during which biological explanations of human behaviour were prevalent. It also was an era of extreme sexual repression and male dominance compared with contemporary North American standards. Freud's theory was greatly influenced by these cultural factors, as reflected in the importance he assigned to sexual motives in explaining behaviour.

According to Freud (1924), human development occurs in three states that reflect different levels of the personality, which he referred to as the *id,* the *ego,* and the *superego.* The **id is the component of personality that includes all the individual's basic biological drives and needs that demand immediate gratification**. For Freud, the newborn child's personality is all id, and from birth the child finds that urges for self-gratification—such as wanting to be held, fed, or changed—are not going to be satisfied immediately. The **ego is the rational, reality-oriented component of personality that imposes restrictions on the innate pleasure-seeking drives of the id**. The ego channels the desire of the id for immediate gratification into the most advantageous direction for the individual. The **superego, or conscience, consists of the moral and ethical aspects of personality**. It is first expressed as the recognition of parental control and eventually matures as the child learns that parental control is a reflection of the values and moral demands of the larger society. When a person is well adjusted, the ego successfully manages the opposing forces of the id and the superego. Figure 3.2 on page 68 illustrates Freud's theory of personality.

Although subject to harsh criticism, Freud's theory made people aware of the importance of early childhood experiences, including abuse and neglect. His theories have also had a profound influence on contemporary mental-health practitioners and on other human-development theories.

Piaget and Cognitive Development

Jean Piaget (1896–1980), a Swiss psychologist, was a pioneer in the field of cognitive (intellectual) development. Cognitive theorists are interested in how people obtain, process, and use information—that is, in how we think. Cognitive development relates to changes over time in how we think.

Piaget (1954) believed that in each stage of development (from birth through adolescence), children's activities are governed by their perception of the world around them. His four stages of cognitive development are organized around specific tasks that, when mastered, lead to the acquisition of new mental capacities, which then serve as the basis for the next level of development. Piaget emphasized that all children must go through each stage in sequence before moving on to the next one, although some children move through them faster than others.

Figure 3.2   **Freud's Theory of Personality**

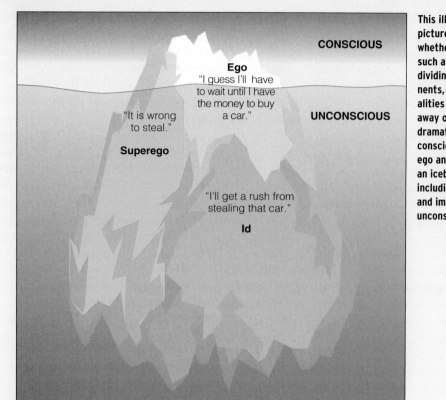

This illustration shows how Freud might picture a person's internal conflict over whether to commit an antisocial act, such as stealing a car. In addition to dividing personality into three components, Freud theorized that our personalities are largely unconscious—hidden away outside our normal awareness. To dramatize his point, Freud compared conscious awareness (portions of the ego and superego) to the visible tip of an iceberg. Most of our personality—including all the id, with its raw desires and impulses—lies submerged in our unconscious.

1. *Sensorimotor stage* (birth to age 2). During this period, children understand the world only through sensory contact and immediate action because they cannot engage in symbolic thought or use language.
2. *Preoperational stage* (age 2–7). In this stage, children begin to use words as mental symbols and to form mental images. However, they still are limited in their ability to use logic to solve problems or to realize that physical objects may change in shape or appearance while still retaining their physical properties. For example, they do not realize that the same amount of water appears at a different level in a narrow glass than it does in a wide glass.
3. *Concrete operational stage* (age 7–11). During this stage, children think in terms of tangible objects and actual events. They can draw conclusions about the likely physical consequences of an action without always having to try it out.
4. *Formal operational stage* (age 12 through adolescence). By this stage, adolescents are able to engage in highly abstract thought and understand

places, things, and events they have never seen. They can think about the future and evaluate different options or courses of action.

Piaget provided useful insights into the emergence of logical thinking through maturation and socialization. However, critics have noted that his approach to cognitive development fails to acknowledge individual differences among children and to provide for cultural differences.

Kohlberg and the Stages of Moral Development

Lawrence Kohlberg (1927–87) elaborated on Piaget's theories of cognitive reasoning by conducting a series of studies in which respondents were presented with a moral dilemma. Based on the responses, Kohlberg (1969, 1981) classified moral reasoning into three sequential levels.

1. *Preconventional level* (age 7–10). Children's perceptions are based on punishment and obedience.

Evil behaviour is that which is likely to be punished; good conduct is based on avoidance of unwanted consequences.

2. *Conventional level* (age 10 through adulthood). At this level, individuals are most concerned with how they are perceived by their peers and with how one conforms to rules.

3. *Postconventional level* (few adults reach this stage). People view morality in terms of individual rights; "moral conduct" is judged by principles based on human rights that transcend government and laws.

Critics have challenged the universality of Kohlberg's stages of moral development. They have also suggested that the elaborate "moral dilemmas" he used are too abstract for children. When questions are made simpler, or when children and adolescents are observed in natural (as opposed to laboratory) settings, they often demonstrate sophisticated levels of moral reasoning (Darley and Shultz, 1990; Lapsley, 1990).

Gilligan's Views on Gender and Moral Development

Psychologist Carol Gilligan (b. 1936) is one of the major critics of Kohlberg's theory of moral development. According to Gilligan (1982), Kohlberg's model was developed solely on the basis of research with male respondents. She suggested that women and men often have divergent views on morality based on differences in socialization and life experiences. Gilligan believes that men become more concerned with law and order but that women tend to analyze social relationships and the social consequences of behaviour. For example, in Kohlberg's story about a man who is thinking about stealing medicine for his critically ill wife, Gilligan argues that male respondents are more likely to use abstract standards of right and wrong whereas female respondents are more likely to be concerned about the consequences his stealing the drug might have on the man and his family. Does this constitute a "moral deficiency" on the part of either men or women? Not according to Gilligan.

To correct what she perceived to be a male bias in Kohlberg's research, Gilligan (1982) examined morality in women by interviewing 28 pregnant women who were contemplating having an abortion. Gilligan concluded that Kohlberg's stages do not reflect the ways many women think about moral problems. As a result, Gilligan identified three stages in female moral development. In stage 1, the woman is motivated primarily by selfish concerns (This is what I want, this is what I need). In stage 2, she increasingly recognizes her responsibility to others. In stage 3, she makes her decision based on her desire to do the greatest good for both herself and others. Gilligan argued that men are socialized to make moral decisions based on abstract principles of justice (What is the fairest thing to do?), whereas women are socialized to make such decisions from a responsibility and care perspective (Who will be hurt least?).

Subsequent research that directly compared women's and men's reasoning with respect to moral dilemmas has supported some of Gilligan's assertions but not others. For example, some researchers have not found that women are more compassionate than men (Tavris, 1993). Overall, however, Gilligan's argument that people make moral decisions according to both abstract principles of justice and principles of compassion and care is an important contribution to our knowledge about moral reasoning.

GENDER SOCIALIZATION

Gender socialization is the aspect of socialization that contains specific messages and practices concerning the nature of being female or male in a specific group or society. Gender socialization is important in determining what we *think* the "preferred" sex of a child should be and in influencing our beliefs about acceptable behaviours for males and females.

Parents may respond differently toward male and female infants; they often play more roughly with boys and talk more lovingly to girls. Throughout childhood and adolescence, boys and girls typically are assigned different types of household chores and given different privileges (such as how late they may stay out at night).

Schools, peer groups, and the media also contribute to our gender socialization. From kindergarten through college or university, teachers and peers reward gender-appropriate attitudes and behaviour. Sports reinforce traditional gender roles through a rigid division of events into male and female categories. The media also are a powerful source of gender socialization; from an early age, children's books, television programs, movies, and music provide subtle and not-so-subtle messages about "masculine" and "feminine" behaviour. Gender socialization is discussed in more depth in Chapter 10.

SOCIALIZATION THROUGH THE LIFE COURSE

Why is socialization a lifelong process? Throughout our lives we continue to learn. Each time we experience a change in status (such as becoming a university student or getting married), we learn a new set of rules, roles, and relationships. Even before we achieve a new status, we often participate in *anticipatory socialization*—**the process by which knowledge and skills are learned for future roles**. Many societies organize social experience according to age. Some have distinct *rites of passage,* based on age or other factors, which publicly dramatize and validate changes in a person's status. In Canada and other industrialized societies, the most common categories of age are infancy, childhood, adolescence, and adulthood (often subdivided into young adulthood, middle adulthood, and older adulthood). See the Census Profile on page 71, which shows the age categories used by Statistics Canada).

Infancy and Childhood

Some social scientists believe that a child's sense of self is formed at a very early age and that it is difficult to change this view later in life. Symbolic interactionists emphasize that during infancy and early childhood, family support and guidance are crucial to a child's developing self-concept. In some families, children are provided with emotional warmth, feelings of mutual trust, and a sense of security. These families come closer to our ideal cultural belief that childhood should be a time of carefree play, safety, and freedom from economic, political, and sexual responsibilities. However, other families reflect the discrepancy between cultural ideals and reality—children grow up in a setting characterized by fear, danger, and risks that are created by parental neglect, emotional abuse, or premature economic and sexual demands (Knudsen, 1992).

Abused children often experience low self-esteem, an inability to trust others, feelings of isolation and powerlessness, and denial of their feelings. However, the manner in which parental abuse affects children's ongoing development is subject to much debate and uncertainty. For example, some scholars and therapists assert that the intergenerational hypothesis—the idea that abused children will become abusive parents—is valid, but others have found little support for this hypothesis.

Adolescence

In industrialized societies, the adolescent (or teenage) years represent a buffer between childhood and adulthood. In Canada, no specific rites of passage exist to mark children's move into adulthood; therefore, young people have to pursue their own routes to self-identity and adulthood. Anticipatory socialization often is associated with adolescence, whereby many young people spend much of their time planning or being educated for future roles they hope to occupy. However, other adolescents (such as 15- and 16-year-old mothers) may have to plunge into adult responsibilities at this time. Adolescence often is characterized by emotional and social unrest. In the process of developing their own identities, some young people come into conflict with parents, teachers, and other authority figures who attempt to restrict their freedom. Adolescents also may find themselves caught between the demands of adulthood and their own lack of financial independence and experience in the job market. The experiences of individuals during adolescence vary according to their ethnicity, class, and gender. Based on their family's economic situation, some young people move directly into the adult world of work. However, those from upper-middle- and upper-class families may extend adolescence into their late 20s or early 30s by attending graduate or professional school, and then receiving additional advice and financial support from their parents as they start their own families, careers, or businesses.

Adulthood

One of the major differences between child and adult socialization is the degree of freedom of choice. If young adults are able to support themselves financially, they gain the ability to make more choices about their own lives. In early adulthood (usually until about age 40), people work toward their own goals of creating meaningful relationships with others, finding employment, and seeking personal fulfillment. Of course, young adults continue to be socialized by their parents, teachers, peers, and the media, but they also learn new attitudes and behaviours. For example, when we marry or have children, we learn new roles

Just as age is a crucial variable in the socialization process, Statistics Canada gathers data about people's age so that the government and other interested parties will know how many individuals residing in this country are in different age categories. This chapter examines how a person's age is related to socialization and life experiences. The table below shows a depiction of the nation's population in the year 2006, separated into three broad age categories (which changed between the 2001 and 2006 censuses).

Age 0–14	Age 15–64	Age 65 and above
17.6%	68.6%	13.7%

Can age be a source of social cohesion among people? Why might age differences produce conflict among individuals in different age groups? What do you think?

as partners or parents. Adults often learn about fads and fashions in clothing, music, and language from their children.

Workplace, or *occupational, socialization* is one of the most important types of adult socialization. Wilbert Moore (1968) divided occupational socialization into four phases: (1) career choice, (2) anticipatory socialization (learning different aspects of the occupation before entering it), (3) conditioning and commitment (learning the ups and downs of the occupation and remaining committed to it), and (4) continuous commitment (remaining committed to the work even when problems or other alternatives may arise). This type of socialization tends to be most intense immediately after a person makes the transition from school to the workplace; however, this process continues throughout our years of employment. Today, many people will experience continuous workplace socialization as a result, having more than one career in their lifetime.

In older adulthood, some people are quite happy and content; others are not. Erik Erikson noted that difficult changes in adult attitudes and behaviour occur in the last years of life, when people experience decreased physical ability, lower prestige, and the prospect of death. Older adults in industrialized societies have experienced *social devaluation*—**wherein a person or group is considered to have less social value than other individuals or groups**. Social devaluation is especially acute when people are leaving roles that have defined their sense of social identity and provided them with meaningful activity (Achenbaum, 1978).

It is important to note that not everyone goes through passages or stages of a life course at the same age. Sociologist Alice Rossi (1980) suggests that human experience is much more diverse than life-course models suggest. She also points out that young people growing up today live in a different world, with a different set of opportunities and problems, than did the young people of previous generations (Epstein, 1988). Rossi further suggests that women's and men's experiences are not identical throughout the life course and that the life course of women today is remarkably different from that of their mothers and grandmothers because of changing societal roles and expectations. Life-course patterns are strongly influenced by ethnicity and social class as well.

RESOCIALIZATION

Resocialization **is the process of learning a set of attitudes, values, and behaviours that is new and different from those in one's previous background and experience**. It may be voluntary or involuntary. In either case, people undergo changes that are much more rapid and pervasive than the gradual adaptations that socialization usually involves. For many new parents, the process of resocialization involved in parenting is the most dramatic they will experience in their lifetime.

Voluntary Resocialization

Resocialization is voluntary when we assume a new status (such as becoming a student, an employee, or a retiree) of our own free will. Sometimes, voluntary resocialization involves medical or psychological treatment or religious conversion, in which case the person's existing attitudes, beliefs, and behaviours must undergo strenuous modification to a new regime and a new way of life. For example, resocialization for adult survivors of emotional/physical child abuse includes extensive therapy in order to form new patterns of thinking and action, somewhat like Alcoholics Anonymous's 12-step program, which has become the basis for many other programs dealing with addictive behaviour (Parrish, 1990).

BOX 3.3	SOCIOLOGY AND THE MEDIA

The Youthful Cry: "Everybody Else Has a Cell Phone! Why Can't I Have One?"

In Canada, 71 percent of young people 12 to 19 years old and 25 percent of 9- to 12-year-olds have cell phones (Schmidt, 2008). As these figures reflect, children and adolescents in high-income nations around the world are increasingly connected with other people by cell phones (referred to as "mobile phones" in some countries), which are not entirely under the control of their parents or other adult supervisors. Increasing numbers of elementary schoolchildren as young as age six view a cell phone as a "must-have techno-toy" and as a status symbol that will impress their friends (Foderaro, 2007). How do cell phones relate to socialization? Child-oriented cell-phone use constitutes a shift from earlier times, when parents or other relatives typically were the most significant agents of socialization in a child's life. When a family had only one land-line telephone in the household, children's interactions with their peers were most often face to face, and their use of the family phone was limited to speaking with "parentally approved" friends for specified times. As a result, parents typically exerted more influence over their children because these adults were the first individuals to whom a child turned when he or she had a question or problem. Now, peers may be the first to hear a child's thoughts or concerns, and parents may be left out of the conversational loop. Many parents have welcomed the use of cell phones by their young children because Mom and Dad view the cell phone as an "electronic security blanket" for their child—as a way to keep in touch with their children and protect them from harm. With many parents' busy schedules, the increasing numbers of two-career households, and split-custody arrangements brought about by divorce, the cell phone seems like an ideal way for parents and kids to be constantly in touch with each other (Foderaro, 2007:E2). Cell phones may serve as *transitional objects* that help young children suffering separation anxiety when they are away from their parents. In turn, some parents believe that the Global Positioning System, the satellite-based navigation network feature available on some cell phones, will help

them keep up with their children's whereabouts. Technological advances—such as the computer, high-speed Internet access, and the cell phone—have not only changed how we communicate with one another, but also necessitated new forms of socialization. Children with cell phones should be socialized to use their phones *wisely* so that they will not become the objects of sexual exploitation or of harassment by bullies. Many parents are particularly concerned about the problem of sexual exploitation. A number of children have "met" another person on an Internet chatroom, exchanged numbers with the person online, and later agreed to meet the individual face to face, only to learn that the other person is much older and perhaps a sexual predator (Magid, 2004).

Socialization for the electronic age is important because, for many people, a cell phone is like a part of their body. As one analyst stated, if you forget your cell phone, "it's like leaving the house without one of your ears" (quoted in Kim, 2006). What do you think are the positive aspects of cell-phone use for children and adults? What are the problems associated with cell-phone use? Do we need new social rules to deal with the new culture that cell phones may be creating around the world?

In our digital age, cell phones make it possible for young people to be connected with other people around the clock. How have cell phones changed our interactions and created new issues in the socialization of young people?

Sources: Foderaro, 2007; Kim, 2006; Schmidt, 2008.

Involuntary Resocialization

Involuntary resocialization occurs against a person's wishes and generally takes place within a **total institution**—**a place where people are isolated from the rest of society for a set period of time and come under the control of the officials who run the institution** (Goffman, 1961). Military boot camps, jails and prisons, concentration camps, and some hospitals for people with mental illnesses are institutions. In these settings, people are stripped of their former selves—or depersonalized—through a *degradation ceremony* (Goffman, 1961). Inmates entering prison, for example, are required to strip, shower, and wear assigned institutional clothing. In the process, they are searched, weighed, fingerprinted, photographed, and given no privacy even in showers and restrooms. Their official identification becomes not a name but a number. In this abrupt break with their former existence, they must leave behind their personal possessions and their family and friends. The depersonalization process continues as they are required to obey rigid rules and to conform to their new environment.

After stripping people of their former identities, the institution attempts to build a more compliant person. A system of rewards and punishments (such as providing or withholding cigarettes and television or exercise privileges) encourages conformity to institutional norms. Some individuals may be rehabilitated; others become angry and hostile toward the system that has taken away their freedom. Although the assumed purpose of involuntary resocialization is to reform persons so that they will conform to societal standards of conduct after their release, the ability of total institutions to modify offenders' behaviour in a meaningful manner has been widely questioned. In many prisons, for example, inmates may conform to the norms of the prison or of other inmates, but little relationship exists between those norms and the laws of society.

SOCIALIZATION IN THE FUTURE

What will socialization be like in the future? The family is likely to remain the institution that most fundamentally shapes and nurtures personal values and self-identity. However, parents increasingly may feel overburdened by this responsibility, especially without societal support—such as high-quality, affordable childcare—and more education in parenting skills. Some analysts have suggested that there will be an increase in known cases of child abuse and in the number of children who experience delayed psychosocial development, learning difficulties, and emotional and behavioural problems. They attribute these increases to the dramatic changes occurring in the size, structure, and economic stability of families.

A central value-oriented issue facing parents and teachers as they attempt to socialize children is the growing dominance of computer technologies such as cell phones (including text messaging, Facebook, and Twitter, which make it possible for children to experience many things outside their own homes and communities (see Box 3.3). Socialization in the future will likely be vastly different in the world of global instant communication than it has been in the past.

CHAPTER REVIEW

■ What is socialization and why is it important?

Socialization is the lifelong process through which individuals acquire their self-identity and learn the physical, mental, and social skills needed for survival in society. The kind of person we become depends greatly on what we learn during our formative years from our surrounding social groups and social environment.

■ To what degree are our unique physical and human characteristics based on heredity and to what degree are they based on social environment?

Each of us is a product of two forces: (1) heredity, referred to as "nature, " and (2) the social environment, referred to as "nurture." Although biology dictates our physical makeup, the social environment largely determines how we develop and behave.

■ What are the most important agents of socialization?

The people, groups, and institutions that teach us what we need to know to participate in society are called agents of socialization. The most important of these are family, schools, peer groups, and the media.

■ How do sociologists understand the development of self-concept?

Charles Horton Cooley developed the image of the looking-glass self to explain how people see themselves through the perceptions of others. Our initial sense of self is typically based on how families perceive and treat us. George Herbert Mead linked the idea of self-concept to role-playing and to learning the rules of social interaction. According to Mead, the self is divided into the "I" and the "me." The "I" represents the spontaneous and unique traits of each person. The "me" represents the internalized attitudes and demands of other members of society.

■ What are the main social psychological theories of human development?

Sigmund Freud divided the self into three interrelated forces: the id, the ego, and the superego. When a person is well adjusted, the three forces act in balance. Jean Piaget identified four cognitive stages of development; at each stage, children's activities are governed by how they understand the world around them. According to Lawrence Kohlberg, certain levels of cognitive development are essential before corresponding levels of moral reasoning may occur. Carol Gilligan suggested that there are male–female differences regarding morality and identified three stages in female moral development.

■ When does socialization end?

Socialization is ongoing throughout the life course. We learn knowledge and skills for future roles through anticipatory socialization. Parents are socialized by their own children, and adults learn through workplace socialization. Resocialization is the process of learning new attitudes, values, and behaviours, either voluntarily or involuntarily.

KEY TERMS

agents of socialization 61
anticipatory socialization 70
ego 67
gender socialization 69
generalized other 66
id 67
looking-glass self 64
peer group 63
resocialization 71
role-taking 66
self-concept 64
significant others 66
social devaluation 71
socialization 56
superego 67
total institution 71

WEB LINKS

For more Web links related to the topic of this chapter, see the Nelson sociology website:
www.sociologyessentials5e.nelson.com

To obtain additional information on the development, care, and education of young children go to the website of Childcare Resource and Research Unit (CRRU):
www.childcarecanada.org

QUESTIONS FOR CRITICAL THINKING

1. Consider the concept of the looking-glass self. How do you think others perceive you? Do you think most people perceive you correctly?
2. What are your "I" traits? What are your "me" traits? Which ones are stronger?

3. Is the attempted rehabilitation of a criminal offender—through boot camp programs, for example—a form of socialization or resocialization?

ONLINE STUDY AND RESEARCH TOOLS

INFOTRAC®

InfoTrac College Edition is included free with every new copy of this text. Explore this online library for additional readings, review, and a handy resource for assignments. Visit **www.infotrac-college.com** to access this online database of full-text articles. Enter the key terms from this chapter to start your search.

CENGAGENOW™ CENGAGENOW

Use CengageNOW™ to help you formulate a customized study plan for this chapter. After you take the Diagnostic Quiz, CengageNOW™ will generate a customized study plan for you. It will identify sections of the chapter you should review.

Social Structure, Social Interaction, and Collective Behaviour

For most homeless persons living on the streets of Canada's major cities, the days end the same way they begin—searching for the basic necessities of life that many of us take for granted: food, shelter, work, and money. These circumstances are captured in the comments of Nancy, who describes her daily routine of survival living on the streets—sleeping "in the rough" (i.e., outdoors), securing food, and panhandling. She also describes the camaraderie among long-term street people:

*It is not always safe. Sometimes you
can get robbed. Sometimes you can get
knocked out even before you wake up.
It is not that safe but when you have
somebody around you we can protect
each other. I have learned to make
street friends. Sometimes, like most
people, we get sick of each other so we
have to look for other friends.*

*If you are panhandling sometimes
people go by and give you money.
Sometimes they just go by. Mostly we
eat at soup kitchens. We go to missions.
Sometimes when you are panhandling,*

people will give you food. In their minds, it is better to give me food than money because money, I might spend on alcohol and drugs. So they buy the food and give it to me. I think these people are smart. Sometimes the police harass you. Sometimes they can be very nice. I had one bring me a sandwich and ask me how I was feeling. I said, "I'm okay and I'm going to be out of here soon. I am about $1.50 short of a sub sandwich." He says "Come with me, I'll buy you one."

Sometimes restaurants won't even serve you. They won't let you pass through the door. That is how we learn to get food from fast-food chains. We can order it out and eat outside without having everyone stare at you or whisper about you under their breath.

I sleep in the park, underneath the overpass or behind the library or downtown beneath the restaurant . . . as long as you find a spot where the cops won't bother you or people won't bother you. . . . Sometimes you have to walk miles to find a spot where you can sleep. I find

good clean cardboard and I always carry my own sleeping bag. The most important thing is to have blankets. We learn to carry those blankets. We learn to because this is our home.
(Neal, 2004:20)

The activities of this homeless woman reflect a specific pattern of social behaviour. All activities in life—including sleeping in the rough or living on the streets—are social in nature. Homeless persons and domiciled persons (those with homes) live in social worlds that have predictable patterns of social interaction. ***Social interaction* is the process by which people act toward or respond to other people and is the foundation for all relationships and groups in society**. In this chapter, we look at the relationship between social structure and social interaction. Homelessness is used as an example of how social problems occur and may be perpetuated within social structures and patterns of interaction.

Social structure **is the stable pattern of social relationships that exists within a particular group or society**. This structure is essential for the survival of society and for the well-being of individuals because it provides a social web of familial support and social relationships that connects each of us to the larger

Chapter Focus Question: How is homelessness related to the social structure of a society?

What are the components of social structure?

Why do societies have shared patterns of social interaction?

What causes people to engage in collective behaviour?

What are some common forms of collective behaviour?

society. Many homeless people have lost this vital linkage. As a result, they often experience a loss of both personal dignity and a sense of moral worth because of their "homeless" condition (Neal, 2004).

Who are the homeless? How is homelessness defined? Before reading on, take the quiz on homelessness in Box 4.1 on page 80. The profile of Canada's homeless has changed dramatically. Although there have always been homeless people, there has been a significant increase in the number of Canadians with no place to live. The homeless category now includes people who have never before had to depend on social assistance for food, clothing, and a roof over their heads. Today's homeless include increasing numbers of women and children, adolescents, and Aboriginal people. The fastest-growing segment of the homeless population is women and children (National Anti-Poverty Organization, 2005). Also startling is the overrepresentation of Aboriginal people in Canada's homeless population. ***Relative homelessness—being housed in a dwelling that fails to meet basic living standards—is disturbingly common in both the urban and rural Aboriginal population***. Refugees and visible minorities are also overrepresented among the homeless (Murphy, 2000; Neal, 2004).

SOCIAL STRUCTURE: THE MACROLEVEL PERSPECTIVE

Social structure provides the framework within which we interact with others. This framework is an orderly, fixed arrangement of parts that together make up the whole group or society (see Figure 4.1). As defined in Chapter 1, a *society* is a large social grouping that shares the same geographical territory and is subject to the same political authority and dominant cultural expectations. At the macrolevel, the social structure of

All activities in life—including panhandling and living "on the streets"—are social in nature.

a society has several essential elements: social institutions, groups, statuses, roles, and norms.

Functional theorists emphasize that social structure is essential because it creates order and predictability in a society (Parsons, 1951). Social structure also is important for our human development. As we saw in Chapter 3, we develop a self-concept as we learn the attitudes, values, and behaviours of the people around us. When these attitudes and values are part of a predictable structure, it is easier to develop that self-concept.

Social structure gives us the ability to interpret the social situations we encounter. For example, we expect our families to care for us, our schools to educate us, and our police to protect us. When our circumstances change dramatically, most of us feel an acute sense of anxiety because we do not know what to expect or what is expected of us. For example, newly homeless individuals may feel disoriented because they do not know how to function in their new setting. The person is likely to wonder, "How will I survive on the

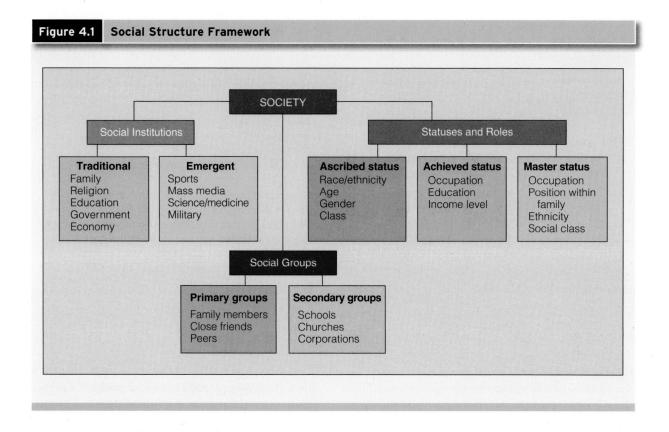

Figure 4.1 Social Structure Framework

streets?" "Where do I go to get help?" and "Where can I get a job?" Social structure helps people make sense out of their environment, even when they find themselves on the streets.

In addition to providing a map for our encounters with others, social structure may limit our options and place us in arbitrary categories not of our own choosing. Conflict theorists maintain that there is more to the social structure than is readily visible and that we must explore the deeper, underlying structures that determine social relations in a society. Karl Marx suggested that the way economic production is organized is the most important structural aspect of any society. In capitalistic societies, where a few people control the labour of many, the social structure reflects a system of relationships of domination among categories of people (e.g., owner–worker, employer–employee).

Social structure creates boundaries that define which persons or groups will be the "insiders" and which will be the "outsiders." *Social marginality* **is the state of being part insider and part outsider in the social structure**. Robert Park (1928) coined this term to refer to persons (such as immigrants) who simultaneously share the life and traditions of two distinct groups. Social marginality can result in stigmatization. A *stigma* **is any physical or social**

attribute or sign that so devalues a person's social identity that it disqualifies that person from full social acceptance** (Goffman, 1963b). A convicted criminal wearing a prison uniform is an example of a person who has been stigmatized; the uniform says that the person has done something wrong and should not be allowed unsupervised outside the prison walls.

COMPONENTS OF SOCIAL STRUCTURE

The social structure of a society includes its social positions, the relationships among those positions, and the kinds of resources attached to each of the positions. Social structure also includes all of the groups that make up society and the relationships among those groups (Smelser, 1988). We begin by examining the social positions that are closest to the individual.

Status

A *status* **is a socially defined position in a group or society characterized by certain expectations,**

BOX 4.1	SOCIOLOGY AND EVERYDAY LIFE

How Much Do You Know about Homelessness?

True	False	
T	**F**	1. Most homeless people choose to be homeless.
T	**F**	2. The number of homeless persons in Canada has gradually declined over the past 30 years.
T	~~F~~	3. Homelessness is often caused by racism and discrimination.
T	**F**	4. Most homeless people are mentally ill.
T	**F**	5. Men over the age of 50 make up most of Canada's homeless population.
T	F	6. The number of homeless adolescents has increased in the past decade.
T	F	7. One out of every four homeless people is a child.
T	**F**	8. There are approximately 20 000 homeless persons in Canada.

Answers on page 82.

rights, and duties. Statuses exist independently of the specific people occupying them (Linton, 1936); the statuses of professional athlete, university student, and homeless person all exist exclusive of the specific individuals who occupy these social positions. For example, although thousands of new students arrive on university campuses each year to occupy the status of first-year student, the status of a university student and the expectations attached to that position have remained relatively unchanged.

Does the term *status* refer only to high-level positions in society? No, not in a sociological sense. Although many people equate the term *status* with high levels of prestige, sociologists use it to refer to *all* socially defined positions—high and low ranking.

Take a moment to answer the question, Who am I? To determine who you are, you must think about your social identity, which is derived from the statuses you occupy and is based on your status set. A ***status set* is made up of all the statuses that a person occupies at a given time**. For example, Marie may be a psychologist, a professor, a wife, a mother, a Catholic, a school volunteer, and a French Canadian. All these socially defined positions constitute her status set.

Ascribed and Achieved Status

Statuses are distinguished by the manner in which we acquire them. An ***ascribed status* is a social position conferred at birth or received involuntarily later in life, based on attributes over which the individual has little or no control**, such as ethnicity, age, and gender. Marie, for example, is a female born to French

Canadian parents; she was assigned these statuses at birth. An ***achieved status* is a social position a person assumes voluntarily as a result of personal choice, merit, or direct effort**. Achieved statuses (such as occupation, education, and income) are thought to be gained as a result of personal ability or competition. Most occupational positions in modern societies are achieved statuses. Not all achieved statuses, however, are positions most people would want to attain; being a criminal, a drug addict, or a homeless person, for example, are negative achieved statuses.

Ascribed statuses have a significant influence on the achieved statuses we occupy. Ethnicity, gender, and age affect each person's opportunity to acquire certain achieved statuses. Those who are privileged by their positive ascribed statuses are more likely to achieve the more prestigious positions in a society. Those who are disadvantaged by their ascribed statuses may more typically acquire negative achieved statuses.

Master Status

If we occupy many different statuses, how can we determine which is the most important? Sociologist Everett Hughes has stated that societies resolve this ambiguity by determining master statuses. **A *master status* is the most important status a person occupies**; it dominates all of the individual's other statuses and is the overriding ingredient in determining a person's general social position (Hughes, 1945). Being poor or rich is a master status that influences many other areas of life, including health, education, and life opportunities.

In the past, a person's status was primarily linked to his or her family background, education, occupation, and other sociological attributes. Today, some sociologists suggest that celebrity status has overtaken the more traditional status indicators.

becomes a master status regardless of the person's other attributes. Homelessness is a stigmatized master status that confers disrepute on its occupant because domiciled people often believe a homeless person has a "character flaw." The circumstances under which someone becomes homeless determine the extent to which that person is stigmatized. For example, individuals who become homeless as a result of natural disasters (such as floods or tornados) are not seen as causing their homelessness or as being a threat to the community; thus, they are less likely to be stigmatized. However, in cases in which homeless persons are viewed as the cause of their own problems, they are more likely to be stigmatized and marginalized by others.

Status Symbols When people are proud of a particular social status they occupy, they often choose to use visible means to let others know about their position. ***Status symbols* are material signs that inform others of a person's specific status.** For example, just as wearing a wedding ring proclaims that a person is married, owning a Rolls-Royce announces that one has "made it." In North American society, people who have "made it" frequently want symbols to inform others of their accomplishments.

In our daily lives, status symbols both announce our statuses and facilitate our interactions with others. For example, in hospitals affiliated with medical schools, the length and colour of a person's uniform indicates the individual's status within the medical centre.

Roles

Role is the dynamic aspect of a status. Whereas we *occupy* a status, we *play* a role (Linton, 1936). A ***role* is a set of behavioural expectations associated with a given status.** For example, a carpenter (employee) hired to remodel a kitchen is not expected to sit down uninvited and join the family (employer) for dinner.

***Role expectation* is a group's or society's definition of the way a specific role ought to be played.** By contrast, ***role performance* is how a person actually plays the role.** Role performance does not always match role expectation. Some statuses have role expectations that are highly specific, such as that of surgeon or university professor. Other statuses, such as friend or significant other, have less structured expectations. The role expectations tied to the status of student are more specific than those for being a friend. Role expectations typically are based on a range of acceptable behaviour rather than on strictly defined standards.

Historically, the most common master statuses for women have related to positions in the family, such as daughter, wife, and mother. For men, occupation usually has been the most important status, although occupation increasingly is a master status for many women as well. "What do you do?" is one of the first questions many people ask when meeting one another. Occupation provides important clues to a person's educational level, income, and family background. An individual's ethnicity also may constitute a master status in a society in which dominant group members single out members of other groups as "inferior" on the basis of real or alleged physical, cultural, or nationality characteristics (see Feagin and Feagin, 2003).

Master statuses confer high or low levels of personal worth and dignity on people. Those are not characteristics that we inherently possess; they are derived from the statuses we occupy. For those who have no residence, being a homeless person readily

BOX 4.1 SOCIOLOGY AND EVERYDAY LIFE

Answers to the Quiz on Homelessness

1. False. This myth is an example of "blaming the victim." Homelessness is the result of a number of social factors, namely poverty, changes in the housing market, and growing rates of unemployment (National Anti-Poverty Organization, 2005).

2. False. Surveys and statistics have shown that the number of homeless in Canada has grown over the past three decades (HRSDC, 2010).

3. True. Approximately one-quarter of homeless persons are Aboriginal. About 15 percent of Toronto's hostel users are immigrants and refugees. Some landlords refuse to rent apartments to families with children or to people on social assistance (Toronto Disaster Relief Committee, 2004).

4. False. Between 20 and 35 percent of homeless people have been treated for a psychiatric disorder (HRSDC, 2003).

5. False. Men over the age of 50 no longer represent the majority of the homeless. Now young men, teenagers, and families with children are predominant among homeless Canadians (HRSDC, 2010).

6. True. The growth in this population of "street youth" has significantly altered the population of homeless Canadians. The majority of these youth report leaving home because of physical and sexual abuse (Layton, 2008, Karabanow, 2008).

7. True. Further, women and children make up the fastest-growing category of homeless people in North America (National Anti-Poverty Organization, 2005).

8. False. Experts estimate the number of homeless persons in Canada at between 300 000 (HRSDC, 2010).

Our roles are relational (or complementary); that is, they are defined in the context of roles performed by others. We can play the role of student because someone else fulfills the role of professor. Conversely, to perform the role of professor, the teacher must have one or more students.

Role ambiguity occurs when the expectations associated with a role are unclear. For example, it is not always clear when the provider–dependent aspect of the parent–child relationship ends. Should it end at the age of 18 or 21? When a person is no longer in school? Different people will answer these questions differently depending on their experiences and socialization, as well as on the parents' financial capability and willingness to continue contributing to the welfare of their adult children.

Role Conflict and Role Strain

Most people occupy a number of statuses, each of which has numerous role expectations attached. For example, Charles is a student who attends morning classes at the university, and an employee at a fast-food restaurant where he works from 3 p.m. to 10 p.m. He also is Stephanie's boyfriend, and she would like to see him more often. On December 7, Charles has a final exam at 7 p.m., when he is supposed to be working. Meanwhile, Stephanie is pressuring him to take her to a movie. To top it off, his mother calls, asking him to fly home because his father is going to have emergency surgery. How can Charles be in all of these places at once? Such experiences of role conflict can be overwhelming.

Role conflict occurs when incompatible role demands are placed on a person by two or more statuses held at the same time. When role conflict occurs, we may feel pulled in different directions. To deal with this problem, we may prioritize our roles and first complete the one we consider to be most important. Or we may *compartmentalize* our lives and "insulate" our various roles (Merton, 1968). That is, we may perform the activities linked to one role for part of the day and then engage in the activities associated with another role later. For example, under routine circumstances, Charles would fulfill his student role for part of the day and his employee role for another part of the day. In his current situation, however, he is unable to compartmentalize his roles.

Role conflict may occur as a result of changing statuses and roles in society. Research has found that women who engage in behaviour that is gender-typed as "masculine" tend to have higher rates of role conflict than those who engage in traditional "feminine" behaviour (Basow, 1992).

Whereas role conflict occurs between two or more statuses (such as being homeless and being a temporary employee of a social-services agency), role strain takes place within one status. **Role strain occurs when incompatible demands are built into a single status that a person occupies** (Goode, 1960). For example, many women experience role strain in the labour force because they hold jobs that are "less satisfying and more stressful than men's jobs since they involve less money, less prestige, fewer job openings, more career roadblocks, and so forth" (Basow, 1992:192). Similarly, married women may experience more role strain than married men, because of work overload, marital inequality with their spouse, exclusive parenting responsibilities, unclear expectations, and lack of emotional support.

Individuals frequently distance themselves from a role they find extremely stressful or otherwise problematic. People use distancing techniques when they do not want others to take them as the "self" implied in a particular role, especially if they think the role is "beneath them." While Charles is working at the fast-food restaurant, for example, he does not want people to think of him as a "loser in a dead-end job." He wants them to view him as a university student who is working there just to "pick up a few bucks" until he graduates.

Role distancing is most likely to occur when people find themselves in roles in which the social identities implied are inconsistent with how they think of themselves or how they want to be viewed by others.

Role Exit   *Role exit* occurs when people disengage from social roles that have been central to their self-identity (Ebaugh, 1988). Helen Rose Fuchs Ebaugh studied this process by interviewing ex-convicts, ex-nuns, retirees, divorced men and women, and others who had exited voluntarily from significant social roles. According to Ebaugh, role exit occurs in four stages. The first stage is doubt, in which people experience frustration or burnout when they reflect on their existing roles. The second stage involves a search for alternatives; here, people may take a leave of absence from their work or temporarily

separate from their marriage partner. The third stage is the turning point at which people realize that they must take some final action, such as quitting their job or getting a divorce. The fourth and final stage involves the creation of a new identity.

Groups

Groups are another important component of social structure. To sociologists, a **social group consists of two or more people who interact frequently and share a common identity and a feeling of interdependence**. Throughout our lives, most of us participate in groups, from our families and childhood friends to our university classes, our work and community organizations, and even our society.

Primary and secondary groups are the two basic types of social groups. A **primary group is a small, less specialized group in which members engage in face-to-face, emotion-based interactions over an extended period**. Primary groups include our family, close friends, and school- or work-related peer groups. By contrast, a **secondary group is a larger, more specialized group in which members engage in more impersonal, goal-oriented relationships for a limited time**. Schools, churches, the military, and corporations are examples of secondary groups. In secondary groups, people have few, if any, emotional ties to one another. Instead, they come together for some specific, practical purpose, such as getting a degree or a paycheque. Secondary groups are more specialized than primary ones; individuals relate to one another in terms of specific roles (such as professor and student) and more limited activities (such as course-related endeavours).

Social solidarity, or cohesion, relates to a group's ability to maintain itself in the face of obstacles. Social solidarity exists when social bonds, attractions, or other forces hold members of a group in interaction over a period (Jary and Jary, 1991). For example, if a local church is destroyed by fire and congregation members still worship together in a makeshift setting, then they have a high degree of social solidarity.

Many of us build social networks from our personal friends in primary groups and our acquaintances in secondary groups. A social network is a series of social relationships that link an individual to others. Social networks work differently for men and women, for different ethnic groups, and for members of different social classes. Traditionally, visible minorities and women have been excluded from powerful

In secondary groups people have few, if any, emotional ties to one another. They come together for some specific, practical purpose, such as getting a degree.

"old boy" social networks. At the middle- and upper-class levels, individuals tap social networks to find employment, make business deals, and win political elections. However, social networks typically do not work effectively for poor and homeless individuals.

A *formal organization* **is a highly structured group formed for the purpose of completing certain tasks or achieving specific goals**. Many of us spend most of our time in formal organizations, such as universities, corporations, or the government. In Chapter 5, we analyze the characteristics of bureaucratic organizations; however, at this point, we should note that these organizations are a very important component of social structure in all industrialized societies. We expect such organizations to educate us, solve our social problems (such as crime and homelessness), and provide work opportunities.

Social Institutions

At the macrolevel of all societies, certain basic activities routinely occur—children are born and socialized, goods and services are produced and distributed, order is preserved, and a sense of purpose is maintained (Aberle et al., 1950; Mack and Bradford, 1979). Social institutions are the means by which these basic needs are met. A *social institution* **is a set of organized beliefs and rules that establish how a society will attempt to meet its basic social needs**. In the past, these needs have centred around five basic social institutions: the family, religion, education, the economy, and the government or politics. Today, mass media, sports, science, medicine, and the military are also considered social institutions.

What is the difference between a group and a social institution? A group comprises specific, identifiable people; an institution is a standardized way of doing something. The concept of "family" helps to distinguish between the two. When we talk about your family or my family, we are referring to *a* family. When we refer to *the* family as a social institution, we are talking about ideologies and standardized patterns of behaviour that organize family life. For example, the family as a social institution contains certain statuses organized into well-defined relationships, such as husband–wife, parent–child, brother–sister, and so forth. Specific families do not always conform to these ideologies and behaviour patterns.

Functional theorists emphasize that social institutions exist because they perform five essential tasks:

1. *Replacing members.* Societies and groups must have socially approved ways of replacing members who leave or die. The family provides the structure for legitimated sexual activity—and thus procreation—between adults.
2. *Teaching new members.* People who are born or move into a society must learn the group's values and customs. The family is essential in teaching new members, but other social institutions educate new members as well.
3. *Producing, distributing, and consuming goods and services.* All societies must provide and distribute goods and services for their members. The economy is the primary social institution fulfilling this need; government is often involved in the regulation of economic activity.
4. *Preserving order.* Every group or society must preserve order within its boundaries and protect itself from attack by outsiders. Government legitimates the creation of law-enforcement agencies to preserve internal order and some form of military for civic and external defence.
5. *Providing and maintaining a sense of purpose.* To motivate people to cooperate with one another, a sense of purpose is needed.

Although this list of functional prerequisites is shared by all societies, the institutions in each society perform these tasks in somewhat different ways, depending on their specific cultural values and norms.

Conflict theorists agree with functionalists that social institutions are organized to meet basic social needs. However, they do not agree that social institutions work for the common good of everyone in society. For example, homeless people lack the power and resources to promote their own interests when they are opposed by dominant social groups. This is a problem not only in Canada and the United States, but also for homeless people, especially homeless youth, throughout the world (see Box 4.2). From the conflict perspective, social institutions such as the government maintain the privileges of the wealthy and powerful while contributing to the powerlessness of others (see Domhoff, 2002). For example, some government policies in urban areas have benefited some people but exacerbated the problems of others. Sometimes, urban renewal and transportation projects caused the destruction of low-cost housing and put large numbers of people "on the street." Similarly, the shift in governmental policies toward people with mental illnesses and people who receive welfare results in more people struggling—and often failing—to find affordable housing. Meanwhile, many wealthy and privileged bankers, investors, developers, and builders benefit at the expense of the low-income casualties of those policies.

BOX 4.2 | SOCIOLOGY IN GLOBAL PERSPECTIVE

Homelessness for Children is an International Problem

The eyes of the homeless, those who really need help, are the same eyes in any country—eyes that can see every door is closed to them.

—Valery Sokolov, a journalist and president of the Nochlyazhka Charitable Foundation in St. Petersburg, Russia, at the time he made this statement, knows what it means to be homeless: During six years of homelessness, he slept in a railroad station and sometimes in the forest (quoted in Spence, 1997).

Homelessness is a widespread problem around the globe. A particularly pressing issue in many countries is the growing number of families with children and the "chronically homeless children," typically between the ages of 12 and 18, who reside on the streets or move between shelters, street life, and squatting (Harrison, 2001). The World Health Organization's Street Children Project identified four categories of young people who experience homelessness:

1. Children living on the streets, whose immediate concerns are survival and shelter.
2. Children who are detached from their families and living in temporary shelter, such as abandoned houses and other buildings (hostels/refuges/shelters), or moving about between friends.
3. Children who remain in contact with their families but because of poverty, overcrowding, or sexual or physical abuse within the family will spend some nights, or most days, on the streets.
4. Children who are in institutional care, who come from a situation of homelessness and are at risk of returning to a homeless existence.

How many children worldwide are homeless or at risk of becoming homeless? Accurate statistics on homelessness in general are difficult to gather.

However, UNICEF estimates there are approximately 100 million street children worldwide, with that number constantly growing. There are an estimated 40 million street children in Latin America, and at least 18 million in India. Many studies have determined that street children are most often boys aged 10 to 14, with increasingly younger children being affected. Young girls who are homeless are more vulnerable to trafficking for commercial sexual exploitation or other forms of child labour (Beasley, 1999). If children are the future of the nations in which they live, what can be said for those children who do not have a home to call their own? Some analysts believe that the homelessness is especially dire in that these children experience alienation and exclusion from society's mainstream structures and systems, including schools, churches, and other organizations that may provide stability and hope to youth. In addition, homeless children may engage in significant antisocial and self-destructive behaviour, and have a profound distrust for social services and welfare systems that might, in some cases, enable them to leave homelessness behind. Whether in England, Australia, Russia, Norway, Canada, the United States, or other nations of the world, homelessness, particularly of children and youth, marks the failure of existing social institutions to adequately provide for the next generation; it also puts people in a devalued master status in which they lack the power and resources to promote their own interests and in which survival becomes their primary objective. Do nations have a responsibility to take care of homeless people within their borders? What about homeless children? When we talk about social responsibility, is there a difference between homeless adults and homeless children?

Sources: Beasley, 1999; Harrison, 2001; Spence, 1997.

SOCIAL INTERACTION: THE MICROLEVEL PERSPECTIVE

So far in this chapter, we have focused on society and social structure from a macrolevel perspective. We have seen how the structure of society affects the statuses we occupy, the roles we play, and the groups and organizations to which we belong. Functionalist and conflict perspectives provide a macrosociological overview because they concentrate on large-scale events and broad social features. By contrast, the symbolic interactionist perspective takes a microsociological approach, examining how social institutions affect our daily lives. We will now look at society from the microlevel perspective, which focuses on social interactions between and among individuals, especially in face-to-face encounters.

Social Interaction and Meaning

When you are with other people, do you often wonder what they think of you? If so, you are not alone! Because most of us are concerned about the meanings others ascribe to our behaviour, we try to interpret their words and actions so that we can plan how we will react toward them (Blumer, 1969). We know that others have expectations of us. We also have certain expectations of them. For example, if we enter an elevator that has only one other person in it, we do not expect that individual to confront us and stare into our eyes. As a matter of fact, we would be quite upset if the person did so.

Social interaction within a given society has certain shared meanings across situations. For instance, our reaction would be the same regardless of *which* elevator we rode in *which* building. Sociologist Erving Goffman (1963b) described these shared meanings in his observation about two pedestrians approaching each other on a public sidewalk. He noted that each will tend to look at the other just long enough to acknowledge the other's presence. By the time they are about 2.5 metres away from each other, both individuals will tend to look downward. Goffman referred to this behaviour as *civil inattention*—the ways in which an individual shows an awareness that others are present without making them the object of particular attention. The fact that people engage in civil inattention demonstrates that interaction does have a pattern, or *interaction order,* which regulates the form and processes (but not the content) of social interaction.

Does everyone interpret social interaction rituals in the same way? No. Ethnicity, gender, and social class play a part in the meanings we give to our interactions with others, including chance encounters on elevators or on the street. Our perceptions about the meaning of a situation vary widely based on the statuses we occupy and our unique personal experiences. For example, Carol Brooks Gardner (1989) found that women frequently do not perceive street encounters to be "routine" rituals. They fear for their personal safety and try to avoid comments and propositions that are sexual in nature when they walk down the street. In another example, members of the dominant classes regard the poor, unemployed, and working class as less worthy of attention, frequently subjecting them to subtle yet systematic "attention deprivation" (Derber, 1983).

The Social Construction of Reality

If we interpret other people's actions so subjectively, can we have a shared social reality? Some interaction theorists believe that there is very little shared reality beyond that which is socially created. Symbolic interactionists refer to this as the ***social construction of reality***—**the process by which our perception of reality is shaped largely by the subjective meaning that we give to an experience** (Berger and Luckmann, 1967). This meaning strongly influences what we "see" and how we respond to situations.

Our perceptions and behaviour are influenced by how we initially define situations: We act on reality as we see it. Sociologists describe this process as the *definition of the situation,* meaning that we analyze a social context in which we find ourselves, determine what is in our best interest, and adjust our attitudes and actions accordingly. This can result in a ***self-fulfilling prophecy***—**a false belief or prediction that produces behaviour that makes the originally false belief come true** (Thomas and Thomas, 1928:72). An example would be a person who has been told repeatedly that he or she is not a good student; eventually, this person might come to believe it to be true, stop studying, and receive failing grades.

People may define a given situation in very different ways. Consider Lesley Harman's initial reaction to her field research site, a facility for homeless women in an Ontario city:

The initial shock of facing the world of the homeless told me much about what I took for granted. . . . The first day I lasted two very long hours. I went home and woke up severely depressed, weeping uncontrollably. (Harman, 1989:42)

In contrast, many of the women who lived there defined the situation of living in a hostel in very different terms. For example, one resident commented, "This is home to me because I feel so comfortable. I can do what I really want, the staff are very nice to me, everybody is good to me, it's home, you know?" (Harman, 1989:91). As these studies show, we define situations from our own frame of reference, based on the statuses that we occupy and the roles that we play.

Dominant group members with prestigious statuses may have the ability to establish how other people define "reality" (Berger and Luckmann, 1967:109). For example, the media often set the tone for our current opinions about homelessness, either with negative stories about the problems the homeless "cause" or with "human interest" stories.

Dramaturgical Analysis

Erving Goffman suggested that day-to-day interactions have much in common with being on stage or in a dramatic production. ***Dramaturgical analysis is the study of social interaction that compares everyday life to a theatrical presentation.*** Members of our "audience" judge our performance (Goffman, 1959, 1963a). Consequently, most of us attempt to play our role as well as possible and to control the impressions we give to others. ***Impression management (presentation of self)* refers to people's efforts to present themselves to others in ways that are most favourable to their own interests or image**.

For example, suppose that a professor has returned graded exams to your class. Will you discuss the exam and your grade with others in the class? If you are like most people, you probably play your student role differently depending on whom you are talking to and what grade you received on the exam. In a study at the University of Manitoba, Daniel and Cheryl Albas (1988) analyzed how students "presented themselves" or "managed impressions" when exam grades are returned. Students who all received high grades ("Ace–Ace encounters") willingly talked with one another about their grades and sometimes engaged in a little bragging about how they had "aced" the test. However, encounters between students who had received high grades and those who had received low or failing grades ("Ace–Bomber encounters") were uncomfortable. The Aces felt as if they had to minimize their own grade. Consequently, they tended to attribute their success to "luck" and were quick to offer the Bombers words of encouragement. On the other hand, the Bombers believed that they had to praise the Aces and hide their own feelings of frustration and disappointment. Students who received low or failing grades ("Bomber–Bomber encounters") were more comfortable when they talked with one another because they could share their negative emotions. They often indulged in self-pity and relied on face-saving excuses (such as an illness or an unfair exam) for their poor performances (Albas and Albas, 1988).

In Goffman's terminology, *face-saving behaviour* refers to the strategies we use to rescue our

Sharply contrasting views of the same reality are evident in these people's views about events after the attacks of September 11th, 2001.

performance when we experience a potential or actual loss of face. When the Bombers made excuses for their low scores, they were engaged in face-saving; the Aces attempted to help them save face by asserting that the test was unfair or that it was only a small part of the final grade. Why would the Aces and Bombers both participate in face-saving behaviour? In most social interactions, all role players have an interest in keeping the "play" going so that they can maintain their overall definition of the situation in which they perform their roles.

Social interaction, like a theatre, has a front stage and a back stage. The *front stage* is the area where a player performs a specific role before an audience. The *back stage* is the area where a player is not required to perform a specific role because it is out of view of a given audience. For example, when the Aces and Bombers were talking with each other at school, they were on the "front stage." When they were in the privacy of their own residences, they were in "back stage" settings—they no longer had to perform the Ace and Bomber roles and could be themselves.

The need for impression management is highest when role players have widely divergent or devalued statuses. As we have seen with Aces and Bombers, the participants often play different roles under different circumstances and keep their various audiences separated from one another. If one audience becomes aware of other roles that a person plays, the impression being given at that time may be ruined. For example, homeless people may lose jobs or the opportunity to get them when their homelessness becomes known. One woman had worked as a receptionist in a doctor's office for several weeks but was fired when the doctor learned that she was living in a shelter (Liebow, 1993). The homeless do not passively accept the roles into which they are cast. For the most part, they attempt—as we all do—to engage in impression management in their everyday lives.

The dramaturgical approach helps us think about the roles we play and the audiences who judge our presentation of self. Like all other approaches, it has its critics. Alvin Gouldner (1970) criticized this approach for focusing on appearances and not on the underlying substance. Others have argued that Goffman's work reduces the self to "a peg on which the clothes of the role are hung" (see Burns, 1992) or have suggested that this approach does not place enough emphasis on the ways in which our everyday interactions with other people are influenced by occurrences within the larger society. Goffman's defenders counter that he captured the essence of society because social interaction "turns out to be not only where most of the world's work gets done, but where the solid buildings of the social world are in fact constructed" (Burns, 1992:380).

According to Erving Goffman, our day-to-day interactions have much in common with a dramatic production.

maureen plainfield/Shutterstock

Nonverbal Communication

In a typical stage drama, the players not only speak their lines but also convey information by nonverbal communication. In Chapter 2, we discussed the importance of language; now we will look at the messages we communicate without speaking. **Nonverbal communication is the transfer of information between persons without the use of speech.** It includes not only visual cues (gestures, appearances) but also vocal features (inflection, volume, pitch) and environmental factors (use of space, position) that affect meanings (Wood, 1999). Facial expressions, head movements, body positions, and other gestures carry as much of the total meaning of our communication with others as our spoken words do (Wood, 1999).

Nonverbal communication may be intentional or unintentional. Actors, politicians, and salespersons may make deliberate use of nonverbal communication to convey an idea or "make a sale." We also may send nonverbal messages through gestures or facial expressions or even our appearance without intending to let other people know what we are thinking.

Functions of Nonverbal Communication

Nonverbal communication often supplements verbal communication (Wood, 1999). Head and facial movements may provide us with information about other people's emotional states, as others receive similar information from us (Samovar and Porter, 1991a). We obtain first impressions of others from various kinds of nonverbal communication, such as the clothing they wear and their body positions.

Our social interaction is regulated by nonverbal communication. Through our body posture and eye contact, we signal that we do or do not want to speak to someone. For example, we may look down at the sidewalk or off into the distance when we pass homeless persons who look as if they are going to ask for money.

Nonverbal communication establishes the relationship between people in terms of their responsiveness to and power over one another (Wood, 1999). For example, we show that we are responsive toward or like another person by maintaining eye contact and attentive body posture and perhaps by touching and standing close. By contrast, we signal to others that we do not want to be near them or that we dislike them by refusing to look them in the eye or stand near them. We can even express power or control over others through nonverbal communication. Goffman (1956) suggested that *demeanour* (how we behave or conduct ourselves) is relative to social power. People in positions of dominance are allowed a wider range of permissible actions than are their subordinates, who are expected to show deference. *Deference* is the symbolic means by which subordinates give a required permissive response to those in power; it confirms the existence of inequality and reaffirms each person's relationship to the other (Rollins, 1985).

Facial Expression, Eye Contact, and Touching

Deference behaviour is important in regard to facial expression, eye contact, and touching. These types of nonverbal communication are symbolic of our relationships with others. Who smiles? Who stares? Who makes and sustains eye contact? Who touches whom? All these questions relate to demeanour and deference; the key issue is the status of the person who is *doing* the smiling, staring, or touching relative to the status of the recipient (Goffman, 1967).

Facial expressions, especially smiles, also reflect gender-based patterns of dominance and subordination in society. Women typically have been socialized to smile and frequently do so even when they are not actually happy (Halberstadt and Saitta, 1987). Jobs held predominantly by women (including flight attendant, elementary-school teacher, and nurse) are more closely associated with being pleasant and smiling than are "men's jobs." In addition to smiling more frequently, many women tend to tilt their heads in deferential positions when they are talking or listening to others. By contrast, men tend to display less emotion through smiles or other facial expressions and instead seek to show that they are reserved and in control (Wood, 1999).

Women are more likely to sustain eye contact during conversations (but not otherwise) as a means of showing their interest in and involvement with others. By contrast, men are less likely to maintain prolonged eye contact during conversations but are more likely to stare at other people (especially men) to challenge them and assert their own status (Pearson, 1985).

Touching is another form of nonverbal behaviour that has many different shades of meaning. Gender and power differences are evident in tactile communication from birth. Studies have shown that touching has variable meanings to parents: boys are touched more roughly and playfully, while girls are handled more gently and protectively (Condry, Condry, and Pogatshnik, 1983). This pattern continues into adulthood, with women touched more frequently than

Nonverbal communication may be thought of as an international language. What message do you receive from the facial expression and gestures of each of these people? Is it possible to misinterpret their messages?

men. Women may hug and touch others to indicate affection and emotional support, while men are more likely to touch others to give directions, assert power, and express sexual interest (Wood, 1999). The "meaning" we give to touching is related to its "duration, intensity, frequency, and the body parts touching and being touched" (Wood, 1999:162).

Personal Space   Physical space is an important component of nonverbal communication. Edward Hall (1966) analyzed the physical distance between people speaking to one another and found that the amount of personal space people prefer varies from one culture to another. ***Personal space is the immediate area surrounding a person that the person claims as private.*** Our personal space is contained within an invisible boundary surrounding our body, much like a snail's shell. When others invade our space, we may retreat, stand our ground, or even lash out, depending on our cultural background (Samovar and Porter, 1991a).

Age, gender, kind of relationship, and social class also have an impact on the allocation of personal space. Power differentials are also reflected in personal space and privacy issues. Adults generally do not hesitate to enter the personal space of a child (Thorne, Kramarae, and Henley, 1983). Similarly, young children who invade the personal space of an adult tend to be tolerated. The need for personal space appears to increase with age (Baxter, 1970; Aiello and Jones, 1971), although it may begin to decrease at about the age of 40 (Heshka and Nelson, 1972).

In sum, all forms of nonverbal communication are influenced by gender, ethnicity, social class, and the personal contexts in which they occur. While it is difficult to generalize about people's nonverbal behaviour, we still need to think about our own nonverbal communication patterns. Learning to understand and respect alternative styles of social interaction increases the range of options we have for communicating with different people in diverse contexts (Wood, 1999).

COLLECTIVE BEHAVIOUR

In the first two sections of this chapter we looked at the impact of social structure on behaviour and at patterns of social interaction among individuals. In this section, we will consider ***collective behaviour, which is voluntary, often spontaneous activity that is engaged in by a large number of people and typically violates dominant group norms and values.*** Unlike the *organizational behaviour* found in corporations and voluntary associations (such as labour unions and environmental organizations), collective behaviour lacks an official division of labour, hierarchy of authority, and established rules and procedures. Unlike *institutional behaviour* (in education, religion, or politics, for example), it lacks institutionalized norms to govern behaviour. Collective behaviour can take various forms, including crowds, mobs, riots, panics, fads, fashions, public opinion, and social movements.

Conditions for Collective Behaviour

Collective behaviour occurs as a result of some common influence or stimulus that produces a response from a collectivity. A *collectivity* is a relatively large number of people who mutually transcend, bypass, or subvert established institutional patterns and structures. Three major factors contribute to the likelihood that collective behaviour will occur: (1) structural factors that increase the chances of people responding in a particular way, (2) timing, and (3) a breakdown in social-control mechanisms and a corresponding feeling of "normlessness" (McPhail, 1991; Turner and Killian, 1993). A common stimulus is an important factor. For example, in 2010 thousands of protestors were arrested at the G-20 global economic summit in Toronto. The exclusive focus on economic issues made it an obvious target for protestors increasingly concerned about the human and social costs of economic globalization. Timing and a breakdown in social-control mechanisms also are important in collective behaviour. Since the 1960s, most urban riots in Canada and the United States have begun in the evenings or on weekends, when most people are off work (McPhail, 1991). As rioting, looting, and arson began to take a toll on certain areas of New Orleans after Hurricane Katrina in 2005, a temporary breakdown in formal social-control mechanisms occurred. In some areas of the city, law enforcement was inadequate to quell the illegal actions of rioters, some of whom began to believe that the rules had been suspended. Following the U.S. invasion of Iraq, rioters and looters destroyed the city of Baghdad as American soldiers were completely unprepared to handle the breakdown in social control.

Distinctions Regarding Collective Behaviour

People engaging in collective behaviour may be divided into crowds and masses. A *crowd* **is a relatively large number of people who are in one another's immediate vicinity** (Lofland, 1993). In contrast, a *mass* **is a number of people who share an interest in a specific idea or issue but who are not in one another's immediate vicinity** (Lofland, 1993). To further distinguish between crowds and masses, think of the difference between a riot and a rumour: people who participate in a riot must be in the same general location; those who spread a rumour may be thousands of kilometres apart, communicating by telephone or the Internet.

Collective behaviour also may be distinguished by the dominant emotion expressed. According to John Lofland (1993:72), the *dominant emotion* refers to the "publicly expressed feeling perceived by participants and observers as the most prominent in an episode of collective behaviour." Lofland suggests that fear, hostility, and joy are three fundamental emotions found in collective behaviour; however, grief, disgust, surprise, or shame also may predominate in some forms of collective behaviour.

Types of Crowd Behaviour

When we think of a crowd, many of us think of *aggregates,* previously defined as a collection of people who happen to be in the same place at the same time but who have little else in common. However, the presence of a relatively large number of people in the same location does not necessarily produce collective behaviour. Sociologist Herbert Blumer (1946) developed a typology in which crowds are divided into four categories: casual, conventional, expressive, and acting. Other scholars have added a fifth category—protest crowds.

Casual Crowds *Casual crowds* **are relatively large gatherings of people who happen to be in the same place at the same time; if they interact at all, it is only briefly.** People in a shopping mall or a bus are examples of casual crowds. Other than sharing a momentary interest, such as a watching a busker perform on the street or observing the aftermath of a car accident, a casual crowd has nothing in common. The casual crowd plays no active part in the event—such as the car accident that would have occurred whether or not the crowd was present; it simply observes.

Conventional Crowds *Conventional crowds* **are made up of people who specifically come together for a scheduled event and thus share a common focus.** Examples include religious services, graduation ceremonies, concerts, and university lectures. Each of these events has established schedules and norms. Because these events occur regularly, interaction among participants is much more likely; in turn, the events would not occur without the crowd, which is essential to the event.

Expressive Crowds *Expressive crowds* **provide opportunities for the expression of some strong emotion (such as joy, excitement, or grief).** People release their pent-up emotions in conjunction with other persons experiencing similar emotions. Examples include worshippers at religious revival services; mourners lining the streets when a celebrity, public official, or religious leader has died; and non-rioting crowds at a sporting event.

Acting Crowds

Acting crowds are collectivities so intensely focused on a specific purpose or object that they may erupt into violent or destructive behaviour. Mobs, riots, and panics are examples of acting crowds, but casual and conventional crowds may become acting crowds under some circumstances. A *mob* is a highly emotional crowd whose members engage in, or are ready to engage in, violence against a specific target—a person, a category of people, or physical property. Mob violence tends to dissipate relatively quickly once a target has been injured, killed, or destroyed.

Compared with mob actions, riots may be of somewhat longer duration. A *riot* is violent crowd behaviour that is fuelled by deep-seated emotions but not directed at one specific target. Riots often are triggered by fear, anger, and hostility. However, not all riots are caused by deep-seated hostility and hatred. People may be expressing joy and exuberance when rioting occurs. Examples include celebrations after sports victories, such as those that occurred in Montreal following a Stanley Cup championship and in Vancouver following a Stanley Cup playoff victory.

A *panic* is a form of crowd behaviour that occurs when a large number of people react to a real or perceived threat with strong emotions and self-destructive behaviour. The most common type of panic occurs when people seek to escape from a perceived danger, fearing that few (if any) of them will be able to get away from that danger.

Panic also can arise in response to events that people believe are beyond their control—such as a major disruption in the economy. Although instances of panic are relatively rare, they receive massive media coverage because they provoke strong feelings of fear in readers and viewers, and because the number of casualties may be large.

Protest Crowds

Clark McPhail and Ronald T. Wohlstein (1983) added protest crowds to the four types of crowds identified by Blumer. *Protest crowds* engage in activities intended to achieve specific political goals. Examples include sit-ins, marches, boycotts, blockades, and strikes. These sometimes take the form of *civil disobedience*—non-violent action that seeks to change a policy or law by refusing to comply with it. Acts of civil disobedience

may become violent, as in a confrontation between protesters and police officers; in this case, a protest crowd becomes an *acting crowd*. Such was the case during the fifth Asia-Pacific Economic Cooperation (APEC) Summit, in Vancouver, when protestors attempted to pull down a fence surrounding the area where economic leaders were meeting. Some protests can escalate into violent confrontations even though that is not the intent of the organizers.

As you will recall, collective action often puts individuals in the position of doing things as a group that they would not do on their own. Does this mean that people's actions are produced by some type of "herd mentality"? Some analysts have answered this question affirmatively; however, sociologists typically do not agree with that assessment.

Explanations of Crowd Behaviour

What causes people to act collectively? How do they determine what types of action to take? One of the earliest theorists to provide an answer to these questions was Gustave Le Bon, a French scholar who focused on crowd psychology in his contagion theory.

Contagion Theory

Contagion theory focuses on the social-psychological aspects of collective behaviour; it attempts to explain how moods, attitudes, and behaviour are communicated rapidly and why they are accepted by others (Turner and Killian, 1993). Le Bon (1841–1931) argued that people are more likely to engage in antisocial behaviour in a crowd because they are anonymous and feel invulnerable. Le Bon (1960/1895) suggested that a crowd takes on a life of its own that is larger than the beliefs or actions of any one person. Because of its anonymity, the crowd transforms individuals from rational beings into a single organism with a collective mind. In essence, Le Bon asserted that emotions such as fear and hate are contagious in crowds because people experience a decline in personal responsibility; they will do things as a collectivity that they would never do when acting alone.

Le Bon's theory is still used to explain crowd behaviour. However, critics argue that the "collective mind" has not been documented by systematic studies.

Convergence Theory

Convergence theory focuses on the shared emotions, goals, and beliefs many people bring to crowd behaviour. Because of their individual characteristics, many people have a predisposition to participate in certain types

Convergence theory adds to our understanding of certain types of collective behaviour by pointing out how individuals may have certain attributes—such as racial hatred or fear of environmental problems that directly threaten them—that initially bring them together. However, this perspective does not explain how the attitudes and characteristics of individuals who take some collective action differ from those who do not.

of activities (Turner and Killian, 1993). From this perspective, people with similar attributes find a collectivity of like-minded persons with whom they can express their underlying personal tendencies. Although people may reveal their "true selves" in crowds, their behaviour is not irrational; it is highly predictable to those who share similar emotions or beliefs.

Convergence theory has been applied to a wide array of conduct, from lynch mobs to environmental movements. In social psychologist Hadley Cantril's (1941) study of one lynching, he found that the participants shared certain common attributes: they were poor and working-class white people who felt that their own status was threatened by the presence of successful African Americans. Consequently, the characteristics of these individuals made them susceptible to joining a lynch mob even if they did not know the target of the lynching.

Emergent-Norm Theory   Unlike contagion and convergence theories, *emergent-norm theory* **emphasizes the importance of social norms in shaping crowd behaviour**. Drawing on the symbolic interactionist perspective, Ralph Turner and Lewis Killian (1993:12) asserted that crowds develop their own definition of a situation and establish norms for behaviour that fit the occasion. According to Turner and Killian (1993:13), emergent norms occur when people define a new situation as highly unusual or see a long-standing situation in a new light.

Sociologists using the emergent-norm approach want to determine how individuals in a given collectivity develop an understanding of what is going on, how they construe these activities, and what type of norms are involved. For example, in a study of audience participation, Steven E. Clayman (1993) found that members of an audience listening to a speech applaud promptly and independently but wait to coordinate their booing with other people; they do not want to "boo" alone. Some emergent norms are permissive—that is, they give people a shared conviction that they may disregard ordinary rules such as waiting in line, taking turns, or treating a speaker courteously.

Emergent-norm theory points out that crowds are not irrational. Rather, new norms are developed in a rational way to fit the immediate situation. However, critics note that proponents of this perspective fail to specify exactly what constitutes a norm, how new ones emerge, and how they are so quickly disseminated and accepted by a wide variety of participants. One variation of this theory suggests that no single dominant norm is accepted by everyone in a crowd; instead, norms are specific to the various categories of actors rather than to the collectivity as a whole (Snow, Zurcher, and Peters, 1981).

Mass Behaviour

Not all collective behaviour takes place in face-to-face collectivities. ***Mass behaviour* is collective behaviour that takes place when people (who often are geographically separated from one another)** respond to the same event in much the same way. For people to respond in the same way, they typically have common sources of information, and this information provokes their collective behaviour. The most frequent types of mass behaviour are rumours, gossip, mass hysteria, public opinion, fashions, and fads. Under some circumstances, social movements constitute a form of mass behaviour. However, we will examine social movements separately because they differ in some important ways from other types of dispersed collectivities.

Rumours and Gossip

***Rumours* are unsubstantiated reports on an issue or subject** (Rosnow and Fine, 1976). While a rumour may spread through an assembled collectivity, rumours may also be transmitted among people who are dispersed geographically. Although they may initially contain a kernel of truth, as they spread, rumours may be modified to serve the interests of those repeating them. Rumours thrive when tensions are high and little authentic information is available on an issue of great concern. People are willing to give rumours credence when no offsetting information is available. Once rumours begin to circulate, they seldom stop unless compelling information comes to the forefront that either proves the rumour false or makes it obsolete.

In industrialized societies with sophisticated technology, rumours come from a wide variety of sources and may be difficult to trace. Print media (newspapers, magazines) and electronic media (radio, television, the Internet), fax machines, cellular networks, satellite systems, and the World Wide Web facilitate the rapid movement of rumours around the globe. In addition, modern communications technology makes anonymity much easier. In a split second, messages (both factual and fictitious) can be disseminated to thousands of people through email or text messaging (see Box 4.3).

Whereas rumours deal with an issue or a subject, ***gossip* refers to rumours about the personal lives of individuals**. Charles Horton Cooley (1962/1909) viewed gossip as something that spread among a small group of individuals who personally knew the person who was the object of the rumour. Today, this often is not the case; many people enjoy gossiping about people they have never met. Tabloid newspapers and magazines such as the *National Enquirer* and *People,* and television "news" programs that purport to provide "inside" information on the lives of celebrities, are sources of contemporary gossip, much of which has not been checked for authenticity.

Mass Hysteria and Panic ***Mass hysteria* is a form of dispersed collective behaviour that occurs when a large number of people react with strong emotions and self-destructive behaviour to a real or perceived threat**. Does mass hysteria actually occur? Although the term has been widely used, many sociologists believe this behaviour is best described as panic with a dispersed audience.

Fads and Fashions ***A fad* is a temporary but widely copied activity enthusiastically followed by large numbers of people**. Some examples of fads are *Twilight* books and movies, and gaming systems such as Wii and Xbox Live. One especially remembered by faculty who have been on campus for several decades was the 1970s fad of "streaking"—students taking off their clothes and running naked in public. Fads can be embraced by widely dispersed collectivities; news networks may bring the latest fad to the attention of audiences around the world.

Fashions tend to last longer. ***Fashion* may be defined as a currently valued style of behaviour, thinking, or appearance**. Fashion can apply to many areas, including child rearing, education, sports, clothing, music, and art. Most sociological research on fashion has focused on clothing, especially women's apparel (Davis, 1992).

Georg Simmel (1904) and French sociologist Pierre Bourdieu viewed fashion as a means of status differentiation among members of different social classes. Simmel suggested a classic "trickle-down" theory (although he did not use those exact words) to describe the process by which members of the lower

BOX 4.3 SOCIOLOGY AND THE MEDIA

Urban Legends: Don't Believe Everything You Read

Consider the following story:

Hi All—

I think you all know that I don't send out hoaxes and don't do the reactionary thing and send out anything that crosses my path. This one, however, is a friend of a friend's and I've given it enough credibility in my mind that I'm writing it up and sending it out to all of you.

My friend's friend was dating a guy from Afghanistan up until a month ago. She had a date with him around 9/6 and was stood up. She was understandably upset and went to his home to find it completely emptied. On 9/10, she received a letter from her boyfriend explaining that he wished he could tell her why he had left and that he was sorry it had to be like that. The part worth mentioning is that he BEGGED her not to get on any commercial airlines on 9/11 and to not go to any malls on Halloween. As soon as everything happened on the 11th, she called the FBI and has since turned over the letter.

This is not an e-mail that I've received and decided to pass on. This came from a phone conversation with a long-time friend of mine last night.

This rumour is an example of an *urban legend*— an unsubstantiated story containing a sensational or unusual plot that is widely circulated and believed. According to urban legend expert Jan Harold Brunvand, the Internet has become a popular medium for transmitting urban legends.

The stories in urban legends are either false, or if they do have some basis in fact, the events being related occurred in the distant past. Urban legends are typically believed because they call up fears or concerns that are real, such as the unpredictable terrorist attacks of September 11, because they describe embarrassing situations that we can imagine ourselves in, or because they relate to some aspect of modern life that we accept but find somewhat disturbing. The Internet has made communication of urban legends faster and easier. In fact, it has been described as the perfect environment for fostering urban legends.

Jan Harold Brunvand also points out that people believe urban legends because they are not that incredible. They are about familiar places such as shopping malls, familiar experiences such as travelling, or worries and fears that are common to most of us (Brunvand, 2001).

According to David Emery, who investigates and debunks urban legends and Internet hoaxes, another reason Internet folklore is so readily accepted is because other sources of information are increasingly regarded with suspicion:

One reason rumour-mongering is rampant is that we don't always trust authorities to tell us the truth, and so you see rumours functioning as a sort of shadow news whereby people share— or think they are sharing—the untold truth. A lot of people have an itchy forward finger, not even bothering to think twice before shooting off unverified rumours to everyone they know. For almost every falsehood transmitted on the Net, the truth is also there to be found. The challenge, I think is for people to accept the personal responsibility that implies. (Christie, 2001:A1)

Have you received any urgent e-mail lately warning of cannibalism, murdering madmen, or traps laid by carjackers? Again, these are Internet-bound urban legends. The world of urban legends is growing so rapidly via the Internet that there are now dozens of websites devoted to debunking these stories. To read about some of the more common urban legends, or to verify whether the e-mail you received about bin Laden's shares in Snapple is true, explore the following urban-legend sites: www.snopes.com and www.scambusters.org.

---

classes emulate the fashions of the upper class. As the fashions descend through the status hierarchy, they are watered down and "vulgarized" so that they are no longer recognizable to members of the upper class, who then regard them as unfashionable and in bad taste (Davis, 1992). Almost 80 years later, Bourdieu (1984) similarly suggested that "matters of taste," including fashion sensibility, constitute a large share of the "cultural capital" (or social assets) possessed by members of the dominant class.

Perhaps one of the best refutations of the trickle-down approach is the way in which fashion today often originates among people in the lower social classes and is mimicked by the elites.

SOCIAL MOVEMENTS

Although collective behaviour is short lived and relatively unorganized, social movements are longer lasting and more organized and have specific goals or purposes. A **social movement is an organized group that acts consciously to promote or resist change through collective action** (Goldberg, 1991). Because social movements have not become institutionalized and are outside the political mainstream, they offer "outsiders" an opportunity to have their voices heard.

Social movements are more likely to develop in industrialized societies than in pre-industrial societies, where acceptance of traditional beliefs and practices makes such movements unlikely. Diversity and a lack of consensus (hallmarks of industrialized nations) contribute to demands for social change, and people who participate in social movements typically lack power and other resources to bring about change without engaging in collective action. Social movements are most likely to spring up when people come to see their personal troubles as public issues that cannot be solved without a collective response.

Social movements make democracy more available to excluded groups. Historically, people in North America have worked at the grassroots level to bring about changes even when elites sought to discourage activism (Adams, 1991). For example, the women's suffrage movement gave a voice to women who had been denied the right to vote (Rosenthal et al., 1985).

Social movements provide people who otherwise would not have the resources to enter the game of politics a chance to do so. We are most familiar with those movements that develop around public-policy issues considered newsworthy by the media, ranging from abortion and women's rights to gun control and environmental justice.

Types of Social Movements

Social movements are difficult to classify; however, sociologists distinguish among movements on the basis of their goals and the amount of change they seek to produce (Aberle, 1966; Blumer, 1974).

Reform Movements   Members of reform movements usually work within the existing system to attempt to change existing public policy so that it more adequately reflects their own value system. Examples of reform movements (in addition to the environmental movement) include labour movements, animal-rights movements, anti-nuclear movements, Mothers Against Drunk Driving, and the disability-rights movement.

Revolutionary Movements   **Movements seeking to bring about a total change in society are referred to as** *revolutionary movements*. These movements usually do not attempt to work within the existing system; rather, they aim to remake the system by replacing existing institutions with new ones. Revolutionary movements range from utopian groups seeking to establish an ideal society to radical terrorists who use fear tactics to intimidate those with whom they disagree ideologically (see Alexander and Gill, 1984; Berger, 1988; Vetter and Perlstein, 1991).

Terrorism **is the calculated unlawful use of physical force or threats of violence against persons or property in order to intimidate or coerce a government, organization, or individual for the purpose of gaining some political, religious, economic, or social objective**. Movements based on terrorism often use tactics such as bombings, kidnappings, hostage taking, hijackings, and assassinations (Vetter and Perlstein, 1991). Over the past 30 years, terrorism has become a global concern. Suicide bombings are regular occurrences in several countries including Afghanistan, Iraq, and Pakistan. The September 11, 2001, terrorist attacks on the World Trade Center and the Pentagon and the crash of a jetliner in Pennsylvania constituted the worst incident of domestic terrorism in U.S. history. These events demonstrated that terrorism continues to pose an ongoing threat to the international community.

Religious Movements   Also referred to as *expressive movements, religious movements* are concerned with renovating or renewing people through "inner change." Fundamentalist religious groups seeking to convert nonbelievers to their belief system are an example of this type of movement. Some religious movements are *millenarian*—that is, they forecast that "the end is near" and assert that an immediate change in behaviour is imperative. Relatively new

These protestors are members of a resistance movement seeking to undo change created by the "gun control" movement.

religious movements in industrialized Western societies have included Hare Krishnas, the Unification Church, Scientology, and the Divine Light Mission, all of which tend to appeal to the psychological and social needs of young people seeking meaning in life that mainstream religions have not provided for them.

Alternative Movements **Movements that seek limited change in some aspect of people's behaviour are referred to as *alternative movements*.** For example, in the early 20th century, the Women's Christian Temperance Union attempted to get people to abstain from drinking alcoholic beverages. More recently, a variety of "New Age" movements have directed people's behaviour by emphasizing spiritual consciousness combined with a belief in reincarnation and astrology. Practices such as vegetarianism, meditation, and holistic medicine often are included in the self-improvement category.

Resistance Movements Also referred to as *regressive movements,* resistance movements seek to prevent change or to undo change that already has occurred. Examples of resistance movements are groups organized to oppose free trade, gun control, gay rights, and restrictions on smoking. Perhaps the most widely known resistance movement, however, is made up of those who label themselves "pro-life" advocates. Protests by some radical anti-abortion groups in Canada and the United States have become violent and have resulted in the deaths of several doctors and clinic workers, thus creating fear among health professionals and patients seeking abortions.

FUTURE CHANGES IN SOCIETY, SOCIAL STRUCTURE, AND INTERACTION

The social structure in North America has been changing rapidly in recent decades. Currently, there are more possible statuses for persons to occupy and roles to play than at any other time in history. Although achieved statuses are very important today, ascribed statuses still have a significant impact on the options and opportunities people have.

Ironically, at a time when we have more technological capability, more leisure activities and types of entertainment, and more quantities of material goods available for consumption than ever before, many people experience high levels of stress, fear for their lives because of crime, and face problems such as homelessness.

Individuals and groups often show initiative in trying to solve some of our pressing problems. However, individual initiative alone will not solve all our social problems. Large-scale, formal organizations must become more responsive to society's needs.

At the microlevel, we need to regard social problems as everyone's problem; even if we do not, they have a way of becoming everyone's problem anyway. In sum, the future of this country rests on our collective ability to deal with major social problems at both the macrolevel and the microlevel of society.

How does social structure shape our social interactions?

The stable patterns of social relationships within a particular society make up its social structure. Social structure is a macrolevel influence because it shapes and determines the overall patterns in which social interaction occurs. Social interaction refers to how people within a society act and respond to one another. This interaction is a microlevel dynamic—between individuals and groups—and is the foundation of meaningful relationships in society. Social structure provides an ordered framework for society and for our interactions with others.

What are the main components of social structure?

Social structure comprises statuses, roles, groups, and social institutions. A status is a specific position in a group or society and is characterized by certain expectations, rights, and duties. Ascribed statuses, such as gender, class, and ethnicity, are acquired at birth or involuntarily later in life. Achieved statuses, such as education and occupation, are assumed voluntarily as a result of personal choice, merit, or direct effort. We occupy a status, but a role is a set of behavioural expectations associated with a given status. A social group consists of two or more people who interact frequently and share a common identity and sense of interdependence. A formal organization is a highly structured group formed to complete certain tasks or achieve specific goals. A social institution is a set of organized beliefs and rules that establish how a society attempts to meet its basic needs.

What are the functionalist and conflict perspectives on social institutions?

According to functionalist theorists, social institutions perform several prerequisites of all societies: replace members; teach new members; produce, distribute, and consume goods and services; preserve order; and provide and maintain a sense of purpose. Conflict theorists, however, note that social institutions do not work for the common good of all individuals. Institutions may enhance and uphold the power of some groups but exclude others, such as the homeless.

What is collective behaviour and when is it most likely to occur?

Collective behaviour is relatively spontaneous, unstructured activity that typically violates established social norms. Collective behaviour occurs when some common influence or stimulus produces a response from a relatively large number of people.

What is a crowd and what causes crowd behaviour?

A crowd is a relatively large number of people who are in one another's immediate vicinity. Social scientists have developed several theories to explain crowd behaviour. Contagion theory asserts that a crowd takes on a life of its own as people are transformed from rational beings into part of an organism that acts on its own. Convergence theory asserts that people with similar attributes find other like-minded persons with whom they can release underlying personal tendencies. Emergent-norm theory asserts that, as a crowd develops, it comes up with its own norms that replace more conventional norms of behaviour.

What are the major types of social movements, and what are their goals?

A social movement is an organized group that acts consciously to promote or resist change through collective action; such movements are most likely to be formed when people see their personal troubles as public issues that cannot be resolved without a collective response. Reform movements seek to improve society by changing some specific aspect of the social structure. Revolutionary movements seek to bring about a total change in society—sometimes by the use of terrorism. Religious movements seek to produce radical change in individuals based on spiritual or supernatural belief systems. Alternative movements seek limited change to some aspect of people's behaviour. Resistance movements seek to prevent change or to undo change that already has occurred.

KEY TERMS

achieved status 80
acting crowd 92
alternative movement 97
ascribed status 80
casual crowd 91
civil disobedience 92
collective behaviour 90
contagion theory 92
conventional crowd 91
convergence theory 92
crowd 91
dramaturgical analysis 87
emergent-norm theory 93
expressive crowd 91
fad 94
fashion 94
formal organization 84

WEB LINKS

For more Web links related to the topic of this chapter, see the Nelson sociology website:
www.sociologyessentials5e.nelson.com

Raising the Roof is a national charity that funds long-term solutions to homelessness in Canada. Its primary activities involve developing, finding, and/or maintaining homes for homeless people. Questions and answers, as well as current articles on homelessness, are available at this site:
www.raisingtheroof.org

QUESTIONS FOR CRITICAL THINKING

1. Think of a person you know well whose behaviour grates on your nerves (it could be a parent, friend, relative, or teacher). First, list that person's statuses and roles. Then, analyze his or her possible role expectations, role performance, role conflicts, and role strains. Does anything you find in your analysis help explain his or her irritating behaviour? (If not, change your method of analysis!) How helpful are the concepts of social structure in analyzing individual behaviour?
2. How does the structure of Canadian society influence the way in which we understand and respond to homelessness, both individually and collectively?
3. You are conducting field research on gender differences in nonverbal communication styles. How will you account for variations among age, ethnicity, and social class?
4. What types of collective behaviour in Canada do you believe are influenced by inequalities based on race/ethnicity, class, gender, age, or disabilities? Why?

ONLINE STUDY AND RESEARCH TOOLS
INFOTRAC®

InfoTrac College Edition is included free with every new copy of this text. Explore this online library for additional readings, review, and a handy resource for assignments. Visit **www.infotrac-college.com** to access this online database of full-text articles. Enter the key terms from this chapter to start your search.

CENGAGENOW™ CENGAGENOW

Use CengageNOW™ to help you formulate a customized study plan for this chapter. After you take the Diagnostic Quiz, CengageNOW™ will generate a customized study plan for you. It will identify sections of the chapter you should review.

Groups and Organizations

Kenneth Payne describes his journey through a bureaucratic maze: "Since November, I have spent six to eight hours a day trying to persuade the authorities to accommodate me, but it just goes around in a circle. . . . It's George Orwell's Big Brother. . . . The bureaucracy is making me prove a negative and it turns 'innocent until proven guilty' on its head. . . . There's no common sense here. It's an inflexible bureaucracy where nobody takes any responsibility" (Reed, 1998:A11).

What is Mr. Payne's problem? The former carpenter wants to be a schoolteacher. He has a degree in education and teaching experience. However, he is unable to get a permanent job teaching because he has a skin disease that causes the skin on his hands to blister and peel. Why should this condition disqualify Mr. Payne from teaching? Because the disease has removed his fingerprints and legislators in his home state of California have passed a law requiring that all teachers be fingerprinted so their criminal records can be checked. Of course, because Mr. Payne has never had proper fingerprints, there would be nothing on file to check against even if they could read

his prints. But this fact has not changed the bureaucrats' minds. Payne has appealed to the state and has offered to prove in other ways that he has no criminal record, but he has been unable to get an exemption from the rule.

Why do people in organizations behave so inflexibly? Some rules are necessary for all organizations to function. Even in small groups, such as families or friendship groups, informal rules help to ensure that people interact smoothly. In a large bureaucracy, an explicit system of rules and regulations means that employees and clients know what is expected of them. These rules can also help to ensure that everyone receives equal treatment from the organization. Unfortunately, adherence to the rules can stifle individual judgment, and some bureaucrats become so inflexible that they hurt the organization and its clients. In Mr. Payne's case, it made sense for the school system to do its best to protect children by establishing background checks for prospective teachers. However, fingerprinting is just one way of ensuring that people with criminal records are not hired as teachers. An official who was concerned with the goal of the policy

(protecting children) rather than with one of the means of achieving that goal (fingerprinting) would have accepted the other ways in which Mr. Payne could have proved he was not an offender.

While Mr. Payne suffered personal hardship, the consequences of bureaucratic inflexibility can be much broader. In August 2005, Hurricane Katrina devastated the city of New Orleans. Tens of thousands of evacuees were not properly cared for, and law and order broke down in the city. The massive failures in planning for the disaster and in coordinating the response after the city was flooded will be studied for years. While the most serious flaw was probably a lack of coordination among the local, state, and federal officials responsible for the emergency, bureaucratic inflexibility was also pervasive.

Several relatively small incidents show that even in the face of the largest natural disaster ever to hit North America, some of the people running bureaucracies were focused more on rules and regulations than on saving lives. Despite the desperate need for water for hurricane survivors, there were incidents where truckloads of water were turned back because the drivers didn't have the proper paperwork (Lipton et al., 2005). A group of doctors were evacuated from their hospital and taken to a New Orleans airport. They offered to help tend the many sick people who had also been taken to the airport, but federal authorities were worried about liability issues and told them they could best help by mopping floors (CNN, 2005). While the doctors cleaned floors, patients died because of the lack of medical care. Another example of inflexibility occurred when hundreds of firefighters from around the United States were forced by the U.S. Federal Emergency Management Agency to delay their deployment into the emergency zone to take several days of community relations and sexual harassment training.

M uch of our time is spent dealing with bureaucratic organizations. Most of us are born in hospitals, educated in schools, fed by restaurants and supermarket chains, entertained by communications companies, employed by corporations, and buried by funeral companies. Some people think of bureaucracies in a negative way because of their red tape and impersonality. However, while they can be inflexible and inhumane, bureaucracies are a very powerful type of social organization and are essential to modern life. Bureaucracies have been the best way of managing large numbers of people who must accomplish a common task, and are an essential part of our industrialized society.

While important and very visible, bureaucracies are just one form of social organization. We spend most of our lives in groups including families, friends, and school and work groups. Humans are social animals so it is important to understand the characteristics and dynamics of social groups ranging from small informal groups to large bureaucracies.

In this chapter, you will learn about different types of groups and organizations, including bureaucracies. As social beings, we live our lives in groups and they constantly affect our behaviour. Before reading on, test your knowledge about bureaucracies by taking the quiz in Box 5.1 on page 104.

QUESTIONS AND ISSUES

Chapter Focus Question: How can we explain the behaviour of people who work in bureaucracies?

What constitutes a social group?

How are groups and their members shaped by group size, leadership style, and pressures to conform?

What purposes does bureaucracy serve?

What are some of the characteristics of bureaucracies?

SOCIAL GROUPS

Three strangers are standing at a street corner waiting for a traffic light to change. Do they constitute a group? Five hundred women and men are first-year students at a university. Do they constitute a group? In everyday usage, we use the word *group* to mean any collection of people. According to sociologists, however, the answer to these questions is no; individuals who happen to share a common feature or to be in the same place at the same time do not constitute social groups.

Groups, Aggregates, and Categories

A *social group* is a collection of two or more people who interact frequently with one another, share a sense of belonging, and have a feeling of interdependence. Several people waiting for a traffic light to change constitute an *aggregate*—a collection of people who happen to be in the same place at the same time but have little else in common. People in aggregates share a common purpose (such as purchasing items or arriving at their destination) but generally do not interact with one another, except perhaps briefly. The first-year students, at least initially, constitute a *category*—**a number of people who may never have met one another but who share a similar characteristic** (such as education level, age, ethnicity, and gender). Men and women make up categories, as do First Nations peoples and victims of sexual harassment. Categories are not social groups because the people in them usually do not create a social structure or have anything in common other than a particular trait.

Occasionally, people in aggregates and categories form social groups. People within the category of "students," become an aggregate when they meet for an orientation. Some of them may form social groups as they interact with one another in classes, find that they have mutual interests and concerns, and develop a sense of belonging to the group.

Social groups can change over time. For example, an aggregate or category of people may become a formal organization with a specific structure and clear-cut goals. A *formal organization* is a structured group formed to achieve specific goals in the most efficient manner. Universities, factories, corporations, and the military are examples of formal organizations. Before we examine formal organizations, we need to know more about groups in general and about how they function.

Types of Groups

Groups have varying degrees of social solidarity and structure. This structure is flexible in some groups and more rigid in others. Some groups are small and personal; others are large and impersonal.

Primary and Secondary Groups
Charles Cooley (1962/1909) used the term *primary group* to describe a small, less specialized group in which members engage in face-to-face, emotion-based interactions over an extended time. We have primary

Private clubs place formal restrictions on group membership.

© Tony Roberts/Corbis

relationships with other individuals in our primary groups—that is, with our *significant others.*

In contrast, a *secondary group* is a larger, more specialized group in which members engage in more impersonal, goal-oriented relationships for a limited time. The size of a secondary group may vary. Twelve students in a university seminar may start out as a secondary group but eventually become a primary group as they get to know one another and communicate on a more personal basis. Formal organizations are secondary groups, but they also contain many primary groups. There are many thousands of primary groups within the secondary-group setting of your university or college.

Ingroups and Outgroups
Groups set boundaries by distinguishing between insiders who are members and outsiders who are not. William Graham Sumner (1959/1906) coined the terms *ingroup* and *outgroup* to describe people's feelings toward members of their own and other groups. An **ingroup is a group to which a person belongs and with which the person feels a sense of identity. An *outgroup* is a group to which a person does not belong and toward which the person may feel a sense of competitiveness or hostility**. Distinguishing between our ingroups and our outgroups helps us establish our individual identity and self-worth. Likewise, groups are solidified by ingroup and outgroup distinctions; the presence of an enemy or hostile group may bind members more closely together (Coser, 1956).

Group boundaries may be formal, with clearly defined criteria for membership. For example, a country club that requires applicants for membership to be recommended by four current members, and to pay a $25 000 initiation fee and $1 000-per-month membership dues has clearly set requirements for its members. The club might even post an entrance sign that states "Members Only" and may use security personnel to ensure that nonmembers do not encroach on its grounds. Boundary distinctions often are reflected in symbols, such as emblems or clothing. These symbols denote that the bearer or wearer is a member of the ingroup; they are status symbols.

Of course, group boundaries are not always as formal as they are in a private club. Friendship groups, for example, usually do not have clear guidelines for membership. Rather, the boundaries tend to be very informal and vaguely defined.

Ingroup and outgroup distinctions may encourage social cohesion among members, but they also may promote racism, classism, sexism, and ageism. Ingroup members typically view themselves positively and

BOX 5.1	SOCIOLOGY AND EVERYDAY LIFE

How Much Do You Know About Bureaucracy?

True	False	
T	(F)	1. Large bureaucracies have existed for about 1000 years.
T	(F)	2. Because of the efficiency and profitability of the new 18th century factory bureaucracies, people were eager to leave the farms to work in the factories.
(T)	F	3. Bureaucracies are deliberately impersonal.
(T)	F	4. In addition to their formal structure, bureaucracies also have an "other face"—an informal structure that is also important in understanding their operation.
(T)	F	5. The rise of Protestantism helped create the social conditions favourable to the rise of modern bureaucracies.
T	(F)	6. Because people in bureaucracies follow the direction of their superiors, bringing about change in large organizations is easy.
(T)	F	7. One of the first modern bureaucratic organizations was the Prussian army.
T	(F)	8. Terrorist groups have been successful because they have established large bureaucratic organizations.
(T)	F	9. The organizational principles used by McDonald's restaurants are being adopted by other sectors of the global economy.
T	(F)	10. Bureaucracies have made it easy for women to move into traditionally male jobs.

Answers on page 105.

may view members of outgroups negatively. These feelings of group superiority, or *ethnocentrism,* can be very detrimental to groups and individuals who are not part of the ingroup. Sexual harassment and racial discrimination are two of the negative consequences of ethnocentrism.

Reference Groups   Ingroups provide us not only with a source of identity but also with a point of reference. A *reference group* **is a group that strongly influences a person's behaviour and social attitudes, regardless of whether that individual is an actual member.** When we attempt to evaluate our appearance, ideas, or goals, we automatically refer to the standards of some group. Sometimes we will refer to our membership groups, such as family or friends. Other times, we will refer to groups to which we do not currently belong but that we might want to join in the future, such as a social club or a profession.

Networks   A *network* **is a web of social relationships that links one person with other people**

and, through them, additional people. Frequently, networks connect people who share common interests but who otherwise might not interact with one another. For example, if A is tied to B and B is tied to C, then a network may be formed among individuals A, B, and C. Think of the experiences that you and your friends have had looking for summer jobs. If your friend works at a company that needs more people, he or she may recommend you to the potential employer. This recommendation helps you get a job, and it gives the employer the assurance that you are likely to be a good employee. Research shows that networks play a very important role in helping graduating students to find employment (Granovetter, 1995).

It's a Small World: Networks of Acquaintances On September 11, 2001, nearly 3000 people died when terrorists crashed planes into the North and South towers of New York's World Trade Center and a third plane into the Pentagon. Many people around the world were surprised to learn that they, or some of

SOCIOLOGY AND EVERYDAY LIFE

Answers to the Sociology Quiz on Bureaucracy

Join In

1. **False.** Many sociologists feel that modern bureaucracies began with the development of large factories in England during the 19th century. Large-scale organizations had existed before this time, but they were not organized on bureaucratic principles. New organizing principles were required in order to manage large organizations.

2. **False.** Commenting on the 18th-century factory, Charles Perrow has observed that "the unnaturalness of working for someone else's profit twelve hours a day, seven days a week was so pronounced that the early factories had to rely on criminals and paupers to do the work" (1986:49).

3. **True.** Bureaucracies are designed to be efficient and productive. To do this, they take a detached approach to clients and employees so personal feelings do not interfere with organizational decisions.

4. **True.** All bureaucracies have an informal structure that is composed of activities and interactions that do not correspond with the official rules and procedures of the bureaucracy.

5. **True.** According to Max Weber, Protestantism, with its emphasis on worldliness and commitment to long-term goals, helped create the social conditions that led to the rise of the modern bureaucracy.

6. **False.** It can be extremely difficult to bring about change in bureaucracies because people become comfortable with the way things have been done in the past.

7. **True.** Napoleon's defeat at Waterloo, in 1815, by the allied armies of Prussia (now part of Germany), Britain, Austria, and Russia, showed that mass armies could not be led in the traditional way, by a single commander responsible for everything (Stark, 1998). The Prussian military, having learned from observing Napoleon's defeat, designed a more effective organization. Field Marshal von Moltke, who took command of the Prussian army in 1857, was responsible for two major innovations. He developed a general staff made up of carefully trained officers who could carry out the leader's commands, and he divided his army into standard-sized "divisions" that could fight as self-sufficient units. These innovations, which still guide contemporary armies, also influenced the development of industrial bureaucracies.

8. **False** Terrorist groups have not set up bureaucracies. Rather, their organizations are based on decentralized networks that are very flexible and highly mobile (Arquilla and Ronfeldt, 2001).

9. **True.** George Ritzer (2000) coined the term "McDonaldization" to describe the highly rationalized business process used by the restaurant chain. This process is characterized by efficiency, an emphasis on speed and quantity rather than quality, predictability, control, and dehumanization. Research suggests this model is spreading to other types of business and to other parts of the world.

10. **False** It has often been very difficult for women to move into traditional male jobs. Many have suffered harassment and other forms of hostility.

their acquaintances, knew someone who had been personally touched by the tragedy. Social scientists were not surprised by this because of a fascinating research project done more than 30 years ago by Stanley Milgram (1967).

Milgram sent packages of letters to people in the Midwestern United States. The objective was to get the letters to one of two target recipients in Boston using personal contacts. Those originating the chain were given the name of the target recipient and told

These Olympic teams graphically illustrate the concept of ingroups and outgroups. Each Olympic team can be seen as an ingroup that gives its members a sense of belonging and identity—feelings that are strengthened by the presence of clearly defined outgroups (competing teams).

Toshifumi Kitamura/AFP/Getty Images

that the person was either a Boston stockbroker or the wife of a Harvard divinity student. They were asked to mail the letter to an acquaintance who they felt would be able to pass it on to another acquaintance even closer to the intended target. Milgram found that it took an average of five contacts to get the letters to the intended recipient.

This research was popularized through the play and movie *Six Degrees of Separation,* and the popular trivia game "Six Degrees of Kevin Bacon, " in which the objective is to link actors to Kevin Bacon using networks. Thus, Nicole Kidman has a Kevin Bacon number of 2, as she appeared in *Eyes Wide Shut* with Tom Cruise, who worked with Kevin Bacon on the movie *A Few Good Men.* Since virtually no American actor has a Bacon number larger than 4, the challenge for movie-trivia experts is to figure out the linkages. (You can find out more about this game at the Oracle of Bacon website at http://oracleofbacon.org).

The "small-world" research has some important implications. Strogatz and Watts (1998) have worked out the mathematics behind the phenomenon and have documented the importance of "bridges"— people who bridge very different social worlds. For example, in Milgram's study the Boston stockbroker received 64 letters, 16 of which were delivered by the owner of a Boston clothing store. Perhaps you can think of friends or acquaintances who come from other countries or who have unusual interests, hobbies, or jobs that would enable them to bridge vast distances or widely different social groups. The study of networks and the role of bridges has important implications for researchers in many fields including *epidemiology,* which is the study of the spread of disease. For example, the spread of HIV/AIDS was reportedly hastened by a Canadian flight attendant ("Patient X") whose travels bridged several different networks of gay males (Saulnier, 1998).

While Milgram's research has been influential, Kleinfeld (2002) found that most of Milgram's letters never reached their intended destination. We do not know if the connections failed because the participants could not think of anyone who could act as the next link in the chain, or simply because they did not bother moving the letter along toward the intended recipient. However, a recent study using e-mail contacts had lower failure rates and had similar results to Milgram's. Dodds and his colleagues (2003) found that those who continued the chain needed an average of five to seven contacts to reach their targets even when in another country.

This research points out an interesting aspect of social networks. Korte and Milgram (1970) found a significantly higher number of completed chains when both the sender and the recipient were the same race, and Dodds et al. (2003) found that people most frequently contacted persons of the same gender. Dodds et al. found that workplace and educational contacts were most likely to be used in completing chains. These findings suggest that members of groups that are less powerful and less educated may be disadvantaged in a world that is increasingly dependent upon geographically dispersed social networks.

Why is this important? We live in a world where many things get done through networks. Granovetter (1995) showed that social networks are very important for employers and for people looking for work. Most people get their jobs through personal contacts rather than through formal job-search mechanisms. Those with strong networks will have an advantage in their search for work, while those without extensive networks or those whose networks are not oriented to the labour market will be at a great disadvantage. If most of your friends are unemployed, they cannot help you find a job. This can perpetuate unemployment among groups, including some visible minorities and women, who may not have had the opportunity to build up strong networks.

Network analysis will become much more important in sociology. For example, e-mail patterns may help us learn how organizations work. How do ideas spread within an organization? Do e-mail messages frequently pass between different levels of an organization, or are communications restricted to one level? Are there cliques that rarely communicate with others or are communications more broadly based? Do women and visible minorities have the same interaction patterns as white males, and are they able to bridge different parts of their organizations? On a broader level, can genuine communities flourish in cyberspace, or does the Internet reduce community by reducing the personal contact between people?

GROUP DYNAMICS

Group Conformity

Groups exert a powerful influence in our lives. To gain and retain our membership in groups, most of us are willing to exhibit a high level of conformity to the wishes of other group members. ***Conformity is the process of maintaining or changing behaviour to comply with the norms established by a society, subculture, or other group.*** We often experience powerful pressure from other group members to conform.

Several researchers have found that the pressure to conform can cause group members to say they see something that is contradictory to what they actually are seeing or to do something they otherwise would be unwilling to do. As we look at two of these studies, ask yourself what you might have done if you had been one of the subjects in this research.

Asch's Research   Pressure to conform is especially strong in small groups in which members want to fit in with the group. In a series of experiments conducted by Solomon Asch (1955, 1956), the pressure toward group conformity was so great that participants were willing to contradict their own judgment rather than be in disagreement with the group.

One of Asch's experiments involved groups of undergraduate men (seven in each group) who ostensibly were recruited for a study of visual perception. All the men were seated in chairs. However, the person in the sixth chair did not know that he was the only actual subject; all the others were assisting the researcher. The participants were first shown a large card with a vertical line on it and then a second card with three vertical lines (see Figure 5.1). Each of the seven participants

Our most intense relationships occur in dyads—groups composed of two members. How might the interaction of these two people differ if they were with several other people?

© Roy Morsch/Zefa/Corbis

was asked to indicate which of the three lines on the second card was identical in length to the "standard line" on the first card.

In the first test with each group, all seven men selected the correct matching line. In the second trial, all seven again answered correctly. In the third trial, however, the subject became uncomfortable when all of the others selected the incorrect line. The subject could not understand what was happening and became even more confused as the others continued to give incorrect responses on 11 out of the next 15 trials.

Although Line 2 is clearly the same length as the line in the lower card, Solomon Asch's research assistants tried to influence subject participants by deliberately picking Line 1 or Line 3 as the correct match. Many of the participants went along rather than disagreeing with the "group."

If you had been in the position of the subject, how would you have responded? Would you have continued to give the correct answer, or would you have been swayed by the others? When Asch (1955)

Figure 5.1	**Asch's Cards**

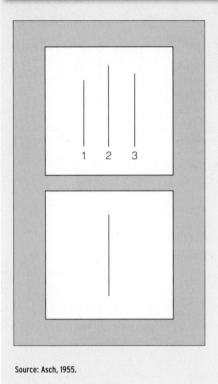

Although Line 2 is clearly the same length as the line in the lower card, Solomon Asch's research assistants tried to influence subject participants by deliberately picking Line 1 or Line 3 as the correct match. Manyof the participants went along rather than disagreeing with the "group."

Source: Asch, 1955.

averaged the responses of the 50 actual subjects who participated in the study, he found that about 33 percent routinely chose to conform to the group by giving the same (incorrect) responses as Asch's assistants. Another 40 percent gave incorrect responses in about half of the trials. Although 25 percent always gave correct responses, even they felt very uneasy and "knew that something was wrong." In discussing the experiment afterward, most of the subjects who gave incorrect responses indicated that they had known the answers were wrong but decided to go along with the group to avoid ridicule or ostracism.

In later studies, Asch found that if even a single assistant did not agree with the others, the subject was reassured by hearing someone else question the accuracy of incorrect responses and was much less likely to give a wrong answer himself. This research shows the power that groups have to produce conformity among members.

Milgram's Research on Authority   How willing are we to do something because someone in a position of authority has told us to do it? How far are we willing to go in following the demands of that individual? Stanley Milgram (1963, 1974) conducted

a series of controversial experiments to find answers to these questions about people's obedience to authority. Milgram wanted to do this research to help him understand atrocities such as the Holocaust, where ordinary citizens behaved brutally when ordered to do so.

Milgram's subjects were men who had responded to an advertisement for participants in an experiment. When the first (actual) subject arrived, he was told that the study concerned the effects of punishment on learning. After the second subject (actually an assistant of Milgram's) arrived, the two men were instructed to draw slips of paper from a hat to get their assignments as either the "teacher" or the "learner." Because the drawing was rigged, the actual subject always became the teacher, and the assistant the learner. Next, the learner was strapped into a chair with protruding electrodes that looked something like an electric chair. The teacher was placed in an adjoining room and given a realistic-looking but nonoperative shock generator. The "generator's" control panel showed levels that went from "Slight Shock" (15 volts) on the left, to "Intense Shock" (255 volts) in the middle, to "DANGER: SEVERE SHOCK" (375 volts), and finally "XXX" (450 volts) on the right.

The teacher was instructed to read aloud a pair of words and then to repeat the first of the two words. At that time, the learner was supposed to respond with the second of the two words. If the learner could not provide the second word, the teacher was instructed to press the lever on the shock generator so that the learner would be punished for forgetting the word. Each time the learner gave an incorrect response, the teacher was supposed to increase the shock level by 15 volts. The alleged purpose of the shock was to determine whether punishment improves a person's memory.

What was the maximum level of shock that a teacher was willing to inflict on a learner? The learner had been instructed (in advance) to beat on the wall between himself and the teacher as the experiment continued, pretending that he was in intense pain. The teacher was told that the shocks might be "extremely painful" but that they would cause no permanent damage. At about 300 volts, when the learner quit responding at all to questions, the teacher often turned to the experimenter to see what he should do next. When the experimenter indicated that the teacher should give increasingly painful shocks, 65 percent of them administered shocks all the way up to the "XXX" (450-volt) level. By this point in the process, the teachers frequently were sweating, stuttering, or biting on their lip:

> . . . subjects showed a reluctance to look at the victim, whom they could see through the glass in front of them. When this fact was brought to their attention they indicated that it caused them discomfort to see the victim in agony. We note, however, that although the subject refuses to look at the victim, he continues to administer shocks (Milgram, 1965: 61).

According to Milgram, the teachers (who were free to leave whenever they wanted to) continued in the experiment because they were being given directions by a person in a position of authority (a scientist wearing a white coat).

What can we learn from Milgram's study? The study suggests that obedience to authority may be more common than most of us would like to believe. None of the "teachers" challenged the process before they had applied 300 volts. Almost two-thirds went all the way to what could have been a deadly jolt of electricity if the shock generator had been real. Some subjects even physically forced the victim's hand onto the shock plate. Burger (2009) has recently conducted a partial replication of Milgram's work and found that rates of obedience were very similar to those of the earlier study. Most people went to the end of the experiment and women were as likely to obey as men.

This research raises questions concerning research ethics (see Chapter 1). Milgram's subjects were deceived about the nature of the study. Many of them found the experiment extremely stressful and some suffered anxiety attacks so severe that their experimental session had to be ended (Milgram, 1963). It would be impossible today to obtain permission to replicate this experiment in a university setting, though such studies were common in the 1960s. Burger's recent partial replication of the study made a number of changes, including stopping the experiment at the 150-volt level, in order to obtain ethics approval. He felt this was justified because in Milgram's work, the vast majority of people who went past this level continued all the way to the end.

In addition to ethical problems, some critics feel that Milgram's study was also methodologically flawed. Brannigan (2004) has raised the issue of whether the subjects actually believed that they were hurting people. The more realistic Milgram made the experiment, the more likely the subjects were to refuse to proceed. One critic explains why he does not take the results of Milgram's study very seriously:

> Every experiment was basically preposterous . . . the entire experimental procedure from beginning to end could make no sense at all, even to the laymen. A person is strapped to a chair and immobilized and is explicitly told he is going to be exposed to extremely painful electric shocks. . . . The task the student is to learn is evidently impossible. He can't learn it in a short time. . . . No one could learn it. . . . This experiment becomes more incredulous and senseless the further it is carried. (Mantell, 1971:110–111)

Because of the artificiality of the laboratory situation, Brannigan is very doubtful that this experiment tells us anything about why German citizens were willing to participate in the atrocities of the Holocaust. The issue of artificiality means that we should always be cautious when we consider the findings of laboratory experiments involving human behaviour.

Groupthink As we have seen, individuals often respond differently in a group context than if they were alone. Irving Janis (1972, 1989) examined group decision making and found that major blunders have been attributed to pressure toward group conformity. To describe this phenomenon, he coined the term **groupthink—the process by which members of a**

cohesive group arrive at a decision that many individual members privately believe is unwise. Why not speak up at the time? Members usually want to be "team players." They may not want to be the ones who undermine the group's consensus or who challenge the leadership. Consequently, members may limit or withhold their opinions and focus on consensus rather than on exploring all the options and making the best decision.

The 1986 launch of the space shuttle *Challenger*, which exploded 73 seconds into its flight, killing all seven crew members, provides an example of groupthink. On the day preceding the launch, engineers at the company that designed and manufactured the rocket boosters became concerned that freezing temperatures at the launch site would interfere with the proper functioning of the O-ring seals in the boosters. But when they expressed their misgivings, they were overruled by higher-level officials at the company and with NASA (the government agency that administers the U.S. space program), where executives were impatient because of earlier delays. A presidential commission that investigated the tragedy concluded that neither the manufacturer nor NASA responded adequately to warnings about the seals (Lippa, 1994).

Why did people agree to the launch despite these safety concerns? After all, it is one thing to doubt your judgment about the length of a line as in the Asch experiments and quite another to send seven people to their deaths. The engineers closest to the situation almost unanimously opposed the launch. However, the decision was ultimately made by managers who were more focused on the schedule than on safety concerns. NASA managers were under great pressure to keep the shuttle flights on schedule because they feared congressional budget cuts. When the contractor suggested delaying the launch until air temperatures were above 12°C, NASA managers responded angrily. One said "My God … when do you want me to launch, next April?" (President's Commission, 1986:96). Another said, "I'm appalled by your recommendation" (President's Commission, 1986:94). Faced with this pressure, the contractor, which was about to begin negotiating a new billion-dollar agreement with NASA, had second thoughts. Senior managers overruled the recommendations of their engineers and recommended launch. NASA managers and the contractor managers risked other people's lives to accomplish their own bureaucratic goals.

Groupthink can be very hard to eliminate. Despite the clear analysis of NASA's errors in the *Challenger* case, groupthink may also have contributed to the 2003 crash of the space shuttle *Columbia*, as administrators did not listen to engineers' concerns about foam that had broken from a fuel tank on seven previous flights. Damage caused by this foam led to the destruction of the shuttle. One of the investigation board members concluded that dissent was still not welcome at NASA, even when concerning matters of safety.

FORMAL ORGANIZATIONS

In earlier times, life was centred on small, informal, primary groups, such as the family and the village. With the advent of industrialization and urbanization,

According to Janis (1972, 1989), prior conditions such as a highly homogeneous group with committed leadership can lead to potentially disastrous "groupthink," which short-circuits careful and impartial deliberation.

people's lives became increasingly dominated by large, formal, secondary organizations. A *formal organization* **is a highly structured secondary group formed for the purpose of achieving specific goals in the most efficient manner.** Formal organizations (such as corporations, schools, and governmental agencies) usually keep their basic structure for many years to meet their specific goals.

Bureaucracies

The bureaucratic model of organization is the most universal organizational form in government, business, education, and religion. A *bureaucracy* **is an organizational model characterized by a hierarchy of authority, a clear division of labour, explicit rules and procedures, and impersonality in personnel matters.**

When we think of a bureaucracy, we may think of "buck passing, " such as occurs when we are directed from one office to the next without receiving an answer to our question or a solution to our problem. We also may view a bureaucracy in terms of red tape because of the situations in which there is so much paperwork and so many incomprehensible rules that no one really understands what to do. However, bureaucracy originally was not intended to be this way; it was seen as a way to make organizations *more* productive and efficient.

Weber (1968/1922) was interested in the historical trend toward bureaucratization that accelerated during the Industrial Revolution. To Weber, bureaucracy was the most efficient means of attaining organizational goals because of its coordination and control.

Formal Characteristics of Bureaucracy Weber set forth several characteristics of bureaucratic organizations. Although real bureaucracies may not feature all of these characteristics, Weber's model highlights the organizational efficiency and productivity to which bureaucracies strive.

Division of Labour Bureaucratic organizations are characterized by specialization, and each member has a specific status with certain assigned tasks to fulfill. This division of labour requires the employment of specialized experts who are responsible for the effective performance of their duties. In a university, for example, a distinct division of labour exists between faculty and the administration.

Hierarchy of Authority Hierarchy of authority, or chain of command, includes each lower office being under the control of a higher one (Perrow, 1986). Hierarchical authority takes the form of a pyramid. Those few individuals at the top have more power and exercise more control than do the many at the lower levels. Hierarchy inevitably influences social interaction. Those who are lower in the hierarchy report to (and often take orders from) those above them in the pyramid. Persons at the upper levels are responsible not only for their own actions but also for those of the individuals they supervise.

Although telephone- and computer-based procedures have streamlined the process, for many students registration exemplifies the worst aspects of academic bureaucracy. Yet students and other members of the academic community depend on the "bureaucracy" to establish and administer procedures that enable the complex system of the university to operate smoothly.

© David Butow/Corbis SABA

Rules and Regulations   Weber asserted that rules and regulations establish authority within an organization. These rules are typically standardized and provided to members in a written format. In theory, written rules and regulations offer clear-cut standards for determining satisfactory performance. They also provide continuity so that each new member does not have to reinvent the necessary rules and regulations.

Qualification-based Employment   Bureaucracies hire staff members and professional employees based on specific qualifications. Favouritism, family connections, and other subjective factors not relevant to organizational efficiency are not acceptable criteria for employment. Promotions are based on merit as spelled out in personnel policies.

Impersonality   A detached approach should prevail toward clients so that personal feelings do not interfere with organizational decisions. Officials must interact with subordinates based on their official status, not on their personal feelings.

Informal Structure in Bureaucracies   When we look at an organizational chart, the official, formal structure of a bureaucracy is readily apparent. In practice, however, a bureaucracy has patterns of activities and interactions that cannot be accounted for by its organizational chart. These patterns have been referred to as *bureaucracy's other face* (Page, 1946).

An organization's **informal structure comprises those aspects of participants' day-to-day activities and interactions that ignore, bypass, or do not correspond with the official rules and procedures of the bureaucracy.** An example is an informal "grapevine" that spreads information (with varying degrees of accuracy) much faster than do official channels of communication, which tend to be slow and unresponsive. The informal structure also includes the ideology and practices of workers on the job. Workers create a work culture to help deal with the constraints of their jobs, and to guide their interactions with co-workers.

Shortcomings of Bureaucracies

Weber's description of bureaucracy was intentionally an idealized model of a rationally organized institution. However, the very characteristics that make up this "rational" model have a dark side that frequently has given this type of organization a bad name (see

Courtesy of Boni Prokopetz

Captain Boni Prokopetz is a Burnaby firefighter who has complained of sexual harassment and discrimination at work. Sociologists have found that women in male-dominated fields are less likely than men to be included in informal networks and more likely to be harassed on the job. Are these two factors related? What steps could be taken to reduce the problems of harassment and exclusion?

Figure 5.2). Three of the major problems of bureaucracies are inefficiency and rigidity, resistance to change, and perpetuation of ethnic, class, and gender inequalities.

Inefficiency and Rigidity   Bureaucracies experience inefficiency and rigidity at both upper and lower levels (see Box 5.2 on page 115). The self-protective behaviour of officials at the top may render the organization inefficient. One type of self-protective behaviour is the monopolization of information in order to maintain control over subordinates and outsiders. Information is crucial for decision making at all levels of an organization. However, those in positions of authority may guard information because it is a source of power for them—others cannot "second-guess" their decisions without access to relevant (and often "confidential") information (Blau and Meyer, 1987).

| Figure 5.2 | Characteristics and Effects of Bureaucracy |

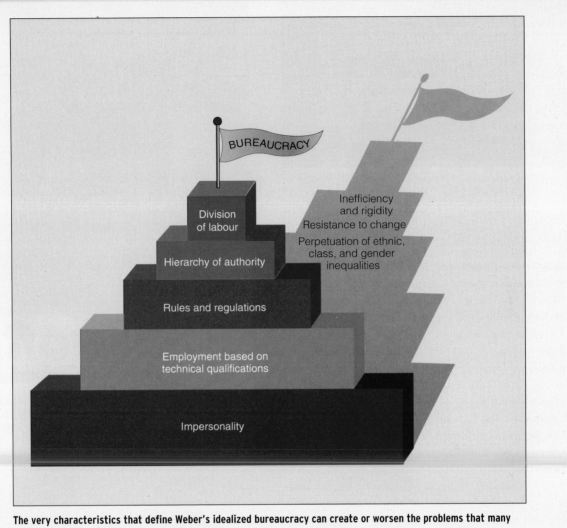

The very characteristics that define Weber's idealized bureaucracy can create or worsen the problems that many people associate with this type of organization.

This information blockage is intensified by the hierarchical arrangement of officials and workers. While those at the top tend to use their power and authority to monopolize information, they also fail to communicate with workers at the lower levels. As a result, they are often unaware of potential problems facing the organization. Meanwhile, those at the bottom of the structure hide their mistakes from supervisors, a practice that ultimately may result in disaster for the organization.

Policies and procedures can also contribute to inefficiency and rigidity. Bureaucratic regulations are often written in greater detail than might seem necessary, to ensure that virtually all conceivable situations are covered (Blau and Meyer, 1987).

Goal displacement **occurs when the rules become an end in themselves rather than a means to an end, and organizational survival becomes more important than achievement of goals** (Merton, 1968). Administrators tend to overconform to the rules because their expertise is knowledge of the regulations, and they are paid to enforce them. They also fear that if they bend the rules for one person, they may be accused of violating the norm of impersonality and engaging in favouritism (Blau and Meyer, 1987).

Bureaucrats may also be inflexible because they fear criticism or liability if they do not follow the rules closely. In the case of Kenneth Payne, the aspiring teacher you read about at the beginning of

The "organization man" of the computer age varies widely in manner and appearance, as shown in the contrast between this casually clad employee at Apple Computer and the dark-suited chairman of Microsoft, Bill Gates.

this chapter, bureaucrats were afraid to waive the fingerprint requirement because of public concern about the possibility of sexual offenders working in the schools. These bureaucrats were able to avoid taking responsibility for their unreasonable decision by saying that they were "just following the rules." Mistakes are blamed on the bureaucracy rather than on the individuals who run it.

Inefficiency and rigidity occur at the lower levels of the organization as well. Workers often engage in ritualism; that is, they become most concerned with "going through the motions" and "following the rules." According to Robert Merton (1968), the term **bureaucratic personality describes those workers who are more concerned with following correct procedures than they are with getting the job done correctly.** Such workers usually are able to handle routine situations effectively but frequently are incapable of handling a unique problem or an emergency. Workers who have reached this point also tend to experience bureaucratic alienation—they really do not care about what is happening around them.

Resistance to Change Resistance to change occurs in all bureaucratic organizations. This resistance can make it very difficult for organizations to adapt to new circumstances. Many workers are reluctant to change because they have adapted their professional and personal lives to the old way of doing their jobs. Also, some workers have seen previous change efforts fail and do not want to commit themselves to the latest effort at transforming their organization. Those trying to implement change can have a difficult time breaking through this resistance.

The hierarchical structure of bureaucracies can make this situation worse. Management is separated from labour, clerical workers from professional workers, and people doing one function from those doing another. This creates structural barriers to communication and to joint problem solving. Information is restricted and problems are dealt with in a segmented way. People are rewarded for not taking risks and punished when they try to make changes. Often people have no structural way of getting innovative ideas from the bottom to the top, so they give up trying. Rosabeth Moss Kanter provides an example of this kind of blockage in a textile company that had been dealing with frequent and costly yarn breakages for decades:

A new plant manager interested in improving employee communication and involvement discovered a foreign-born worker with an ultimately successful idea for modifying the machine to reduce breakage—and was shocked to learn that the man had wondered about the machine modification for thirty-two years. "Why didn't you say something before?" the manager asked. The reply: "My supervisor wasn't interested and I had no one else to tell it to." (Kanter, 1983:70)

BOX 5.2 SOCIOLOGY AND THE MEDIA

Dilbert and the Bureaucracy

Our experiences with red tape and other bureaucratic inefficiencies have been satirized by cartoonist (and disillusioned bureaucrat) Scott Adams. In the late 1980s, Adams began passing his humorous cartoons around the office at Pacific Bell. Since then, *Dilbert* has become a phenomenal success and is read in more than 2000 papers in 70 countries. *Dilbert* ridicules many of the worst features of bureaucracy, including stupid bosses, reliance on technology instead of people, cubicles, management consultants, pointless meetings, and inflexibility. (For examples of the cartoon, go to http://dilbert.com/strips.)

Dilbert strikes a responsive chord with workers. The cartoons are posted on doors, walls, and desks in thousands of offices, and many of Adams's ideas come from readers' suggestions. The British magazine *The Economist* attributes *Dilbert's* popularity to the fact that the comic strip taps into three trends that trouble workers:

1. Employees are forced to work harder to compensate for the effects of downsizing.
2. Workers are afraid of being laid off and see their wage increases falling far behind those of their managers.
3. New management fads have led to constant reorganization but have had little impact on efficiency or on job satisfaction.

Ironically, although many workers feel *Dilbert* says what they feel about ineffective and uncaring managers, the leaders of many of North America's largest corporations have used the cartoons for training and corporate communications.

Sources: *The Economist*, 1997; Whitaker, 1997. *Dilbert* © Scott Adams/Dist. by United Feature Syndicate, Inc.

Organizations that resist change rather than adapt to it may not survive and certainly will not flourish. Thus, leaders of many different organizations face the task of developing new organizational models that are better suited to today's environment. Consider the challenges faced by leaders of corporations such as those discussed in Box 5.3 on page 116.

Perpetuation of Gender, Race, and Class Inequalities

Bureaucracies can perpetuate inequalities of gender, race, and class. Power at the top of most North American bureaucracies still remains in the hands of affluent white men. These inequalities can be perpetuated by the "dual labour market" in which bureaucracies provide different career paths for different categories of workers. Middle- and upper-class employees are more likely to have careers characterized by job security, and opportunities for advancement. By contrast, poor and working-class employees (who are also more likely to be women and members of racial minorities) work in occupations characterized by a lack of job security, and few opportunities for promotion. The "dual labour market" not only reflects class, race, and gender inequities but also helps to perpetuate them.

While the situation has improved over the past several decades, women and members of racial minorities may also find themselves excluded from

BOX 5.3   SOCIOLOGY AND THE MEDIA

The Internet and the Organization

Do you enjoy going to the grocery store, standing in line at the checkout counter, and carrying your groceries to the car? What if you could order your groceries on the Internet and have them delivered to your home for less than what it would cost to buy them at the store? The Internet may have a major impact on the organizational structure of many businesses, including the food industry, by simplifying product distribution. One company, Grocery Gateway (www.grocerygateway.com), sells groceries over the Internet in Ontario, and other Canadian grocers, including Loblaws, are considering the idea. If large numbers of people shop on the Internet, we may see what some analysts have called *disintermediation*—the removal of the intermediary. An Internet transaction can be made directly between the producer and the consumer. The Internet will allow manufacturers to sell their products faster and more cheaply without going through wholesalers and retailers. This change may have a major impact on the structure of organizations that deal with consumer goods.

The greeting-card business shows us how the Internet can provide new ways of serving customer needs. For the past century, companies have designed and produced greeting cards and have sold the cards to wholesalers who distributed them to retail outlets. Customers bought the cards, bought stamps, and mailed them to the recipient through Canada Post. The new approach taken by Blue Mountain (www.bluemountain.com) eliminates the need for printing material and for wholesalers and retailers. Rather than using the mail, Blue Mountain cards are sent electronically over the Internet. Online cards have contributed to flattened sales of greeting cards over the past five years. Christmas mail volumes have also declined in Canada and the U.S. over the same period (Krashinsky, 2009).

Electronic commerce has become common in areas such as banking, purchasing travel services, buying and selling stocks, and in selling goods such as automobiles, flowers, and pizza. It is much cheaper for these organizations to transact business over the Internet. What do you think will happen to the jobs of those who sell stocks and work in banks and travel agencies? How will the change affect the bureaucracies in which they work?

Internet commerce now represents a relatively small but growing portion of consumer sales. However, several factors suggest that Internet commerce will continue to expand rapidly: use of the Internet is growing, those who use the Internet tend to be well-educated people with high incomes who are attractive to marketers, and secure payment mechanisms are making people more comfortable about providing their credit-card numbers. Thus merchandising organizations of the future will likely look very different than traditional bureaucracies.

The Internet also provides opportunities for illegal transactions. For example, the music industry claims to be threatened by the development of technology that allows people to download music without paying royalties to the companies or musicians. Many different programs can be used to download music that can then be played on conventional stereo systems, stored on players designed to hold such files, or recorded on a customized CD. Although some people use this technology to purchase music online or to download songs that are in the public domain, many others use it to copy music illegally. Services such as iTunes have been successful in selling music over the Internet, but unauthorized downloading will be difficult to stop. Ian Clarke, the developer of Freenet, has said he thinks that in 20 to 40 years people will "look at the idea that you can own information in the same way as gold or real estate the way we look at witch burning today" (Markoff, 2000:B14).

Even if there were no illegal copying, the music industry is still threatened by the fact that Internet technology allows artists to sell their music directly to the public without going through the intermediary of the music companies.

Source: Markoff, 2000.

---

informal networks. Kanter (1977) conducted an important study of the difficulties faced by workers who did not fit the white male stereotype. There are enormous pressures on "tokens"—group members who were different from the dominant group members. Tokens were singled out and were often viewed as representatives of their group rather than as individual workers. These pressures led to higher turnover rates and to reduced performance by those in the token groups.

To counteract these pressures, organizations must establish policies that ensure supportive environments for members of disadvantaged groups. Pryor and McKinney (1991) have demonstrated how people respond to environments that condone sexist behaviour. Their experiments examined the dynamics of sexual harassment on university campuses. In one experiment, a graduate student (actually a member of the research team) led research subjects to believe that they would be training undergraduate women to use a computer. The actual purpose of the experiment was to observe whether the trainers (subjects) would harass the women if encouraged to do so. By design, the graduate student purposely harassed the women (who were also part of the research team), setting an example for the subjects to follow.

Pryor found that when the "trainers" were led to believe that sexual harassment was condoned and then were left alone with the women, they took full advantage of the situation in 90 percent of the experiments. One of the women who participated as a member of the research team felt vulnerable because of the permissive environment created by the men in charge:

> So it kind of made me feel a little bit powerless as far as that goes because there was nothing I could do about it. But I also realized that in a business setting, if this person really was my boss, that it would be harder for me to send out the negative signals or whatever to try to fend off that type of thing. (Pryor, 1995)

A real-life version of this experiment occurred in Winnipeg where two male employees were fired from a bread plant because of sexual harassment against female employees. One of the men allegedly exposed himself and stalked a female employee. The other man was accused of repeatedly making lewd and suggestive comments to female employees and inappropriately touching them. There were reports that 10 or 12 women on the work floor had taken stress leave from work over a five-year period because of the abuse. Men outnumbered women on the shop floor by about eight to one. The United Food and Commercial Workers union spokesperson explained that "the system of dealing with sexual-harassment complaints failed in this case because of the influential position one of the accused men held with the union." These incidents were not brought to the attention of the union management. Female employees say that the atmosphere at the plant discouraged women from coming forward to report incidents of harassment (Owen, 1996, n.p.).

Contemporary Applications of Weber's Theory

How well do Weber's theory of rationality and his ideal-type characteristics withstand the test of time? Over 100 years later, organizational theorists are still modifying and extending Weber's perspective.

McDonaldization   Weber's work on bureaucracy was based on his view that rationalization was an inexorable part of the social world. George Ritzer has updated Weber's work by looking at what he calls *McDonaldization*—"the process by which the principles of the fast-food restaurant are coming to dominate more and more sectors of American society, as well as of the rest of the world" (2004:1). Ritzer thinks that McDonald's restaurants perfectly embody the principles of rationalization and establish a model that has been emulated by many other types of organizations. To Ritzer, fast-food restaurants go beyond Weber's model of bureaucracy. The basic elements of McDonaldization are as follows:

Efficiency   Fast-food restaurants operate like an assembly line. Food is cooked, assembled, and served according to a standardized procedure. Customers line up or move quickly past a drive-through window. Despite the old McDonald's slogan, "We do it all for you," it is the customer who picks up the food, takes it to the table, and cleans up the garbage at the end of the meal.

Calculability   The emphasis is on speed and quantity rather than quality. Cooking and serving operations are precisely timed and the emphasis on speed often results in poor employee morale and high rates of turnover. Restaurants are designed to encourage customers to leave quickly.

Predictability   Standard menus and scripted encounters with staff make the experience predictable for customers. The food is supposed to taste the same wherever it is served.

Control   Fast-food restaurants have never allowed much discretion on the part of individual employees, who must follow very detailed procedures. The degree of control has been enhanced through technology. For example, automatic french-fry cookers and other devices ensure a standardized product. Nobody pretends to be a chef in a fast-food restaurant.

Irrationalities of Rationality Fast-food restaurants are dehumanizing for both customers and employees. The examples of bureaucratic inflexibility used at the beginning of this chapter are examples of this dehumanization because the real human concerns of people like the New Orleans hurricane victims were subordinated to the rules of organizations. Rather than encouraging innovation and creativity, McDonaldization can stifle these characteristics and can actually contribute to inefficiency and control.

Ritzer feels that McDonaldization is expanding to other parts of our lives and to other parts of the world. Many universities process huge numbers of students by giving them classes in large lecture theatres and testing them using machine-graded, multiple-choice exams. The questions on these examinations are often taken from test banks provided by the textbook publishers who also provide instructors with many of their teaching aids. Students who are more interested in efficiency than in learning can purchase their term papers online so they don't have to spend time writing them even though this may result in course failure or expulsion. Recent increases in the number of babies born via surgery, using cesarean sections rather than waiting for a natural birth, indicates that even the birth process is being rationalized. Families and doctors may welcome the predictability associated with scheduling birth on a specific day during normal working hours. We can see that characteristics such as efficiency and calculability have spread to many different settings, including government, health care, and the business world. Can you think of examples from your own experience?

ORGANIZATIONS OF THE FUTURE: THE NETWORK ORGANIZATION

The form of organizations has changed over time to accommodate social change. While we can never be certain about the future, broad social trends, such as globalization, technological innovation, and the increased prevalence of a service economy make it likely that *networks* will be the dominant organization of the future. One of the leading proponents of this view is Manuel Castells, who argues that "the old order, governed by discrete individual units in the pursuit of money, efficiency, happiness, or power, is being replaced by a novel one in which motives,

decisions, and actions flow from ever more fluid, yet ever-present networks. It is networks, not the firm, bureaucracy, or the family that gets things done" (Esping-Anderson, 2000:68).

You can learn how global networks operate by reading about the structure of terrorist organizations in Box 5.4, or by thinking about the ways in which illicit drugs get from the coca fields of Colombia and the poppy fields of Thailand to users on the streets of Halifax, Toronto, and Victoria. Large bureaucracies are not involved in either of these complex global enterprises, as terrorists and drug dealers operate very effectively through decentralized global networks. One reason drug-suppression strategies have not succeeded is that there is no company called Global Drugs Incorporated that can be easily located and destroyed by law enforcement agencies. Instead there are shifting, fluid networks of people who are difficult to identify and who are easily replaced when the legal system takes them out of the network. Similar problems face those who are trying to deal with the threat of terrorism.

Another example of the operation of a flexible global network is the production of open-source software, such as the Linux operating system and the Firefox Internet browser. Such software was not produced by a large profit-making corporation, like Microsoft, but by networks of people working together with no expectation of profit. The product is available freely to anyone who wishes to download it, and programmers all over the world can contribute to improvements in the software. While some coordination is necessary to develop a product that can be used by the public, no large bureaucracy is required and individual users are free to modify programs to suit their own needs.

Networks have always had an advantage over other organizational forms because they are highly agile and can quickly adapt to new circumstances. However, the ability to coordinate network activities has been very weak compared with hierarchical bureaucratic organizations that have well-specified lines of communication and means of coordination. This has given bureaucracies a competitive advantage in handling complex tasks (Castells, 2000b). However, modern information and communication technology has now provided networks with a competitive advantage. Each part of a network can communicate instantly with other parts and those responsible for the network can constantly monitor performance even if the network is globally distributed. With this technology, the network can quickly shift and change, as pieces can be eliminated if they are no longer useful or can be temporarily set aside if they are not needed for a particular project (Castells, 2000b). It is more difficult to centrally control a network than a traditional hierarchical organization because once the network has been programmed and set in motion it may be difficult for anyone, even those who started the network, to shut it down. With no central communication and control system, parts of the network can continue to operate even if the central core is eliminated. Thus, opponents of al Qaeda could not shut down the network by simply closing down some of its pieces. Even Osama bin Laden would have difficulty closing down the network or changing its goals if other members of al-Qaeda and its affiliated groups around the world wanted to continue with their activities.

Krebs (2002) analyzed the relationships between the hijackers responsible for the September 11, 2001, attacks on the United States. Mohamed Atta, who was the leader of the attacks, had contacts with each of the teams of hijackers. However, most of the others had no contact with teams other than their own. The strategy of minimizing ties among members of the network is deliberate—if security personnel identify or apprehend one or two members of the network, they can provide only limited information about other members so the entire network would not be jeopardized. In a videotape that was found at an al-Qaeda training camp in Afghanistan, Osama bin Laden said that "Those who were trained to fly didn't know the others. One group of people did not know the other group" (Department of Defense, 2001, quoted in Krebs, 2002:46). It is very difficult for those opposing such networks to be able to target more than a limited part of the terrorist organization.

Castells (2000a, 2000b) speaks of a new type of economic organization, called the network enterprise.

| BOX 5.4 | SOCIOLOGY IN GLOBAL PERSPECTIVE |

The Structure of Terrorist Networks

The growth of large armies such as the Prussian army contributed to the development of the bureaucratic form of organization. These large armies represented the governments of established states. Recent terrorist attacks in the United States, Spain, Russia, England, and elsewhere, and the difficulties in fighting the insurgency in Afghanistan have drawn attention to what military planners refer to as *asymmetrical warfare*. This term refers to attacks by small groups of people, who usually do not represent states or governments, upon much larger and stronger opponents. Terrorists do not directly confront their opponents since they would be quickly defeated in such a confrontation. Rather, they use covert tactics, such as car bombs and suicide bombings, which are difficult to prevent.

In order to fight successfully against larger and more powerful opponents, terrorist groups must develop organizational structures that are difficult to identify and combat. Rather than forming large hierarchical armies, terrorist groups such as al-Qaeda have evolved sophisticated network structures. These networks are made up of loosely coupled cells, each of which has only a few members. This structure allows for a high level of secrecy, flexibility, and innovation. Participants in the network operate in a coordinated way because they have relationships with other members of the network with whom they share a common vision of the future, not because they are controlled by a bureaucracy. Al-Qaeda-network members are linked by a common religious background and philosophy, and through the leadership of Osama bin Laden and his associates.

The figure on page 120 is a simplified diagram of the al-Qaeda network (Marion and Uhl-Bien, 2003). This structure is very different from the hierarchical organization charts of the military and security organizations that are trying to defeat al-Qaeda. This loose and flexible network structure makes it difficult to defeat terrorist organizations. For example, the network has roots in many different countries, and information and funds can flow relatively freely from one jurisdiction to another. On the other hand, security and intelligence agencies are based in individual countries and, for a variety of reasons, find it very difficult to work cooperatively (Arquilla and Ronfeldt, 2001). You can contrast the fluid network of al-Qaeda shown in the figure with the hierarchical, vertical structure of the armies and governments opposing it. Using modern communications technology, including the Internet, information can flow to all parts of the network much more easily than can information that must be filtered through national governments and their internal bureaucracies.

BOX 5.4   SOCIOLOGY IN GLOBAL PERSPECTIVE

The Structure of Terrorist Networks (Continued)

Simplified Representation of the al-Qaeda Network

Subcategories identify the given component's functions; arrows indicate direction of moderately to tightly coupled dependency. Al-Qaeda refers to bin Laden's leadership core. Each component comprises numerous aggregates linked in loose to tightly coupled networks of interdependency.

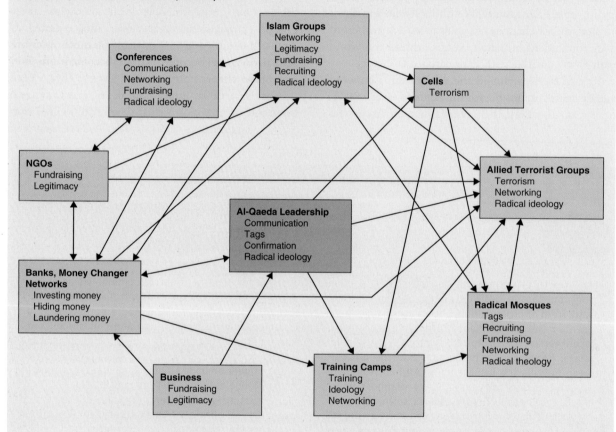

Source: Marion, Russ and Mary Uhl-Bien, 2003, "A Complexity Theory and Al-Qaeda: Examining Complex Leadership" © *Emergence* 5 (1): 54–76.

Businesses, which may be companies or parts of companies, join for specific projects that become the focus of the network. This structure gives those responsible for the network a great deal of flexibility, as they can select and change network partners based upon factors such as cost, efficiency, and technological innovation. The Dell laptop computer that you may be working on is also the product of a network enterprise (Friedman, 2005). Dell sells its products over the Internet and by telephone rather than in stores, so your order may be taken by a person in Bangalore, India, rather by a clerk in your own city. The hardware that makes up the computer was manufactured by companies in Israel, the Philippines, Malaysia, Costa Rica, China, Taiwan, South Korea, Germany, Japan, Mexico, Singapore, Indonesia, India, and Thailand. The computers are assembled in Dell factories located in Ireland, China, Brazil, Malaysia, and the United States. Thomas Friedman describes how the company fills its orders:

> "In an average day, we sell 140 000 to 150 000 computers," explained Dick Hunter, one of Dell's three global production managers. "Those orders come over Dell.com or over the telephone. As soon as these orders come in, our suppliers

know about it. They get a signal based on every component in the machine you ordered, so the supplier knows just what he has to deliver. If you are supplying power cords for desktops, you can see minute by minute how many power cords you are going to have to deliver." Every two hours, the Dell factory in Penang [Malaysia] sends an e-mail to the various SLCs [supplier logistics centres] nearby, telling each one what parts and what quantities of those parts it wants delivered within the next ninety minutes—and not one minute later. Within ninety minutes, trucks from the various SLCs around Penang pull up to the Dell manufacturing plant and unload the parts needed for all those notebooks ordered in the last two hours. This goes on all day, every two hours. As soon as those parts arrive at the factory, it takes thirty minutes for Dell employees to unload the parts, register their bar codes, and put them into bins for assembly. "We know where every part in the SLC is in the Dell system at all times," said Hunter. (2005:415)

This system is a major reason that Dell has helped to dramatically reduce retail computer prices over the past decade.

A critical factor in the development of widely dispersed network organizations has been the development of modern communications technology. Networks are held together by the rapid flow of information rather than by bricks and mortar and a rigid organizational chart like that of the industrial organization. The globalized production processes used by companies such as Toyota and Dell would not be possible without instant global communication. It is worth noting that the Internet itself is a decentralized and loosely coupled structure. The Internet was originally designed as a way of ensuring that communications systems could survive a military attack targeted at the central hubs of information systems. Instead of flowing from a central hub, information on the Internet is transmitted in small packets that can follow a wide range of electronic routes and are put together at the destination computer (Castells, 2000a). Nobody owns the Internet, so it is universally accessible to anyone who has a computer and a connection. While the Internet is vulnerable to a variety of threats, including computer hacking, it would be almost impossible to completely shut it down. This flexibility and resilience is what makes the Internet such a valuable tool for networks. (See Box 5.3 on page 116 for a discussion of how the Internet is transforming the retail industry.)

However, Castells (2004) points out that it is not simply the technology that is critical, but also the cultural and organizational means of using the technology. This means that just having computers is not enough to guarantee access to the networked global economy. Countries with ineffective systems of government, few trained workers, and no entrepreneurial culture that supports innovation will be excluded from these networks. India has been very successful in getting involved in network enterprises because of an entrepreneurial culture, a democratic government, and the presence of a well-educated workforce with English language skills, while many parts of Africa and Latin America have almost no involvement in the new economy.

Sociologists are also concerned with the impact of network enterprises on people. While this network structure can help corporations to become more profitable, the impact upon workers has not always been as positive. For example, unions lose much of their bargaining power when production at one plant can be quickly moved to another part of the network in a different country. Thus, a strike may result in the permanent closure of a factory and the movement of jobs offshore. You will read about the impact of these changes upon the workforce in Chapter 8. It is quite likely that the future work lives of today's university and college students will be affected in many ways—some positive but others negative—by the shift to networked organizations. Because network enterprises are very fluid and can quickly transform themselves, you should anticipate that your working lives might also change very rapidly after you enter the labour market.

Finally, there are inherent dangers in networked organizations. These dangers were illustrated in August 2003 when the power went off for several days in much of Ontario because of a power outage in Ohio that cascaded through the transmission networks covering the Northeastern United States and Ontario. A similar network failure led to the global financial crisis in 2008 in which lax California mortgage practices affected the pensions of workers in Canada and Europe who had not even invested in these mortgages (Watts, 2009). Our reliance on complex physical and social networks places us at risk and these risks are not always predictable. Global transportation networks facilitate the spread of disease; e-mail viruses threaten our computers; a moment of indiscretion can be spread around the globe through YouTube; and any disruption of traffic between Detroit and Windsor would have a serious impact on North American automobile production because of the system of parts manufacture and supply. Governments will be challenged in the future to determine ways of minimizing this risk.

■ How do sociologists define social groups?

Sociologists define a social group as a collection of two or more people who interact frequently, share a sense of belonging, and depend on one another.

■ How do sociologists classify groups?

Primary groups are small and personal, and members engage in emotion-based interactions over an extended period. Secondary groups are larger and more specialized, and members have less personal and more formal, goal-oriented relationships. Ingroups are groups to which we belong and with which we identify. Outgroups are groups we do not belong to or perhaps feel hostile toward.

■ What do experiments on conformity show about the importance of groups?

Groups may have a significant influence on members' values, attitudes, and behaviours. To maintain ties with a group, many members are willing to conform to norms established and reinforced by group members.

■ What are the strengths and weaknesses of bureaucracies?

A bureaucracy is a formal organization characterized by hierarchical authority, division of labour, explicit procedures, and impersonality. According to Max Weber, a bureaucracy supplies a rational means of attaining organizational goals because it contributes to coordination and control. A bureaucracy also has an informal structure that includes the daily activities and interactions that bypass official rules and procedures. Bureaucracies, however, may be inefficient and resistant to change.

■ What form will large organizations likely take in the future?

While we can never be certain about the future, broad social trends, such as globalization, technological innovation, and the increased prevalence of a service economy, make it likely that networks will be the dominant organization of the future. Networked organizations, which are made possible by modern communications technology, are highly flexible and can respond quickly to social change.

KEY TERMS

aggregate 102
bureaucracy 111
bureaucratic personality 114
category 103
conformity 107
formal organization 111
goal displacement 113
groupthink 109
informal structure 112
ingroup 103
network 104
network enterprise 119
outgroup 103
reference group 104

WEB LINKS

For more Web links related to the topic of this chapter, see the Nelson sociology website:
www.sociologyessentials5e.nelson.com

Government is a very complex bureaucracy. To see the number of departments in the Canadian federal government, go to:
www.canada.gc.ca

The Public Service Commission of Canada has an extensive bibliography of material on group leadership:
http://psc-cfp.gc.ca/library/guide/leadership_e.htm

Read more about Stanley Milgram's work on obedience and hear audio clips from one of his experiments:
http://elvers.stjoe.udayton.edu/history/people/Milgram.html

To read an interview with George Ritzer concerning his view of the "McDonaldization" of society, go to:
www.mcspotlight.org/peopleinterviews/ritzer_george.html

QUESTIONS FOR CRITICAL THINKING

1. Who might be more likely to conform in a bureaucracy, those with power or those wanting more power?
2. Despite extensive debate about what is and what is not sexual harassment, it has been difficult to reach a clear consensus on what behaviours and actions are acceptable. What are some specific ways both women and men can avoid contributing to an atmosphere of sexual harassment in organizations? Consider team relationships, management and mentor relationships, promotion policies, attitudes, behaviour, dress and presentation, and after-work socializing.

3. Many students have worked at a McDonald's or at some other fast-food restaurant. Relate your experience (or that of your friends) to George Ritzer's analysis of "McDonaldization."

4. Downloading music and movies from the Internet has become very popular in Canada and in other countries. The film and music industries are trying hard to convince the government to pass new legislation to combat this downloading. What are the arguments of those who think that this material should be widely available on the Internet? What are the counterarguments of those who wish to see downloading regulated? Which side do you support in this debate?

ONLINE STUDY AND RESEARCH TOOLS

INFOTRAC®

InfoTrac College Edition is included free with every new copy of this text. Explore this online library for additional readings, review, and a handy resource for assignments. Visit **www.infotrac-college.com** to access this online database of full-text articles. Enter the key terms from this chapter to start your search.

CENGAGENOW™ CENGAGENOW

Use CengageNOW™ to help you formulate a customized study plan for this chapter. After you take the Diagnostic Quiz, CengageNOW™ will generate a customized study plan for you. It will identify sections of the chapter you should review.

Deviance and Crime

Maurice "Mom" Boucher was the most powerful Hells Angels leader in Canada. President of the Quebec-based Nomads chapter, Boucher decided to go to war against the justice system in 1997. His first act in this war was to order the killing of some prison guards. Stephane Gagné was ordered to carry out the killings. Gagné was a member of the Rockers, a Hells Angels puppet gang that did much of the Angels' dirty work. Gagne enforced drug debts, served as a bodyguard, and did other jobs for the Hells Angels. In two separate operations, Gagné and another gang member killed guards Diane Lavigne and Pierre Rondeau. Gagné was eventually arrested and confessed to the murders. In exchange for some relatively minor concessions, he agreed to testify against Mom Boucher for ordering the murders.

In 1998 Boucher was acquitted but the Crown successfully appealed and Boucher was convicted at a second trial in 2002, Boucher is currently serving a life sentence.

At Boucher's first trial, Gagné testified about his leader's role in the killing of the prison guards. In his cross-examination, Boucher's lawyer, Jacques Larochelle, tried to discredit Gagné's testimony by highlighting his criminal

past. Gagné's responses illustrate the brutality of organized crime:

"During this entire time, you evidently had no respect for authority?"

"No."

"No respect for other people's property."

"No."

"No respect for the truth?"

"No."

Larochelle then tried to show Gagné's readiness to do anything he thought would please the Hells Angels. He recalled a hunger strike at Sorel prison that Mom ordered because he was sick of eating shepherd's pie. One inmate broke ranks and ate the meal.

"And without anyone asking you to do it," Larochelle asked, "you went over and beat him up?"

"Yes."

"In fact you courageously waited until he was asleep and you went to attack him in his bed, is that correct?"

"Yes."

"You hit him so hard with your fist that the bone came out his nose—all so that you would be noticed, is that correct?"

"Yes."

Larochelle also elicited the details of Gagné's attempted murder of drug dealer Christian Bellemare. He showed how Gagné acted alone, deciding to kill him because he owed him money.

"The first two bullets hit Bellemare in the throat or in that area. But the other bullets didn't fire, and Bellemare was still alive?" Larochelle said, taking the jurors back to the scene of the crime.

"Yes," Gagné agreed.

"You went running up to Bellemare and you put your fingers around his neck, your two hands around his neck, and squeezed?"

"Yes."

"He tries to talk, is that correct?" Larochelle pushed. "You have a good idea of what he is trying to tell you, I imagine?"

"Yes."

"Don't kill me, or something like that?" the lawyer suggested.

"Something like that, yes," said Gagné.

"That didn't impress you?"

"I had a job to do," he admitted. (Sher and Marsden, 2003:147-148)

Despite the Hells Angels' attempts to convince the public that they are just a social club, supporting the community through events such as toy runs, they are one of Canada's most powerful criminal organizations. The violence of Stephane Gagné is typical of the methods used by organized criminals and explains why one in every four Canadian homicides—138 killings in 2008—was gang-related (Beattie, 2009).

The problem of organized crime is certainly not unique to Canada. Organized crime has existed for centuries, and today operates around the world. Organized crime is one of a wide range of behaviours that society has defined as deviant and/or criminal. Sociologists have asked many important questions about crime and deviance: What is deviant behaviour, and how does it differ from criminal behaviour? Why are some people considered "deviants" or "criminals" while others are not? In this chapter, we look at the relationship between conformity, deviance, and crime. Before reading on, take the quiz on organized crime, deviance, and crime in Box 6.1.

QUESTIONS AND ISSUES

Chapter Focus Question: What are the causes and consequences of organized crime in Canada?

What is deviant behaviour?

How do sociologists explain deviant and criminal behaviour?

When is deviance considered a crime?

How do sociologists classify crime?

How does the criminal justice system deal with crime?

How can we reduce crime?

WHAT IS DEVIANCE?

How do societies determine what behaviour is acceptable and unacceptable? All societies have norms that govern acceptable behaviour. If we are to live and to work with others, these rules are necessary. We must also have a reasonable expectation that other people will obey the rules. Think of the chaos that would result if each driver decided which side of the road she would drive on each day, or which stop sign he would decide to obey. Most of us usually conform to the norms our group prescribes. Of course, not all members of the group obey all the time. All of us have broken rules, sometimes even important ones. These violations are dealt with through various mechanisms of *social control—* **systematic practices developed by social groups to encourage conformity and to discourage deviance.** One form of social control takes place through socialization whereby individuals *internalize* societal norms and values. A second form of social control involves the use of negative sanctions to punish rule breakers.

We can illustrate mechanisms of social control by looking at how organizations control intellectual property such as music and movies. Many companies and individuals try to control their intellectual property through legal means, which is a *formal* type of social control. For example, the Walt Disney Company requires permission to use a picture of Winnie the Pooh, and taking a video recorder into a theatre to film the latest hit movie may result in prosecution. Most of the time, though, *informal* means of social control shape our behaviour.

Loshin (2007) has provided an interesting example of how behaviour can be controlled without resort to the formal legal system. Magicians have not been able to protect their intellectual property—the techniques behind their magic tricks—by using the law. A magician can spend decades working out a new illusion, but be unable to prosecute or sue someone who steals the trick. Instead, magicians have worked out an informal social control system to protect their secrets. Within the community of magicians, there is much sharing but universal disapproval of sharing the secrets behind magic tricks with the public. The norm of "never exposing a secret to a non-magician" applies even to a magician's own secrets. Magicians who violate the rules will be ostracized. Loshin describes how the rule was enforced against a magic trick manufacturer who stole a magician's design:

BOX 6.1 SOCIOLOGY AND EVERYDAY LIFE

How Much Do You Know About Crime and Organized Crime?

J⬥inIn™

True	False	
T	**F**	1. Official statistics accurately reflect the amount of crime in Canada.
T	**F**	2. Most organized criminals are affiliated with the Italian Mafia.
T	F	3. Organized crime exists largely to provide goods and services demanded by "respectable" members of the community.
T	**F**	4. Rates of murder and other violent crimes have been steadily rising for the past 20 years.
T	**F**	5. Because of their connection with a variety of charitable causes, biker gangs such as the Hells Angels have become less of a social threat.
T	**F**	6. Gang-related killings have been declining at the same rate as other types of homicide.
T	F	7. One of Canada's most prolific killers was a Hells Angel who was convicted of killing 43 people but served only seven years of a sentence for manslaughter.
T	F	8. Many organized crime groups are made up of people from the same ethnic group.
T	F	9. In Russia, organized crime is so pervasive that it is a threat to the future economic and political life of that country.
T	**F**	10. Most of the money made by organized criminals comes from gambling and loan sharking.

Answers on page 128.

[A] company in England ... was selling still another rip-off of my illusion. When I protested to the owner ... he told me there was no court in the world which could stop him.... I explained I had no intention of going to court. I instead simply told my many friends in [London's] Magic Circle about it. When the word spread [the owner] 'had a problem'. As things turned out, there was indeed a court which promptly put him out of business ... the bankruptcy court." (Loshin, 2007: 32)

While social control generally ensures some level of conformity, all societies still have some degree of **deviance—any behaviour, belief, or condition that violates significant social norms in the society or group in which it occurs.**

We are most familiar with *behavioural* deviance; a person may engage in intentional deviance by drinking too much or shoplifting, or in inadvertent deviance by losing the rent money at a video lottery terminal or laughing during a solemn occasion.

While we usually think of deviance as a type of behaviour, people may be considered deviant if they express *radical* or *unusual beliefs.* For example,

members of cults (such as Moonies and Satanists) and of far-right or far-left-wing political groups may be considered deviant when their religious or political beliefs become known to people with more conventional views.

Defining Deviance

According to sociologists, deviance is *relative*— an act becomes deviant when it is socially defined as such. Definitions of deviance vary widely from place to place and from group to group. For example, in some countries female genital mutilation is conforming behaviour, but in Canada, where cultural and legal norms are different, proponents will find that the practice is considered deviant. Definitions also change over time. You may have played a "Pick 3" lottery. To win, you must pick a three-digit number matching the one drawn by a government lottery agency. Television commercials encourage us to risk our money on this game, from which the government profits. Several years ago, another version of this game was known as the "numbers racket" and was the most popular form of gambling in many

BOX 6.1 | **SOCIOLOGY AND EVERYDAY LIFE**

Answers to the Sociology Quiz on Crime and Organized Crime

Join In

1. False.   Official crime statistics reflect only crimes that are *reported* to police, not all the offences that are *committed*. Less than half of all crimes are reported to the police (Evans and Himelfarb, 2009).

2. False.   The Italian Mafia has a global influence on organized crime. However, it is only one of many organized crime groups (Stamler, 2009).

3. True.   If not for public demand for illegal drugs, gambling, tax-free liquor, and cigarettes, and the other goods and services supplied by organized crime, illegal profits would largely disappear (Stamler, 2009).

4. False.   While violent crime rates generally rose through the 1980s, they declined steadily throughout the 1990s and continue to decline (Evans and Himelfarb, 2009).

5. False.   The Hells Angels have used high-profile activities such as toy runs for children to improve their public image. However, they are one of the most ruthless and profitable criminal organizations in North America.

6. False.   Gang-related homicides have been increasing, while other homicide types have declined. Between 1993 and 2007, the number of gang-related homicides increased by 700 percent to a total of 117 (Li, 2008).

7. True.   Yves ("Apache") Trudeau was a contract killer who received a lenient sentence in exchange for information about other Montreal underworld figures (Lavigne, 1987). (For more on this case, see Box 6.4, on page 149.)

8. True.   Many different nationalities are involved in Canadian organized crime, including Russian, Iranian, Chinese, Vietnamese, Colombian, Jamaican, and Italian. Restricting membership has many advantages. Interpersonal ties based on ethnic communities and language differences make it difficult for law-enforcement officials to infiltrate the groups. Ethnic ties also facilitate the development of international crime networks (Stamler, 2009).

9. True.   After the fall of communism, the lack of meaningful economic institutions and the failure of the criminal justice system created conditions favourable to organized crime. Organized criminals control many of the new businesses in Russia and have powerful links to the government (Jamieson, 2001).

10. False.   The importation and distribution of illegal drugs is the main source of funds for organized crime (Stamler, 2009).

low-income neighbourhoods. The two main differences between now and then are that the game used to be run by organized criminals and these criminals paid winners a higher share of the take than the government does. While the profits now go to social services rather than to the pockets of criminals, the example shows that the way societies define behaviour can be more important than the harm caused by that behaviour, as legalized gambling involves far more people suffering losses than was the case when gambling was illegal.

Definitions of deviance are continually changing. Several hundred thousand "witches" were executed in Europe during the Middle Ages; now witchcraft as a crime doesn't exist. Racist comments used to be socially acceptable; now they are not. Tattoos and piercings are now common among students, but 30 years ago they were almost unknown.

Deviance can be difficult to define. "Deviant" and "nondeviant" are not two distinct categories. They overlap, and the line between them can be ambiguous. For example, how do we decide that someone is

Montreal La Presse/The Canadian Press/Alain Roberge

Many different groups are involved in organized crime in Canada. Here, Nicolo Rizzuto, patriarch of a Montreal Mafia family, leaves the courtroom after his 2010 conviction for tax fraud. Rizzuto's son Vito is in a U.S. prison because his involvement in several murders, and his grandson Nick was killed in a gang hit in 2009. Nicolo Rizzuto was shot in front of his family later in 2010 at the age of 86.

mentally ill? What if your brother begins to behave in a strange fashion? He occasionally yells at people for no apparent reason and keeps changing topics when you talk to him. He begins to wear clothes that don't match and calls you in the middle of the night to talk about people who are threatening him. How would you respond to this change in behaviour? Would it make any difference if you knew that your brother was drinking heavily at the time or that he was under a lot of stress at work? Would it make a difference if he behaved this way once a year or twice a week? When would you decide that he had a problem and should seek help? What is the difference between someone who is eccentric and someone who has a mental illness? These questions reflect the difficulty we have in defining deviance. The issue of definition becomes even more problematic when you realize that individuals who are considered "deviant" by one group of people may be seen as "conformists" by another group. You can find many people on the Internet who support child pornography and others who praise anorexia and suicide.

Deviant behaviour also varies in its seriousness, ranging from mild transgressions of folkways, through more serious infringements of mores, to quite serious violations of the law. Have you kept a library book past its due date or cut classes? If so, you have violated folkways. Others probably view your infraction as relatively minor; at most, you might have to pay a

fine or receive a lower grade. Violations of mores—such as falsifying a university or college application or cheating on an examination—are viewed as infractions that are more serious and are punishable by stronger sanctions, such as academic probation or expulsion. Some forms of deviant behaviour are officially defined as *crimes*—**behaviours that violate criminal law and are punishable with fines, jail terms, and other sanctions**. Crimes range from minor offences (such as running an illegal bingo game or telling fortunes) to major offences (such as sexual assault and murder).

FUNCTIONALIST PERSPECTIVES ON DEVIANCE

Strain Theory: Goals and the Means to Achieve Them

According to Robert Merton (1938, 1968), in a smoothly functioning society, deviance will be limited because most people share common cultural goals and agree on the appropriate means for reaching them. However, societies that do not provide sufficient avenues to reach these goals may also lack agreement about the appropriate means by which people achieve their aspirations. Deviance may be common in such societies because people may be willing to use whatever means they can to achieve their goals. According to *strain theory*, **people feel strain when they are exposed to cultural goals that they are unable to reach because they do not have access to culturally approved means of achieving those goals**. The goals may be material possessions and money; the approved means may include an education and jobs. When denied legitimate access to these goals, some people seek access through deviant means.

Typically, strain theory has been used to explain the deviance of the lower classes. Denied legitimate access to the material goods that are such an important part of North American culture, some individuals may turn to illegal activities to achieve their goals. However, not only the poor turn to illegal ways of achieving their goals. Some sociologists feel that strain theory can help explain upper-class deviance as well. In 2007, Conrad Black, one of Canada's wealthiest and most influential businessmen, was convicted of misappropriating millions of dollars from the newspaper chain he once headed and sentenced to 6.5 years in prison. Despite his wealth, Black took money from the Hollinger company that rightfully belonged to shareholders. A committee established to investigate Black's activities concluded that "Black and [his partner] Radler were motivated by a ravenous appetite for cash ... and Hollinger International, under their reign 'lost any sense of corporate purpose, competitive drive or internal ethical concerns' as the two executives looked for ways to 'suck cash' out of the company" (McNish and Stewart, 2004:288).

Opportunity Theory: Access to Illegitimate Opportunities

Expanding on Merton's strain theory, Richard Cloward and Lloyd Ohlin (1960) suggested that for deviance to occur people must have access to **illegitimate opportunity structures—circumstances that provide an opportunity for people to acquire through illegitimate activities what they cannot get through legitimate channels**. For example, members of some communities may have insufficient legitimate means to achieve conventional goals of status and wealth but greater access to illegitimate opportunity structures—such as theft, drug dealing, or robbery—through which they can achieve these goals.

According to Cloward and Ohlin (1960), three different forms of delinquent subcultures—criminal, conflict, and retreatist—emerge based on the type of illegitimate opportunities available in a specific area. The criminal subculture focuses on economic gain and includes acts such as theft, extortion, and drug dealing. Elijah Anderson (1990) suggested that the "drug economy [is like an] employment agency superimposed on the existing gang network" for many young men who lack other opportunities. For young men who grow up in a gang subculture, running drug houses and selling drugs on street corners becomes a source of illegitimate opportunity. Using the money from these "jobs," they can support themselves and their families as well as purchase material possessions to impress others. When illegitimate economic opportunities are not available, gangs may become conflict subcultures that fight over territory and adopt a value system of toughness, courage, and similar status-enhancing qualities. Those who lack the opportunity or ability to join one of these gangs may turn to retreatist activities, such as drinking and drug use.

Opportunity theory expands strain theory by emphasizing the relationship between deviance and the availability of illegitimate opportunity structures. Some gang studies have supported this theory by showing that gang membership provides some women and men in low-income central-city areas with an illegitimate means to acquire money, entertainment, refuge, physical protection, and escape from living like their parents (Jankowski, 1991; Esbensen and Huizinga, 1993).

Control Theory: Social Bonding

Like strain theory, social control theory has its roots in Durkheim's anomie theory. In *Suicide* (1964b/1897), Durkheim pointed out the importance of social bonds to the understanding of deviant behaviour. Anomic suicide occurs when a lack of social regulation, caused by factors such as rapid economic change, creates a situation in which social organization is weak and the individual lacks moral guidance. Early social control theories explained how some types of social structures led to high rates of deviance. Communities characterized by poverty, physical deterioration, and internal conflict were too disorganized to exert effective control over residents' behaviour and often had high rates of suicide, mental illness, substance abuse, and crime.

While most of the research documenting the relationship between community disorganization and crime has been done in large, urban areas, Linda Deutschmann (2002) has applied the theory to frontier areas. Many small Canadian communities were created solely to develop an economic resource and have grown up around mines, railroads, pulp mills, and hydro dams. Deutschmann notes that in these towns' early stages, the absence of controls from institutions such as families and churches means that deviant behaviour, including fighting and alcohol abuse, may be common. In later stages of development, the strains of a booming town may also cause deviance.

While work in this tradition continues, much of the recent work on control theory has focused on the individual rather than on the community. In doing so, it has posed the fundamental question about causes of deviance in a new way. Most theories of deviance ask the question: Why do they do it? Control theorists reverse this question. They ask: Why don't we *all* do it? Or, put another way, they wonder: Why do some people *not* engage in deviant behaviour? To answer this question, Travis Hirschi (1969) suggested that deviant behaviour is minimized when people have strong bonds that tie them to families, school, peers, churches, and other social institutions.

Social bond theory holds that the probability of deviant behaviour increases when a person's ties to society are weakened or broken. According to Hirschi, social bonding consists of (1) *attachment* to other people; (2) *commitment* to conventional lines of behaviour, such as schooling and job success; (3) *involvement* in conventional activities; and (4) *belief* in the legitimacy of conventional values and norms. The variables of attachment and commitment are much more strongly related to delinquency than involvement and belief. Although Hirschi did not include females in his study, others who have replicated it with both females and males have found that the theory explains the delinquency of both (Linden and Fillmore, 1981).

While Hirschi's theory did not differentiate between bonds to conventional and to deviant others, several researchers have suggested that the probability of deviance increases when a person's social bonds are weak and when peers promote antisocial values and deviant behaviour (Linden and Fillmore, 1981). Gang members may bond with one another rather than with persons who subscribe to dominant cultural values. As one gang member explains:

> Before I joined the gang, I could see that you could count on your boys to help in times of need and that meant a lot to me. And when I needed money, sure enough they gave it to me. Nobody else would have given it to me; my parents didn't have it, and there was no other place to go. The gang was just like they said they would be, and they'll continue to be there when I need them. (Jankowski, 1991:42).

SYMBOLIC INTERACTIONIST PERSPECTIVES ON DEVIANCE

Symbolic interactionists focus on how people develop a self-concept and learn conforming behaviour through the process of socialization. According to symbolic interactionists, deviance is learned in the same way as conformity—through interaction with others.

Differential Association Theory

Edwin Sutherland (1939) developed a theory to explain how people learn deviance through social interaction. **Differential association theory states that individuals have a greater tendency to deviate from societal norms when they frequently associate with people who favour deviance over conformity.** According to Sutherland, people learn the necessary techniques and the motives, drives, rationalizations, and attitudes of deviant behaviour from people with whom they associate.

Differential association is most likely to result in criminal activity when a person has extensive interaction with rule-breakers. Ties to other deviants can be particularly important in the world of organized crime, where the willingness of peers to stand up for one another can be critical in maintaining power in the face of violent opposition from competitors. Daniel Wolf, an anthropologist who rode with the Rebels, an Edmonton biker gang, describes this solidarity:

> For an outlaw biker, the greatest fear is not of the police; rather, it is of a slight variation of his own mirror image: the patch holder [full-fledged member] of another club. Under slightly different circumstances those men would call each other "brother." But when turf is at stake, inter-club rivalry and warfare completely override any considerations of the common bonds of being a biker—and brother kills brother. None of the outlaws that I rode with enjoyed the prospect of having to break the bones of another biker. Nor did they look forward to having to live with the hate–fear syndrome that dominates a conflict in which there are no rules. I came to realize that the willingness of an outlaw to lay down his life in these conflicts goes beyond a belligerent masculinity that brooks no challenge. When a patch holder defends his colours, he defends his personal identity, his community, his lifestyle. When a war is on, loyalty to the club and one another arises out of the midst of danger, out of apprehension of possible injury, mutilation, or worse. Whether one considers this process as desperate, heroic, or just outlandishly foolish and banal does not really matter. What matters is that, for patch holders, the brotherhood emerges as a necessary feature of their continued existence as individuals and as a group. (1996a:11)

Group ties are not just important in highly organized crime groups such as motorcycle gangs. Think of the different subcultural groups that are involved in deviant activities in many Canadian high schools. Whether the focus of the group is graffiti, body piercing, punk music or dress, or the use of illegal drugs, the encouragement and support of peers is vital to recruiting and teaching new members and to sustaining the group.

Differential association theory contributes to our knowledge of how deviant behaviour reflects the individual's learned techniques, values, attitudes, motives, and rationalizations. However, critics question why many individuals who have had extensive contact with people who violate the law still conform most of the time. They also assert that the theory does not adequately assess possible linkages between social inequality and criminal behaviour.

Labelling Theory

Two processes are involved in defining deviance. First, some people act (or are believed to act) in a manner contrary to the expectations of others. Second, others disapprove of and try to control this contrary behaviour. Part of this social control process involves labelling people as deviants. An important contribution to the study of deviance was made by sociologists who asked the question "Why are some people labelled as deviants while others are not?" **Labelling theory suggests that deviants are those people who have been successfully labelled as such by others**. The process of labelling is directly related to the power and status of those persons who *do* the labelling and those who are *being* labelled. To the labelling theorist, behaviour is not deviant in and of itself; it is defined as such by a social audience (Erikson, 1962). Labels are applied most easily to those who lack the power to resist them.

Robert Rosenhan demonstrated the power of a deviant label in a study in which he and seven other people admitted themselves to mental hospitals. As pseudo-patients, they reported hearing voices saying things like "empty" and "hollow." Other than this faked symptom, which is consistent with a diagnosis of schizophrenia, the "patients" told the truth about their life histories. These histories were distorted by hospital staff to fit the schizophrenia diagnoses. Thus a normal relationship between a man and his parents became psychopathological: "[he] manifests a long history of considerable ambivalence in close relationships which began in early childhood. . . . Affective stability is absent[.]" (Rosenhan, 1973:254.)

Once admitted to hospital, the "patients" acted completely normally. However, their sanity went undetected by staff, though many of their fellow patients realized they were sane. Rosenhan said other patients commonly made comments such as "You're not crazy. You're a journalist, or a professor. . . .

You're checking up on the hospital" (Rosenhan, 1973:253). The pseudo-patients spent an average of nineteen days in hospital before being released. When they were released, it was with the diagnosis "schizophrenic in remission"; none were appraised as "sane."

Stigmatizing labels such as "mentally ill" or "criminal" can last a long time and may make it difficult for the labelled person to reintegrate into society. These labels can hurt employment opportunities and may affect relationships with friends and acquaintances.

According to Lemert (1951), *primary deviance is the initial act of rule breaking. Secondary deviance occurs when a person who has been labelled a deviant accepts that new identity and continues the deviant behaviour* (see Figure 6.1). For example, a person may shoplift, not be labelled as deviant, and subsequently not shoplift in the future. Secondary deviance occurs if the person shoplifts, is labelled a "shoplifter," accepts that label, and then continues to steal. The concept of secondary deviance is important to labelling theory because it suggests that when people accept a negative label that has been applied to them, the label may contribute to the recurrence of the behaviour it was meant to control (Figure 6.1).

Labelling theorists have made an important contribution to our understanding of the process by which society defines behaviours and individuals as deviant and of the consequences of that definition.

Think of the impact that labels can have on a person's self-concept and on life chances. The label "drug addict" can lead to difficulties in getting a job even after successful treatment. If the label prevents the former addict from reintegrating into the conventional community, he or she may accept the deviant status and return to friends in the drug world. Other deviant labels bring similar problems. Many of us have done things in the past that others would not approve of, but if we have not been labelled, then we will not suffer some of the consequences of our behaviour. The impact of the label of "mental illness" is described by Tom, an ex-patient:

> Having been diagnosed as a psychiatric patient with psychotic tendencies is the worst thing that has ever happened to me. It's shitty to be mentally ill; it's not something to be proud of. It makes you realize just how different you are from everybody else—they're normal and you're not. Things are easy for them; things are hard for you. Life's a ball for them; life's a bitch for you. I'm like a mental cripple! I'm a failure for life! (Herman, 1997:310)

Not everyone passively submits to the labelling process—some people successfully resist the

Figure 6.1   Labelling Theory

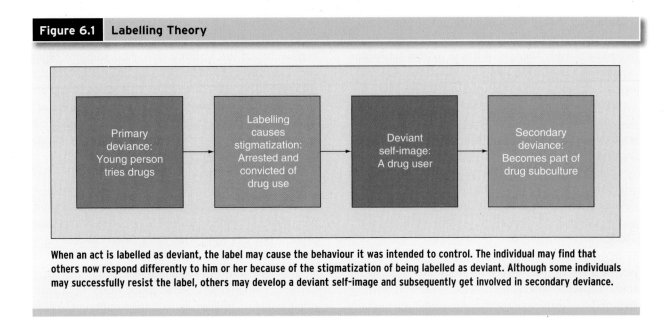

When an act is labelled as deviant, the label may cause the behaviour it was intended to control. The individual may find that others now respond differently to him or her because of the stigmatization of being labelled as deviant. Although some individuals may successfully resist the label, others may develop a deviant self-image and subsequently get involved in secondary deviance.

imposition of a label. This can be done individually or by collectively. The leader of an Ontario group of former psychiatric patients described the aims of his group:

> Simply put, we're tired of being pushed around. We reject everything society says about us, because it's just not accurate. . . . We don't like the meaning of the words [people] use to describe us—"mentals" and "nuts." We see ourselves differently, just as good and worthy as everybody out there. In our newsletter, we're trying to get across the idea that we're not the stereotypical mental patients you see in movies. We're real people who want to be treated equally under the Charter of Rights. We're not sitting back, we're fighting back! (Herman, 1997:323)

The idea that deviance is socially defined raises the question of why some behaviours are defined as deviant and others are not. One answer to this question highlights the role of *moral entrepreneurs—* **persons who use their own views of right and wrong to establish rules and label others as deviant** (Becker, 1963). Think of the role that groups such as Mothers Against Drunk Driving (MADD) have played in getting governments to increase the penalties for drunk driving and in educating the public about the dangers of this behaviour. Similarly, in recent years health advocates have stigmatized cigarette smoking and communities have passed legislation banning smoking in most public places. A few decades ago, there was little opposition to smoking; people smoked on buses, in airplanes, in classrooms,

in offices, and in virtually all other public places. When the health risks of smoking became better known, an antismoking movement grew that was able to overcome the lobbying of tobacco companies and convince governments to restrict smoking. Now, smoking is not only banned in public places, but there seems to be a new definition of the smoker as a deviant who is threatening public health (Tuggle and Holmes, 2000). Thus smoking has moved from a normative behaviour to a stigmatized behaviour over a period of about 30 years.

Moral entrepreneurs often create *moral crusades—***public and media awareness campaigns that help generate public and political support for their causes**. The moral entrepreneurs promoting the Canadian anti-drug movement in the 1920s focused most of their attention on nonwhite immigrants. Chinese and black residents were labelled as villainous threats to Canada. The racist rhetoric of some of Canada's most prominent citizens made it much easier for members of the public to stigmatize these racial minorities and to impose harsh penalties for drug use.

In recent years, we have seen attempts to create moral crusades against abortion providers, wife abusers, "squeegee kids," prostitutes, and a wide variety of other real or perceived threats to society. Some crusades have been more successful than others. The campaign by women's groups for zero-tolerance policies mandating arrest in domestic violence cases has been successful. Anti-abortion groups have received attention, but have not been able to bring about legal change.

Labelling theory has had an important impact on the justice system. It has led to an increased use of diversion outside the formal justice system for minor offences to avoid a formal label. The Youth Criminal Justice Act does not allow the public to learn the names of young offenders to protect them from stigmatization and mandates that most youth court records be destroyed so that youthful offences do not have a negative impact on young offenders' later lives.

Critics argue that labelling theory does not explain what causes the original acts that make up primary deviance nor provide insight into why some people accept deviant labels and others do not (Cavender, 1995).

Symbolic interactionists are concerned with how people learn deviant behaviour, identities, and social roles through interaction with others. Labelling theory has addressed the question of how certain kinds of people and behaviour, and not others, come to be defined as deviant. This issue is also the main focus of conflict theories of deviance and crime.

CONFLICT PERSPECTIVES ON DEVIANCE

Who determines what behaviours are deviant or criminal? Conflict theorists feel that people in positions of power maintain their advantage by using the law to protect their interests. Conflict theorists suggest that lifestyles considered deviant by political and economic elites often are defined as illegal. The activities of poor and lower-income individuals are more likely to be defined as criminal than those of persons from middle- and upper-income backgrounds. For example, those who commit welfare fraud are more likely to face criminal charges than are professionals whose misconduct is generally dealt with by disciplinary committees of their peers rather than by the criminal courts. The relative social harm caused by either of these groups seems to have little relevance in the determination of who is defined as a criminal. What matters more is the power of some groups to resist sanctions.

The Conflict Approach

Karl Marx wrote very little about deviance and crime but his ideas influenced a critical approach based on the assumption that the criminal justice system protects the power and privilege of the capitalist class.

Marx based his critique of capitalism on the inherent conflict that he believed existed between capitalists and the working class. According to Marx, social institutions (such as law, politics, and education) make up a superstructure in society that legitimizes the class structure and maintains the capitalists' superior position in it. Crime is an expression of the individual's struggle against the unjust social conditions and inequality produced by capitalism.

According to Quinney (1980), people with economic and political power define behaviour that threatens their own interests as criminal. People with power use the law to control those who are without power. For example, the drug laws enacted early in the 20th century were passed and enforced in an effort to control immigrant workers, particularly Chinese workers, who were more likely than most other residents of Canada to smoke opium. The laws were motivated by racism more than by a real concern over drug use (Cook, 1969). By contrast, while the Canadian government passed anti-combines legislation in 1889 in response to concerns expressed by labour and small business people about the growing power of monopoly capitalists, the law had no impact. Large companies still engaged in price-fixing and other means of limiting competition. Having symbolic anti-combines laws on the books merely made the government appear responsive to public concerns about big business (Smandych, 1985).

Why do people commit crimes? Some conflict theorists believe that the affluent commit crimes because they are greedy. Corporate and white-collar crimes such as price-fixing and stock market manipulation often involve huge sums of money and harm many people. By contrast, street crimes, such as robbery and assault, generally involve small sums of money and cause harm to limited numbers of victims (Bonger, 1969). According to conflict theorists, the poor commit street crimes in order to survive; they cannot afford the necessary essentials such as food, clothing, shelter, and health care. Thus, some crime represents a rational response by the poor to the unequal distribution of resources in society (Gordon, 1973). Further, living in poverty may lead to violent crime and victimization *of the poor by the poor*. For example, violent gang activity may be a collective response of young people to seemingly hopeless poverty (Quinney, 1979).

In sum, the conflict approach argues that the law protects the interests of the affluent and the powerful. The way laws are written and enforced benefits the capitalist class by ensuring that individuals at the bottom of the social-class structure do not take property from or threaten the safety of those at the top (Reiman, 1984).

This theory explains some types of laws but not others. People of all classes share a consensus about the criminality of certain acts. For example, laws that prohibit murder, rape, and armed robbery protect not only middle- and upper-income people, but also low-income people, who frequently are the victims of such violent crimes (Klockars, 1979). While some laws do protect the rich and powerful, others reflect the interests of all citizens.

Feminist Perspectives on Crime and Deviance

Can theories developed to explain male behaviour help us understand female deviance and crime? According to some feminist scholars, the answer is no. The few early studies that were conducted on "women's crimes" focused almost exclusively on prostitution and attributed the cause of this crime to women's biological or psychological "inferiority." As late as the 1980s, researchers were still looking for unique predisposing factors that led women to commit crime, which was often seen as individual psychopathology rather than as a response to their social environment. These theories reinforce existing female stereotypes and have had a negative impact on our understanding and treatment of female offenders.

A new interest in women's deviance developed in 1975, when two books—Freda Adler's *Sisters in Crime* and Rita James Simons's *Women and Crime*—declared that women's crime rates were going to increase as a result of the women's liberation movement. Although this so-called *emancipation theory* of female crime has been strongly criticized by subsequent analysts (Comack, 2009), Adler's and Simons's works encouraged feminist scholars to examine the relationship between gender, deviance, and crime more closely.

Recent feminist scholars have concluded that the roots of female criminality lie in a social structure that is "characterized by inequalities of class, race, and gender" (Comack, 2009:192). Women's deviance and crime are rational responses to gender discrimination experienced in work, marriage, and interpersonal relationships. Some female crimes are attributed to women's lack of job opportunities and to stereotypical expectations about appropriate roles for women. For example, a woman is even less likely to be a big-time drug dealer or an organized crime boss than she is to be a corporate director (Daly and Chesney-Lind, 1998; Simpson, 1989). Other theorists propose that

women are exploited by capitalism and patriarchy. Most females have had relatively low-wage jobs and few economic resources, so some turned to minor crimes such as prostitution, shoplifting, and passing bad cheques to earn money or to acquire consumer products. Increases in women's criminality during the 1970s and 1980s reflect the fact that the number of single female parents living in poverty grew significantly during this period.

Some of the most interesting work on female criminality has focused on the simultaneous effects of race, class, and gender on deviant behaviour. Arnold (1990) attributes many of the women's offences to living in families in which sexual abuse, incest, and other violence left them few choices except deviance. Economic marginality and racism also contributed to their victimization.

These conclusions are supported by the work of Elizabeth Comack who examined the relationship between women's victimization and their subsequent involvement in Manitoba's criminal justice system. Prior victimization was pervasive among the 24 women she interviewed in a provincial jail. The abuse suffered by the women was connected to their criminal behaviour in several ways. Some women turned to crime as a means of coping with their abuse. "Meredith" had been sexually abused by her father since the age of four or five. She was in jail for fraud and had been involved in drug use and prostitution:

> Some people are violent, some people take it out in other ways, but that was my only way to release it. It was like, it's almost orgasmic, you know, you'd write the cheques, and you'd get home and you'd go through all these things and it's like, "There's so much there. I have all these new things to keep my mind off. I don't have to deal with the old issues." And so you do it. And it becomes an escape. (Comack, 1996b:86)

Others break the law in the course of resisting abuse. "Janice" had been raped as a teenager and turned to alcohol as a means of coping. Serving time for manslaughter, she recounts the circumstances of the offence:

> [W]ell I was at a party, and this guy, older, older guy, came, came on to me. He tried telling me, "Why don't you go to bed with me. I'm getting some money, you know." And I said, "No." And then he started hitting me and then he raped me and then (pause) I lost it. Like I just, I went, I got very angry and I snapped. And I started hitting him. I threw a coffee table on top of his head and then I stabbed him, and then I left. (Comack, 1996b:96)

While abuse was strongly related to the women's law violations, Comack also found that race and class were factors contributing to their criminal behaviour—most were Aboriginal and poor.

Feminist theorists feel that women who violate the law are not "criminal women" but "criminalized women" (Laberge, 1991). This means that they commit crimes and acts of deviance because they have been forced into difficult situations that are not of their own making. The women interviewed by Comack faced many social pressures caused by race, class, and gender and had few options for escaping their situations and improving their lives.

Postmodern Perspectives on Deviance

How do postmodernists view deviance and social control? Although the works of French social theorist Michel Foucault are difficult to categorize, *Discipline and Punish* (1979) can be considered postmodern in its approach to explaining the intertwining nature of power, knowledge, and social control. In his study of prisons from the mid-1800s to the early 1900s, Foucault found that many penal institutions ceased torturing prisoners who disobeyed the rules and began using new surveillance techniques to maintain social control. Although prisons appeared to be more humane in the post-torture era, Foucault contends that the new means of surveillance impinged more on prisoners and brought greater power to prison officials. To explain, he described the *Panopticon*—a structure that gives prison officials the possibility of complete observation of criminals at all times. The Panopticon might be a tower located in the centre of a circular prison, from which guards can see all the cells. Although the prisoners know they can be observed at any time, they do not actually know when their behaviour is being scrutinized. As a result, prison officials can use their knowledge as a form of power over the inmates. Eventually, the guards would not even have to be present all the time because prisoners would believe that they were under constant scrutiny by officials in the observation post. Social control and discipline are based on the use of knowledge, power, and technology.

How does Foucault's perspective explain social control in the larger society? Technologies such as the Panopticon make widespread surveillance and disciplinary power possible in many settings, including streets, factories, schools, and hospitals. Current technology has the potential to expand surveillance far more broadly than Foucault could have imagined. The computer acts as a modern Panopticon that gives workplace supervisors virtually unlimited capabilities for surveillance over subordinates (Zuboff, 1988). Lashmar has described recent technological developments that will broaden the capacity of governments and corporations to control our behaviour:

> A Japanese company has already developed a toilet—targeted for use in large companies—that can analyse whether an employee has recently used illegal recreational drugs, such as cocaine or heroin. Numberplate recognition cameras are in place in a number of key British motorways, enabling police to track suspect or stolen vehicles. Facial recognition for [closed circuit surveillance television] is still in the early stages of development but has already been tried out in the London borough of Newham. . . . Leeds University's Institute for Transport Studies has developed a communication box that could be fitted to all vehicles to regulate traffic speed and flow. (2004:1)

These technologies can be valuable tools in improving public safety. Closed-circuit television cameras in the public transportation system were used to identify the people who carried out the July 2005 bombings that took more than 50 lives in London. Licence plate recognition cameras have enabled the police to get many auto thieves and suspended drivers off the road. DNA technology has freed many people who had been unjustly convicted of serious crimes and has enabled the justice system to imprison others who had committed crimes such as sexual assault and murder. A system that would allow us to log on to our computers by scanning our eyes or our fingerprints would eliminate the confusing number of passwords that each of us must remember.

While there are benefits, these technologies raise important issues of privacy and individual rights. As these technologies continue to develop, society will have to decide the degree to which greater protection is worth the loss of our personal privacy. What are your views on this issue? Where should the balance lie between collective security and individual rights?

We have examined functionalist, symbolic interactionist, critical, feminist, and postmodern perspectives on deviance and crime (see Concept Table 6.1). These explanations help us understand the causes and consequences of certain kinds of behaviour and provide us with guidance concerning how we might reduce crime and deviance.

Concept Table 6.1	THEORETICAL PERSPECTIVES ON DEVIANCE	
	THEORY	KEY ELEMENTS
Functionalist Perspectives		
Robert Merton	Strain theory	Deviance occurs when access to the approved means of reaching culturally approved goals is blocked.
Richard Cloward/Lloyd Ohlin	Opportunity theory	For deviance to occur, people must have the opportunity. Access to illegitimate opportunity structures varies, and this helps determine the nature of the deviance in which a person will engage.
Travis Hirschi	Social control/social bonding	Social bonds keep people from becoming criminals. When ties to family, friends, and others become weak, an individual is most likely to engage in criminal behaviour.
Symbolic Interactionist Perspectives		
Edwin Sutherland	Differential association	Deviant behaviour is learned in interaction with others. A person becomes delinquent when exposure to law-breaking attitudes is more extensive than exposure to law-abiding attitudes.
Howard Becker	Labelling theory	Acts are deviant or criminal because they have been labelled as such. Powerful groups often label less powerful individuals.
Edwin Lemert	Primary/secondary deviance	Primary deviance is the initial act. Secondary deviance occurs when a person accepts the label of "deviant" and continues to engage in the behaviour that initially produced the label.
Critical Perspectives		
Karl Marx, Richard Quinney	Conflict approach	The powerful use law and the criminal justice system to protect their own class interests.
Feminist Perspectives		
Kathleen Daly, Meda Chesney-Lind, Elizabeth Comack	Feminist approach	Current feminist theories suggest that structured inequalities of race, class, and gender condition lead to the criminalization of women.
Postmodern perspectives		
Michel Foucault	Knowledge as power	Power, knowledge, and social control are intertwined. In prisons, for example, new means of surveillance that make prisoners think they are being watched all the time give officials knowledge that inmates do not have. Thus, the officials have a form of power over the inmates.

CRIME CLASSIFICATION AND STATISTICS

How Sociologists Classify Crime

Sociologists categorize crimes based on how they are committed and how society views the offences. We will examine three types: (1) street crime; (2) occupational, or white-collar, and corporate crime; and (3) organized crime. As you read about these types of crime, ask yourself how you feel about them. Should each be a crime? How severe should the sanctions be against each type?

Street Crime   When people think of crime, they most commonly think of **street crime, which**

includes offences such as robbery, assault, and break and enter. These crimes occupy most of the time of the criminal justice system. All street crime does not occur on the street; it frequently occurs in bars, the home, workplace, and other locations.

Violent crime involves force or the threat of force against others, including murder, sexual assault, robbery, and assault. Violent crimes are probably the most anxiety provoking of all criminal behaviour. Victims are physically injured or even killed, and the psychological trauma may last for years (Parker, 1995). Violent crime receives the most attention from law-enforcement officials and the media (see Box 6.2). While much media coverage is given to the violent stranger, the vast majority of violent-crime victims are harmed by someone whom they know: family members, friends, neighbours, or co-workers (Silverman and Kennedy, 1993).

Property crimes include break and enter, theft, motor-vehicle theft, and arson. While violent crime receives the most publicity, property crime is much more common. In most property crimes, the primary motive is to obtain money or some other valuable.

Morals Crimes These involve an illegal action voluntarily engaged in by the participants, such as prostitution, illegal gambling, illegal drugs, and illegal pornography. Many people feel that such conduct should not be labelled as a crime. These offences often are referred to as "victimless crimes" because they involve exchanges of illegal goods or services among willing adults (Schur, 1965). However, morals crimes can also involve practices such as child pornography that can be very harmful to victims.

Occupational and Corporate Crime

Occupational, or white-collar, crime consists of **illegal activities committed by people in the course of their employment or financial dealings**. Much white-collar crime involves the violation of positions of trust. These activities include employee theft of company property, soliciting bribes or kickbacks, and embezzling. Some white-collar criminals set up businesses for the sole purpose of victimizing the public, engaging in activities such as land swindles, securities thefts, and consumer fraud.

In addition to acting for their own profit, some white-collar offenders become involved in criminal activities to improve the market share or profitability of their companies. This is known as ***corporate crime*—illegal acts committed by corporate employees on behalf of the corporation and with**

its support. Examples include anti-trust violations; false advertising; infringements on patents, copyrights, and trademarks; price-fixing; and financial fraud. These crimes are a result of deliberate decisions made by corporate personnel to enhance resources or profits at the expense of competitors, consumers, and the general public.

The cost of white-collar and corporate crimes far exceeds that of street crime. Tax evasion costs Canadians billions of dollars a year. In one of the world's biggest white-collar crimes, investors in Calgary's Bre-X gold-mining company lost around $5 billion when it was learned that a company geologist had added gold to core samples to make a worthless property look like the world's biggest gold find. At the individual level, while few bank robbers get away with more than a few thousand dollars, Earl Jones, an investment advisor, defrauded Canadians of over $50 million in order to support his lavish lifestyle. Many investors trusted Jones with their life savings and were financially devastated by his actions (Sutherland, 2009).

Corporate crimes can be very costly in terms of death and injury. Laureen Snider (1988) found that occupational deaths were the third leading cause of

Conrad Black is one of Canada's best known white-collar criminals. Black once controlled the world's third-largest newspaper chain and was admitted to the British House of Lords as Lord Black of Crossharbour. In 2007, Black was convicted of taking money from his company that rightfully belonged to shareholders and for obstruction of justice and was sentenced to six years in prison by a U.S. court. In 2010, he was released on bail after the U.S. Supreme Court raised questions about the law underlying three of the four charges for which he was convicted.

BOX 6.2 SOCIOLOGY AND THE MEDIA

"If It Bleeds, It Leads": Fear of Crime and the Media

Most Canadians learn about crime through the media. Stories on television and radio and in newspapers, magazines, and books shape our views about crime and criminals. However, the media do not simply "report" the news. Editors and reporters select the crime news and construct the way this news is presented to us.

Unfortunately, the picture of crime we receive from the media is not accurate. For example, most crime is property crime but most media stories deal with violent crime. Gabor (1994) reviewed all the crime-related stories reported over two months in an Ottawa newspaper. More than half the stories focused on violent crimes, particularly murders. However, violent crimes made up only 7 percent of reported crimes in Ottawa, and the city averaged just six murders per year. While violent crimes were overreported, property crimes rarely received much attention, and white-collar and political crimes were almost never written about. Between 1990 and 1996, the homicide rate in Canada declined by almost 20 percent while murder coverage on CBC and CTV national news programs increased by 300 percent. Calgary had 12 murders in 1996, a year in which the *Calgary Herald* published 1,667 murder-related stories (National Media Archive, 1997).

Why do the media misrepresent crime? The primary goal of the media is to make profits by selling advertising. Stories about violent crime boost ratings and circulation, even if these stories do not represent reality. The informal media rule "If it bleeds, it leads" reflects the fact that the public are fascinated by sensationalized, bloody stories, such as those of mass murders. Commenting on his experience with the media, the executive director of a provincial legal society said, "If there's no blood and gore, or there's no sex, it's not newsworthy. And if it falls into the category of being newsworthy, then they have to show the dead body. They've got to show the corpse" (McCormick, 1995:182).

The media's misrepresentation of crime has several consequences. First, Canadians greatly overestimate the amount of violent crime and have a fear of crime that is higher than the risk of victimization justifies. Our fears are reinforced by the global coverage of violence. Television can instantly bring us events from anywhere and violent crimes, such as mass murders in Australia and in Scotland, are reported as immediately and as thoroughly as if they had happened in our own communities.

The media also provide a distorted stereotype of offenders. Violent crimes are most often committed by relatives, friends, and acquaintances, not by the anonymous stranger so many of us fear. Corporate and white-collar criminals are responsible for a great deal of social harm, but except for the most dramatic cases—such as Conrad Black in Canada, and Martha Stewart in the United States—their activities rarely receive much attention in the media. Reporting of these cases is typically limited to the business section rather than the headlines.

Some have blamed the media for failing to cover the story of large numbers of missing women in Canada until Robert Pickton was charged with 26 murders. While a missing child from a middle-class home will generate an avalanche of publicity, the stories of dozens of missing lower-class women – many of whom were sex-trade workers – were not seen as important. Robert Pickton's trial generated international coverage but the media focused on the gruesome crimes and did not consider larger social issues such as legal policies that endanger sex trade workers, the structural reasons why so many of the victims were Aboriginal, and the role of the state in producing socially impoverished neighbourhoods such as Vancouver's Downtown Eastside where Pickton found most of his victims (Hugill, 2010).

Members of the media pursue a vehicle containing convicted murderer Karla Homolka following a court hearing.

death in Canada. She attributes at least half of these deaths to unsafe and illegal working conditions. Working conditions in the mining industry have been especially dangerous. Decades ago, large numbers of Canadian miners died because their employers failed to protect them from mine hazards. Coal miners died of black lung, a condition caused by inhaling coal dust, and fluorspar miners died from the effects of inhaling silica dust in unventilated mineshafts. Not only did mine owners fail to provide safe working conditions, but also company doctors were told not to tell the miners of the seriousness of their illnesses (Leyton, 1997).

One reason many employers have not implemented required safety measures is that the penalties for violating workplace health and safety laws are so light. Typically, companies have been fined only a few thousand dollars even when employees died because of their employers' negligence.

Although people who commit occupational and corporate crimes can be arrested, fined, and sent to prison, many people do not regard such behaviour as "criminal." In Canada, punishment for such offences is usually a fine or a relatively brief prison sentence at a minimum-security facility. In the United States, however, penalties have become much more severe in the past decade.

The concept of white-collar crime also fits some people who wear blue collars. Thus, *occupational crime* may be a more accurate term. Many tradespeople defraud the government by doing work "off the books" in order to avoid provincial sales tax and the Goods and Services Tax (GST) or Harmonized Sales Tax (HST), and some blue-collar businesses such as auto repair have bad reputations for consumer fraud.

Organized Crime   *Organized crime* is a business operation that supplies illegal goods and services for profit. Organized crime includes drug trafficking, prostitution, liquor and cigarette smuggling, loan sharking, money laundering, and large-scale theft, such as truck hijacking. No single organization controls all organized crime, but many groups operate at all levels of society. Organized crime thrives because there is great demand for illegal goods and services. This public demand has produced illicit supply systems with global connections. These activities are highly profitable, since groups that have a monopoly over goods and services the public strongly desires can set their own prices. Legitimate competitors are excluded because of the illegality; illegitimate competitors are controlled by force.

Gang-related killings have been increasing in Canada. The deadly nature of organized crime was shown in Metro Vancouver. In early 2009 there were 16 gang-related shootings, seven of them fatal, in less than a month. Many of the shootings took place in public places, including streets and mall parking lots. In one incident, a woman was fatally shot one morning while driving her car with a four-year-old child in the back seat. Arrests in such incidents are rare.

Along with their illegal enterprises, organized crime groups have infiltrated legitimate business. Linkages with organized crime exist in many businesses including immigration consulting, real estate, garbage collection, vending-machine businesses, construction, and trucking. Law enforcement and governmental officials may be corrupted through bribery, campaign contributions, and favours intended to buy them off, although this has been much less of a problem in Canada than in many other countries.

Crime Statistics

It is difficult to gather statistics about crime and to get access to the social worlds of criminals. While citizens, police, and policy makers all wish to know how much crime there is and how these crimes occur, those who commit crimes normally try to conceal their actions. Thus our information about crime will always be incomplete and we can never be certain of its accuracy. Our main sources of information about crime are police statistics and victimization surveys.

Official Statistics   Our most important source of crime data is the *Canadian Uniform Crime Reports* (CUCR) system, which summarizes crimes reported to all Canadian police departments. Most of our public information about crime comes from the CUCR. When we read that the homicide rate in British Columbia is higher than the national average, or that in 2008 nearly 2.2 million criminal offences were reported to police, this information is based on CUCR data. Figure 6.2 shows trends in violent and property crimes, and Figure 6.3 (on page 142) shows Canada's homicide rates. While most Canadians think crime is increasing, these charts show that it has declined in the past 20 years. The decline is particularly significant in the case of homicide, where rates are now the lowest they have been in 35 years.

Crime figures should be interpreted cautiously. We can have confidence in homicide and auto theft statistics but the accuracy of other crime statistics is

| Figure 6.2 | Canadian Crime Rates, 1962–2009 |

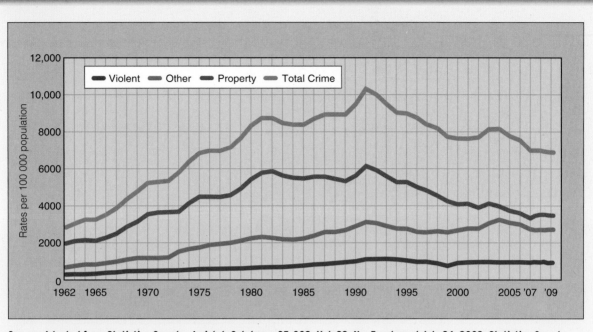

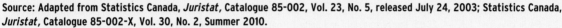

Source: Adapted from Statistics Canada, *Juristat*, Catalogue 85-002, Vol. 23, No. 5, released July 24, 2003; Statistics Canada, *Juristat*, Catalogue 85-002-X, Vol. 30, No. 2, Summer 2010.

less certain and it is important to recognize their limitations.

The major weakness is that police statistics always underreport the actual amount of crime. The vast majority of offences reported in the CUCR come to the attention of the police from reports by victims of crime, and victims do not report all crimes. Crime reporting is also inconsistent. For example, serious assaults are more likely to be reported than minor ones and offences by strangers are more likely to be reported than offences by family members.

Official crime rates are the result of a criminal act, a complaint by a victim or witness, and a response by the criminal justice system. A change in any of these will lead to an increase or decrease in crime rates. For example, Figure 6.2 shows that rates of reported violent crimes increased significantly during the late 1980s and early 1990s. We know that most of this increase was due to a change in police charging practices. Many provincial governments implemented policies requiring police agencies to lay charges in all suspected domestic violence cases (Linden, 1994). Rates of reported violent crime jumped after this policy change. We also know that many white-collar crimes are dealt with by administrative bodies or civil courts or are never reported to avoid negative publicity for the companies involved. As a result, many elite crimes are never classified as "crimes" nor are the businesspeople who commit them labelled as "criminals."

Victimization Surveys

The weaknesses of police-reported crime statistics have led to the development of other methods of measuring crime, the most important of which is the *victimization survey*. Because many people do not report their victimization to police, some governments carry out large surveys in which members of the public are directly asked whether they have been victims of crime. In the largest Canadian survey, less than 42 percent of the victimizations reported by respondents had been reported to police (Evans and Himelfarb, 1996). Thus, reported crimes reveal only the "tip of the iceberg." People told interviewers they did not report crimes because they considered the incident too minor, because they felt it was a personal matter, because they preferred to deal with the problem in another way, or because they did not feel the police could do anything about the crime. Victimization surveys provide us with information about crimes that have not been officially reported, so they provide more accurate statistics of crime than do police records. However, these surveys also have weaknesses: people may not remember minor types

| **Figure 6.3** | **Canadian Homicide Rates, 1961–2009** |

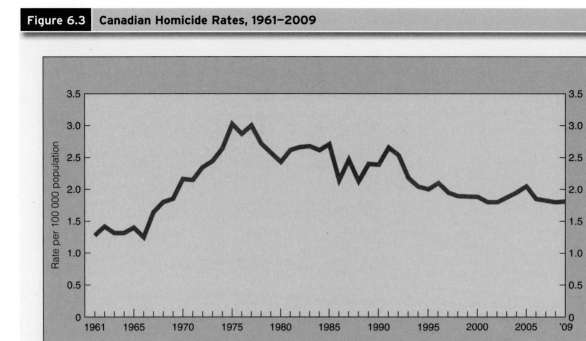

Source: "Canadian Homicide Rates, 1962–2002," adapted from the Statistics Canada publication "Juristat," Catalogue 85-002, Vol. 23, No.5, released July 24, 2003; Dauvergne, Mia and John Turner. 2010. Police-Reported Crime Statistics in Canada, 2009. *Juristat* 30 (Summer). Ottawa: Statistics Canada.

of victimization; they may not report honestly to the interviewer; and the surveys do not provide information about "victimless crimes" such as drug use and illegal gambling. Despite these flaws, victimization surveys have shed new light on the extent of criminal behaviour. They are a valuable complement to other ways of counting crimes.

Street Crimes and Criminals

Given the limitations of official statistics, is it possible to determine who commits crimes? We have much more information available about conventional or street crime than elite crime. Therefore, statistics do not show who commits all types of crime. Age, gender, class, and race are important factors in official statistics pertaining to street crime. These are known as *correlates of crime.* That is, they are factors associated with criminal activity. One method of testing theories of crime is to see how well they explain these correlates.

Age and Crime

The offender's age is one of the most significant factors associated with crime and most other kinds of deviance. Arrests increase from early adolescence,

peak in young adulthood, and steadily decline with age. There is some variation—for example, violent crimes peak at a later age than property crimes—but the general pattern is usually the same. Crime is a young person's game.

Possible explanations for the decline in crime and deviance after early adulthood are the physical effects of aging, which make some criminal activity more difficult, and the realization by older chronic offenders that further arrests will result in long jail sentences. Perhaps the best explanation for maturational reform, though, reflects the different social positions of youth and adults. Adolescents are between childhood and adult life. They have few responsibilities and no clear social role. Adolescence is also a time when young people are breaking away from the controls of their parents and others and preparing to live on their own. However, as we move out of adolescence, we begin to acquire commitments and obligations such as spouses and children that limit our freedom to choose a lifestyle that includes crime and other forms of deviance.

Gender and Crime

Another consistent correlate of crime is gender. Most crimes are committed by males. Females are more

| Figure 6.4 | Percentages of Adults Charged with Selected Criminal Offences by Sex, 2002 |

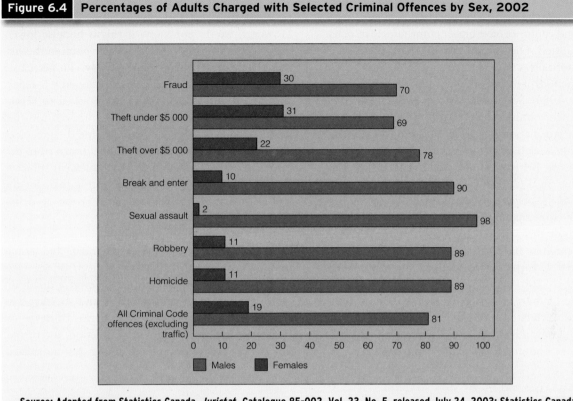

Source: Adapted from Statistics Canada, *Juristat*, Catalogue 85-002, Vol. 23, No. 5, released July 24, 2003; Statistics Canada, *Juristat*, Catalogue 85-002-X, Vol. 30, No. 2, Summer 2010.

likely to be victims than offenders. As with age and crime, this relationship has existed in almost all times and cultures. However, while the age distribution is remarkably stable, there is considerably more variation in male/female crime ratios in different places, at different times, and for different types of crime.

Men make up more than 80 percent of those charged with Criminal Code offences in Canada. The degree of involvement of males and females varies substantially for different crimes (see Figure 6.4). The most important gender difference in arrest rates is the proportionately greater involvement of men in violent crimes and major property offences.

The difference between male and female crime rates has narrowed over the past three decades. Hartnagel (2009) found that the percentage of Criminal Code offences committed by females nearly doubled, from 9 to 17 percent, between 1968 and 2000. While there was virtually no change in the percentage of homicides committed by women (11 percent versus 10 percent), women's involvement in serious theft (9 percent versus 23 percent), fraud (11 percent versus 30 percent), and minor theft (22 percent versus 28 percent) increased substantially. While female crime

rates have increased more rapidly than male crime rates, it is important to remember that the numbers seem more dramatic than they are because the percentage changes are based on very low numbers of female crimes in earlier decades. Women have a long way to go to reach equality in crime with men.

Social Class and Crime

Many theories assume that crime is economically motivated and that poverty will lead to criminal behaviour. However, the evidence concerning the impact of economic factors on crime is not entirely clear. We know that persons from lower socioeconomic backgrounds are more likely to be arrested for violent and property crimes. However, we also know that these types of crimes are more likely to come to the attention of the police than are the white-collar and corporate crimes that are more likely to be committed by members of the upper class. Because the vast majority of white-collar and corporate crimes are never reported, we lack the data to adequately assess the relationship between class and crime.

Before looking at some of the data on social class and crime we do have, let us consider several other economic variables. Does crime increase during times of high unemployment? Do poor cities, provinces, territories, and countries have higher crime rates than richer communities? The answer to both these questions is no. Historically, crime rates are at least as likely to rise during periods of prosperity as during recessionary times (Nettler, 1984). We are also as likely to find high crime rates in rich countries as in poor ones. Within Canada, the poor provinces of Newfoundland and Labrador and New Brunswick have crime rates far lower than the rich provinces of British Columbia and Alberta (see Map 6.1). Hartnagel (2009) has concluded that the *degree of inequality*—poverty amid affluence—is a better predictor of crime than is the amount of poverty.

Little of this research has been done in Canada, but researchers have found that homicide rates are correlated with the degree of inequality of provinces (Daly et al., 2001) and cities (Kennedy et al., 1991). The size of the gap between rich and poor is more strongly correlated with homicide rates than are income levels. Thus, relative deprivation is a better predictor of homicide than absolute deprivation.

We know that lower-class people are overrepresented in arrest and prison admission statistics. However, we do not know if this is because lower-class people commit more crimes or because the justice system treats them more harshly. To get closer to actual behaviour, researchers developed self-report surveys in which respondents were asked to report the number of deviant acts they had committed during a specified time. There is some disagreement about the conclusions that should be drawn from this research, most of which has used adolescent subjects. However, the most likely conclusion is that, for the vast majority of people, class and crime or delinquency are not related.

However, while people from all classes break the law, at least occasionally, the most frequent and serious offenders come from the very bottom of the class ladder—from an underclass that is severely disadvantaged economically, educationally, and socially. The evidence also suggests that other forms of deviance, such as suicide, alcoholism, drug addiction, and mental illness, are also more common among this underclass.

| Map 6.1 | 2005 Crime Rates per 100 000 Population (Criminal Code Excluding Traffic Offences) |

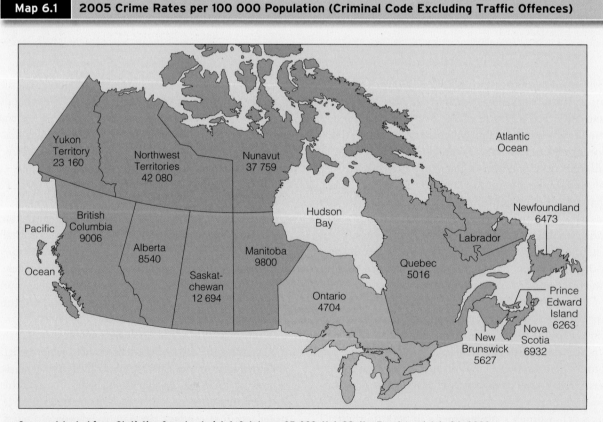

Source: Adapted from Statistics Canada, *Juristat*, Catalogue 85-002, Vol. 23, No. 5, released July 24, 2003.

This conclusion is supported by field studies conducted among street youth in several countries. U.S. research has focused on the role of chronic unemployment and discrimination in the development of street gangs in Hispanic (Vigil, 1990) and African-American (Anderson, 1994) communities. Subcultures that encourage and facilitate crime have developed in response to the long-term poverty so common in many American communities. Compared to the bleak legitimate opportunities available to them, criminal opportunities, particularly from the drug trade, can be very attractive. Studies of street youth in Toronto (Hagan and McCarthy, 1992) and Edmonton (Baron, 1994) found that many street youth came from lower-class families and were on the streets because of poor relationships at home and at school. Their life on the streets often leads to delinquency because of the need to survive and because engaging in crime provides them with a sense of control they do not experience in other facets of their lives.

A unique victimization survey also shows a relationship between deviance and the underclass. More than 12 000 Canadian women were interviewed for the national Violence Against Women Survey (Johnson, 1996a). Several findings from this study supported the view that violence is greatest in the lowest class. First, men with only high-school educations assaulted their wives at twice the rate of men with university degrees. Second, men who were out of work committed assaults at twice the rate of men who were employed. Third, men in the lowest income category (less than $15 000 a year) assaulted their wives at twice the rate of men with higher incomes. However, above this $15 000 level there was no relationship between income and crime. This again suggests that the highest crime rates can be found at the very bottom of the economic ladder, but that above this level there is no relationship.

Race and Ethnicity and Crime

In societies with culturally heterogeneous populations, some ethnic and racial groups will have higher crime rates than others. For example, in the United States, African Americans, and Hispanics are overrepresented in arrest data. However, because Statistics Canada does not routinely collect data about racial and ethnic correlates of crime, we know relatively little about the situation in Canada.

In addition to data about Aboriginal Canadians, which will be discussed later, there have been four studies dealing with minorities and crime in Canada. The first of these examined race and ethnicity in the federal prison system. Offenders from non-Aboriginal, visible ethnic minorities were *underrepresented* in the federal correctional system's population (Thomas, 1992). Specifically, the study found that in 1989 5.2 percent of the federal corrections population were members of ethnic minority groups, while these groups made up more than 6.3 percent of the general population. The second study, which examined provincial youth and adult correctional centres in British Columbia, arrived at similar findings. Only 8.2 percent of the prison population were members of non-Aboriginal, visible ethnic minorities, yet these groups made up 13.5 percent of the province's population (Gordon and Nelson, 1993). The third study, which was conducted for the Commission on Systemic Racism in the Ontario Criminal Justice System (1995) reported that the rate of imprisonment for black adults in Ontario was five times higher than the rate for white adults. Black adults were also more likely to be imprisoned while awaiting trial, particularly for discretionary charges, such as drug possession and drug trafficking. Most recently, the *Toronto Star* used Canada's criminal records database to show that 16.7 percent of people with a criminal record in Canada were "non-white." This is below the percentage of visible minorities and Aboriginal people in the Canadian population, which is 20 percent (Rankin and Powell, 2008).

While statistics on other minorities are limited, there are extensive data on Aboriginal peoples. This is due in part to special inquiries held to find out whether actions toward Aboriginal people by the justice system in several provinces have been discriminatory. Many studies have demonstrated the *overinvolvement* of Aboriginal people (Hartnagel, 2009). For example, while Aboriginal people made up about 4 percent of the population in 2006, they made up about 24 percent of admissions to provincial prisons and 18 percent of admissions to federal prisons (Landry and Sinha, 2008). They also made up 23 percent of those accused of homicide between 1997 and 2004 (Brzozowski et al, 2006). It is important to note that there is much variation in Aboriginal crime rates among different communities and parts of the country (Wood and Griffiths, 2000).

What is the reason for these racial and ethnic differences in crime rates? One answer is that there has often been discrimination by the justice system against minority groups. The racist treatment of blacks in South Africa and in the southern United States throughout much of the 19th and 20th centuries is an obvious example. Discrimination against Aboriginal peoples in Canada, Australia, and New

Zealand has also been well documented by commissions of inquiry. Members of economically disadvantaged minority groups may go to prison for minor offences if they are unable to pay fines. While this type of discrimination may be unintentional, it is nonetheless real. The justice system also tends to focus on the types of crimes that are committed by low-income people rather than on white-collar crimes, so members of poor minority groups may be overrepresented in crime statistics. Discrimination likely accounts for some, but not all, of the high rates of criminality of some minority groups.

To provide a further explanation, consider again the case of Canada's Aboriginal people. Their situation is, of course, unique, but the same kinds of factors may apply to other groups. While a number of theories have been advanced to explain Aboriginal over-involvement in crime (Hartnagel, 2004; Wood and Griffiths, 2000), consider the following explanation, which has been drawn from conflict and social control theories. Canada's Aboriginal people have far less power and fewer resources than other Canadians. They must cope with systems of education and religion that have been imposed on them from outside their cultural communities and that are incompatible with their customs and traditions. In the past, forced attendance at residential schools and forced adoption outside the community weakened family ties. Crippling rates of unemployment in many areas, particularly on isolated reserve communities, mean no job ties, and school curricula that are irrelevant to the lives of Aboriginal students mean that children do not become attached to their schools. Under these conditions, strong social bonds are difficult to develop and high rates of crime can be predicted. As Manitoba's Aboriginal Justice Inquiry concluded: "From our review of the information available to us ... we believe that the relatively high rates of crime among Aboriginal people are a result of the despair, dependency, anger, frustration and sense of injustice prevalent in Aboriginal communities, stemming from the cultural and community breakdown that has occurred over the past century" (Hamilton and Sinclair, 1991b:91).

Region and Crime Crime is not evenly distributed around the globe. Different countries have very difference practices of reporting and recording crime, so international comparisons are difficult. The most reliable measure for comparison is homicide rates, which are reported in a reasonably similar fashion in most countries. Canada's homicide rate of about 1.8 per 100 000 people is relatively low by world standards. It is about one-third of the U.S. rate, but about one-and-a-half times that of the United Kingdom.

There are major regional differences in crime rates within Canada. Map 6.1 on page 144 shows that crime rates are highest in the West and the North and lowest in Central Canada. Crime rates used to be lowest in Atlantic Canada, but have increased in those provinces over the past few years.

THE CRIMINAL JUSTICE SYSTEM

The criminal justice system includes the police, the courts, and prisons. However, the term *criminal justice system* is misleading because these institutions do not usually work together as a system and each has considerable autonomy.

The Police

Most people think the main function of the police is to enforce the law. That is indeed one of their functions, but there are several others, including order maintenance and the provision of social services. Order maintenance refers to keeping the peace. Stopping arguments, controlling the areas where homeless

Does the justice system discriminate against members of racial minority groups? Former Toronto Raptors' star Dee Brown was involved in a legal case that raised the issue of racial profiling by the Toronto Police Service. (See Box 6.3 on page 148.)

alcoholics drink, and making a group of boisterous teenagers move away from the parking lot of a convenience store are all order-maintenance activities. While the main concern in law enforcement is arresting a suspect, the main concern in order maintenance is restoring peace in the community. The service role is also important and consists of many different activities, including finding lost children, counselling crime victims, and notifying next of kin in fatal accidents.

Two questions you might ask are these: Why do the police have such a broad range of responsibilities? What ties these diverse activities together? To answer the first question, there are several reasons why the police have the broad responsibilities they do (Cumming et al., 1965):

1. The police are one of the few public agencies open 24 hours a day.
2. In many cases, the police are serving clients that other agencies may not be interested in. The poor, the homeless, and the mentally ill may become police clients almost by default. If no other agency will look after intoxicated people who pass out on downtown streets, the police must do it.
3. The police may not be well informed about or have access to other agencies that could handle some of their cases.

The second question—What ties these diverse activities together?—is best answered by looking at two dimensions of the police role. First, the police have the *authority* (and often the duty) to intervene in situations where something must be done immediately. This authority is the same whether the incident is an armed robbery in progress, a naked man standing on a busy street screaming at people, or a complaint that someone's pet boa constrictor has just appeared in someone else's bedroom. Second, the authority is backed up by *non-negotiable force.* If someone refuses to go along with what a police officer suggests, the officer can use force (usually arrest) to back up his or her demands. Even professional caregivers may need to call the police when clients refuse to cooperate with them. Egon Bittner has summed up the patrol officer's role: "What policemen do appears to consist of rushing to the scene of any crisis whatever, judging its needs in accordance with canons of common sense reasoning, and imposing solutions upon it without regard to resistance or opposition" (1980:137).

The Courts

Criminal courts decide the guilt or innocence of those accused of committing a crime. In theory, justice is determined in an adversarial process in which the prosecutor (a lawyer representing the state) argues that the accused is guilty and the defence lawyer asserts that the accused is innocent. Proponents of the adversarial system feel this system best provides a just decision about guilt or innocence (see Box 6.4 on page 149).

The essence of the adversarial system can be seen in the defence lawyer's role, which is to defend the accused. This role was described by Lord Brougham, a defence lawyer in a case that could have had disastrous consequences for the British government had his defence been successful:

> An advocate, in the discharge of his duty, knows but one person in all the world, and that person is his client. To save that client by all means and expedients, and at all hazards and costs to their persons, and amongst them, to himself, is his first and only duty; and in performing this duty he must not regard the alarm, the torments, the destruction which he may bring upon others. Separating the duty of a patriot from that of an advocate, he must go on reckless of the consequences, though it should be his unhappy fate to involve his country in confusion. (Quoted in Greenspan, 1982:201)

We can add to Lord Brougham's comment that in an adversarial system the defence lawyer is obliged to fulfill this duty to the client without concern for the client's actual guilt or innocence.

Most of those working in the courts strongly defend the adversarial system and see it as one of the cornerstones of a free and democratic society. Many of the procedures that seem to restrict the ability of the court to get at the "truth," such as the rule that accused persons cannot be forced to testify against themselves, were adopted to prevent the arbitrary use of state power against the accused. However, some critics feel that this system does not deal adequately with crime because it places more emphasis on winning than on doing what is best for the accused, for the victim, and for society. The plea bargaining described in Box 6.4 on page 149 is one aspect of our court system that has often been criticized.

Punishment

***Punishment* is any action designed to deprive a person of things of value (including liberty) because of some offence the person is deemed to have committed** (Barlow, 1987:421). Punishment can serve four functions:

BOX 6.3   CRITICAL THINKING

The Police and Racial Profiling: Do Police Actions Help to Explain Race Differences in Criminality?

On November 1, 1999, former Toronto Raptors' basketball star Dee Brown was stopped by a member of the Toronto Police Service and charged with impaired driving. Brown was initially found guilty, but his conviction was overturned by higher courts.

The controversy in Brown's case related to the reason why the police stopped him in the first place. The arresting officer said that he had stopped Brown because he was speeding in his Ford Expedition (Tyler, 2003). However, Brown was never charged with speeding; his lawyers maintained there was no legal reason for the stop and that Brown was pulled over because he was a young black man in an expensive vehicle. The Ontario Court of Appeal ruled that the arrest was unconstitutional because of racial profiling and a new trial was ordered.

Racial profiling refers to the practice of subjecting some people to greater scrutiny than others because of their race. In the United States, many police forces have been accused of stopping black and Hispanic drivers for trivial reasons, and then searching their vehicles for drugs, weapons, or other illegal items. As a result, blacks and Hispanics were more likely to be charged with drug and weapons offences than whites were. Profiling is not just a police issue, as there were complaints in many countries that airline-security personnel and customs and immigration officials were profiling young Muslim males following the destruction of the World Trade Center on September 11, 2001.

Following the Dee Brown case, the *Toronto Star* used police data to show that in Toronto blacks charged with simple drug possession were more likely to be taken into custody than whites charged with the same offence and that black suspects were more likely to be held overnight than white suspects. The *Star* also found that blacks were more likely than whites to receive nonmoving traffic violations (such as driving with an invalid driver's licence or insurance certificate) (Rankin et al., 2002). This research was supported by survey data collected by Wortley and Tanner (cited in Rankin et al., 2002), who found that 28 percent of a sample of black Toronto residents reported having been stopped by the police in the previous two years, compared with 14.6 percent of whites and 18.2

percent of Chinese. The difference was even greater in a study of high school students conducted by the same researchers (Rankin et al., 2002).

Although some law-enforcement and security agencies have accepted the results of research suggesting that profiling was occurring and have tried to change these practices, others deny that profiling takes place. The police claim that although they may stop minorities more often than nonminorities, this is justified because it reflects racial differences in their likelihood of committing crimes (Melchers, 2003).

In Canada, blacks are not the only group that has raised complaints of racial profiling. Aboriginal people have also alleged that the police often single them out for special attention. Perhaps the best-known case that involved allegations of profiling was that of Manitoba Aboriginal leader J.J. Harper, who was shot and killed in a scuffle with a Winnipeg police officer. The officer had stopped Harper on suspicion of car theft, even though Harper did not resemble the suspect. The Manitoba Aboriginal Justice Inquiry, which was established in response to this shooting, concluded that racial profiling was a major factor in this death:

> Racial stereotyping motivated the conduct of [Constable] Cross. He stopped a "native" person walking peaceably along a sidewalk merely because the suspect he was seeking was native. This then leads to the conclusion that race was a major contributing factor in the death of J. J. Harper. Race was one of the facts included in the description broadcast of the car-theft suspect for whom the police were looking. If Harper had not been a native person, Cross would have ignored him. (Hamilton and Sinclair, 1991:86)

The debate about the extent of racial profiling is difficult to resolve, as the interaction between police and citizens often has a low visibility and is not subject to public scrutiny. However, there is little doubt that being more frequently stopped does contribute to the perception of police harassment felt by many visible minorities and Aboriginal people.

1. *Retribution* imposes a penalty on the offender based on the premise that the punishment should fit the crime. For example, a person who murders should be punished more severely than one who steals.
2. *Social protection* results from restricting offenders so they cannot commit further crimes. If someone is in prison, he or she is no longer a threat to those on the outside.
3. *Rehabilitation* seeks to return offenders to the community as law-abiding citizens.
4. *Deterrence* seeks to reduce criminal activity by instilling a fear of punishment.

There is no question that the law can deter. You do not deliberately park where you know your car will be towed away, and you do not speed if you see a police car behind you. However, the law does not deter as well as we might hope because the *certainty* of being arrested and convicted for most crimes is low. Most crimes do *not result* in arrests and most arrests do not result in convictions. It is difficult to increase the certainty of punishment, so governments tinker with the severity of punishment instead. Most "law and order" politicians talk about getting tough on crime by increasing penalties rather than by making punishment more certain. However, increasing the average penalty for robbery by a year will not reduce robbery rates if most robberies do not result in a conviction or a jail sentence.

BOX 6.4   CRITICAL THINKING

Let's Make a Deal: Bargaining for Justice

The image most of us have of the court process is that those who are charged will go to trial. However, this image is far from the truth. Trials are relatively rare and most cases are decided by guilty pleas. A high proportion, probably the majority, of these guilty pleas result from plea bargaining.

Plea bargaining is the process of negotiating a guilty plea. Informal, private discussions are held between the defence and the prosecution in an attempt to reach a mutually agreeable outcome in which both parties receive concessions. For the accused, plea bargaining may mean that the severity of the penalty will be reduced. For the prosecution, plea bargaining saves time, which is crucial in our overloaded courts. If all cases went to trial, the backlog would be endless. The prosecutor may also bargain if the prosecution's case is weak.

Plea bargaining has been widely criticized on the grounds that it subverts the aims of the criminal justice system by rewarding the guilty and penalizing those who elect to maintain their innocence and go to trial.

Plea bargaining has been particularly criticized in cases where guilty people are given light sentences in exchange for testimony against their partners in crime. The 12-year sentence given to Karla Homolka in exchange for her testimony against Paul Bernardo is an example of this type of bargaining. Although the Homolka case was controversial because of her direct involvement with Bernardo's killings, some cases are even more questionable. For example, someone heavily involved in criminal activity can receive a lenient disposition in exchange for information about others who are less involved.

Consider the case of Yves ("Apache") Trudeau (Lavigne, 1987). A former Hells Angel of the notorious Laval, Quebec, chapter, Trudeau is probably the most prolific contract killer in Canada's history. Trudeau admitted to 43 gang-related killings and was able to negotiate a plea bargain in which the Crown accepted guilty pleas to 43 counts of manslaughter and agreed that he would be released with a new identity after serving seven years in jail. Trudeau agreed to cooperate with the police after learning he was the target of other Hells Angels who had already killed six members of his chapter. In exchange for police protection, a comfortable cell, and a light sentence, Trudeau agreed to tell what he knew about the operation of the Hells Angels and other Montreal organized crime groups. His testimony led to the convictions of five Hells Angels who received life sentences. While prosecutors would argue that plea bargaining was the only way to convict other Hells Angels and to reduce the influence of the gang, the practice of making deals with killers raises some difficult moral and ethical questions.

What are your views about plea bargaining? Do you think that justice is served when deals are made?

Many Canadians think that longer sentences and tougher prisons are the best way to reduce crime. However, the evidence tells us that prevention programs will do more than prisons to reduce our crime rates.

AP/Wide World Photos

Restorative Justice

For many years, we have relied on the formal justice system to deal with crime. Community members have been discouraged from participating in their own protection and have had little say in the services they received. After the victim called the police, the police would soon arrive to take care of the problem, and if an arrest was made, case processing was left to the formal justice system. Some of those found guilty were removed from the community and sent to jail. Professionals controlled each step in the system, and victims and other community members had little involvement.

While most people have come to accept this as the proper way of dealing with crime, some feel the system has failed them. Victims feel left out, as their role as the aggrieved party is forgotten and they are relegated to the role of witnesses. Offenders are also dealt with impersonally and are rarely reminded of the personal harm they have done. Instead, many offenders are sent to prisons where their stays may result more in alienation than rehabilitation. Finally, the public is often dissatisfied with a justice system that does not respond to their concerns.

Some reformers have advocated a justice system that will help to restore social relationships rather than simply punishing offenders (Church Council on Justice and Corrections, 1996). Advocates of *restorative justice* seek to return the focus of the justice system to repairing the harm that has been done to the victim and to the community. A key element of restorative justice is the involvement of the victim and other members of the community as active participants in the process in order to reconcile offenders with those they have harmed, and to help communities to reintegrate victims and offenders.

Restorative justice has its roots in traditional societies where the restoration of order was crucial to society's survival. In Canada, Aboriginal communities are leading the way in the return to the use of restorative justice practices.. They have used a variety of different methods, including *circle sentencing*, which brings an offender together with the victim and other community members to resolve disputes.

Restorative justice has been particularly emphasized for young offenders. Separate courts that are governed by the Youth Criminal Justice Act deal with people younger than 18 years of age. The underlying philosophy of this legislation mandates the use of restorative justice for many young offenders to avoid stigmatizing them and to try to reintegrate them back into their communities.

DEVIANCE AND CRIME IN THE FUTURE

Among the questions pertaining to deviance and crime in the future are: Is the solution to our "crime problem" more law and order? What impact will the global economy have on crime? How will technology change the nature of crime in the future?

BOX 6.5   SOCIOLOGY IN GLOBAL PERSPECTIVE

The Globalization of Crime

Crime is becoming a global phenomenon. Consider the following examples:

- Con men in Amsterdam sell bogus U.S. securities by telephone to Germans; the operation is controlled by an Englishman residing in Monaco whose profits go to a bank based in Panama. (United Nations Development Programme, 1999:104).

- When Yugoslavia disintegrated during the 1990s, the predominantly Albanian province of Kosovo sought to break free of Serbian control. The United Nations intervened, but the agreement ending the fighting did not provide for a functioning justice system (Linden et al., 2007). Instead, United Nations personnel were responsible for policing, and the rest of the justice system was barely functioning. It was not clear what criminal laws would apply. The Kosovo Liberation Army took advantage of this situation to become a major global player in trafficking heroin to many different countries and used its profits to buy weapons to help support its political cause (Dishman, 2001).

- Somalia is a failed state with no functioning government. Some Somalis, many of whom are fishermen whose livelihoods have been affected by overfishing by other countries, have taken advantage of this lack of governance to engage in piracy. Using speedy small boats, in 2009 they attacked 214 ships and captured 47 to hold for ransom. These vessels ranged in size from large oil tankers to personal yachts. Once they have boarded their target ships the pirates sail them back to the port of Eyl to await the payment of ransom. In 2010, the pirates received as much as $5.5 million ransom payment for one ship (a Greek oil tanker) and this money has made Eyl a prosperous community by Somali standards. Somalia will not prosecute the pirates or help owners recover their ships. Even when pirates are captured at sea, they are often released because international law does not provide a clear basis for prosecution. Kenya has agreed to establish an international tribunal to try pirates, but even if this is successful it is very difficult for the world's navies to patrol the vast distances over which the pirates operate.

These examples show how international criminal activity poses challenges not only for its victims but also for the governmental agencies that are mandated to control crime. Among these issues are questions such as: Which police forces should investigate? In which jurisdiction should a prosecution be mounted? How can we facilitate cooperation among justice agencies from different countries?

Global crime **refers to the networking of powerful criminal organizations and their associates in shared activities around the world** (Castells, 1998). Global networks are fluid and are constantly changing. There have been formal alliances between groups, such as the Sicilian Mafia and the Medellin drug cartel in Colombia (Jamieson, 2001), but typically relationships are less formal. Many global crime networks are involved in smuggling things, including drugs, weapons, endangered animal and plant species, illegal immigrants, and toxic waste. Such smuggling requires groups to have a presence in a number of countries or to form alliances with local groups.

There has also been a blurring of the boundaries between organized crime and terrorism (Jamieson, 2001). Many terrorist groups use transnational crime such as drug smuggling to raise money to fund their other activities. Al-Qaeda–linked networks in Canada have used credit-card fraud and forgery to fund their operations. For example, Ahmed Ressam had been given political asylum in Canada in 1994 and in December 1999 was arrested at the U.S. border with a car full of explosives that he intended to detonate at the Los Angeles airport to mark the millennium on January 1, 2000. Ressam later testified about some of his fund raising activities:

> Q. How did you support yourself during that four-year period [when you lived in Montreal]?
> A. I lived on welfare and theft.
> Q. What do you mean by "theft"?
> A. I used to steal tourists [sic], rob tourists. I used to go to hotels and find their suitcases and steal them when they're not paying attention.
> Q. And what would you do with the contents of those suitcases?
> A. I used to take the money, keep the money, and if there are passports, I would sell them, and if there are Visa credit cards, I would use them up, and if there were any traveler's checks, I would use them or sell them. (PBS, 2001:2)

Ressam and his accomplices had equipment to counterfeit credit cards and to forge cheques. They were also involved in passport-fraud networks that were linked with Osama bin Laden's terrorist training camps in Afghanistan.

Political and corporate corruption plays a major role in global crime. When governments failed in places such as the Soviet Union and Yugoslavia, power vacuums were created; the vacuums were quickly filled by organized criminals. In the economic chaos that followed these political events, those who were willing and able to use force could make huge amounts of money and influence the political process through bribery and threats of violence. In Russia, organized criminals may still control as much as half the economy, and they are using their secure base in Russia to expand their networks to many other countries, including Canada.

Global crime will continue to prosper. The opportunities to make money are simply too great and the global justice system is too weak to deter potential criminals. The fight against global organized crime "pits bureaucracies against networks" (Naim, 2003:35), and law-enforcement agencies have not been able to keep up with the criminals. As with the terrorist groups you read about in Chapter 5, the networks are so flexible that if one part is closed the rest of the network can make small adjustments and continue to operate. To make things even more difficult, international policing organizations are reluctant to cooperate with one another, and their countries are often more concerned with protecting their own sovereignty than with breaking up crime networks.

Figure 6.5   International Maritime Crime Bureau Piracy Map, 2009

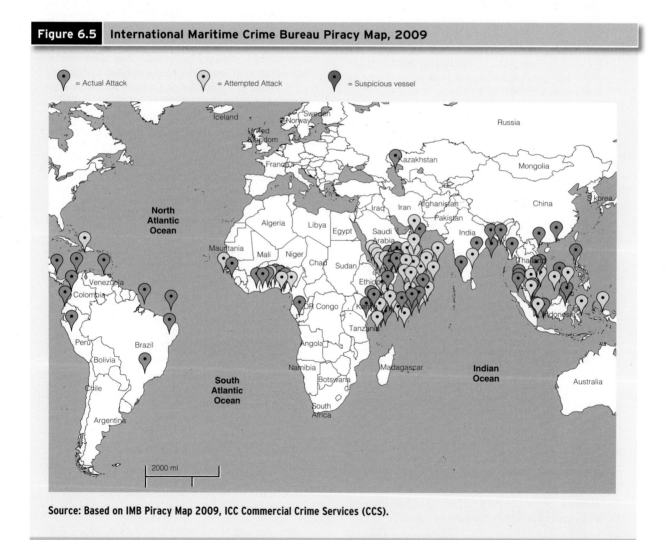

Source: Based on IMB Piracy Map 2009, ICC Commercial Crime Services (CCS).

Although many Canadians agree that crime is an important problem, they are divided over what to do about it. One thing is clear: the existing criminal justice system cannot solve the "crime problem." If most crimes do not result in arrest, if most arrests do not result in convictions, and if most convictions do not result in a jail term, the "lock 'em up and throw away the key" approach has little chance of succeeding. Nor does the high rate of recidivism among those who have been incarcerated speak well for the rehabilitative efforts of our correctional facilities. We can look to the United States to see the results of a very expensive social experiment. Massive numbers of people are being locked up for very long periods of time, and prison populations have increased much more rapidly than in other countries. Several states have passed "three strikes and you're out" laws that impose a mandatory life sentence for anyone convicted of a third felony. Each inmate convicted under these laws will cost about $1.5 million to keep in prison for the rest of his or her life. In many U.S. states, particularly California, the prison systems are so overcrowded and underfunded that the courts have ordered increased spending to pay for improvements or have ordered that prisoners be released. Crime rates have declined in the United States, but no more than in Canada, where the incarceration rate is about one-seventh that of the United States.

An alternative to this approach begins with the knowledge that the best way to deal with crime is to ensure that it doesn't happen. Instead of longer sentences, military-style boot camps, or other stop-gap measures, *structural solutions*—such as more and better education and jobs, affordable housing, more equality and less discrimination, and socially productive activities—are needed to reduce street crime in the future. The best approach for reducing delinquency and crime ultimately is prevention: working with young people *before* they become juvenile offenders by helping them establish family relationships, build self-esteem, choose a career, and get an education that will help them pursue that career. Until these long-term measures can be implemented, there are many different preventive measures—including better policing strategies—that are much more likely to reduce crime than passing tougher sentencing laws (Sherman et al, 1998).

A major trend that will affect the type of crime we will see in the future is globalization. Organized crime has spread from one country to another because the drug trade is a vast international business. With the aid of satellites and computers, financial crimes can be committed from anywhere in the world and may be almost impossible to punish because of competing jurisdictions and different laws. The reduction of border controls in trading alliances such as the European Union makes it easier for criminals to move from one country to another. For a more detailed look at global crime, see Box 6.5 on page 151.

Finally, much of the future growth of crime lies in the Internet and other new technologies. Computer hackers are responsible for viruses and for attacks intended to shut down specific websites. Hackers may also use the Internet to steal people's identifying information and credit-card numbers in order to obtain money by fraud. The Internet has also proved to be a very effective way of distributing pornography, including child pornography, and to engage in cyber-stalking. These crimes are difficult to deal with because technology provides an anonymity that is not present in many other types of offences. The global nature of the Internet means that many jurisdictions can be involved, some of which refuse to investigate their own citizens. The nature of many of these crimes and the expertise required to investigate them mean that investigations are expensive.

The potential for criminals to exploit other new technologies, such as biotechnology and nanotechnology, means that we have only begun to see the potential of new discoveries to shape the crimes of the future.

CHAPTER REVIEW

■ What is deviance?

Deviant behaviour is any act that violates established norms. Deviance varies from culture to culture and in degrees of seriousness. Crime is seriously deviant behaviour that violates written laws and is punishable by fines, incarceration, or other sanctions.

■ What is the strain theory of deviance?

Strain theory says that the structure of a society can produce pressures that result in deviant behaviour. When denied legitimate access to cultural goals, such as a good job or nice home, people may engage in illegal behaviour to obtain them. Opportunity theory suggests that access to illegitimate opportunity structures varies, and this access helps determine the nature of the deviance in which a person will engage.

■ How does social control theory explain crime?

According to social control theory, everyone is capable of committing crimes, but social bonding keeps many from doing so. People bond to society through their attachments to family and to other social institutions, such as the church and school. When a person's bonds to society are weakened or broken, the probability of deviant behaviour increases.

■ How do symbolic interactionists view the causes of crime?

Differential association theory states that individuals have a greater tendency to deviate from societal norms when they frequently associate with persons who tend toward deviance instead of conformity. According to labelling theory, deviant behaviour is that which is labelled deviant. The process of labelling is related to the relative power and status of those persons who do the labelling and those who are labelled. Those in power may use their power to label the behaviour of others as deviant.

■ How do conflict and feminist perspectives explain deviance?

Conflict perspectives on deviance examine inequalities in society. According to the critical approach, the legal order protects those with political and economic power and exploits persons from lower classes. Feminist approaches to deviance examine the relationship between gender and deviance.

■ How do postmodern theorists approach crime and deviance?

Some postmodern theorists focus on social control and discipline based on the use of knowledge, power, and technology. While most social control agencies no longer use harsh methods of social control, such as torture, newer techniques allow constant surveillance over individuals. The techniques that began in prison now exist in many parts of society, including factories, schools, and hospitals.

■ What are the major types of crime?

Street crime includes violent crimes, property crimes, and morals crimes. Occupational, or white-collar, crimes are illegal activities committed by people in the course of their employment or financial dealings. Other major types are corporate crimes, which are illegal acts committed by company employees on behalf of the corporation and with its support, and organized crime, which is an illicit business operation that supplies illegal goods and services for profit.

■ What are our main sources of crime statistics?

Official crime statistics are taken from the Canadian Uniform Crime Reporting survey, which lists crimes reported to the police. We also conduct victimization surveys that interview households to determine the incidence of crimes, including those not reported to police. Many more crimes are committed than are officially reported.

■ How are age, sex, and social class related to crime?

Persons under 25 have the highest rates of crime. Persons arrested for assault and homicide and white-collar criminals are generally male. Women have much lower rates of crime than men. Persons from lower socioeconomic backgrounds are more likely to be arrested for violent and property crimes while corporate crime is more likely to occur among upper socioeconomic classes.

■ How is discretion used in the justice system?

The criminal justice system includes the police, the courts, and prisons. These agencies have considerable discretion in dealing with offenders. The police often use discretion in deciding whether to act on a situation. Prosecutors and judges use discretion in deciding which cases to pursue and how to handle them.

KEY TERMS

corporate crime 138
crime 129
deviance 127
differential association theory 131
global crime 151

WEB LINKS

For more Web links related to the topic of this chapter, see the Nelson sociology website: **www.sociologyessentials5e.nelson.com**

Blue Line magazine is intended for police audiences and looks at a variety of issues concerning Canadian policing; see: **www.blueline.ca**

Many jurisdictions still have outdated or strange laws on their books. Read some of them at: **www.dumblaws. com**

Look at Canada's Criminal Code. You can read the way each offence is defined and look at the maximum penalties at: **http://laws.justice.gc.ca/en/C-46/index. html**

Read recent news about criminal justice and Canadian research in policing and corrections at the website of Public Safety and Emergency Preparedness Canada: **www.psepc-sppcc.gc.ca**

See also the site for the Correctional Service of Canada: **www.csc-scc.gc.ca**

For the Canadian government's perspectives on terrorism, go to: **www.publicsafety.gc.ca/prg/ns/ index-eng.aspx**

QUESTIONS FOR CRITICAL THINKING

1. Consider the role of power in defining what acts are deviant and what acts are not. Can you think of examples where the definition of deviance has been changed because formerly stigmatized groups have achieved the power necessary to resist being labelled as deviant?

2. Should so-called victimless crimes, such as prostitution and recreational drug use, be decriminalized? Do these crimes harm society?

3. Several commissions have recommended that Aboriginal people should have a separate justice system. Do you agree? How do you think such a system would operate?

4. As a sociologist armed with a sociological imagination, how do you propose to deal with the problem of crime in Canada? What programs would you suggest enhancing? What programs would you reduce?

ONLINE STUDY AND RESEARCH TOOLS

INFOTRAC®

InfoTrac College Edition is included free with every new copy of this text. Explore this online library for additional readings, review, and a handy resource for assignments. Visit **www.infotrac-college.com** to access this online database of full-text articles. Enter the key terms from this chapter to start your search.

CENGAGENOW™ CENGAGENOW

Use CengageNOW™ to help you formulate a customized study plan for this chapter. After you take the Diagnostic Quiz, CengageNOW™ will generate a customized study plan for you. It will identify sections of the chapter you should review.

Social Stratification in Canada

Financial wealth—or, in more technical terms, "net worth"—is an important element of Canadian society. Most Canadians aspire for it in order to live long and well. Others seek it to help the less fortunate. Whether it is fair or not, wealth is also one of the ways used to measure people and their achievements. Advertisers push "the dream" of wealth, and what it can bring. For some, the dream and the reality do become one. There are more than 1 million millionaire households in Canada, and the richest 10 percent of Canadian households control close to 60 percent of the country's wealth (Chawla, 2008).

For many, however, the dream never does become reality. Their reality regarding wealth may consist of having enough to live just above the poverty line. The poorest 10 percent of Canadian households have a median net worth of only $150. The bottom half of all households control less than 10 percent of the wealth (Morissette and Zhang, 2006). Grade 4 and 5 students in North Bay, Ontario, were asked to respond to the question "What does poverty mean?" The following are their responses:

© Ted Horowitz/Corbis

Poverty is...

Not being able to go to McDonald's.

Getting a basket from the Santa Fund.

Feeling ashamed when my dad can't get a job.

Not buying a book at the book fair.

Not getting to go to birthday parties.

Hearing my mom and dad fight over money.

Not ever getting a pet because it costs too much.

Wishing you had a nice house.

Not being able to go camping.

Not getting a hot dog on hot dog day.

Not getting pizza on pizza day.

Not being able to have your friends sleep over.

Pretending you forgot your lunch.

Being afraid to tell your mom that you need gym shoes.

Not having breakfast sometimes.

Not being able to play hockey.

Sometimes really hard because my mom gets scared and she cries.

Not being able to go to Cubs or play soccer.

Not being able to take swimming lessons.

Not being able to afford a holiday.

Not having pretty barrettes for your hair.

Not having your own private backyard.

Being teased for the way you are dressed.

Not getting to go on school trips.

(Interfaith Social Assistance Reform Coalition, 1998:107)

Source: *Our Neighbours' Voices: Will We Listen?* By The Interfaith Social Assistance Reform Coalition. Toronto: James Lorimar & Co. Ltd. Reprinted with permission.

In Canadian society we are socialized to believe that hard work is the key to personal success. Conversely, we are also taught that individuals who fail—who do not achieve success—do so as a result of their own personal inadequacies. Poverty is attributable to personal defect and it is up to the individual to find a way to break the "cycle of poverty." Do you agree? Or do you think structural factors in Canadian society affect the degree of success individuals achieve?

In this chapter, we will examine systems of social stratification and how the Canadian class system may make it easier for some individuals to attain (or maintain) top positions in society while others face significant obstacles in moving out of poverty. Before reading on, test your knowledge of wealth and poverty in Canada by taking the quiz in Box 7.1. on page 158.

QUESTIONS AND ISSUES

Chapter Focus Question: How are the lives of Canadians affected by social inequality?

How do prestige, power, and wealth determine social class?

How are social stratification and poverty linked?

What is the extent of social inequality in Canada?

SOCIAL STRATIFICATION

Social stratification **is the hierarchical arrangement of large social groups based on their control over basic resources** (Feagin and Feagin, 2008). Stratification involves patterns of structural inequality that are associated with membership in each of these groups, as well as the ideologies that support inequality. Sociologists examine the social groups that make up the hierarchy in a society and seek to determine how inequalities are structured and persist over time.

Max Weber's term *life chances* **refers to the extent to which individuals have access to important societal resources such as food, clothing, shelter, education, and health care.** According to sociologists, more-affluent people typically have better life chances than the less affluent because they have greater access to quality education, safe neighbourhoods, high-quality

nutrition and health care, police and private security protection, and an extensive array of other goods and services. In contrast, persons with low- and poverty-level incomes tend to have limited access to these resources. Resources are anything valued in a society, ranging from money and property to medical care and education; they are considered to be scarce because of their unequal distribution among social categories. If we think about the valued resources available in Canada, for example, the differences in life chances are readily apparent. Our life chances are intertwined with our class, race, gender, and age.

All societies distinguish among people by age. Young children typically have less authority and responsibility than older persons. Older persons, especially those without wealth or power, may find themselves at the bottom of the social hierarchy. Similarly, all societies differentiate between females and males: Women are often treated as subordinate to men. From society to society, people are treated differently as a result of their religion, race/ethnicity, appearance, physical strength, disabilities, or other distinguishing characteristics. All of these differentiations result in inequality. However, systems of stratification are also linked to the specific economic and social structure of a society and to a nation's position in the system of global stratification, which is so significant for understanding social inequality that we will devote Chapter 8 to this topic.

SYSTEMS OF STRATIFICATION

Around the globe, one of the most important characteristics of systems of stratification is their degree of flexibility. Sociologists distinguish among such systems based on the extent to which they are open or closed. In an *open system,* the boundaries between levels in the hierarchies are more flexible and may be influenced (positively or negatively) by people's achieved statuses. Open systems are assumed to have some degree of social mobility. **Social mobility is the movement of individuals or groups from one level in a stratification system to another** (Rothman, 2001). This movement can be either upward or downward. *Intergenerational mobility* **is the social movement experienced by family members from one generation to the next.** By contrast, *intragenerational mobility* **is the social movement of individuals within their own lifetime.** Both intragenerational mobility and intergenerational mobility may be downward as well as upward. In a *closed system,* the boundaries between levels in the hierarchies of social stratification are rigid, and people's positions are set by ascribed status.

Open and closed systems are ideal-type constructs; no actual stratification system is completely open or closed. The systems of stratification that we will examine—slavery, caste, and class—are characterized by different hierarchical structures and varying degrees of mobility.

Slavery

Slavery is an extreme form of stratification in which some people are owned by others. It is a closed system in which people designated as "slaves" are treated as property and have little or no control over their lives. According to some social analysts,

throughout recorded history only five societies have been slave societies—those in which the social and economic impact of slavery was extensive: ancient Greece, the Roman Empire, the United States, the Caribbean, and Brazil (Finley, 1980). Others suggest that slavery also existed in the Americas prior to European settlement, and throughout Africa and Asia (Engerman, 1995).

Many Canadians are not aware of the legacy of slavery in our own country. Beginning in the 1600s, slaves were forcibly imported to both Canada and the United States as a source of cheap labour. Slavery existed in Quebec, New Brunswick, Nova Scotia, and Ontario until the early nineteenth century. (Satzewich, 1998) As practised in North America, slavery had four primary characteristics: (1) it was for life and was inherited (children of slaves were considered to be slaves); (2) slaves were considered property, not human beings; (3) slaves were denied rights; and (4) coercion was used to keep slaves "in their place" (Noel, 1972).

The Caste System

Like slavery, caste is a closed system of social stratification. A *caste system* **is a system of social inequality in which people's status is permanently determined at birth based on their parents' ascribed characteristics.** Vestiges of caste systems exist in contemporary India and South Africa.

In India, caste is based in part on occupation; thus, families typically perform the same type of work from generation to generation. By contrast, the caste system of South Africa was based on racial classifications and the belief of white South Africans (Afrikaners) that they were morally superior to the black majority. Until the 1990s, the Afrikaners controlled the government, the police, and the military by enforcing *apartheid*—the separation of the races. Blacks were denied full citizenship and restricted to segregated hospitals, schools, residential neighbourhoods, and other facilities. Whites held almost all of the desirable jobs; blacks worked as manual labourers and servants.

In a caste system, marriage is endogamous, meaning that people are allowed to marry only within their own group. In India, parents traditionally select marriage partners for their children. In South Africa, interracial marriage was illegal until 1985.

Cultural beliefs and values sustain caste systems. Hinduism, the primary religion of India, reinforced the caste system by teaching that people should

Hulton Archive/Getty Images

© SuperStock

Arthur Tilley/Getty Images

Systems of stratification include slavery, caste, and class. As shown in these photos, the life chances of people living in each of these systems differ widely.

BOX 7.1 | SOCIOLOGY AND EVERYDAY LIFE

Answers to the Sociology Quiz on Wealth and Poverty Join In

1. **False.** Despite the House of Commons' unanimous decision to "eliminate child poverty among Canadian children by the year 2000," there is more child poverty now than there was then (Campaign 2000, 2006).

2. **False.** As a group, children have a higher rate of poverty than the elderly. Government programs such as Old Age Security are indexed to inflation, while many of the programs for the young have been scaled back or eliminated. However, many elderly individuals do live in poverty (Canadian Council on Social Development, 2009).

3. **False.** Women, not men, account for two out of three impoverished adults in Canada. Reasons for this include the lack of job opportunities for women, lower pay for women than men for comparable jobs, lack of affordable daycare for children, sexism in the workplace, and a number of other factors (Statistics Canada, 2006e)

4. **False.** Just over half of the children in low-income families lived in two-parent families. The average female lone parent is living close to $10, 000 below the poverty line (Campaign 2000, 2006).

5. **True.** Groups that are older, such as senior families, naturally tend to have more wealth since they have had more years to accumulate assets and pay off debt (Sauvé, 2007g).

6. **False.** The richest 10 percent of all households held 58 percent of all wealth. This has increased from their share of 52% of all wealth in 1984 (Morissette and Zhang, 2006).

7. **False.** In 2005 there were 1.1 million millionaires in Canada. This millionaire group represents approximately 9 percent of all households (Chawla, 2006).

8. **True.** While the average incomes of the poorest 10 percent of Canadian families have increased by 18 percent, the richest 10 percent of families saw average income increases of 46 percent in a 10-year period (Campaign 2000, 2006).

accept their fate in life and work hard as a moral duty. However, caste systems grow weaker as societies industrialize: The values reinforcing the system break down, and people start to focus on the types of skills needed for industrialization.

The Class System

The **class system is a type of stratification based on the ownership and control of resources and on the type of work people do** (Rothman, 2001). At least theoretically, a class system is more open than a caste system because the boundaries between classes are less distinct than the boundaries between castes. In a class system, status comes at least partly through achievement rather than entirely by ascription.

In class systems, people may become members of a class other than that of their parents through both intergenerational and intragenerational mobility, either upward or downward. *Horizontal mobility* occurs when people experience a gain or loss in position and/or income that does not produce a change in their place in the class structure. For example, a person may get a pay increase and a more prestigious title but still not move from one class to another. By contrast, movement up or down the class structure is *vertical mobility.*

Ascribed statuses such as race/ethnicity, gender, and religion also affect people's social mobility. Sometimes, the media portray upward social mobility as something that is easily achieved by a few lucky people regardless of their ascribed or achieved statuses. We will return to the ideals versus the realities of social mobility when we examine the Canadian class structure later in the chapter.

INEQUALITY IN CANADA

Throughout human history, people have argued about the distribution of scarce resources in society. Disagreements often concentrate on whether the share we get is a fair reward for our effort and hard work. Social analysts have recently pointed out that the old maxim "the rich get richer" continues to be valid in Canada. To understand how this happens, we must take a closer look at income and wealth inequality in this country.

Money is essential for acquiring goods and services. People without money cannot purchase food, shelter, clothing, legal services, education, nor the other things they need or desire. Money—in the form of both income and wealth—is unevenly distributed in Canada (see the Census Profile). Among the industrialized nations of North America and Europe, Canada has one of the worst records of income inequality, following only the United States and the United Kingdom (Picot and Myles, 2004).

Income Inequality

***Income* is the economic gain derived from wages, salaries, income transfers (e.g., governmental aid), and ownership of property** (Beeghley, 2000). Sociologist Dennis Gilbert (2003) compares the distribution of income to a national pie that has been cut into portions ranging from stingy to generous, for distribution among segments of the population. In 2007, the wealthiest 20 percent of households received approximately 70 percent of the total income "pie," while the poorest received only 4 percent of all income (Statistics Canada, 2009d). Analysts further report that incomes have remained remarkably stable over time. Using inflation-adjusted dollars, average family income was $52 756 in 1989, and by 2007 it increased only slightly, to $61 000 (Sauvé, 2008). However, a closer examination of the data reveals that focusing on the overall average family income tends to conceal wide variations between different segments of the populations and hides increasing

Census Profile   REGIONAL VARIATION IN ANNUAL FAMILY INCOME, 2005

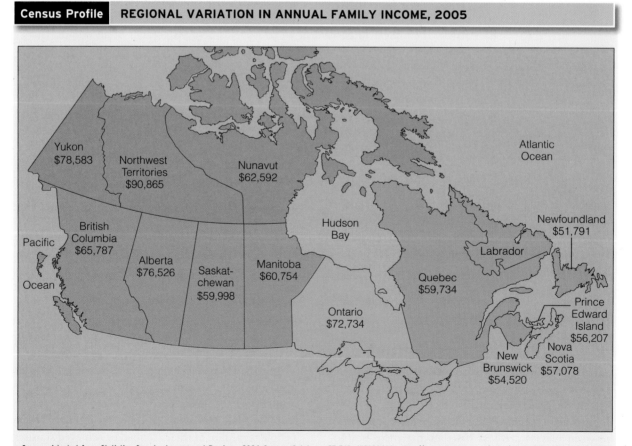

Source: Adapted from Statistics Canada, *Income and Earnings, 2006 Census*, Catalogue 97-563- XIE2006001, http://www.statcan.gc.ca/bsolc/olc-cel/olc-cel?catno=97-563-XIE2006001&lang=eng, Retrieved November 29, 2010.

inequities in the distribution of income in Canada. Overall, the average family income of the three lowest income groups has declined in the past decade, while that of the two highest income groups continues to increase (Sauvé, 2008; Statistics Canada, 2009d).

There is also considerable regional variation in income across the country. As shown in the Census Profile, family income is highest in the Northwest Territories, Yukon, Ontario, and Alberta, and lowest in the Atlantic provinces (Statistics Canada, 2008g). There is also significant income variation among particular racial/ethnic groups. For example, recent statistics indicate that 40 percent of visible minorities are in the low-income group, as compared to 20 percent of the general population. The data also clearly demonstrate the inequities in income distribution experienced by Aboriginal peoples in Canada, whose average income is less than two-thirds the average income of the general population (Henry and Tator, 2006).

People's life chances are enhanced by access to important societal resources, such as education. How will the life chances of students who have the opportunity to pursue a university degree differ from those of young people who do not have the chance to go to university?

Wealth Inequality

Wealth **includes property, such as buildings, land, farms, houses, factories, and cars, as well as other assets, such as money in bank accounts, corporate stocks, bonds, and insurance policies.** Wealth is computed by subtracting all debt obligations and converting the remaining assets into cash. The terms *wealth* and *net worth,* therefore, are used interchangeably. For most people in Canada, wealth is invested primarily in property that generates no income, such as a house or a car. In contrast, the wealth of an elite minority often is in the form of income-producing property.

Research on the distribution of wealth in Canada reveals that wealth is more unevenly distributed among the Canadian population than is income. Although the term *wealthy,* like the term *poor,* is a relative one, analysts generally define the wealthy as those whose total assets after debt payments are more than $250 000. Now 1.1 million households can claim millionaire status because their net worth is at least one million dollars. (Chawla, 2008).

Most of the wealthiest people in Canada are inheritors, with some at least three or four generations removed from the original fortune. As shown in Table 7.1 on page 164, the combined wealth of Canada's richest families, totals approximately $68 billion (Heaven, 2010). Clearly, a limited number of people own or control a very large portion of the wealth in Canada.

A recent survey of wealth concluded that there is "gross and persistent inequality in the distribution of wealth in Canada. A surprisingly small number of Canadians have huge slices of the wealth pie, and a surprisingly large number of Canadians have no more than a few crumbs" (Kerstetter, 2002:6).

Whether we consider distribution of income or wealth, though, it is relatively clear that social inequality is a real, consistent, and enduring feature of life in Canadian society.

CLASSICAL PERSPECTIVES ON SOCIAL CLASS

Early sociologists grappled with the definition of class and the criteria for determining people's location within the class structure. Both Karl Marx and Max Weber viewed class as an important determinant

Table 7.1	WEALTHIEST CANADIANS, 2010	
NAME		**WEALTH ($ BILLION)**
David Thomson		19.5
Galen Weston & Family		7.4
James (J.R.), Arthur, and John (Jack) Irving		4.1
James (Jimmy) Pattison		4.1
Paul Desmarais Sr.		4
Bernard (Barry) Sherman		3.9
David Azrieli & family		2.6
Robert Miller		2.6
Guy Laliberte		2.6
Emanuele (Lino) Saputo		2.5

Source: Heaven, 2010.

of social inequality and social change, and their works have had a profound influence on contemporary class theory.

Karl Marx: Relation to Means of Production

According to Karl Marx, class position is determined by people's work situation, or relationship to the means of production. As previously discussed, Marx suggested that capitalistic societies comprise two classes—the capitalists and the workers. The *capitalist class*, or *bourgeoisie,* **consists of those who own the means of production**—the land and capital necessary for factories and mines, for example. The *working class,* or *proletariat,* **consists of those who must sell their labour to the owners in order to earn enough money to survive**.

According to Marx, class relationships involve inequality and exploitation. The workers are exploited as capitalists maximize their profits by paying workers less than the resale value of what they produce but do not own. This exploitation results in workers' *alienation*—**a feeling of powerlessness and estrangement from other people and oneself**. In Marx's view, alienation develops as workers manufacture goods that embody their creative talents, but the goods do not belong to them. Workers are also alienated from the work itself because they are forced to perform it in order to live. Because the workers' activities are not their own, they feel self-estrangement. Moreover, the workers are separated from others in the factory because they individually sell their labour power to the capitalists as a commodity.

In Marx's view, the capitalist class maintained its position at the top of the class structure by control of society's *superstructure,* which comprises the government, schools, churches, and other social institutions that produce and disseminate ideas perpetuating the existing system of exploitation. Marx predicted that the exploitation of workers by the capitalist class ultimately would lead to **class conflict—the struggle between the capitalist class and the working class.** According to Marx, when the workers realized that capitalists were the source of their oppression, they would overthrow the capitalists and their agents of social control, and this would lead to the end of capitalism. The workers would then take over the state and create a more egalitarian society.

Why has no workers' revolution occurred? According to Ralf Dahrendorf (1959), capitalism may have persisted because it has changed significantly since Marx's time. Individual capitalists no longer own and control factories and other means of production; today, ownership and control largely have been separated. For example, contemporary multinational corporations are owned by a multitude of stakeholders but run by paid officers and managers.

Marx had a number of important insights into capitalist societies. First, he recognized the economic basis of class systems (Gilbert, 2003). Second, he noted the relationship between people's location in the class structure and their values, beliefs, and behaviour. Finally, he acknowledged that classes may have opposing (rather than complementary) interests. For example, capitalists' best interests are served by a decrease in labour costs and other expenses and a corresponding increase in profit; workers' best interests are served by well-paid jobs, safe working conditions, and job security.

The Canadian Press/Moe Doiron

The attempt by workers to improve their place in the stratification system has led to numerous labour strikes. Here, Ontario public-sector workers fight with police in an attempt to move their protests to the provincial legislature.

Max Weber: Wealth, Prestige, and Power

Max Weber's analysis of class builds upon earlier theories of capitalism (particularly those of Marx). Living in the late 19th and early 20th centuries, Weber was in a unique position to see the transformation that occurred as individual, competitive, entrepreneurial capitalism went through the process of shifting to bureaucratic, industrial, corporate capitalism. As a result, Weber had more opportunity than Marx did to see how capitalism changed over time. Weber agreed with Marx's assertion that economic factors are important in understanding individual and group behaviour. However, he emphasized that no one factor (such as economic divisions between capitalists and workers) was sufficient for defining people's location within the class structure. For Weber, the access that people have to important societal resources (such as economic, social, and political power) is crucial in determining people's life chances. To highlight the importance of life chances for categories of people, Weber developed a multidimensional approach to social stratification that reflects the interplay among wealth, prestige, and power. In his analysis of these dimensions of class structure, Weber viewed the concept of "class" as an *ideal type* (which can be used to compare and contrast various societies), rather than as a specific category of "real" people (Bourdieu, 1984).

Weber placed people who have a similar level of wealth and income in the same class. For example, he identified a privileged commercial class of *entrepreneurs*—wealthy bankers, ship owners, professionals, and merchants who possess similar financial resources. He also described a class of *rentiers*—wealthy individuals who live off their investments and do not have to work. According to Weber, entrepreneurs and rentiers have much in common. Both are able to purchase expensive consumer items, control other people's opportunities to acquire wealth and property, and monopolize costly status privileges (such as education) that provide contacts and skills for their children.

Weber divided those who work for wages into two classes: the middle class and the working class. The middle class consists of white-collar workers, public officials, managers, and professionals. The working class consists of skilled, semiskilled, and unskilled workers.

The second dimension of Weber's system of social stratification is *prestige*—**the respect with which a person or status position is regarded by others.** Fame, respect, honour, and esteem are the most common forms of prestige. A person who has a high level of prestige is assumed to receive deferential and respectful treatment from others. Weber suggested that individuals who share a common level of social prestige belong to the same status group regardless of their level of wealth. They tend to socialize with one another, marry within their own group of social equals, spend their leisure time together, and safeguard their status by restricting outsiders' opportunities to join their ranks (Beeghley, 1996). Style of life, formal education, and occupation are often significant factors in establishing and maintaining prestige in industrial and post-industrial societies.

The other dimension of Weber's system is *power*—**the ability of people or groups to achieve**

their goals despite opposition from others. The powerful shape society in accordance with their own interests and direct the actions of others (Tumin, 1953). According to Weber, social power in modern societies is held by bureaucracies; individual power depends on a person's position within the bureaucracy. Weber suggested that the power of modern bureaucracies was so strong that even a workers' revolution (as predicted by Marx) would not lessen social inequality (Hurst, 1998).

Wealth, prestige, and power are separate continuums on which people can be ranked from high to low. As shown in Figure 7.1, individuals may be high in one dimension while being low in another. For example, people may be very wealthy but have little political power (e.g., a recluse who has inherited a large sum of money). They also may have prestige but not wealth (e.g., a university professor who receives teaching excellence awards but lives on a relatively low income). In Weber's multidimensional approach, people are ranked in all three dimensions. Sociologists often use the term *socioeconomic status* (SES) to refer to a combined measure that attempts to classify individuals, families, or households in terms of factors such as income, occupation, and education to determine class location.

What important insights does Weber provide in regard to social stratification and class? Weber's analysis of social stratification contributes to our understanding by emphasizing that people behave according to both their economic interests and their values. He also added to Marx's insights by developing a multidimensional explanation of the class structure and identifying additional classes.

POVERTY IN CANADA

When many people think about poverty, they think of people who are unemployed or on welfare. However, many hard-working people with full-time jobs live in poverty. Canada has no official definition of poverty, no official method of measuring poverty, and no official poverty line (Pohl, 2002). As a result, there is ongoing and contentious debate with respect to how prevalent and how serious the problem of poverty is in Canada. The most accepted and commonly used definition of poverty is Statistics Canada's before-tax *low-income cutoff*—the income level at which a family may be in "straitened circumstances" because it spends considerably more on the basic necessities of life (food, shelter, and

| Figure 7.1 | Weber's Multidimensional Approach to Social Stratification |

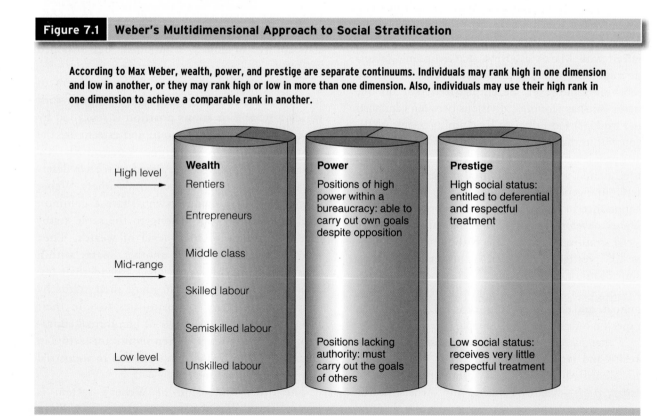

According to Max Weber, wealth, power, and prestige are separate continuums. Individuals may rank high in one dimension and low in another, or they may rank high or low in more than one dimension. Also, individuals may use their high rank in one dimension to achieve a comparable rank in another.

clothing) than the average family. According to this measure, any individual or family that spends more than 70 percent of its income on the necessities of life—food, clothing, and shelter—is considered to be living in poverty. There is no single cutoff line for all of Canada because living costs vary by family size and place of residence. When sociologists define poverty, they distinguish between absolute and relative poverty.

Absolute poverty **exists when people do not have the means to secure the most basic necessities of life**. Absolute poverty often has life-threatening consequences, such as when a homeless person freezes to death on a park bench. By comparison, *relative poverty* **exists when people may be able to afford basic necessities but are unable to maintain an average standard of living** (Lee, 2000). The relative approach is based on equality—that is, on some acknowledgment of the extent to which a society should tolerate or accept inequality in the distribution of income and wealth. This definition recognizes that someone who has so little that they stand out in relation to their community will feel poor (Canadian Council on Social Development, 1996).

Who Are the Poor?

Poverty in Canada is not randomly distributed, but rather is highly concentrated among certain groups of people—specifically, women, children, persons with disabilities, and Aboriginal peoples. When people belong to more than one of these categories, for example, Aboriginal children, their risk of poverty is even greater.

Age Today, children are at much greater risk of living in poverty than are older persons. Increased government transfer payments and an increase in the number of elderly individuals retiring with private pension plans has led to an decline in poverty among the elderly.

Recent statistics indicate that while the overall poverty rate is about 14 percent, the rate for children under age 18 is approximately 17 percent. More than

---

| BOX 7.2 | SOCIOLOGY IN GLOBAL PERSPECTIVE |

How Does Child Poverty in Canada Compare with Child Poverty in Other Nations?

The UNICEF report *Child Poverty in Rich Nations* ranks Canada a low 14 (see the figure on page 166) out of the 23 rich nations belonging to the Organisation for Economic Cooperation and Development (OECD).

The international rankings show that a nation's level of wealth does not predetermine its ability to prevent children from falling into poverty. Countries with higher economic growth do not necessarily have a lower poverty ranking. Many of the countries with the lowest poverty rates have relatively lower wealth rankings. The wealthiest nation, the United States, has the second-highest poverty ranking. The contention that child poverty can be addressed only through increased economic growth is contradicted by the available evidence.

UNICEF states that the difference between how countries are able to address child poverty with such varying degrees of success is related to how each chooses to set priorities according to its wealth.

Most of the nations that have been more successful than Canada at keeping low levels of child poverty are willing to counterbalance the effects of unemployment and low-paid work with substantial investments in family policies. The comprehensive approach to the well-being of children adopted by many European countries includes generous income security and unemployment benefits, national affordable housing programs, as well as widely accessible early childhood education and care.

The contrast of early childhood education and care services in Canada and in Europe is instructive. A recent OECD review of 12 nations found that early childhood education and care had experienced a "surge of policy attention" in Europe during the past decade. This has not been true in Canada. While the nations of Western Europe now provide universal full-day early childhood education and care for all three- to five-year-olds, Canada has not even begun to consider this. Yet there is widespread agreement, including among Canadian researchers, that early childhood education and care is a critical component of comprehensive family policy and of an effective anti-poverty strategy.

Source: Campaign 2000, 2002b; UNICEF Innocenti Research Centre, 2000.

1 million Canadian children are living in poverty and a large number of children hover just above the poverty line (Canadian Council on Social Development, 2009).

Despite the promise made by the House of Commons in 1989 to alleviate child poverty by the year 2000, the future for poor children does not look bright. These children are poor because their parents are, and one of the main reasons for poverty among adults is a lack of good jobs. Government cuts to unemployment-insurance benefits, employment programs, income supports, and social services for families and children will affect not only those who need these services but also the children of these individuals. See Box 7.2 on page 167 for a comparison of child poverty rates in Canada with other wealthy nations.

Gender   About two-thirds of all adults living in poverty in Canada are women. Women in all categories (married, divorced, widowed, and single) are at greater risk for poverty than men, but the risk is particularly significant for single-parent families headed by women (Naiman, 2008). As Figure 7.2 shows, in 2007 single parent families headed by women had a 45 percent poverty rate, compared with a rate

of 10 percent for two-parent families. Furthermore, women are among the poorest of the poor. Poor single mothers with children under 18 are the worst off, struggling on incomes more than $9 000 below the low-income cutoff (Campaign 2000, 2002a). Diana Pearce (1978) coined a term to describe this problem: the ***feminization of poverty* refers to the trend in which women are disproportionately represented among individuals living in poverty**. Women have a higher risk of being poor because they bear the major economic burden of raising children as single heads of households but earn only 70 cents for every dollar a male worker earns—a figure that has changed little over four decades. More women than men are unable to obtain regular, full-time, year-round employment, and the lack of adequate, affordable daycare exacerbates this problem (Schellenberg and Ross, 1997).

Does the feminization of poverty explain poverty in Canada today? Is poverty primarily a women's issue? On one hand, these questions highlight a genuine problem—the link between gender and poverty. On the other hand, several major problems exist with this argument. First, women's poverty is not a new phenomenon. Women have always been more susceptible

Figure 7.2   Poverty Rate by Family Type, 2007

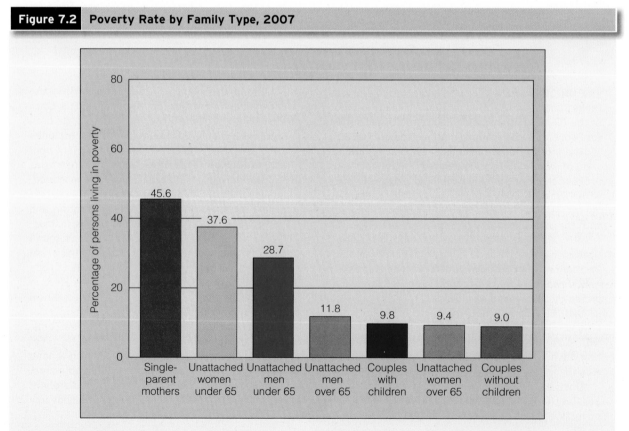

Source: Adapted from Canadian Council on Social Development, 2009

Child Poverty in Selected OECD Nations, 2007

This bar graph shows the percentage of children (0–17 years) in households with equivalent income less than 50 percent of the medium.

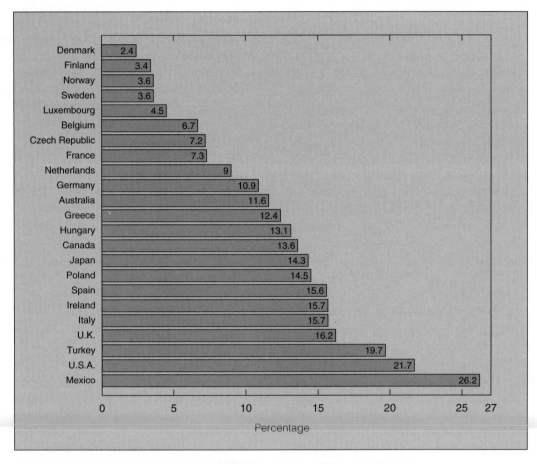

Nation	Percentage
Denmark	2.4
Finland	3.4
Norway	3.6
Sweden	3.6
Luxembourg	4.5
Belgium	6.7
Czech Republic	7.2
France	7.3
Netherlands	9
Germany	10.9
Australia	11.6
Greece	12.4
Hungary	13.1
Canada	13.6
Japan	14.3
Poland	14.5
Spain	15.6
Ireland	15.7
Italy	15.7
U.K.	16.2
Turkey	19.7
U.S.A.	21.7
Mexico	26.2

Source: Sourced from OECD publication *Starting Strong II Early Childhood Education and Care: 2006*. Reprinted with permission.

to poverty (see Katz, 1989). Second, all women are not equally susceptible to poverty. For example, some women experience what has been described as *event-driven poverty* as a result of marital separation, divorce, or widowhood (Bane, 1986). Third, event-driven poverty does not explain the realities of poverty for many visible-minority women, who instead may experience *reshuffled poverty*—a condition of deprivation that follows them regardless of their marital status or the type of family in which they live. Some women experience *multiple jeopardies,* a term that refers to the even greater risk of poverty experienced by women who are immigrants, visible minorities, or Aboriginal, or by women who have disabilities (Gerber, 1990).

Poverty is everyone's problem, not just women's. When women are impoverished, so are their children. Moreover, many of the poor in our society are men, especially the chronically unemployed, seniors, the homeless, people with disabilities, and men who are members of visible minorities. Many have spent their

The 'feminization of poverty' refers to the fact that two out of three impoverished adults in North America are women. Should we assume that poverty is primarily a women's issue? Why or why not?

adult lives without hope of finding work (Ross, Scott, and Smith, 2000).

Race and Ethnicity According to some stereotypes, most of the poor and virtually all welfare recipients are visible minorities. Such stereotypes are perpetuated, however, because a disproportionate percentage of the impoverished in Canada are Aboriginal peoples and recent immigrants. Aboriginal peoples in Canada are among the most severely disadvantaged persons. About one-half live below the low-income cutoff, and some live in conditions of extreme poverty. The average income for Aboriginal peoples is just over $15 000—$11 000 below the national average income of $26 000 (Gionet, 2009). According to a recent study, the quality of life for Aboriginal peoples living on reserves ranks worse than in countries such as Mexico and Thailand. For those Aboriginal peoples who live off reserves, the quality of life is slightly better (Tjepkema, 2002).

People with Disabilities Awareness that people with disabilities have been discriminated against in the job market has increased in recent years. As a result, they now constitute one of the recognized "target groups" in efforts to eliminate discrimination in the workplace and have more opportunities to work than they had a decade ago. However, although over 50 percent of people with disabilities are now in the labour force, many continue to be excluded, not because of their disabilities, but because of workplace environmental barriers (Galarneau and Radulescu, 2009). The effects of this systemic discrimination continue to be felt by people with disabilities as they are still, as a group, vulnerable to poverty. Adults with disabilities have significantly lower incomes than non-disabled Canadians. Recent estimates indicate that close to half of employed persons with disabilities had annual incomes below $10 000 (Canadian Council on Social Development, 2002). Once again, when gender and disability are combined, we find that women with disabilities are doubly disadvantaged (Galarneau and Radulescu, 2009).

Economic and Structural Sources of Poverty

Poverty has both economic and structural sources. The low wages paid for many jobs is the major cause:

half of all families living in poverty are headed by someone who is employed either full- or part-time (Naiman, 2008). In 1972, minimum-wage legislation meant that a worker who worked 40 hours a week, 52 weeks a year could earn a yearly income that was 20 percent over the poverty line. By today's standards, the same worker would have to earn more than $10 per hour simply to reach the low-income cutoff. Minimum wages across Canada range from $8.00 per hour to a high of $10.25 per hour. In other words, a person with full-time employment in a minimum-wage job cannot keep a family of four above the low-income cutoff.

Structural problems contribute to both unemployment and underemployment. Today, a rapid world wide transformation is changing our society's technological base from being industrially based to being "informationally" based. Automation in the industrial heartland of Quebec and Ontario has made the skills and training of thousands of workers obsolete. Many of these workers have become unemployable and poor. Corporations have been deinvesting in Canada, and millions of people have lost their jobs as a result. Economists refer to this displacement as the *deindustrialization* of North America (Bluestone and Harrison, 1982). Even as they have closed their Canadian factories and plants, many corporations have opened new facilities in other countries, where cheap labour exists because people of necessity will work for lower wages. ***Job deskilling*—a reduction in the proficiency needed to perform a specific job that leads to a corresponding reduction in the wages paid for that job**—has resulted from the introduction of computers and other technology (Hodson and Parker, 1988). The shift from manufacturing to service occupations has resulted in the loss of higher-paying positions and their replacement with lower-paying and less secure positions that do not offer the wages, job stability, or advancement potential of the disappearing manufacturing jobs. Consequently, there are simply not enough good jobs available in Canada to enable families to lift themselves out of poverty. In addition, the lack of affordable high-quality daycare for women who need to earn an income means that many jobs are inaccessible, especially to women who are single parents. The problems of unemployment, underemployment, and poverty-level wages are even greater for visible minorities and young people (Canadian Council on Social Development, 2009).

CONSEQUENCES OF INEQUALITY

Income and wealth are not simply statistics; they are intricately related to our individual life chances. People with a high income or substantial wealth have more control over their lives. They have greater access to goods and services; they can afford better housing, more education, and a wider range of medical services. Similarly, those with greater access to economic resources fare better when dealing with the criminal-justice system. People with less income, especially those living in poverty, must spend their limited resources to acquire the basic necessities of life.

Physical and Mental Health and Nutrition

People who are wealthy and well educated and who have high-paying jobs are far more likely to be healthy than are poor people. As people's economic status increases, so does their health status. The poor have shorter life expectancies and are at greater risk for chronic illnesses such as diabetes, heart disease, and cancer, as well as for infectious diseases such as tuberculosis.

A recent report by Professor Dennis Raphael at York University concluded that the economic and social conditions under which Canadians live their lives are greater determinants of whether they develop heart disease than medical and lifestyle factors (such as poor diet, lack of activity, and smoking). If all Canadians had the cardiovascular health of the wealthiest Canadians, there would be approximately 6000 fewer deaths a year from heart disease. According to Raphael's (2001) report, the economic and social conditions that most contribute to heart disease are poverty and low income. Specifically, poverty and low income lead to heart disease in three ways:

1. People on low incomes live under conditions of material deprivation that produce a cardiovascular heart burden that accumulates over the life span.
2. Living on low incomes creates excessive stress that damages the cardiovascular system.
3. The stressful conditions associated with having a low income lead to unhealthy behaviours such as smoking.

Children born into poor families are at much greater risk of dying during their first year of life. Some die from disease, accidents, or violence. Others are unable to survive because they are born with low birth weight, a condition linked to birth defects and increased probability of infant mortality (Canadian Institute of Child Health, 1994; Health Canada, 1997). Low birth weight in infants is attributed, at least in part, to the inadequate nutrition received by many low-income pregnant women. Most of the poor do not receive preventive medical and dental checkups; many do not receive adequate medical care after they experience illness or injury. Furthermore, many high-poverty areas lack an adequate supply of doctors and medical facilities. The higher death rates among Aboriginal peoples in Canada are partly attributable to unequal access to medical care and nutrition.

Although the precise relationship between class and health is not known, analysts suggest that people with higher income and wealth tend to smoke less, exercise more, maintain a healthy body weight, and eat more nutritious meals than poorer people. As a category, affluent people also tend to be less depressed and face less psychological stress, conditions that tend to be directly proportional to income, education, and job status (Ross and Roberts, 1997). Good health is basic to good life chances, and adequate amounts of nutritious food are essential for good health. Hunger is related to class position and income inequality. After spending 60 percent of their income on housing, low-income families are often unable to provide enough food for their children. Consider the following comments by a mother on her attempts to manage her food budget:

> I remember opening up the fridge just to see what was in there. There was a green pepper, an onion in the drawer and a bag of frozen rhubarb in the freezer, and that was all the food we had in the entire house. We used to eat peanut butter by the spoonful, if we had any peanut butter. We used to make rhubarb soup. And we'd throw in whatever we could find. (Canadian Council on Social Development, 1996:21)

A report of the Canadian Association of Food Banks (2009) shows that twice as many people go to food banks now than in 1989. Close to 800 000 Canadians now rely on food banks each month to make ends meet. This increase clearly indicates that many Canadians are unable meet their nutritional needs.

Education

Educational opportunities and life chances are directly linked. Some functionalist theorists view education as the "elevator" to social mobility. Improvements in the educational achievement levels (measured in number of years of schooling completed) of the poor, visible minorities, and women have been cited as evidence that students' abilities now are more important than their class, race, or gender. From this perspective, inequality in education is declining, and students have an opportunity to achieve upward mobility through achievements at school. Functionalists generally see the education system as flexible, allowing most students the opportunity to attend university if they apply themselves (Ballantine, 2001).

In contrast, most conflict theorists stress that schools are agencies for reproducing the capitalist class system and perpetuating inequality in society From this perspective, education perpetuates poverty. Parents with limited income are not able to provide the same educational opportunities for their children as are families with greater financial resources. Today, greater disparities exist in the distribution of educational resources. Because funding for education comes primarily from local property taxes, school districts in wealthy communities generally have newer buildings and state-of-the-art equipment. By contrast, schools in poorer areas have a limited funding base. Poverty exacts such a toll that many young people will not have the opportunity to finish high school, much less enter university, which subsequently affects job prospects, employment patterns, and potential earnings.

SOCIOLOGICAL EXPLANATIONS OF SOCIAL INEQUALITY

Obviously, some people are disadvantaged as a result of social inequality, but is inequality always harmful to society? See Table 7.2 for an overview of the different theoretical explanations of social inequality.

Functionalist Perspectives

According to Kingley Davis and Wilbert Moore (1945), inequality is not only inevitable but also necessary for the smooth functioning of society. **The *Davis-Moore thesis*, which has become the definitive functionalist explanation for social inequality**, can be summarized as follows:

1. All societies have important tasks that must be accomplished and certain positions that must be filled.
2. Some positions are more important for the survival of society than others.
3. The most important positions must be filled by the most qualified people.
4. The positions that are the most important for society and that require scarce talent, extensive training, or both, must be the most highly rewarded.
5. The most highly rewarded positions should be those that are functionally unique (no other position can perform the same function) and on which other positions rely for expertise, direction, or financing.

Table 7.2	SOCIOLOGICAL EXPLANATION OF SOCIAL INEQUALITY
PERSPECTIVE	**KEY ELEMENTS**
Functionalist	Inequality is necessary for the smooth functioning of society. Social stratification leads to meritocracy: a hierarchy in which all positions are rewarded based on ability and credentials.
Conflict	Dominant groups maintain and control the distribution of rewards, resources, privileges, and opportunities at the expense of others. Marxist conflict theorists explain that growing inequality is a result of the surplus value, profit that is generated when the cost of labour is less than the cost of the goods and services being produced.
Symbolic Interactionist	Focus is on the microlevel effects of wealth and poverty on people's social interactions. For example, in its various forms deference confirms inequality between individuals in differing social-class positions.
Feminist	Class and gender reinforce one another and create inequalities and oppressions for women "within" different social classes.

Davis and Moore use the physician as an example of a functionally unique position. Doctors are important to society and require extensive training, but individuals would not be motivated to go through years of costly and stressful medical training without incentives to do so. The Davis-Moore thesis assumes that social stratification results in **meritocracy— a hierarchy in which all positions are rewarded based on people's ability and credentials**.

Critics have suggested that the Davis-Moore thesis ignores inequalities based on inherited wealth and intergenerational family status (Rossides, 1986). The thesis assumes that economic rewards and prestige are the only effective motivators for people and fails to take into account other intrinsic aspects of work, such as self-fulfillment (Tumin, 1953). It also does not adequately explain how such a reward system guarantees that the most qualified people will gain access to the most highly rewarded positions.

Conflict Perspectives

From a conflict perspective, people with economic and political power are able to shape and distribute the rewards, resources, privileges, and opportunities in society for their own benefit. Conflict theorists do not believe that inequality serves as a motivating force for people; they argue that powerful individuals and groups use ideology to maintain their favoured positions at the expense of others. Core values in Canada emphasize the importance of material possessions, hard work, individual initiative to get ahead, and behaviour that supports the existing social structure. These same values support the prevailing resource-distribution system and contribute to social inequality.

Conflict theorists note that laws and informal social norms also support inequality in Canada. For the first half of the 20th century, for example, both legalized and institutionalized segregation and discrimination reinforced employment discrimination and produced higher levels of economic inequality. Although laws have been passed to make these overt acts of discrimination illegal, many forms of discrimination still exist in educational and employment opportunities.

Feminist Perspectives

According to feminist scholars, the quality of individuals' life experiences is a reflection of both their class position and their gender. Feminist analysis examines the secondary forms of inequality and oppression occurring *within* each class that have been overlooked by the classical theorists. Feminist theorists focus on the combined effect that gender has on class inequality. Some feminist scholars view class and gender as reinforcing one another, creating groups that are "doubly oppressed." This combined effect of one's class and gender may result in exploitation in the workplace or the home, or both. Subsequently, feminist authors have identified such terms as the "double ghetto" (Armstrong and Armstrong, 1994), the "double shift," or the "second shift" (Hochschild, 1989) to describe women's experiences in the segregated workforce or the home (see Chapters 11 and 15). Rather than male and female spouses maintaining similar class positions within a family unit, women hold a subordinate position. A feminist perspective emphasizes that within any class, women are less advantaged than men in their access to material goods, power, status, and possibilities for self-actualization. The causes of the inequality lie in the organization of capitalism itself (Ritzer, 1996:321) For example, upper-class women are wealthy but often remain secondary to their husbands in terms of power. Middle-class women may be financially well off, but often lack property or labour force experience and are vulnerable to financial instability in cases of divorce or separation. The position of working-class women varies based on their participation in the paid labour force.

Typically the working-class woman has little income, primary responsibility for the household work, and an inferior position in terms of power and independence to her husband. As a result, the female spouse may become "the slave of a slave" (Mackinnon, 1982:8), allowing the working-class male to compensate for his lower-class position in society. The family is viewed as an institution that supports capitalism and encourages or exacerbates the exploitation of women.

Symbolic Interactionist Perspectives

Symbolic interactionists focus on microlevel concerns and usually do not analyze larger structural factors that contribute to inequality and poverty. However, many significant insights on the effects of wealth and poverty on people's lives and social interactions can be derived from applying a symbolic interactionist approach. Using qualitative research methods and being influenced by a symbolic interactionist approach, researchers have collected the personal narratives of people across all social classes, ranging from the wealthiest to the poorest people.

A few studies provide rare insights into the social interactions between people from vastly divergent classes. Judith Rollins's (1985) study of the relationship between household workers and their employers is one example. Based on in-depth interviews and participant observation, Rollins examined rituals of deference that were often demanded by elite white women of their domestic workers, who were frequently women of colour. According to Erving Goffman (1967), *deference* is a type of ceremonial activity that functions as a symbolic means whereby appreciation is regularly conveyed to a recipient. In fact, deferential behaviour between nonequals (such as employers and employees) confirms the inequality of the relationship and each party's position in the relationship relative to the other. Rollins identified three types of linguistic deference between domestic workers and their employees; use of the first names of the workers, contrasted with the titles and last names (e.g., "Mrs. Adams") of the employers; use of the term *girls* to refer to household workers regardless of their age; and deferential references to employers, such as "Yes, ma'am." Spatial demeanour, including touching and how close one stands to another, is an additional factor in deference rituals across class lines.

What could you learn about class-based inequality in Canada by using a symbolic interactionist approach to examine a setting with which you are familiar?

SOCIAL STRATIFICATION IN THE FUTURE

Will social inequality in Canada increase in the future? Many social scientists predict that existing trends point to an increase. First, the purchasing power of the dollar has stagnated or declined since the early 1970s. As families started to lose ground financially, more family members (especially women) entered the labour force in an attempt to support themselves and their families (Gilbert, 2003). Economist Robert Reich (1993:145) has noted that the employed have been travelling on two escalators—one going up and the other going down—in recent years. The gap between the earnings of workers and the income of managers and top executives has widened. Second, wealth continues to become more concentrated at the top of the Canadian class structure. As the rich have grown richer, more people have found themselves among the ranks of the poor. Third, federal tax laws in recent years have benefited corporations and wealthy families at the expense of middle- and lower-income families. Finally, structural sources of upward mobility are shrinking while the rate of downward mobility has increased.

Are we sabotaging our future if we do not work constructively to eliminate poverty? It has been said that a chain is no stronger than its weakest link. If we apply this idea to the problem of poverty, it is to our advantage to see that those who cannot find work or do not have a job that provides a living wage receive adequate training and employment. Children of today—the adults of tomorrow—need education, health care, and nutrition as they grow up.

Canada's response to poverty has been contradictory. One would expect that in working toward eliminating poverty, action would be taken to address the structural causes of poverty: high unemployment and an inadequate set of child and family social policies. Instead, the federal government has cut federal social supports (such as subsidized daycare, unemployment benefits, and family allowance), leaving families to bear the burden of poverty.

As Greg deGroot-Maggetti, a socioeconomic-policy analyst for Citizens for Public Justice, so poignantly concludes in his report *A Measure of Poverty in Canada* (2002:16):

> Ultimately, the discussion of poverty lines reflects the values we hold for our society. Do we value a society in which all people possess the means to participate fully in the life of their communities? Are we comfortable with having large differences in income levels? Are we willing to accept increasing reliance on emergency food and shelter by a growing proportion of the population? What social outcomes do we value—do they include improved prospects for long-term health? The measure of poverty we choose can serve as an indicator of how close or far we are as a society from meeting objectives. However, it does not provide a road map for reaching those objectives. That remains a challenge to all levels of society— from businesses and households, to local communities, municipalities, and provincial and federal governments.

How does income differ from wealth?

Whereas income is the economic gain derived from wages, salaries, income transfers (governmental aid), and ownership of property, wealth is the value of all of a person's or family's economic assets, including income, personal property, and income-producing property.

How did classical sociologists Karl Marx and Max Weber view social class?

Marx and Weber acknowledged social class as a key determinant of social inequality and social change. For Marx, people's relationship to the means of production determines their class position. Weber developed a multidimensional concept of stratification that focuses on the interplay of wealth, prestige, and power.

How do sociologists define poverty?

Sociologists distinguish between absolute poverty and relative poverty. Absolute poverty exists when people do not have the means to secure the basic necessities of life. Relative poverty exists when people may be able to afford basic necessities but still are unable to maintain an average standard of living.

Who are the poor in Canada?

Age, gender, race, ethnicity, and disability tend to be factors in poverty. Children have a greater risk of being poor than do the elderly, while women have a higher rate of poverty than do men. Although whites account for approximately two-thirds of those below the low-income cutoff, Aboriginal peoples and visible minorities each account for a share of the impoverished in Canada that is disproportionate to their numbers.

What are some of the consequences of inequality in Canada?

The stratification of society into different social groups results in wide discrepancies in income and wealth and in variable access to available goods and services. People with high incomes or wealth have greater opportunity to control their own lives. People with lower incomes have fewer life chances and must spend their limited resources to acquire basic necessities.

What is the functionalist view of social inequality?

According to the Davis-Moore thesis, stratification exists in all societies, and some inequality is not only inevitable but also necessary for the ongoing functioning of society. The positions that are most important within society and that require the most talent and training must be highly rewarded.

What is the conflict view of social inequality?

Conflict perspectives on the Canadian class structure are based on the assumption that social stratification is created and maintained by one group in order to enhance and protect its own economic interests. Conflict theorists measure class according to people's relationships with others in the production process.

KEY TERMS

absolute poverty 167
alienation 164
bourgeoisie 164
capitalist class 164
caste system 159
class conflict 164
class system 161
Davis-Moore thesis 172
feminization of poverty 168
income 162
intergenerational mobility 159
intragenerational mobility 159
job deskilling 170
life chances 158
low-income cutoff 166
meritocracy 173
power 165
prestige 165
proletariat 164
relative poverty 167
slavery 159
social mobility 159
social stratification 158
socioeconomic status (SES) 166
wealth 163
working class 164

WEB LINKS

For more Web links related to the topic of this chapter, see the Nelson sociology website:
www.sociologyessentials5e.nelson.com

The Canadian Council on Social Development is one of the leading organizations speaking for Canada's poor:
www.ccsd.ca

Campaign 2000 produces an annual report card on the fight to end child and family poverty. The reports can be found at:

http://www.campaign2000.ca/reportcards. html

QUESTIONS FOR CRITICAL THINKING

1. Based on the functionalist model of class structure, what is the class location of each of your 10 closest friends or acquaintances? What is their location in relation to yours? To one another? What does their location tell you about friendship and social class?
2. Should employment be based on merit, need, or employment-equity policies?
3. If the gap between rich and poor continues to widen, what might happen in Canada in the future?

ONLINE STUDY AND RESEARCH TOOLS

INFOTRAC®

InfoTrac College Edition is included free with every new copy of this text. Explore this online library for additional readings, review, and a handy resource for assignments. Visit **www.infotrac-college.com** to access this online database of full-text articles. Enter the key terms from this chapter to start your search.

CENGAGENOW™ CENGAGENOW

Use CengageNOW™ to help you formulate a customized study plan for this chapter. After you take the Diagnostic Quiz, CengageNOW™ will generate a customized study plan for you. It will identify sections of the chapter you should review.

Global Stratification

This is an excerpt from a letter a mother in the Philippines wrote to her daughters explaining her commitment to political activism:

> Today, both of you are in University. In less than five years, you will join the ranks of the 40–50 percent unemployed and underemployed Filipinos. If you are lucky and do find jobs, you will painfully experience the discrepancy between the daily cost of living at 354 pesos and the minimum wage pegged by the government at 150 pesos. I won't be surprised if you find yourselves in the 70 percent of the population considered below the poverty line and the 40 percent below the food threshold. Even now, that is what we see happening.
>
> I fear that very soon, even the environment will no longer be a dependable support system. What with biologically dead rivers, contaminated drinking water, and depleted marine resources because of the mine tailings spewed by mining companies, the likes of Marcopper and its Canadian partner, Placer Dome,

what with dry rice fields that have to be abandoned due to the lack of water for irrigation brought about by open pit mining operations of giant establishments. . . . What with 2/3 of the whole Cordillera region apportioned to Australian, American and Canadian mining companies [.]

This government has launched a grandiose plan it calls Philippines 2000. President Fidel Ramos. . . wants to take the Philippines down the road to NIC-hood [Newly Industrialized Country] by the year 2000. That is why our agricultural lands which 75 percent of our population was tilling have now been converted into industrial enclaves, called Regional Industrial Centers. Is it any wonder, then, that thousands of peasants have been displaced?

The road is long that leads to progress—too long in fact, that hope could easily be snuffed out. But this one thing I

can say, Mitzi May and Lily Joyce: I have not lost hope. This is why I have opted to leave you for a while—to join the many hopeful Filipinos who have put their lives on the line. And I will continue to put my life on the line for as long as this insensitive government rides roughshod on our people's God-given rights. (Sharon Ruiz-Duremdes, Anglican Church of Canada [personal communication])

You might be surprised to learn that of all the narratives that we used to open the 16 chapters in this book, this was the most difficult to find. The world's poorest people have little voice. Even researchers who study global stratification rarely let them tell their own stories. Books are full of statistics that describe nations that cannot feed their citizens and provide researchers' compassionate descriptions of the lives of people living at the margins of survival. However, the poor themselves remain faceless. If not for the haunting images of famine or civil war that we see on television news programs, or the occasional story about problems in low-income countries on the radio or in the newspaper, most of us would know nothing about the more than 1 billion people who live in abject poverty. They are also invisible to the global corporations and the international organizations whose decisions have life and death consequences for those at the bottom of the global stratification system.

Even the quotation we did select is not representative of the world's poor. The writer is educated, articulate, and a political activist. Although her country, the Philippines, is poor, it is far wealthier than many other nations. However, her letter does articulate many of the problems of people in poor countries, including unemployment, foreign control of resources, environmental degradation, economic restructuring, and political discontent.

In this chapter, we examine global stratification and inequality and discuss the perspectives that have been developed to explain this problem. It is often difficult to connect the lives of people living in poverty in distant countries to our own lives in one of the world's wealthiest countries. When television shows us thousands of people starving in Somalia or babies being treated for dehydration at aid stations in Darfur, it is sometimes hard to realize that the people we see are individual human beings just like us and our friends. The global stratification system determines who will live long, prosperous lives and who will live short, miserable lives, eking out a marginal existence in subsistence agriculture and subject to the vagaries of rain, floods, and political instability.

Why do these inequities persist? In this chapter, you will learn why the life prospects of billions of people remain dismal. When you read the explanations of global stratification, you should remember that these are not just dry, academic theories. Rather, these are the ideas shaping the way governments and international organizations such as the United Nations deal with the problem of global poverty. As you will see, decisions based on the wrong theories can be disastrous for the poor.

Before reading on, test your knowledge of global wealth and poverty by taking the quiz in Box 8.1 on page 181.

QUESTIONS AND ISSUES

Chapter Focus Question: What is global stratification, and how does it contribute to economic inequality?

How are global poverty and human development related?

What is modernization theory, and what are its stages?

How do conflict theorists explain patterns of global stratification?

What is world-systems theory?

How does the new system of global trade affect people in poor countries?

WEALTH AND POVERTY IN GLOBAL PERSPECTIVE

Global Stratification *Global stratification* **refers to the unequal distribution of wealth, power, and prestige on a global basis, resulting in people having vastly different lifestyles and life chances.** Just as Canada can be divided into classes, the world can be divided into unequal segments characterized by extreme differences in wealth and poverty. Gaps in social and economic inequality are even more pronounced in other countries than in Canada. *High-income countries* have highly industrialized economies; technologically advanced industrial, administrative, and service occupations; and relatively high levels of income. In contrast, *low-income countries* are undergoing the transformation from agrarian to industrial economies and have lower levels of per capita income. Within some nations, the poorest one-fifth of the population has an income that is only a small fraction of the country's overall per capita income. For example, in Brazil, less than 3 percent of total national income goes to the poorest one-fifth of the population (World Bank, 2003).

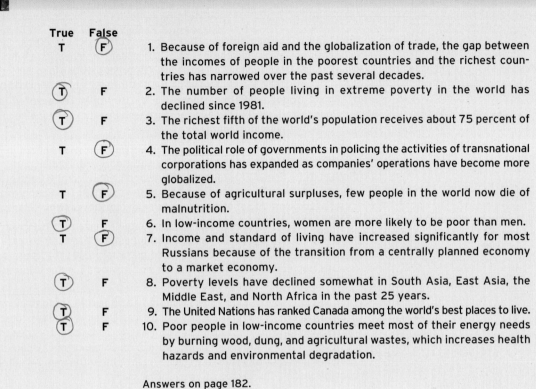

BOX 8.1 SOCIOLOGY AND EVERYDAY LIFE

How Much Do You Know about Global Wealth and Poverty?

True	False	
T	F	1. Because of foreign aid and the globalization of trade, the gap between the incomes of people in the poorest countries and the richest countries has narrowed over the past several decades.
T	F	2. The number of people living in extreme poverty in the world has declined since 1981.
T	F	3. The richest fifth of the world's population receives about 75 percent of the total world income.
T	F	4. The political role of governments in policing the activities of transnational corporations has expanded as companies' operations have become more globalized.
T	F	5. Because of agricultural surpluses, few people in the world now die of malnutrition.
T	F	6. In low-income countries, women are more likely to be poor than men.
T	F	7. Income and standard of living have increased significantly for most Russians because of the transition from a centrally planned economy to a market economy.
T	F	8. Poverty levels have declined somewhat in South Asia, East Asia, the Middle East, and North Africa in the past 25 years.
T	F	9. The United Nations has ranked Canada among the world's best places to live.
T	F	10. Poor people in low-income countries meet most of their energy needs by burning wood, dung, and agricultural wastes, which increases health hazards and environmental degradation.

Answers on page 182.

Where you are born has a huge influence on your life chances. A World Bank report (2006) contrasts the prospects of two children, Nthabiseng, born in a rural area of South Africa, and Sven, born in Sweden. The chance of Sven dying in his first year of life is only 0.3 percent, compared with the 7.2 percent risk faced by Nthabiseng. Sven will likely complete 11.4 years of schooling, while Nthabiseng will have less than one year of formal education. Sven will have access to clean water, good housing, proper food, and excellent medical care, while Nthabiseng may have none of these advantages. As a result, Sven will likely live to the age of 80, while Nthabiseng will likely die before she is 50.

Many people have tried to determine how to reduce world poverty. However progress has been slow despite a great deal of talk and billions of dollars in "foreign aid" flowing from high- to low-income nations. The notion of "development" has become the primary means used to try to reduce social and economic inequalities and to alleviate global poverty. Often, the nations that have been unable to reduce poverty are blamed for not establishing the necessary social and economic reforms to make change possible. However, as some analysts have suggested, the *problem* of inequality lies not in poverty, but in excess. "The problem of the world's poor," defined more accurately, turns out to be "the problem of the world's rich." This means that the solution to the problem is not a massive change in the culture of poverty so as to place it on the path of development, but a massive change in the culture of superfluity in order to place it on the path of counter-development. It does not call for a new value system forcing the world's majority to feel shame at their traditionally moderate consumption habits, but for a new value system forcing the world's rich to see the shame and vulgarity of their overconsumption habits, and the double vulgarity of standing on other people's shoulders to achieve those consumption habits. (Lummis, 1992:50)

The increasing interdependency of all the world's nations was largely overlooked until increasing emphasis was placed on the global marketplace and

BOX 8.1 | **SOCIOLOGY AND EVERYDAY LIFE**

Answers to the Sociology Quiz on Global Wealth and Poverty

J in

1. False. Since 1960, the gap between the incomes of the richest 20 percent of the world's population and the poorest 20 percent has been steadily growing. The ratio of the income of the top 20 percent of the population to that of the poorest 20 percent rose from 30:1 in 1960 to 74:1 in 2000 (United Nations Development Programme, 2001, 2003a). More recently, this trend has levelled off, largely because of increased incomes in China and India, the world's most populous countries.

2. True. The World Bank found that the percentage of the world's people living in absolute poverty has declined since the mid-1980s, particularly in Asia. Between 1981 and 2001, about 400 million people climbed out of extreme poverty (living on less than $1 per day). However, 1.1 billion people, or 21 percent, of the world's population remain below this level (World Bank, 2005a).

3. True. According the United Nations Development Programme, the richest one-fifth receive 75 percent of total world income, while the poorest one-fifth receive only 1.5 percent of world income. The poorest 40 percent of the world's population receive only 5 percent of world income (United Nations Development Programme, 2005:36).

4. False. As companies have globalized, governments have less control over their activities. Transnational corporations can easily sidestep restrictions imposed by individual governments. For example, if a country tries to impose environmental restrictions on a manufacturer, that company can just move production to another country that does not have the same environmental regulations.

5. False. Millions of people still die of malnutrition. For example, about 10 million children under five years of age die each year and about half these deaths are linked to malnutrition (United Nations Development Programme, 2005).

6. True. In almost all low-income countries (as well as most other countries), poverty is a greater problem for women due to sexual discrimination, resulting in a lack of educational and employment opportunities (United Nations Development Programme, 2005).

7. False. Not all Russians have shared equally in the transition to the market economy. Some have become billionaires while most of the population have seen their living standards decline.

8. True. These have been the primary regions in which poverty has decreased somewhat and infant mortality rates have fallen. Factors such as economic growth, oil production, foreign investment, and overall development have been credited with the decrease in poverty in East Asia, South Asia, the Middle East, and North Africa (United Nations Development Programme, 2005).

9. True. The latest Human Development Index rankings rate Canada as the fourth best country to live in after Iceland, Norway, and Australia (United Nations Development Program, 2008).

10. True. Poor people in low-income countries do meet most of their energy needs by burning wood, dung, and agricultural wastes. Although these fuels are inefficient and harmful to health, many low-income people have no other options (United Nations DPCSD, 1997).

Vast inequalities in income and lifestyle are shown in this photo of slums and nearby upper-class housing in Mumbai, India. Do similar patterns of economic inequality exist in other nations?

© Viviane Moos/CORBIS

the global economy. The linkage between consumption and global poverty is explored in more detail in Box 8.2 on page 184.

Inequality and Individuals

The disparity between rich and poor is highlighted by the difference between the wealth amassed by a few individuals and the poverty of the poorest nations. The income of the 500 wealthiest people in the world is greater than the 416 *million* poorest people (United Nations Development Programme, 2005:4). Only a small fraction of their incomes would be required each year to achieve reproductive health care for all women and basic education, basic medical care, and adequate food, water, and sanitation for all. According to the UN, in 1998 the wealth of the three richest people (Microsoft owner Bill Gates, investor Warren Buffett, and the oil-rich Sultan of Brunei) was greater than the gross domestic product of the 48 least-developed countries (United Nations Development Programme, 1998).

DEFINING GLOBAL INEQUALITY

During the past 50 years, major changes have occurred in the way inequality is defined by organizations such as the UN. Most definitions of *inequality* are based on comparisons of levels of economic development.

The Levels of Development Approach

Describing world poverty and global stratification has become quite controversial. Terminology based on levels of development includes concepts such as developed nations, developing nations, less-developed nations, and underdevelopment. Let's look at the contemporary origins of the idea of "underdevelopment" and "underdeveloped nations."

Following World War II, the concept of *underdeveloped nations* emerged out of the Marshall Plan, which provided massive sums of money in aid and loans to rebuild the European economic base destroyed during World War II. Given the Marshall Plan's success in rebuilding much of Europe, U.S. political leaders decided that Southern Hemisphere nations that had recently been released from European colonialism could also benefit from a massive financial infusion and rapid economic development. Leaders of the developed nations argued that problems such as poverty, disease, and famine could be reduced through the transfer of finance, technology, and experience from developed to less-developed countries. From this viewpoint, economic development is the primary way to solve the poverty problem. Hadn't economic growth brought the developed nations to their own high standard of living? Moreover, "self-sustained development" in a nation would require that people in the less-developed nations accept the beliefs and values of people in the developed nations, so the development movement had an explicitly political component.

BOX 8.2   SOCIOLOGY IN GLOBAL PERSPECTIVE

Consumption and Global Poverty

The annual United Nations *Human Development Report* has drawn attention to the need to eradicate poverty. One edition showed how consumption has affected global stratification. Excessive consumption in developed countries threatens the environment, depletes natural resources, and wastes money that might otherwise provide for the needs of the desperately poor in developing countries.

Global consumption is concentrated among the wealthy. The wealthiest 20 percent of the world's people account for 86 percent of private consumption (see the figure below), while the poorest 20 percent account for only 1.3 percent. While some argue that money now used to buy luxuries might be better spent on the world's poor, others claim that conspicuous consumption does buy happiness for those who can afford it. The limited evidence available does not support the view that consumption beyond basic needs necessarily makes people happier. According to the Human Development Report, the percentage of Americans who describe themselves as "happy" peaked in 1957, even though consumption has increased by several times since then. Unfortunately, as we spend more, we find more things to spend on. If we can keep up with the Joneses next door, we shift our horizons to the rich and famous, whose lifestyles we know about from the media. When American consumers were asked in 1986 how much they would need to earn annually to "fulfill all their dreams" the answer was US$50 000. By 1994, this had increased to US$102 000 (United Nations Development Programme, 1998). Theoretically, at least, our wants are limitless.

However, Nobel Prize–winning economist Daniel Kahneman found that above a minimal level, money doesn't bring happiness (Kahneman et al., 2006). What is important is *relative* income—how much you make compared with your peers. People may be pleased by a pay increase, but that pleasure passes when their peers also move ahead and when they get used to the new things that they buy. People may actually become *less* happy because the extra money may come at the cost of leisure time. Our society is focused on earning and spending more—even though this does not make us any happier—instead of helping the world's poor move out of life-threatening poverty.

Why has consumption become so important? Several changes have spurred our desire to consume more (Lock and Ikeda, 2005).

- First, the development of the department store made consumer goods much more available. Shopping in these stores, and later in shopping malls, became an important social activity.
- Second, the development of advertising and marketing encouraged what Veblen (1967) had called "conspicuous consumption." Conspicuous consumption fills not only basic needs such as food and shelter, but also symbolic needs for status and prestige. The young woman who told the *Winnipeg Free Press* Style section (2009: F9) that her fashion essential was "Shoes, mostly heels. I buy, like, two pairs a week" was not just protecting her feet from the elements.
- Third, consumer credit allowed people to spend money they did not have.
- Finally, consumption was encouraged by the idea of fashion. People feel that a pair of shoes or a suit still in good condition needs replacement because they are no longer fashionable, or that a functioning television set may be discarded because it is not a high-definition flat screen model.

Canadians spend $21 billion on clothing (Lin, 2003); much of this is spent keeping up with changes in style. Spending even a small part of this money on disease prevention or education rather than on fashion trends could keep hundreds of thousands of low-income people alive.

But aren't the needs so great that channelling some of the money we now spend on excessive consumption could have little impact on the lives of the world's poor? Surprisingly, the amount of money required to meet some basic human needs is not that great. *The Hindu*, an Indian newspaper, put these needs in perspective:

Consumers in Europe and the U.S. spend [US]$17 billion every year on pet foods. Yet, the world cannot find the additional [US]$13 billion that is needed every year to provide basic health services to all people in developing countries. Consumers in Europe and the U.S. annually spend [US]$12 billion on perfumes. This is the additional amount needed to meet the basic reproductive health needs of the women in developing countries. Consumers in Europe spend [US]$11 billion every year buying ice cream, which is more than the extra [US]$9 billion required to provide universal access to drinking water and sanitation in the developing countries. (*The Hindu*, 1998:25)

BOX 8.2 SOCIOLOGY IN GLOBAL PERSPECTIVE

Consumption and Global Poverty (Continued)

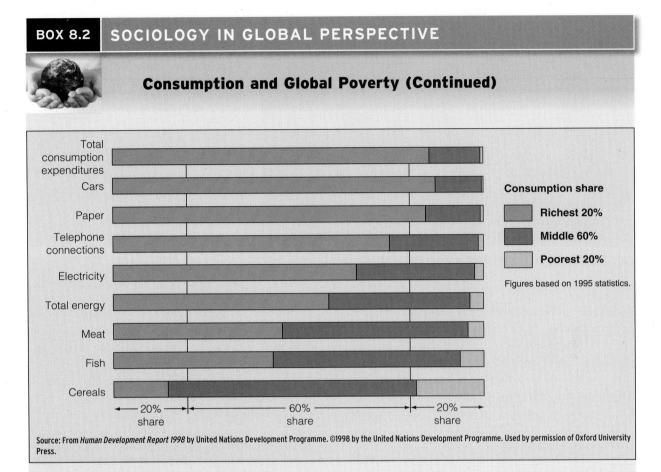

Consumption share

- Richest 20%
- Middle 60%
- Poorest 20%

Figures based on 1995 statistics.

Source: From *Human Development Report 1998* by United Nations Development Programme. ©1998 by the United Nations Development Programme. Used by permission of Oxford University Press.

Excessive consumption hurts the poor in another way. Rising consumption is harmful to the environment, and the poor are more vulnerable than the wealthy to environmental damage. Environmental degradation in countries where people depend on subsistence agriculture can mean malnutrition and starvation for huge numbers of people.

As we consume more, there is less for people in poor countries. Do you think we will ever have the political will to donate more of our surplus wealth to low-income countries?

Source: United Nations Development Programme, 1998; *The Hindu*, 1998.

Ideas regarding *underdevelopment* were popularized by U.S. President Harry S. Truman in his 1949 inaugural address. According to Truman, the nations in the Southern Hemisphere were "underdeveloped areas" because of their low *gross national income* (GNI)—a term that refers to all the goods and services produced in a country in a given year, plus the income earned outside the country by individuals or corporations. If nations could increase their GNI, then social and economic inequality within the country could also be reduced. Accordingly, Truman believed that it was necessary to help the people of economically underdeveloped areas to raise their *standard of living,* by which he meant material well-being that can be measured by the quality of goods and services that may be purchased by the per capita national income (Latouche, 1992).

After several decades of economic development fostered by organizations such as the UN and the World Bank, it became apparent by the 1970s that improving a country's GNI did *not* tend to reduce the poverty of the poorest people in that country. In fact, global poverty and inequality were increasing, and hopes of a speedy end to underdevelopment faded. Even in developing countries that had achieved economic growth, the gains were not shared by everyone. For example, the poorest 20 percent of the Brazilian population receives less than 3 percent of the total national income, whereas the richest 20 percent of the population receives more than 63 percent (World Bank, 2003).

Why did inequality increase even with greater economic development? Many attribute this to the actions of the industrialized countries. These actions

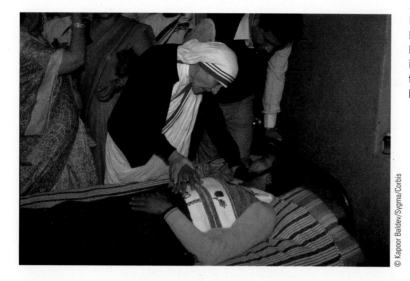

In 1997, people around the world were saddened by the death of Mother Teresa, who had dedicated her life to ministering to the poor and unfortunate in low-income nations, especially India. According to Mother Teresa, people who are not poor could learn much from the poor.

include the impact of foreign aid programs and debt-control policies, which will be discussed later in this chapter. Some analysts have also linked growing global inequality to relatively high rates of population growth taking place in the poorest nations. Organizations such as the UN and the World Health Organization stepped up their efforts to provide family-planning services to the populations so that they could control their own fertility.

CLASSIFICATION OF ECONOMIES BY INCOME

Another way of describing the global stratification system is simply to measure a country's per capita income. The World Bank (2008) classifies nations into four economic categories: *low-income economies* (a GNI per capita of US$935 or less), *lower-middle-income economies* (a GNI per capita between $936 and $3705), *upper-middle-income economies* (a GNI per capita between $3706 and $11 455), and *high-income economies* (a GNI per capita of $11 456 or more). See Map 8.1.

Low-Income Economies

About half of the world's population lives in the 49 low-income economies, where most people engage in agricultural pursuits, reside in nonurban areas, and are impoverished (World Bank, 2008). As shown in Map 8.1, low-income economies are found primarily in Asia and Africa. Included are nations such as Ethiopia, Nigeria, Cambodia, Afghanistan, and Bangladesh. Caribbean and Latin American nations with low-income economies include Haiti and Nicaragua.

Women and children are particularly affected by poverty in low-income economies. Many poor women worldwide do not have access to commercial credit and have been trained only in low-wage traditionally female skills. These factors have contributed to the *global feminization of poverty,* whereby women tend to be more impoverished than men (Durning, 1993). Despite some gains, the income gap between men and women continues to widen in many low-income, developing nations.

Middle-Income Economies

About one-third of the world's population resides in the 95 nations with middle-income economies, which can be divided into lower-middle and upper-middle income (World Bank, 2008). Countries classified as lower-middle income include the Latin American nations of Colombia, El Salvador, and Honduras. However, even though these countries are referred to as "middle income," more than half of the people residing in many of these countries live in poverty, defined as US$1.25 per day in purchasing power (World Bank, 2008).

Other lower-middle-income economies include Russia, Ukraine, and Romania. These countries had centrally planned (i.e., socialist) economies until dramatic political and economic changes occurred in the late 1980s and early 1990s. Since then, these nations have been going through transitions to market

| Map 8.1 | High-, Middle-, and Low-Income Economies in Global Perspective |

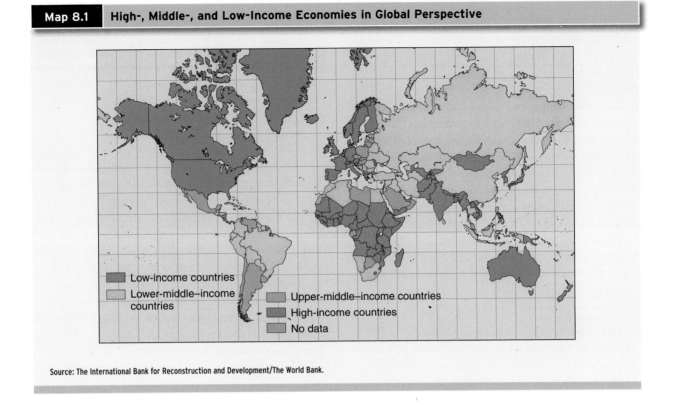

Low-income countries
Lower-middle–income countries
Upper-middle–income countries
High-income countries
No data

Source: The International Bank for Reconstruction and Development/The World Bank.

economies. Some nations have been more successful than others in making the change and achieving a higher standard of living. Several factors, including high rates of inflation, the growing gap between rich and poor, low life-expectancy rates, and homeless children show the problems in the transition toward a free-market economy in countries such as Russia.

Nations having upper-middle-income economies typically have a higher standard of living and export diverse goods and services, ranging from manufactured goods to raw materials and fuels. Upper-middle-income economies include Saudi Arabia, Chile, Hungary, and Mexico. Many of these countries have high levels of indebtedness, leaving them with few resources for economic development and fighting poverty.

High-Income Economies

There are 65 high-income nations, including Canada, the United States, Japan, and Germany (World Bank, 2008). High-income nations dominate the world economy.

The only significant group of middle- and lower-income economies to close the gap with the high-income economies over the past few decades have been the nations of East Asia. South Korea has been

reclassified from a middle-income to a high-income economy and other Asian countries, including China, have grown dramatically over the past two decades. Despite its recent economic growth, the East Asian region remains home to approximately 260 million poor people (United Nations Development Programme, 2004).

THE IMPACT OF DEBT AND FOREIGN AID

Debt and Global Stratification

The gap between rich and poor countries has grown over the past 50 years. The problem of debt has made it almost impossible for some countries to move out of poverty. Private banks, governments, and international organizations have lent more money to poor countries than these countries can repay. Much of the borrowed money was spent on military hardware and other nonproductive investments, rather than on building the productive capacity that would have helped development. Many countries were forced by the International Monetary Fund (IMF) and the

World Bank to restructure their economies by cutting back on social spending, devaluing their currencies, and reducing the funds spent on economic development. These governments have lost whatever power they once had to control their own economic destinies because they were forced to follow the demands of the lenders. This happened to most Latin American economies during the 1980s and to many East Asian and Eastern European economies during the late 1990s.

In many countries, this externally imposed structural adjustment has had disastrous consequences. Debt repayment takes money that could otherwise be used to provide social services and health care, and to expand the country's economic base. Debt repayment and economic restructuring have caused massive unemployment, reduced incomes, and soaring prices that have led to drastically reduced living standards, declines in investment, and political instability. The problem has been summarized by Michel Chossudovsky:

> The movement of the global economy is "regulated" by "a world wide process of debt collection" which constricts the institutions of the national state and contributes to destroying employment and economic activity. In the developing world, the burden of external debt has reached two trillion [U.S.] dollars: entire countries have been destabilized as a consequence of the collapse of national currencies, often resulting in the outbreak of social strife, ethnic conflicts and civil war [1997:15]. . . . Internal purchasing power has collapsed, famines have erupted, health clinics and schools have been closed down, hundreds of millions of children have been denied the right to a primary education. In several regions of the developing world, the reforms have been conducive to resurgence of infectious diseases including tuberculosis, malaria, and cholera. (1997:33)

Many countries, particularly in sub-Saharan Africa, have no chance of progressing economically unless the burden of debt repayment is eased by the debt-holding countries.

In 2005, the wealthy countries agreed to cancel US$40 billion in debt to allow some of the poor countries to spend money on education, agriculture, health care, and infrastructure that would otherwise have gone to interest payments. While this was a significant step, hundreds of billions of dollars in debt remain to be repaid and between 2005 and 2007 overall foreign aid declined from $107 billion to $104 billion largely because of a reduction in debt relief (United Nations, 2008). Also, some of the most indebted nations, including Nigeria, Sudan, and Congo, were not included in the deal because their governments were considered too corrupt, and the donor countries were concerned that the benefits of debt cancellation would go to a few powerful rulers rather than to the poorest citizens.

Foreign Aid and Global Stratification

We have all been moved by the plight of starving people in developing countries where droughts or floods have destroyed the annual harvest. Most of us support the emergency exports of food to these countries to prevent famine. However, some analysts have questioned whether this type of aid hurts more than it helps. For example, consider Somalia, one of the world's poorest and most politically

Jeff Robbins/AP/CP Picture Archive

Based on the assumption that economic development is the primary way to reduce poverty in low-income nations, the United Nations has funded projects such as this paper company in Nepal.

Many people around the world have protested globalization. This is part of a crowd marching in the streets of Toronto during G8 and G20 summits in 2010.

unstable countries. Although Somalia's troubles are commonly blamed on drought and clan rivalries, some analysts feel that economic restructuring and food aid are also causes (Chossudovsky, 1997). Because of droughts and other internal problems, food aid to Somalia increased dramatically from the mid-1970s to the mid-1980s. This donated food was sold into local markets very cheaply and undercut the price of locally grown food. At the same time, currency devaluation demanded by the International Monetary Fund made the cost of farm equipment and fuel more expensive. The financial restructuring and the lower food prices virtually destroyed Somalia's agricultural system. Although we normally think that a shortage of food is the cause of starvation, the global oversupply of grain may actually have contributed to famine by destroying the agricultural base of developing countries, making them vulnerable to future food shortages (Chossudovsky, 1997).

Foreign aid can damage low-income countries in other ways. First, aid can be tied to specific projects or objectives that meet the interests of the donor country more than the interests of the recipients. Military aid does little to help the poor and may do them great harm. Similarly, aid devoted to large infrastructure projects such as dams may cause more problems than it solves. Second, aid may be given to achieve political objectives. The Soviet Union provided aid to Cuba to maintain an ally just off the coast of the United States. The United States did the same thing in countries of strategic interest, including several Latin American countries. This aid is dependent on the low-income country's continuing political support for the donor country's

activities. This can severely limit the power of governments to make decisions based on their own national interests. Third, even when aid is targeted to individuals, it may not filter down to the poor. For example, donor countries may intend food aid to go to the poor, but elites may simply take the food, sell or trade it, and keep the proceeds.

Finally, there is not enough aid. According to the United Nations (2008), foreign-aid donations from the world's wealthiest countries declined from a high of $107 billion in 2005 to $104 billion in 2007 despite the enormous growth of their economies over that time. During the 1990s, Canada's foreign aid budget declined by about 20 percent. While aid has increased since then, Canada donated 0.3 percent of GDP in 2008 compared to the official target of 0.7 percent of GDP.

Not only is there not enough aid, but also the aid that is provided is often not spent effectively. However, there are signs of change. Many aid agencies have changed their focus away from large infrastructure programs such as dams and railroads to programs that focus directly on the poor. New ideas include using labour-intensive technologies and other strategies to create employment; providing basic social services such as health care, nutrition, and education; and giving assistance directly to the poorest people in low-income countries (Martinussen, 1997). Above all, the poor themselves must have a say in aid programs and should be empowered to make decisions about how aid money is spent. Otherwise, foreign aid can create more problems than it solves.

High-income countries need to change trade policies that are often devastating to the economies of poor countries and can negate the benefits of the aid that is provided. For example, in the mid-1990s Canada gave an average of $44 million per year in aid to Bangladesh. However, Canadian quotas (which have now been removed) that restricted the export of textiles from Bangladesh cost $36 for every $1 in aid that we provided (Oxfam, 2001). These quotas protected Canadian manufacturers from foreign competition, but they prevented low-income nations from building a viable economic base. Even worse, high-income countries often force poor countries to liberalize their own trade laws and then sell heavily subsidized products into the poor countries' internal markets. The United States seriously harmed Haiti's rice farmers by forcing Haiti to reduce its tariffs on imported rice and then selling Haiti huge quantities of subsidized American-grown rice. This depressed local prices and resulted in a 40 percent reduction in Haitian rice production (Oxfam, 2001). In 2002, the United States and the countries making up the European Union were spending more than $450 billion to subsidize their farmers, making it impossible for farmers in poor countries to compete (United Nations Development Programme, 2003). At the same time, the aid given by wealthy countries was only $75 billion. These policies need to be changed to achieve the goal of alleviating global poverty. However, as of 2010 negotiations conducted through the World Trade Organization had not convinced wealthy countries to lower their agricultural subsidies. Figure 8.1 illustrates the size of agricultural subsidies in the European Union, Japan, and the United States compared with the average income in sub-Saharan Africa and the aid given to these countries.

Despite these problems, some progress is being made in improving the lives of the world's poor. For many years, development programs such as the "structural adjustment" programs of the IMF and the World Bank had an economic focus. The assumption was that if economies could be turned around, other benefits would follow. Recently, work by the Nobel Prize–winning economist Amartya Sen has helped to create a philosophy of development that may be more effective. Sen believes that human development is a vital prerequisite of economic development (Sen,

1993; Anand and Sen, 2000). Building new roads and dams would not have any significant impact on development unless a country had the human capacity to take advantage of these infrastructure improvements. Sen drew attention to the role of people both as a source of development and as the beneficiaries of development.

Based on this work, the United Nations Development Programme established the Millennium Development Compact, which sets global development priorities to try to make aid and other development initiatives more effective. The compact sets out six policy clusters that will help to break the structural conditions that prevent growth (2003a:4):

1. Invest early and ambitiously in basic education and health while fostering gender equity. These are preconditions to sustained economic growth. Growth, in turn, can generate employment and raise incomes.
2. Increase the productivity of small farmers in unfavourable environments.
3. Improve basic infrastructure, such as ports, roads, power, and communications, to reduce the costs of doing business and overcome geographic barriers.
4. Develop an industrial development policy that nurtures entrepreneurial activity and helps diversify the economy away from dependence on commodity exports.
5. Promote democratic governance and human rights to remove discrimination, secure social justice, and promote well-being.
6. Ensure environmental sustainability and sound urban management so that development improvements are long term.

Because these clusters are based on evidence from successful development initiatives around the globe, living standards may improve if this work is supported by the global community.

A young Hong Kong woman wearing a dust mask sews in a garment sweatshop under poor conditions.

© Paul A. Saunders/Corbis

GLOBAL POVERTY AND HUMAN DEVELOPMENT ISSUES

Most of the early work on global stratification focused on incomes as a measure of well-being. However, income disparities are not the only factor that defines poverty and its effect on people. Work by economists such as Amartya Sen has led to a shift toward human welfare as a measure of development.

Figure 8.1 Cows and Cotton Receive More Aid than People, 2000

In order to protect their agricultural industries, high-income countries provide enormous subsidies to farmers and to large agricultural corporations. In the United States, the subsidy provided to cotton growers is greater than the cash value of the entire cotton crop. The amount provided in subsidies by high-income countries to their own farmers far exceeds the foreign aid donated to the low-income countries and can have devastating effects on countries that are heavily dependent upon the export of commodities.

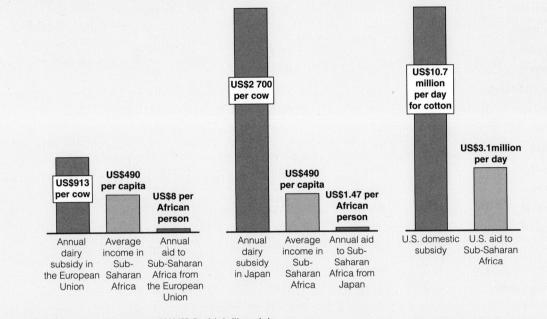

Source: United Nations Development Programme, 2003:155. Reprinted with permission.

In 1990, the United Nations Development Programme introduced the Human Development Index (HDI), establishing three new criteria—in addition to GNI—for measuring the level of development in a country: life expectancy, education, and living standards.

Table 8.1 shows the difference between Canada and several other countries on the HDI. While Canadians can be justifiably proud that they are close to the top of the Index, the picture is not all positive. The United Nations Development Programme also publishes a Human Poverty Index for industrial countries that measures the percentage of people not expected to survive to age 60, the percentage of the population that is functionally illiterate, the population below the poverty line, and the percentage of the labour force that has suffered long-term unemployment. Canada ranks only eighth on this index, because of a relatively high rate of functional illiteracy and a high proportion of the population with incomes below the poverty level. The UN has been critical of the quality of life among Canada's Aboriginal people, who rank far below other Canadians on the HDI.

Life Expectancy

Although some advances have been made regarding life expectancy, major problems remain. On the positive side, average life expectancy has increased by about a third in the past three decades and is now more than 70 years in 87 countries (United Nations Development Programme, 2003). However, the average life expectancy at birth in the 20 countries ranked highest on human development is about 80 years, compared with 49 years in the bottom 20 countries (United Nations Development Programme, 2008). Especially striking are the declines in life expectancies in sub-Saharan Africa, where estimated life expectancy has dropped in many countries, largely because of HIV/AIDS.

One cause of shorter life expectancy in low-income nations is the high rate of infant mortality. The infant-mortality rate is more than eight times higher in low-income countries than in high-income ones (World Bank, 2003). Low-income countries typically have higher rates of illness and

Table 8.1	HUMAN DEVELOPMENT INDEX

COUNTRY	RANK	INDEX	PER CAPITA GDP*
Iceland	1	.968	36,510
Norway	2	.968	41,420
Australia	3	.962	31,794
Canada	**4**	**.961**	**33, 375**
Ireland	**5**	**.959**	**38,505**
Sweden	6	.956	32,525
United States	12	.951	41,890
Mexico	52	.829	10,751
Russia	67	.802	10,845
Brazil	70	.800	8,402
Thailand	78	.781	8,677
China	81	.777	6,757
Turkey	84	.775	8,407
India	128	.619	3,452
Kenya	148	.521	1,240
Nigeria	158	.470	1,128
Sierra Leone	177	.336	806

*In comparing GDP, the *Human Development Report* uses purchasing power parities (PPP) in U.S. dollars. PPP is a measure that accounts for different levels of purchasing power within different countries.

Source: United Nations Development Programme, 2008.

disease, and they lack adequate health care facilities. Nearly 1 billion people suffer from chronic malnutrition, and over 9 million people die each year from hunger-related causes (World Food Program, 2009). About 10 million children under five years of age die each year, and about half these deaths are linked to malnutrition (United Nations Development Programme, 2005). However, some progress has been made. Since 1955 life expectancy has increased from 46 years to 67 years and infant mortality has been cut in half in low-income countries through simple measures such as basic immunization and malaria nets (World Health Organization, 2003, 2009).

Health

Health is defined by the World Health Organization as "a state of complete physical, mental and social well-being, and not merely the absence of disease or infirmity" (Smyke, 1991:2). Many people in low-income nations do not have physical, mental, and social well-being. Of the 4.6 billion people who live in low-income countries, 2.7 billion do not have proper sanitation and 1.2 billion do not have safe water. Many do not have adequate housing or access to modern health services (United Nations Development Programme, 2004). About 12 million people die each year from diarrhea, malaria, tuberculosis, and other infectious and parasitic illnesses (World Health Organization, 2004). Infectious diseases persist in many nations because of unsanitary and overcrowded living conditions and a lack of basic health care. Despite these problems, progress has been made and over the past 30 years significant improvements were made in life expectancy at birth, infant mortality, and malnutrition. Most of this improvement has been in poorer countries. (United Nations Development Programme, 2001)

Malnutrition is a widespread health problem in many low-income nations.

Education and Literacy

We know that education is fundamental to reducing both individual poverty and national poverty. Thus school enrolment is used as a measure of human development. The United Nations Educational, Scientific, and Cultural Organization (UNESCO) defines a *literate* person as "someone who can, with understanding, both read and write a short, simple statement on their everyday life" (United Nations, 1997a:89). The adult-literacy rate in low-income countries is about half that of the high-income nations, and for women in these countries the rate is even lower (United Nations, 1997a).

Gender and Equality

Women suffer more than men from global inequality:

Women have an enormous impact on the well-being of their families and societies—yet their potential is not realized because of discriminatory social norms, incentives, and legal institutions. And while their status has improved in recent decades, gender inequalities remain pervasive.

Gender inequality starts early and disadvantages women throughout their lives. In some countries, infant girls are less likely to survive than infant boys because of parental discrimination and neglect. Girls are more likely to drop out of school than boys because of discrimination, education expenses, and household duties (World Bank, 2004:1).

Although more women have paid employment than in the past, many women still live in poverty because of increases in single-person and single-parent households headed by women, and because low-wage work is often the only source of livelihood available to them. According to an analyst for the Inter-American Development Bank, women experience sexual discrimination in employment and also in wages:

In Honduras, for example, coffee and tobacco farmers prefer to hire girls and women as laborers because they are willing to accept low wages and are more reliable workers. Especially in poor countries, female labor is primarily sought for low-paid positions in services agriculture, small-scale commerce, and in the growing, unregulated manufacturing and agribusiness industries, which pay their workers individual rather than family wages, offer seasonal or part-time employment, and carry few or no benefits. Hence, this explains the seemingly contradictory trends of women's increased economic participation alongside their growing impoverishment. (Buvinic, 1997:47)

Researchers have found that women play a critical role in development. Women's education is particularly important because it has an impact on many other factors that contribute to human development (United Nations Development Programme, 2003). Figure 8.2 (on page 194) illustrates how educated girls marry later and have smaller families. They also do a better job feeding their families and getting medical care, so more of their children survive. The children of illiterate mothers have an under-five mortality rate that is twice as high as the mortality rate for the children of mothers who have a middle-school education (United Nations Development Programme, 2005:31). Higher child survival rates lead to a reduction in birth rates, which allows better child care and less strain on the educational system. In societies where educated women are allowed to work outside the home, they make a significant contribution to family income.

Some progress is being made in improving women's education. Between 1990 and 2001, the ratio of literate females to literate males in low-human-development countries increased from 70 women per 100 men to 81 women, and between 1990 and 2000 the ratio of girls to boys in primary education rose from 86 girls per 100 boys to 92 girls. However, it will take many years to achieve gender equality (United Nations Development Programme, 2003). While most countries have seen improvement in women's education, some countries, such as India, Afghanistan, Ethiopia, and Pakistan, have ratios that are far below average and this will hamper their future development. Literacy is crucial for women because it has been closely linked to decreases in fertility, improved child health, and increased earnings potential (Hauchler and Kennedy, 1994).

THEORIES OF GLOBAL INEQUALITY

Why is the majority of the world's population growing richer while the poorest 20 percent are so poor that they are excluded from even a moderate standard of living? Social scientists have developed many theories, which view the causes and consequences of global inequality somewhat differently. We will examine the development approach and modernization theory, dependency theory, world systems theory, and the new international division of labour theory. Modernization theory is part of the functionalist tradition, while the other perspectives are rooted in conflict theory. These approaches are depicted in Figure 8.3.

Development and Modernization Theories

According to some social scientists, global wealth and poverty are linked to a society's industrialization and economic development. These theorists maintain that low-income nations have progressed less than the wealthier industrial countries. They feel that industrialization and economic development are essential steps that nations must go through to reduce poverty and to improve the living conditions of their citizens.

The most widely known development theory is ***modernization theory**—a perspective that links global inequality to different levels of economic development and suggests that low-income economies can move to middle- and high-income economies by achieving self-sustained economic growth.* According to Langdon, modernization theory holds that undeveloped countries must follow the road travelled by successful Western capitalist, democratic societies:

> The usually implicit assumption was that economic development and growth involved a process of becoming like those societies and would be achieved essentially as those societies had achieved it: through economic change focused around industrialization, through social changes that would introduce Western institutions based on universalism and merit/achievement, and through political changes marked by secularization and the bureaucratic efficiency of the state. (1999: 41)

Just as Weber had concluded that the adoption of a "spirit of capitalism" facilitated economic development, modernization theorists felt that the development process would be accompanied by changing beliefs, values, and attitudes toward work. With modernization, the values of people in developing

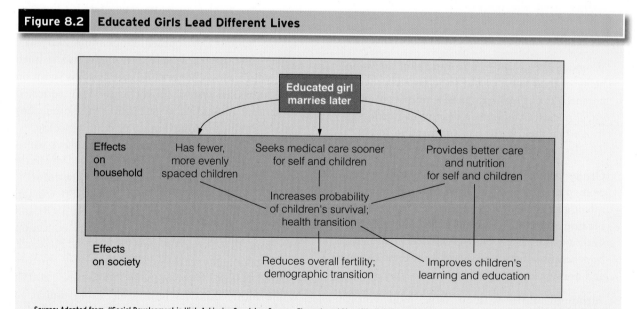

Figure 8.2 **Educated Girls Lead Different Lives**

Educated girl marries later

Effects on household

Has fewer, more evenly spaced children

Seeks medical care sooner for self and children

Provides better care and nutrition for self and children

Increases probability of children's survival; health transition

Effects on society

Reduces overall fertility; demographic transition

Improves children's learning and education

Source: Adapted from "Social Development in High-Achieving Countries: Common Elements and Diversities" by Santosh Mehrotra, Mehrotra, S., Jolly, R., eds. *Development with a human face: experiences in social achievement and economic growth*, (1998), as appearing in the United Nations Development Report for 2003.

Figure 8.3 Approaches to Studying Global Inequality

What causes global inequality? Social scientists have developed a variety of explanations, including the four theories shown here.

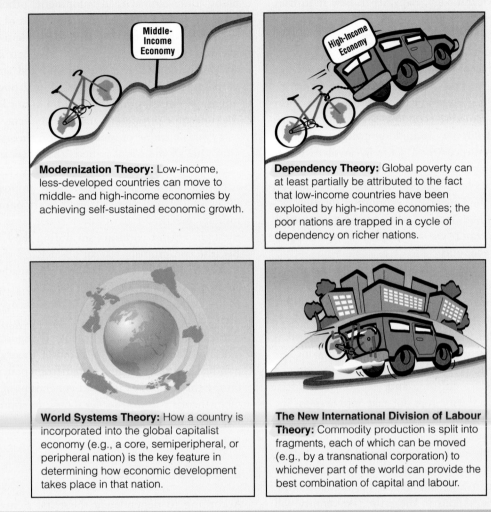

Modernization Theory: Low-income, less-developed countries can move to middle- and high-income economies by achieving self-sustained economic growth.

Dependency Theory: Global poverty can at least partially be attributed to the fact that low-income countries have been exploited by high-income economies; the poor nations are trapped in a cycle of dependency on richer nations.

World Systems Theory: How a country is incorporated into the global capitalist economy (e.g., a core, semiperipheral, or peripheral nation) is the key feature in determining how economic development takes place in that nation.

The New International Division of Labour Theory: Commodity production is split into fragments, each of which can be moved (e.g., by a transnational corporation) to whichever part of the world can provide the best combination of capital and labour.

countries would become more similar to those of people in high-income nations.

Perhaps the most widely known modernization theory is that of Rostow (1971, 1978). To Rostow, one of largest barriers to development in low-income nations was the traditional cultural values held by people, particularly fatalistic beliefs such as viewing extreme hardship and economic deprivation as inevitable and unavoidable facts of life. Fatalistic people do not see any need to work in order to improve their lot in life: it is predetermined for them, so why bother? According to modernization theory, poverty can be attributed to people's cultural failings, which are reinforced by governmental policies interfering with the operation of the economy.

Rostow suggested that all countries go through four stages of economic development with identical content, regardless of when these nations started the process of industrialization. He compares the stages of economic development to an airplane ride. The first stage is the *traditional stage,* in which people do not think about changing their circumstances. The second stage is the *takeoff stage*—a period of economic growth accompanied by a growing belief in individualism, competition, and achievement. People start to look toward the future, to save and invest money, and to discard traditional values. According to Rostow, the development of capitalism is essential for the transformation from a traditional, simple society to a modern, complex one. With the financial help and advice of high-income countries, low-income nations eventually will be able to "fly" and enter the third stage of economic development in which the country moves toward *technological maturity*. The country improves its technology, reinvests in new industries, and embraces the beliefs, values, and social institutions of the developed nations. In the fourth and final stage, the country reaches the phase of *high mass consumption* and a corresponding high standard of living.

According to proponents, studies have supported the assertion that economic development occurs more rapidly in a capitalist economy. The countries that have moved from low- to middle-income status typically have been those most centrally involved in the global capitalist economy. For example, many East Asian countries have successfully made the transition from low- to higher-income economies through factors such as a high rate of savings, an aggressive work ethic among employers and employees, and support for a market economy.

Critics of modernization theory point out that it tends to be Eurocentric in its analysis of low-income countries, which it implicitly labels as backward (see Evans and Stephens, 1988). In many respects, modernization was equated with westernization, as modernization theorists assumed that the problems of low-income countries would be alleviated only once they adopted Western values, culture, and economic models. Modernization theory does not take into account the possibility that all nations do not industrialize in the same manner. Allahar (1989) points out that leading industrial countries such as the United States, Britain, and Japan followed different paths to industrialization. Thus, we might also assume that the modernization of low-income nations in the early 21st century will require novel policies, sequences, and ideologies that are not accounted for by Rostow's theory (Gerschenkron, 1962). The theory also does not tell us what actually causes the move from one stage to another, but simply assumes that they are natural stages that must be followed as societies advance economically and socially.

One of the most influential critics of modernization theory was Andre Gunder Frank (1969). Frank's research in Latin America convinced him that modernization theory was badly flawed. While Rostow felt that all societies had to move in a linear fashion from underdevelopment to industrialization, Frank pointed out that underdevelopment was not an original stage but a condition created by the imperial powers that had created dependency during the colonial era through actions such as the deindustrialization of India, the damage incurred by African societies during the years of the slave trade, and the

destruction of indigenous civilizations in Central and Latin America (Hettne, 1995). All societies were *un*developed at one time, but not all became *under*developed. While some countries moved from being undeveloped to development, others moved from being undeveloped to a condition of underdevelopment in which they were dependent on other nations. These dependent countries had structures and institutions that effectively blocked any further development (Allahar, 1989). Colonial powers were interested in exploiting their colonies, not in helping them become prosperous and independent.

Frank's critique of modernization theory was also a critique of the social policies that grew out of the theory. Frank believed that the Western powers, particularly the United States, were imposing their views of development through both political and military means. Modernization theory was linked to the fight against communism during the Cold War. Because communism was an obstacle on the road to modernization, it was necessary to persuade or force countries to adopt alternative forms of government. Many critics felt that modernization theory contributed to underdevelopment by encouraging policies that perpetuated global inequality (Langdon, 1999). The inadequacies of modernization theory and the political injustices that resulted from policies based on the theory moved the next generation of development theorists to *dependency theory*, an approach that was based on the conflict perspective.

Dependency Theory

According to dependency theorists, rich countries have an interest in maintaining the dependent status of poor countries, since this ensures them a source of raw materials and a captive market for manufactured goods exported to the dependent nations. Business and political leaders in the poor nations find it in their interests to accept dependence and willingly work with the advanced nations to impose policies that maintain the dependent relationship. Any surpluses created in the dependent country will be taken by the affluent capitalist country rather than being used to build up production infrastructure or raise the standard of living in the dependent nations. Unless this changes, poor countries will never reach the sustained economic growth patterns of the more advanced capitalist economies.

Dependency theory states that global poverty can at least partially be attributed to the fact that low-income countries have been exploited by

high-income ones. Analyzing events as part of the expansion of global capitalism, dependency theorists see the greed of the rich countries as a source of increasing impoverishment of the poorer nations and their people. Dependency theory disputes the notion of the development approach—and modernization theory specifically—that economic growth is the key to meeting important human needs in societies. Instead, dependency theorists see poorer nations as trapped in a cycle of structural dependency on the richer nations due to their need for infusions of foreign capital and external markets for their raw materials, which makes it impossible for the poorer nations to pursue their own economic and human-development agendas. Frank and other scholars believed that the best way for low-income countries to move ahead was to break their links with the industrialized countries and to establish independent, socialist governments.

Dependency theory has been most often applied to the newly industrializing countries (NICs) of Latin America, but scholars examining the NICs of East Asia have found that dependency theory has little or no relevance to that part of the world. According to Gereffi (1994), differences in outcome are probably associated with differences in the timing and sequencing of a nation's relationship with external entities such as foreign governments and transnational corporations.

Dependency theory has contributed to our understanding of global poverty by pointing out that "underdevelopment" is not necessarily the cause of inequality. Rather, this theory points out that exploitation of one country by another and also of countries by transnational corporations may limit or retard economic growth and human development in some nations.

What remains unexplained is how some East Asian countries had successful "dependency management"

A variety of factors—such as foreign investment and the presence of transnational corporations—have contributed to the economic growth of nations such as Singapore.

whereas many Latin American countries did not (Gereffi, 1994). In fact, between 1998 and 2005 the annual economic growth in emerging East Asian countries averaged 9 percent, which was much higher than growth in the West (Gill and Kharas, 2007).

Dependency theory has contributed to our understanding of global stratification but even its proponents feel it is no longer adequate. In addition to the problem of explaining the success of the East Asian economies that were closely linked with global capitalist structures, the dependency theorists' faith in development through socialist revolution has been shaken by the failure of many socialist economies, including that of the Soviet Union (Frank, 1981). Most have concluded that the global economy is so pervasive that it is impossible for low-income countries to disconnect themselves from the industrialized world and proceed with their own development (Martinussen, 1997).

World Systems Theory

Drawing on Karl Marx, world systems theory suggests that what exists under capitalism is a truly global system held together by economic ties. From this perspective, global inequality does not emerge solely as a result of the exploitation of one country by another. Instead, economic domination involves a complex world system in which the industrialized, high-income nations benefit from other nations and exploit the citizens of those countries. Wallerstein (1979, 1984), believed that a country's mode of incorporation into the capitalist work economy is the key feature in determining how economic development takes place in that nation. According to his *world systems theory,* **the capitalist world economy is a global system divided into a hierarchy of three major types of nations—core, semiperipheral, and peripheral—in which upward or downward mobility is conditioned by the resources and obstacles that characterize the international system.**

Core nations **are dominant capitalist centres characterized by high levels of industrialization and urbanization.** Core nations such as the United States, Japan, and Germany possess most of the world's capital and technology. This allows them to exert massive control over world trade and economic agreements across national boundaries.

Most low-income countries in Africa, South America, and the Caribbean are *peripheral nations—* **nations that are dependent on core nations for capital, have little or no industrialization (other** than what may be brought in by core nations), and have uneven patterns of urbanization. According to Wallerstein (1979, 1984), the wealthy in peripheral nations benefit from the labour of poor workers and from their economic relations with core nation capitalists, which they uphold in order to maintain their own wealth and position. At a global level, uneven economic growth results from capital investment by core nations. Disparity between the rich and the poor within the major cities in these nations is increased in the process.

The United States–Mexico border is an example of disparity and urban growth: transnational corporations have built *maquiladora* plants just over the border in Mexico so that goods can be assembled by low-wage workers to keep production costs down. Because of the demand for low-wage workers, thousands of people have moved from the rural regions of Mexico to urban areas along the border in hope of earning a higher wage. This influx has pushed already overcrowded cities far beyond their capacity. Many people live on the edge of the city in shantytowns made from discarded materials or in low-cost rental housing in central-city slums because their wages are low and affordable housing is nonexistent (Flanagan, 1995).

Semiperipheral nations are more developed than peripheral nations but less developed than core nations. These nations typically provide labour and raw materials to core nations within the world system. They constitute a midpoint between the core and peripheral nations that promotes the stability and legitimacy of the three-tiered world economy. These nations include South Korea and Taiwan in East Asia, Brazil in Latin America, India in South Asia, and Nigeria and South Africa in Africa. According to Wallerstein, semiperipheral nations exploit peripheral nations, just as the core nations exploit both the semiperipheral and the peripheral.

Even Wallerstein (1991) acknowledges that world systems theory is an "incomplete, unfinished critique" for long-term, large-scale social change that influences global inequality. However, most scholars acknowledge that nations throughout the world are influenced by a relatively small number of cities and transnational corporations that have prompted a shift from an international to a more global economy (see Knox and Taylor, 1995; Wilson, 1997).

The New International Division of Labour Theory

According to the *new international division of labour theory,* commodity production is being split into fragments that can be assigned to whichever part of the world can provide the most profitable combination of capital and labour. Consequently, the new international division of labour has changed the pattern of geographic specialization between countries, whereby high-income countries have become dependent on low-income nations for cheap labour. Low-income countries allow transnational corporations to pay lower wages and taxes and face fewer regulations regarding workplace conditions and environmental protection (Waters, 1995).

This new division of labour is part of a global economy based on free trade among countries. Multilateral trade agreements such as the General Agreement on Tariffs and Trade (GATT) and the North American Free Trade Agreement (NAFTA) allow the freer transfer of goods and services among countries, and global corporations now view all countries both as potential markets and as potential locations for production.

These trade-liberalization agreements appear to be beneficial for poor countries, as the movement of production into developing countries brings jobs to countries with chronically high unemployment. However, few of the profits stay in these countries. For example, a study of garment manufacturing in Bangladesh found that less than 2 percent of the final value of the product went to production workers and that 1 percent went to the local producer. The rest of the money went to profit those who owned the company and to pay expenses such as shipping and storage costs, customs duties, and sales taxes in high-income countries (Chossudovsky, 1997). There is little hope of higher wages for workers, since the jobs are unskilled and can quickly be moved to another poor country if workers begin to put pressure on the companies (Klein, 2000).

Many corporations have global operations. Typically, labour-intensive manufacturing operations, ranging from textiles to computers, are established in low-wage countries. Even service industries—such as completing income-tax forms, booking airline flights, and processing insurance claims forms have become exportable through electronic transmission and the Internet (see Box 8.3 on page 200). These activities make up *global commodity chains,* a complex pattern of international labour and production processes that results in a finished commodity ready for sale in the market place.

Commodity chains are most common in labour-intensive consumer-goods industries such as toys, garments, and footwear (Gereffi, 1994). Athletic-footwear companies such as Nike and Reebok and clothing companies such as The Gap and Liz Claiborne are examples of this model. Manufacturing these products is labour intensive so the factory system is very competitive and globally decentralized. Workers in commodity chains are often exploited by low wages, long hours, and poor working conditions. In fact, most workers cannot afford the products they make. Tini Heyun Alwi, who works on the assembly line of a shoe factory in Indonesia that makes Reebok sneakers, is an example: "I think maybe I could work for a month and still not be able to buy one pair" (quoted in Goodman, 1996:F1). Since Tini earned only 2 600 Indonesian rupiah ($1.28) per day working a ten-hour shift six days a week, her monthly income was less than the retail price of the shoes (Goodman, 1996).

We live in a world where "(1) the political unit is *national*, (2) industrial production is *regional*, and (3) capital movements are *international*. The rise of Japan and the East Asian [NICs] in the 1960s and 1970s is the flip side of the "deindustrialization" that occurred in the United States and much of Europe. Declining

Tiger Woods makes more money for endorsing Nike shoes than the combined salaries of thousands of the workers who manufacture the products. According to Nike's chief executive officer, marketing is more important to the company's success than is the manufacturing of its products (Klein, 2000).

Scott McDermott/Corbis

industries in North America have been the growth industries in East Asia" (Gereffi, 1994: 225).

These changes have had a mixed impact upon people living in these countries. For example, Indonesia has been able to attract foreign business into the country, but workers remain poor despite working full-time in factories making consumer goods such as Nike shoes (Gargan, 1996). As employers feel pressure from workers to raise wages, clashes erupt between the workers and managers or owners. Governments in these countries fear that rising wages and labour strife will drive away the business, leaving behind workers who have no other hopes for employment to become more impoverished than they previously were. What will be the future of global inequality given this current set of conditions in countries such as Indonesia?

The "Flying Geese" Model of Development

The "flying geese" model was developed by Japanese economist Akamatsu Kaname and is a type of international division of labour theory. The model has been used to explain the rapid development of East Asian economies following World War II (Korhonen, 1994). This process involves one country—in this case Japan—leading other less-developed countries into more prosperous times. The countries go through the sequential steps of importing goods, manufacturing to serve domestic markets, and finally exporting goods. Factors such as labour costs lead production to shift from advanced to less advanced economies. This boosts the standard of living of the less advanced economies, raises wages, and this in turn leads to a shift in production to countries that are even less developed. In the 1960s, Japan was the only developed economy in Asia but was then followed by the "Asian tigers," Singapore, Hong Kong, Taiwan, and South Korea. Development in these countries was followed by industrialization in Malaysia, Indonesia, the Philippines, and Thailand and most recently by China and India.

One example of this process has been in textiles, where Japan had a thriving export business for a number of years. When wages in Japan became globally uncompetitive, production shifted to the next tier of countries while Japan moved into the production of higher-technology goods such as automobiles and electronics. Production of these goods has also moved to lower-tier countries that have upgraded their technological skills. Companies such as South Korea's Hyundai and Samsung are now producing very high-quality, high-technology products that are displacing some Japanese products in global markets.

BOX 8.3 | SOCIOLOGY AND THE MEDIA

The Digital Third World

Information and communications technologies are changing our world, but there is considerable debate about the impact of these technologies on the poor. Some feel that the ability to share information from around the globe will hasten development, as low-income countries will be able to become knowledge societies that can compete with the industrialized nations. For example, technology can speed up educational reform and help to build a more participatory civil society through the sharing of information and ideas. India has generated hundreds of thousands of jobs based on new information and communication technologies (Friedman, 2005).

However, there is also a danger that the move to a world linked by new information and communications technology will lead to a greater polarization between the rich who can exploit the new technologies and the poor who do not even have access to them. The poor may be excluded from the global information society—and this includes the poor in industrialized countries, as the "digital Third World" does not follow international borders.

There are many barriers to the spread of information and communications technology. The major obstacle is cost. To become part of the "digital world," low-income countries must build very expensive communications infrastructures. Because of these costs, high-income residents of high-income countries are most likely to have access to the Internet. In 2009, 74 percent of North Americans had access to the Internet, compared with 17 percent of people in Asia and only 5.6 percent of residents of Africa. One positive sign is that there has been growth in Internet use in low-income countries. Even though usage is still very low in Africa, it increased by 1100 percent between 2000 and 2008 (Internet World Stats, 2009).

In a world in which global communications and access to the Internet are becoming critical to business and trade, countries that cannot afford to build communications networks or to train people in how to use computers will be at a great competitive disadvantage. For example, the World Bank (2008) found that mobile phone use is associated with increased productivity in low-income countries. It is difficult for deeply indebted countries with other pressing needs, such as health care and nutrition, to create a communications infrastructure without a great deal of help. It is hard to think of the "wired classroom" in a country that cannot afford to build schools or train teachers.

Language issues act as a barrier to Internet access in many parts of the world. Most of the content on the Internet is in English. Without multilingual sites, the name "the World Wide Web" will never be accurate. A Web that is dominated linguistically by English and technologically and culturally by the United States does not reflect the point of view of people in low-income countries. (For a rare example of an Internet site that uses several African languages, see the Channel Africa site at www.channelafrica.org.). The magnitude of this problem was demonstrated by Charles Kenny (2003), who searched for Web pages in Igbo, a language spoken by 17 million Nigerians. The Internet would be of little use to these people, as he found only five sites that used the Igbo language.

Government censorship also limits access to modern communications technology. Totalitarian countries are afraid of the free flow of information and restrict access to ensure that their citizens are unable to share ideas with each other and with people in other countries. Many governments, including China, Iran, and Algeria, have restricted their citizens' access to new forms of communications technology, particularly the Internet.

While low-income countries continue to fall further behind in the development of information technology, some small steps are reducing the gap. One model project has been undertaken by Canada's International Development Research Centre (IDRC). Project Acacia is an international effort led by the IDRC to provide sub-Saharan communities with the ability to apply information and communication technologies to their own social and economic development (see http://www.idrc.ca/acacia). Partners in the project include the African Information Society Initiative, which provides an African perspective on the opportunities and challenges of that continent in an emerging information age. This perspective is important for cultural, as well as economic, reasons. A global Internet culture controlled by industrialized countries is a great threat to the cultural identity of groups whose perspectives are not represented.

While this project is promising, it is a very small step toward the solution of a very large problem. Much more must be done if low-income countries are to build on-ramps to the information superhighway.

However, if basic infrastructure can be developed, information technology can provide significant development opportunities for low-income countries. For example, India has recently been successful in creating software development and information-processing industries and a number of U.S. and European companies, including Microsoft, U.S. Hospitals, and British Airways, have moved some of their operations to India in order to reduce wage costs (Chandrasekhar, 2001). In addition to providing significant financial gains, this will also help India to further develop its information technology sector.

This perspective provides a dynamic picture of the global division of labour that gives us some reason for optimism as we see technology being transferred from more-industrialized to less-industrialized countries. However, it is not clear that the flying geese model will apply outside East Asia, or whether unique circumstances led to the pattern of development in those countries.

The Foxconn Suicides In May, 2010, the Apple corporation became the world's largest technology company when its value jumped over that of Microsoft. The same month, a worker at a Foxconn factory in Shenzhen, China, became the ninth worker in 2010 to jump to his death from one of the company's buildings. The connection between these two events is that the Foxconn factory is one of the largest producers of Apple products, including iPods, iPhones, and iPads. It also produces items for other companies including Dell, Microsoft, and Sony.

Like many of its competitors, Apple manufactures most of its products outside North America because of lower wages offshore. Foxconn is a Taiwan-based company that has large factories in mainland China. The Shenzhen plant, which employs over 400 000 people, is modern and working conditions are much better than in the sweatshops that exist in many poor countries. However, the pay was only $130 per month and workers are pressured to work long hours of overtime. Many of the workers are rural young people who migrated to Shenzhen to get jobs and who live in company dormitories where they have little contact with their families and friends. The workers who have killed themselves may have seen little in their futures except endless hours on an assembly line.

In response to the suicides, Foxconn has significantly increased salaries and has also placed netting around its buildings to prevent workers from jumping. At the same time, unprecedented strikes in China, including at several Honda factories, have resulted in large wage hikes for workers and dissatisfaction seems to be growing across the country over low wages and poor working conditions. It is too soon to know if this unrest will spread to other companies.

The Foxconn situation illustrates the flying geese model. Work sent offshore from North America might at one time have been done in Foxconn's home country of Taiwan but is now done in the lower-wage environment of China. If Chinese workers succeed in getting higher wages, some low-skill work will likely move from China to poorer countries where workers are still desperate for jobs.

The suicides raise another issue. Labour costs make up very little of the final cost of most high-technology products. About $4 of the cost of a $299 iPod can be attributed to the labour costs of final assembly in China (Linden, Kraemer, and Dedrick, 2007). Doubling or tripling these wages would mean that you would have to pay a few dollars more for these products or that Apple would make slightly less profit. Would you feel better about the technology you use if you knew that the people who manufactured it were being paid a living wage? Are purchasers who continue to buy these devices complicit in a system that has these consequences on workers?

GLOBAL INEQUALITY IN THE FUTURE

Social inequality is a major issue within and among the countries of the world. Even in high-income nations where wealth is highly concentrated, many poor people coexist with the affluent. In middle- and low-income countries, there are small pockets of wealth in the midst of poverty and despair.

What are the future prospects for greater equality across and within nations? Not all social scientists agree on the answer to this question. Depending on their theoretical framework, they may see either an optimistic or a pessimistic future scenario.

In some regions, economic development has stalled and persistent and growing poverty continues to undermine human development and possibilities for change. According to the United Nations, "For many countries the 1990s were a decade of despair. Some 54 countries are poorer now than in 1990. In 21, a larger proportion of people is going hungry. In 14, more children are dying before age five. In 12, primary school enrolments are shrinking. In 34, life expectancy has fallen. Such reversals in survival were previously rare" (United Nations Development Programme, 2003:2). Most of the countries where human development worsened were in sub-Saharan Africa and in Eastern Europe. Many have been affected by the HIV/AIDS epidemic or were adjusting to the collapse of the Soviet Union and then hurt by the global recession of 2009. Others have suffered from low prices for the agricultural products that are their main source of income. Coffee farmers illustrate how low-income producers can fail to benefit from rising prices in high-income countries. Canadians have become used to paying $2 or $3 for a cup of coffee at chains such as Second Cup and Starbucks. Many of us assume that the people who grow the coffee receive a fair share of this price. However, according to the UN, since 1990 the retail value of coffee sold in high-income countries has increased from US$30 billion to US$80 billion (United Nations Development Programme, 2005). Over the same period, the income received by coffee exporters dropped from US$12 billion to US$5.5 billion even though the amount of coffee exported has increased. The farmer receives only one cent of each dollar you pay for your cup of coffee. This income reduction had devastating effects on human development in countries such as Ethiopia, Uganda, and Nicaragua, which rely heavily on coffee exports. At the same time, the coffee chains have been enormously profitable because they can charge high prices while paying almost nothing for their raw materials. While consumers in North America and Europe are content to pay high prices for their double-espresso low-fat lattes, coffee retailers took advantage of an oversupply of coffee beans to reduce their costs.

In the future, continued population growth, urbanization, and environmental degradation will threaten even the meagre living conditions of people in low-income nations. Environmental problems will be catastrophic if billions of people in countries such as China and India begin to live like middle-class North Americans as we are setting an example that is very wasteful and resource intensive.

On the other hand, a more optimistic scenario is also possible. The United Nations Development Programme (2001) showed many positive changes between 1970 and 2000. Levels of development have increased, most countries are at least formally recognizing human rights, health is better, a higher proportion of people are educated, incomes have increased, far more females are enrolled in schools, and more countries are holding democratic elections. Most of this improvement has been in East Asia—particularly in China—where the number of people living in absolute poverty was reduced by nearly half during the 1990s (United Nations Development Programme, 2003), and it will be challenging to maintain these gains and to make similar progress in areas such as sub-Saharan Africa, which have largely been left behind. These improvements show it will be possible to reduce global poverty, but only if the practices of foreign aid donors, global corporations, and international lending organizations focus on the needs of low-income countries rather than solely on the demands of the marketplace.

These needs were formally recognized in 2000, when most of the world's heads of state adopted the UN Millennium Declaration that committed countries to make dramatic improvements in the lives of the poor. The declaration contains a series of specific goals and targets that are being monitored to track the progress made (see Figure 8.4).

The UN has suggested six broad types of policy changes that will help low-income countries to improve their situations (United Nations Development Programme, 2003:4):

- Investing in basic education and health and encouraging the equality of women will help to encourage economic growth;
- Helping to improve the productivity of small farmers;
- Improving roads, ports, communications systems, and the other infrastructure necessary for production and trade;
- Promoting the development of small- and medium-sized businesses to help countries move away from dependence on exporting commodities;

Figure 8.4   **Millennium Development Goals and Targets**

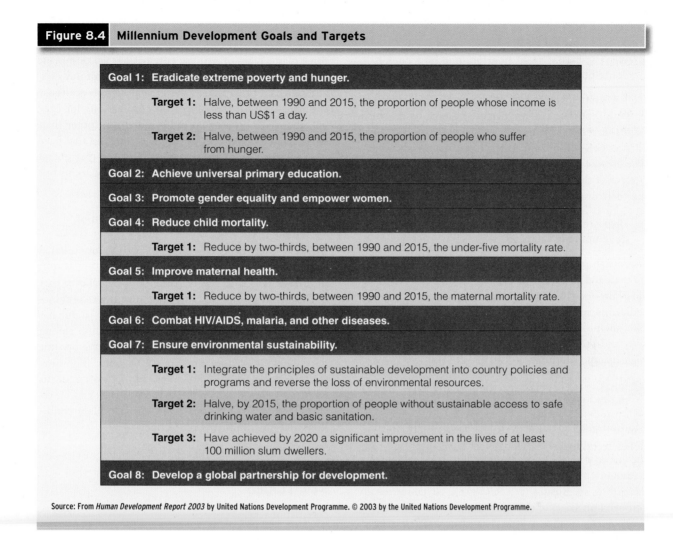

Goal 1:   Eradicate extreme poverty and hunger.

Target 1: Halve, between 1990 and 2015, the proportion of people whose income is less than US$1 a day.

Target 2: Halve, between 1990 and 2015, the proportion of people who suffer from hunger.

Goal 2:   Achieve universal primary education.

Goal 3:   Promote gender equality and empower women.

Goal 4:   Reduce child mortality.

Target 1: Reduce by two-thirds, between 1990 and 2015, the under-five mortality rate.

Goal 5:   Improve maternal health.

Target 1: Reduce by two-thirds, between 1990 and 2015, the maternal mortality rate.

Goal 6:   Combat HIV/AIDS, malaria, and other diseases.

Goal 7:   Ensure environmental sustainability.

Target 1: Integrate the principles of sustainable development into country policies and programs and reverse the loss of environmental resources.

Target 2: Halve, by 2015, the proportion of people without sustainable access to safe drinking water and basic sanitation.

Target 3: Have achieved by 2020 a significant improvement in the lives of at least 100 million slum dwellers.

Goal 8:   Develop a global partnership for development.

Source: From *Human Development Report 2003* by United Nations Development Programme. © 2003 by the United Nations Development Programme.

- Promoting democratic governance and human rights, which will help to ensure that economic growth benefits the poorest people within low-income countries rather than just the elite;
- Ensuring environmental sustainability and urban planning.

Making these changes is beyond the capability of the poorest countries, so progress will depend on the willingness of the rest of the world to work with them to meet the Millennium Development Goals. Achieving these goals is important to the world's poor. To give just one example, if the goals are not met, 41 million more children will die before their fifth birthday between 2005 and 2015 than would be the case if the goals were achieved (United Nations Development Programme, 2005).

We will continue to focus on issues pertaining to global inequality in subsequent chapters as we discuss topics such as race, gender, education, health and medicine, population, urbanization, social change, and the environment.

CARE water trucks, like this one, help provide clean drinking water to more than a quarter-million residents of Kabul, Afghanistan.

CHAPTER REVIEW

What is global stratification, and how does it contribute to economic inequality?

Global stratification refers to the unequal distribution of wealth, power, and prestige on a global basis, which results in people having vastly different lifestyles and life chances both within and among the nations of the world. The income gap between the richest and the poorest 20 percent of the world population continues to widen and hundreds of millions of people are living in abject poverty.

How are global poverty and human development related?

Income disparities are not the only factor that defines poverty and its effect on people. The UN's HDI measures the level of development in a country, through indicators such as life expectancy, the infant-mortality rate, the proportion of underweight children under age five, and the adult-literacy rate for low-, middle-, and high-income countries.

What is modernization theory, and what stages did Rostow believe all societies go through?

Modernization theory links global inequality to different levels of economic development and suggests that low-income economies can move to middle- and high-income economies by achieving self-sustained economic growth. According to Rostow (1971, 1978), all countries go through four stages of economic development: (1) the traditional stage, with very little social change; (2) the takeoff stage, a period of economic growth accompanied by a growing belief in individualism, competition, and achievement; (3) technological maturity, a period of improving technology, reinvesting in new industries, and embracing the beliefs, values, and social institutions of the high-income, developed nations; and (4) the phase of high mass consumption, accompanied by a high standard of living.

How does dependency theory differ from modernization theory?

Dependency theory states that global poverty can at least partially be attributed to the fact that low-income countries have been exploited by high-income ones. Whereas modernization theory focuses on how societies can reduce inequality through industrialization and economic development, dependency theorists see the greed of the rich countries as a source of increasing impoverishment of the people in poorer nations.

What is world systems theory, and how does it view the global economy?

According to world systems theory, the capitalist world economy is a global system divided into a hierarchy of three major types of nations: core nations are dominant capitalist centres characterized by high levels of industrialization and urbanization; peripheral nations are those countries that are dependent on core nations for capital, that have little or no industrialization (other than what may be brought in by core nations), and that have uneven patterns of urbanization; and semiperipheral nations are more developed than peripheral nations but less developed than core nations.

What is the new international division of labour theory?

The new international division of labour theory is based on the assumption that commodity production is split into fragments that can be assigned to whichever part of the world can provide the most profitable combination of capital and labour. This division of labour has changed the pattern of geographic specialization among countries, whereby high-income countries have become dependent on low-income ones for labour. The low-income countries provide transnational corporations with a situation in which they pay lower wages and taxes and face fewer regulations regarding workplace conditions and environmental protection.

KEY TERMS

core nations 197
dependency theory 196
global stratification 180
high-income economies 186
low-income economies 186
lower-middle-income economies 186
modernization theory 194
new international division of labour theory 198
peripheral nations 197
semiperipheral nations 198
upper-middle-income economies 186
world systems theory 197

WEB LINKS

For more Web links related to the topic of this chapter, see the Nelson sociology website:
www.sociologyessentials5e.nelson.com

For an interesting way of presenting data about global stratification take a look at the Miniature Earth website, which presents the world as if it had only 100 people. For a look at this interesting video go to:
www.miniature-earth.com

The United Nations Development Programme has done an excellent job in focusing public attention on global inequality issues. To find out more about the world's poorest people and to learn what can be done to help them, visit the program's website: **www.undp.org**

The *World Factbook* contains demographic information from around the globe:
www.odci.gov/cia/publications/ factbook

You can monitor the progress the world is making toward achieving the Millennium Development Goals at: **www.un.org/millenniumgoals**

A number of reports from the World Bank are available at: **www.worldbank.org**

Boycotts have been held against Nike and Reebok because of their treatment of their workers in low-income countries. Read about reasons for the boycott at: **http://www.viet.net/~nike/**

QUESTIONS FOR CRITICAL THINKING

1. You have decided to study global wealth and poverty. How would you approach your study? What research methods would provide the best data for analysis? What might you find if you compared your research data with popular presentations—such as films and advertising—of everyday life in low- and middle-income countries?
2. What are some of the positive aspects of globalization? How might the globalization of manufacturing and service industries benefit the world's poorest people?
3. Discuss why educating women is such an important strategy for improving the lives of people living in poor countries that it is one of the Millennium Development Goals.
4. Using the theories discussed in this chapter, devise a plan to alleviate poverty. Assume that you have the necessary wherewithal, including wealth, political power, and natural resources. Share your plan with others in your class and create a consolidated plan that represents the best ideas and suggestions presented.

ONLINE STUDY AND RESEARCH TOOLS

INFOTRAC®

InfoTrac College Edition is included free with every new copy of this text. Explore this online library for additional readings, review, and a handy resource for assignments. Visit **www.infotrac-college.com** to access this online database of full-text articles. Enter the key terms from this chapter to start your search.

CENGAGENOW™ CENGAGENOW

Use CengageNOW™ to help you formulate a customized study plan for this chapter. After you take the Diagnostic Quiz, CengageNOW™ will generate a customized study plan for you. It will identify sections of the chapter you should review.

Ethnic Relations and Race

Professor Carl James has more than 15 years' experience teaching at colleges and universities in southern Ontario. In the following personal narrative, he discusses how the preconceived ideas of students inform their expectations of and interactions with him as a member of racial minority (2001:153–154):

Within either the first hour of my class or the first two weeks, students usually ask me, "Where are you from?" or "Are you from Jamaica?" In earlier years I used to say, "I am from the Caribbean," and to the Jamaica question I would say, "I'm not from Jamaica." And when I ask, "Why the question?" or "Why do you assume that I am not Canadian, but an immigrant?" the response is, "Because you have an accent."

Nowadays usually I do not answer the question, because I want to challenge the tendency of students, like many other Canadians, to associate being Black with being an immigrant. That tendency is an example of how individuals, consciously or unconsciously, reaffirm difference and

CP Picture Archive/The Canadian Press/Paul Chiasso

remind those of us who are constructed as "other"—because we do not "look and/or sound Canadian"—of our "outsider status." Is it any wonder, then, that, when asked, we mention our ethnocultural origins, hyphenate our identities, and/or continue to identify ourselves as immigrants rather than Canadians? In doing so, we avoid the further question, "But where are you really from?"

In some circles the question "Where are you from?" is considered a "friendly" way of initiating a conversation, of indicating an interest in the background and experiences of the person, and/or of showing that the questioner sees the "difference" and is not "colour-blind." I am aware that students sometimes ask this question because they are interested in establishing a "friendly" rapport with me. But my response (or nonresponse) to the question does not mean that I am being unfriendly; rather, it is a way to have students, and whites in particular, recognize that all of our

interactions, and indeed the educational process we engage in, are mediated by our race and other identities—their own as well as mine. Race and racial difference, then, are not the only, or even the most, significant factors around which interactions are built. I am not suggesting that students ignore our differences with regard to race—surely, we all see colour—but I want them to recognize, in my reactions to the question, my resistance to how my "otherness" is reinscribed and the not-so-subtle ways in which they make evident their privilege and power in our encounters.

In my experience with racial minority students, and Blacks in particular, the question is sometimes a way of establishing a connection or creating distance. In attempting to create distance, the question would be a way of demonstrating to their peers that there is a difference between us—I talk with an "accented" voice and they do not, because they are Canadian (born).

anada is a diverse and complex society composed of racially and ethnically different groups. Our country has a reputation as a tolerant and compassionate country whose success in race and ethnic relations has received worldwide admiration (Fleras & Elliot, 2003). Canada is widely renowned for its "cultural democracy" and "harmonious" ethnic diversity (James, 2005) Without question, significant gains have been made in the past 50 years for "visible" and "non-visible" minority groups in Canada (Hier and Singh Bolaria, 2007). From a distance, Canada maintains its enviable status. However, upon closer examination, we see a more complex picture in terms of race and ethnic relations. Despite our claims that Canadians are "colour-blind", racist ideas and practices affect individuals and groups in very real ways. Racism is not only part of Canada's history, but also an important part of some racial and ethnic groups' present-day reality (Satzewich and Liodakis, 2007). In this chapter, racism will be central to the discussion of race and ethnicity. Before reading on, test your knowledge about racism in Canada by taking the quiz in Box 9.1.

QUESTIONS AND ISSUES

Chapter Focus Question: What is the significance of race in Canadian society?

How do race and ethnicity differ?

How does discrimination differ from prejudice?

How are racial and ethnic relations analyzed according to the main theoretical perspectives?

What are the unique experiences of racial and ethnic groups in Canada?

March 21 is recognized annually as the International Day for the Elimination of Racial Discrimination. On that day in 1960, police opened fire and killed 69 people at a peaceful demonstration against apartheid in South Africa.

RACE AND ETHNICITY

What is "race"? Some people think it refers to skin colour (the *Caucasian race*); others use it to refer to a religion (the *Jewish race*), nationality (the *British race*), or the entire human species (the *human race*) (Marger, 2000). Popular usages of race have been based on the assumption that a race is a grouping or classification based on *genetic* variations in physical appearance, particularly skin colour. However, social scientists and biologists dispute the idea that biological race is a meaningful concept (Johnson, 1995). In fact, the idea of race has little meaning in a biological sense because of the enormous amount of interbreeding that has taken place within the human population. For these reasons, sociologists sometimes place "race" in quotation marks to show that categorizing individuals and population groups on biological characteristics is neither accurate nor based on valid distinctions between the genetic makeup of differently identified "races" (Marshall, 1998). Today, sociologists emphasize that race is a *socially constructed reality,* not a biological one (Hier and Singh Bolaria, 2006). From this approach, the social significance that people accord to race is more significant than any biological differences that might exist among people who are placed in arbitrary categories.

BOX 9.1 SOCIOLOGY AND EVERYDAY LIFE

How Much Do You Know about Racial and Ethnic Relations in Canada?

J⇒in|n™
on TurningPoint®

True	False	
T	**F**	1. Canadians are significantly less racist than Americans.
T	F	2. The majority of Canadians support multiculturalism.
T	**F**	3. Racism in Canada is a result of immigration of nonwhites.
T	**F**	4. Racism occurs only in times of economic decline and recession.
T	**F**	5. Canada continues to employ racial criteria in the selection of new immigrants.
T	**F**	6. No civil rights movement has ever existed in Canada.
T	**F**	7. Employment-equity programs directed at hiring visible minorities are a form of reverse discrimination.
T	**F**	8. Slavery has never existed in Canada.

Answers on page 210.

A *race* is a category of people who have been singled out as inferior or superior, often on the basis of real or alleged physical characteristics, such as skin colour, hair texture, eye shape, or other subjectively selected attributes (Feagin and Feagin, 2003). Categories of people frequently thought of as racial groups include Asian Canadians, African Canadians, and Aboriginal peoples. This classification is rooted in 19th-century distinctions made by some biologists who divided the world's population into three racial categories: *Caucasian*—people characterized as having relatively light skin and fine hair; *Negroid*—people with darker skin and coarser, curlier hair; and *Mongoloid*—people with yellow or brown skin and distinctively shaped eyelids. However, racial categorization based on phenotypical differences (such as facial characteristics or skin colour) does not correlate with genotypical differences (differences in genetic makeup). As anthropologists and biologists have acknowledged for some time, most of us have more in common genetically with individuals from another "race" than we have with most people from our own. Moreover, throughout human history, extensive interbreeding has made such classifications unduly simplistic.

How do you classify yourself with regard to race? For an increasing number of people, this is a difficult question to answer. What if you were asked about your ethnic origin or your ethnicity? The Canadian census, unlike that of the United States, collects information on ethnic origin rather than race. Race refers only to *physical* characteristics, but the concept of ethnicity refers to *cultural* features. An **ethnic group is a collection of people distinguished, by others or by themselves, primarily on the basis of cultural or nationality characteristics** (Feagin and Feagin, 2003). Ethnic groups share five main characteristics: (1) *unique cultural traits,* such as language, clothing, holidays, or religious practice; (2) *a sense of community;* (3) *a feeling of ethnocentrism;* (4) *ascribed membership from birth;* and (5) *territoriality, or a tendency to occupy a distinct geographic area.*

Although some people do not identify with any ethnic group, others participate in social interaction with the individuals in their group and feel a sense of common identity based on cultural characteristics such as language, religion, or politics. Ethnicity provides individuals with a sense of identity and belonging based on not only their perception of being different, but also on others' recognition of their uniqueness.

The Social Significance of Race and Ethnicity

How important are race and ethnicity in Canada? It is easy to suggest that race is insignificant if one is not a member of a racial minority. But, whether we like to acknowledge it or not, race does matter. It matters because it provides privilege and power for some. Fleras and Elliott (1999:33) discuss the significance of being white and enjoying what has sometimes been referred to as *white privilege:*

BOX 9.1   **SOCIOLOGY AND EVERYDAY LIFE**

Answers to the Sociology Quiz on Racism

JoinIn™
on TurningPoint®

1. **False.**   A comparative study of public opinion in both countries revealed that Canadians and Americans are roughly similar in their attitudes and behaviour toward racial minorities.

2. **True.**   A recent poll indicated that over 80 percent of Canadians agree that the government should support the preservation of the multicultural heritage of Canadians (ACS/Environics, 2002).

3. **False.**   The argument here is that if immigration is curbed, racism will decrease. However, even before Canada began allowing large-scale immigration, racism existed in the relationship between white colonial settlers and Aboriginal peoples (Henry and Tator, 2006).

4. **False.**   Racism has been practised systematically in Canada since this country was formed—even in times of economic prosperity. For example, in the early 1950s, despite an economic boom, Chinese and Japanese citizens were regarded as "enemy aliens" (Henry and Tator, 2006).

5. **False.**   Canada officially abandoned racial criteria in the selection of new immigrants in the mid-1960s, when the points system was first introduced (Henry and Tator, 2006).

6. **False.**   In the 1940s and 1950s, organizations such as the Windsor Council on Group Relations, the National Unity Association of Chatham-Dresden-North Buxton, and the Negro Citizens' Association of Toronto fought segregation in housing and employment, as well as fighting racist immigration laws (Fleras and Elliot, 2003).

7. **False.**   For employment-equity policies to be a form of reverse discrimination, they would have to require employers to discriminate against better-qualified whites and give an unfair advantage to visible minorities. Employment equity is directed not at discrimination, but at the elimination of a long history of employment practices that result in preferential treatment toward white candidates (Fleras and Elliot, 2003)

8. **False.**   Indeed, slavery was legal and practised by Europeans in Canada since almost the first European settlement of New France. Sixteen legislators in the first Parliament of Upper Canada owned slaves. Slavery existed in Quebec, New Brunswick, Nova Scotia, and Ontario until the early 19th century (Satzewich, 1998).

Think for a moment about the privileges associated with whiteness, many of which are taken for granted and unearned by accident of birth. Being white means you can purchase a home in any part of town and expect cordial treatment rather than community grumblings about the neighborhood "going to pot." Being white saves you the embarrassment of going into a shopping mall with fears of being followed, frisked, monitored, or finger printed. Being white means you can comment on a variety of topics without someone questioning your objectivity or second-guessing your motives. Being white provides a peace of mind in that your actions are judged not as a betrayal of or a credit to your race, but in terms of individual idiosyncrasies. . . . Finally, being white ensures one the satisfaction of socializing at night, without being pulled over by the police or patted down.

Ethnicity, like race, is a basis of hierarchical ranking in society. John Porter (1965) described Canada as a "vertical mosaic," made up of different ethnic groups wielding varying degrees of social and economic power, status, and prestige. Porter's extensive analysis of ethnic groups in Canada revealed a significant degree of ethnic stratification, with some ethnic groups heavily represented in the upper strata, or elite, and other groups heavily represented in the lower strata. The dominant group holds power over other (subordinate) ethnic groups. A more recent analysis by Jason and Matthews (2005) reported that the vertical mosaic might now resemble more of a "coloured mosaic." After controlling for level of education and other relevant social variables, they reported that Aboriginal peoples were still at the bottom of the income hierarchy. Similarly disadvantaged were almost all Asian groups and most of those of Latin American and Middle Eastern ethnicity (Lian and Matthews, 2005:134). Perhaps this revised mosaic is a more a reflection of minority-group status than the ethnicity of particular disadvantaged groups in society.

Majority and Minority Groups

The terms *majority group* and *minority group* are widely used, but what do they actually mean? To sociologists, a **majority (or *dominant*) group is one** **that is advantaged and has superior resources and rights in a society** (Feagin and Feagin, 2003). In Canada, whites with northern European ancestry (often referred to as Euro-Canadians, white Anglo-Saxon Protestants, or WASPs) are considered a majority group. A **minority (or *subordinate*) group is one whose members, because of physical or cultural characteristics, are disadvantaged and subjected to unequal treatment by the dominant group and who regard themselves as objects of collective discrimination**. All visible minorities and white women are considered minority-group members in Canada. The term **visible minority refers to an official government category of nonwhite, non-Caucasian individuals**. Included in this category are black people, Chinese, Japanese, Koreans, Filipinos, Indo-Pakistanis, West Asians and Arabs, Southeast Asians, Latin Americans, and Pacific Islanders (Statistics Canada, 2008). Aboriginal people form a separate category. Between 2001 and 2006, the visible minority population increased over 27 percent, five times faster than the increase for the population as a whole (see the Census profile given below) Today, over five million Canadians—close to one in six—identified themselves as members of a visible minority (Statistics Canada, 2008e).

Census Profile   **Number and Share of Visible Minority Persons in Canada, 1981–2006**

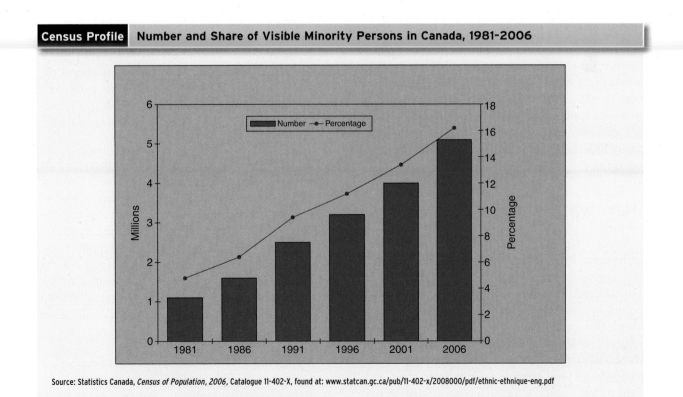

Source: Statistics Canada, *Census of Population, 2006*, Catalogue 11-402-X, found at: www.statcan.gc.ca/pub/11-402-x/2008000/pdf/ethnic-ethnique-eng.pdf

Although the terms *majority group* and *minority group* are widely used, their actual meanings are not clear. In the sociological sense, *group* is misleading because people who merely share ascribed racial or ethnic characteristics do not constitute a group. Further, *majority* and *minority* have meanings associated with both numbers and domination. Numerically speaking, *minority* means that a group is smaller in number than a dominant group. However, in countries such as South Africa and India, this has not historically been true. Those running the country were of a race (in South Africa) or caste (in India), with far fewer members than the masses that they ruled. Consequently, the use of these terms from a standpoint of dominance is more accurate. In this context, majority and minority refer to relationships of advantage/disadvantage and power/exploitation.

PREJUDICE

Prejudice is a negative attitude based on preconceived notions about members of selected groups. The term *prejudice* comes from the Latin words *prae* ("before") and *judicium* ("judgment"), which means that people may be biased either for or against members of other groups before they have had any contact with them. Although prejudice can be either *positive* (bias in favour of a group—often our own) or *negative* (bias against a group—one we deem less worthy than our own), it most often refers to the negative attitudes people may have about members of other racial or ethnic groups. *Racial prejudices* involve beliefs that certain racial groups are innately inferior to others or have a disproportionate number of negative traits.

Stereotypes

Prejudice is rooted in stereotypes and ethnocentrism. As discussed in Chapter 2, *ethnocentrism* refers to the tendency to regard one's own culture and group as the standard, and thus superior, whereas all other groups are seen as inferior. Ethnocentrism is maintained and perpetuated by *stereotypes*—overgeneralizations about the appearance, behaviour, or other characteristics of members of particular groups. The term *stereotype* comes from the Greek word *stereos* ("solid"), and refers to a fixed mental impression (Cashmore, 1996). Although all stereotypes are hurtful, negative stereotypes are particularly harmful to members of minority groups. Consider the following conversation:

Sabra: So, you think I'm not like the rest of them.

Alex: Yes, you are different. Well, you know what I mean.

Sabra: No, I don't. Tell me exactly what you do mean.

Alex: Well, when I see you, I don't see your colour. I don't see you as a South Asian. You're not like the rest of them. I'd like to think that I judge you though my own personal experiences with you. I don't judge you on the basis of your culture, colour, or class for that matter. I refuse to see you as being different. You're just another human being.

Sabra: First you tell me that I'm different, and then you say that you refuse to see me as being different. So which is it? Let's try to unravel this.

Alex: Well, I meant that you're more like me, you know, like one of us.

Sabra: Oh, so, I'm more like you and less like, should I say it, "a real South Asian." You see, although you're not saying it, your statement reveals that you have some preconceived ideas of South Asians, the people that I'm supposed to be so unlike. This means that whatever your preconceived ideas are of South Asians, they make South Asians less acceptable, less attractive, and less appealing to you than I. Well, this is not just stereotyping, it is racist stereotyping. (Desai, 2001:241–242)

How do people develop these stereotypes? As discussed in Box 9.2, the media are a major source of racial and ethnic stereotypes. Another source of stereotypes is ethnic jokes, which portray minorities in a derogatory manner. Take a moment and think of an ethnic joke you have heard recently. Do youthink this joke is harmful? Would you tell the joke to the member of the ethnic group that the joke is about? Paul, a student in a race and ethnic-relations course at a Canadian university, discusses this issue:

I laugh at a joke that uses a Black . . . because I associate a stereotype with what has been said, I am a bigot. For example, what do you call a Black guy in a new car? A thief. Funny, eh? No, the joke itself is not funny, but it makes

BOX 9.2 SOCIOLOGY AND THE MEDIA

Racism in the Media

The media are one of the most powerful sources of information in society, influencing the way we look at the world, how we understand it, and the manner in which we experience and relate to it. In other words, the media provide a "window on the world." For many Canadians, the media are the primary source of information about racial and ethnic groups. Racial minorities have accused Canada's mass media of slanted coverage; descriptions of the coverage have ranged from unfair and inadequate to overtly racist. These charges are not as obvious as we might expect. Rather, one's evaluation of media racism is contingent upon how racism is defined. The following vignettes from *Media and Minorities: Representing Diversity in a Multicultural Canada* (Fleras and Kunz, 2001) provide some insight into the complexity of racism when applied to media representations of minority men and women.

1. Diversity rules? On the basis of 114 hours of TV viewing by a *Toronto Star* television critic, minorities remain underrepresented in relation to their population and relative to whites. Advertisers justify this discrepancy on the grounds that minority images may offend their mainstream customers.
2. A six-month study of five major Canadian papers confirmed how the mainstream media routinely stereotype Muslims as barbaric fanatics.

Muslims were repeatedly typecast as violent persons or terrorists who happen to believe in a fundamentalist religion that condones acts of inhumanity.

3. A CTV newscaster accidentally blurted out a self-deprecating employment-equity "joke" about lesbians, blacks, people with disabilities, and stutterers. She was subsequently fired for her impertinent remarks. For some, this incident was proof that racism was alive and well in Canada's mainstream media; for others, the draconian response simply confirmed the degree of political correctness that was compromising society, despite Canada's reputation as one of the world's most tolerant countries. For still others, the issue was not about the attitude of one broadcaster, but a reflection of a bias that pervades the structure and culture of media organizations (Tator and Henry, 1999).

What do these vignettes have in common? In each of these media-related incidents, the media have been accused of reflecting, reinforcing, and advancing mainstream racism. Exactly what is meant by racism in the media? Are media racist, and, if so, how? Is it more accurate to say that media are the sites of racist incidents by racist individuals? Or are media racist by definition, given their priorities, agenda, operational values, and practices?

Source: Fleras and Kunz, 2001.

---

reference to a stereotype about Blacks that they're all thieves, which I do not find funny. . . . That kind of joke is not funny. It does not point out a funny stereotype of a certain race . . . it is pure malice and cruelty against a specific group. (James, 2001:107)

Measuring Prejudice

To measure levels of prejudice, some social scientists use the concept of *social distance,* **which refers to the extent to which people are willing to interact and establish relationships with members of racial and ethnic groups other than their own** (Park and Burgess, 1921). Sociologist Emory Bogardus (1925, 1968) developed a scale to measure social distance

in specific situations ranging from minimal contact to marriage. He concluded that some groups were consistently ranked as more desirable than others for close interpersonal contacts. A more study showed that Canadian-born respondents reported greater levels of "comfort" when interacting with Canadians of British, Italian, French, Ukrainian, German, and Jewish origin. Respondents reported significantly less comfort when interacting with Canadians of West Indian, black, Muslim, Arab, Indo-Pakistani, and Sikh origin or religion (Angus Reid, 1991).

Can prejudice really be measured? Existing research does not provide us with a conclusive answer to this question. Most social-distance research has examined the perceptions of whites; few studies have measured the perceptions of people of colour about their interactions with members of the dominant group.

DISCRIMINATION

Whereas prejudice is an attitude, ***discrimination involves actions or practices of dominant-group members (or their representatives) that have a harmful impact on members of a subordinate group (Feagin and Feagin, 2003)***. For example, people who are prejudiced toward East Indians, Jews, or Aboriginal peoples may refuse to hire them, rent an apartment to them, or allow their children to play with children belonging to those groups. In these instances, discrimination involves the differential treatment of minority-group members not because of their ability or merit, but because of irrelevant characteristics such as skin colour or language preference. Discriminatory actions vary in severity from the use of derogatory labels to violence against individuals and groups. Discrimination takes two basic forms: *de jure,* or legal discrimination, which is encoded in laws; and *de facto,* or informal discrimination, which is entrenched in social customs and institutions. *De jure* discrimination has been backed by explicitly discriminatory laws, such as the Chinese Exclusionary Act, which restricted immigration to Canada on the basis of race, or the Nuremberg laws passed in Nazi Germany, which imposed restrictions on Jews. The Indian Act of Canada provides other examples of *de jure* discrimination. According to the act, an Aboriginal woman who married a non-Native man automatically lost her Indian-status rights and was thus no longer authorized to live on a reserve. The Indian Act also specified that Native people who graduated from university, or who became doctors, lawyers, or ministers before 1920 were forced to give up their status rights. An amendment to the Indian Act in 1985 (Bill C-31) ended this legally sanctioned discrimination. The *Charter of Rights and Freedoms* prohibits discrimination on the basis of race, ethnicity, or religion. As a result, many cases of *de jure* discrimination have been eliminated. *De facto* discrimination is more subtle and less visible to public scrutiny, and, therefore, much more difficult to eradicate.

Prejudicial attitudes do not always lead to discriminatory behaviour. This was demonstrated in a classic study conducted in the early 1930s. Richard LaPiere travelled around the United States with a Chinese couple, stopping at more than 250 restaurants and hotels along the way. The pervasive anti-Asian prejudice of the time led LaPiere to assume that the travellers would be refused service in most of the hotels and restaurants at which they intended to stop. However, LaPiere was wrong—only one establishment refused service to LaPiere and his friends. Several months later LaPiere sent letters to all the establishments they had visited, asking if they would serve "members of the Chinese race" as guests in their establishments. Ninety-two percent of the establishments that had earlier accepted LaPiere and his guests replied that Chinese people would not be welcome. This study is one of many examples of sociological research that reveals the discrepancy between what people say and what they do (Robertson, 1977).

RACISM

***Racism* is a set of ideas that implies the superiority of one social group over another on the basis of biological or cultural characteristics, together with the power to put these beliefs into practice in a way that denies or excludes minority members** (Fleras and Kunz, 2001).

Racism involves elements of prejudice, ethnocentrism, stereotyping, and discrimination. For example, racism is present in the belief that some racial or ethnic groups are superior while others are inferior; this belief is a prejudice. Racism may be the basis for unfair treatment toward members of a racial or ethnic group. In this case the racism involves discrimination.

Fleras and Elliott (1999) make distinctions between a number of diverse types of racism. ***Overt racism may take the form of public statements about the "inferiority" of members of a racial or ethnic group This form of racism is often described as "red-necked" racism or "hate racism."*** Examples of overt racism although rare, occur in Canada. In 2009, a Winnipeg case made national headlines when family service agencies removed two children from their home because their parents were teaching the children racist views. Social workers became aware when the young girl attended school with white supremacist symbols and slogans drawn all over her skin. The girl informed social workers that she watched violent racist videos in her home and her parents regularly discussed killing minorities. This type of overt racism is becoming increasingly unacceptable in Canadian society, and few people today will tolerate the open expression of racism. In fact, overt acts of discrimination are now illegal. The *Criminal Code,* the *Charter of Rights and Freedoms*, and human-rights legislation have served to limit the expression of racist ideology or active racial discrimination.

***Polite racism* is an attempt to disguise a dislike of others through behaviour that outwardly is**

nonprejudicial. This type of racism may be operating when members of visible minority groups are ignored or turned down for jobs or promotions on a regular basis. Polite racism may consist of subtle remarks or a "look" that has the effect of making visible minorities feel different, inferior, and out of place in Canadian society (Fleras and Elliott, 2003). A number of studies over the past two decades have demonstrated the extent to which this type of racism manifests itself in the workplace (Kunz et al., 2000; Henry, 2006). Researchers have found that members of particular visible minority groups are often ignored; assigned unpleasant tasks at work; turned down for interviews, jobs, and promotions; or excluded from the inner circle of their workplace. Consider the comments from a focus-group participant in a recent study conducted by the Canadian Race Relations Foundation:

I've called for jobs and had people say "come down for an interview" and when I get there, I get the feeling they are surprised to see that I'm black, because I sound like the average guy on the telephone. They've said "oh, the job has just been filled," or during the interview they will say that I'm overqualified or ask me questions like "Are

you sure you want to work at this type of job?" (Kunz et al., 2000:30)

Polite racism may be more subtle or hidden in our "politically correct" society, but the effects on victims are similar to the more overt forms of the past—control, exclusion, and exploitation (Fleras and Elliott, 2003:70).

Subliminal racism **involves a subconscious racism that occurs when there is a conflict of values.** Subliminal racism is not directly expressed but is demonstrated in opposition to progressive minority policies (such as Canada's immigration policy) or programs (such as employment equity). For example, after the 9/11 terrorist attacks, there were insinuations that Canada's "weak" immigration policies allowed the terrorists to enter the United States (Dench, 2001). Subliminal racism, more than any other type of racism, demonstrates the ambiguity concerning racism. Values that support racial equality are publicly affirmed while, at the same time, resentment at the prospect of moving over and making space for newcomers is also present (Fleras and Elliott, 2003).

Institutionalized racism **is made up of the rules, procedures, and practices that directly or indirectly promote, sustain, or entrench differential advantage or privilege for dominant group members.** The practice of word-of-mouth recruitment is an example of an institutional practice that has the result of excluding racial minorities from the hiring selection process.

Institutionalized racism may also be reflected in organizational practices, rules, or procedures that have the unintended consequences of excluding minority group members. For example, occupations such as police officer and firefighter had minimum weight, height, and educational requirements for job applicants. These criteria resulted in discrimination because they favoured white applicants over members of many minority groups, as well as males over females. Other examples of this type of institutional racism include the requirement of a college or university degree for nonspecialized jobs, employment regulations that require people to work on their Sabbath, and the policy of recognizing only university degrees and trade diplomas obtained in North America.

Institutionalized racism is normally reflected in the statistical underrepresentation of certain groups within an institution or organization. For example, a given group may represent 15 percent of the general population but only 2 percent of those promoted to upper-management positions in a large company. Efforts to eliminate this kind of disproportionate

Recent anti-Semitic attacks on Jewish synagogues are an unfortunate reminder that some forms of overt racism still exist.

AFP/Getty Images

Table 9.1	THE FACTS OF RACISM			
	WHAT: CORE SLOGAN	WHY: DEGREE OF INTENT	HOW: STYLE OF EXPRESSION	WHERE: MAGNITUDE AND SCOPE
Overt racism	"X" get out	Conscious	Personal and explicit	Interpersonal
Polite racism	"Sorry, the job is taken."	Moderate	Discreet and subtle	Personal
Subliminal racism	"I'm not racist, but . . ."	Ambivalent	Oblique	Cultural
Institutionalized racism	"We treat everyone the same here"	Unintentional or intentional	Impersonal	Institutional and societal

Source: *Unequal Relationships: An Introduction to race, Ethnic and Aboriginal Dynamics in Canada, 2nd Ed*, Fleras and Elliot, 1996, p. 84, Prentice Hall, reprinted with permission by Pearson Canada Inc.

representation are the focus of employment-equity legislation. The target groups for employment equity in Canada are visible minorities, women, people with disabilities, and Aboriginal peoples. Strategies include modified admissions tests and requirements, enhanced recruitment of certain target groups, establishment of hiring quotas for particular minority groups, or specialized training or employment programs for specific target groups. Consideration of employment-equity strategies inevitably leads to claims of reverse discrimination by some individuals who enjoy majority-group status. For a detailed examination of this claim, see Box 9.3 on page 217. See Table 9.1 on this page for a summary of the types of racism.

SOCIOLOGICAL PERSPECTIVES ON ETHNIC RELATIONS AND RACE

Symbolic interactionists, functionalists, conflict analysts, feminists, and postmodernists examine race and ethnic relations in different ways. Functionalists focus on the macrolevel intergroup processes that occur between members of majority and minority groups in society. Conflict theorists analyze power and economic differentials between the dominant group and subordinate groups. Interactionists examine how microlevel contacts between people may produce either greater racial tolerance or increased levels of hostility. Feminists highlight the interactive effects of racism and sexism on the

exploitation of women who are members of visible minority groups. Postmodernists focus on the fluid nature of racial and ethnic identities and examine how these concepts are socially constructed.

Symbolic Interactionist Perspectives

What happens when people from different racial and ethnic groups come into contact with one another? In the *contact hypothesis*, interactionists point out that contact between people from divergent groups should lead to favourable attitudes and behaviour when certain factors are present. Members of each group must (1) have equal status, (2) pursue the same goals, (3) cooperate with one another to achieve their goals, and (4) receive positive feedback when they interact with one another in positive, nondiscriminatory ways (Allport, 1958; Coakley, 2004).

What happens when individuals meet someone who does not conform to their existing stereotype? Frequently, they ignore anything that contradicts the stereotype, or interpret the situation to support their prejudices (Coakley, 2004). For example, a person who does not fit the stereotype may be seen as an exception—"You're not like other [persons of a particular race]."

When a person is seen as conforming to a stereotype, he or she may be treated simply as one of "you people." Former Los Angeles Lakers basketball star Earvin "Magic" Johnson (1992:31–32) described how he was categorized along with all other African Americans when he was bused to a predominantly white school:

BOX 9.3   CRITICAL THINKING

Can Minorities be Racist?

One of the most common questions asked by students when they first examine the issue of racism and its diverse forms concerns reverse racism. Class discussions regarding employment equity and equality rights inevitably provoke a discussion about whether members of minorities can also be racist. For example, can ethnic minorities be racist toward other ethnic minorities? Is it a case of reverse racism when non-Aboriginal writers are discouraged from filming or writing fiction about Aboriginal themes? Is it racist for Aboriginal people to accuse whites of genocide because of the dominant society's undermining of the political, social, and cultural structure of Aboriginal society? Is it racist for black militants to openly display hatred toward whites as an inferior race? Are black leaders who make defamatory remarks about Jews acting in a racist manner (D'Sousa, 1996)? According to sociologist Augie Fleras, these difficult questions may never be answered to everyone's satisfaction, but the very asking promotes a clearer understanding of racism.

Consider the suggestion of reverse racism when the Writers' Union of Canada sponsored a conference in Vancouver in 1994 that barred white Canadians from some activities. This conference, Writing Thru "Race": A Conference for First Nations Writers and Writers of Colour, sought a forum for minorities to explore the experiences of racism in a world where, national myths notwithstanding,

race matters. The conference justified its decision to exclude whites from one session on the grounds of improving dialogue among the historically oppressed, in the same way women's consciousness-raising movements excluded men. Critics saw this as a reverse discrimination on the basis of race. They resented the idea that people could be singled out and denied participation on the basis of race.

Would you agree that this is a case of reverse racism? Is it possible for minorities to be racist? Your answer will depend largely on how you define racism—as biology or power. An understanding of racism as biology suggests that anyone who approaches, defines, or treats someone else on the basis of race is a racist. Thus, minorities can be racist if they criticize or deny whites because of their whiteness ("reverse racism").

However, reference to racism as power points to a different conclusion. Accusations of reverse racism must go beyond superficial appearances. There is a world of difference between using race to create equality (employment equity) and using it to limit opportunity (discrimination), even if the rhetoric sounds the same. Emphasis must be instead on the context of the actions and on their social consequences. Racism is not about treating others differently because they are different; rather, it involves different treatment in colour-conscious contexts of power that limit opportunities or privileges for racial minorities.

Source: Fleras and Elliott, 2003, pp. 62–63.

On the first day of [basketball] practice, my teammates froze me out. Time after time I was wide open, but nobody threw me the ball. At first I thought they just didn't see me. But I woke up after a kid named Danny Parks looked right at me and then took a long jumper. Which he missed.

I was furious, but I didn't say a word. Shortly after that, I grabbed a defensive rebound and took the ball all the way down for a basket. I did it again and a third time, too.

Finally Parks got angry and said, "Hey, pass the [bleeping] ball."

That did it. I slammed down the ball and glared at him. Then I exploded. "I knew this would

happen!" I said. "That's why I didn't want to come to this [bleeping] school in the first place!"

"Oh, yeah? Well, you people are all the same," he said. "You think you're gonna come in here and do whatever you want? Look, hotshot, your job is to get the rebound. Let us do the shooting."

The interaction between Johnson and Parks demonstrates that when people from different racial and ethnic groups come into contact with one another, they may treat one another as stereotypes, not as individuals.

Symbolic interactionist perspectives make us aware of the importance of inter-group contact and the fact that it may either intensify or reduce racial and ethnic stereotyping and prejudice.

Functionalist Perspectives

How do members of subordinate racial and ethnic groups become a part of the dominant group? To answer this question, early functionalists studied immigration and patterns of majority- and minority-group interaction.

Assimilation   *Assimilation* **is a process by which members of subordinate racial and ethnic groups become absorbed into the dominant culture.** To functionalist analysts, assimilation is beneficial because it contributes to the stability of society by minimizing group differences that otherwise might result in hostility and violence. Assimilation occurs at several distinct levels, including the cultural, structural, biological, and psychological levels.

Cultural assimilation, or *acculturation,* occurs when members of an ethnic group adopt dominant-group traits, such as language, dress, values, religion, and food preferences. Cultural assimilation in this country initially followed an "Angloconformity" model; members of subordinate ethnic groups were expected to conform to the culture of the dominant white Anglo-Saxon population (Gordon, 1964). However, some groups, such as Aboriginal peoples and the Québécois, refused to be assimilated and sought to maintain their unique cultural identity.

Structural assimilation, or *integration,* occurs when members of subordinate racial or ethnic groups gain acceptance in everyday social interaction with members of the dominant group. This type of assimilation typically starts in large, impersonal settings, such as schools and workplaces, and only later (if at all) results in close friendships and intermarriage.

Biological assimilation, or *amalgamation,* occurs when members of one group marry those of other social or ethnic groups. Biological assimilation has been more complete in some other countries, such as Mexico and Brazil, than in Canada.

Psychological assimilation involves a change in racial or ethnic self-identification on the part of an individual. Rejection by the dominant group may prevent psychological assimilation by members of some subordinate racial and ethnic groups, especially those with visible characteristics, such as skin colour or facial features, that differ from those of the dominant group.

Ethnic Pluralism   Instead of complete assimilation, many groups share elements of the mainstream culture while remaining culturally distinct from both the dominant group and other social and ethnic groups. *Ethnic pluralism* **is the coexistence of a variety of distinct racial and ethnic groups within one society.** *Equalitarian pluralism,* **or** *accommodation,* **is a situation in which ethnic groups co-exist in equality with one another.**

Has Canada achieved equalitarian pluralism? The Canadian Multiculturalism Act of 1988 stated that "all Canadians are full and equal partners in Canadian society." The Department of Multiculturalism and Citizenship was established in 1991 with the goal of encouraging ethnic minorities to participate fully in all aspects of Canadian life and, at the same time, maintain their distinct ethnic identities and cultural practices. The objective of multiculturalism is to "promote unity through diversity." Multiculturalism programs provide funding for education, consultative support, and a range of activities, including heritage language training, race-relations training, ethnic policing and justice, and ethnic celebrations. In recent years, multiculturalism policies have been under increasing attack. Neil Bissoondath, author of *Selling Illusions: The Cult of Multiculturalism in Canada* (1994), suggests that multiculturalism does not promote equalitarian pluralism. Rather, he argues, multiculturalism serves to discourage differences, and it alienates people from mainstream society, which detracts from national unity.

Inequalitarian Pluralism, or Segregation

Inequalitarian pluralism or segregation exists when specific ethnic groups are set apart from the dominant group and have unequal access to power and privilege (Marger, 2000). *Segregation* **is the spatial and social separation of categories of people by race, ethnicity, class, gender, and/or religion.** Segregation may be enforced by law (*de jure*) or by custom (*de facto*). An example of *de jure* segregation was the *Jim Crow laws,* which legalized the separation of the races in all public accommodations (including hotels, restaurants, transportation, hospitals, jails, schools, churches, and cemeteries) in the Southern United States after the American Civil War (Feagin and Feagin, 2003).

De jure segregation of Blacks is also part of the history of Canada. Blacks in Canada lived in largely segregated communities in Nova Scotia, New Brunswick, and Ontario, where racial segregation was evident in the schools, government, workplace, residential housing, and elsewhere. Segregated schools continued in Nova Scotia until the 1960s. Residential segregation was legally enforced through the use of racially restrictive covenants attached to deeds and leases. Separation and refusal of service were common in restaurants, theatres, and recreational facilities (Henry et al., 2006).

One of the most blatant examples of segregation in Canada is the federal reserve system for status Indians, by which Aboriginal peoples were segregated on reserves in remote areas.

Although legally sanctioned forms of racial segregation have been all but eliminated, *de facto* segregation, which is enforced by custom, still exists.

Conflict Perspectives

Why do some ethnic groups continue to experience subjugation after many years? Conflict theorists focus on economic stratification and access to power in their analysis of race and ethnic relations.

Internal Colonialism
Conflict theorists use the term *internal colonialism* to refer to a situation in which members of a racial or ethnic group are conquered or colonized and forcibly placed under the economic and political control of the dominant group. Groups that have been subjected to internal colonialism often remain in subordinate positions longer than groups that have voluntarily migrated to North America.

Aboriginal peoples in Canada were colonized by Europeans and others who invaded their lands and conquered them. In the process, Aboriginal peoples lost property, political rights, aspects of their culture, and often their lives (Frideres and Gadacz, 2005). The capitalist class acquired cheap labour and land through this government-sanctioned racial exploitation. The effects of past internal colonialism are reflected today in the number of Aboriginal peoples who live in extreme poverty on government reserves (Fleras and Elliott, 2003).

The experiences of internally colonized groups are unique in three ways: (1) they have been forced to exist in a society other than their own; (2) they have been kept out of the economic and political mainstream, so that it is difficult for them to compete with dominant-group members; and (3) they have been subjected to severe attacks on their own culture, which may lead to its extinction (Blauner, 1972).

The Split-Labour-Market Theory
Who benefits from the exploitation of visible minorities? The split-labour-market theory states that both white workers and members of the capitalist class benefit from the exploitation of visible minorities. The *split labour market* refers to the division of the economy into two areas of employment: a primary sector, or upper tier, composed of higher-paid (usually dominant-group) workers in more secure jobs, and a secondary sector, or lower tier, made up of lower-paid (often subordinate-group) workers in jobs with little security and hazardous working conditions (Bonacich, 1972, 1976). According to this perspective, white workers in the upper tier may use racial discrimination against non-whites to protect their positions. These actions most often occur when upper-tier workers feel threatened by lower-tier workers hired by capitalists to reduce labour costs and maximize corporate profits. In the past, immigrants were a source of cheap labour that employers could use to break strikes and keep wages down. Agnes Calliste (1987) applied the split-labour-market theory in her study, "Sleeping Car Porters in Canada." Calliste found a doubly submerged split labour market, with three levels of stratification in this area of employment. Although "white" trade unions were unable to restrict access to porter positions on the basis of race, they were able to impose differential pay scales. Consequently, black porters received less pay than white porters did, even though they were doing the same work. Furthermore, the labour market was doubly submerged because black immigrant workers from the United States received even less pay than did both black and white Canadian porters. Throughout history, higher-paid workers have responded with racial hostility and joined movements to curtail immigration and thus do away with the source of cheap labour (Marger, 2000).

Feminist Perspectives

Minority women (women of colour, immigrant women, and Aboriginal women) are doubly disadvantaged because of their gender. The term *gendered racism* refers to the interactive effect of racism and sexism in the exploitation of women of colour. According to social psychologist Philomena Essed (1991), women's particular position must be explored within each racial or ethnic group because their experiences will not have been the same as the men's in each grouping.

All workers are not equally exploited by capitalists. Gender and race or ethnicity are important in this exploitation. For example, jobs are race-typed and gender-typed. Consider a registered nurse and a custodian in a hospital. What race and gender are they likely to be? Did a white woman and a man of colour come to mind? Most jobs have similar race and gender designations. Often, the jobs people hold are linked to their class, race, and gender. Consequently, the effect of class on our life chances is inseparable from the effects of our gender and race or ethnicity. The split labour market, then, involves not only class but also race, ethnicity, and gender (Amott and Matthaei, 1991).

Historically, the high-paying primary labour market has been monopolized by white men. People of colour and most white women more often hold lower-tier jobs (Arat-Koc, 1999). Below that tier is the underground sector of the economy, characterized by illegal or quasi-legal activities such as drug trafficking, prostitution, and working in sweatshops that do not meet minimum wage and safety standards. Many undocumented workers and some white women and people of colour attempt to earn a living in this sector (Amott and Matthaei, 1991).

Postmodern Perspectives

Conventional theories of race and ethnicity tend to see racial or ethnic identities as organized around social structures that are fixed and closed, such as nations, tribes, bands, and communities. As such, there is little movement in or out of these groups. Postmodern perspectives, in contrast, view ethnic and racial identities as largely a consequence of personal choice (agency) and subjective definition. Ethnic and racial identities are socially constructed and given meaning by our fragmented society These identities are constantly evolving and subject to the continuous interplay of history, power, and culture.

A postmodernist framework may ask how social actors come to understand who they are in "race" terms. Central to a postmodern perspective on race is the concept of *discourse*. Based on the work of Michel Foucault, discourse is used to refer to "different ways of structuring knowledge and social practice" (Fiske, 1994, cf. Henry and Tator, 2006). Postmodernists view reality as constructed through a broad range of discourses, which includes all that is written, spoken, or otherwise represented through language and communication systems (Anderson, 2006:394). Analysts

The effects of past colonialism are reflected in the poor housing conditions of many Aboriginal persons living on reserves today.

using this perspective will therefore focus on *deconstructing—meaning analyzing the assumptions and meanings embedded in scientific works* (Anderson, 2006).

Postmodernist scholars use this perspective to shift the frame of analysis away from race relations to an intense examination (deconstruction) of racist discourse. *Racist discourse* or *racialized discourse* is defined as a collection of words, images, and practices through which racial power is directed against ethnic and racial minority groups. An analysis of racist discourse is central to understanding the ways in which a particular society gives a voice to racism and advances the interests of whites.

Frances Henry and Carol Tator (2006) have identified examples of racist discourse that serve to sustain or perpetuate racism in our society. For example, the *discourse of denial* suggests that racism simply does not exist in our Canadian democratic society. When racism is shown to exist, the discourse of denial will explain it away as an isolated incident. There are numerous examples of the discourse of denial in policing agencies across the country. Despite numerous complaints of racism directed at visible minority groups and Aboriginal persons, top police administrators continue to respond to allegations with "we do not have a problem with racism within our organization" or "I have never witnessed a racist incident."

A postmodern perspective not only examines how identities of racial and ethnic minorities are formed but also asks the same question about white identities. For example, a second related discourse identified by Henry and Tator is the *discourse of colour-blindness*, in which white people insist that they do not notice the skin colour of a racial-minority person. By claiming to be colour blind, members of the dominant white majority are able to ignore the power differentials they experience as a result of their "whiteness" while at the same time negating the racialized experiences of visible minority persons. (2006:25)

An Alternative Perspective: Critical Race Theory

Emerging out of scholarly law studies on racial and ethnic inequality, critical race theory derives its foundation from the civil-rights tradition and the writing of persons such as Martin Luther King, Jr., W. E. B. Du Bois, Malcolm X, and Cesar Chavez. The growth of critical race theory began in Canada in the 1980s. It is based on the same theoretical foundation as its American counterpart—that is, a growing

dissatisfaction with the failure to acknowledge and recognize the critical roles that race and racism have played in the political and legal structures of Canadian society (Aylward, 1999).

Critical race theory has several major premises, including the belief that racism is such an ingrained feature of North American society that it appears to be ordinary and natural to many people (Delgado, 1995). As a result, civil-rights legislation and employment equity may remedy some of the more overt, blatant forms of racial injustice but have little effect on subtle, business-as-usual forms of racism that people of colour experience as they go about their everyday lives. According to this approach, the best way to document racism and ongoing inequality in society is to listen to the lived experiences of people who have experienced such discrimination. In this way, we can learn what actually happens in regard to racial oppression and the many effects it has on people, including alienation, depression, and certain physical illnesses (Razack, 1998).

Central to this argument is the belief that *interest convergence* is a crucial factor in bringing about social change. According to the legal scholar Derrick Bell, white elites tolerate or encourage racial advances for people of colour *only* if the dominant-group members believe that their own self-interest will be served in so doing (cited in Delgado, 1995). From this approach, civil-rights laws typically have benefited white North Americans as much (or more) as people of colour because these laws have been used as mechanisms to ensure that "racial progress occurs at just the right pace: Change that is too rapid would be unsettling to society at large; change that is too slow could prove destabilizing" (Delgado, 1995:xiv).

Critical race theory is similar to postmodernist approaches in that it calls our attention to the idea that things are not always as they seem. Formal equality under the law does not necessarily equate to actual equality in society. This theory also makes us aware of the ironies and contradictions in civil-rights law, which some see as self-serving laws.

Concept Table 9.1 outlines the key aspects of each sociological perspective.

ETHNIC GROUPS IN CANADA

How do racial and ethnic groups come into contact with one another? How do they adjust to one another and to the dominant group over time? Sociologists

Concept Table 9.1	SOCIOLOGICAL PERSPECTIVES ON RACE AND ETHNIC RELATIONS

PERSPECTIVE	FOCUS	THEORY/HYPOTHESIS
Symbolic Interactionist	Microlevel contacts between individuals	Contact hypothesis

Functionalist	Macrolevel intergroup processes	Assimilation
		  cultural
		  biological
		  structural
		  psychological
		Ethnic pluralism
		  equalitarian pluralism
		  inequalitarian pluralism (segregation)

Conflict	Power/economic differentials between dominant and subordinate groups	Caste perspective Class perspective Internal colonialism Split labour market
Feminist	Gendered racism	Minority women are doubly disadvantaged as a result of their gender.
Postmodern	Racialized and racist discourse	Racist discourse serves to sustain and reinforce patterns of discrimination against racial and ethnic minorities.
Critical Race Theory	Racism as an ingrained feature of society that affects everyone's daily life	Laws may remedy overt discrimination but have little effect on subtle racism. Interest convergence is required for social change.

have explored these questions extensively; however, a detailed historical account of each group is beyond the scope of this chapter. Given the diversity of our population, imposing any kind of conceptual order on a discussion of ethnic groups in Canada is difficult. We will look briefly at some of the unique ethnic groups in Canada and examine a history of racism with respect to each group.

Aboriginal Peoples

Canada's Aboriginal peoples are believed to have migrated to North America from Asia an estimated 40 000 years ago (Dyck, 2008). Native peoples are an extremely diverse group with varying access to resources, development levels, and social health. Today, the terms *Native, First Nations,* and *Aboriginal* refer to approximately 55 sovereign peoples, including the Inuit, Cree, Mi'kmaq, Blackfoot,

Iroquois, and Haida. Other categories of Aboriginal peoples are also classified as status Indians (those Indians with legal rights under the Indian Act), non-status Indians (those without legal rights), Métis, and Inuit. Those who settled in the southern part of Canada, Yukon, and the Mackenzie Valley can be termed *North American Indians.* Those located in the eastern Arctic and northern islands, who were formerly referred to as Eskimos, are now referred to as *Inuit.* A third category, *Métis,* who live mostly on the Prairies, are descendants of Indian and non-Indian unions (primarily French settlers and Indian women).

When European settlers arrived on this continent, the Aboriginal inhabitants' way of life was changed forever. Experts estimate that between 1 million and 12 million Aboriginal people lived in North America at that time; however, by 1900 their numbers had been reduced to under 240 000 (Churchill, 1994). What factors led to this drastic depopulation?

Genocide, Forced Migration, and Forced Assimilation   Native people have been the victims of genocide and forced migration. Many Native Americans either were killed or died from European diseases (such as typhoid, smallpox, and measles) and starvation (Wagner and Stearn, 1945; Cook, 1973). In battle, Native people often were no match for the Europeans, who had the latest weaponry (Amott and Matthaei, 1991). Europeans justified their aggression by stereotyping the Natives as "savages" and "heathens" (Frideres and Gadacz, 2004).

Entire Aboriginal nations were forced to move in order to accommodate the white settlers. The "Trail of Tears" was one of the most disastrous of the forced migrations to occur in North America. In the coldest part of the winter of 1832, more than half of the Cherokee Nation died during or as a result of their forced relocation from the southeastern United States to the Indian Territory in Oklahoma (Thornton, 1984)

Indian rights were clearly defined in the Royal Proclamation of 1763, which divided up the North American territory acquired by Britain. In a large area called Indian Territory, the purchase or settlement of land was forbidden without a treaty. However, the government broke treaty after treaty as it removed Aboriginal peoples in order to clear the land for settlement by white pioneers (Green, 1977; Churchill, 1994). The Canadian government then passed the Indian Act of 1876, which gave the federal government control of almost every aspect of Indian life. For example, Aboriginal people were prohibited from owning land, voting, and purchasing and consuming alcohol or leaving the reserves without permission (Frideres and Gadacz, 2005).

Aboriginal children were placed in residential boarding schools to facilitate their assimilation into the dominant culture. The Jesuits and other missionaries who ran these schools believed that Aboriginal peoples should not be left in their "inferior" natural state and considered it their mission to replace Aboriginal culture with Christian beliefs, values, rituals, and practices (Bolaria and Li, 1988). Many of the children who attended these schools were sexually, physically, and emotionally abused. They were not allowed to speak their language or engage in any of their traditional cultural practices. The coercive and oppressive nature of the residential school experience is one of the worst examples of institutionalized racism in Canadian history (Henry et al., 1995:62).

Aboriginal Peoples Today   According to the 2006 census, over one million people reported having Aboriginal ancestry, including almost 700 000 Native American Indians, 300 000 Métis, and 50 000 Inuit. These numbers represent approximately 4 percent of Canada's total population (Statistics Canada, 2008b). See figure 9.2 the Census Profile on this page 226.

Although the majority of registered Indians live on reserves, the majority of the total Aboriginal population live off reserves. The Aboriginal population is unevenly distributed across Canada, with the heaviest concentrations of Aboriginal Canadians in Western and Northern Canada.

In terms of income, employment, housing, nutrition, and health, Aboriginal peoples are the most disadvantaged racial or ethnic group in Canada (Frideres, 2007). The life chances of Aboriginal peoples who live on reserves are especially limited. They have the highest rates of infant mortality and death by exposure and malnutrition. They also have high rates of depression, tuberculosis, alcoholism, and suicide.

Figure 9.1	Aboriginal Identity Population

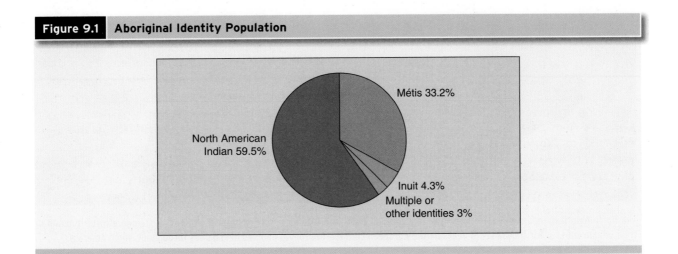

The overall life expectancy of Aboriginal Canadians is five years less than that of non-Natives; this is largely due to poor health services and inadequate housing on reserves. Aboriginal peoples also have had limited educational opportunities (the functional illiteracy of Aboriginal peoples is 45 percent, compared with the overall Canadian rate of 17 percent) and they have an unemployment rate about 29 percent, nearly three times the Canadian rate (Indian and Northern Affairs, 2005). Approximately one-third of Aboriginal persons in Canada live in poverty (Frideres, 2007).

Despite the state's efforts to assimilate Aboriginal peoples into Canadian culture, many Aboriginal people have successfully resisted oppression. National organizations such as the Assembly of First Nations, Inuit Tapirisat, the Native Council of Canada, and the Métis National Council have been instrumental in bringing the demands of those they represent into the political and constitutional arenas. Of these demands, the major ones have been and still are self-government, Aboriginal rights, and the resolution of land claims (see Frideres and Gadacz, 2005).

The Québécois

The European colonization of Canada began with the exploration and settlement of New France. In 1608, the first permanent settlement in New France was established at Quebec City. France's North American empire extended from Hudson Bay to Louisiana.

Following the British conquest of the French in Canada in the Seven Years' War (1756–1763), Canada became a British dominion and the French here found themselves in an inferior position

The North American Indigenous Games, held in Vancouver in 2008, are a reflection of Aboriginal persons' sustained efforts to maintain their unique culture. For thousands of years before European contact, Aboriginal peoples held games throughout North America.

CP Photo/Winnipeg Free Press - Jeff de Booy

(Weinfeld, 1995). The French were able to maintain French civil law, language, and religion. However, the overall economic, social, and political power passed to English Canada.

The British North America Act formally acknowledged the rights and privileges of the French and British as the founding or charter groups of Canadian society. With Confederation, it was assumed that in the future French- and English-speaking groups would coexist and complement one another. However, during the period between Confederation and World War II, the French struggled for cultural survival because English-speaking Canadians controlled the major economic institutions in both English Canada and Quebec.

In the 1960s, Quebec nationalism grew and francophones in Quebec began to believe that their language and culture were threatened (see Chapter 12). As a result of two referendums held in 1980 and in 1995, Quebeckers rejected sovereignty, but the issue remains contentious.

French Canadians Today   Today, approximately 22 percent of the Canadian population is francophone, 85 percent of whom are located in Quebec (Statistics Canada, 2007a). Many Quebec nationalists now see independence or separation as the ultimate protection against cultural and linguistic assimilation, as well as the route to economic power. As political scientist Rand Dyck comments:

> [G]iven its geographic concentration in Quebec and majority control of a large province, and given their modern-day self-consciousness and self-confidence, the French fact in Canada cannot be ignored. If English Canada wants Quebec to remain a part of the country, it cannot go back to the easy days of pre-1960 unilingualism. (2000:97)

French Canadians have at least forced Canada to take its second language and culture seriously, which is an important step toward attaining cultural pluralism.

Canada's Multicultural Minorities

Home to approximately 6 million foreign-born immigrants, Canada is well described as a land of immigrants. Approximately 75 percent of immigrants arriving in Canada today are members of a visible minority group (Statistics Canada, 2008a). Canada's policies toward some of these groups have been far from exemplary. In fact, initial Canadian immigration policies have been described as essentially racist in orientation, assimilationist in intent, and exclusionary in outcome (Fleras and Elliott, 2003). A "racial pecking order" sorted out potential immigrants on the basis of racial characteristics and capacity for assimilation (Walker, 1997). As much energy was expended in keeping out certain "types" as was put into encouraging others to settle (Whitaker, 1991). A preferred category was that of *white ethnics*—a term coined to identify immigrants who came from European countries other than England, such as Scotland, Ireland, Poland, Italy, Greece, Germany, Yugoslavia, and Russia and other former Soviet republics. Immigration from "white" countries was encouraged to ensure the British character of Canada. With the exception of visa formalities, this category of "preferred" immigrants was virtually exempt from entry restrictions. On the other hand, Jews and Mediterranean populations required special permits for entry, and Asian populations were admitted only because they could provide cheap labour. The restrictions regarding the Chinese, Japanese, and Jews highlighted the racist dimension of Canada's early immigration policies (Satzewich, 1998).

Chinese Canadians   The initial wave of Chinese migrants came to Canada in the 1850s, when Chinese men were attracted to emigrate by the gold rush in British Columbia and employment opportunities created by expansion of a national railroad The work was brutally hard and dangerous, living conditions were appalling, food and shelter were insufficient, and there was a high fatality rate from scurvy and smallpox. These immigrants were "welcomed" only as long as there was a shortage of white workers. However, they were not permitted to bring their wives and children with them or to have sexual relations with white women because of the fear they would spread the "yellow menace"—a term used to describe individuals with Asian racial origins (Henry and Tator, 2006).

The Chinese were subjected to extreme prejudice and were referred to by derogatory terms such as "coolies," "heathens," and "Chinks." In 1885, the federal government passed its first anti-Chinese bill, the purpose of which was to limit Chinese immigration. Other hostile legislation included a range of racist, exclusionary policies, including prohibiting the Chinese from voting, serving in public office, serving on juries, participating in white labour unions, and working in the professions of law and pharmacy. In 1885 a $50 head tax was imposed on all Chinese males arriving in Canada. In 1903, the tax was raised to $500 in a further attempt to restrict entry to Canada (Satzewich and Loidakis, 2007). These discriminatory policies were not removed from the Immigration Act until after World War II. After immigration laws were further relaxed in the 1960s, the second and largest wave of Chinese immigration occurred, with immigrants coming primarily from Hong Kong and Taiwan (Henry and Tator, 2006).

Japanese Canadians   Japanese immigrants began arriving in Canada in large numbers after Chinese immigration tapered off. The Japanese were also viewed as a threat by white workers and became victims of stereotyping and discrimination.

In 1907, an organization known as the Asiatic Exclusion League was formed with the mandate of restricting the admission of Asians to Canada. Following the arrival of a ship carrying more than a thousand Japanese and a few hundred Sikhs, the league carried out a demonstration that precipitated a race riot. A "gentlemen's agreement," negotiated in 1908, permitted entry of only certain categories of Japanese persons. Later, Japanese Canadians experienced one of the most vicious forms of discrimination ever sanctioned by Canadian law; during World War II, when Canada was at war with Japan, nearly 23 000 people of Japanese ancestry—13 300 of whom were Canadian born—were placed in internment camps, forced to work, and had their property confiscated. They were not released until two years after the war ended. Only the Japanese were singled out for such harsh treatment; German immigrants avoided this fate even though Canada was at war with both countries. After the war, restrictions were placed on where Japanese Canadians could settle and some were forcibly sent back to Japan. Forty years later, the Canadian government issued an apology for its actions and agreed to pay $20 000 to each person who had been placed in an internment camp (Henry and Tator, 2006).

South Asians   South Asians also had to deal with discriminatory immigration laws. One of these laws was the "continuous passage" rule of 1908, which specified that South Asians could immigrate only if they came directly from India and did not stop at any ports on the way. This law made it almost impossible for them to enter the country, since no ships made direct journeys from India. South Asians who did manage to immigrate to Canada faced hostile employers and distrustful citizens. Their property and businesses were frequently attacked, and they were denied citizenship and the right to vote in British Columbia until the mid-1900s (Henry and Tator, 2006).

Jewish Canadians   Many Jews sought refuge from the persecution of the Nazis between 1933 and 1945. During this time Canada admitted fewer Jewish refugees as a percentage of its population than any other Western country. In 1942, a ship carrying Jewish refugees from Europe attempted to land in Halifax and was denied entrance., Jews who did immigrate experienced widespread discrimination in employment, business, and education. Other indicators of anti-Semitism included restrictions on where Jews could live, buy property, and attend university. Signs posted along Toronto's beaches warned "No dogs or Jews allowed." Many hotels and resorts had policies prohibiting Jews as guests (Abella and Troper, 1982, cited in Henry et al., 2000:80).

Immigration Trends Post World War II to Present   Changes to the Immigration Act in 1962 opened the door to immigration on a nonracial basis. Education, occupation, and language skills replaced race or national origin as the criteria for admission. In 1967, a *points system* was introduced whereby immigrants were rated according to the totals of points given for the following: job training, experience, skills, level of education, knowledge of English or French, degree of demand for the applicant's occupation, and job offers (Henry and Tator, 2006). Although this act opened the doors to those from previously excluded countries, critics have suggested that it maintained some of the same racist policies. In 2002, in response to the numerous concerns of continued exclusionary and racist immigration practices, the Immigration and Refugee Protection Act was implemented. This act recognizes three classes of immigrant: economic, family class, and refugee, and reflects a more open policy with selection criteria based on language skills, education, age, employment experience, and a category called "adaptability" (Henry and Tator, 2006:78).

RACIAL AND ETHNIC INEQUALITY IN CANADA IN THE FUTURE

Racial and ethnic diversity are increasing in Canada. This changing demographic pattern is largely the result of the elimination of overtly racist immigration policies and the opening up of immigration to developing countries. Canada has evolved from a country largely inhabited by whites and Aboriginal peoples to a country made up of people from more than 70 countries. Today, people born outside Canada make up more than 20 percent of the total population of Canada. Newcomers from Asia make up the largest proportion of immigrants followed by newcomers from Europe (Chi, Tran, and Maheux, 2007).

Almost all immigrants to Canada live in cities, with the majority of recent immigrants living in Toronto, Montreal, or Vancouver. Today, nearly half of the population of Toronto and almost two-fifths of the population of Vancouver is composed of immigrants (Statistics Canada, 2008e).

What effect will these changes have on racial and ethnic relations? Several possibilities exist. On the one hand, conflict between whites and minority groups may become more overt and confrontational. Certainly, the concentration of visible minorities will mean that these groups will become more visible than ever in some Canadian cities. Increasing contact may lead to increased intergroup cohesion and understanding or it may bring on racism or prejudice. Rapid political changes and the global economy have made people fearful about their future and may cause some to blame "foreigners" for their problems. Inter-ethnic tensions among members of subordinate groups in urban areas may increase as subordinate groups continue to face economic deprivation and discrimination. People may continue to use *discourses of denial*, such as "I am not racist" or "I have never discriminated against anyone"—even when these are inaccurate perceptions (Henry and Tator, 2006). Concerns about violence, crime, welfare, education, housing, and taxes may be encompassed in the larger issue of race (Edsall and Edsall, 1992).

On the other hand, there is reason for cautious optimism. Throughout Canadian history, subordinate racial and ethnic groups have struggled to gain the freedom and rights that previously were withheld from them. Today, employment-equity programs are alleviating some of the effects of past discrimination against minority groups as well as addressing institutional racism that exists in employment. Movements made up of both whites and members of visible minorities continue to oppose racism in everyday life, seek to heal divisions among racial groups, and teach children about racial tolerance (Rutstein, 1993). Many groups hope not only to affect their own countries but also to contribute to worldwide efforts to end racism.

How do race and ethnicity differ?

A race is a category of people who have been singled out as socially different often on the basis of real or alleged physical characteristics, such as skin colour, hair texture, eye shape, or other subjectively selected characteristics. An ethnic group is a collection of people distinguished, by others or by themselves, primarily on the basis of cultural or nationality characteristics.

Why are race and ethnicity important?

Race and ethnicity are ingrained in our consciousness. They often form the basis of hierarchical ranking in society and determine who gets what resources: employment, housing, education, and social services.

What is prejudice?

Prejudice is a negative attitude based on preconceived notions about members of selected groups. Prejudice is often reinforced by stereotypes and is present in ethnocentric attitudes.

What is discrimination and how does it differ from prejudice?

Discrimination involves actions or practices of dominant-group members that have a harmful impact on members of a subordinate group. Whereas prejudice involves attitudes, discrimination involves actions. Discriminatory actions range from name calling to violent actions. Discrimination can be either *de jure* (encoded in law) or *de facto* (informal).

What is racism and what form does it take?

Racism refers to an organized set of beliefs about the innate inferiority of some racial groups combined with the power to discriminate on the basis of race. There are many different ways in which racism may manifest itself including overt racism, polite racism, subliminal racism, and institutionalized racism.

How do sociologists view racial and ethnic group relations?

Interactionists suggest that increased contact between people from divergent groups should lead to favourable attitudes and behaviour when members of each group (1) have equal status, (2) pursue the same goals, (3) cooperate with one another to achieve goals, and (4) receive positive feedback when they interact with one another. Functionalists stress that members of subordinate groups become absorbed into the dominant culture.

Conflict theorists focus on economic stratification and access to power in race and ethnic relations. Feminist analysts highlight the fact that women who are members of racial and ethnic minorities are doubly disadvantaged as a result of their gender. There is an interactive effect of racism and sexism on the exploitation of women of colour. Postmodernists view racial and ethnic identities as fluid and examine how these concepts are socially constructed.

How have Canada's immigration policies past and present affected the composition of Canada's racial and ethnic population?

Canada's early immigration policies were described as racist and included exclusionary policies directed at Asian populations, including Chinese and Japanese, and South Asians and Jews. "White ethnics" who came from European countries comprised the preferred category of immigrants. Changes to the Immigration Act in 1962 involving the implementation of a points system opened the door to immigration on a nonracial basis. In 2002, the Immigration and Refugee Protection Act was implemented with selection criteria based on human-capital attributes and skills of potential immigrants.

KEY TERMS

accommodation 218
assimilation 218
discrimination 214
equalitarian pluralism 218
ethnic group 209
ethnic pluralism 218
institutionalized racism 215
internal colonialism 219
majority (dominant) group 211
minority (subordinate) group 211
overt racism 214
polite racism 214
prejudice 212
race 209
racial prejudices 212
racism 214
segregation 218
social distance 213
split labour market 219
stereotypes 212
subliminal racism 215
visible minority 211

QUESTIONS FOR CRITICAL THINKING

1. Do you consider yourself defined more strongly by your race, your ethnicity, or neither of these concepts? Explain.
2. Given that minority groups have some common experiences, why is there such deep conflict between certain minority groups?
3. Is it possible for members of racial minorities to be racist?
4. What would need to happen both individually and collectively for a positive form of ethnic pluralism to flourish in our society?

WEB LINKS

For more Web links related to the topic of this chapter, see the Nelson sociology website:

www.sociologyessentials5e.nelson.com

The most comprehensive site for information, publications, policies, and programs that address racism is the Canadian Race Relations Foundation at:

www.crr.ca

ONLINE STUDY AND RESEARCH TOOLS

INFOTRAC®

InfoTrac College Edition is included free with every new copy of this text. Explore this online library for additional readings, review, and a handy resource for assignments. Visit **www.infotrac-college.com** to access this online database of full-text articles. Enter the key terms from this chapter to start your search.

CENGAGENOW™ CENGAGENOW

Use CengageNOW™ to help you formulate a customized study plan for this chapter. After you take the Diagnostic Quiz, CengageNOW™ will generate a customized study plan for you. It will identify sections of the chapter you should review.

CHAPTER 10

Sex and Gender

Professor Ted Cohen describes an exercise he uses in his gender studies class to demonstrate the significance of gender in the lives of men and women.

Let's try a little exercise that I use with students in my gender classes. Close your eyes and think carefully about what you believe life must be like for the "opposite sex." Then complete the following statements:

1. *"The best thing(s) about being a (male/ female) in this society must surely be . . ."*
2. *"The worst thing(s) about being (male/ female) in this society must surely be . . ."*

There is one catch: Males reading these questions must answer them about being female, and females must answer about being male. . . . If you are like most of my students, your responses are something like those that follow. Understand that these are not the "correct answers." They are just the ones my students most often mention, summarized and rephrased here.

Andrew Paterson/Alamy

Women's Views of the Best and Worst Things About Being Male

Best

- Higher pay; access to higher status positions
- Respect
- Freedom of movement; less fear about safety and less concern about the possibility of rape
- No monthly periods, no PMS, no cramps
- Not having to worry about pregnancy, childbirth, and childcare
- Less concern for one's appearance

Worst

- Need to be stoic and emotionally strong, and tendency to be inexpressive
- Pressure to be the breadwinner or devote oneself to work
- Depleted emotional or physical health; earlier death
- Restricted intimacy (included relations with children and loss of custody after divorce)

Men's Views of the Best and Worst Things About Being Female

Best

- Freedom to show feelings, especially feelings of vulnerability or of affection towards friends and loved ones
- Ability to choose—though within limits—whether to seek employment outside the home or raise children
- Depth of connection felt in relationships
- Giving birth
- Longer life span

Worst

- Being sexually harassed, assaulted, or objectified
- Being judged by and related to so much in terms of one's appearance
- Being underpaid, occupationally segregated, discriminated against
- Having so much responsibility for children, families, and households
- Having to think so much about one's safety and potential vulnerability
- Being trivialized in conversation and patronized in relationships

No matter how closely your own ideas matched those above, the task itself is an instructive one. . . . People often find it hard to look at life through the eyes and experiences of others whose life seems fundamentally unlike their own. . . . This exercise also reminds us that we are all both benefited and harmed because of our being male or female. In fact, comparing or combining the "best" and "worst" list reveals an interesting cross-gender consensus. . . . To further your sense of the constraining and enabling effects of gender, answer this last question that I also ask my students:

1. Imagine and describe how your life would differ if you had been born and were living as the opposite sex. (Cohen, 2001:2-3)

As Professor Cohen knows, addressing these questions is a good starting point for an examination of the social significance of gender in our lives. In this chapter we will examine in greater detail the effects of gender on the lives of both men and women in today's society.

Gender is a social construction with important consequences in everyday life. Just as stereotypes regarding race/ethnicity have built-in notions of superiority and inferiority, gender stereotypes hold that men and women are inherently different in attributes, behaviour, and aspirations. Specific ideas of femininity and masculinity are inescapable producers of the society we live in. Although significant changes have occurred in the last half of the 20th century in terms of work and family, notions of gender remain firmly embedded in social institutions and relationships. Gender is so much a part of who we are that it often goes unexamined. In this chapter we examine the issue of gender: what it is and how it affects us. Before reading further, test your knowledge of gender inequality by taking the quiz in Box 10.1.

QUESTIONS AND ISSUES

Chapter Focus Question: What effect does gender inequality have on men and women?

How do a society's resources and economic structure influence gender stratification?

What are the primary agents of gender socialization?

How does the contemporary workplace reflect gender stratification?

How do functionalist, conflict, feminist, and symbolic interactionist perspectives on gender stratification differ?

SEX: THE BIOLOGICAL DIMENSION

Whereas the word *gender* is often used to refer to the distinctive qualities of men and women (masculinity and femininity) that are culturally created, *sex* refers to the biological and anatomical differences between females and males. At the core of these differences is the chromosomal information transmitted when a child is conceived. The mother contributes an X chromosome and the father either an X (which produces a female embryo) or a Y chromosome (which produces a male embryo). At birth, male and female infants are distinguished by *primary sex characteristics: the genitalia used in the reproductive process*. At puberty, an increased production of hormones results in the development of *secondary sex characteristics: the physical traits (other than reproductive organs) that identify an individual's sex*. For

BOX 10.1 SOCIOLOGY AND EVERYDAY LIFE

How Much Do You Know About Gender Inequality? Join In

True	False	
(T)	F	1. The average earnings of employed women are still substantially lower than those of men, even when they are employed full-time.
T	(F)	2. Men continue to outnumber women in Canadian universities.
(T)	F	3. The proportion of women working in female-dominated occupations has declined significantly in the past 20 years.
(T)	F	4. Most Canadians living in poverty are women.
(T)	F	5. Men have a shorter life expectancy than women.
T	(F)	6. Married couples today who both work full-time tend to share the "unpaid labour" fairly equally.
(T)	F	7. Women make up the majority of persons living in poverty in the world.
(T)	F	8. Approximately half of all victims of violent crime are male.

Answers on page 234.

women, these include larger breasts, wider hips, and narrower shoulders; a layer of fatty tissue throughout the body; and menstruation. For men, they include development of enlarged genitals, a deeper voice, greater height, a more muscular build, and more body and facial hair.

Hermaphrodites/Transsexuals

Sex is not always clear-cut. Occasionally, a hormone imbalance before birth produces a **hermaphrodite— a person in whom sexual differentiation is ambiguous or incomplete.** Hermaphrodites tend to have some combination of male and female genitalia. In one case, for example, a chromosomally normal (XY) male was born with a penis just one centimetre long with a urinary opening similar to that of a female (Money and Ehrhardt, 1972). In another case, a newborn male had his penis irreversibly damaged during a circumcision and had his gender "reassigned" to female (see Box 10.2 on page 237).

Some people may be genetically of one sex but have a gender identity of the other. That is true for a **transsexual, a person in whom the sex-related structures of the brain that define gender identity are opposite from the physical sex organs of the person's body.** Consequently, transsexuals often feel that they are the opposite sex from that of their sex organs. Some transsexuals are aware of this conflict between gender

identity and physical sex as early as the preschool years. Some transsexuals take hormone treatments or have a sex-change operation to alter their genitalia in order to achieve a body congruent with their sense of sexual identity (Basow, 1992). Many transsexuals who receive hormone treatments or undergo surgical procedures go on to lead lives that they view as being compatible with their true sexual identity.

Western societies acknowledge the existence of only two sexes; some other societies recognize three—men, women, and *berdaches* (or *hijras* or *xaniths*), biological males who behave, dress, work, and are treated in most respects as women. The closest approximation of a third sex in Western societies is a **transvestite, a male who lives as a woman or a female who lives as man but who does not alter the genitalia.** Although transvestites are not treated as a third sex, they often "pass" for members of the other sex because their appearance and mannerisms fall within the range of what is expected from members of the other sex (Lorber, 1994).

Transsexuality may occur in conjunction with homosexuality, but this is frequently not the case. Some researchers believe that both transsexuality and homosexuality have a common prenatal cause such as a critically timed hormonal release due to stress in the mother or the presence of certain hormone-mimicking chemicals during critical steps of fetal development. Researchers continue to examine this issue and debate the origins of transsexuality and homosexuality.

SOCIOLOGY AND EVERYDAY LIFE

Answers to the Sociology Quiz on Gender Inequality

1. True. Women working on a full-time, full-year basis had average earnings of $36 500, or 71 cents for every dollar their male counterparts made (Statistics Canada, 2006h). As well, the gap between the earnings of women and men has not changed substantially in the past decade.

2. False. Close to 60 percent of university graduates are female. (Statistics Canada, 2006g).

3. True. Two-thirds of all employed women were working in teaching, nursing and related health occupations, clerical or other administrative positions, and sales and service occupations. In fact, there has been virtually no change in the proportion of women employed in these traditionally female-dominated occupations over the past decade (Statistics Canada, 2006e).

4. True. This pattern, referred to as the "feminization of poverty," has changed little in recent decades. Families headed by female single parents and unattached women are particularly likely to have low incomes.

5. True. Although gender differences in life expectancy are shrinking, males continue to have higher rates of heart disease, homicide, drug- and alcohol-induced deaths, suicide, and firearm and motor-vehicle accidents (Naiman, 2008).

6. False. Regardless of their employment status, women continue to do the majority of "unpaid labour" (home maintenance, childcare, and elder care) (Statistics Canada, 2006e).

7. True. Seventy percent of the two billion people living in poverty globally are women (Naiman, 2008)

8. True. Men and women have roughly similar rates of violent crime (Statistics Canada, 2008m).

Sexual Orientation

Sexual orientation **refers to an individual's preference for emotional–sexual relationships with members of the opposite sex (heterosexuality), the same sex (homosexuality), or both (bisexuality)** (Lips, 2001). Some scholars believe that sexual orientation is rooted in biological factors than are present at birth (Pillard and Weinrich, 1986); others believe that sexuality has both biological and social components and is not preordained at birth.

The terms *homosexual* and *gay* are most often used in association with males who prefer same-sex relationships; the term *lesbian* is used in association with females who prefer same-sex relationships. Heterosexual individuals, who prefer opposite-sex relationships, are sometimes referred to as *straight*. However, it is important to note that heterosexual

people are much less likely to be labelled by their sexual orientation than are people who are gay, lesbian, or bisexual.

What criteria do social scientists use to classify individuals as gay, lesbian, or homosexual? In a definitive study of sexuality in the mid-1990s, researchers at the University of Chicago established three criteria for identifying people as homosexual or bisexual: (1) *sexual attraction* to persons of one's own gender, (2) *sexual involvement* with one or more persons of one's own gender, and (3) *self-identification* as a gay, lesbian, or bisexual (Michael et al., 1994). According to these criteria, then, having engaged in a homosexual act does not necessarily classify a person as homosexual. In fact, many respondents in the University of Chicago study indicated that although they had at least one homosexual encounter when they were younger, they were no longer involved in homosexual

BOX 10.2 SOCIOLOGY AND CRITICAL THINKING

Gender Reassignment: "As Nature Made Him"

On April 27, 1966, in Winnipeg, Manitoba, an infant boy's routine circumcision went terribly wrong. Through a medical error, eight-month-old Bruce Reimer was left without a penis. The circumcision of his twin brother, Brian, had gone smoothly and his male genitalia remained intact. In desperation, the twins' parents consulted John Money, medical director of the Gender Identity Clinic at the world renowned Johns Hopkins University. Based on his research, Money asserted that a person's gender identity and sexual orientation were not biologically determined but rather were the result of socialization. Tragically, Bruce Reimer became the "test case" used to prove this theory.

Dr. Money convinced Bruce's parents to have their son surgically transformed into a girl (he was renamed Brenda), based on his assurance that with appropriate parenting she would grow up to be a feminine, heterosexual woman (LeVay, 2000:1). John Money monitored Brenda and her identical twin, Brian, during their childhood, and he reported extensively in books, journals, and lectures that this "experiment" had been a complete success. According to Money, Brenda had grown up happily feminine, displaying many of the stereotypical traits associated with being female: she was shy, neat, and pretty, and she enjoyed playing with dolls and cooking. Most important, Brenda's own gender identity was that of a female, supporting Money's theory that gender was malleable.

This "test case" gave Money enormous professional acclaim and success. The case was cited repeatedly for 30 years as proof that our sense of being female or male is not inborn but primarily the result of how we are raised. The case also established a medical precedent for the gender reassignment of thousands of other newborns who were similarly injured during circumcision or who were born with ambiguous genitals.

This "experiment" was, in fact, a failure from the start, and had disastrous results for the Reimer family. The truth was that "Brenda" did not see herself as female, nor did her peers. She preferred to play with her twin brother's toys. She was tormented at school, nicknamed "Cavewoman," and teased for her masculine qualities. Finally, when Brenda was a teenager, after years of depression and a suicide attempt, her parents told her the truth about her gender reassignment. In response, Brenda assumed a male gender identity and underwent surgery to create a cosmetic penis. He changed his name to David (in reference to David and Goliath) and eventually married a woman who had three children.

Dr. Money failed to report this final outcome and claimed that he had lost track of the Reimer family, despite the fact that they had never moved (Nussbaum, 2003:1). In 1996, sexologist Milton Diamond from the University of Hawaii found David and revealed the truth to the medical community, destroying Money's professional reputation. The true facts of this case have been particularly helpful in dealing with the treatment of hermaphroditic infants, who in the past were "normalized" to female. Evidence now shows that many, like David, had rejected their medically created gender and had been traumatized by the medical intervention. Tragically, on May 4, 2004, David Reimer committed suicide at the age of 38.

What conclusions do you draw about gender identity from David Reimer's case? Consider the formation of your own gender identity. What factors have contributed to your being a female or a male? What role does society play in the formulation of gender identity, both in general and in your own life in particular?

Sources: LeVay, 2000; Nussbaum, 2003; Colapinto, 2001.

conduct and never identified themselves as gay, lesbian, or bisexual.

More recent studies have examined how sexual orientation is linked to identity. For example, Kristin G. Esterberg (1997) interviewed lesbian and bisexual women to determine how they "perform" lesbian or bisexual identity through daily activities such as choice of clothing and hairstyles, as well as how they use body language and talk. According to Esterberg (1997), some of the women viewed themselves as being "lesbian from birth," whereas others had experienced shifts in their identities, depending on social surroundings, age, and political conditions at specific periods in their lives.

The term *transgender* was created to describe individuals whose appearance, behaviour, or self-identification does not conform to common social rules of gender expression. "Transgenderism" is sometimes used to refer to those who cross-dress, to transsexuals, and to others outside mainstream categories. Although some gay and lesbian advocacy groups oppose the concept of transgender as being somewhat meaningless, others applaud the term as one that might help unify diverse categories of people based on sexual identity. Various organizations of gays, lesbians, and transgendered persons have been unified in their desire to reduce hate crimes and other forms of **homophobia—extreme prejudice directed at gays, lesbians, bisexuals, and others who are perceived as not being heterosexual.**

Gender can be ambiguous, and individuals whose appearance, behaviour, or self-identification does not conform to common social rules of gender expression are often referred to as being transgendered.

GENDER: THE CULTURAL DIMENSION

Gender refers to the culturally and socially constructed differences between females and males found in the meanings, beliefs, and practices associated with "femininity" and "masculinity." Although biological differences between women and men are very important, in reality most "sex differences" are socially constructed "gender differences" (Gailey, 1987). According to sociologists, social and cultural processes, not biological "givens," are most important in defining what females and males are, what they do, and what sorts of relations do or should exist between them (Ortner and Whitehead, 1981; Lott, 1994). Judith Lorber (1994:6) summarizes the importance of gender:

> Gender is a human invention, like language, kinship, religion, and technology; like them, gender organizes human social life in culturally patterned ways. Gender organizes social relations in everyday life as well as in the major social structures, such as social class and the hierarchies of bureaucratic organizations.

Virtually everything social in our lives is *gendered:* People continually distinguish between males and females and evaluate them differentially. Gender is an integral part of the daily experiences of both women and men (Mackie, 1995; Mandell, 2001).

A microlevel analysis of gender focuses on how individuals learn gender roles and acquire a gender identity. **Gender role refers to the attitudes, behaviour, and activities that are socially defined as appropriate for each sex and are learned through** the socialization process (Lips, 2001). For example, in North American society, males are traditionally expected to demonstrate aggressiveness and toughness, whereas females are expected to be passive and nurturing. **Gender identity is a person's perception of the self as female or male.** Typically established between 18 months and 3 years of age, gender identity is a powerful aspect of our self-concept (Lips, 2001). Although this identity is an individual perception, it is developed through interaction with others. As a result, most people form a gender identity that matches their biological sex: Most biological females think of themselves as female, and most biological males think of themselves as male.

Body consciousness is a part of gender identity. **Body consciousness is how a person perceives and feels about his or her body**; it also includes an awareness of social conditions in society that contribute to this self-knowledge (Thompson, 1994). Consider, for example, these comments by Steve Michalik, a former Mr. Universe:

I was small and weak, and my brother Anthony was big and graceful, and my old man made no bones about loving him and hating me . . . The minute I walked in from school, it was, "You worthless little s—t, what are you doing home so early?" His favourite way to torture me was to tell me he was going to put me in a home. We'd be driving along in Brooklyn somewhere, and we'd pass a building with iron bars on the windows, and he'd stop the car and say to me, "Get out. This is the home we're putting you in." I'd be standing there sobbing on the curb—I was maybe eight or nine at the time. (quoted in Klein, 1993:273)

As we grow up, we become aware that the physical shape of our bodies subjects us to the approval or disapproval of others. Although being small and weak may be considered positive attributes for women, they are considered negative characteristics for "real men."

A macrolevel analysis of gender examines structural features, external to the individual, that perpetuate gender inequality. These structures have been referred to as *gendered institutions,* meaning that gender is one of the major ways by which social life is organized in all sectors of society. Gender is embedded in the images, ideas, and language of a society and is used as a means to divide up work, allocate resources, and distribute power. For example, every society uses gender to assign certain tasks—ranging from child-rearing to warfare—to females and to males.

These institutions are reinforced by a *gender belief system* that includes all of the ideas regarding masculine

Sociologists highlight that our bodies are objectified with both compulsive dieting and bodybuilding. Recently, a variation of eating disorders known as exercise bulimia has been identified, as both men and women struggle to attain the socially defined ideal of the "perfect" body.

© Fabio Cardoso/zefa/Corbis

and feminine attributes that are held to be valid in a society. This belief system is legitimated by religion, science, law, and other societal values (Lorber, 2001). For example, gendered belief systems may change over time as gender roles change. Many fathers take care of young children today, and there is a much greater acceptance of this change in roles. However, popular stereotypes about men and women, as well as cultural norms about gender-appropriate appearance and behaviour, serve to reinforce gendered institutions in society (Mandell, 2001).

Sexism

Sexism **is the subordination of one sex, usually female, based on the assumed superiority of the other sex.** Sexism directed at women has three components: (1) negative attitudes toward women; (2) stereotypical beliefs that reinforce, complement, or justify the prejudice; and (3) discrimination—acts that exclude, distance, or keep women separate (Lott, 1994).

Can men be victims of sexism? Although women are more often the target of sexist remarks and practices, men can be victims of sexist assumptions. According to social psychologist Hilary M. Lips (2001), an example of sexism directed against men is the mistaken idea that it is more harmful for female soldiers to be killed in battle than male soldiers.

Like racism, sexism is used to justify discriminatory treatment. When women participate in what are considered gender-inappropriate endeavours in the workplace, at home, or in leisure activities, they often find that they are the targets of prejudice and discrimination. Obvious manifestations of sexism are found in the undervaluing of women's work, and in hiring and promotion practices that effectively exclude women from an organization or confine them to the bottom of the organizational hierarchy. Women who attempt to enter nontraditional occupations (such as fire-fighting, welding, and steel working) or professions (such as dentistry and architecture) often encounter hurdles that men do not face. Likewise, men who enter female-dominated occupations such as nursing face challenges in overcoming sexist attitudes.

Sexism is interwoven with *patriarchy*—**a hierarchical system of social organization in which cultural, political, and economic structures are controlled by men.** By contrast, *matriarchy* **is a hierarchical system of social organization in which cultural, political, and economic structures are controlled by women;** however, few (if any) societies have been organized in this manner. Patriarchy is reflected in the way men may think of their position as men as a given, while women may deliberate on what their position in society should be (see Box 10.3).

GENDER STRATIFICATION IN HISTORICAL AND CONTEMPORARY PERSPECTIVES

How do tasks in a society come to be defined as "men's work" or "women's work"? Three factors are important in determining the gendered division of labour in a society: (1) the type of subsistence base, (2) the supply of and demand for labour, and (3) the extent to which women's child-rearing activities are compatible with certain types of work. Subsistence refers to the means by which a society gains the basic necessities of life, including food, shelter, and clothing (Nielsen, 1990). You may recall that societies are classified based on subsistence as hunting-and-gathering societies, horticultural and pastoral societies, agrarian societies, industrial societies, or postmodern societies.

Pre-industrial Societies

The earliest known division of labour between women and men is in hunting-and-gathering societies. While the men hunt for wild game, women gather roots and berries. A relatively equitable relationship exists because neither sex has the ability to provide all of the food necessary for survival. When wild game is nearby, both men and women may hunt. When it is far away, hunting becomes incompatible with child rearing (which women tend to do because they breast-feed their young), and women are placed at a disadvantage in terms of contributing to the food supply (Lorber, 1994). In most hunting-and-gathering societies, women are full economic partners with men; relations between them tend to be cooperative and relatively egalitarian (Chafetz, 1984; Bonvillain, 2001). Little social stratification of any kind is found because people do not acquire a food surplus.

In horticultural societies, which first developed 10 000 to 12 000 years ago, a steady source of food becomes available. People are able to grow their own food because of hand tools such as the digging stick and the hoe. Women make an important contribution to food production because hoe cultivation is compatible with childcare. A fairly high degree of gender equality exists because neither sex controls the food supply

When inadequate moisture in an area makes planting crops impossible, *pastoralism*—the domestication of large animals to provide food—develops. Herding is primarily done by men, and women contribute relatively little to subsistence production in such societies. In some herding societies, women have relatively low status; their primary value is their ability to produce male offspring so that the family lineage can be preserved and enough males will exist to protect the group against attack (Nielsen, 1990).

In agrarian societies, which first developed about 8 000 to 10 000 years ago, gender inequality and male dominance become institutionalized. Agrarian societies rely on agriculture—farming done by animal-drawn or energy-powered plows and equipment. Because agrarian tasks require more labour and greater physical strength than horticultural ones, men become more involved in food production. It has been suggested that women are excluded from these tasks because they are viewed as too weak for the work and because childcare responsibilities are considered incompatible with the full-time labour that the tasks require (Nielsen, 1990). Most of the world's population currently lives in agrarian societies in various stages of industrialization.

Industrial Societies

An *industrial society* is one in which factory or mechanized production has replaced agriculture as the major form of economic activity. As societies industrialize, the status of women tends to decline further. Industrialization in Canada created a gap between the nonpaid work performed by women at home and the paid work that increasingly was performed by men and unmarried women (Krahn et al., 2008).

In Canada, the division of labour between men and women in the middle and upper classes became much more distinct with industrialization. The men were responsible for being "breadwinners," while the women were seen as "homemakers." In this new "cult of domesticity" (also referred to as the "cult of true womanhood"), the home became a private, personal sphere in which women created a haven for the family. Those who supported the cult of domesticity argued that women were the natural keepers of the domestic sphere and that children were the mother's responsibility. Meanwhile, the "breadwinner" role

BOX 10.3 | SOCIOLOGY IN GLOBAL PERSPECTIVE

The Rise of Islamic Feminism in the Middle East

I would like for all of the young Muslim girls to be able to relate to Iman, whether they wear the hijab [head scarf] or not. Boys will also enjoy Iman's adventures because she is one tough, smart girl! Iman gets her super powers from having very strong faith in Allah, or God. She solves many of the problems by explaining certain parts of the Koran that relate to the story.

Rima Khoreibi, an author from Dubai (United Arab Emirates), explaining that she has written a book about an Islamic superhero who is female because she would like to dispel a widely held belief that sexism in her culture is deeply rooted in Islam (see http://theadventuresofiman.com, 2007; Kristof, 2006)

Although Rima Khoreibi and many others who have written fictional and nonfictional accounts of girls and women living in the Middle East typically do not deny that sexism exists in their region or that sexism is deeply interwoven with patriarchy around the world, they dispute the perception that Islam is inherently misogynistic (possessing hatred or strong prejudice toward women). As defined in this chapter, *patriarchy* is a hierarchical system of social organization in which cultural, political, and economic structures are controlled by men. The influence of religion on patriarchy is a topic of great interest to contemporary scholars, particularly those applying a feminist approach to their explanations of why persistent social inequalities exist between women and men and how these inequalities are greater in some regions of the world than in others.

According to some gender studies specialists, a newer form of feminist thinking is emerging among Muslim women. Often referred to as "feminist Islam" or "Islamic feminism," this approach is based on the belief that greater gender equality may be possible in the Muslim world if the teachings of Islam, as set forth in the Koran (or *Qur'an*)—the Islamic holy book—are followed more closely. Islamic feminism is based on the principle that Muslim women should retain their allegiance to Islam as an essential part of their self-determination and identity, but that they should also work to change patriarchal control over the basic Islamic world view (Wadud, 2002). According to journalist Nicholas D. Kristof (2006), both Islam and evangelical Christianity have been on the rise in recent years because both religions provide "a firm moral code, spiritual reassurance and orderliness to people vexed by chaos and immorality around them, and they offer dignity to the poor" (p. A22).

Islamic feminists believe that the rise of Islam might contribute to greater, rather than less, equality for women. From this perspective, stories about characters such as Iman may help girls and young women realize that they can maintain their deep religious convictions and their *hijab* while, at the same time, work for greater equality for women and more opportunities for themselves. In *The Adventures of Iman,* the female hero always wears a pink scarf around her neck, and she uses the scarf to cover her hair when she is praying to Allah. Iman quotes the Qur'an when she is explaining to others that Muslims are expected to be tolerant, kind, and righteous. For Iman, religion is a form of empowerment, not an extension of patriarchy.

Islamic feminism is quite different from what most people think of as Western feminism (particularly in regard to issues such as the wearing of the *hijab* or the fact that in Saudi Arabia, a woman may own a motor vehicle but may not legally drive it). However, change is clearly underway in many regions of the Middle East and other areas of the world as rapid economic development and urbanization quickly change the lives of many people.

Why is women's inequality a complex issue to study across nations? What part does culture play in defining the roles of women and men in various societies? How do religious beliefs influence what we think of as "appropriate" or "inappropriate" behaviors for men, women, and children?

placed enormous pressure on men to support their families—being a good provider was considered a sign of manhood. However, this gendered division of labour increased the economic and political subordination of women. The cult of true womanhood not only increased white women's dependence on men but also became a source of discrimination against visible-minority women, based on both their race and the fact that many of them had to work in order to survive. Employed working-class white women were similarly stereotyped—they became economically dependent on their husband because their wages were so much lower.

Post-industrial Societies

A *post-industrial society* is one in which technology supports a service- and information-based economy. In such societies, the division of labour in paid employment is increasingly based on whether people provide or apply information or are employed in service jobs, such as fast-food restaurant counter help or health-care workers. For both women and men in the labour force, formal education is increasingly crucial for economic and social success. However, as some women have moved into entrepreneurial, managerial, and professional occupations, many others have remained in the low-paying service sector, which affords few opportunities for upward advancement.

How does the division of labour change in families in post-industrial societies? For a variety of reasons, more households today are headed by women with no adult male present. This means that women in these households truly have a double burden, both from family responsibilities and the necessity of holding gainful employment in the labour force.

In post-industrial societies such as Canada, over 80 percent of adult women are in the labour force. This reality means that despite living in an information and service-oriented economy, women will continue to bear the heavy burden of finding time to care for children, helping aging parents, and meeting the demands of the workplace (Marshall, 2006).

How people accept new technologies and the effect these technologies have on gender stratification are related to how people are socialized into gender roles. However, gender-based stratification remains rooted in the larger social structures or society, which individuals have little ability to control.

GENDER AND SOCIALIZATION

We learn gender-appropriate behaviour through the socialization process. Our parents, teachers, friends, and the media all serve as gendered institutions that communicate to us our earliest, and often most lasting, beliefs about the social meanings of being male or female and thinking and behaving in masculine or feminine ways. Some gender roles have changed dramatically in recent years; others remain largely unchanged over time.

Some parents prefer boys to girls because of stereotypical ideas about the relative importance of males and females to the future of the family and society. Although some parents prefer boys to girls because they believe old myths about the biological inferiority of females, research suggests that social expectations also play a major role in this preference. We are socialized to believe that it is important to have a son, especially as a first or only child. For many years it was assumed that a male child could support his parents in their later years and carry on the family name.

Across cultures, boys are preferred to girls, especially when the number of children that parents can have is limited by law or economic conditions. For example, in China, which strictly regulates the allowable number of children to one per family, a disproportionate number of female fetuses are aborted (Basow, 1992). In India, the practice of aborting female fetuses is widespread, and female infanticide occurs frequently. As a result, both India and China have a growing surplus of young men who will face a shortage of women their own age.

Parents and Gender Socialization

From birth, parents act toward children on the basis of the child's sex. Baby boys are perceived to be less fragile than girls and tend to be treated more roughly by their parents. Girl babies are thought to be "cute, sweet, and cuddly" and receive more gentle treatment. Parents strongly influence the gender-role development of children by passing on—both overtly and covertly—their own beliefs about gender (Wharton, 2004).

Children's toys reflect their parents' gender expectations. Gender-appropriate toys for boys include computer games, trucks and other vehicles, sports equipment, and war toys such as guns and soldiers.

From an early age, a number of societal influences encourage us to learn gender-appropriate behaviour.

Girls' toys include Barbie dolls, play makeup, and homemaking items. One study found that although parents gender-stereotyped toys for boys and girls of all ages, they are less likely to do so with infants and toddlers (Campenni, 1999)

When children are old enough to help with household chores, they often are assigned different tasks. Maintenance chores (such as mowing the lawn) are assigned to boys, while domestic chores (such as shopping, cooking, and cleaning the dinner table) are assigned to girls. Chores also may become linked with future occupational choices and personal characteristics. Girls who are responsible for domestic chores such as caring for younger brothers and sisters may learn nurturing behaviours that later translate into employment as a nurse or schoolteacher. Boys may learn about computers and other types of technology that lead to different career options.,

Many parents are aware of the effect that gender socialization has on their children and make a conscientious effort to provide nonsexist experiences for them. For example, one study found that mothers with nontraditional views encourage their daughters to be independent (Brooks-Gunn, 1986). Many fathers also take an active role in socializing their sons to be thoughtful and caring individuals who do not live by traditional gender stereotypes. However, peers often make nontraditional gender socialization much more difficult for parents and children.

Peers and Gender Socialization

Peers help children learn prevailing gender-role stereotypes as well as gender-appropriate and -inappropriate behaviour. During the school years, same-sex peers have a powerful effect on how children see their gender roles; during adolescence, they often are more influential agents of gender socialization than adults (Maccoby and Jacklin, 1987).

Male peer groups place more pressure on boys to do "masculine" things than female peer groups place on girls to do "feminine" things. For example, girls wear jeans and other "boy" clothes, play soccer and softball, and engage in other activities traditionally associated with males. But, if a boy wears a dress, plays hopscotch with girls, and engages in other activities associated with being female, he will be ridiculed by his peers. This distinction between the relative value of boys' and girls' behaviours strengthens the cultural message that masculine activities and behaviour are more important and more acceptable.

Peers are thought to be especially important in boys' development of gender identity (Maccoby and Jacklin, 1987). Male bonding that occurs during adolescence is believed to reinforce masculine identity (Gaylin, 1992) and to encourage gender-stereotypical attitudes and behaviour (Huston, 1985; Martin, 1989). For example, male peers have a tendency to ridicule and bully others about their appearance, size, and weight. One woman painfully recalled walking down the halls at school when boys would flatten themselves against the lockers and cry, "Wide load!" At lunchtime, the boys made a production of watching her eat lunch and frequently made sounds like pig grunts or moos (Kolata, 1993). Because peer acceptance is so important for both males and females during their first two decades, such actions can have very harmful consequences for the victims.

As young adults, men and women still receive many gender-related messages from peers. Among university students, for example, peers play an important role in career choices and in the establishment of long-term, intimate relationships (Holland and Eisenhart, 1990). In a study that followed a number of women students at two universities, anthropologists Dorothy C. Holland and Margaret A. Eisenhart (1990) found that the peer system propelled women into a world of romance in which their attractiveness to men counted most. Although peers initially did not influence the women's choices of majors and careers, they did influence whether the women continued to pursue their initial goals, changed their course of action, or were "derailed" (Holland and Eisenhart, 1981, 1990).

Teachers, Schools, and Gender Socialization

From kindergarten through university, schools operate as gendered institutions. Teachers provide important messages about gender through both the formal content of classroom assignments and informal interaction with students. Sometimes gender-related messages from teachers and other students reinforce gender roles that have been taught at home; however, teachers may also contradict parental socialization. During the early years of a child's schooling, the teachers' influence is very powerful; many children spend more hours per day with their teachers than they do with their parents.

Research conducted during the 1990s found extensive evidence of gender bias in virtually all educational settings. ***Gender bias* consists of showing favouritism toward one gender over the other**. Gender bias is displayed in a number of different ways in academic settings through teacher–student interactions, biased or stereotyped resources, and responses to male and female interactions. Although there is evidence that girls are becoming more academically successful than boys, close examination of what goes on in our classrooms shows that girls and boys continue to be socialized in ways that work against gender equality (Chapman, 2003).

Subsequent research on the marginalization of girls in the education system has produced contradictory evidence. For example, a survey of 1 300 students and 1 000 teachers reported that girls were more likely to have higher educational aspirations than boys, more likely to value a good education, and less likely to believe that their teachers didn't listen to them (Sommers, 2000). Teachers also influence how students treat one another during school hours. Many teachers use sex segregation as a way of organizing students, resulting in unnecessary competition between females and males. In addition, teachers may also take a "boys will be boys" attitude when females complain of sexual harassment. As a result, the school setting can become a hostile environment rather than a site for learning (Sadker and Sadker, 1994).

As a result of research evidence of the destructive impact of gender bias in the classroom and political lobbying, positive changes have been made. Ministries of education across the country appointed advisory groups to screen resources being used in the classroom, issued nonsexist guidelines, and developed and published alternative materials. As a result, there are more diverse and less stereotyped materials used in classroom curricula today, and more awareness of gender bias in teacher–student interactions (Gaskell, McLaren, and Novogradsky, 1995). We are beginning to see some results of these changes in the educational system. As shown in Figure 10.1 (on page 245), there has been a dramatic increase in the proportion of women with a university degree in Canada in recent decades. Indeed, social scientists describe this as one of the real success stories for Canadian women. In 1971, only 3 percent of women had a university degree, compared with 15 percent of women today (Statistics Canada, 2006:89). The mix of men and women in professions that in the past have been male dominated is now relatively equal. For example, women now make up over half of all law and medicine students in Canadian universities.

These recent trends should be reflected in further reductions in the wage gaps still seen in these professions.

Mass Media and Gender Socialization

The media are a powerful source of gender stereotyping. While some critics argue that the media simply reflect existing gender roles in society, others point out that the media have a uniquely persuasive ability to shape ideas. Think of the impact that television has on children, who are estimated to spend one-third of their waking time watching it.

From children's cartoons to adult shows, television programs offer more male than female characters. Furthermore, the male characters act in a strikingly different manner from female ones. Male characters in both children's programs and adult programs are typically more aggressive, constructive, and direct, and are rewarded for their actions while some female characters defer to others or manipulate them by acting helpless, seductive, or deceitful.

In prime-time television, a number of significant changes in the past three decades have reduced gender stereotyping; however, men still outnumber women as leading characters, and they are often in charge in any setting where both men and women are portrayed. In the popular series *Grey's Anatomy* for example, the number of women's and men's roles is evenly balanced, but the male characters typically are the top surgeons, whereas the female characters are residents, interns, or nurses. In shows with predominantly female characters, such as *Desperate Housewives*, the women are typically attractive, thin, and ultimately either hysterical or compliant when dealing with male characters (Stanley, 2004).

Whether on television and billboards or in magazines and newspapers, advertising can send out persuasive messages about gender roles. The intended message is clear to many people: If they embrace traditional notions of masculinity and femininity, their personal and social success is assured; and if they purchase the right products and services, they can enhance their appearance and gain power over other people. For example, one study of television commercials reflects that men's roles are portrayed differently from women's roles. As such, television commercials may act as agents of socialization, showing children and others what women's and men's designated activities are (Kaufman, 1999).

CONTEMPORARY GENDER INEQUALITY

According to feminist scholars, women experience gender inequality as a result of past and present economic, political, and educational discrimination (Luxton, 1980; Smith, 1987; Eichler, 1997). Women's position in the Canadian workforce reflects their overall subordination in society.

Gendered Division of Paid Work

Where people are located in the occupational structure of the labour market has a major impact on their earnings (Kemp, 1994). The workplace is another example of a gendered institution. ***Gender-segregated work* refers to the concentration of women and men in different occupations, jobs, and places of work** (Reskin and Padavic, 2002). Gender-segregated work is most visible in occupations that remain more than 90 percent female (e.g., secretary, registered nurse, and bookkeeper/auditing clerk) or more than 90 percent male (e.g., carpenter, construction worker, mechanic, truck driver, and electrical engineer) (Statistics Canada, 2006e). In 2005, for example, more than 85 percent of all clerical staff in Canada were women; close to 90 percent of all engineers were men (Statistics Canada, 2006e). To eliminate gender-segregated jobs in North America, more than half of all men or all women workers would have to change occupations. Moreover, women are severely underrepresented at the top Canadian corporations, at only about 14 percent of the corporate officers in the Financial Post 500 list (comprising the 500 largest companies in Canada). Of these, only about 7 percent hold the highest corporate-officer titles, and only 19 women are chief executive officers (Catalyst, 2009). Despite some gains, "the story of women's advancement in corporate leadership in Canada continues to be one of disturbingly slow growth" (Catalyst, 2005:1). Based on current rates of change, the number of women reaching the top ranks of corporate Canada will not reach a target level of 25 percent until 2025. See Table 10.1 (on page 244) for more on gender segregation by occupation.

Gender-segregated work affects both men and women. Men often are kept out of certain types of jobs. Those who enter female-dominated occupations often have to justify themselves and prove that they are "real men." They have to fight stereotypes (gay, wimpy, and passive) about why they are

What stereotypes are associated with men in female-oriented occupations? With women in male-oriented occupations? Do you think such stereotypes will change in the near future?

Table 10.1	**GENDER SEGREGATION BY OCCUPATION**

PERCENTAGE OF WOMEN IN THE TEN HIGHEST-PAYING OCCUPATIONS

Judges	23%
Specialist physicians	26%
General practitioners and family physicians	26%
Dentists	18%
Senior managers (goods production, utilities, transportation, construction)	9%
Senior managers (financial, communications, other business)	17%
Lawyers	37%
Senior managers (trade, broadcasting, other services)	14%
Primary production managers	6%
Securities agents, investment dealers, traders	33%

PERCENTAGE OF WOMEN IN THE TEN LOWEST-PAYING OCCUPATIONS

Sewing machine operators	92%
Cashiers	84%
Ironing, pressing, and finishing occupations	70%
Artisans and craftspersons	52%
Bartenders	56%
Harvesting labourers	54%
Service station attendants	20%
Food service attendants and food preparers	75%
Food and beverage servers	76%
Babysitters, nannies, and parents' helpers	98%

Source: UN Platform for Action Committee, 2005.

interested in such work (Williams, 2004). Even if these assumptions do not push men out of female-dominated occupations, they affect how the men manage their gender identity at work. For example, men in occupations such as nursing emphasize their masculinity, attempt to distance themselves from female colleagues, and try to move quickly into management and supervisory positions (Williams, 2004).

Occupational gender segregation contributes to stratification in society. Job segregation is structural; it does not occur simply because individual workers have different abilities, motivations, and material needs. As a result of gender and racial segregation, employers are able to pay many visible-minority males and females less money, promote them less often, and provide fewer benefits. If they demand better working conditions or wages, workers often are reminded of the number of individuals (members of Marx's "reserve army") who would like to have their jobs.

THE GENDER WAGE GAP

Occupational segregation contributes to a second form of discrimination—the *wage gap,* **a term that refers to the disparity between women's and men's earnings.** It is calculated by dividing women's earnings by men's to yield a percentage, also known as the *earnings ratio* (Krahn, Lowe, and Hughes, 2008). There has been some improvement in this earnings ratio over the past two decades, but the progress has been slow. Today, women who worked full-time for the whole year still earned just over 70 cents for each dollar earned by their male counterparts (Statistics Canada, 2006). A recent study found that the majority of this wage gap is explained by differences in worker characteristics such as experience, type of occupation, and workplace characteristics (Drolet, 2002). Marital status has a dramatic impact on the wage gap. The wage gap is smallest between single, never-married men and women (94 percent) and greatest between married men and women (65 percent) (Statistics Canada, 2008i). As shown in Figure 10.1, the gender wage gap also exists for all levels of education. Although higher education clearly narrows the wage gap between men and women, a woman with a university degree earns approximately $15 000 less than a man with one. Once again, this gap is partially attributable to occupational segregation. The majority of female university students enrol in degree programs in education, health professions, fine arts, and the humanities, while males continue to dominate in the fields of science and engineering. Even within occupations that require specialized educational credentials, the wage gap does not disappear—for every dollar earned by men, women earned 65 cents as dentists,

68 cents as lawyers, and 77 cents as university professors (Statistics Canada, 2008i).

Because women's overall pay relative to men's has increased by about a penny a year for the past 10 years, it might seem that women's earnings have taken a noticeable move upward. However, this decrease in the wage gap can be partially attributed to the fact that men's earnings have declined since the 1970s, while women's have climbed slowly (Drolet, 2001c).

Pay Equity and Employment Equity

A number of strategies have been implemented in an attempt to achieve greater gender equality in the labour market. *Pay equity* attempts to raise the value

---

Figure 10.1 The Wage Gap

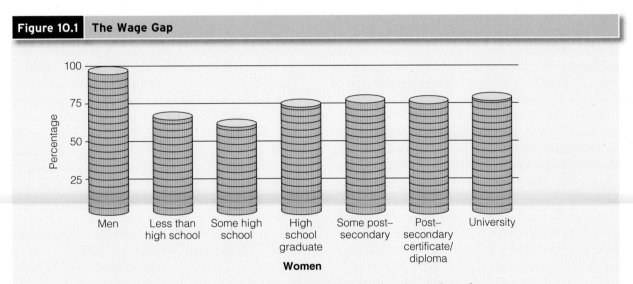

a. Across all levels of education, men's earnings are higher than the earnings of women. The wage gap does narrow slightly for women with higher levels of education.

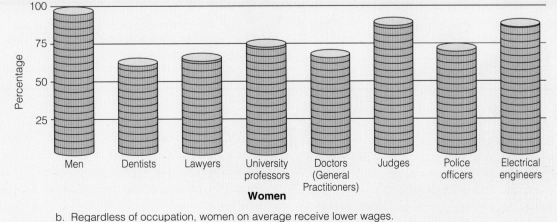

b. Regardless of occupation, women on average receive lower wages.

Sources: Statistics Canada, 2001f; UN Platform for Action Committee, 2005.

of the work traditionally performed by women. *Employment-equity* strategies focus on ways to move women into higher-paying jobs traditionally held by men (Creese and Beagan, 1999). Since the 1980s, the federal government, some provincial governments, and a number of private companies have implemented pay-equity and employment-equity policies (Lowe, 1999).

Pay equity—or, as it is sometimes called, comparable worth—reflects the belief that wages ought to reflect the worth of a job, not the gender or race of the worker (Kemp, 1994). How can the comparable worth of different kinds of jobs be determined? One way is to compare the actual work of women's and men's jobs and see if there is a disparity in the salaries paid for each. To do this, analysts break a job into components—such as the education, training, and skills required; the extent of responsibility for others' work; and the working conditions—and then allocate points for each (Lorber, 1994). For pay equity to exist, men and women in occupations that receive the same number of points should be paid the same. In short, pay equity promotes the principle of equal pay for work of equal value.

A second strategy for addressing inequality in the workplace is *employment equity*—a strategy to eliminate the effects of discrimination and to fully open the competition for job opportunities to those who have been excluded historically (Krahn, Lowe, and Hughes, 2007). The target groups for employment equity are visible minorities, people with disabilities, Aboriginal peoples, and women. In comparison with pay equity, which addresses wage issues only, employment equity covers a range of employment issues, such as recruitment, selection, training, development, and promotion. Employment equity also addresses issues pertaining to conditions of employment, such as compensation, layoffs, and disciplinary action (Boyd, 1995). Critics of employment-equity policies have pointed out that the Employment Equity Act of 1995 has jurisdiction over a very small percentage of the population; it covers only federal government employers or companies that have contracts with the federal government. Although these policies represent a start in the right direction, male resistance and poor regulation and enforcement have resulted in minimal progress toward gendered employment equity (Nelson, 2006).

Paid Work and Family Work

As previously discussed, the first big change in the relationship between family and work occurred with the Industrial Revolution and the rise of capitalism. The cult of domesticity kept many middle- and upper-class women out of the workforce during this period, primarily because working-class and poor women were the ones who had to deal with the work/family conflict. Today, however, the issue spans the entire economic spectrum. The typical married woman in Canada combines paid work in the labour force and family work as a homemaker.

While dramatic changes have occurred in women's participation in the workforce, men's entry into housework has been gradual, prompting some to refer to the latter as a "stalled revolution" (Cooke,

According to the human-capital model, women earn less in the labour market because of their child-rearing responsibilities. What other explanations are offered for the lower wages that women receive?

2004 c.f. Marshall, 2006: 16). Recent time-use surveys have confirmed that the burden of unpaid work continues to rest disproportionally on women. Even when women work full time, most maintain primary responsibility for child care, elder care, housework, shopping, and meal preparation. Among couples, the woman does close to two hours per day more housework than her male partner.

Consequently, many women have a "double day" or "second shift" because of their dual responsibilities for paid and unpaid work (Hochschild, 1989, 2003). Working women have less time to spend on housework; if husbands do not participate in routine domestic chores, some chores simply do not get done or get done less often.

Many working women care not only for themselves, their husbands, and their children, but also for elderly parents or in-laws. Some analysts refer to these women as "the sandwich generation"—caught between the needs of their young children and elderly relatives. Many women try to solve their time crunch by foregoing leisure time and sleep. When Arlie Hochschild interviewed working mothers, she found that they talked about sleep "the way a hungry person talks about food" (1989:9). In more research, Hochschild (1997) learned that some married women with children found more fulfillment at work and that they worked longer hours because they liked work better than facing the pressures of home.

Although the transition into housework has been slow for men, there is room for optimism as the household–work gender gap slowly narrows. Gender differences in the division of labour remain, but they are slowly diminishing. Since 1986, as women have increased their participation in paid work, men have increased their time spent on housework. In particular, men have made significant changes in their participation in core housework, such as meal preparation and cleanup, cleaning, and laundry. For couples with children, there have also been noticeable changes in men's participation in meeting childcare responsibilities and duties (Marshall, 2006).

PERSPECTIVES ON GENDER STRATIFICATION

Sociological perspectives on gender stratification vary in their approach to examining gender roles and power relationships in society (see Concept Table 10.1 on page 248). Some focus on the roles of women and men in the domestic sphere; others note the inequalities arising from a gendered division of labour in the workplace. Still others attempt to integrate both the public and private spheres into their analyses.

Functionalist Perspectives and Neoclassical Economic Perspectives

As seen earlier, functionalist theory views men and women as having distinct roles that are important for the survival of the family and society. The most basic division of labour is biological: men are physically stronger while women are the only ones able to bear and nurse children. Gendered belief systems foster assumptions about appropriate behaviour for men and women and may have an impact on the types of work women and men perform.

The Importance of Traditional Gender Roles
According to functional analysts such as Talcott Parsons (1955), women's roles as nurturers and caregivers are even more pronounced in contemporary industrialized societies. While the husband performs the *instrumental* tasks of providing economic support and making decisions, the wife assumes the *expressive* tasks of providing affection and emotional support for the family. This division of family labour ensures that important societal tasks will be fulfilled; it also provides stability for family members.

This view has been adopted by a number of conservative analysts who assert that relationships between men and women are damaged when changes in gender roles occur, and family life suffers as a consequence. From this perspective, the traditional division of labour between men and women is the natural order of the universe.

The Human-Capital Model
Functionalist explanations of occupational gender segregation are similar to neoclassical economic perspectives, such as the human-capital model (Horan, 1978; Kemp, 1994). According to this model, individuals vary widely in the amount of human capital they bring to the labour market. *Human capital* is acquired through education and job training; it is the source of a person's productivity and can be measured in terms of the return on the investment (wages) and the cost (schooling or training) (Stevenson, 1988; Kemp, 1994).

From this perspective, what individuals earn is the result of their own choices (the kinds of training, education, and experience they accumulate, for example) and of the labour-market need (demand) for and availability (supply) of certain kinds of workers at specific points in time. For example, human-capital analysts argue that women diminish their human capital when they leave the labour force to engage in childbearing and childcare activities. While women are out of the labour force, their human capital deteriorates from nonuse. When they return to work, women earn lower wages than men because they have fewer years of work experience and have "atrophied human capital" because their education and training may have become obsolete (Kemp, 1994:70).

Evaluation of Functionalist and Neoclassical Economic Perspectives

Although Parsons and other functionalists did not specifically endorse the gendered division of labour, their analysis views it as natural and perhaps inevitable. However, critics argue that problems inherent in traditional gender roles, including the personal-role strains of men and women and the social costs to society, are minimized by this approach. For example, men are assumed to be "money machines" for their families when they might prefer to spend more time in child-rearing activities. Also, the woman's place is assumed to be in the home, an assumption that ignores the fact that many women hold jobs due to economic necessity.

In addition, the functionalist approach does not take a critical look at the structure of society (especially the economic inequalities) that make educational and occupational opportunities more available to some than to others. Furthermore, it fails to examine the underlying power relations between men and women or to consider the fact that the tasks assigned to women and to men are unequally valued by society (Kemp, 1994).

Similarly, the human-capital model is rooted in the premise that individuals are evaluated based on their human capital in an open, competitive market, where education, training, and other job-enhancing characteristics are taken into account. From this perspective, those who make less money (men who are visible minorities and all women) have no one to blame but themselves.

Conflict Perspectives

According to many conflict analysts, the gendered division of labour within families and in the workplace

Concept Table 10.1	THEORETICAL PERSPECTIVES ON GENDER	
PERSPECTIVE	**KEY TERMS**	**KEY ELEMENTS**
Functionalist	Instrumental and expressive tasks	Division of labour by gender ensures stability.
Neoclassical Economic	Human capital	Gender inequality in the labour market results from women's diminished human capital.
Conflict	Gendered division of labour	The gendered division of labour at home and work is the result of male control of women and resources.
Feminist		
Liberal Feminism	Equal rights	Women's equality is equated with equality of opportunity.
Radical Feminism	Patriarchy	Patriarchy must be abolished for gender equality to be achieved.
Socialist Feminism	Gendered job segregation	Capitalism must be eliminated and a socialist economy established to obtain gender equality.
Multicultural Feminism	Double or triple jeopardy	Race, class, and gender simultaneously oppress women.
Postmodernist Feminism	Deconstructing gender	Categories of male and female and man and woman are artificial and malleable. People create, maintain, and modify their gender through their everyday interactions.

results from male control of and dominance over women and resources. Differentials between men and women may exist in terms of economic, political, physical, and/or interpersonal power. The importance of a male monopoly in any of these arenas depends on the significance of that type of power in a society (Richardson, 1993). In hunting-and-gathering and horticultural societies, male dominance over women is limited because all members of the society must work in order to survive (Collins, 1971; Nielsen, 1990). In agrarian societies, however, male sexual dominance is at its peak. Male heads of household gain a monopoly not only on physical power but also on economic power, and women become sexual property.

Although men's ability to use physical power to control women diminishes in industrial societies, men still remain the heads of household and control the property. In addition, men gain more power through their predominance in the most highly paid and prestigious occupations and the highest elected offices. In contrast, women have the ability to trade their sexual resources, companionship, and emotional support in the marriage market for men's financial support and social status; as a result, however, women as a group remain subordinate to men (Collins, 1971; Nielsen, 1990).

All men are not equally privileged; some analysts argue that women and men in the upper classes are more privileged, because of their economic power, than men in lower-class positions and members of some minority groups (Lorber, 1994). In industrialized societies, people who occupy elite positions in corporations, universities, the mass media, and government, or who have great wealth, have the most power (Richardson, 1993). Most of these are men, however.

Conflict theorists in the Marxist tradition assert that gender stratification results from private ownership of the means of production; some men not only gain control over property and the distribution of goods, but also gain power over women. According to Marx and Engels, marriage serves to enforce male dominance. Men of the capitalist class instituted monogamous marriage (a gendered institution) so that they could be certain of the paternity of their offspring, especially sons, whom they wanted to inherit their wealth. Feminist analysts have examined this theory, among others, as they have sought to explain male domination and gender stratification.

Feminist Perspectives

Feminism—the belief that women and men are equal and that they should be valued equally and

have equal rights—is embraced by many men as well as women. Gender is viewed as a socially constructed concept that has important consequences in the lives of all people (Craig, 1992). According to Ben Agger (1993), men can be feminists and propose feminist theories; both women and men have much in common as they seek to gain a better understanding of the causes and consequences of gender inequality.

Although all feminist perspectives begin with the assumption that the majority of women occupy a subordinate position to men, they often diverge in terms of their explanations of how and why women are subordinate and the best strategies to achieve equality for women (Chunn, 2000). Feminist perspectives vary in their analyses of the ways in which norms, roles, institutions, and internalized expectations limit women's behaviour. Taken together, they all seek to demonstrate how women's personal control operates even within the constraints of a relative lack of power (Stewart, 1994).

Liberal Feminism In liberal feminism, gender equality is equated with equality of opportunity. Liberal feminists assume that women's inequality stems from the denial to them of equal rights (Mandell, 2001). Only when these constraints on women's participation are removed will women have the same chance of success as men. This approach notes the importance of gender-role socialization and suggests that changes need to be made in what children learn from their families, teachers, and the media about appropriate masculine and feminine attitudes and behaviour. Liberal feminists fight for better childcare options, a woman's right to choose an abortion, and the elimination of sex discrimination in the workplace.

Radical Feminism According to radical feminists, male domination causes all forms of human oppression, including racism and classism (Tong, 1989). Radical feminists often trace the roots of patriarchy to women's child-bearing and child-rearing responsibilities, which make them dependent on men (Firestone, 1970; Chafetz, 1984). In the radical feminist view, men's oppression of women is deliberate, and ideological justification for this subordination is provided by other institutions, such as the media and religion. For women's condition to improve, radical feminists claim, patriarchy must be abolished. If institutions currently are gendered, alternative institutions—such as women's organizations seeking better health care and daycare and shelters for victims of domestic violence and sexual assault—should be developed to meet women's needs.

Socialist Feminism

Socialist feminists suggest that women's oppression results from their dual roles as paid *and* unpaid workers in a capitalist economy. In the workplace, women are exploited by capitalism; at home, they are exploited by patriarchy (Kemp, 1994). Women are easily exploited in both sectors; they are paid low wages and have few economic resources. Gendered job segregation is "the primary mechanism in capitalist society that maintains the superiority of men over women, because it enforces lower wages for women in the labour market" (Hartmann, 1976:139). As a result, women must do domestic labour either to gain a better-paid man's economic support or to stretch their own wages (Lorber, 1994). According to socialist feminists, the only way to achieve gender equality is to eliminate capitalism and develop a socialist economy that would bring equal pay and rights to women.

Multicultural Feminism

During the "second wave of feminism" (1970–90), the mainstream feminist movement was criticized for ignoring the experiences of poor women, women of colour, and women with disabilities. Feminism in its various forms described middle-class white women's experiences as the norm, and other women's experiences were treated as "different" (Cassidy, Lord, and Mandell, 2001). Recently, academics and activists have been attempting to address these criticisms and working to include the experiences of women of colour and Aboriginal women. Anti-racist feminist perspectives are based on the belief that women of colour experience a different world than middle-class white women because of multilayered oppression based on race/ethnicity, gender, and class (Khayatt, 1994). Building on the civil-rights and feminist movements of the late 1960s and early 1970s, contemporary feminists have focused on the cultural experiences of marginalized women, such as women of colour, immigrant women, and Native women. An assumption central to this analysis is that race, class, and gender are forces that simultaneously oppress some women (Hull, Bell-Scott, and Smith, 1982). The effects of these statuses cannot be adequately explained as "double" or "triple" jeopardy (class plus race plus gender) because these ascribed characteristics are not simply added to one another. Instead, they are multiplicative in nature (race times class times gender); different characteristics may be more significant in one situation than another. For example, a wealthy white woman (class) may be in a position of privilege as compared with people of colour (race) and men from lower socioeconomic positions (class), yet be in a subordinate position as compared with a white man (gender) from the capitalist class (Andersen and Collins, 1998). Feminists who analyze race, class, and gender suggest that equality will occur only when all women, regardless of race/ethnicity, class, age, religion, sexual orientation, or ability (or disability), are treated more equitably (Cassidy, Lord, and Mandell, 2001).

Postmodernist Feminism

One of the more recent feminist perspectives to emerge is *postmodernist feminism.* Postmodern feminists argue that the various feminist theories—including liberal, Marxist, radical, and socialist—which advocate a single or limited number of causes for women's inequality and oppression are flawed, inadequate, and typically based upon suppression of female experiences. In keeping with the assumptions of postmodernist theory, postmodernist feminists resist making generalizations about "all women." Rather, they attempt to acknowledge the individual experiences and perspectives of women of all classes, races, ethnicities, abilities, sexualities, and ages. To postmodernist feminists, a singular feminist theory is impossible because there is no essential "woman." The category *woman* is seen as a social construct that is "a fiction, a non-determinable identity" (Cain, 1993, cf. Nelson, 2006:94).

Given that the category "woman" is regarded as socially constructed, the challenge of postmodernist feminism is to "deconstruct" these notions of the natural or essential woman. For example, the traditional sciences, in particular medicine, have viewed "reproduction" as a central construct of "woman." As Phoenix and Woolett (1991:7) have argued, "women continue to be defined in terms of their biological functions" such that "motherhood and particularly childbearing continues to be defined as the supreme route to physical and emotional fulfillment and as essential for all women." Postmodernist feminists challenge the concept of the reproductive woman as essential and highlight the oppressive nature of such so-called scientific knowledge.

Postmodern feminists argue that the various feminist theories—including liberal, Marxist, radical, and socialist—which advocate a single or limited number of causes for women's inequality and oppression are flawed, inadequate, and typically based upon suppression of female experiences. In keeping with the assumptions of postmodernist theory, postmodernist feminists resist making generalizations about "all women." Rather, they attempt to acknowledge the individual experiences and perspectives of women of all classes, races, ethnicities, abilities, sexualities, and ages. To postmodernist feminists, a singular feminist theory is impossible because there is no essential "woman." The category *woman* is seen as a social construct that is "a fiction, a non-determinable identity" (Cain, 1993, cf. Nelson, 2006:94).

Given that the category "woman" is regarded as socially constructed, the challenge of postmodernist feminism is to "deconstruct" these notions of the natural or essential woman. For example, the traditional sciences, in particular medicine, have viewed "reproduction" as a central construct of "woman." As Phoenix and Woolett (1991:7) have argued, "women continue to be defined in terms of their biological functions" such that "motherhood and particularly childbearing continues to be defined as the supreme route to physical and emotional fulfillment and as essential for all women." Postmodernist feminists challenge the concept of the reproductive woman as essential and highlight the oppressive nature of such so-called scientific knowledge.

Postmodernist feminists argue that there is nothing that is essentially male or female. In fact, they go so far as to challenge the idea of any real biological categories of male or female—suggesting, rather, that our understanding of biological differences between the sexes is of socially constructed categories that have emerged from specific cultural and historical contexts. Some scholars view the distinction between sex and gender as false because it is based on the assumption of biological differences as real (Anderson, 2006:395). In sum, the categories of male and female, man and woman, are best understood by postmodernist feminists as fluid, artificial, and malleable.

Evaluation of Conflict and Feminist Perspectives
Conflict and feminist perspectives provide insights into the structural aspects of gender inequality in society. While functionalist approaches focus on the characteristics of individuals, the conflict and feminist approaches emphasize factors external to individuals that contribute to the oppression of women. These approaches also examine the ways in which the workplace and the home are gendered.

Conflict theory has been criticized for emphasizing the differences between men and women without taking into account their commonalities. Feminist approaches have been criticized for their emphasis on

male dominance without a corresponding analysis of the ways in which some men also may be oppressed by patriarchy and capitalism.

A Symbolic Interactionist Perspective

In contrast to functionalist, conflict, and feminist theorists, who focus primarily on macrolevel analysis of structural and systemic sources of gender differences and inequities, symbolic interactionists focus on a microlevel analysis that views a person's identity as a product of their social interactions. From this perspective, people create, maintain, and modify gender as they go about their everyday lives. Candace West and Don Zimmerman (1991) utilized a symbolic interactionist perspective to explain what they refer to as "doing gender"—a term used to describe an individual interacting with another in a way that displays characteristics of a particular gender. This perspective views gender not as fixed in biology or social roles, but rather as something that is "accomplished" through interactions with others (1991:16).

In illustrating the concept of "doing gender," West and Zimmerman refer to a case study of Agnes, a transsexual raised as a boy until she adopted a female identity at age 17. Although Agnes eventually underwent a sex-reassignment operation several years later, she had the challenging task of displaying herself as female even though she had never experienced the everyday interactions that women use to attach meaning to the concept of being female. Agnes had to display herself as a woman while simultaneously learning what it was to be a woman. To make matters more difficult, she was attempting to do so when most people at that age "do gender" virtually without thinking. As West and Zimmerman explain, this does not make Agnes's gender artificial:

> She was not faking what real women do naturally. She was obliged to analyze and figure out how to act within socially constructed circumstances and conceptions of femininity that women born with the appropriate biological credentials take for granted early on. . . . As with others who must "pass" . . . Agnes's case makes visible what culture has made invisible—the accomplishment of gender. (1991:18)

Can you think of ways in which you "do gender" in your daily interactions?

Evaluation of the Symbolic Interactionist Perspective Using a symbolic interactionist perspective helps us to understand how we create, sustain, or change the gender categories that constitute being a man or a woman in our society. Symbolic interactionists emphasize that socialization into gender roles is not simply a passive process whereby people simply internalize others' expectations, but rather that the people can choose to "do gender" to varying degrees. In doing so, we are able to continually change the social definition of gender (Messner, 2000, cf. Anderson, 2006). The symbolic interactionist perspective has been criticized for failing to address the power differences between men and women as well as the significant economic and political advantages that exist in the larger social structure (Anderson, 2006).

GENDER ISSUES IN THE FUTURE

In the past 30 years, women have made significant progress in the labour force. Laws have been passed to prohibit sexual discrimination in the workplace and school. Employment-equity programs have made women more visible in education, government, and the professional world.

Many men have joined movements to raise their consciousness not only about men's concerns but also about the need to eliminate sexism and gender bias. Many men realize that what is harmful to women also may be harmful to men. For example, women's lower wages in the labour force suppress men's wages as well; in a two-paycheque family, women who are paid less contribute less to the family's finances, thus placing a greater burden on men to earn more money.

In the midst of these changes, many gender issues remain unresolved. In the labour force, gender segregation and the wage gap are still problems. Although the wage gap is narrowing, women continue to make significantly less than their male counterparts. The pay gap between men and women should continue to shrink, but this may be due in part to decreasing wages paid to men during the recent economic crisis. What can be done to address the gendered division of unpaid work? Strategies include improved government supports such as low-cost daycare and better maternity- and paternity-leave provisions. Employers also need to create more "family-friendly" programs such as on-site daycare, flex-time, and family leave, as well as decreasing demands for overtime. Finally, although men are involved in a greater share of the unpaid work in the home than ever before, the division of labour is still far from equal. Until significant changes are made in the distribution of unpaid work, gender segregation in lower-paying jobs will likely remain a reality for most Canadian women (Creese and Beagan, 2008).

▓ How do sex and gender differ?

Sex refers to the biological categories and manifestations of femaleness and maleness; *gender* refers to the socially constructed differences between females and males. In short, sex is what we (generally) are born with; gender is what we acquire through socialization.

▓ What are gender roles and gender identity?

Gender role encompasses the attitudes, behaviours, and activities that are socially assigned to each sex and that are learned through socialization. Gender identity is an individual's perception of his or her self as either female or male.

▓ How does the nature of work affect gender equity in different societies?

In most hunting-and-gathering societies, fairly equitable relationships exist because neither sex has the ability to provide all of the food necessary for survival. In horticultural societies, a fair degree of gender equality exists because neither sex controls the food supply. In agrarian societies, male dominance is very apparent; agrarian tasks require more labour and physical strength, and women often are excluded from these tasks because they are viewed as too weak or too tied to child-rearing activities. In industrialized societies, a gap exists between non-paid work performed by women at home and paid work performed by men and women. A wage gap also exists between women and men in the marketplace. In post-industrial societies, the division of labour in paid employment is increasingly based on whether people provide or apply information or are employed in service jobs.

▓ What are the key agents of gender socialization?

The key agents of gender socialization are parents, peers, teachers and schools, sports, and the media, all of which tend to reinforce stereotypes of appropriate gender behaviour.

▓ What causes gender inequality in Canada?

Gender inequality results from economic, political, and educational discrimination against women. In most workplaces, jobs are either gender segregated or the majority of employees are of the same gender.

▓ How is occupational segregation related to the pay gap?

Many women work in lower-paying, less prestigious jobs than men. This occupational segregation leads to a disparity, or pay gap, between women's and men's earnings. Even when women are employed in the same job as men, on average they do not receive the same, or comparable, pay.

▓ How do functionalist and conflict theorists differ in their views of the gendered division of labour?

According to functional analysts, women's roles as caregivers in contemporary industrialized societies are crucial in ensuring that key societal tasks are fulfilled. While the husband performs the instrumental tasks of economic support and decision making, the wife assumes the expressive tasks of providing affection and emotional support to the family. According to conflict analysts, the gendered division of labour within families and the workplace—particularly in agrarian and industrial societies—is caused by male control and dominance over women and resources.

▓ How do the various feminist perspectives explain gender inequality?

Although feminist perspectives vary in their analyses of women's subordination, they all advocate social change to eradicate gender inequality. In liberal feminism, gender equality is connected to equality of opportunity. In radical feminism, male dominance is seen as the cause of oppression. According to socialist feminists, women's oppression is the result of their dual roles as paid and unpaid workers. Multicultural feminists focus on including knowledge and awareness of the lives of marginalized women in the struggle for equality. Finally, postmodern feminists regard the category "woman" as a social construct and strive to deconstruct traditional notions of male and female.

KEY TERMS

body consciousness 236
employment equity 246
feminism 249
gender 236
gender bias 242
gender identity 236
gender role 236
gender-segregated work 243
hermaphrodite 233
homophobia 236
matriarchy 237
patriarchy 237
pay equity 245

WEB LINKS

For more Web links related to the topic of this chapter, see the Nelson sociology website:
www.sociologyessentials5e.nelson.com

The Canadian Women's Internet Association (CWIA) contains hundreds of links to sites relevant to women, with a special focus on Canadian content:
www.herplace.org/

The National Organization for Men Against Sexism (NOMAS) has a pro-feminist stance that seeks to end sexism and an affirmative stance on the rights of gay men and lesbians. Go to: **www.nomas.org**

QUESTIONS FOR CRITICAL THINKING

1. Do the media reflect societal attitudes on gender, or do the media determine and teach gender behaviour? (As a related activity, watch television for several hours and list the roles women and men play in the shows watched and in the advertisements.)

2. Examine the various academic departments at your university. What is the gender breakdown of the faculty in selected departments? What is the gender breakdown of undergraduates and graduates in those departments? Are there major differences among the social sciences, sciences, and humanities departments? How can you explain your observations?

3. As discussed throughout this chapter, gender may be viewed as a social construction. "Doing gender," whether you are male or female, is something you have learned through a process of socialization. What changes would you have to make in your "gender performance" if you were to wake up one morning as the opposite gender?

ONLINE STUDY AND RESEARCH TOOLS

INFOTRAC®

InfoTrac College Edition is included free with every new copy of this text. Explore this online library for additional readings, review, and a handy resource for assignments. Visit **www.infotrac-college.com** to access this online database of full-text articles. Enter the key terms from this chapter to start your search.

CENGAGENOW™   CENGAGENOW

Use CengageNOW™ to help you formulate a customized study plan for this chapter. After you take the Diagnostic Quiz, CengageNOW™ will generate a customized study plan for you. It will identify sections of the chapter you should review.

Health, Health Care, and Disability

Rae Lewis-Thornton describes her experience with HIV/AIDS in the following way:

The day I found out [I was HIV-positive] I was so calm. . . . I walked out of the . . . Red Cross office and into the . . . sunshine, flagged a cab and went back to work. I worked late that night . . . I was 24. I'd just been given a death sentence. . . . I am the quintessential Buppie. I'm young. . . . Well educated. Professional. Attractive. Smart. I've been drug and alcohol-free all my life. I'm a Christian. I've never been promiscuous. Never had a one-night stand. And I am dying of AIDS.

I've been living with the disease for nine years, and people still tell me that I am too pretty and intelligent to have AIDS. But I do. I discovered I was HIV-positive when I tried to give blood at the office. I have no idea who infected me or when it happened. Still, there is one thing I am absolutely certain of; I am dying now because I had one sexual partner too many. And I'm here to tell you one is all it takes. (Lewis-Thornton, 1994:63)

AIDS Memorial

AIDS is a significant global problem, taking its toll on individuals, families, cities, and nations. The disease known as AIDS (acquired immunodeficiency syndrome) is caused by HIV, the human immunodeficiency virus, which gradually destroys the immune system by attacking the white blood cells, making the person with HIV more vulnerable to other types of illnesses. While we do not know the actual number of people infected with HIV—some countries lack adequate diagnostic equipment or centralized reporting systems—the United Nations estimated that in 2008, 33.4 million people were infected with HIV/AIDS (including 2.1 million children under 15) and that 2 million people died of AIDS (UNAIDS, 2009). Some countries are being devastated by HIV/AIDS; in Botswana and Zimbabwe, more than 25 percent of the adult population is infected. In Canada, 65 000 people were living with HIV (Public Health Agency of Canada, 2009), and more than 22 000 had died of AIDS by 2008 (Public Health Agency of Canada, 2009). Map 11.1 on page 258 outlines the global distribution of HIV.

Because of a massive global effort, progress has been made in the fight against AIDS. The number of annual AIDS deaths has been slowly declining—from 2.2 million in 2005 to 2 million in 2008—and the number of new infections declined from 3 million in 2001 to 2.7 million in 2008 (UNAIDS, 2009).

HIV/AIDS has nonetheless had a devastating impact in sub-Saharan Africa, which has 67 percent of all AIDS cases and 70 percent of AIDS deaths (UNAIDS, 2009).

Half of all new infections in Africa are among people of ages 15 to 24, and many newborns are being infected by their mothers. This means that the disease is destroying much of Africa's future. The average life expectancy in many African countries has dropped by as much as 17 years, and the cost of providing even minimal treatment for the disease is taking away many of the hard-won economic gains of some countries.

The problem of AIDS illustrates how sociology can apply to what, at first glance, appears to be a purely medical phenomenon. As Karen Grant explains, AIDS is a social phenomenon as much as a disease:

AIDS demonstrates that disease not only affects health, but one's definition of self, relations with others, and behaviours. As well, AIDS has had a significant impact on social institutions. The health-care system has been most directly affected, requiring assessments of the adequacy of research, treatment modalities, and health-care facilities. Legal scholars and legislators have wrestled with issues of privacy and human rights protections for people with AIDS. AIDS has resulted in social and sexual mores and lifestyles being reassessed. (Grant, 1993:395)

QUESTIONS AND ISSUES

Chapter Focus Question: What effect has HIV/AIDS had on the health of the global population?

Why is HIV/AIDS referred to as a global/human problem?

In what ways do sociological factors influence health and disease?

How do functionalist, symbolic interactionist, conflict, feminist, and postmodern theories differ in their analyses of health?

How does social inequality affect health and health care?

What are some of the consequences of disability?

What is the state of the health-care system in Canada today, and how could it be improved?

| Map 11.1 | Numbers of HIV-Positive People around the World, 2009 |

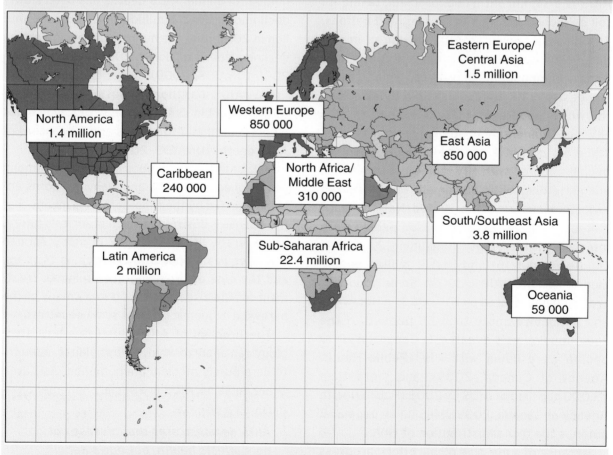

Source: Data from UNAIDS. 2009. *AIDS Epidemic Update*, December 2009. Geneva: World Healt Organization.

SOCIOLOGY AND EVERYDAY LIFE

How Much Do You Know about HIV/AIDS?

True	False	
T	F	1. Worldwide, most people with AIDS are gay men.
T	F	2. In Canada, you can be sent to jail if you knowingly transmit HIV to another person.
T	F	3. HIV is spreading rapidly among women in some nations.
T	F	4. Young people are particularly vulnerable to HIV.
T	F	5. Bill Gates, the Microsoft founder who is the world's richest person, is one of the leaders in the fight against AIDS.
T	F	6. People can get HIV from sharing toilets, toothbrushes, eating utensils, or razors.
T	F	7. People infected with HIV may not show any physical symptoms for ten years or longer and can infect others without realizing it.
T	F	8. AIDS is now a curable disease.
T	F	9. In Canada, the majority of new HIV cases occur among men who have sex with men.
T	F	10. One of the major concerns of AIDS activists is reducing the stigmatization of HIV/AIDS victims.

Answers on page 260.

In this chapter, we will explore the dynamics of health and health care. In the process, we will periodically focus on HIV/AIDS and on its impact on society. Although we will use HIV/AIDS as an example throughout this chapter, you should be aware that globally several other causes of death are more common. The leading cause of death is heart disease (12.2 percent), followed by cerebrovascular disease (9.7 percent), lower respiratory infections (7.0 percent), chronic obstructive pulmonary disease (5.1 percent), diarrhoeal diseases (3.6 percent), and HIV/AIDS (3.5 percent) (World Health Organization, 2009). Before reading on, test your knowledge about HIV/AIDS by taking the quiz in Box 11.1.

HEALTH AND MEDICINE

What does the concept of health mean to you? If you were asked whether you are healthy, how would you respond? Although the definition of health may appear to be obvious, consensus on its definition remains elusive. Health was once considered simply the absence of disease. The World Health Organization (WHO) provides a more inclusive definition of *health,* **calling it a state of complete physical, mental, and social well-being**. This definition of health has several dimensions; physical, social, and psychological factors are all important. Health does not depend solely on the absence of disease or sickness. Health is socially defined, and therefore varies over time and between cultures. For example, in our society obesity is viewed as unhealthy, while in other times and places it signalled prosperity and good health.

Medicine **is an institutionalized system for the scientific diagnosis, treatment, and prevention of illness**. Medicine forms a vital part of the broader concept of *health care,* **which is any activity intended to improve health**. In North America, medicine typically is used when there is a failure in health. When people get sick, they seek medical attention to make them healthy again. The field of *preventive medicine*—**medicine that emphasizes a healthy lifestyle in order to prevent poor health before it occurs,** is receiving increasing attention.

| BOX 11.1 | SOCIOLOGY AND EVERYDAY LIFE |

Answers to the Sociology Quiz on HIV/AIDS

Join In on TurningPoint®

1. False.   Although AIDS has taken a devastating toll on the gay population in North America, globally, heterosexual contact is the most common way of transmitting HIV/AIDS.

2. True.   No specific law forbids this behaviour. However, in 1998, the Supreme Court of Canada ruled that a person was guilty of assault if they did not tell their sexual partners they had HIV/AIDS or other sexually transmitted diseases. In 2009, a Hamilton man was convicted of two counts of first-degree murder for knowingly infecting seven women, two of whom died. He is now serving a life sentence in prison (see Box 11.2 on page 262).

3. True.   Globally, nearly half of all people living with HIV are women (UNAIDS, 2009). In Canada, women accounted for 26 percent of newly diagnosed cases of HIV/AIDS in 2008 (Public Health Agency of Canada, 2009).

4. True.   AIDS is found disproportionately among young people, a consequence of the fact that they are more likely to engage in sexually promiscuous behaviour and/or to be intravenous drug users. Twenty-seven percent of HIV cases in Canada were found among people ages 15 to 29 (Public Health Agency of Canada, 2007).

5. True.   Through his charitable foundation, Gates has given billions of dollars to fight AIDS. One of his priorities is to develop a vaccine that would immunize people against HIV/AIDS. Gates has funded a University of Manitoba project studying Kenyan prostitutes who have not contracted AIDS despite repeated exposure to HIV. Understanding their immunity may help to find a vaccine (see www.gatesfoundation.org).

6. False.   AIDS is caused by HIV (human immunodeficiency virus), which is transmitted to men or women through unprotected sexual contact with an infected partner (either male or female), through sharing a contaminated hypodermic needle with someone who is infected, through exposure to contaminated blood or blood products (usually from a transfusion), and through the passing on of the virus by an infected woman to her child during pregnancy, childbirth, or breast-feeding.

7. True.   Without an HIV-antibody test it may be impossible for an individual to tell whether he or she has been infected with HIV. It can take from three to six months from the time a person is infected for the virus to show up on the test.

8. False.   HIV/AIDS is a fatal disease. While new drug treatments have extended the lives of many people with HIV/AIDS, there is no cure.

9. False.   In 2008, 44 percent of newly diagnosed HIV infections occurred among men who have sex with men, 36 percent were attributed to heterosexual transmission, and 17 percent were due to injection drug use (Public Health Agency of Canada, 2009).

10. True.   Many AIDS victims have suffered hostility and discrimination because of their illness. Educational programs and political lobbying by AIDS activists have tried to reduce this stigmatization.

SOCIOLOGICAL PERSPECTIVES ON HEALTH AND MEDICINE

Functionalist Perspectives on Health: The Sick Role

Functionalists view society as a complex, stable system. Therefore, the normal state of affairs is for people to be healthy and to contribute to their society. Talcott Parsons viewed illness as dysfunctional both for the individual who is sick and for the larger society (Parsons, 1951). Sick people may be unable to fulfill their necessary social roles, such as parenting, or working in the paid labour force. Thus, illness can cause the social system to malfunction. Societies must therefore establish definitions of who is legitimately sick. Societies also hold the expectation that those who are sick will get well so they can once again contribute to the healthy functioning of the social system. According to Parsons, all societies have a *sick role*—**patterns of behaviour defined as appropriate for people who are sick**. This definition implies that illness is a social role that is defined by a culture. The characteristics of the sick role are:

1. The sick person is temporarily exempt from normal social responsibilities. For example, when you are sick you are not expected to go to work or school.
2. The sick person is not responsible for his or her condition. Individuals should not be blamed or punished because sickness is not their fault.
3. The sick person must want to get well. The sick role is temporary. The person who does not do everything possible to return to a healthy state is no longer a legitimately sick person and may be considered a hypochondriac or a malingerer.
4. The sick person should seek technically competent help and cooperate with health-care practitioners to hasten his or her recovery.
5. Physicians are the "gate keepers" who maintain society's control over people who enter the sick role.

Critics of Parsons's model, and more generally of the functionalist view of health and illness, argue that it places too much responsibility for illness on the sick people, neglecting the fact that often the actions of other people may be the cause of someone's illness. For example, a child may be born with fetal alcohol syndrome because the mother consumed alcohol during pregnancy. Individuals living in poverty may become sick because of inadequate food and shelter.

Also, contrary to the functionalist view, individuals may be blamed for their illness, as people who contract HIV or lung cancer often are.

Conflict Theory: Inequalities in Health and Health Care

The conflict approach emphasizes the political, economic, and social forces that affect health and the health-care system and the inequities that result from these forces. Among the issues of concern for conflict theorists are the ability of all citizens to obtain health care; the impact of race, class, and gender on health and health care; the relative power of doctors compared with other health workers; and the dominance of the medical model of health care.

While we will consider several of these issues later in this chapter, the role of conflict in the provision of health care is clearly illustrated in the debate over the allocation of money for research and treatment for different diseases. There is competition among advocates for different diseases; money spent doing research on cancer cannot be spent on heart disease. Conflict also exists among those who take different approaches to research and treatment of a particular disease. Should funds be spent on treatment or prevention? Should nontraditional treatment methods be studied or is the medical model the only legitimate way of responding to disease?

Understandably, groups representing victims of particular types of diseases have lobbied governments and medical groups to give their problem more funding. Thus, the priority given to research, prevention, and medical care for particular types of diseases may reflect the power of lobby groups as well as the seriousness of the problem. AIDS activists have been particularly successful in having their concerns reflected in policy. Gay men have worked together to form a lobby that has had a powerful impact on securing government support and funding for AIDS research and treatment. As you will learn from reading Box 11.2 on page 262, AIDS activists have also been concerned with reducing the stigmatization of HIV/AIDS victims.

BOX 11.2   CRITICAL THINKING

AIDS and Public Health

In 2009, a Hamilton jury found Johnson Aziga guilty of 2 counts of first-degree murder and 10 counts of aggravated sexual assault. Aziga, a former research analyst for the Ontario Attorney-General's department, was the first person convicted of murder in Canada (and possibly in the world) for knowingly infecting others with HIV. Despite being diagnosed with HIV, Aziga had unprotected sex with 13 women. Seven of these women contracted HIV and two died.

Aziga learned he had HIV in 1996. He was counselled to tell potential sexual partners of his disease and to avoid unprotected sex. However, despite several warnings and a Health Protection and Promotion order, he continued to have unprotected sex with multiple partners and he did not tell his partners that he was HIV positive. The public health system could not protect Aziga's victims from HIV/AIDS.

Canada has no specific law against knowingly infecting others with a sexually transmittable disease, though such laws do exist in several other countries. However, the Supreme Court of Canada determined that if someone does not disclose HIV, they do not have their partner's consent and can be found guilty of assault. Almost 100 men and women have been charged with criminal offences for exposing partners to HIV. Perhaps the best-known case was that of former Saskatchewan Roughriders linebacker Trevis Smith who was sentenced to six years in prison for having unprotected sex with two women.

Controlling the spread of HIV is controversial. The normal steps taken in dealing with infectious diseases include routine testing for infection, reporting the names of those who have positive tests, and tracing contacts to inform them they have been exposed to the disease. Quarantine has even been used to prevent the spread of disease. In 2003, quarantines were used to control the SARS outbreak in Toronto. In Ontario, 12 diseases, including syphilis, gonorrhea, and tuberculosis, are defined as virulent, and people with these diseases can be forced to stay in a hospital or jail for up to four months for treatment. However, HIV/AIDS is not included in this category. Because it is incurable, health authorities have reasoned, it does not make sense to force victims to have treatment. When Dr. Richard Schabas, Ontario's former medical officer of health, suggested classifying HIV/AIDS as a virulent disease in order to control rare, irresponsible victims who knowingly spread the disease, AIDS activists burned Dr. Schabas in effigy and he was given police protection after he received death threats. More recently, several people, including Dr. Mark Wainberg, the former head of the International AIDS Society, were critical of the use of the criminal law in cases like Aziga's.

Why do some feel that the criminal law should not be used in HIV/AIDS transmission cases and oppose treating HIV/AIDS like other communicable diseases? Dr. Wainberg feels that these cases will discourage people from getting tested, thus increasing the chances of further transmission of the disease. He also feels that prosecutions will further stigmatize HIV/AIDS victims. There is no question that HIV/AIDS victims have been stigmatized and to some AIDS activists, Dr. Schabas's suggestion that AIDS victims could be involuntarily detained raised the possibility of homophobic governments locking up large numbers of gay men simply because they were ill.

What are your views on this issue? Should all known partners of HIV victims be informed of their risk? Because new drugs can slow the progress of HIV, should more effort go into identifying those with HIV so that they can be treated? Can attitudes be changed so that the consequences of being labelled an HIV/AIDS victim are less severe? Should it be a crime to knowingly spread HIV, or should the problem be dealt with outside the criminal courts?

Feminist Perspectives on Health and Illness

Feminist scholars have studied many different aspects of health and health care. One of the first problems they identified was that most medical research was centred on males and ignored diseases that primarily affected females. Other feminist researchers have studied the discrimination against women working in a health-care system that has traditionally been dominated by male doctors. Women were relegated to subservient roles and have lacked access to leadership roles within the system. Some of the most important work by feminist scholars has looked at the ways in which the process of medicalization has affected women.

The Medicalization of Women's Lives The term *medicalization* **refers to the process whereby an object or condition becomes defined by society as a physical or psychological illness.** Medicalization has been a focus of feminist researchers because women's health issues, including those having to do with childbirth, menopause, PMS, and contraception, have been particularly susceptible to medicalization, something that has not necessarily served the interests of women. Historically, women's health needs, including pregnancy and childbirth, were looked after by other women in their communities (Findlay and Miller, 2002). The era of women looking after women ended when the male profession of medicine successfully challenged midwives and other traditional health practitioners and claimed exclusive jurisdiction over conditions such as childbirth and menopause, which were redefined as medical problems. Medical doctors won this struggle despite the fact that traditional practices often had more favourable outcomes than those of the new profession of medicine. Findlay and Miller conclude that healing became "men's work." While this development helped to raise the status of the medical profession, it reduced women's control over their own bodies. Medicalization had a profound effect on the practices of childbirth, child rearing, and mothering.

Feminist researchers have also questioned the role of medicine in shaping the ways in which women view their physical appearance: "Certain sociocultural forces invite an excessive concern for 'feminine beauty' and medical rhetoric itself acts to exacerbate the already powerful cultural demands on women to overemphasize their bodily appearance" (Findlay and Miller, 2002:197).

A 1989 paper by the American Society for Plastic and Reconstructive Surgery provides a rather extreme example of this medical rhetoric. This society, the major professional organization representing plastic surgeons, wanted the U.S. government to loosen its restrictions on the use of breast implants. The society based its case on the view that having small breasts constituted a disease. It alleged that this disease (called *micromastia*) resulted in "feelings of inadequacy, lack of self-confidence, distortion of body image, and a total lack of well-being due to a lack of self-perceived femininity" (cited in Weitz, 1996:123). Of course, this "disease" could be cured if the victims received expensive, potentially dangerous breast implants from the plastic surgeons. It is not difficult to imagine the harm that the plastic surgeons' lobbying effort encouraging women to think of their biologically normal bodies as "diseased" might have on some women's self-images. For example, press reports of a Penticton, B.C., contest in which 36 women competed for a chance to win breast implants said that many of the losers had "lost a chance at gaining self-confidence" (Carmichael, 2005). That breast size is still a measure of these young women's sense of self-worth, and that many aspects of physical appearance have come under medical control, is a clear indication of the degree to which women's appearance has become medicalized.

Findlay and Miller feel that the medicalization of women's lives individualizes and depoliticizes their problems, and by blaming them on the women "leaves the dominant patriarchal conceptions of femininity untouched" (2002:201). Medicalization also forces women to conform to a set of traditional social norms, and "limits women's options—in behaviour, in appearance, and in relationships" (2002:201). However, they believe that the medical model is so dominant that women will not be able to develop an alternative. Rather, they will continue to make incremental changes that will reduce some of the negative effects of medicalization while retaining the benefits of the modern medical system. Women have made great headway in re-establishing midwifery and natural childbirth methods that return some of the control over the birthing process to the mother. Women have also forced the medical profession to share more information and to empower clients in many other ways.

Symbolic Interactionist Theory: The Social Construction of Illness

Interactionists try to understand the specific meanings and causes that we attribute to particular events. In studying health, interactionists focus on how the meaning that social actors give their illness or disease will affect their self-concept and their relationships with others. The interactionist approach is illustrated by society's response to AIDS.

We often try to explain disease by blaming it on those who are ill. This practice reduces the uncertainty of those of us who fear the disease. Nonsmokers who learn that a cancer victim had a two-pack-a-day habit feel comforted that the guilty have been punished and that the same fate is unlikely to befall them. Because of the association of their disease with homosexuality and intravenous drug use, victims of AIDS have particularly suffered from blame. How is a person's self-concept affected when he or she is diagnosed with AIDS? How does this diagnosis affect the relationships the person has with others in his or her social world?

In the case of AIDS, the social definition of the illness can have as profound an impact on the AIDS patient as the medical symptoms. AIDS is an example of illness as stigma (Giddens, 1996). A *stigma* is any physical or social attribute or sign that so devalues a person's social identity that it disqualifies that person from social acceptance. Unlike other illnesses that may provoke sympathy or compassion, an illness such as AIDS is perceived by some people as dishonourable or shameful, and sufferers are rejected by the healthy population. Children with AIDS have been driven from their schools; homes of people with AIDS have been burned by people afraid of getting the disease; employees have been fired; and medical professionals have refused treatment to AIDS patients. These events have happened despite the fact that AIDS cannot be transmitted by casual, everyday contact. However, the social definition of an illness is not always based on medical fact. The incidents of hostility and discrimination directed at individuals with AIDS have a profound impact on their self-concept, social relationships, and ability to cope with the illness.

The Social Definition of Health and Illness: The Process of Medicalization

Most of us would agree that conditions such as heart disease and cancer are illnesses because of their biological characteristics. However, even in these cases there is a subjective component to the way illness is defined. This subjective component is very important when we look at conditions that are more ambiguous than cancer or a broken bone. For example: a child who has difficulty learning may be diagnosed as having attention deficit/hyperactivity disorder (ADHD); a man who occasionally behaves strangely may be called mentally ill; and a woman going through menopause may be defined as having a hormonal deficiency disease. Alternatively, we could view these conditions as part of the range of normal human behaviour. The child might be seen as a poor student, the man as a bit odd, and the woman as a person going through the normal aging process. The way we view these individuals will depend on our cultural perspectives, which can change over time.

Medicalization usually entails the application of medical technology in the diagnosis and treatment of the condition (Grant, 1993). Conrad and Schneider (1992) found that medicalization is typically the result of a lengthy promotional campaign conducted by interest groups, often culminating in legislative or other official changes that institutionalize a medical treatment for the new "disease." The interest groups may include scientists acting on the results of their research; those who have the disease, and who are seeking either a cure; and members of the medical industry interested in increasing their profits.

Conrad and Schneider (1980) emphasize that many behaviours that were at one time defined as "badness" have been redefined as "sicknesses" or "illnesses." Conrad (1975) describes how the disruptive behaviour of children in schools became medicalized. Until a medical condition was established and given the name attention-deficit/hyperactivity disorder (ADHD), children who had difficulty sitting still, concentrating, or who were impulsive and full of energy were labelled "active" or "energetic, "or they were called "problem children" (Conrad, 1975). In the early 1970s, the medical profession began to treat such children as deviant. The "discovery" of the illness now known as ADHD coincided with the development of Ritalin, a drug that suppresses hyperactive behaviours and medication became the accepted treatment for this condition. For schools, the social construction of this illness results in fewer disruptive students and more manageable classrooms; the illness also creates a large new patient population for doctors and a profitable new market for the pharmaceutical industry. For the children whose problem behaviour is organically based, Ritalin enables them to concentrate and function better in the classroom. However, for children whose disruptive behaviour is a reflection of their acting "like children" rather than symptomatic of ADHD, it results in unnecessary medication.

Behaviours can also be *demedicalized.* For many years, homosexuality was defined as a mental illness, and gays and lesbians were urged to seek psychiatric treatment. Gay activists fought for years to convince the American Psychiatric Association to remove homosexuality from the association's psychiatric diagnostic manual. At the same time, women's groups have been trying to demedicalize childbirth and menopause, and redefine them as natural processes rather than as illnesses.

Postmodern Perspectives on Health: The Crossroads of Biology and Culture

David Morris has proposed a postmodern perspective on health that understands disease and illness "whatever [their] particular causes, as created in the convergences between biology and culture" (1998:76). While most of us are aware of the biological dimensions of disease and illness, culture is a factor in health in many ways. Human activities such as coal mining and the pollution caused by burning fossil fuels have health implications for workers and for the general population. Culture also affects the way in which we experience illness. The experience of having cancer—part of which involves the "sick role" described by Parsons—is very different for someone in a poor village in Uganda than in a wealthy city in North America. While the biological factors may be identical, the understanding of the illness, the treatment available, the suffering experienced by the patient, and the likelihood of survival differ greatly between the two cultural contexts. According to Morris, another characteristic of postmodern illness is an ambiguity about the nature of some disorders. Patients and doctors have contested the existence of ailments such as chronic fatigue syndrome, post-traumatic stress disorder, ADHD, male menopause, and even some types of addictions. Our understanding of, and experience with, health and illness is socially constructed and is not simply a matter of biology.

Postmodern culture has a fixation on health. Health-related products are heavily advertised, every new development in health research is widely reported in the media—often long before results have been validated—and health care is been one of Canada's most important political issues. While 16th-century explorers sailed the world searching for the Fountain of Youth, people in postmodern societies search for immortality through medical research, plastic surgery, fitness programs, miracle cures and even cryonics—freezing the body in hopes of bringing the person back to life when a cure is found for the disease that caused death. In this search for perfection, "our culture has declared war on biology" (Morris, 1998:2).

One aspect in this war on biology is the belief in the perfectability of the body. People now have "the option of transforming bodies into a facsimile of their own ideal vision" (Morris, 1998: 138). The desire for bodily perfection is manifested in many ways, including cosmetic surgery, legal and illegal drugs used by athletes to enhance their performance, the very different body types attained by competitive bodybuilders and by anorexics, and the burgeoning occupation of personal trainer. While these measures may change the look of the body, the search for perfection may also be harmful. The premature deaths caused by anorexia and steroid use and the psychological consequences of realizing that no matter what one does perfection is not attainable, show the futility of pursuing a vision of bodily perfection. This utopian vision is ultimately contradicted by the biology of aging and the inevitability of death. When old age is seen as just another stage in an active life rather than as a time when one prepares for the end, physical decline is an embarrassment and there is often a denial of death.

Even when death is imminent, postmodern patients are trapped between two conflicting realities. The first is the ability of biomedicine to keep failing bodies alive almost indefinitely; the second is the public pressure in many cultures to allow doctor-assisted suicide in order to alleviate suffering and to provide a dignified death at a time of the patient's choosing. Doctors, patients, and policy makers find it difficult to resolve this impasse.

While Morris feels that modernist Western biomedicine is being challenged by the postmodern emphasis on culture, the future of our culture's understanding of health and illness is not yet clear:

> It is an untold, unnoticed story in which the cultural fantasy of living forever—or at least pushing back death through an unending series of medical purchases—creates sickly lives obsessed with heartburn, bowels, megavitamins, and miracle cures. This new postmodern narrative, in short, represents for us the confusing historical moment we are living through when the biomedical model has begun to reveal its inherent limitations but when a biocultural model . . . has not yet proven its power to constitute a satisfying and coherent replacement. (Morris, 1998: 278)

Concept Table 11.1. outlines the major theoretical perspectives on health and illness.

SOCIAL FACTORS IN HEALTH: AGE, SEX, AND SOCIAL CLASS

We often think of health in only physical terms. However, the health of any group is a product of the interaction of a wide range of physiological, psychological, spiritual, historical, sociological, cultural, economic, and environmental factors (Waldram et al., 1995). In this section, we will see how these factors

Concept Table 11.1	THEORETICAL PERSPECTIVES ON HEALTH AND ILLNESS	
PERSPECTIVE	**THEORY**	**KEY ELEMENTS**
Functionalist Parsons	Functional Theory	Illness is dysfunctional both for the individual who is sick and for the larger society. All societies have a sick role—patterns of behaviour defined as appropriate for people who are sick.
Conflict Inequalities in Health Care	Inequalities in Health Care	Among the issues for conflict theorists are the ability of all citizens to obtain health care; the impact of race, class, and gender on health care; the relative power of doctors and the medical model in the health-care system; and the role of profit in the health-care system.
Feminist Findlay and Miller	Medicalization of Women's Lives	Medicalization blames women for their problems. It also forces women to conform to traditional role expectations and limits their freedom of behaviour, appearance, and relationships.
Symbolic Interactionist Conrad and Schneider	Medicalization Theory	All illnesses have a subjective component. Medicalization is the process whereby an object or a condition becomes defined by society as a physical or psychological illness.
Postmodern Morris	Biology and Culture	Modernist Western biomedicine is being challenged by the postmodern emphasis on culture, but the future of our culture's understanding of health and illness is not yet clear.

affect the health of people of different ages, genders, and classes in Canada.

A basic premise of conflict theory is that groups compete with one another for access to scarce resources. Conflict theorists would predict that because of this competition, the quality of health and health care would vary by age, sex, class, and race. Indeed, there are dramatic differences in the health of people in these different social categories.

Age

Rates of illness and death are highest among the very old and the very young. Mortality rates drop shortly after birth and begin to rise significantly during the middle years. After age 65, rates of chronic illness and mortality increase rapidly. This has not only obvious implications for individuals and their families, but also an impact on Canadian society.

Canada is an aging society (see Chapter 16). Today, about 12 percent of the population is age 65 or over; by 2036, this will double to about 25 percent. Because health-care costs are high for some older people, these costs will continue to rise as the baby boomers age. Concern with future costs is one of the factors behind attempts by provincial and federal governments to restructure the health-care system. For example, the number of cases of one of the most debilitating conditions among the elderly, *senile dementia*—**a term for diseases, such as Alzheimer's, that involve a progressive impairment of judgment and memory**—is forecast to triple by 2031 to nearly 800 000 people (Lipovenko, 1997). Many of these people will require costly institutional care unless changes are made to improve the support available for community care.

Sex

Prior to the 20th century, women had shorter lives than men because of high mortality rates during pregnancy and childbirth. Preventive measures have

Michael Lea/CP Picture Archive

In the summer of 1997, 650 people met in Kingston, Ontario, for the first World Conference on Breast Cancer. The major political goal of the conference was "to do for breast cancer what happened to AIDS in the 1980s—to put breast cancer on the centre stage" (Driedger, 1997).

greatly reduced this cause of female mortality and women now live longer than men. Females born in Canada in 2007 could expect to live about 83 years, compared with 78 years for males (Statistics Canada, 2010a). Waldron (1994) has identified three factors leading to this sex difference in mortality rates. First, differences in gender roles mean that females are less likely than males to engage in risky behaviour such as using alcohol and drugs, driving dangerously, and fighting. Males are also more likely to work in dangerous occupations such as commercial fishing, mining, and construction. Second, females are more likely to seek medical care and so may have problems identified at an earlier, more treatable stage than men. Third, biological differences may contribute, as females have higher survival rates than males at every stage from fetus to old age.

As the social roles played by females become more like those of males, the mortality gap has narrowed. Women in traditionally male-dominated occupations, such as farming and policing, face the same risks as their male counterparts, and the number of such women is steadily increasing. As female rates of behaviour such as smoking approach those of males, females have begun to pay the price in illness and early death. About four decades ago, smoking among

women began to increase. Predictably, rates of lung cancer among women have tripled since 1975, while rates for men are dropping because male smoking rates have declined since the 1960s (Canadian Cancer Society, 2008).

Women live longer than men, but they also have higher rates of disease and disability. While men at every age have higher rates of fatal diseases, women have higher rates of nonfatal chronic conditions (Waldron, 1994).

One other important issue is the lack of medical research on women. Much of the research on diseases such as heart disease, that affect both sexes, has excluded women. However, these studies are the basis for the diagnosis and treatment of both sexes, even though there appear to be sex differences in the diseases. Most funding agencies now require researchers to include both men and women subjects unless there are clear reasons for limiting the study to one sex. However, much of our existing medical knowledge is based on the earlier male-centred research.

ALAN ODDIE/PHOTOEDIT

Alzheimer's disease is a tragedy for the afflicted individuals and for their families. As our population ages, such debilitating conditions will also increasingly place a burden on our health-care system and on the taxpayers who fund it.

Figure 11.1   **Children with Lower Functional Health, by Average Household Income[1]**

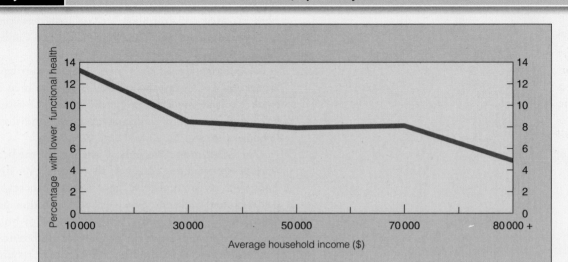

Children from low-income families are more likely to have health problems than children whose families have higher incomes.

[1]Statistics Canada has based functional health on eight attributes: vision, hearing, speech, mobility, dexterity, cognition, emotion, and pain and discomfort.

Note: Two-parent families with children aged 4–11.

Sources: Prepared by the Canadian Council on Social Development, using the National Longitudinal Survey of Children and Youth, 1994–1995. Reprinted by permission.

Social Class

The poor have worse health and die earlier than the rich. This is also true of poor and rich countries as illness and mortality rates are far higher in low-income countries than in high-income nations. In Canada, males living in the highest-income neighbourhoods have a life expectancy almost five years greater than males in the lowest-income neighbourhoods. For women the difference is about two years (Statistics Canada, 2002g).

There are similar differences between people in the highest- and lowest-income neighbourhoods for other health indicators. For example, the infant mortality rate in Canada's poorest urban neighbourhoods was over 50 percent higher than that in the richest neighbourhoods (Statistics Canada, 2002f).

The National Population Health Survey found that low-income Canadians had higher rates of major chronic diseases, such as emphysema and high blood pressure than those with middle and upper incomes. Low-income Canadians also had much higher mortality rates (Statistics Canada, 1998). The National Longitudinal Survey of Children and Youth found that children from low-income families were more than twice as likely as those from families in the highest income category to have functional health problems (see Figure 11.1).

While poverty is correlated with poor health, good health-care policy can help reduce its effects. Providing the poor with access to medical advice and treatment through universal medicare is one way of doing this. A study comparing cancer survival rates for the poorest one-third of Toronto residents, who all had government-funded health care, with their counterparts in Detroit, who typically had little or no health insurance, showed the benefits of providing adequate health care for the poor (Gorey et al., 1997). Survival rates were higher in Toronto for 12 of the 15 most common types of cancer. For many of these types of cancer, survival rates after five years were 50 percent higher among the poor in Toronto than among those in Detroit. The benefits of government-funded care go particularly to the poor, as this study found no difference among middle- or high-income patients in the two countries.

If access to medical care improves the health of the poor, why are Canada's poor less healthy than its middle and upper classes? The answer is that medical care cannot compensate for the other disadvantages of poverty such as poor housing, hazardous employment, inadequate diet, greater exposure to disease, and the psychological stresses of poverty. The poor are more likely to engage in unhealthy behaviours such as smoking and excessive drinking. A recent study found that class differences in smoking accounted for over half the difference in death rates between upper and lower classes (Jha et al., 2006).

The poor also lack knowledge of preventive strategies and services. For example, college- or university-educated women are twice as likely as women who have not graduated from high school to have mammograms, which means that less-educated women are at a higher risk of dying of breast cancer. Finally, when they are ill, the poor are less likely to visit doctors (Roos et al., 2004).

While differences remain between rich and poor, the gap in life expectancy between people living in the highest- and lowest-income neighbourhoods has declined substantially (Statistics Canada, 2002g). One reason for this is that the difference in infant mortality rates between high- and low-income neighbourhoods declined from 9.8 deaths per 1000 births in 1971 to 2.4 deaths per 1000 births in 1996 and has remained low since then.

Race, Class, and Health: Canada's Aboriginal Peoples

We have looked at the relationship between class and health. The experience of Canada's Aboriginal peoples illustrates how the disadvantages of race can interact with those of class to cause health problems.

Health Problems Among Aboriginal Peoples in Canada   Aboriginal people have a history of serious health problems that begins with their early contact with Europeans. ***Epidemics—sudden, significant increases in the numbers of people contracting a disease***—of contagious diseases such as tuberculosis, measles, smallpox, and influenza broke out in the early years of this contact. These epidemics occurred partly because Aboriginal people had no immunity to these European diseases. They were also caused by new patterns of trade that led to contact with more diverse groups of people than had occurred before European settlement. Tuberculosis epidemics were particularly devastating in the late 19th century when Aboriginal people were moved to reserves. Crowded, and lacking proper sanitation

facilities, the reserves were an ideal setting for the spread of disease, and mortality rates for tuberculosis remained high until the 1950s.

While their mortality rates have improved significantly, Aboriginal people still have shorter lives than other Canadians. Infant mortality rates among Aboriginal people have declined significantly since the 1970s, but are still well above the Canadian average. The infant mortality rate for First Nations people is about twice the Canadian average and for the Inuit, it is four times the national average (Smylie and Adomako, 2009). Life expectancy is seven years less than average for First Nations men and five years less for First Nations women (Health Canada, 2005). While infectious diseases among Aboriginal peoples have been brought under control (though their rates remain higher than those of other Canadians), their health problems now comprise chronic diseases such as heart disease, respiratory problems, and diabetes. HIV/AIDS is also now beginning to affect the Aboriginal community, where rates of HIV are nearly four times higher than for other Canadians. The majority contracted HIV through intravenous drug use (Public Health Agency of Canada, 2009).

What are the reasons for the poorer health of Aboriginal peoples? A major factor is poverty. Aboriginal people are among the poorest in Canada and suffer from the poor nutrition and other social conditions that go with poverty. Food is expensive in isolated communities, and the cost of a well-balanced diet can be too high for poor families. Many of the diseases that affect Aboriginal peoples can also be traced to the inadequate housing, crowding, and poor sanitary conditions common on reserves and in the other communities where they live. For example, in 2008 93 reserves were put under orders to boil their water because it was not safe to drink (Eggertson, 2008). The isolation of many Aboriginal communities is also a factor; an illness that could be easily treated in a city hospital can be fatal in a community 800 kilometres from the nearest doctor.

Aboriginal people also have high rates of violent death, with rates of death by murder and suicide higher than those of other Canadians. Rates of adolescent suicide are particularly high, especially in Nunavut. Accidental death rates, particularly by motor vehicle accidents and drowning, are also higher for Aboriginal people.

Finally, the legacy of colonialism still affects Aboriginal peoples' health. Anastasia Shkilnyk (1985), who studied the Ojibwa community of Grassy Narrows in northwestern Ontario, attributes the high rates of suicide, violent death, and health problems on the reserve to colonial actions such as the destruction of Aboriginal language and religion, family breakdown caused by enforced attendance at residential schools, and forced relocation of the community by the Department of Indian Affairs. Environmental destruction by local industries that dumped methyl mercury into the lakes and rivers around the reserve was another contributor. This toxic substance had a direct impact on the health of Grassy Narrows residents and also an indirect impact by destroying the traditional fishery that was the foundation of the community's way of life.

DISABILITY

The medical definition of a disability focuses on the physical condition of the individual—the problem is within the body (Albrecht, 1992). However, this definition is too narrow. Many people have vision problems that would make it difficult for them to read. Do these people have a disability? The answer is no, because eyeglasses or contact lenses can restore most people's vision and make it possible for them to function normally. Thus, the definition of a disability must have a social component.

Think of how your life would change if you woke up tomorrow and were unable to use your legs. Your ability to function would be *impaired,* but would you consider yourself to have a *disability?* What is the difference between the two terms (Oliver, 1990)? *Impairment* in this case would mean that your legs did not function, while a **disability is a physical or health condition that reduces a person's ability to perform tasks one would normally do at a given stage in life and that may result in stigmatization or discrimination against the person with the disability**. In other words, the notion of disability is based not only on physical conditions but also on social attitudes and the social and physical environments in which people live. All too often, people with disabilities are treated as if they were not fully human. Laurie Krever Karmona, the mother of a daughter with cerebral palsy, experienced this herself when she was temporarily forced to use a wheelchair:

> My sister wheeled me to my local Shoppers Drug Mart where I shop at least once a week. I recognize the clerks and, I thought, they recognize me. When we got to the cashier, she asked my sister, "Does she have an Optimum card?" and then,

"How does she wish to pay for her purchases?" I was looking around for the "she" until I realized she meant me ... The equation, I realize, goes something like this: one sprained ankle plus one broken ankle must equal one totally brain-injured person. (Karmona, 2001:A16)

The classification of a condition as a disability involves a labelling process. Those who have the power to resist being classified as being "disabled" will be able to avoid the negative consequences of that label. Accommodation of physical differences—through technological means or through allowing people to fill roles that are appropriate to their abilities—can also reduce the impact of those differences.

According to Blackford (1996), society has failed to provide the universal access that would allow people with impairments to participate fully in all aspects of life. For example, many buildings are not accessible to persons using a wheelchair. In this context, disability derives from a lack of accommodation, not simply from someone's physical condition. Oliver (1990) used the term *disability oppression* to describe the barriers that exist for people with disabilities. These include economic hardship (from the additional costs of accessibility devices, transportation, and attendant care; or from employment discrimination), inadequate government-assistance programs, and negative social attitudes toward people with disabilities. According to disability-rights advocates, disability must be thought of in terms of how society causes or contributes to the problem—not in terms of what is "wrong" with the person with a disability.

Sociological Perspectives on Disability

How do sociologists view disability? Functionalists often apply Parson's sick role model, which is referred to as the *medical model* of disability. According to the medical model, people with disabilities become chronic patients under the supervision of doctors and other medical personnel, subject to a doctor's orders or a program's rules, and not to their own judgment (Shapiro, 1993). From this perspective, disability is deviance.

The deviance framework is also apparent in some symbolic interactionist perspectives. According to symbolic interactionists, people with disabilities experience *role ambiguity* because many people equate disability with deviance (Murphy et al., 1988). By labelling individuals with disabilities as "deviant,"

Steven Fletcher, the Minister of State for Democratic Reform, is the first quadriplegic to be elected to Canada's House of Commons. After being injured in an automobile accident, Fletcher began his political career by serving two terms as president of the University of Manitoba's Students' Union while completing his MBA degree.

other people can avoid them or treat them as outsiders. Society marginalizes people with disabilities because they have lost old roles and statuses and are labelled as "disabled" persons.

According to Eliot Freidson (1965), the nature of this label results from three factors: (1) the person's degree of responsibility for their impairment, (2) the apparent seriousness of their condition, and (3) the perceived legitimacy of the condition. Freidson concluded that the definitions of and expectations for people with disabilities are socially constructed factors.

Tanya Titchkosky is critical of the prevailing view that disability is "an individual incapacity—an inability to do things" (2003: 15). Like Freidson, she feels that disability can be understood only by considering its social and cultural context. A main feature of this context is "the fact that disability is necessarily an experience of marginality" (2003: 232). Titchkosky describes how the arrival of a guide dog affected her partner, a professor whose sight had been deteriorating for years, but who was usually able to pass as a sighted person:

> I had not anticipated that acquiring a guide dog would also mean acquiring a new identity. Rod arrived home with a beautiful new dog and an expert guide. But there was more. With Smokie, Rod was seen as blind. Staring, grabbing, helping, offers of prayers or medical advice, groping for words or even a voice are some of the many ways in that sighted people show that they are seeing a blind person. Through these interactions, Rod was given the identity—blind person. (2003: 82)

Finally, from a conflict perspective, persons with disabilities are members of a subordinate group in conflict with persons in positions of power in the government, in the health-care industry, and in the rehabilitation business, all of whom are trying to control the destinies of people with disabilities (Albrecht, 1992). Those in positions of power have created policies and artificial barriers that keep people with disabilities in a subservient position (Asch, 1986; Hahn, 1987). In a capitalist economy, disabilities are big business. When people with disabilities are defined as a social problem and public funds are spent to purchase goods and services for them, rehabilitation becomes a commodity that can be bought and sold by the medical-industrial complex (Albrecht, 1992). From this perspective, persons with disabilities are objectified. They have an economic value as consumers of goods and services that will allegedly make them "better" people. Many persons with disabilities endure the same struggle for resources faced by people of colour, women, and older people. Individuals who hold more than one of these ascribed statuses, combined with experiencing disability, are doubly or triply oppressed by capitalism.

Disability in Contemporary Society

An estimated 4.4 million people aged 15 and over, representing 14 percent of the adult population in Canada, have one or more physical or mental disabilities (Statistics Canada, 2007d). This number is increasing for several reasons. First, with advances in medical technology, many people who formerly would have died from an accident or illness now survive, although with an impairment. Second, as more people live longer, they are more likely to experience disabling diseases such as arthritis (Albrecht, 1992). Third, people born with serious disabilities are more likely to survive infancy because of medical technology. Finally, there is some indication that people are now more willing to report disabilities (Statistics Canada, 2007d).

Some people are more likely to become disabled than others. Aboriginal people have higher rates of disability, especially serious disabilities, than other Canadians. Persons with lower incomes also have higher rates of disability (Bolaria and Bolaria, 1994).

Environment, lifestyle, and working conditions may all contribute to disability. For example, air pollution and smoking lead to a higher incidence of chronic respiratory disease and lung damage. In industrial societies, workers in many types of low-status jobs are at the greatest risk for certain health hazards and disabilities. Employees in data-processing and service-oriented jobs may be affected by work-related disabilities such as lower-back pain and carpal tunnel syndrome.

In 2001, one in eight Canadians experienced "limitations in their everyday activities because of physical, psychological or health conditions" (Statistics Canada, 2004a: 15) followed by chronic pain (2.4 million people), agility difficulties (2.3 million people), hearing difficulties (1 million people), vision difficulties (590 000 people), and speech-related difficulties (360 000 people).

People with disabilities have been kept out of the mainstream. They have often been denied equal educational opportunities by being consigned to special education classes or special schools. Many have been restricted from entry into schools and the workforce, not due to their own limitations, but by societal barriers. Why are people with disabilities excluded? Susan Wendell offers an explanation:

> In a society which idealizes the body, the physically disabled are often marginalized. People learn to identify with their own strengths (by cultural standards) and to hate, fear, and neglect their own weaknesses. The disabled are not only de-valued for their de-valued bodies; they are constant reminders to the able-bodied of the negative body—of what the able-bodied are trying to avoid, forget, and ignore. . . . In a culture which loves the idea that the body can be controlled, those who cannot control their bodies are seen (and may see themselves) as failures. (1995:458)

Among persons who acquire disabilities through disease or accidents later in life, the social significance of their disability can be seen in how they initially respond to their symptoms and diagnosis, how they view the immediate situation and their future, and how the illness and disability affect their lives. According to Wendell:

> Disabled people can participate in marginalizing ourselves. We can wish for bodies we do not have, with frustration, shame, self-hatred. We can feel trapped in the negative body; it is our internalized oppression to feel this. Every (visibly or invisibly) disabled person I have talked to has felt this; some never stop feeling it. (1995:458)

The combination of a disability and society's reaction to the disability has an impact on the lives of many people. People with disabilities often suffer from stereotyping; for example, movies are given to depicting villains as individuals with disabilities (think of the villains in the Batman movies such as the *Dark Knight*, in which both the Joker and the former District Attorney Harvey Dent were driven to commit crimes by serious disfigurement). Charitable organization fundraising campaigns may contribute to the perception of people with disabilities as persons who are to be pitied. Prejudice against persons with disabilities may result in either subtle or overt discrimination. According to Asch (2004:11):

> Many commentators note that people with disabilities are expected to play no adult social role whatsoever; to be perceived as always, in every social interaction, a recipient of help and never a provider of assistance; and to be more disliked by nondisabled others if they are clearly competent than if they are perceived as incompetent at a task.

While the situation has improved in recent years, compared with nondisabled adults a much smaller proportion of the disabled population is employed. Statistics Canada found that only about 25 percent of working-age people who had received care at home because of a long-term health problem or physical limitation were in the labour force. The care-receivers who had jobs were younger, better educated, and healthier than those who did not (Cranswick, 1999). Overall, the unemployment rate of adults aged 25 to 64 with disabilities was almost double that of people without disabilities, and many people were not in the labour force at all because of their disabilities (Statistics Canada, 2008f). Without jobs, people with disabilities were more likely to be poor (Statistics Canada, 2004a). Many people with disabilities feel they are disadvantaged in terms of employment and that they have been discriminated against in the workplace (Statistics Canada, 2008f).

Ensuring equality for people with disabilities is not just a matter for governments. While legislation is important, social attitudes also must change. Adrienne Asch, a blind university professor, says that even her close friends do not treat her in the same way as they treat others. For example, they "do not feel comfortable accepting my offers to pick up food as part of a dinner we plan to have . . . or who would prefer that a high-school-age stranger take care of their six-year-old son for an evening than have me do it, even though I have known their son and their home ever since his birth" (2004:11). Thus equality isn't just a matter of ending discrimination against people with disabilities, but rather of ensuring full integration into mainstream society.

SOCIAL DEVELOPMENT AND HEALTH: A GLOBAL PERSPECTIVE

Earlier in this chapter you learned how poverty and colonialism have affected the health of Canada's Aboriginal peoples. These factors also operate on a global scale. For example, Hunt (1989) attributes the rapid spread of diseases, such as HIV/AIDS in Africa, to the underdevelopment and dependency that is the legacy of colonialism. The underlying roots of this health problem lie in the economic and social marginalization of most African people.

The difference between rich and poor countries is dramatically reflected in infant mortality rates. While about five out of every 1000 infants in Canada die before their first birthday, infant mortality rates in the world's poorest countries are far higher. Afghanistan, Nigeria, and Rwanda, for instance, have infant mortality rates of 152, 94, and 82 per 1000 live births (CIA, 2009). Life expectancy is correspondingly low; for persons born in Canada in 2007, life expectancy at birth was about 81 years, compared with less than 45 years in many poor African nations. Most deaths in less-developed countries are caused by infectious and parasitic diseases that are now rare in the industrialized world.

A UNICEF (2009) report on the health of the world's children puts the situation in even more stark terms. More than 9 million children die each year. This figure is the equivalent of 60 Boeing 747 crashes each day of the year—and most of these deaths could be easily prevented. Most child deaths are caused by malnutrition and by the childhood diseases of measles, diarrhea, malaria, and pneumonia. As Sharma and Tulloch tell us, "Children in rich countries do not die from the common, preventable diseases of childhood. Children in poor countries do" (1997:1).

Tremendous progress has nevertheless been made in saving the lives of children. The number of child deaths is now less than half the 20 million who died in 1960 (UNICEF, 2008b). Measures such as immunization, rehydration therapy for diarrhea, increased breast-feeding, and child mosquito nets save millions of children each year. However, millions more deaths could be prevented through simple measures such as improved sanitation, clean water, better immunization programs, and better local health services.

Of course, not only children in poor countries are dying. Each year more than 500 000 women— virtually all of them in poor countries—die of

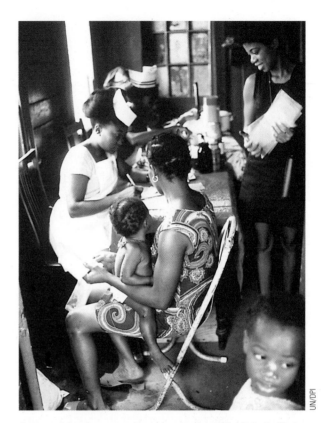

A nurse interviews a mother at a rural health clinic in Sierra Leone. With the support of the WHO, these clinics were established to reduce infant mortality and to improve the health of mothers and their children.

complications arising from pregnancy and childbirth. Virtually all of these deaths take place in poor countries. In Niger, 1 in 7 women will die in childbirth compared with 1 in 8 000 women in high-income countries (UNICEF, 2009).

We have described how AIDS has become an epidemic in developing countries (see Box 11.3 on page 274 for more on the spread of AIDS in Africa.). The new methods of treatment that have extended the lives of those with AIDS in the developed world are unaffordable in developing countries, where average annual incomes are only a fraction of the cost of these treatments. Financial considerations also mean that drug companies are not interested in developing cures for diseases such as malaria, as residents of the poor countries where these diseases are epidemic cannot afford to pay high prices for such drugs.

Despite these problems, significant progress has been made in saving the lives of children and adults. Since 1955 the average life expectancy in the world has increased from 46 years to 67 years (World Health Organization, 2003, 2009). Life expectancy at birth has risen to more than 70 years in 84 countries, up from only 55 countries in 1990. This increase has

BOX 11.3   SOCIOLOGY IN GLOBAL PERSPECTIVE

The AIDS Epidemic in Africa

RAKAI, UGANDA—From the shadows of this mud hut, the gaunt and weary young man stares outside at the pigs playing in the dust under the banana palms. His chest is covered with open sores; skin rashes have left his ebony arms looking as if they are covered in chalk; his army fatigues hang loosely around his waist.

Outside, Charles Lawanga glances toward his ailing second son and lowers his voice. Last year, when the Ugandan army gave him his medical furlough, his son was sick, but at least he could walk, says Lawanga.

Lawanga's brows are furrowed; he has the face of a man who is watching his son die. His eyes sharpen when he hears that an American journalist knows many of the Western doctors working on the disease. He knows that the United States is a country of immense wealth and that the medicine that will save his country and his son will probably come from there. Tears gather in his brown eyes, and he asks, "When will it come? When will there be the cure?" (Shilts, 1988:621).

By the mid-1990s, Uganda had the highest number of recorded HIV cases in Africa—around 1.5 million—and AIDS has touched virtually all families in this country. However, Uganda was the first African country to make major gains in the fight against HIV/AIDS. One key indicator was the infection rate of pregnant women: Between 1992 and 1998, this rate dropped from 31 to 14 percent in the capital city of Kampala and from 21 to 8 percent in the rest of the country. The rate among men attending clinics for sexually transmitted diseases dropped from 46 to 20 percent over the same period (Global Health Council, 2002).

The fight against HIV/AIDS was personally led by Uganda's President Museveni. The government worked with community partners to implement a program involving sex education in the schools that encouraged abstinence but also promoted condom use for those who were sexually active; quick treatment of other sexually transmitted diseases; and

same-day results for HIV tests and immediate counselling for those who were tested. Uganda developed the "ABC" approach to AIDS prevention: **A**bstinence; **B**e faithful to one partner; and use **C**ondoms. This program was implemented through grassroots organizations throughout the country and received funding from the World Bank and the United States (Avert, 2005).

Unfortunately, few other countries have followed Uganda's lead. Successful programs in Thailand and Senegal have also been based on encouraging condom use and discouraging risky sexual behaviour, such as casual sex and sex with prostitutes (Global Health Council, 2002). However, many countries deny they have a problem and others reject modern treatment methods. South Africa's former president, Thabo Mbeki, denied that AIDS was caused by HIV and his government refused to provide treatment to pregnant women to prevent the transmission of HIV to their children. His health minister promoted garlic and beetroot as remedies for AIDS. These policies resulted in hundreds of thousands of needless deaths before the government changed.

In other countries, public discussion of sexual behaviour is so taboo that governments and other leaders refuse to address rising infection rates. Even in Uganda, progress was slowed because under former President Bush, U.S.-based funding organizations discouraged the promotion of condoms and advocated "abstinence-only" programs. In response, President Museveni condemned condom use as immoral and the safe-sex advertising campaign and the free distribution of condoms were drastically curtailed. There is clear evidence that condom use is a vital component of successful AIDS prevention programs and that abstinence-only programs do not work, so the ideology of the faith-based organizations that helped deliver U.S. funding jeopardized the lives of millions of Ugandans (Avert, 2005; *The New York Times*, 2005).

been attributed to a number of factors, one of the most important of which is the development of a safe water supply. The percentage of the world's population with access to safe water nearly doubled between 1990 and 2000 (United Nations Development Programme, 2003).

Health Care in Canada

Health care is an important social and political issue in Canada. Health care costs are increasing steadily, while governments are being forced to make cuts in other areas including support for university and

| Figure 11.2 | Canada: Satisfaction with the Health-Care System, 1988, 1998, 2001, and 2007 |

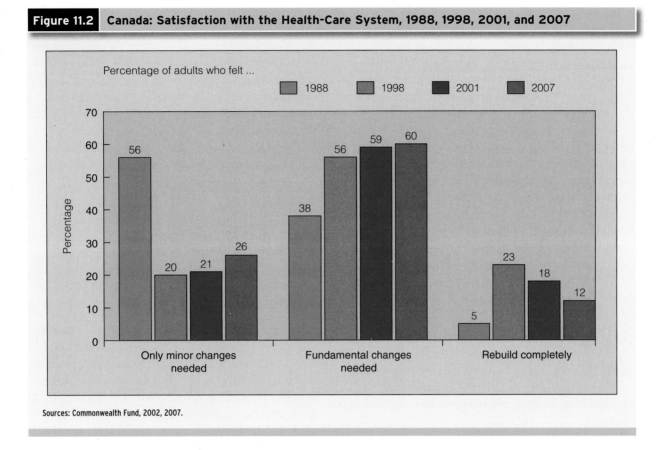

Percentage of adults who felt ...

■ 1988   ■ 1998   ■ 2001   ■ 2007

Sources: Commonwealth Fund, 2002, 2007.

college students. However, attempts by governments to make changes in the way health care is provided usually meet with great resistance from the public and from those who work in the health-care system. In the early 1990s, medical-school enrolments were reduced and nurses and health-care workers were laid off. Because of these and other cuts, waiting times for medical procedures increased. Opinion polls show how these changes led to public concern about medical care, a concern that continues today. An international health survey found that in 1988 only 5 percent of Canadians believed their health-care system required major rebuilding. By 2001, 18 percent felt that major changes were needed (Blendon et al., 2002). However, by 2007 that number had dropped to 12 percent, suggesting that the billions of dollars that have been invested in the system since 2000 have helped improve health care (see Figure 11.2).

Public pressure stopped the erosion of health services. The provinces put new money into health care, and the federal government placed health-care funding at the top of the spending priority list. However, health-care costs continue to increase

rapidly and major changes must be made if quality care is to remain affordable.

Universal Health Care

Canadians have a *universal health-care system, that is, one in which all citizens receive medical services paid for through taxation revenues.* Prior

Soaring health care costs and personnel shortages have made salaries very contentious. In this photo, Vancouver nurses cheer the fact that 95 percent of their colleagues have voted to support a strike.

to the early 1960s, Canadians had a user-pay system, in which people had paid for health care directly out of their pockets. Individuals who did not have health insurance and who required expensive medical procedures or long-term care, or who developed a chronic illness, often suffered severe financial losses. Under our universal system, if you are sick, you have the right to receive quality medical care regardless of your ability to pay. Individuals do not pay doctor or hospital costs directly, but they are responsible for at least part of the costs of other health services, such as prescription drugs, ambulances, and dental care.

Health care is a provincial and territorial responsibility, and each province and territory has its own medical-insurance plan. However, the federal government contributes billions of dollars to the provinces for health care and enforces basic standards that each province must follow. Provincial plans must meet the following requirements:

1. *Universality*—all Canadians should be covered on uniform terms and conditions.
2. *Comprehensiveness*—all necessary medical services should be guaranteed, without dollar limit, and should be available solely on the basis of medical need.
3. *Accessibility*—reasonable access should be guaranteed to all Canadians.
4. *Portability*—benefits should be transferable among provinces and territories.
5. *Public administration*—the system should be operated on a nonprofit basis by a public agency or commission (Grant, 1993:401).

Canada spends about 10 percent of its gross domestic product on health care. While this is low compared with the rate in the United States (see Table 11.1), it is higher than those of most other industrialized countries. Canada's 2008 health-care expenditures were $172 billion (Canadian Institute for Health Information, 2008). Of this amount, $120 billion came from government funding, while the remainder came from individuals and medical insurance companies for services not covered by medicare. Health care costs are rising much faster than government revenues and governments.

One cause of increasing costs is overutilization of health care services. According to Karen Grant:

> Canadians have an almost insatiable appetite for medical services, because they do not pay for health services when received, and because they have no knowledge of the actual costs of care, they inappropriately use the system. Frequenting emergency rooms for routine care is perhaps the most common illustration of this problem. (Grant, 1993:401)

While members of the public may not always make the most economical choices, many of the costs of our system are controlled by doctors, who prescribe drugs, admit patients to hospitals, determine patients' lengths of stay in hospital, order tests and examinations, determine the course of treatment that will be used, and recommend follow-up visits. Since patients will do almost anything to ensure their health and since they do not pay directly, they have no incentive to question doctors' recommendations. On the other hand, doctors have a financial interest in providing more treatment. Ensuring that doctors make decisions about treatment only on medical grounds is a major challenge faced by taxpayer-funded health-care systems.

Another reason for the high costs of health care is the system's focus on hospitals and doctors. There has been an imbalance in our national health-care

Table 11.1	LIFE EXPECTANCIES AND HEALTH CARE–VARIOUS COUNTRIES[1]		
Countries in Order of Life Expectancy	Life Expectancy at Birth, 2008, in Years	Total Expenditure on Health, % of GDP, 2008	Expenditure on Health, per Capita, 2008[1]
Japan	83	8.1	$2869
Canada	81	10.4	$4079
France	81	11.2	$3696
U.K.	80	8.7	$3129
Germany	80	10.5	$3737
U.S.	78	16	$7538

[1]Adjusted for cost of living differences in U.S. dollars.

Source: Data from OECD, 2010.

system in its emphasis on acute care and its lack of funding for community care. Cheaper forms of non-institutional health care, such as home-care services, are not subject to national standards, so these services vary widely across the country and may not be available even when they are the most cost-effective type of care. Thus, people who need minimal care may be housed in expensive, acute-care hospital beds costing more than $1 000 per day because community alternatives are not available. Acute care costs also mean that funding is not available for preventive measures, such as promoting healthy diets and exercise, which could lower costs in the longer term.

While our health-care system has many problems, in many respects it is far better than that of the United States, the only major industrialized country without a health-care system that provides universal coverage to all citizens. While Canada and Western European countries treat health care as a basic human right, the United States treats it as a market commodity. Although there is government coverage for seniors, people with disabilities, and some of the poor in the United States, approximately 15 percent of the population—47 million people—have no medical coverage (U.S. Census Bureau, 2008). Many others lack adequate coverage and the expense incurred in treating serious medical conditions such as cancer or a stroke, can lead to financial ruin. Medical expenses are the leading cause of personal bankruptcy in the United States (Himmelstein et al., 2005). While per capita costs in the U.S. system are almost double those in Canada (see Table 11.1), Canadians are healthier than Americans, have better treatment outcomes, and are more satisfied with their health-care system.

APPROACHES TO HEALTH CARE

The Medical Model of Illness

The medical model has been the predominant way of thinking about illness in Western industrialized societies for many years. The medical model has five basic assumptions: that illness is "(1) deviation from normal, (2) specific and universal, (3) caused by unique biological forces, (4) analogous to the breakdown of a machine whose parts can be repaired, and (5) defined and treated through a neutral scientific process" (Weitz, 1996:129). Acceptance of this

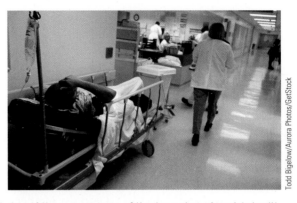

One of the consequences of the demands on Canada's health care system has been hospital overcrowding. In some hospitals patients are forced to spend time in emergency room hallways because no rooms are available.

model has given greater power to doctors, who are viewed as the experts in diagnosing and treating illness. Doctors have gone to great lengths to protect their role at the centre of the health-care system. For example, they have actively resisted those with conflicting views such as midwives, advocates of natural healing methods, and those more concerned with preventing disease than with treating it.

Technology and Medicine

An important trend is the increasing role of technology in health care. Technology has raised the cost of health care, because technological devices such as diagnostic scanners are very expensive to purchase and to operate. Although new medical technology does help in diagnosis and treatment, it may draw funds from other important areas, such as public health and preventive medicine, which may provide even greater benefits.

Technology also has sociological consequences. For example, Helman (2000) concluded that technology has changed the way we think of the human body. Among "the new bodies of the twentieth century" are:

1. The composite body. We can alter our bodies for aesthetic purposes through devices such as breast implants or make them function more effectively by replacing defective body parts with artificial hips, knees, and heart valves. We can also receive transplanted organs including hearts and kidneys from other people. This blurs the distinction between what is "self" and what is "nonself."
2. The cyborg. Cyborgs are part human and part machine. Technologists can now provide people

with machines such as heart pacemakers and dialysis machines, and more sophisticated machines such as artificial hearts will likely be available in the near future.

3. The brain. Although many cultures locate the self within the body as a whole, technology has helped to shift the image of the self to the brain. Thus, in many countries, death is defined as brain death and the rest of the body can be harvested for use in transplant surgery.

4. The external womb. New reproductive technologies mean that a baby can have three mothers: "the genetic mother, the carrying mother, and the nurturing mother" (Helman, 2000:27).

These new conceptualizations of the human body will shape peoples' expectations of the health-care system in the future.

Alternative Approaches

Despite the many successes of modern medicine, the medical model of illness is losing some of its dominance. While medical care is an important part of the health-care system, Canadians are recognizing that their health needs cannot be met by medical services alone and that more medical care does not necessarily lead to better health (Grant, 1993). In 1986, the federal government explicitly adopted a health-promotion policy, which emphasized prevention of disease and promoted healthy lifestyles and an increase in informal and community-based care (Crichton et al., 1997). Rising medical costs have led the federal government to implement programs emphasizing environment and lifestyle in health promotion. For example, education about the hazards of smoking combined with more effective legislation against the use and advertising of tobacco products can improve public health and save the money now used to treat victims of smoking-related diseases such as emphysema and lung cancer. Responsibility for health care is shifting away from the government and the health-care system toward the individual and the family.

Issues of cost and benefit to patients have also led to a move toward community-based care in most provinces and territories. Programs such as home care, community health clinics, and alternative care for the elderly have saved costs by reducing the need for more expensive hospital care. These community programs also enhance people's quality of life by allowing them to remain in their communities.

The popularity of the holistic health care movement is a further indication of the move toward a new definition of health. Holism reflects the orientations of many ancient therapeutic systems including that of Canadian Aboriginal peoples. Modern scientific medicine has been criticized for focusing on diseases and injuries rather than preventing illness and promoting overall well-being. Holistic medicine advocates say the medical model looks at problems in a mechanical fashion without considering their context, while the holistic approach emphasizes the interdependence of body, mind, and environment (Northcott, 1994).

Holism is adaptable to more conventional medical practice and is being adopted by some medical doctors and nurses as well as by practitioners of alternative health care, including chiropractors, osteopaths, acupuncturists, and naturopathic doctors. Supporters of the holistic health movement encourage people to take greater individual responsibility for their health and health care, especially with regard to lifestyle-related diseases and disabilities. They also urge health-care providers to pay more attention to clients in diagnosing and treating illness, and to develop a greater sensitivity to cultural differences in the ways in which people define and react to illness.

The holistic approach's emphasis on the role of social factors in illness is now beginning to receive support in research done by traditional practitioners. For example, authors of a *Journal of the American Heart Association* article found that middle-aged men with high levels of despair had a 20 percent greater chance of developing atherosclerosis—narrowing of the arteries—than more optimistic men with similar physiological risk factors. This was a difference in the risks for heart disease as great as that between a nonsmoker and a pack-a-day smoker (Cable News Network, 1997). Research on the health of older adults has shown that nonmedical factors, such as isolation, the death of a family member or a friend, and the loss of status after retirement have a major influence on health. Thus, programs for the elderly must deal with these issues as well as with physical problems (Crichton et al., 1997).

The National Population Health Survey found that many Canadians were making use of alternative medicine. While about 20 percent of those surveyed had consulted an alternative practitioner within the previous year, very few had relied exclusively on alternative medicine (Statistics Canada, 2005f). Thus it seems that alternative medicine is being used as a complement to traditional medicine rather than as a replacement. Of the groups surveyed, college- and university-educated young adults were most likely to use alternative health care. It was also found that women were more likely than men to use alternative health care (Statistics Canada, 2005f).

Christopher Fries (2008) has described some of the factors that have facilitated the integration of traditional medicine and alternative techniques. He reports that people no longer accept the dominance of traditional medicine and shop around for whatever combination of treatment they feel meets their physical and psychological needs. Their goal is not only to avoid sickness, but also to achieve a state of well-being. This individualized view of consuming health care is reinforced by the government's attempt to encourage people to take responsibility for their own health rather than relying on the health-care system.

While its use is growing, some types of alternative medicine have been criticized. Psychologist Barry Beyerstein has summarized the most pointed criticism, saying that some of the claims of alternative medical practice have not been empirically verified. He blames the acceptance of such claims on the fact that most people know little about science:

> [E]ven an elementary understanding of chemistry should raise strong doubts about the legitimacy of homeopathy; a passing familiarity with human anatomy would suggest that "subluxations" of the vertebrae cannot cause all the diseases that chiropractors believe they do; and a quite modest grasp of physiology should make it apparent that a coffee enema is unlikely to cure cancer. But when consumers have not the foggiest idea of how bacteria, viruses, carcinogens, oncogenes, and toxins wreak havoc on bodily tissues, then shark cartilage, healing crystals, and pulverized tiger penis seem no more magical than the latest

breakthrough from the biochemistry laboratory. (1997:150)

Beyerstein does see some benefits in alternative medicine, however. It has, he says, added a comforting human component to a medical world that has become increasingly impersonal and technological. Many alternative healers offer sound advice about prevention and a healthy lifestyle, and some alternative practices do have scientific backing. However, he fears that some alternatives can divert sick people from more effective treatment. People will need to be sufficiently well informed about the variety and nature of the options available to make sound treatment choices in the future. These options will certainly grow in number as alternative therapies become more widely accepted and as more become integrated with conventional medicine.

HEALTH-CARE ISSUES IN THE FUTURE

Health and health care will continue to change in the years to come. Scientific developments such as the mapping of human genes and the new reproductive technologies have already begun to affect our lives. These changes will improve the lives of many but will also create some very difficult social and ethical problems. For example, the ability to determine the sex of our children may lead to an imbalance between males and females. This imbalance would have a major impact on courtship and marriage as some in the larger sex group would have no chance to marry, while those in the smaller group would be very much in demand. Can you predict some of the possible consequences this might have on family structure and social relationships?

In the absence of major economic problems, Canadians will likely see continued increases in funding to health care. The evolution from hospital-based care to prevention and community care will continue. This change should be a positive one. Most of you have many years to live before you reach old age, but think ahead to that time. If you become unable to perform some household tasks such as cooking and cleaning, would you prefer to sell your home and move into institutional care or to receive daily home-care visits that would enable you to continue living independently? The political power of aging baby boomers and the cost of caring

Canadians are increasingly using alternative health-care methods such as acupuncture.

Cora Reed/Shutterstock

for growing numbers of elderly people will force governments to give more serious attention to home-care programs.

Attention is not enough, however. The shift to community-based health care will not improve matters unless governments put adequate resources into community care. The deinstitutionalization of people with mental illnesses during the 1970s and 1980s illustrates this danger. Ending the warehousing of people with mental illnesses in institutions was positive. However, rather than providing sufficient funding for community services for the deinstitutionalized patients, governments spent the savings on other things. As a result, many former patients became a burden on their communities and were put at risk because the proper support was not available. If home care is not properly funded, the burden of care will be transferred from the state to relatives who already have busy lives (Armstrong et al., 1997). More than one in eight Canadians are already providing care to people with long-term health problems. Many of these caregivers have reported that providing this help has hurt their jobs, finances, or health (Statistics Canada, 1997b). While many of the caregivers surveyed were willing and able to provide support, government assistance will be necessary for those caregivers who lack the resources to do it alone and for individuals who do not have a network of family and friends to assist them.

As medical costs continue to take up an increasing share of government and personal revenues, we will continue to see a debate over the level of health care that Canadians will receive and the type of services that are funded by the government. There has been pressure from some provinces to privatize some medical services. Proponents of privatization claim that it would provide services more cheaply and reduce waiting lists for diagnostic tests and treatment. Those who oppose privatization fear it would be the first step toward a two-tier health care system, in which those who can afford to pay would receive a different level of service than those who cannot pay for private treatment.

The health of Canadians will likely continue to improve in the future, but at the global level there is some cause for concern. You have read about the impact of AIDS on people in low-income nations and about the precarious health of many of the world's children. Medical authorities now fear the return of infectious diseases, such as cholera, malaria, and tuberculosis, that were once controlled by antibiotics, vaccines, and by public-health programs such as improved sanitation. The reasons for the renewed threat from these diseases include environmental change, the public-health consequences of poverty in the developing world, and the fact that global travel has helped bacteria and viruses move easily from one place to another (Taylor, 1997). In 2003, an outbreak of SARS (severe acute respiratory syndrome) spread within days from China to Toronto where it spread quickly, largely among people who were connected to hospitals, including several nurses. Forty-four people died of SARS in Ontario, and because of worldwide concern about the disease, it had a major economic impact on Toronto. Most experts are concerned that a more serious global outbreak will occur. Many believe that *avian influenza,* which has been epidemic among domestic birds in several Asian countries, may spread to humans and become a pandemic that will kill millions of people. In 2010 there was great concern that H1N1 virus would become a pandemic, and Canada and other countries implemented massive vaccination programs.

The resurgence of diseases such as malaria and tuberculosis, and the rapid spread of HIV/AIDS, show that health is a social issue as much as it is a medical one. Social factors such as economic inequality, geographic mobility, societal values, human settlement patterns, and the overuse of pesticides and antibiotics all contribute to the spread of disease. Improving the health of the world's population will require social change as well as improved ways of treating the sick.

▥ What is health?

Health is often defined as a state of complete physical, mental, and social well-being.

▥ What is the relationship among health care, medicine, and preventive medicine?

Medicine is an institutionalized system for the scientific diagnosis, treatment, and prevention of illness. Medicine forms a vital part of the broader concept of health care, which is any activity intended to improve health. Preventive medicine is medicine that emphasizes a healthy lifestyle that will prevent poor health from occurring.

▥ What are the functionalist, conflict, feminist, symbolic interactionist, and postmodern perspectives on health and health care?

Functionalists view society as a complex, stable system; therefore, the normal state of affairs is for people to be healthy and to contribute to their society. Illness is seen as dysfunctional for both the individual who is sick and for society. Sickness may result in an inability on the part of the sick person to fulfill his or her necessary social roles. The conflict approach to health and illness considers the political and social forces that affect health and the health-care system, and the inequities that result from these forces. Feminist scholars have studied a variety of issues, including the manner in which medicalization has affected the lives of women and the male-centred focus of medical research. Symbolic interactionists attempt to understand the specific meanings and causes that we attribute to particular events. In studying health, interactionists focus on the way the meaning that social actors give their illness or disease will affect their self-concept and their relationships with others. Finally, postmodern theorists have examined the relationship between biology and culture.

▥ How do age, sex, and social class affect health?

Rates of illness and death are highest among the old and the very young. Mortality rates drop shortly after birth and begin to rise significantly during the middle years. After age 65, rates of chronic illnesses and mortality increase rapidly. Women now live longer than men do, but have higher rates of disease and disability. The poor have worse health and die earlier than the rich. Illness and mortality rates are far higher for less developed countries than for developed nations.

▥ What is a disability?

A disability is a physical or health condition that reduces a person's ability to perform tasks one would normally do at a given stage of life and that may result in stigmatization or discrimination against the person.

▥ What is the difference between a universal health-care system and one in which the user pays for health services?

Canadians have a universal health-care system in which all Canadians receive medical services that are paid for through the tax system. If you are sick, you have the right to receive quality medical care regardless of your ability to pay. Before the early 1960s, Canadians had a "user pay" system, which meant that many people had to pay for health care directly out of their own pockets. Individuals without health insurance who required expensive medical procedures, long-term care, or who developed a chronic illness often suffered severe financial losses.

KEY TERMS

disability 270
epidemics 269
health 259
health care 259
medicalization 263
medicine 259
preventive medicine 259
senile dementia 266
sick role 261
universal health-care system 275

WEB LINKS

For more Web links related to the topic of this chapter, see the Nelson sociology website:
www.sociologyessentials5e.nelson.com

Read about a wide variety of diseases including HIV/AIDS at the website of the Centers for Disease Control and Prevention:
www.cdc.gov/hiv/pubs/facts.htm

Health Canada has established a comprehensive database on health and health care issues called the Canadian Health Network; see
www.canadian-health-network.ca

For recent information about the problems of HIV/AIDS, see the website of the Joint UN Programme on HIV/AIDS at:
www.unaids.org

Learn about global health issues and some possible solutions at the website of the World Health Organization: **www.who.int/en**

The website of the Society for Women's Health Research discusses the sex differences between women and men that affect the prevention, diagnosis, and treatment of disease: **www.womenshealthresearch.org**

For comparative health-care data from a variety of countries, see the International Health Policy and Practice section of the Commonwealth Fund website: **http://www.commonwealthfund.org/Topics/International-Health-Policy-2009.aspx**

The article by Gail Fawcett titled "Canada's Untapped Workplace Resource: People with Disabilities" deals with the issue of barriers to employment faced by people with disabilities: **http://www.ccsd.ca/perception/214/per_214a.htm**

The Council of Canadians with Disabilities advocates for the right of Canadians with disabilities to be centrally involved in the decision-making processes that affect their lives, and for the removal of barriers to their full participation in matters affecting their lives. The organization has a website at: **http://www.ccdonline.ca**

For information about health care in Canada, visit the Canadian Institute for Health Information website: **www.cihi.ca**

QUESTIONS FOR CRITICAL THINKING

1. How do you think governments should balance their needs for financial savings and the public need for quality health care? Should everyone receive unlimited health services regardless of cost, or should priorities be set based on provincial and federal budgets?

2. What is the best way for society to control diseases such as lung cancer and HIV/AIDS that sometimes can be controlled by changing people's behaviour?

3. What is the role of alternative therapies in health care? Have you or your friends and relatives made use of alternative treatments?

4. In your view, what constitutes a disability? How do you think that Canadians and Canadian government policies need to change so that people with disabilities can participate more fully in society?

ONLINE STUDY AND RESEARCH TOOLS

INFOTRAC®

InfoTrac College Edition is included free with every new copy of this text. Explore this online library for additional readings, review, and a handy resource for assignments. Visit **www.infotrac-college.com** to access this online database of full-text articles. Enter the key terms from this chapter to start your search.

CENGAGENOW™ CENGAGENOW

Use CengageNOW™ to help you formulate a customized study plan for this chapter. After you take the Diagnostic Quiz, CengageNOW™ will generate a customized study plan for you. It will identify sections of the chapter you should review.

CHAPTER 12

Families and Intimate Relationships

The following is a brief excerpt from an article titled "Out Family Values" by Professor James Miller from the University of Western Ontario:

> The family I live in as a father is also the family I live out in as a gay man. I call it an "out family" for three reasons: its openness to homosexual membership; its opposition to heterosexist conformity (the prejudicial assumption of heterosexuality as normal and proper); and its overtness within the contemporary lesbian and gay movement.
>
> Mine is a family that opens out, steps out, and stands out. It opens out to people traditionally excluded from the charmed circle of Home; it steps out beyond the polite and policed borders of the Normal; and it stands out as a clear new possibility on the horizon of what used to be called—in the heady days following Pierre Trudeau's decriminalization of homosexuality in Canada (1969)—the Just Society.
>
> . . . . When I first came out to my children in January of 1990, they immediately wanted to know whether they were

gay, too. Not necessarily, I told them, trying to allay their time-honoured fears without compromising my newfound sense of pride. Yet was I not outing them by outing myself? For better or worse, I realized my uncloseted gayness was bound to be socially projected onto all who lived with me. Whatever my children's sexual orientations might be, their close association with me would effectively gay them in the eyes of straight society and queer their cultural outlook. So look out, I warned them, the World likes to see things straight.

They have taken my warning to heart by setting the record straight about me and them ("Our Dad's gay, but we're probably not") for any curious soul who comes into our domestic space. . . . An out family must learn to speak about itself in unaccustomed ways, develop its own outlandish frontier lingo, for its members are always proudly, if at times also painfully, aware of their strategic positioning outside the normative vision of heterosexual monogamy. . . . My out family bravely resists the exclusionary

pressures of heterosexist institutions and their defenders simply by existing as such, by brazenly occupying hallowed spaces like "family rooms" and "family cottages" and even "family restaurants" where we're not supposed to exist. (Miller, 2003:104)

James Miller's family is one of millions around the globe redefining what the concept of family means in our modern society. Fifty years ago, the majority of Canadian families consisted of two adults in a permanent union that produced three to five children. Other kinds of families were the exception. Today, when we think of families, we think of diversity and change, and exceptions are the rule.

Other variations on what has been described as a "traditional" family are also common. Separation and divorce, remarriage, and blended or reconstituted families are a reality for many Canadians. Despite these changes, family life continues to be a source of great personal satisfaction and happiness. A recent opinion poll of Canadians indicated that more than 97 percent of respondents believed that family life was essential to their personal well-being (Bibby, 2004).

In this chapter, we examine the diversity and complexity of families and intimate relationships. Before reading on, test your knowledge about the changing family by taking the quiz in Box 12.1 on page 287.

QUESTIONS AND ISSUES

Chapter Focus Question: How is social change affecting the Canadian family?

Why is it difficult to define family?

How do marriage patterns vary across cultures?

What are the key assumptions of functionalist, conflict, feminist, and symbolic interactionist and postmodern perspectives on families?

What significant trends affect many Canadian families today?

FAMILIES IN GLOBAL PERSPECTIVE

Defining Family

What is a family? Although we all have a family of some form or another, and we all understand the concept of family, it is not an easy concept to define. More than ever, this term means different things to different people. As the nature of family life and work has changed in high-, middle-, and low-income nations, the issue of what constitutes a "family" has been widely debated. For example, Hutterite families in Canada live in communal situations, in which children from about the age of three spend most of their days in school. The children also eat their meals in a communal dining hall, away from their parents. In this case, the community is the family, as opposed to a traditional nuclear family.

Some Aboriginal families in Canada also tend to have a much broader idea of family membership. Children are often cared for by relatives in the extended family. Because a social worker may define a family as consisting of parents and children only, some Aboriginal parents may be perceived as neglecting their children, when the parents believe the children are safe and well cared for by "their family"—that is, by uncles, grandparents, or other relatives (Castellano, 2002).

Similarly, gay men and lesbians often form unique family forms. Many gay men and lesbians have ***families we choose***—**social arrangements that include intimate relationships between couples and close familial relationships with other couples and with other adults and children** (Ambert, 2005b).

In a society as diverse as Canada's, talking about "a family" as though a single type of family exists or ever did exist is inaccurate. In reality, different groups will define their family lives in unique ways, depending on a number of factors such as their socioeconomic

Despite the idealized image of "the family," North American families have undergone many changes in the past century as exemplified by the case of Nadya Suleman who had eight babies using assisted reproductive technologies.

background, immigrant status, religious beliefs, or cultural practices and traditions (Baker, 2005).

For many years, a standard sociological definition of *family* has been a group of people who are related to one another by bonds of blood, marriage, or adoption, and who live together, form an economic unit, and bear and raise children (Benokraitis, 1999). Many people believe that this definition should not be expanded—that social approval should not be extended to other relationships simply because the persons in those relationships want to consider themselves a family. However, others challenge this definition because it simply does not match the reality of family life in

BOX 12.1 SOCIOLOGY AND EVERYDAY LIFE

How Much Do You Know about the Changing Family in Canada?

Join In
on TurningPoint®

True	False	
T	**F**	1. Today, people in Canada are more inclined to get married than at any time in history.
T	**F**	2. Men are as likely as women to be single parents.
T	**F**	3. One out of every two marriages ends in divorce.
T	F	4. Almost half of young persons aged 20–29 still live at home.
T	**F**	5. The number of extended families living together in the same home has decreased in the past 20 years.
T	F	6. There are more single adults in Canada than married persons.
T	**F**	7. Most Canadians remain opposed to same-sex marriage.
T	F	8. Fertility rates in Canada are lower than those in the United States, France, and the United Kingdom.

Answers on page 288.

contemporary society (Eichler, 1981; Bibby, 2004; Ambert 2006a). Today's families include many types of living arrangements and relationships, including single-parent households, unmarried couples, lesbian and gay couples, and multiple generations (such as grandparents, parents, and children living in the same household). To accurately reflect the reality of family life, we need an encompassing definition of what constitutes a family. Accordingly, we will define *families* **as relationships in which people live together with commitment, form an economic unit, care for any young, and consider their identity to be significantly attached to the group**. Sexual expression and parent–children relationships are a part of most, but not all, family relationships (based on Benokraitis, 2002; Lamanna and Riedmann, 2003).

In our study of families, we will use our sociological imagination to see how our personal experiences are related to the larger happenings in our society. At the microlevel, each of us has our own "biography," based on our experience within a family; at the macrolevel, our families are embedded in a specific social context that has a major impact on them (Aulette, 1994). We will examine the institution of the family at both of these levels, starting with family structure and characteristics.

Family Structure and Characteristics

In pre-industrial societies, the primary form of social organization is through kinship ties. ***Kinship* refers to a social network of people based on common ancestry, marriage, or adoption**. Through kinship networks, people cooperate so that they can acquire the basic necessities of life, including food and shelter. Kinship systems can also serve as a means by which property is transferred, goods are produced and distributed, and power is allocated.

In industrialized societies, other social institutions fulfill some of the functions previously taken care of by the kinship network. For example, political systems provide structures of social control and authority, and economic systems are responsible for the production and distribution of goods and services. Consequently, families in industrialized societies serve fewer and more specialized purposes than do families in pre-industrial societies. Contemporary families are primarily responsible for regulating sexual activity, socializing children, and providing affection and companionship for family members.

Families of Orientation and Procreation

During our lifetime, many of us will be members of two different types of families—a family of orientation and a family of procreation. The ***family of orientation* is the family into which a person is born and in which early socialization usually takes place**. Although most people are related to members of their family of orientation by blood ties, those who are adopted have a legal tie that is patterned after a blood relationship. The ***family of procreation* is the**

BOX 12.1 | **SOCIOLOGY AND EVERYDAY LIFE**

Answers to the Sociology Quiz on the Changing Family in Canada

J♦in In

1. **False.** According to census data, the marriage rate has gone down by about one-third since 1960. The marriage rate today remains at a record low of 4.7 per 1000 population, well below the peak in 1988 of 7.0 per 1000 population (Statistics Canada, 2007c).

2. **False.** Eighty-one percent of single-parent families in Canada are headed by a mother (Statistics Canada, 2007c).

3. **False.** Current estimates are that about one-third of marriages will end in divorce (Vanier Institute of the Family, 2008).

4. **True.** Today, 44 percent of people aged 20–29 live at home compared to 32 percent 20 years ago. (Turcotte, 2008)

5. **False.** A growing number of grandparents are sharing their home with their children and grandchildren. These extended families are formed as a result of cultural, economic, and social needs (Statistics Canada, 2007c).

6. **True.** For the first time ever, married persons in Canada are in the minority. Fifty-one percent of the adult population today are never married, divorced, separated, widowed, or living common-law (Statistics Canada, 2007c).

7. **False.** A 2002 survey indicated that approximately two-thirds of Canadians support same-sex marriage. (Mawhinney, 2002)

8. **True.** On average, Canadian women will have 1.5 children as compared to the United States (2.0), France (1.9), and the United Kingdom (1.7) (Vanier Institute of the Family, 2008).

family that a person forms by having or adopting children (Benokraitis, 2002). Both legal and blood ties are found in most families of procreation. The relationship between a husband and wife is based on legal ties; however, the relationship between a parent and child may be based on either blood or legal ties, depending on whether the child has been adopted (Aulette, 1994).

Although many young people leave their family of orientation as they reach adulthood, finish school, or get married, recent studies have found that many people maintain family ties across generations, particularly as older persons have remained actively involved in relationships with their adult children.

Extended and Nuclear Families Sociologists distinguish between extended and nuclear families based on the number of generations that live within a household. An **extended family is a family unit composed of relatives in addition to parents and children who live in the same household**. These families often include grandparents, uncles, aunts, or other relatives who live in close proximity to the parents and children, making it possible for family members to share resources (see Box 12.2 on page 292). In horticultural and agricultural societies, extended families are extremely important; having a large number of family members participate in food production may be essential for survival. Today, extended families are becoming more common across North America and Britain. This trend is related to an increase in the number of families caring for aging parents, an increase in the number of grandparents with children and grandchildren living with them for economic reasons, and an increase in immigration from countries where extended family living is the norm (Andreatta, 2007).

A **nuclear family is a family composed of one or two parents and their dependent children, all of whom live apart from other relatives**. A traditional definition specifies that a nuclear family is made up of a "couple" and their dependent children; however, this definition has become outdated as significant changes have occurred in the structure of families. As shown in the Census Profile (on page 290), in 2006,

Although the relationship between a husband and wife is based on legal ties, relationships between parents and children may be established either by blood ties or by legal ties.

approximately 41 percent of all households were composed of couples with children under the age of 18, as compared with 57 percent in 1981. Today, for the first time ever, the largest family type, at almost 43 percent, were couples without children living at home. This group consists of childless couples and couples whose children no longer lived at home (empty-nesters) (Statistics Canada, 2007c).

Nuclear families are smaller than they were 20 years ago; whereas the average family size in 1971 was 3.7 persons, in 2006 it was 2.5 persons (Statistics Canada, 2007c). This decrease has been attributed to decisions to delay or forego child-bearing and increases in divorce rates.

Marriage Patterns

Across cultures, families are characterized by different forms of marriage. *Marriage* **is a legally recognized and/or socially approved arrangement between two or more individuals that carries certain rights and obligations and usually involves sexual activity.**

In Canada the only legally sanctioned form of marriage is *monogamy*—**a marriage to one person at a time**. For some people, marriage is a lifelong commitment that ends only with the death of a partner. For others, marriage is a commitment of indefinite duration. Through a pattern of marriage, divorce, and remarriage, some people practise *serial monogamy*—a succession of marriages in which a person has several spouses over a lifetime but is legally married to only one person at a time.

Polygamy **is the concurrent marriage of a person of one sex with two or more members of**

the opposite sex **(Marshall, 1998).** The most prevalent form of polygamy is *polygyny*—**the concurrent marriage of one man with two or more women.** Polygyny has been practised in a number of Islamic societies, including in some regions of contemporary Africa and southern Russia. How many wives and children might a polygynist have at one time? According to one report, Rodger Chilala of southern Zambia claimed to have 14 wives and more than 40 children; he stated that he previously had 24 wives but found that he could not afford the expenses associated with that many spouses. Some analysts believe that the practice of polygamy contributes to the likelihood that families will live in poverty (Chipungu, 1999).

The second type of polygamy is *polyandry*—**the concurrent marriage of one woman with two or more men.** Polyandry is very rare; when it does occur, it is typically found in societies where men greatly outnumber women because of high rates of female infanticide or where marriages are arranged between two brothers and one woman (fraternal polyandry). According to recent research, polyandry is never the only form of marriage in society: whenever polyandry occurs, polygyny co-occurs (Trevithick, 1997). Although Tibetans are the most frequently studied population where polyandry exists, anthropologists have also identified the Sherpas, Paharis, Sinhalese, and various African groups as sometimes practising polyandry (Trevithick, 1997). A recent anthropological study of Nyinba, an ethnically Tibetan population living in northwestern Nepal, found that fraternal polyandry (two brothers sharing the same wife) is the normative form of marriage and that the practice continues to be highly valued culturally (Levine and Silk, 1997).

Census Profile | **Changes in Family Structure**

Changes to the family structure include a decline in marriages, an increase in common-law unions, and an increase in single-parent families.

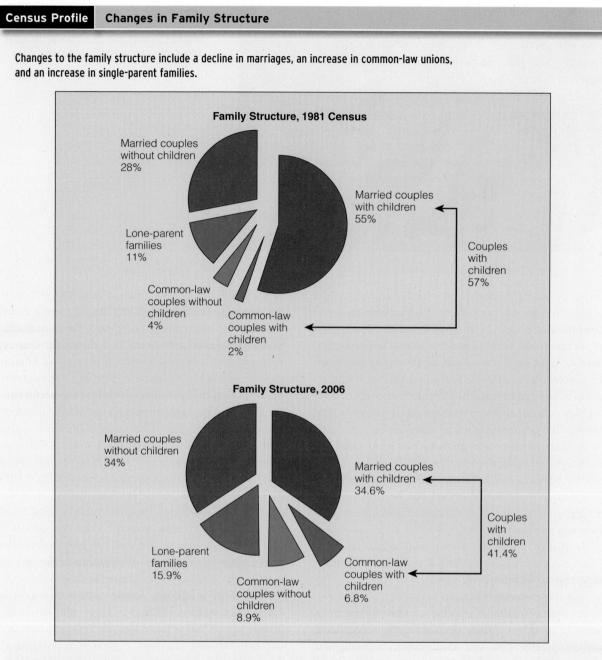

Source: Statistics Canada, *Families and Households Highlight Tables. 2006 Census.* Catalogue No. 97-553-XWE2006002. Ottawa. Released September 12, 2007. http://www.statcan.gc.ca/bsolc/olc-cel/olc-cel?catno=97-553-XWE2006002&lang=eng&lang=eng, Retrieved November 29, 2010.

Patterns of Descent and Inheritance

Even though a variety of marital patterns exist across cultures, virtually all forms of marriage establish a system of descent so that kinship can be determined and inheritance rights established. In pre-industrial societies, kinship is usually traced through one parent (unilineally). The most common pattern of unilineal descent is **patrilineal descent**—a system of tracing **descent through the father's side of the family**. Patrilineal systems are set up in such a manner that a legitimate son inherits his father's property and sometimes his position upon the father's death. In nations such as India, where boys are seen as permanent patrilineal family members while girls are seen as only temporary family members, girls tend to be considered more expendable than boys (O'Connell, 1994). Even with the less common pattern of *matrilineal descent*—a system of tracing descent through the mother's side of the family—women may not control property. However, inheritance of property and position usually is traced from the maternal uncle (mother's brother) to his nephew (mother's son). In some cases, mothers may pass on their property to daughters.

By contrast, in industrial societies, kinship usually is traced through both parents (bilineally). The most common form is *bilateral descent*—a system of tracing descent through both the mother's and father's sides of the family. This pattern is used in Canada for the purpose of determining kinship and inheritance rights; however, children typically take the father's last name.

Power and Authority in Families

Descent and inheritance rights are intricately linked with patterns of power and authority in families. The most prevalent forms of familial power and authority are patriarchy, matriarchy, and egalitarianism. A *patriarchal family* is a family structure in which authority is held by the eldest male (usually the father). The male authority figure acts as head of the household and holds power and authority over the women and children as well as over other males. A *matriarchal family* is a family structure in which authority is held by the eldest female (usually the mother). In this case, the female authority figure acts as head of the household. Although there has been a great deal of discussion about matriarchal families, scholars have found no historical evidence to indicate that true matriarchies ever existed.

The most prevalent pattern of power and authority in families is patriarchy. Across cultures, men are the primary (and often sole) decision makers regarding domestic, economic, and social concerns facing the family.

Moreover, some economists believe that the patriarchal family structure (along with prevailing market conditions and public policy) limits people's choices in employment. According to this view, the patriarchal family structure has remained largely unchanged in this country, even as familial responsibilities in the paid labour market have undergone dramatic transformation. In the postindustrial age, for example, gender-specific roles may have been reduced; however, women's choices remain limited by the patriarchal tradition in which women do most of the unpaid labour, particularly in the family. Despite dramatic increases in the number of women in the paid workforce, there has been a lack of movement toward gender equity, which would equalize women's opportunities (Lindsay, 2008).

An *egalitarian family* is a family structure in which both partners share power and authority equally. In egalitarian families, issues of power and authority may be frequently negotiated as the roles and responsibilities within the relationship change over time. Recently, a trend toward more egalitarian relationships has been evident in a number of countries as women have sought changes in their legal status and increased educational and employment opportunities. Some degree of economic independence makes it possible for women to delay marriage or to terminate a problematic marriage (Ward, 2005). However, one study of the effects of egalitarian values on the allocation and performance of domestic tasks in the family found that changes were relatively slow in coming. According to the study, fathers were more likely to share domestic tasks in nonconventional families where members held values that are more egalitarian. Similarly, children's gender-role stereotyping was more closely linked to their parents' egalitarian values and nonconventional lifestyles than to the domestic tasks they were assigned (Weisner, Garnier, and Loucky, 1994).

DEVELOPING INTIMATE RELATIONSHIPS AND ESTABLISHING FAMILIES

It has been said that North Americans are "in love with love." Why is this so? Perhaps the answer lies in that our ideal culture emphasizes "romantic love," which refers to a deep emotion, the satisfaction of significant needs, a caring for and acceptance of the person we love, and involvement in an intimate relationship (Lamanna and Riedmann, 2003). Although the methods we employ to pursue romance may have changed, we are certainly no less enthralled with the idea (see Box 12.3 on page 294).

Love and Intimacy

How have Canadians viewed love and intimacy in the past? During the Industrial Revolution, and into the late 19th century, people came to view work and home as separate spheres in which different feelings

BOX 12.2 SOCIOLOGY IN A GLOBAL PERSPECTIVE

Buffering Financial Hardship: Extended Families in the Global Economy

- Day after day, Nang Pajik sews collars on workshirts at a factory in Vientiane, Laos, so that she can send money home to her six brothers and sisters and her extended family in her home village (Bradsher, 2006).
- Odilon Hernandez bought a television and several appliances from La Curacao, a Los Angeles store, for his parents in Puebla, Mexico. La Curacao delivers items directly to the extended families of U.S. immigrant workers from the store's warehouse in Mexico, which was set up for that purpose (Associated Press, 2006).
- A United Kingdom building society estimates that the number of homes containing three generations of a family will triple in England during the next 20 years because of rising levels of debt and the high cost of property. According to a Skipton Building Society spokesperson, "These issues are likely to get worse and so combining incomes and sharing mortgage repayments may well be the only alternative for some families" (BBC News, 2004).

Although many people think of the extended family as primarily a thing of the past, current evidence suggests that the extended family is far from becoming obsolete. What unique benefits do extended families offer? The answer is quite simple: Extended families offer a financial safety net that is unavailable in the typical nuclear family. For many families in the United Kingdom, purchasing a house is a possibility only if multiple generations combine their incomes and share their living expenses and mortgage payments. However, as the cost of child care rises in the United Kingdom, extended family residential patterns are important not only for house purchases but also for child care because expenditures are greatly reduced when grandparents serve as live-in childminders (BBC News, 2004).

In low-income and immigrant families, the extended family is particularly important: pooling resources often means economic survival for the family. In the poorest of nations, such as Laos, some family members remain in the home village to tend the family's rice plot while other members migrate to the city to earn money that can be shared with relatives at home.

To people in high-income nations, the thought of earning wages of $50 a month for factory work is unheard of; however, for individuals with few educational opportunities or little experience using machines, moving from a village to the city to work in a factory constitutes a major economic improvement (even if it is only temporary) in the standard of living for their entire family.

The stories above could be repeated in many nations. In Africa, for example, extended family systems help buffer inequality through the exchanges of resources and fostering of children across nuclear family units. At this time, it does not appear that globalization or greater exposure to other cultural norms of family life will change this pattern significantly. The African HIV/AIDS epidemic has left many children dependent on relatives for their survival. Like children, many older adults benefit from extended family patterns. In a study of elderly Asians living in Britain, researchers found that the grandmothers in their study had better mental health (were "better adjusted") when they resided in an extended family rather than in a nuclear family (Guglani, Coleman, and Sonuga-Barke, 2000).

What conclusions might we draw from this brief look at extended families in the global economy? Apparently, extended families meet specific needs that are not easily met by nuclear families, and current evidence suggests that extended family patterns are not likely to disappear in the near future. Do you or someone you know live in an extended family? What are the strengths and limitations of this arrangement?

---

and emotions were appropriate (Coontz, 1992). The public sphere of work—men's sphere—emphasized self-reliance and independence. In contrast, the private sphere of the home—women's sphere—emphasized the giving of services, the exchange of gifts, and love. Accordingly, love and emotions became the domain of women, and work and rationality the domain of men (Lamanna and Riedmann, 2003).

Although the roles of women and men have changed dramatically in the 20th century, men and women still do not always share the same perspectives about romantic love. According to Francesca Cancian (1990), women tend to express their feelings verbally, whereas men tend to express their love through nonverbal actions, such as running an errand for someone or repairing a child's broken toy.

Love, intimacy, and sexuality are closely intertwined. Intimacy may be psychic ("the sharing of minds") or sexual, or both. Although sexuality is an integral part of many intimate relationships, perceptions about sexual activities vary from one culture to the next and from one era to another. For example, kissing is found primarily in Western cultures; many African and Asian cultures view kissing negatively (Reinisch, 1990).

For more than 40 years, the work of biologist Alfred C. Kinsey was considered the definitive research on human sexuality, even though some of his methodology had serious limitations. Recently, the work of Kinsey and his associates has been suoerceded by the National Health and Social Life Survey. Based on interviews with more than 3400 men and women aged 18 to 59, this random survey in 1949 tended to reaffirm the significance of the dominant sexual ideologies. Most respondents reported that they engaged in heterosexual relationships, although 9 percent of the men said they had had at least one homosexual encounter resulting in orgasm. Although 6.2 percent of men and 4.4 percent of women said that they were at least somewhat attracted to others of the same gender, only 2.8 percent of men and 1.4 percent of women identified themselves as gay or lesbian. According to the study, persons who engaged in extramarital sex found their activities to be more thrilling than those with their marital partner, but they also felt guilty. Persons in sustained relationships such as marriage or cohabitation found sexual activity to be the most satisfying emotionally and physically.

Cohabitation

Cohabitation refers to a couple's living together without being legally married. Attitudes about cohabitation have changed in the past three decades. This was reflected in the Census Profile on page 290. In Canada, cohabitation has become increasingly popular. The census defines _common-law_ partners as two persons of the opposite sex who are not legally married but live together as husband and wife. The growth of common-law families is the strongest of all family structures. Since the early 1980s, the number of persons living common-law has nearly doubled, going from 700 000 in 1981 to 1.4 million in 2006. Almost half of common-law-couple families include children, whether born to the current union or brought to the family from previous unions. The proportion of people in common-law unions varies considerably by province. In Quebec,

In Canada, the notion of romantic love is deeply intertwined with our beliefs about how and why people develop intimate relationships and establish families. Not all societies share this concern with romantic love.

one in three couples live common-law, making it the province with the highest rate of common-law families (Statistics Canada, 2007c).

Those most likely to cohabit are young adults between the ages of 25 and 29; one out of every six Canadians in this age group lives in a common-law union. Cohabitation is even more common among Canadian university and college students, an estimated 25 percent of whom report having cohabited at some time. Although "living together" or living common-law is often a prelude to marriage for young adults, common-law unions are also becoming a popular alternative both to marriage and to remarriage following divorce or separation (Ambert, 2005c; Statistics Canada, 2007c).

Today, some people view cohabitation as a form of "trial marriage." Some people who have cohabited do eventually marry the person with whom they have been living whereas others do not. A recent study of 11 000 women found that there was a 70 percent marriage rate for women who remained in a cohabiting relationship for at least five years. However, of the women in that study who cohabited and then married their partner, 40 percent became divorced within a 10-year period (Bramlett and Mosher, 2001). Whether these findings will be supported by

© Dick Hemingway

BOX 12.3   SOCIOLOGY AND THE MEDIA

Cyber-Dating: Love and Intimacy Online

A recent survey by Internet demographers reported that the number of Internet users in Canada and the United States has reached close to 230 million. Global use is estimated at over 1 billion people (Canada is, per capita, one the most "wired" countries in the world, along with the United States, Japan, and Australia [Internet World Statistics, 2006]). Because of the availability of this technology, our interpersonal relationships have also been transformed. Relationships that previously involved face-to-face interaction or some other form of direct personal contact are now mediated through new forms of technology (such as e-mail, voice mail, and fax). As a result, on any given day, we can "interact" with numerous people in our professional and personal lives and yet never have any contact with them. As the pace of our daily lives continues to accelerate and free time becomes an increasingly scarce commodity, it becomes necessary to explore new avenues for social interaction. The Internet is one such avenue (Merkle and Richardson, 2000).

Who uses these sites? You name it: teenagers, seniors, heterosexuals, homosexuals, single parents, and yes, university and college students. One online research firm estimates the number of regular users of Internet dating services at 4 million (Brym and Lenton, 2001). Although cyber-dating is most popular with North American users, it is becoming popular globally. In China, the practice is challenging the tradition of parents selecting their child's spouse. In Britain, an estimated one in five singles used the Net or dating agencies to find romantic partners. One expert predicts this number will "explode over the next five years as globalization brings American-length workdays to the rest of the world" (Stone, 2001:46).

A telephone survey of 1200 Canadians revealed the popularity of this new venue for dating. Specifically the study reported the following:

- Four main social forces appear to be driving the rapid growth of online dating:
  - A growing proportion of the population comprises singles, the main pool for online dating.
  - Career and time pressures are increasing, so people are looking for more efficient ways of meeting others for intimate relationships.

  - Single people are more mobile because of the demands of the job market, so it is more difficult for them to meet people for dating.
  - Workplace romance is on the decline because of growing sensitivity about sexual harassment.
- In Canada, Internet users are younger, better educated, more likely to be employed in the paid labour force, and more likely to earn higher income than Canadians in general.
- Most people use online dating services mainly to find dates and establish a long-term relationship, not to flirt online, find a marriage partner, or find a sexual partner.
- People use online dating services mainly because they:
  - create the opportunity to meet people one would otherwise never meet,
  - offer privacy and confidentiality, and
  - are more convenient than other ways of trying to meet people.
- The main perceived disadvantage of online dating is that people sometimes do not tell the truth about themselves.
- A quarter of online daters have misrepresented themselves online. There were almost no differences between men and women in their propensity to misrepresent themselves.
- Online dating seems to be safer than conventional dating. Although 10 percent of people who went out on a date with someone they met online reported being frightened at least once, this was not sufficiently serious to change their favourable attitude toward online dating.
- Embarrassment is not a major factor inhibiting Canadians from using online dating services. The main inhibiting factors are control related (some people believe it is too risky) and pragmatic (some people do not believe it is effective, others think there are better ways to meet people for dating, and still others have simply not yet found a suitable date). However, if a friend has used an online dating service, and especially if the friend's experience was positive, these inhibitions are considerably reduced (Brym and Lenton, 2001:3).

What do you think about using the Internet to find a date or a romantic partner? What are the potential hazards of this new form of relationship building?

subsequent research remains to be seen. But we do know that studies over the past decade have supported the proposition that couples who cohabit before marriage do not necessarily have a stable relationship following marriage (Clark and Crompton, 2006).

Marriage

Why do people get married? Couples get married for a variety of reasons. Some do so because they are "in love," desire companionship and sex, want to have children, feel social pressure, are attempting to escape from a bad situation in their parents' home, or believe that they will have more money or other resources if they get married. These factors notwithstanding, the selection of a marital partner actually is fairly predictable. Most people in Canada tend to choose marriage partners who are similar to themselves. **Homogamy refers to the pattern of individuals marrying those who have similar characteristics, such as race/ethnicity, religious background, age, education, or social class**. However, homogamy provides only the general framework within which people select their partners; people are also influenced by other factors. For example, some researchers claim that people want partners whose personalities match their own in significant ways. As a result, people who are outgoing and friendly may be attracted to people with those same traits. However, other researchers claim that people look for partners whose personality traits differ from but complement their own.

Regardless of the individual traits of marriage partners, research indicates that communication and emotional support are crucial to the success of marriages. Common marital problems include lack of emotional intimacy, poor communication, and lack of companionship. One study concluded that for many middle- and upper-income couples, women's paid work was critical to the success of the marriages. People who have a strong commitment to their work have two distinct sources of pleasure—work and family. For members of the working class, however, work may not be a source of pleasure. For all women and men, balancing work and family life is a challenge (Marshall, 2009b).

Housework and Childcare Responsibilities

Thirty years ago, most Canadian families relied on one wage earner. Today approximately 70 percent of all families in Canada are **dual-earner families—families in which both partners are in the labour force**. More than half of all employed women hold full-time, year-round jobs. Even when their children are very young, most working mothers work full-time (Statistics Canada, 2006f). Moreover, as discussed in Chapter 10, many married women leave their paid employment at the end of the day and go home to perform hours of housework and childcare. Difficulty in balancing work and family is the defining feature of family life today. Parents must make difficult decisions—decisions often driven by economic necessity—between the amount of time they spend at work and the amount of time they can be at home with their children (Marshall, 2006; Barrette, 2009). Arlie Hochschild (1989, 2003) refers to this as the **second shift—the domestic work that employed women perform at home after they complete their workday on the job**. Thus, many married women today contribute to the economic well-being of their families and also meet many, if not all, of the domestic needs of family members by cooking, cleaning, shopping, taking care of children, and managing household routines. In households with small children or many children, the amount of housework increases. Hochschild points to the second shift in many families as a sign that the gender revolution has stalled:

> The move of masses of women into the paid workforce has constituted a revolution. But the slower shift in ideas of "manhood," the resistance of sharing work at home, the rigid schedules at work make for a "stall" in this gender revolution. It is a stall in the change of institutional arrangement of which men are the principal keepers. (2003:28)

As Hochschild points out, the second shift remains a problem for many women in dual-earner marriages.

However, recent time-use surveys of Canadian households indicate that the "stalled" revolution may be picking up the pace. Gendered differences persist in the division of labour, but they are slowly diminishing. As women's participation in the paid labour market has increased, men's involvement in housework and child care has risen also. In the mid-1980s, only half of men with or without children participated in daily housework. Today approximately seven out of ten men do so. Even when husbands share some of the household responsibilities, however, they typically spend much less time on these activities than do their wives. For example, married women with children do about 1.5 times more housework per day than married men (Marshall, 2006). Couples with more egalitarian ideas about women's and men's roles tend to share more equally in food preparation, housework, and childcare.

Women employed full-time who are single parents probably have the greatest burden of all; they have complete responsibility for the children and the household, often with little or no help from ex-husbands or relatives. Recent statistics indicate that female single parents with full-time employment work about 11 hours per day when paid and unpaid work are combined (Vanier Institute of the Family, 2009).

CHILD-RELATED FAMILY ISSUES AND PARENTING

Not all couples become parents. Those who decide not to have children often consider themselves to be "child-free," whereas those who do not produce children through no choice of their own may consider themselves "childless."

Deciding to Have Children

Cultural attitudes about having children and about the ideal family size began to change in North America in the late 1950s. Today, the fertility rate—an estimate of the average number of children women aged 15 to 49 will have in their lifetime—sits at a record low of just under 1.5 (Statistics Canada, 2007c). Advances in birth-control techniques over the past four decades—including the birth-control pill and contraceptive patches and shots—now make it possible for people to decide whether they want to have children, how many they want to have, and (at least somewhat) the spacing of their births. Sociologists suggest, however, that fertility is linked not only to reproductive opportunities but also to women's beliefs that they do or do not have other opportunities in society that are viable alternatives to childbearing (Lamanna and Riedmann, 2003).

Today, the concept of reproductive freedom includes both the desire *to have* or *to not have* one or more children. According to Leslie King and Madonna Harrington Meyer (1997), many women spend up to one-half of their life attempting to control their reproductive systems. Many diverse reasons were given as to why they chose not to have children,

Geostock/Getty Images

Dual-earner marriages are a challenge for many children as well as their parents. While parents are at work, latchkey children often are at home alone.

including never having wanted them, not finding themselves in the right circumstances, and religious or environmental concerns. However, the desire not to have children often comes in conflict with society's *pro-natalist bias,* which assumes that having children is the norm and can be taken for granted, whereas those who choose not to have children must justify their decision to others (Stobert and Kemeny, 2003).

Some couples experience the condition of *involuntary infertility,* whereby they want to have a child but find that they are physically unable to do so. **Infertility is defined as an inability to conceive after a year of unprotected sexual relations**. A leading cause of infertility is sexually transmitted infections, especially those in cases that develop into pelvic inflammatory diseases. Although roughly half of those who seek fertility treatments can be helped, some remain unable to conceive despite expensive treatments such as in vitro fertilization, which costs as much as $12 000 per attempt (Norris, 2001).

People who are involuntarily childless may choose to become parents by adopting a child.

Adoption

Adoption is a legal process through which the rights and duties of parenting are transferred from a child's biological or legal parents to new legal parents. This procedure gives the adopted child all of the rights of a biological child. In most adoptions, a new birth certificate is issued, and the child has no further contact with the biological parents. In Canada, adoption is regulated provincially. Therefore, adopted persons' access to information regarding their biological parents varies, as does their desire to access this information (Jackson, 1993).

Matching children who are available for adoption with prospective adoptive parents can be difficult. The available children have specific needs, and the prospective parents often set specifications on the type of child they want to adopt. There are fewer infants available for adoption today than in the past because better means of contraception exist, abortion is more readily available, and more single parents decide to keep their babies. As a result, many prospective parents pursue international adoptions from countries including China, Haiti, South Korea, and India (Vanier Institute of the Family, 2008).

Assisted Reproductive Technologies

The availability of a variety of reproductive technologies is having a dramatic impact on traditional concepts of the family and parenthood. Since the first "test tube" baby was born in 1978, there has been an explosion of research, clinical practice, and experimentation in the area of reproductive technology. Procedures used in the creation of new life, such as artificial insemination and in vitro fertilization, are referred to as methods of assisted reproduction (Achilles, 1996). These procedures have raised some controversial ethical issues in terms of what role medical science should play in the creation of human life (Marquardt, 2006).

Artificial insemination is the oldest, simplest, and most common type of assisted reproduction. The most common form of artificial insemination is intrauterine insemination, which involves a physician inserting sperm directly into the uterus near the time of ovulation. Insemination may be performed with donor sperm.

There are several complex issues concerning the moral, legal, and social implications of artificial insemination. In most cases, the woman is given no information about the donor and the donor is not told whether a pregnancy has occurred. The result of this anonymity is that neither the mother nor the individuals conceived through donor insemination will have access to information regarding the biological father. With the exception of Quebec and Yukon, the law does not provide protection for the participants in this procedure. In Quebec, a child born through intrauterine insemination is legally considered to be the child of the *social* father, that is, the father who rears the child. In the Yukon, donors are protected from possible legal action by offspring or donor-sperm recipients (Achilles, 1996).

In light of all the assisted reproductive technologies available, what does the term *parent* mean? How many *parents* does the child have? Is *mother* an accurate term for the gestational surrogate mother? How do the children conceived with assisted reproductive technologies define their families? There are over a million donor-conceived children in the world. Now that they are able to speak for themselves, these children have raised some difficult questions about the rights of the child, biology, identity, and families. Some of these issues are highlighted in the following commentary:

> Is it right to deprive people of knowing who their natural parents are? What happens to your sense of identity when one of your biological parents is missing? Is there a difference when you're raised by "social" rather than biological parents? What if those parents are two women, or two men, or perhaps three people? Are children's understandings of parenthood as flexible as we would like to think? How do kids feel about all this? And do their feelings matter? (Wente, 2006:A21)

In 2004 legislation was enacted to regulate assisted reproductive technologies in Canada. This legislation forbids human cloning, sex selection, and buying or selling of human embryos and sperm. It further specifies that the practices of surrogate motherhood, donation of human sperm and embryos, and the use of human embryos and stem cells for scientific research are allowed (Department of Justice, 2009). The issues raised by this legislation have complex legal, social, moral, and ethical implications. However, the availability of these assisted reproductive technologies have enabled some infertile couples to become parents.

Single-Parent Households

Single parenting is not a new phenomenon in Canada. However, one of the most significant changes in Canadian families is the dramatic increase in single-parent families. Today, there are more than a million single-parent families, the majority of which (more than 80 percent) are headed by women. In the past, most single-parent families were created when one parent died. The major causes of single parenthood today are separation and divorce. Even for a person with a stable income and a network of friends and family to help with child-care, raising a child alone can be an emotional and financial burden. Children in single-parent families are more likely than children in two-parent families to exhibit poor academic achievement, higher school absentee and dropout rates, higher early marriage and early parenthood rates, and higher divorce rates, as well as being more likely to abuse drugs and alcohol (Ambert, 2006). Does living in a one-parent family cause all of this? Certainly not! Many other factors—including discrimination, unsafe neighbourhoods, and high crime rates—contribute to these problems.

Single fathers who do not have custody of their children may play a relatively limited role in the lives of those children. Although some remain actively involved in their children's lives, others may become less involved, spending time with their children around recreational activities and on special occasions. Sometimes this limited role is by choice, but more often it is caused by workplace demands on time and energy, the location of the ex-wife's residence, and the limitations placed on the visitation arrangements. Currently, men head close to one-fifth of single-parent families; among many of these men, a pattern of "involved fatherhood" has emerged (Vanier Institute of the Family, 2009b).

Remarriage

Most people who divorce get remarried (Ambert, 2005b), and most divorced people remarry others who have been divorced. Remarriage rates, however, vary by gender. At all ages, a greater proportion of men than women remarry (an estimated 70 percent of men and 58 percent of women), but both often do so relatively soon after their divorce (Ambert, 2005b). Among women, the older a woman is at the time of divorce, the lower the likelihood of her remarrying. Women who have not graduated from high school and have young children tend to remarry relatively quickly; by contrast, women with a university degree and without children are less likely to remarry (Clark and Kennedy, 2006).

Some of these remarriages involve children from a previous relationship, thus creating stepfamilies or *blended families,* which consist of a husband and wife, children from previous marriages, and children (if any) from the new marriage. Canada had just over 500 000 step-families in 2001, accounting for almost 12 percent of all couples with children (Ambert 2005b).

TRANSITIONS AND PROBLEMS IN FAMILIES

Families go through many transitions and experience a wide variety of problems, ranging from separation and divorce, to unplanned pregnancy, to family violence. These all-too-common experiences highlight two important facts about families: (1) for good or ill, families are central to our existence; and (2) the reality of family life is far more complicated than the idealized image found in the media and in many political discussions. Whereas some families provide their members with love, warmth, and satisfying emotional experiences, other families may be hazardous to the individual's physical and mental well-being. Because of this dichotomy in family life, sociologists have described families as both a "haven in a heartless world" (Lasch, 1977) and a "cradle of violence" (Gelles and Straus, 1988).

Family Violence

Violence between men and women in the home is often referred to as spousal abuse or domestic violence. *Spousal abuse* refers to the violence or mistreatment that a woman or a man experiences at the hands of a marital, common-law, or same-sex partner. Forms of spousal abuse include physical abuse, sexual abuse, and economic or financial abuse (Department of Justice, 2002b). As discussed in Chapter 3, *child abuse* refers to physical abuse, sexual abuse, or neglect by a parent or caregiver.

How much do we know about violence in families? Women, as compared to men, are more likely to be victims of violence perpetrated by intimate partners. Recent statistics indicate that women are five times more likely than men to experience such violence and that many of these women live in households with children witnessing the violence (Ogrodnik, 2008). Experts suggest that the prevalence of family violence may be much higher than this figure, given that these sources cannot capture all incidents of violence in the home. Self-report data indicates that many abuse victims do not—or cannot—report their experiences to the police.

Children who are raised in an environment of violence suffer profoundly, even if they are not the direct targets. Their own physical and emotional needs are often neglected, and they may learn by example to deal with conflict through violence (Dauvergne and Johnson, 2001).

Why has our society been slow to respond to the problem of domestic violence, whether in the form of child or spouse abuse? Until recently, individuals and law-enforcement officials have followed a policy of *nonintervention,* which was based on a strong reluctance to interfere in other people's family matters. Only within the past few decades have various forms of domestic violence been defined as intolerable criminal offences. Historically, domestic abuse was seen as a private family matter. Police reacted to calls for assistance with frustration or apathy, viewing responses to "domestic" calls as a waste of valuable time and resources. The general perception was that battered women could simply leave an abusive relationship if they so wanted.

The women's movement was largely responsible for challenging these misconceptions and bringing the issue of wife abuse into the public and political arenas.

Divorce

Divorce is the legal process of dissolving a marriage that allows former spouses to remarry if they so choose. Before 1968 it was difficult to obtain a divorce in Canada; a divorce was granted only on the grounds of adultery. In 1968, the grounds for divorce were expanded to include marital breakdown (i.e., desertion, imprisonment, or separation of three or more years) and marital offences (physical or mental cruelty). In 1985, the Divorce Act introduced "no fault" provisions that made marital breakdown the sole ground for divorce. Under no-fault divorce laws, proof of "blameworthiness" is no longer necessary. However, when children are involved, the issue of "blame" may assume greater importance in the determination of parental custody.

Have you heard statements such as "One out of every two marriages ends in divorce"? Statistics might initially appear to bear out this statement. In 2005, for example, 148 439 Canadian couples married and 71 269 divorces were granted (Statistics Canada,

2009c). However, comparing the number of marriages with the number of divorces from year to year can be misleading. The couples that divorce in a given year are unlikely to come from the group that married that year. In addition, in years when the economy is in a recession people may delay getting married but not divorced. Some people also may go through several marriages and divorces, thus skewing the divorce rate. The likelihood of divorce goes up with each subsequent marriage in the serial monogamy pattern (Clark and Crompton, 2006).

In order to assess the probability of a marriage ending in divorce, it is necessary to use what is referred to as a *cohort approach.* This approach establishes probabilities based on assumptions about how the various age groups (cohorts) in society might behave, given their marriage rate, their age at first marriage, and their responses to various social, cultural, and economic changes. Canadian estimates based on a cohort approach are that 35 to 40 percent of marriages will end in divorce (Ambert, 2005b)

Causes of Divorce   Why do divorces occur? As you will recall from Chapter 1, sociologists look for correlations (relationships between two variables) in attempting to answer questions such as this. Existing research has identified a number of factors at both the macrolevel and microlevel that make some couples more or less likely to divorce. At the macrolevel, societal factors contributing to higher rates of divorce include changes in social institutions, such as religion, the family, and the legal system. Some religions have taken a more lenient attitude toward divorce, and the social stigma associated with divorce has lessened. Further, as we have seen in this chapter, the family institution has undergone a major change that has resulted in less economic and emotional dependency among family members—and thus reduced a barrier to divorce. And, as Figure 12.1 (on page 300) demonstrates, the liberalization of divorce laws in Canada has had a dramatic impact on the divorce rate.

At the microlevel, a number of factors contribute to a couple's "statistical" likelihood of becoming divorced. Some of the primary risk factors for divorce include (Ambert, 2005b):

- youthful marriage,
- low incomes and poverty, as well as rapid upward social mobility,
- cohabitation prior to marriage,
- remarriage,
- parents who are divorced or have unhappy marriages,

■ low religiosity, and

■ the presence of children (depending on their gender and age at the beginning of the marriage).

The interrelationships of these and other factors are complicated. For example, the effect of age is intertwined with economic resources: persons from families at the low end of the income scale tend to marry earlier than those at more affluent income levels. Thus, the question becomes whether age itself is a factor or whether economic resources are more closely associated with divorce.

Consequences of Divorce   Divorce may have a dramatic economic and emotional impact on family members. The exact number of children affected by divorce in Canada is difficult to determine because no official information is available on out-of-court custody decisions. A conservative estimate for 2001 of the number of children who have experienced the separation and divorce of their parents in Canada is around two million (Wichmann, 2005). Every year, approximately 40 000 Canadian children are involved in custody disputes. In just over 50 percent of these

cases, the mother will be awarded custody (Statistics Canada, 2002h). Parental joint custody is awarded for some divorcing couples. When joint custody is a voluntary arrangement and when there is motivation to make it work, it has benefits for both children and parents (Ambert, 2005b). However, this arrangement may also create unique problems for children, who must adjust to living in two homes and to the fact that their parents no longer live together. The worst thing that can happen to a child after a divorce is that his or her parents remain in conflict (Buchanan, Maccoby, and Dornbush, 1996).

DIVERSITY IN FAMILIES

Gay and Lesbian Families

Lesbians and gay men grow up in families; establish long-lasting, committed, emotional relationships; and sometimes become parents. Nevertheless, until recently, discussions of gay and lesbian relationships

| **Figure 12.1** | **Divorces in Canada** |

The consequences of divorce are not entirely negative. There is no doubt that some children are better off after their parents' divorce. For some people, divorce may be an opportunity to terminate destructive relationships. For others, it may represent a means to achieve personal growth by enabling them to manage their lives and social relationships and establish their own identity.

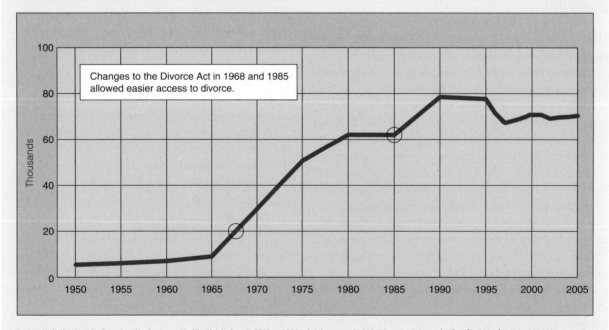

Source: Statistics Canada, *Report on the Demographic Situation in Canada 2003 and 2004*, Catalogue no. 91-209-XIE, www.statcan.gc.ca/pub/91-209-x/91-209-x2003000-eng.pdf

The issue of same-sex marriage remains a hotly debated topic in Canada.

Adoption is a complex legal process for most parents; it can be even more complicated for gay and lesbian couples.

and families have been excluded from discussions of the family. These relationships were considered by many as threatening to notions of the traditional family. Notions of the family that are limited to unions between members of the opposite sex are examples of *heterosexism*—**an attitude in which heterosexuality is considered the only valid form of sexual behaviour, and gay men, lesbians, and bisexuals are inferior to heterosexual people**.

In Canada, the law grants particular rights, benefits, and privileges only to heterosexual relationships, especially legally married partners. Until recently, gay and lesbian couples have been prohibited from jointly adopting children, sponsoring their partner's immigration to Canada, obtaining custody of their children, or receiving spousal benefits and survivor's pensions. Until very recently, same-sex couples were prohibited from legally marrying in Canada. This lack of recognition has had emotional, legal, and economic consequences for same-sex families.

In contrast to stereotypes of same-sex relationships as short term, promiscuous, and noncommitted, research on homosexual relationships indicates that partnerships lasting 20 years or more are not uncommon (Ambert, 2005a). In fact, the breakup rates of married or cohabiting heterosexual couples and lesbian and gay couples have been found to be approximately equal. However, studies have found that lesbian and gay relationships are more egalitarian than heterosexual relationships. This finding is in part attributable to the fact that in virtually all lesbian and gay relationships both partners are wage earners (Ambert, 2005a).

An increasing number of lesbian and gay males form families with children. In the 2006 census, over 45 000 couples identified themselves as same-sex married or common-law couples (Statistics Canada, 2007c). In many cases, lesbian mothers and gay fathers may have children from a previous marriage or relationship. However, not all children in same-sex families are products of previous heterosexual relationships. Lesbians may become pregnant through *alternative insemination* (sexual relations as a means to get pregnant) or artificial insemination (Epstein, 2003). Lesbian mothers and gay fathers may also form families through fostering or adoption. Unlike many heterosexual families in which both mother and father have genetic links to their children, gay and lesbian families always have a nonbiological parent. These nonbiological parents are often not regarded as parents either socially or legally. For example, nonbiological parents may not be granted admission to parent–teacher interviews or may be denied permission to make important medical decisions for their children if the biological parent is unavailable. Anne, a lesbian mother, describes one of her encounters with the medical profession:

> You can tell the doctor three times, "Talk to me like I'm his mother; so is she," and they don't get it. Sometimes they really say, "I don't know what you're talking about." [And we'll answer,] "We're two lesbians, we're both the mother." "Huh. No, I'll talk to the one with the dress, that's safe."
> (Quoted in Rachel Epstein, 1996:123)

Many people believe that being parented by same-sex couples is emotionally unhealthy for children and can cause them confusion about their own sexuality. However, research has consistently shown that the children of lesbians and gay men are as well adjusted as children who grow up in heterosexual households. In addition, these children experience no psychological damage, and they are no more likely to be homosexual than are children raised by heterosexual parents (Ambert, 2005a). According to Rachel Epstein (2003), there can be positive effects of being raised by lesbian or gay parents, such as a greater appreciation of diversity and increased tolerance of individual differences.

Diversity among Singles

Although marriage at increasingly younger ages was the trend in Canada during the first half of the 20th century, by the 1960s the trend had reversed itself, and many more adults were remaining single. In 1971, close to half of Canadians aged 20 to 24 were already married. Today, almost 90 percent of Canadians in the same age group were single (Statistics Canada, 2007c). Currently, approximately 25 percent of households in Canada are single-person households. However, this estimate includes people who are divorced, widowed, and those who have never married. Given that nine out of ten Canadians marry at some time in their lives, single status is often temporary. Only an estimated 10 percent of the population will remain single throughout their lives Some never-married singles remain single by choice. Reasons include more opportunity for a career (especially for women), the availability of sexual partners without marriage, the belief that the single lifestyle is full of excitement, and the desire for self-sufficiency and freedom to change and experiment (Stein, 1976, 1981). Some scholars have concluded that individuals who prefer to remain single hold more individualistic values and are less family-oriented than those who choose to marry. Friends and personal growth tend to be valued more highly than marriage and children (Alwin, Converse, and Martin, 1985; Nett, 1993; Turcotte, 2006). Other never-married singles remain single out of necessity. Being single is an economic necessity for those who cannot afford to marry and set up their own household (Turcotte, 2006)

Aboriginal Families

It is difficult to discuss Aboriginal families given that Aboriginal peoples in Canada are by no means a homogeneous group. Aboriginal peoples are composed of many distinct nations with different histories, cultures, economic bases, and languages (Das Gupta, 2000). However, in all Aboriginal families, the extended family was seen as central to both the individual and the community. The concept of family was defined very broadly. For example, to the Ojibwa, *family* referred to individuals who worked as a unit and were bound together by responsibility and friendship as well as kinship ties. Family size averaged between 20 and 25 persons (Shkilnyk, 1985). A band member describes the economic cooperation and sharing that once existed within the Ojibwa family:

> Trapping kept the family together because everyone in the family had something to do; the man had to lay traps and check them; the woman skinned the animals, cooked, and looked after the kids. The grandparents helped with the kids; they taught them manners, how to behave, and told them stories about our people. The kids, if they were old enough, had work to do. (Shkilnyk, 1985:81)

Under this extended and cooperative family system, Aboriginal families were extremely successful in ensuring the survival and well-being of their members.

Four hundred years after contact with the European settlers, the current state of family disruption is evident when you consider the following data: Aboriginal children represent 40 percent of children placed in care in Canada; the rate of wife abuse among Aboriginal peoples is five times the national average; and the suicide rate of Aboriginal peoples is double the rate of the general population (Ogrodnik, 2008; Assembly of First Nations, 2008). How did this happen? Aboriginal family life was profoundly changed as a result of interventionist strategies employed by the Canadian church and state. Families were displaced from their traditional lands, moved to reserves, and denied access to the resources that were central to the economic survival of the extended family unit. Aboriginal children were removed from their families and placed in residential schools (where they were often sexually and physically abused) or adopted by non-Aboriginal families. Generations of Aboriginal children were separated from their families and their communities, and this separation also served to sever links with Aboriginal culture and languages.

After generations of cultural and spiritual destruction, Aboriginal peoples are now reclaiming their culture. They have also united behind the goal of self-government, especially in the areas of social services and child welfare (Castellano, 2002). Aboriginal peoples believe in maintaining the ties between children and their natural parents, as well as caring for children within their Aboriginal communities. They see this as essential to the rebuilding of Aboriginal families in Canada. Many Aboriginal communities are striving to return to the practices and values that traditionally nourished Aboriginal family life: respect for women and children, mutual responsibility, and, above all, the general creed of sharing and caring (Royal Commission on Aboriginal Peoples, 1995:81).

THEORETICAL PERSPECTIVES ON FAMILIES

The *sociology of family* **is the subdiscipline of sociology that attempts to describe and explain patterns of family life and variations in family structure**. Functionalist perspectives emphasize the functions that families perform at the macrolevel of society, while conflict and feminist perspectives focus on families as a primary source of social inequality. By contrast, symbolic interactionists examine microlevel interactions that are integral to the roles of different family members. Finally, postmodern theorists emphasize that families today are diverse and variable.

Functionalist Perspectives

Functionalists emphasize the importance of the family in maintaining the stability of society and the well-being of individuals. According to Emile Durkheim, marriage is a microcosmic replica of the larger society; both marriage and society involve a mental and moral fusion of physically distinct individuals (Lehmann, 1994). Durkheim also believed that a division of labour contributed to greater efficiency in all areas of life—including marriages and families—even though he acknowledged that this division imposed significant limitations on some people.

Talcott Parsons was a key figure in developing a functionalist model of the family. According to Parsons (1955), the husband/father fulfills the *instrumental role* (meeting the family's economic needs, making important decisions, and providing leadership) while the wife/mother fulfills the *expressive role* (running the household, caring for children, and meeting the emotional needs of family members).

Contemporary functionalist perspectives on families derive their foundation from Durkheim and Parsons. Division of labour makes it possible for families to fulfill a number of functions that no other institution can perform as effectively. In advanced industrial societies, families serve four key functions:

1. *Sexual regulation.* Families are expected to regulate the sexual activity of their members and thus control reproduction so that it occurs within specific boundaries. At the macrolevel, incest taboos prohibit sexual contact or marriage between certain relatives. For example, virtually all societies prohibit sexual relations between parents and their children and between brothers and sisters.
2. *Socialization.* Parents and other relatives are responsible for teaching children the necessary knowledge and skills to survive. The smallness and intimacy of families make them best suited for providing children with the initial learning experiences they need.
3. *Economic and psychological support.* Families are responsible for providing economic and psychological support for members. In pre-industrial societies, families are economic production units; in industrial societies, the economic security of families is tied to the workplace and to macrolevel economic systems. In recent years, psychological support and emotional security have been increasingly important functions of the family
4. *Provision of social status.* Families confer social status and reputation on their members. These statuses include the ascribed statuses with which individuals are born, such as race/ethnicity, nationality, social class, and sometimes religious affiliation. One of the most significant and compelling forms of social placement is the family's class position and the opportunities (or lack thereof) resulting from that position. Examples of class-related opportunities include access to quality health care, higher education, and a safe place to live.

Conflict Perspectives

Both conflict and feminist analysts view functionalist perspectives on the role of the family in society as idealized and inadequate. Rather than operating harmoniously and for the benefit of all members, families are sources of social inequality and conflict over values, goals, and access to resources and power (Benokraitis, 2002).

In his classic work *The Origin of the Family, Private Property and the State* (1972/1884), Friedrich Engels argued that the family in a capitalist society is an exploitive social institution that oppresses women. According to conflict theorists, families in capitalist economies are similar to workers in a factory. Women are dominated by men in the home in the same manner that workers are dominated by capitalists and managers in factories. Although childbearing and childcare for family members in the home contribute to capitalism, these activities also reinforce the subordination of women through unpaid (and often devalued) labour. As a result, husbands—like capitalists—enjoy more power and privilege within the family. Engels predicted that the oppression of women would end when women moved out of the private sphere of the home and into the paid workforce. As discussed in Chapter 10, women's oppression has not disappeared as a result of the dramatic increases in the number of women in the paid workforce; in many ways, it has become more prevalent as women struggle with issues of gender inequality in pay and benefits, job advancement, and balancing career and home responsibilities. Other conflict analysts are concerned with the effect that class conflict has on the family. The exploitation of the lower classes by the upper classes contributes to family problems such as high rates of divorce and overall family instability.

Feminist Perspectives

The contributions of feminist theorists have resulted in radical changes in the sociological study of families. Feminist theorists have been primarily responsible for redefining the concept of "the family," focusing on the diversity of family arrangements. Some feminist scholars reject the "monolithic model of the family" (Eichler, 1981:368), which idealizes one family form—the family with a male breadwinner and stay-at-home wife and children—as the normal family arrangement. Feminist theorists argue that limiting our concept of family to this traditional form means ignoring or undervaluing diverse family forms, such as single-parent families, childless families, gay or lesbian families, and stepfamilies. Roles within the family are viewed by feminist theorists as primarily socially constructed rather than biologically determined. Feminist scholars have challenged a number of common assumptions about family life and the roles we fulfill within families. For example, they question whether all "real" women want to be mothers, or whether the inequality between

traditional husbands and wives is "natural" (Mandell and Duffy, 2005).

Feminist perspectives on inequality focus on **patriarchy—a hierarchical system of social organization in which cultural, political, and economic structures are controlled by men**. From this viewpoint, men's domination over women existed long before private ownership of property and capitalism (Mann, 1994). Women's subordination is rooted in patriarchy and men's control over women's labour power (Hartmann, 1981). Although the division of labour may appear to be an equal pooling of contributions within the family unit, feminist scholars view women as giving much but receiving less in return. According to Patricia Mann, "Male power in our society is expressed in economic terms even if it does not originate in property relations; women's activities in the home have been undervalued at the same time as their labour has been controlled by men" (1994:42).

Feminist perspectives on families primarily focus on the problems of dominance and subordination inherent in relationships. Specifically, feminist theorists have acknowledged what has been described as the "dark side of the family," focusing on research efforts on issues such as child abuse, wife abuse, and violence against the elderly. Feminist explanations take into account the unequal political relationship between women and men in families and outside families (Ambert, 2001; Comack, 1996b; Smith, 1985; Hamilton, 1988).

Symbolic Interactionist Perspectives

Early symbolic interactionists viewed the communication process in families as integral to the roles that different family members play. Symbolic interactionists examine the roles of husbands, wives, and children as they act out their own parts and react to the actions of others. From this perspective, what people think, as well as what they say and do, is important in understanding family dynamics.

According to Peter Berger and Hansfried Kellner (1964), interaction between marital partners contributes to a shared reality. Although newlyweds bring separate identities to a marriage, over time they construct a shared reality as a couple. In the process, the partners redefine their past identities to be consistent with new realities. Development of a shared reality is a continuous process, taking place not only in the family but also in any group in which the couple participates. Divorce is the reverse of this process; couples may start with a shared reality and, in the process of uncoupling, gradually develop separate realities (Vaughan, 1985).

Symbolic interactionists explain family relationships in terms of the subjective meanings and everyday interpretations people give to their lives. Sociologist Jessie Bernard (1982/1973) pointed out that women and men experience marriage differently, and a marriage, in effect, contains two marriages: "his marriage" and "her marriage." While a husband may see his marriage very positively, his wife may feel less positive about her marriage, and vice versa. Researchers have found that husbands and wives may give rather different accounts of the same event, and their two "realities" frequently do not coincide (Safilios-Rothschild, 1969).

Postmodern Perspectives

Although postmodern theorists disparage the idea that a universal theory can be developed to explain social life, a postmodern perspective might provide insights on questions such as this: How is family life different in the Information Age? Social scientist David Elkind (1995) describes the postmodern family as *permeable*—capable of being diffused or invaded in such a manner that an entity's original purpose is modified or changed. According to Elkind (1995), if the nuclear family is a reflection of the age of modernity, the permeable family reflects the postmodern assumptions of difference, particularity, and irregularity. Difference is evident in that the nuclear family is now only one of many family forms. Similarly, the idea of romantic love under modernity has given way to the idea of consensual love: Individuals agree to have sexual relations with others whom they have no intention of marrying, or, if they marry, do not necessarily see the marriage as having permanence. Maternal love has also been transformed into shared parenting, which includes not only mothers and fathers but also caregivers, who may be either relatives or nonrelatives (Elkind, 1995).

Urbanity is another characteristic of the postmodern family. The boundaries between the public sphere (the workplace) and the private sphere (the home) are becoming more open and flexible. In fact, family life may be negatively affected by the decreasing distinction between what is work time and what is family time. As more people are becoming connected "24/7," the boss who before would not have called at 11:30 p.m. or when an employee is on vacation may send an e-mail asking for an immediate response to some question that has arisen while the person is away with family members (Leonard, 1999). According to

some postmodern analysts, this is an example of the "power of the new communications technologies to integrate and control labour despite extensive dispersion and decentralization" (Haraway, 1994:439).

Social theorist Jean Baudrillard's idea that the simulation of reality may come to be viewed as "reality" by some people can be applied to family interactions in the Information Age. Does the ability to contact someone anywhere and anytime provide greater happiness and stability in families? Or is "reach out and touch someone" merely an ideology promulgated by the consumer society? Journalists have written about the experience of watching a family gathering at an amusement park, restaurant, mall, or other location only to see family members pick up their cell phones to receive or make calls to individuals not present, rather than spending "face time" with those family members who are present.

Concept Table 13.1 (on page 306) summarizes these sociological perspectives on the family. Taken together, these perspectives on the social institution of families help us understand both the good and bad sides of familial relationships. Now we shift our focus to love, marriage, intimate relationships, and family issues in Canada.

FAMILY ISSUES IN THE FUTURE

As we have seen, families and intimate relationships have changed dramatically over the last century. Some people believe that family as we know it is doomed. Others believe that a return to traditional values will save this important social institution and create greater stability in society. Family diversity is perceived as an indication that Canadian families are in "decline" or "crisis." In reality, family diversity is the norm in Canadian society, past and present. The diversity in Canadian families has simply taken on new forms, with increases in common-law unions, gay and lesbian families, and single-parent and blended families.

One of the most notable changes in the past 50 years has been the increase in dual-wage earner families. The labour-force participation rate of women, particularly married women, has increased dramatically. However, regardless of women's labour-force participation, women are still primarily responsible for childcare, senior care, and domestic chores (Marshall, 2009b). The gap between men and women in the division of labour still exists; but it is getting narrower. The absence of adequate, affordable childcare; inflexible work hours; and parental leave policies means that work is structured in ways that are not "family friendly" (Friendly and Prentice, 2009). With an aging population, the "sandwich generation" is growing. The term refers to an increasing number of Canadians who are sandwiched between aging parents who need care and their own children. A challenge for families is to find ways to reconcile family and work contradictions. As gender roles continue to change, we can expect to see a greater degree of egalitarianism within the family.

Regardless of problems facing families in the future, the family remains the central institution in the lives of most Canadians. A recent national opinion poll found that over three-quarters of Canadians regard the family as the most important thing in their lives, more important than their career or religion. Ninety-two percent of the respondents with young children at home indicated that the family is becoming more important to them. Finally, an overwhelming majority demonstrated their faith in the family by indicating that they want to marry and have children (although fewer children than in the past) (Bibby, 2004). Individuals in families are now freer to establish the kinds of family arrangements that best suit them.

Concept Table 12.1   THEORETICAL PERSPECTIVES ON FAMILIES

PERSPECTIVE	FOCUS	KEY POINTS	PERSPECTIVE ON FAMILY PROBLEMS
Functionalist	Role of families in maintaining stability of society and individuals' well-being	In modern societies, families serve the functions of sexual regulation, socialization, economic and psychological support, and provision of social status.	Family problems are related to changes in social institutions, such as the economy, religion, education, and law/government.
Conflict	Families as sources of conflict and social inequality	Families both mirror and help perpetuate social inequalities based on class and gender.	Family problems reflect social patterns of dominance and subordination.
Feminist	Families are patriarchal institutions	Women's subordination is rooted in patriarchy and men's control over women's labour power.	Family problems, such as child abuse, wife abuse, and elder abuse are the result of attempts to control women and perpetuate gender inequality.
Symbolic Interactionist	Family dynamics, including communication patterns and subjective meanings people assign to events	Interactions within families create a shared reality.	How family problems are perceived and defined depends on patterns of communication, the meanings people give to roles and events, and individuals' interpretations of family interactions.
Postmodern	Permeability of families	In postmodern societies, families are diverse and fragmented. Boundaries between workplace and home are blurred.	Family problems are related to cyberspace, consumerism, and the hyper-real in an age increasingly characterized by high-tech "haves" and "have-nots."

What is a family?

Families may be defined as relationships in which people live together with commitment, form an economic unit and care for any young, and consider their identity to be significantly attached to the group.

What pattern of marriage is legally sanctioned in Canada?

Monogamy, marriage to one person at a time, is the only form of marriage sanctioned by law in Canada.

What are the functionalist, conflict, feminist, symbolic interactionist, and postmodern perspectives on families?

Functionalists emphasize the importance of the family in maintaining the stability of society and the well-being of its individuals. Functions of the family include sexual regulation, socialization, economic and psychological support, and provision of social status. Both conflict and feminist perspectives view the family as a source of social inequality and as an arena for conflict over values, goals, and access to resources and power. Conflict theorists view the family in a capitalist society as an exploitive institution that is primarily responsible for women's oppression. Feminist scholars focus on patriarchy as the source of inequality between men and women. Symbolic interactionists explain family relationships in terms of the subjective meanings and everyday interpretations people give to their lives. Postmodern analysts view families as permeable, reflecting the individualism, particularity, and irregularity of social life in the Information Age.

How are Canadian families changing?

Cohabitation has increased significantly in the past two decades. With the rise in dual-earner marriages, women increasingly have been burdened by the second shift—the domestic work that employed women perform at home after they complete their paid workday. The number of single-parent families has also increased dramatically.

KEY TERMS

bilateral descent 291
cohabitation 293
dual-earner families 295
egalitarian family 291
extended family 288
families 287
families we choose 286
family of orientation 287

family of procreation 287
heterosexism 301
homogamy 295
infertility 296
kinship 287
marriage 289
matriarchal family 291
matrilineal descent 291
monogamy 289
nuclear family 288
patriarchy 304
patriarchal family 291
patrilineal descent 290
polyandry 289
polygamy 289
polygyny 289
second shift 295
sociology of family 303

WEB LINKS

For more Web links related to the topic of this chapter, see the Nelson sociology website:
www.sociologyessentials5e.nelson.com

The Vanier Institute of the Family provides the most comprehensive information on Canadian families:
www.vifamily.ca

PFLAG (Parents and Friends of Lesbians and Gays) is a national organization promoting the health and well-being of gay, lesbian, bisexual, and transgendered persons and their families and friends:
www.pflag.ca

QUESTIONS FOR CRITICAL THINKING

1. In your own thinking, what constitutes an ideal family? How might functionalist, conflict, feminist, symbolic interactionist, and postmodern perspectives describe the ideal family?
2. Based on your understanding of the term *family*, should the following be considered families?
   - man, woman, no children; married but living apart;
   - woman, woman, child of one woman; living together (women are a same-sex couple);
   - man, his biological child and woman (not his wife) with whom he has a sexual relationship; living together; or
   - four adults; sharing a household for many years (none are a same-sex couple).

3. Do you think reproductive technology should be allowed to help people pre-select the sex of a fetus? Why or why not? Do you think pre-selection of sex would have an impact on the number of children couples had? What effect might this have on the sex ratio in Canada and other countries?

ONLINE STUDY AND RESEARCH TOOLS

INFOTRAC®

InfoTrac College Edition is included free with every new copy of this text. Explore this online library for additional readings, review, and a handy resource for assignments. Visit **www.infotrac-college.com** to access this online database of full-text articles. Enter the key terms from this chapter to start your search.

CENGAGENOW™ CENGAGENOW

Use CengageNOW™ to help you formulate a customized study plan for this chapter. After you take the Diagnostic Quiz, CengageNOW™ will generate a customized study plan for you. It will identify sections of the chapter you should review.

CHAPTER

13

Politics

Compared to most other nations, Canada has had a peaceful political history. However, there have been instances of political violence. During the 1960s and early 1970s, a group called the Front de Libération du Québec (FLQ) committed a number of terrorist acts, which culminated in the kidnapping of a British diplomat and the murder of a Quebec cabinet minister. One of the intellectual leaders of the FLQ was Pierre Vallières. In *White Niggers of America*, a book he wrote in prison following his arrest for the murder of a woman who died in one of the terrorist bomb attacks carried out by the FLQ, Vallières outlined some of the grievances of the Quebec separatists:

In writing this book I claim to do no more than bear witness to the determination of the workers of Quebec to put an end to three centuries of exploitation, of injustices borne in silence, of sacrifices accepted in vain, of insecurity endured with resignation; to bear witness to their new and increasingly energetic determination to take control of their economic, political, and social affairs and to transform into a more just and fraternal society this country, Quebec, which is theirs, this country where they have always been the overwhelming majority of citizens and producers of the "national" wealth, yet where they never have enjoyed the economic power and social freedom to which their numbers and labor entitle them. (1971:17)

While this sounds much like the rhetoric of present-day Quebec separatists, FLQ members also believed in a revolutionary Marxist ideology, which justified violence. Vallières, who saw himself as a political prisoner rather than as a "common criminal," described the two goals of his movement in this way:

The FLQ is . . . the armed avant-garde of the exploited classes of Quebec: the workers, the farmers, the petty white-collar workers, the students, the unemployed, and those on welfare—that is, at least 90 percent of the population. The FLQ is struggling not only for the political independence of Quebec, but also and inseparably for the revolution, a total revolution which will give all power

to the workers and students in a free, self-administering, and fraternal society. Only a total revolution will make it possible for the Québécois, in collaboration with the other peoples of the earth, to build a Quebec that is truly free, truly sovereign. (1971:258–259)

Many Quebeckers still dream of independence, though few now share Vallières's views about the need for a violent revolution. Feeling their culture threatened by the influence of English-speaking North America, separatists believe they can fulfill their destiny only as a distinct "people" through political independence. Although the separatists lost the October 1995 referendum by the narrowest of margins and were supported by a large majority of French-speaking voters, the feelings of Quebeckers remain ambivalent. A poll conducted after the referendum found that two-thirds of Quebeckers wanted their province to remain part of Canada. However, the same poll showed that 55 percent would vote for separation. These data reflect Quebec comedian Yvon Deschamps's perception that what Québécois really want is an independent Quebec within a strong and united Canada. The data also suggest that some flexibility from the other provinces concerning Quebec's

Two solitudes: In the 1990s, then Quebec Premier Lucien Bouchard and then Prime Minister Jean Chrétien were the two people responsible for Canada's future as a nation. Does the body language in this photo suggest that cooperation was likely?

Shaun Best/Reuters/Landov

place in Canada would ensure that our country stays together, as many Quebeckers would clearly prefer constitutional reform to separation.

Interestingly, Vallières reflected these two different strains of political thought in Quebec. After his release from prison, he disavowed violence and became a member of the separatist Parti Québécois. Prior to his death in 1998, however, he rejected separatism, fearing it would lead to ethnic and linguistic apartheid. (Late in his life, Vallieres had been horrified by the ethnic violence in the former Yugoslavia.)

This chapter is about politics and politics is about power. Our political and state institutions are the means through which that power is exercised. Those who control these institutions can implement policies that reflect their interests and values. There are constant tensions as different groups compete to gain the power they need to change social policy.

Modern nations face tremendous political challenges. Resolving the future of Quebec is just one of the political issues facing Canadians. In this chapter, we will discuss some of these issues and describe the political system through which Canadians will deal with them. We will also examine other systems of government. Before reading on, test your knowledge about political issues and state institutions by taking the quiz in Box 13.1.

QUESTIONS AND ISSUES

Chapter Focus Question: Can the aspirations of Aboriginal people and French-speaking Quebeckers be accommodated within the Canadian political system?

What is the relationship between power and authority? Why do people accept authority?

What are the major political systems?

Whose interests are reflected in political decisions?

How is government shaped by political parties and political attitudes?

Why is nationalism such an important force in the world today?

What is the place of democracy in the 21st century?

POLITICS, POWER, AND AUTHORITY

Political participation, measured by indicators such as the percentage of people who vote in elections, have

been steadily declining. Many Canadians, particularly young people, seem to feel that politics is irrelevant to their lives. However, politics is vitally important to all of us, and many things about your future will be affected by political decisions. At the extreme, we can look at "failed states" such as Somalia and Haiti,

SOCIOLOGY AND EVERYDAY LIFE

How Much Do You Know About Political and State Institutions?

J⭘in

True	False	
(T)	F	1. Organizations in which authority is based on the charismatic qualities of particular leaders can be unstable, and these kinds of organizations often fail.
T	(F)	2. In Canada, our constitutional right to freedom of speech means that pornography and hate literature can be legally distributed.
(T)	F	3. While authoritarian governments still exist in many countries, democratic government has become more widespread throughout the world during the past 20 years.
T	(F)	4. In Canada, members of the governing party are free to vote against the government in Parliament whenever they wish.
T	(F)	5. Canada's Aboriginal peoples have been able to vote in federal elections since Confederation in 1867.
T	(F)	6. All citizens have an equal say in government decisions.
(T)	F	7. Canada has had a female prime minister.
(T)	F	8. Canada is one of the few nations in the world that has had as its official opposition in Parliament a political party dedicated to the breakup of the country.
T	(F)	9. A higher proportion of Canadians vote in federal elections than do the citizens of other industrialized countries.
T	(F)	10. Under most proposals for Aboriginal self-government, Aboriginal groups in Canada would have total control over their territory and would be considered sovereign nations.

Answers on page 314.

where politics has failed and where most people live miserable lives on the edge of starvation. Even in Canada, political decisions affect almost all aspects of our lives. Parenti has described the impact of politics:

> The taxes and prices we pay and the jobs available to us, the chances that we will live in peace or perish in war, the costs of education and the availability of scholarships, the safety of the airliner or highway we travel on, the quality of the food we eat and the air we breathe, the availability of affordable housing and medical care, the legal protections against racial and sexual discrimination—all the things that directly affect the quality of our lives are influenced in some measure by politics. (1996:7–8)

Politics has a major impact on our daily lives. During much of the 1990s governments sought to reduce the role of government, and many of its functions were cut or contracted out to private companies. However, disasters such as destruction of financial markets in 2008, the water-contamination deaths of people in Walkerton, Ontario, and the 2003 SARS outbreak are reminders of the important role that governments must play in protecting the public from harm.

Politics is the social institution through which power is acquired and exercised by some people and groups. In contemporary societies, the government is the primary political system. **Government is the formal organization that has the legal and political authority to regulate the relationships among members of a society and between the society and those outside its borders.** Some social scientists refer to government as the *state*—**the political entity that possesses a legitimate monopoly over the use of force within its territory to achieve its goals.**

Power and Authority

Power is the ability of people or groups to carry out their will despite opposition from others (Weber, 1968/1922). Through the use of persuasion, authority, or force, some people are able to get others

BOX 13.1   SOCIOLOGY AND EVERYDAY LIFE

Answers to the Sociology Quiz on Political Issues and State Institutions

1. True. Many political and religious movements that are held together by the personal qualities of their leader fail when the leader dies, retires, or is found to be "ordinary."

2. False. While the Canadian Charter of Rights and Freedoms does guarantee the freedom of speech, all freedoms are subject to "reasonable limits." Our courts have interpreted this to allow governments some powers of censorship.

3. True. The movement toward democratic government sped up dramatically with the fall of the Berlin Wall in 1989 and the subsequent breakup of the Soviet Union. A number of countries in Africa and in Central and South America have also become democracies since that time, but this progress has stalled in recent years (Freedom House, 2009).

4. False. In the United States, members of Congress who belong to the same party as the president often vote against the president. However, in Canada party discipline is often imposed on those who vote against their leader.

5. False Aboriginal people did not have voting rights in federal elections until 1960.

6. False. Special-interest groups and various elites in society have far more influence on government policy than do average citizens.

7. True. Kim Campbell was prime minister of Canada in 1993. When Brian Mulroney retired from politics, Campbell took over the leadership of the Progressive Conservative Party and automatically became prime minister. However, she was defeated in an election held a few months later, so we have still never had a woman elected prime minister.

8. True. In 1993, the Bloc Québécois won the second-highest number of seats in the federal election and became the official opposition. The main purpose of the Bloc is to promote the separation of Quebec from Canada (www.danielturp.org).

9. False. Canada's voter turnout rate is higher than that of the United States, but lower than that of most other industrialized countries.

10. False. Some Aboriginal groups, including some Quebec Mohawks, do argue that they have the status of sovereign nations, but most Aboriginal people have a more limited view of self-government (Boldt, 1993).

to acquiesce to their demands. Consequently, power is a *social relationship* that involves both leaders and followers. Power also is a dimension in the structure of social stratification. People in positions of power control valuable resources of society—including wealth, status, comfort, and safety—and are able to influence the actions of others by awarding or withholding those resources (Dye and Zeigler, 1993).

The most basic form of power is force or military might. Initially, force may be used to seize and hold power. Max Weber suggested, however, that force is not the most effective long-term means of gaining compliance, because those who are being ruled do not accept coercive rulers as legitimate. Consequently, most leaders do not want to base their power on force alone; they seek to legitimize their power by turning it into **authority—power that people accept as legitimate rather than coercive**.

Ideal Types of Authority

Under what circumstances are people likely to accept authority as legitimate and adhere to it? People have a greater tendency to accept authority as legitimate if they are economically or politically dependent on those who hold power. They also may accept authority more readily if it reflects their own beliefs and values (Turner, Beeghley, and Powers, 1995). *Legitimation* refers to the process by which power is institutionalized and given a moral foundation to justify its existence. Weber outlined three *ideal types* of authority—charismatic, traditional, and rational-legal—each of which has a different basis of legitimacy and a different means of administration. These three types of authority are summarized in Concept Table 13.1.

Charismatic Authority

According to Weber, **charismatic authority is power legitimized on the basis of a leader's exceptional personal qualities or accomplishments**, which inspire loyalty and obedience from followers. Charismatic leaders may be either a tyrants or heroes. Thus, charismatic authority has been attributed to such diverse historical figures as Jesus Christ, Napoleon, Julius Caesar, Adolf Hitler, Winston Churchill, and Martin Luther King, Jr. Former prime minister Pierre Trudeau was one of the most charismatic leaders in Canadian politics but few of our current leaders are known for their charismatic qualities.

Charismatic authority generally tends to be temporary and unstable; it derives primarily from individual leaders (who may change their minds, leave, or die) and from an administrative structure usually limited to a small number of faithful followers. For this reason, charismatic authority often becomes routinized. The *routinization of charisma* occurs when charismatic authority is

Concept Table 13.1 — WEBER'S THREE TYPES OF AUTHORITY

Weber's three types of authority are shown here in global perspective. Charismatic authority is exemplified by former prime minister Indira Gandhi of India. King Gyanendra of Nepal is an example of traditional authority sanctioned by custom. The Canadian House of Commons represents rational-legal authority, which depends on established rules and procedures.

	DESCRIPTION	EXAMPLES
Charismatic	Based on leaders' personal qualities / Temporary and unstable	Napoleon / Adolph Hitler / Indira Gandhi
Traditional	Legitimized by long-standing custom	Authority resides in traditional leader supported by larger social structures, as in old British monarchy
	Subject to erosion as traditions weaken	Patriarchy (rule by men occupying traditional positions of authority, as in the family)
Rational-legal	Legitimized by rationally established rules and procedures	Modern British Parliament
	Authority resides in the office, not the person	Canadian prime minister, Parliament, federal bureaucracy

NEL

succeeded by a bureaucracy controlled by a rationally established authority or by a combination of traditional and bureaucratic authority (Turner et al, 1995). However, charisma cannot always be successfully transferred to organizations. Many organizations, particularly religious ones, fail when the leader departs.

Traditional Authority

Traditional authority **is power that is legitimized by respect for long-standing custom**. In pre-industrial societies, the authority of traditional leaders, such as kings, queens, pharaohs, emperors, and religious dignitaries, was usually grounded in religious beliefs and established practices. For example, British kings and queens historically claimed that their authority came from God. Members of subordinate classes obey a traditional leader's edicts out of economic and political dependency and, sometimes, personal loyalty. However, custom and religious beliefs are sufficient to maintain traditional authority only as long as people share similar backgrounds and accept this type of authority as legitimate.

As societies industrialize, traditional authority is challenged by a more complex division of labour and by a wider diversity of people. In industrialized societies, people do not share the same viewpoint on many issues and tend to openly question traditional authority. Weber felt that traditional authority inhibited the development of capitalism, which he felt worked best in systems of rational-legal authority (Weber, 1968/1922).

Rational-Legal Authority

Rational-legal authority **is power legitimized by law or by written rules and regulations**. Rational-legal authority is also called *bureaucratic authority*. As you learned in Chapter 5, bureaucracies are characterized by a clear-cut division of labour, hierarchy of authority, formal rules, impersonal enforcement of rules, and job security based on a person's technical qualifications. In rational-legal authority, power is legitimized by procedures; if leaders obtain their positions in a procedurally correct manner (such as by election or appointment), they have the right to act.

For example, Canada's political system gives rational-legal authority to the office of the prime minister by specifying the procedures by which persons hold the office as well as its duties and limitations. Rational-legal authority also is held by other elected or appointed government officials and by officers in formal organizations. Authority is invested in

the *office*, not in the *person* who holds the office, however. For example, when the Liberals lost the 2006 federal election, Paul Martin passed on the power of the office of prime minister to Stephen Harper and no longer had any involvement in government.

GLOBAL POLITICAL SYSTEMS

In the earliest societies, politics was not an entity separate from other aspects of life. However, all groups have some means of legitimizing power. Hunting-and-gathering societies do not have political institutions as such because they have very little division of labour or social inequality. Leadership and authority are centred in the family and clan. Individuals acquire leadership roles because of personal attributes such as great physical strength, exceptional skills, or charisma (Lenski, Lenski, and Nolan, 1991).

Political institutions first emerged in agrarian societies as they acquired surpluses and developed greater social inequality. Elites took control of politics and used custom or traditional authority to justify their position. When cities developed, the *city-state*—a city whose power extended to adjacent areas—became the centre of political power.

Nation-states, as we know them, began to develop in Spain, France, and England between the 12th and 15th centuries (see Tilly, 1975). A *nation-state* is a unit of political organization that has recognizable national boundaries and whose citizens possess specific legal rights and obligations. Nation-states emerge as countries develop specific geographic territories and acquire greater ability to defend their borders. Improvements in communication and transportation make it possible for people in a larger geographic area to share a common language and culture. As charismatic and traditional authority are superseded by rational-legal authority, legal standards come to prevail in all areas of life, and the nation-state claims a monopoly over the legitimate use of force (Kennedy, 1993).

There are currently about 195 nation-states in the world. Four main types of political systems are found in them: monarchies, authoritarian systems, totalitarian systems, and democracies.

Monarchies

A *monarchy* **is a political system in which power resides in one person or family and is passed from** generation to generation through lines of inheritance. Monarchies are most common in agrarian societies and are associated with traditional authority patterns. The power of monarchs has varied. *Absolute monarchs* claim a hereditary right to rule (based on membership in a noble family) or a divine right to rule (a God-given right to rule). In *limited monarchies,* rulers depend on powerful members of the nobility to retain their thrones. Unlike absolute monarchs, limited monarchs are not considered to be above the law. In *constitutional monarchies,* the royalty serve as symbolic rulers or heads of state while actual authority is held by elected officials in national parliaments. In such present-day monarchies as the United Kingdom, Sweden, Japan, and the Netherlands, members of royal families primarily perform ceremonial functions.

Authoritarian Systems

An *authoritarian political system* is controlled by rulers who deny popular participation in government. Some authoritarian regimes are absolute monarchies in which rulers claim a hereditary right to their position. Today, Saudi Arabia and Kuwait are examples of authoritarian absolute monarchies. *Dictatorships,* in which power is gained and held by a single individual, also are authoritarian. Pure dictatorships are rare, as all rulers need the support of the military and the backing of business elites. *Military juntas* result when military officers seize power from the government. Some countries, such as Myanmar, have been under military rule for many years.

Totalitarian Systems

In a *totalitarian political system* the state seeks to regulate all aspects of people's public and private lives. The National Socialist (Nazi) party in Germany was a totalitarian regime during World War II, as leaders sought to control all aspects of national life, not just government operations.

To keep people from rebelling, totalitarian governments enforce conformity. People are denied the right to assemble for political purposes; access to information is strictly controlled; and secret police enforce compliance, creating an environment of constant fear and suspicion. North Korea is one contemporary example of a totalitarian regime; another was the Taliban regime that ruled Afghanistan until it was forced out by an American-led coalition following the September 11, 2001, terrorist attacks in the United States. The Taliban regime maintained absolute

Kim Jong-II has been the leader of North Korea's totalitarian government since 1994. He took over this position after the death of the previous leader, his father Kim Il Sung. Kim Jong-Il is in poor health and will likely pass on leadership to his son, Kim Jung-Un. In 2010, Kim Jung-Un was made a four-star general in the army at the age of 26.

control over the Afghan people in most of that country. For example, it required that all Muslims take part in prayer five times each day and that men attend prayer at mosques, where women were forbidden (Marquis, 2001). All facets of daily life were regulated according the Taliban leaders' interpretation of Muslim law. Although the Taliban regime was difficult for many people, it was particularly oppressive for women, who were viewed by this group as being "biologically, religiously and prophetically" inferior to men (McGeary, 2001:41). The regime banned women from public life and essentially kept them isolated at home.

Democracies

A *democracy* is a political system in which the people hold the ruling power either directly or through elected representatives. In an ideal-type democracy, people would actively and directly rule themselves. *Direct participatory democracy* requires that citizens be able to meet regularly to debate and decide the issues of the day. Historical examples of direct democracy might include ancient Athens or a town meeting in colonial New England. This type of democracy is not feasible in large-scale societies and in most democratic countries, including Canada, people have a voice in the government through *representative democracy,* whereby citizens elect representatives to run the government. Elected representatives are supposed to convey the concerns and interests of those they represent, and the government is expected to be responsive to the wishes of the people. Elected officials are held accountable to the people through elections.

However, representative democracy is not always equally accessible to all people in a nation. Throughout Canada's history, for example, members of subordinate groups have been denied full participation in the democratic process. Aboriginal peoples, women, and South and East Asians have in the past been prohibited from voting. Today, the *Charter of Rights and Freedoms* guarantees that all Canadians have the right to democratic participation.

During the past two decades, democracy has spread very rapidly, particularly in formerly communist states. Communism was a one-party system that often maintained its power through repressive means. Since the fall of the Berlin Wall in 1989, the countries of the former Soviet bloc in Eastern Europe, as well as others, such as Nicaragua and Zambia, have established democratic governments. While communist governments remain in a number of countries, including China and Cuba, pressures for democratization are strong around the globe. Between 1990 and 2005, the number of countries that are considered free based upon their human rights and civil liberties has increased from 65 to 89, and 119 countries are electoral democracies. This number did not increase between 2003 and 2009 (Freedom House, 2009). New democracies may be fragile; Zimbabwe has become what the United Nations has called a "pseudo-democracy," as President Robert Mugabe turned to authoritarian rule in order to maintain power. In 2005, Freedom House reclassified Russia from "partly free" to "not free" because of governmental interference in elections and control of the media.

PERSPECTIVES ON POWER AND POLITICAL SYSTEMS

Is political power in Canada concentrated in the hands of the few or distributed among the many? Sociologists and political scientists have suggested

many different answers to this question; however, two prevalent models of power have emerged: pluralist and elite.

Functionalist Perspectives: The Pluralist Model

The pluralist model is rooted in a functionalist perspective, which assumes that people share a consensus on central concerns, such as freedom and protection from harm, and that the government serves important functions in society that no other institution can fulfill. Functionalists see four main functions of government: (1) maintaining law and order; (2) planning and directing society; (3) meeting social needs; and (4) handling international relations, including warfare.

If government is responsible for these functions, what role do people play in the political system? What keeps the government from becoming

In addition to direct contact with legislators, special-interest groups such as the "gun lobby" try to influence policy making by mobilizing constituents and stirring up public opinion. Recent years have seen a proliferation of single-issue groups like those on both sides of the gun-control issue. The strong feelings of gun owners are shown in this Ottawa rally.

all-powerful? What happens when people do not agree on specific issues or concerns? Functionalists suggest that divergent viewpoints lead to a system of political pluralism in which the government functions as an arbiter between competing interests and viewpoints. According to the *pluralist model,* **power in political systems is widely dispersed throughout many competing interest groups** (Dahl, 1961). Many of these are *special-interest groups*—**political coalitions comprising individuals or groups that share a specific interest they want to protect or advance with the help of the political system** (Greenberg and Page, 1993). Examples of special-interest groups are the Business Council on National Issues, the Canadian Labour Congress, the National Action Committee on the Status of Women, and the Assembly of First Nations.

From a pluralist perspective, representative democracy (coupled with the checks and balances provided by our legal system, and the division of governmental powers between a central government and smaller units such as provinces, territories, and municipalities) ensures that no one group can overpower the others and that individual rights are protected.

Special-Interest Groups

Special-interest groups help people advocate their own interests and further their causes. Of the thousands of special-interest groups in Canada, some (such as consumer groups) seek a collective good while others (such as the cigarette manufacturers' lobby) have a relatively narrow focus. Categories of special-interest groups include banking, business, education, energy, the environment, health, labour, persons with disabilities, religious groups, retired persons, and women. Obviously, many groups overlap in interests and membership. Despite their claims to objectivity, members of the media may also represent interest groups. Box 13.2 (on page 320) shows how the media portray different sides in the separatism debate.

Advocates of the pluralist model point out that special-interest groups provide a voice for people who otherwise might not be heard by elected officials at the national, provincial, and local level. However, many special-interest groups (such as the Canadian Bankers' Association) represent very powerful interests and are part of Canada's elites.

Some feel that people are choosing to work through pressure groups rather than through the normal political party system. Our country is so large and so diverse that we have always had a highly pluralistic society, and pluralism will become even more important in the future. Our ethnic diversity is growing

(see Chapter 9), and groups representing women, French-speaking Quebeckers, Aboriginal peoples, ethnic Canadians, and many others are challenging the elitism of the past. Interest groups are now part of our political culture.

While a pluralistic system ensures the voice of many groups will be heard, it does not always work as fairly as political theorists might wish. For example, there are many more groups representing business interests than there are groups representing the interests of the lower class (Dyck, 2004). While this does not mean that government actions always reflect the interests of the powerful, it does mean that the weak must work much harder to be heard. Another potential problem with a highly pluralistic system is that if people turn away from broad social values to those of particular economic, cultural, racial, and gender groups—a process known as *identity politics*—society may become too fragmented.

Over the past two decades, special-interest groups have become more involved in "single-issue politics," in which political candidates often are supported or rejected solely on the basis of their views on a specific issue—such as abortion, gun control, gay and lesbian rights, or the environment. Single-issue groups derive their strength from the intensity of their beliefs; leaders have little room to compromise on issues. Some of these groups have been very effective; about two decades ago, a quickly organized group of seniors was able to make the government back down on its plans to change the law that provided automatic cost-of-living increases to old-age pensioners.

Interest groups have also been effective on the international level. In recent years, Canada played a major role in passing two important international agreements. The first was to ban the use of landmines; the second was to set up a permanent war-crimes tribunal. While these agreements were signed by governments, citizens' groups in many different countries were instrumental in convincing those governments to take action. The 1997 Nobel Peace Prize was awarded to one of these groups, the International Campaign to Ban Landmines, which coordinated the activities of over 1000 nongovernmental organizations in more than 60 countries. These efforts culminated in the landmines treaty that was signed in Ottawa in 1997.

Conflict Perspectives: Elite Models

Although conflict theorists acknowledge that the government serves important purposes for everyone, they

BOX 13.2 | SOCIOLOGY AND THE MEDIA

The Media and Separatism

The mass media have a major influence on politics. Most of us are aware that the media can distort events; this is particularly true of television, which is Canadians' main source of political information. Television news is very brief—items rarely last more than a minute or two—and producers try to show pictures that are interesting, exciting, and visually appealing. Since most political issues are very complex, they are inevitably oversimplified and distorted by television.

Media bias is a particular problem when reporters favour one side of a political debate. This has been the case in the battle over Quebec separatism. Many of those who work in Quebec's French-language media are ardent nationalists and their stories reflect their political views.

On the other side, most of the English-language media oppose Quebec sovereignty and their work reflects a pro-unity position. That the French and English media in Quebec can differ dramatically in their reporting of the same event was shown in their coverage of a June 1996 rally of federalists on Parliament Hill in Ottawa. *The Gazette*, Montreal's leading English-language newspaper, reported that 12 000 people had attended a federalist "love-in." Their front-page photo showed a girl in front of the flag-waving crowd. In the girl's hand was a sign saying "Separation: It's Over." Contrast this with *Le Devoir*, a French-language paper, which reported that 6 000 people had attended the rally. On the front page was a photo of a protester wearing a Lucien Bouchard mask and carrying a cane. Another man appeared to be kicking him in the leg.

(Bouchard, a leader of the separatist forces, had recently had his leg amputated.) The spin the media put on events, as in this case, makes it difficult to separate reality from media bias.

In 1989, a group of protesters in Brockville, Ontario, stomped on the Quebec provincial flag. A film and photographs of this event played a prominent role in the 1995 referendum campaign. However, the pro-separatist media did not balance this coverage by showing pictures of the many Canadian flags that have been burned by Quebec nationalists.

Sources: Panitch and Swartz, 1993; Wieler, 1986.

---

assert it exists for the benefit of wealthy or politically powerful elites who use it to impose their will on the masses. According to the ***elite model*, power in political systems is concentrated in the hands of a small group of elites and the masses are relatively powerless**.

Early Italian sociologists Vilfredo Pareto (1848–1923) and Gaetano Mosca (1858–1941) were among the first to show that concentration of power may be inevitable within societies. Pareto first used the term *elite* to refer to "the few who rule the many" (Marshall, 1994). Similarly, Karl Marx claimed that

under capitalism the government serves the interests of the ruling (or capitalist) class that controls the means of production.

From this perspective, a few of the "best and brightest" among the masses may rise to elite positions by acquiring the requisite education, experience, leadership skills, and other attributes of the elite (Dye and Zeigler, 2006). However, those who do not share the attitudes, political philosophy, gender, or race of the elites will not succeed in this way. The pluralist and elite models are compared in Figure 13.1.

Figure 13.1 **Pluralist and Elite Models**

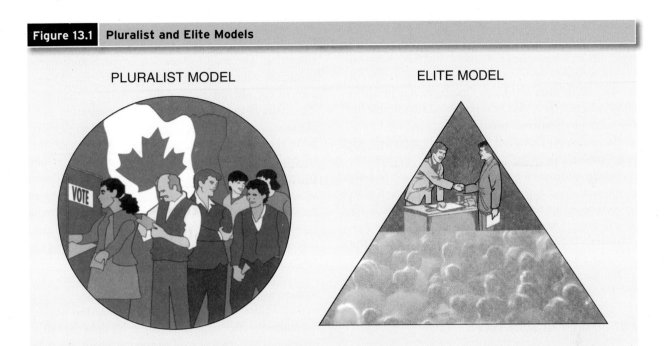

PLURALIST MODEL

ELITE MODEL

- Decisions are made on behalf of the people by leaders who engage in bargaining, accommodation, and compromise.
- Competition among leadership groups makes abuse of power by any one group difficult.
- Power is widely dispersed and people can influence public policy by voting.
- Public policy reflects a balance among competing interest groups.

- Decisions are made by a small group of elite people.
- Consensus exists among the elite on the basic values and goals of society.
- Power is highly concentrated at the top of a pyramid-shaped social hierarchy.
- Public policy reflects the values and preferences of the elite.

C. Wright Mills and the Power Elite

C. Wright Mills (1959a) was among the most important contributors to our knowledge of power elites. The *power elite* **comprises leaders at the top of business, the executive branch of the federal government, and the military**. Mills speculated that the "corporate rich" (the highest-paid officers of the biggest corporations) were the most powerful elites because of their unique ability to turn the vast economic resources at their disposal into political power. The legislative branch of government, special-interest groups, and local opinion leaders were at the middle level of the pyramid. The bottom (and widest layer) of the pyramid is occupied by the unorganized masses, which are relatively powerless and vulnerable to economic and political exploitation.

Mills emphasized that individuals who make up the power elite have similar class backgrounds and interests; many of them also interact on a regular basis. They are able to influence many important decisions, including government policies.

G. William Domhoff and the Ruling

Class According to Domhoff (1978), the *ruling class* is made up of the corporate rich, who make up less than 1 percent of the population. Domhoff uses the term *ruling class* to signify a relatively fixed group of privileged people who wield sufficient power to constrain political processes—who *governs* is much less important than who *rules*—and serve underlying capitalist interests.

Like Mills, Domhoff believed that the upper echelon consists of members of a business class that owns and controls large corporations (Domhoff, 1983). The intertwining of the upper class and the corporate community produces economic and social cohesion. Members of the ruling class have business ties and are also socially linked. They attend the same schools, and belong to the same clubs and the same corporate boards. Consider the example of Power Corporation, which is controlled by Paul Desmarais, a close friend of former prime ministers Brian Mulroney and Jean Chrétien; in fact, Desmarais's son is married to Chrétien's daughter.

Another former prime minister, Paul Martin, used to work for Power Corporation and many politicians and government bureaucrats move back and forth between senior Power Corporation positions and government service. With these contacts, Desmarais has no difficulty in having his views heard by those responsible for Canada's governmental policy.

According to Domhoff (1983), the corporate rich influence the political process in three ways. First, they help to finance campaigns and provide favours to political candidates. Second, through participation in the special-interest process, the corporate rich are able to obtain favours, tax breaks, and favourable regulatory rulings. Finally, they may gain access to the policy-making process through their appointments to governmental bodies such as the Senate.

Feminist Perspectives

Political theorists have focused much attention on class issues. Mary McIntosh (1978) was among the first to argue that gender issues were also important. McIntosh felt that the state supported a system in which women were controlled in the household, where they performed unpaid labour that helped supply a cheap workforce for the capitalist system. Until they achieved some political power, women would inevitably be subordinated by the patriarchal state.

Women have long been excluded from the political process. The Elections Act of 1903 said that "No woman, criminal, or lunatic can vote," and Canadian women were not permitted to vote in federal elections until 1918. Most provinces began allowing women to vote at around this time, though in Quebec women were not enfranchised until 1940. With the vote, women also received the right to run for election. However, few ran, and even fewer were successful. Only 27 women were elected to the federal Parliament between 1921 and 1968, and, as late as 1980, only 5 percent of members of Parliament were women. Since that time, significant progress has been made; 22 percent of the members of Parliament elected in 2008 were women, although this proportion has not increased for the past 15 years and women have not yet reached the highest political positions. Although Canada has had one female prime minister (Kim Campbell) and two provincial premiers, only one of these three, Catherine Callbeck of Prince Edward Island, was actually elected to the position. Women have been much more successful at the municipal level; many of Canada's mayors

are women. The low representation of women in Canadian political office is typical of most Western countries. The major exception is the Scandinavian countries, where women make up more than 35 percent of the membership of the national parliaments. The issue is not simply one of representation. The absence of women in our legislatures has meant that many gender-related issues have not received sufficient attention. Issues such as daycare policy, pay equity, the feminization of poverty, and violence against women and children have only recently begun to receive the attention they deserve. In theory, male legislators, whose constituents are more than 50 percent women, could have pursued these issues, but for many years they did little.

A recent U.S. study showed the difference that women's participation in the electoral process can make. Miller (2008) looked at legislation passed immediately after women received the right to vote in each state. Within a year of women receiving the right to vote, public health spending increased by about 37 percent. The improvement in hygienic conditions and the subsequent decline in infectious diseases led to a decrease in child mortality of 8 to 15 percent in various states.

Interactionist Perspectives on the Political Process

The symbolic interactionist perspective is useful because politics is very much a human process and interactionist insights can help to understand why people behave the way they do in the political arena. Gusfield's 1963 work on the importance of symbolic action in politics provides an example of these insights.

Gusfield and Symbolic Crusades   In 2005, many interest groups, including the Catholic Church and various family organizations, spent a great deal of time and money trying to defeat the federal Liberal government's same-sex marriage legislation. At the same time, in the United States, the National Rifle Association was fighting proposed laws that would prevent people whose names were listed on terrorist watch lists from buying weapons. To many of us, these battles might not seem worth the effort. Allowing gays and lesbians to marry should not affect other Canadians, especially because at the time the legislation was being considered same-sex marriage was already permitted in eight provinces and territories, and could not be regulated by the federal government without invoking the notwithstanding clause in the Charter of Rights and Freedoms. In the security-conscious United States, denying suspected terrorists access to weapons would seem a prudent thing to do and it is difficult to see any social benefit in allowing them to legally purchase guns. However, for many North Americans these issues were vitally important.

Why do interest groups spend so much time and energy on issues such as same-sex marriage and gun control?

About 50 years ago Joseph Gusfield (1963) asked this question about the temperance movement. He was interested in learning why people became intensely involved in trying to ban the consumption of alcohol. In the early part of the 20th century, the temperance movement succeeded in having alcohol sales prohibited for several years in the United States and in most Canadian provinces. Gusfield concluded that the movement was a *symbolic crusade* in which the recognition of the crusaders' values by the government was at least as important as achieving the instrumental goal of prohibiting alcohol use. At a time when the United States was urbanizing, many of the temperance advocates were rural Protestants who felt that their importance in American society was declining and that their values were being replaced with a more indulgent urban-oriented value system. For many, this change threatened their place in American society as well as their religious and moral values:

> In response, many in [the Protestant group] fought to reassert the dominance of their lifestyle by pressing for adherence to its values regarding alcohol consumption. However, the movement's alcohol orientation did not simply highlight preferences regarding liquid refreshments; more important, it provided the symbolic means for proclaiming one's membership in a status group that valued self-control and industriousness. Furthermore, the inability to enforce Prohibition was of small consequence to the crusaders. What these crusaders defined as important was that other rival status groups had to modify their drinking habits according to "our" law. (Snow, 2003:141)

Gusfield's work highlights the dynamics of the legislative process. Not all laws are passed for symbolic reasons; many are deemed necessary in order to keep society running smoothly. However, many laws do have a symbolic component, and passage of these laws reassures various groups that their views are important and are recognized by the government. For example, in 2009, faced with rising gang violence in British Columbia, the federal government announced some modest changes in the Criminal Code that could not possibly have any impact on crime. Nonetheless, the "get tough" rhetoric communicated the symbolic message that the government was responding to public concerns by doing something about the gang problem. Political campaigns rely heavily on symbolism to appeal emotionally to voters because these symbols have the power to bring people together and to unite them behind a political movement (Hall, 1972). Can you think of other political positions or laws that are primarily symbolic? Can you think of other positions or laws that might change society but which have little symbolic impact?

Postmodern Perspectives on Government

Postmodernist scholars have contributed to our understanding of government by broadening the concept to include the means by which the state, and organizations working above and below the interests of the state, influence the behaviour of the citizenry. They refer to this as *governmentality* or *governance*. Rather than taking the traditional view that governments and other organizations rule through top-down commands, postmodernists propose that the state seeks to control people in a less repressive fashion by providing them with incentives and by enlisting members of the community to encourage conforming behaviour. Ideally, conformity becomes part of each individual's self-identity, so people essentially govern themselves.

This concept of governance has been applied in a wide variety of contexts. For example, Tannis Peikoff (2000) used Foucault's (1991) framework to analyze the non-state techniques of governance that were used to control Aboriginal people in the Red River settlement during the mid-1800s. Her research focused on Anglican missionaries, who were not part of the government but who played a significant role in the colonization of Aboriginal peoples. The missionaries sought to convert the Aboriginal peoples to Christianity and a Christian way of life, and to establish an indigenous Anglican clergy who would lead their own congregations. These changes required a break with traditional forms of Aboriginal spirituality and profound changes in practices in areas such as family life and education.

The missionaries were surprised to find strong resistance to their attempts to convert Aboriginal peoples to Christianity and to convince them to shift to European values and practices in other parts of their lives. While the missionaries had no direct power over Aboriginal people, they tried to overcome this resistance by breaking down Aboriginal peoples' traditional way of life, spirituality, and sense of self in order to change them from "barbarous Indians" into good Christians. Some of the methods they used included trying to discredit Aboriginal spiritual leaders and trying to convince parents that their children were at risk unless they agreed to religious conversion. The latter approach is illustrated by the comments of the missionary William Cockran to the parents of a child who had just died: "Trifle not with the Master of Life, or He will touch you again. You have more children; you have an only son; perhaps he shall be next, who shall be taken if your reformation is not effected by the present warning" (Peikoff, 2000:105).

Ultimately, the efforts of the missionaries were not very successful and they decided they should focus educating the children. When this tactic also failed, they began to establish residential schools where they could isolate children from their families and from their cultural traditions to resocialize them.

POLITICS AND GOVERNMENT IN CANADA

The Canadian political process consists of formal elements, such as the duties of the prime minister and the legislative process, and informal elements, such as the role of political parties in the election process. We will examine these informal elements, including political parties, and individual aspects of politics including political socialization, political attitudes, and participation in politics.

Political Parties

A *political party* is an organization whose purpose is to gain and hold legitimate control of government; it is usually composed of people with similar attitudes, interests, and socioeconomic status. A political party (1) develops policy positions, (2) educates voters about issues and simplifies the choices for them, and (3) recruits candidates who agree with those policies, helps those candidates win office, and holds the candidates responsible for implementing the party's policy positions.

The party that wins the most seats in an election forms the government; the party with the

next largest number of seats becomes the official Opposition. Since Confederation, two political parties, the Liberals and the Progressive Conservatives (now the Conservative Party, after a merger with the Canadian Alliance party in 2004), have dominated the Canadian political system. Although one party may control the government for several terms, eventually political control shifts. From time to time, other parties have gained some strength but rarely enough to replace the two major parties. However, in the 1993 election, after being in power for nine years, the Progressive Conservatives were reduced to only two seats and the Liberals assumed power. To the shock of many, the Bloc Québécois, a party that favours breaking up Canada through the separation of Quebec, became the official Opposition in the federal parliament.

Individuals and Politics

Why do some people vote while others do not? How do people come to think of themselves as being conservative, moderate, or liberal? Key factors include

Former Governor-General Michaelle Jean offers a piece of cake to Sasha Dobson of Iqaluit, Nunavut, after her father Vincent Dobson (right), originally of Trinidad and Tobago, was presented with his Canadian Citizenship certificate during a ceremony at the Supreme Court of Canada, in Ottawa.

The Canadian Press/Fred Chartrand

The swearing in of the new cabinet after the 2006 election. In our system of parliamentary democracy, power rests in the hands of the prime minister and the cabinet. Individual members of Parliament have little influence on government policy.

individuals' political socialization, attitudes, and participation.

Political Socialization

Political socialization **is the process by which people learn political attitudes, values, and behaviour.** The family is the primary agent of political socialization, and children tend to learn and hold many of the same opinions as their parents (Burnham, 1983). As they grow older, other agents of socialization, including peers, teachers, and the media, begin to affect children's political beliefs. These other agents may cause people's political attitudes and values to change, and people may cease to identify with the political party of their parents. Even for adults, political socialization continues through the media, friends, neighbours, and colleagues in the workplace.

Political Attitudes

People's socioeconomic status affects their political attitudes, values, beliefs, and behaviour. For example, individuals who are poor or who are unable to find employment tend to believe that society has failed them, and therefore are often indifferent toward the political system (Zipp, 1985). They tend not to vote because they do not feel that casting a ballot would make any difference in their lives.

Voters tend to select candidates and political parties based on social and economic issues they consider important to their lives. *Social issues* are those relating to moral judgments or civil rights, ranging from abortion rights to equal rights for homosexuals. *Economic issues* fall into two broad categories: (1) the amount that should be spent on government programs and (2) the extent to which these programs should encourage a redistribution of income and assets.

Social class is correlated with political attitudes. Upper-class people tend to be more conservative on economic issues and more liberal on social issues. They generally favour equality of opportunity but do not want their own income and assets taxed heavily to abolish poverty or societal problems that they believe some people bring upon themselves. Most of Canada's social programs, such as pensions and medicare, faced opposition from corporate and upper-class interests, and some of these groups led the call for cuts to these programs in the 1990s. By contrast, Canadians in the lower classes tend to be conservative on social issues, such as capital punishment or abortion rights, but liberal on economic issues, such as increasing the minimum wage and expanding social programs.

Despite these tendencies, there is probably less of a connection between voting behaviour and social class in Canada than in many other industrialized countries. The Liberal Party has typically attracted voters from all classes. While the left-wing NDP gets a high proportion of its support from skilled and unskilled labour, more of these workers usually vote for other parties than they do for the NDP. Canadian voters, moreover, tend to be fickle at the polls and frequently switch parties (Pammett, 1993).

Political Participation

The voting rate for federal elections has declined from 75 percent in 1988 to a record low of 59 percent in 2008. This is much lower than the voting rates in most Western European countries. Voting rates are particularly low among young Canadians. Why do you think young people show so little interest in the formal political process?

Nevitte (2000) has studied the decline in political participation and concluded that the way in which Canadians relate to their structures of governance has changed over the past two decades. For Nevitte, the institutions of democratic governance that were designed in the Industrial Age no longer reflect the way in which citizens are connected to the state. In addition to lower rates of voting, signs of stress in the political systems of a number of Western democracies included lower levels of attachment to political parties and shifting patterns of support for political parties. In Canada, public confidence in political institutions, particularly in the federal Parliament, has eroded. Only one in ten Canadians says they are "very satisfied" with government and one-third report "little satisfaction" with government. A majority of people (53 percent) feel they have little say in the actions of the government (Nevitte, 2000). Young people are particularly negative about government and have a weaker attachment to Canada.

As their attachment to government declines, citizens are becoming more involved in alternate forms of political behaviour such as demonstrations, boycotts, and other forms of political expression. The anti-globalization movement is a good example of political action taken outside the regular political system. Frustrated by the determination of most Western governments to pursue an agenda of globalized free trade through agreements such as the North American Free Trade Agreement (NAFTA) and the rules of the World Trade Organization (WTO), thousands of activists from around the globe have organized major protests during meetings of world leaders. In Canada, we have seen these demonstrations in several cities, most recently during the 2010 G20 summit meetings in Toronto. Thus, people are still interested in political matters but believe that the political system cannot or will not respond to their concerns. This challenges Canada's political parties to find ways of relating more effectively with their constituents to reconnect citizens to the political process.

MAJOR POLITICAL ISSUES IN CANADA: QUEBEC SEPARATISM AND ABORIGINAL SELF-GOVERNMENT

The Quiet Revolution and Quebec Nationalism

Because of the dissatisfaction of many Quebec nationalists with the current political structure,

constitutional matters have been very prominent in Canada. Events from the early 1960s onward set the stage for the very close results of the 1995 referendum on separation. More than 15 years after the referendum, these factors continue to play a major role in the political, economic, and social life of Canada.

The constitutional crises of the 1980s and 1990s were set in motion by the Quiet Revolution, which began in Quebec in the 1960s. The term of Premier Jean Lesage (1960–66) saw a dramatic change. Before 1960, Quebec had been a very traditional society. The Roman Catholic Church and the family were at the core of French Canadian society, and economic power in the province was in the hands of English Canadians. However, in a brief time Quebec dramatically transformed itself into a secular, urban society with a modern educational system, strong public health and welfare programs, and a provincially controlled electric-power system. A new sense of nationalism was used as a core ideology to justify the expanded role of the state. This nationalism was clearly expressed in the 1962 Liberal campaign slogan *maîtres chez nous* ("masters in our own house"). Economic and social reform would strengthen French culture. The state would replace the church at the heart of Quebec society. The Quebec government began demanding, and receiving, more control over matters traditionally managed by the federal government.

As Quebec became more like the rest of North America in most other respects, language became increasingly important. English was the language of business in the province, and French Canadian owners and managers were rare. In a series of legislative steps beginning in the 1960s, the provincial government moved to ensure that French became the language of business.

By any measure, the Quiet Revolution has been a success. Legislation now protects the French language in Quebec. Regulations requiring immigrant children to attend French-language schools and restrictions on the use of English on commercial signs have reinforced the dominant role of the French language in Quebec. Quebeckers have gained control over their province's economy and over its other major social institutions including culture, politics, and government.

While the transformation of Quebec was remarkably rapid, it was not rapid enough for some. Nationalist groups, which began to emerge in the 1960s, saw independence as the only means by which Quebec could fulfill its destiny. At the same time, another vision was offered by Quebeckers such as Pierre Trudeau, who believed that Quebec's aspirations could best be fulfilled within Canada. For

Trudeau, cultural survival did not depend on political sovereignty. A strong federal government that actively promoted bilingualism was the best guarantee that French would survive in a predominantly English North America. As prime minister, Trudeau passed the Official Languages Act in 1969, which made the federal public service bilingual. This provided opportunities for francophones and helped to ensure that Canadians in all parts of the country could receive services in either language. The government also began to encourage French-immersion programs in schools in English Canada.

These changes were met with vociferous resistance from some English Canadians. Consider matters from the perspective of those opposed to bilingualism. As Quebec was becoming more autonomous and less bilingual, the need for bilingualism was being promoted throughout the rest of the country (Dyck, 2004). Unilingual anglophone civil servants had to learn French to be promoted, and bilingualism was clearly a major part of the federal political agenda. Many felt that Quebec was blackmailing the federal government at the expense of the other provinces and territories. With extreme Quebec nationalists on one side and those in the rest of Canada who were tired of "having French forced down their throats" on the other, the stage was set for several decades of constitutional debate.

After the 1995 referendum, which the separatists lost by the narrow margin of 50.6 percent to 49.4 percent, separatist sentiment has gradually waned in Quebec. However, in 2005, findings of the Gomery Inquiry into bribery and corruption by the federal Liberals in Quebec led to outrage among many Quebeckers, and support for sovereignty once again began to climb. In a gesture to Quebecers, Prime Minister Stephen Harper passed a motion in Parliament in 2006 stating that the Quebecois constituted a nation within a united Canada. However, this move did not result in greater support for Harper's Conservatives in the 2008 federal election and the separatist Bloq Quebecois remained the most popular federal party in Quebec.

Aboriginal Self-Government

Canada's constitutional debate has largely focused on the role of our "two founding peoples"—the English and the French. Aboriginal peoples have strongly objected to this view of Canadian history. Anthropologist Olive Dickason, a Métis, has pointed out that when the Europeans first came to North America, 55 Aboriginal First Nations were already on the continent. Each of these nations had its own government, territory, culture, and language. Aboriginal objections to the notion of two founding peoples also focus on the issue of which groups will have political power in the future. Quebec claims a special status that entitles it to certain powers to govern its own people, and also certain rights within the federation, such as having three Quebec members of the Supreme Court. Aboriginal peoples also claim a unique status based on their position as Canada's First Nations and have pursued their right to self-government.

While the issue of self-government is complex, some background will help in understanding the issue. In 1763, the British government issued a royal proclamation that formed the basis for the negotiation of treaties with Aboriginal groups. Without a background in European law, Aboriginal peoples did not realize that title to the land had passed to the Crown. They were, however, still entitled to the use and benefit of that land through their "Aboriginal title" (Boldt, 1993). Following Confederation, Aboriginal peoples came under the control of the federal government. The mechanism for this control, the Indian Act, was passed in 1876 and gave government bureaucrats almost total control over Aboriginal peoples. The act even went so far as to define a "person" as "an individual other than an Indian" (Hamilton and Sinclair, 1991b).

The consequences of the Indian Act were profound. For example, Aboriginal children were forced to attend residential schools (which meant that generations of children were not raised with their families and were not allowed to speak or to learn their Aboriginal languages); traditional religious practices were restricted; Aboriginal peoples did not fully control their own land and could not sell agricultural products off the reserve; and the government imposed a "pass system," which restricted the right of Aboriginal peoples to travel off their reserves. Aboriginal peoples did not have full voting rights in federal elections until 1960. As Menno Boldt has observed, contemporary "Indian powerlessness has its roots in Canada's Indian policies" (1993:xvii).

In the 1960s, the federal government began to review its policies concerning Aboriginal peoples. A 1969 government policy paper proposed assimilation of Aboriginal peoples. Treaties were to be dropped, reserves were to become like neighbouring non-Aboriginal communities, and Aboriginal rights and Aboriginal land titles were to be discarded. The "Aboriginal problem" would disappear, it was thought, if Aboriginal peoples became, in Pierre

Two of Canada's most influential Aboriginal leaders are Shawn Atleo, Chief of the Assembly of First Nations, and Justice Murray Sinclair, Chair of the Indian Residential Schools Truth and Reconciliation Commission.

Trudeau's words, "Canadians as all other Canadians" (Boldt, 1993). Reaction to this paper marked a watershed in Aboriginal politics. A national campaign, which ultimately forced the government to drop its proposals, became a countrywide movement and led to the formation of several pan-Indian organizations, including the Assembly of First Nations (Hamilton and Sinclair, 1991b). Rather than accepting the federal government's assimilationist model, Aboriginal leaders embraced nationalism. Self-government, Aboriginal rights, and land claims became the rallying points of the movement.

Some Aboriginal leaders, particularly among the Mohawks, view their bands as separate nations that have sovereign control over their lands. However, most proponents of Aboriginal self-government take a more limited view. They understand that their First Nations status gives them the "inherent" right to self-government within the Canadian federation (Boldt, 1993). They feel their status as Canada's first people, who were never conquered and who signed voluntary treaties with the Crown, entitles them to self-determination and to protection of their culture and customs. They believe these rights are not *granted* by the Canadian government but are inherently theirs. On the other hand, the federal, provincial, and territorial governments have taken the position that the right to self-determination could

be extended only as powers delegated to Aboriginal peoples by government through legislation or constitutional change. Further, the powers that would be granted by government would extend only to powers now held by municipal governments rather than the much broader powers sought by Aboriginal peoples. It is difficult to predict where the current process of ending the colonial rule of Aboriginals will lead. Two major changes occurred in 1999. First, Inuit took over government of the newly created Nunavut Territory, encompassing more than 350 000 km² of land in the northern and eastern Arctic. The second major achievement was the signing of a treaty with the Nisga'a people, who had been seeking recognition of Aboriginal title to their land for more than 100 years. This treaty gave the Nisga'a a large land settlement in north-western British Columbia and significant powers of self-government similar to those of municipal governments.

Although the federal government accepted the inherent nature of Aboriginal peoples' right to self-government in 1995 and is committed to dismantling the Department of Indian Affairs and Northern Development, the future form of that government is not at all clear—not even among Aboriginal peoples. Many problems must be solved, including decisions about how the growing number of urban Aboriginals will be included, the applicability of the Canadian

Charter of Rights and Freedoms to Aboriginal communities, and sources of funding for this new order of government.

POLITICS AND THE ECONOMY

Politics and the economy are so closely intertwined that many social scientists speak of the two as a single entity, the political economy. Sociologists have studied Canadian society using the political economy framework, which "investigates the relationship between economy and politics as they affect the social and cultural life of societies" (Clement and Williams, 1989:6). For example, economic globalization and international trade agreements such as the North American Free Trade Agreement (NAFTA) have an impact on Canada's political sovereignty and on our culture and social institutions.

Clement and Drache have outlined some of the issues that Canadian sociologists and economists have addressed using the political economy perspective:

1. The implications of external relations for internal development, especially early colonial ties with France and the United Kingdom and the current dependence on the United States in many economic, political, and military activities;
2. The origin of Canadian capitalism in a staple economy, its movement into commercial and financial specialization, and its continued reliance on resource extraction;
3. The dependence on external markets, both as outlets for raw materials (making Canada vulnerable to world conditions) and as capital sources (which ultimately act as a drain on investment capital);
4. The effect of technology and the ownership of that technology, especially patent rights, in shaping the economy and labour force;
5. The continued survival of two nations within a single state—the conquered French and the conquering English—and the demise of the Native people, along with the reactions of these repressed minorities (1978: iv–v).

Each of these issues highlights the interdependence of economic and political factors. The way in which a society is organized to produce goods and services and the political structure of that society have an impact on all of our social institutions. To help understand the linkage between politics and the economy, you need to understand the nature of global economic systems.

GLOBAL ECONOMIC SYSTEMS

Capitalism and socialism have been the principal economic models in industrialized countries over the past 100 years. Sociologists often use two criteria—property ownership and market control—to distinguish between types of economies. Keep in mind, however, that no society has a purely capitalist or socialist economy.

Capitalism

Capitalism **is an economic system characterized by private ownership of the means of production, from which personal profits can be derived through market competition and without government intervention**. Most of us think of ourselves as "owners" of private property because we own a car, a television set, or other possessions. However, most of us are not capitalists; we *spend money* on the things we own, rather than *making money* from them. Capitalism is not simply the accumulation of wealth, but also the "use of wealth . . . as a means for gathering more wealth" (Heilbroner, 1985:35). Relatively few people own the means of production and the rest of the workers in the private sector are paid to work for these "capitalists." "Ideal" capitalism has four distinctive features: (1) private ownership of the means of production, (2) pursuit of personal profit, (3) competition, and (4) lack of government intervention.

Private Ownership of the Means of Production Capitalist economies are based on the right of individuals to own income-producing property, such as land, mines, and factories, and to "buy" people's labour.

The early Canadian economy was based on the sale of *staples*—goods associated with primary industries including lumber, wheat, and minerals. The economy was driven by the demands for raw materials from the colonial powers of France and Britain (Innis 1984/1930). This began early in Canada's history; in 1670 a British royal charter gave the privately held Hudson's Bay Company exclusive control over much of what is now Western Canada, which was the source of the very lucrative fur trade.

In the early stages of industrial capitalism (1850–1890), virtually all investment capital was individually owned, and a few individuals and families controlled all the major trade and financial organizations in Canada. Under early monopoly capitalism (1890–1940), most ownership rapidly shifted from individuals to huge *corporations*—**large-scale organizations that have legal powers, such as the ability to enter into contracts and buy and sell property, separate from their individual owners**. Major industries came under the control of a few corporations owned by shareholders. For example, the automobile industry in North America came to be dominated by the "Big Three"—General Motors, Ford, and Chrysler. Industrial development in Canada lagged behind that of many other countries as business focused on exporting raw materials and importing finished products. Many of the industries that did establish themselves in Canada were branch plants of large American and British corporations whose profits flowed back to their home countries. By 1983, Canada was receiving more direct foreign investment than any other country (Laxer, 1989). Economist Kari Levitt (1970) was among the first to show that this foreign private investment posed a threat to Canadian sovereignty as fundamental economic decisions were made outside the country. Although foreign investment has declined, many of our industries are still controlled by foreign parent corporations, such as Honda and Walmart.

Today, *multinational corporations*—**large companies that are headquartered in one country and have subsidiaries or branches in other countries**—play a major role in the economies and governments of many nations. Multinational corporations also are referred to as *transnational corporations* because they sell and produce goods abroad. The largest of these corporations have sales that are greater than the economies of many countries. For example, Walmart's sales are greater than the economies of all but 18 countries. These corporations are not dependent on the labour, capital, or technology of any one country and may move their operations to countries where wages and taxes are lower and potential profits are higher. For example, Nike produces virtually all of its sports shoes and other equipment in countries such as Vietnam and Indonesia, where workers are willing to work long hours in cramped factories for low wages.

Pursuit of Personal Profit A tenet of capitalism is the belief that people are free to maximize their individual gain through personal profit; in the process, the entire society will benefit from their activities (Smith, 1976/1776). Economic development is assumed to benefit both capitalists and workers, and the general public also benefits from public expenditures (such as for roads, schools, and parks) made possible through an increase in business tax revenues.

During the period of industrial capitalism, however, specific individuals and families (not the general public) were the primary recipients of profits. For many generations, descendants of some of the early industrial capitalists have benefited from the economic deeds (and misdeeds) of their ancestors. For example, the Seagram company fortune (controlled by the Bronfman family) was partly based on the profits made from bootlegging during Prohibition.

Competition In theory, competition acts as a balance to excessive profits. When producers compete for customers, they must be able to offer innovative goods and services at competitive prices. However, the trend has been toward less, rather than more, competition among companies; profits are higher when there is less competition. For example, Microsoft so dominates certain areas of the computer software industry that it has virtually no competitors.

How do large companies restrict competition? Many competing companies simply get together and agree on the prices all will charge. Many of Canada's largest corporations have been convicted of this offence, which is known as price-fixing.

What appears to be competition among producers *within* an industry actually may be "competition" among products, all of which are produced and distributed by relatively few corporations. An *oligopoly* **exists when several companies overwhelmingly control an entire industry**. An example is the music industry, in which a few giant companies are behind many of the labels and artists known to consumers. Most of the beer in Canada is produced by Molson Coors and Labbatt, which make and distribute a wide variety of different brands of beer and are partly competing against themselves.

Corporations with control both within and across industries often are formed by a series of mergers and acquisitions across industries. These corporations are referred to as *conglomerates*—**combinations of businesses in different commercial areas, all of which are owned by one holding company**. Media ownership is a case in point: companies such as Time Warner have extensive holdings in radio and television stations, cable television companies, book publishing firms, and film production and distribution companies.

Lack of Government Intervention

Proponents say that capitalism works best without government intervention in the marketplace. Despite this ideal of free enterprise, the notion of unregulated markets benefiting all citizens has seldom been realized. Individuals and companies have run roughshod over weaker competitors in the pursuit of higher profits, and small businesses have grown into large monopolistic corporations. Accordingly, governments implemented regulations to try to curb the excesses of the marketplace. While its effectiveness can be debated, Canada has a Competition Bureau to ensure that corporations compete fairly.

Ironically, much of what is referred to as government intervention has been in the form of *aid* to business. Canadian governments have always provided financial support to business. To encourage settlement of the West, the government gave subsidies and huge tracts of land to the Canadian Pacific Railway for the construction of a national railway. Many corporations receive government assistance in the form of public subsidies and protection from competition by tariffs, patents, and trademarks. Governments provide billions of dollars in tax credits for corporations, large subsidies and loan guarantees to manufacturers, and subsidies and tariff protection for farmers. While most corporations have gained much more than they have lost as a result of government involvement in the economy, the free enterprise mythology still persists.

Socialism

Socialism **is an economic system characterized by public ownership of the means of production, the pursuit of collective goals, and centralized decision making.** Like "pure" capitalism, "pure" socialism does not exist. Marx described socialism as a temporary stage en route to an ideal communist society.

Although the terms *socialism* and *communism* are often are used interchangeably, they are not identical. Marx defined communism as an economic system characterized by common ownership of all economic resources (Marshall, 1994). In *The Communist Manifesto* and *Das Kapital,* he predicted that the working class would become increasingly impoverished and alienated under capitalism. As a result, the workers would become aware of their own class interests, revolt against the capitalists, and overthrow the entire system. After the revolution, private property would be abolished and capital would be controlled by collectives of workers who would own the means of production (Marx and Engels, 1967/1848; Marx, 1967/1867). Marx felt that after the revolution government would no longer would be necessary, but over the years state control was added as an organizing principle for communist societies. "Ideal" socialism has three distinctive features: (1) public ownership of the means of production, (2) pursuit of collective goals, and (3) centralized decision making.

Public Ownership of the Means of Production

In a socialist economy, the means of production are owned and controlled by the state, not by private individuals or corporations. Prior to the early 1990s, the state owned all the natural resources and almost all the capital in the Soviet Union. At least in theory, goods were produced to meet the needs of people. Access to housing and medical care were considered a right.

In the 1990s, leaders of the former Soviet Union and other Eastern European nations abandoned government ownership and control of the means of production because the system was so inefficient. Shortages and widespread unrest led to the reform movement headed by Soviet President Mikhail Gorbachev.

Pursuit of Collective Goals

Ideal socialism is based on the pursuit of collective goals, rather than on personal profits. Equality in decision making replaces hierarchical relationships (such as between owners and workers or political leaders and citizens). Everyone shares in the goods and services of society, especially necessities such as food, clothing, shelter, and medical care based on need, not on ability to pay. In reality, however, few societies can or do pursue purely collective goals.

Centralized Decision Making

Another tenet of socialism is centralized decision making. In theory, economic decisions are based on the needs of society and the government is responsible for facilitating the production and distribution of goods and services. Central planners set wages and prices. When problems such as shortages and unemployment arise, they can be dealt with quickly and effectively by the central government (Boyes and Melvin, 1994).

In the former Soviet Union, broad economic policy decisions were made by the highest authorities of the Communist Party. The production units (the factories and farms) at the bottom of the structure had little voice in the decision-making process. Wages and prices were based on political priorities and eventually came to be completely unrelated to actual supply and demand. Thus while some factories kept producing goods that nobody wanted, there were chronic shortages of other goods.

The collapse of state socialism in the former Soviet Union was due partly to the declining ability of the Communist Party to act as an effective agent of society and partly to the growing incompatibility of central planning with the requirements of a modern economy (see Misztal, 1993).

Mixed Economies

No economy is truly capitalist or socialist; most economies have elements of both. A *mixed economy* **combines elements of a market economy (capitalism) with elements of a command economy (socialism)**. There is significant variation in the degree of government involvement in the economy in different countries. For example, in Sweden the government owns railroads, mineral resources, a bank, and liquor and tobacco operations (Feagin and Feagin, 1994). All residents have health insurance, housing subsidies, child allowances, paid parental leave, and daycare subsidies. Public funds help subsidize cultural institutions, such as theatres and orchestras ("General Facts on Sweden," 2005; Kelman, 1991). Most Western European countries have more government involvement in their economies than in North America, and government in Canada plays a greater role in the economy than in the United States. For example, while Canada provides medical care to all its citizens, 47 million Americans have no medical coverage (U.S. Census Bureau, 2008) (see Chapter 11).

POLITICAL ISSUES FOR THE FUTURE

Economic agreements, such as the North American Free Trade Agreement (NAFTA) and the European Union, are helping to create a single market for capital and services. This will inevitably lead to closer relationships between the countries involved. At the same time, budget cuts have reduced the role of governments in providing services to their citizens, and globalization of financial markets has dramatically reduced the ability of governments to control their own economic destinies. Many economic decisions are made by international organizations, such as the WTO and the World Intellectual Property Organization. Multinational corporations, some of which are larger economic entities than many of the world's countries, also have an impact on global economic policy that may not reflect the interests of any nation-state. These developments have led many people to ask if the governments of modern nation-states will become obsolete. People have little influence over multinational corporations and international trade agreements. People can vote only within their own countries, yet many of the decisions that affect their lives and their futures are made outside their borders.

The nature of the new challenges facing many governments makes it increasingly difficult for them to control events. For example, how do nations deal with terrorism within their borders, such as the 2001 attacks on the World Trade Center and the Pentagon that resulted in the deaths of almost 3000 people, and the terrorist attacks carried out in England by the Irish Republican Army? In the aftermath of tragedies such as these, governments' responsibility for protecting citizens but not violating their basic freedoms is widely examined in national debates that inevitably will continue into the future. (For a Canadian perspective on terrorism, see Box 13.3.)

Likewise, how are nations to deal with the proliferation of arms and nuclear weapons in other countries? Will some of the missiles and warheads fall into the hands of terrorists? What should be done with the masses of nuclear waste being produced? No easy answers are forthcoming but without some form of effective international control it will be impossible to ensure that future generations are protected from environmental threats such as global warming and water and air pollution.

While international agreements are necessary, it is likely that these agreements will be reached in different ways and involve different participants from those in the past. The way in which hundreds of groups came together with governments to create the treaty banning landmines is increasingly becoming a model for involving more grassroots organizations in such negotiations. The Internet has made it much easier for such widely scattered organizations to work effectively together.

BOX 13.3   SOCIOLOGY IN GLOBAL PERSPECTIVE

Terrorism in Canada

Some of you may have been surprised to read about political terrorism in Canada in the chapter introduction. While most Canadians rightly feel that Canada is a very peaceful country, there have been a significant number of terrorist incidents here over the past 50 years.

Using a database developed by the federal government, Anthony Kellett (2004) studied acts of terrorism that occurred in Canada between 1960 and 1992. Defining terrorism as "comprising acts of serious violence, planned and executed clandestinely, and committed with clear intention to achieve political ends" (2004:286), Kellett found more than 400 incidents and 13 deaths during this period. While this might seem like a large number, it is much lower than in many European countries where groups like the Irish Republican Army and the Basque separatist group ETA have been active for many years.

Almost 85 percent of the incidents involved Canadian-based groups attacking domestic targets, while the remainder involved either foreign terrorists or foreign targets in Canada. The number of incidents peaked in the 1960s, when several secessionist groups were active in Quebec and the Sons of Freedom Doukhobor sect was engaged in bombings and other acts of terrorism in British Columbia. Together, these groups accounted for most of the terrorist attacks in the database, which largely explains why 97 percent of the total number of attacks occurred in the provinces of Quebec and British Columbia.

You read earlier about the role played by Pierre Vallières in events in Quebec. Terrorist acts began in the early 1960s and ended about a decade later. Kellett estimates that only about 100 people were ever members of the FLQ. Most were young and single, and many were students. Like many contemporary terrorist groups, members financed their political activities by engaging in crimes such as credit-card fraud and robbery.

While the FLQ had many similarities to other terrorist organizations, the Sons of Freedom Doukhobors were quite unique. Members of the Sons of Freedom, one branch of the pacifist Christian Doukhobor group that came to Canada in the late 19th century, rejected any government involvement in their lives. They refused to send their children to school, pay taxes, or register births and deaths. While most Doukhobors eventually accepted the role of government, some members of the Sons of

Jacques Rose, Paul Rose, Francis Simard, and Bernard Lortie were the members of the Montreal-based Chénier cell of the FLQ that kidnapped and murdered Quebec cabinet minister Pierre Laporte in 1970.

Freedom sect did not. There were many clashes between sect members and the government, and in the 1950s the B.C. government took children away from their communities and forced them to live in residential schools until they were 15 years of age. The protests of the sect between 1960 and 1962 resulted in 107 incidents of arson and bombings of public facilities, such as schools, power lines, bridges, and the property of other Doukhobors. The terrorist acts ended when many of the perpetrators were imprisoned.

Besides the political attacks in Quebec and the religious terrorism of some members of the Sons of Freedom, the only other category that had a substantial number of terrorist incidents between 1960 and 1989 was that of émigré groups. These included attacks by anti-Castro Cubans on Cuban targets in Canada, attacks on Turks in Canada by Armenian

BOX 13.3   SOCIOLOGY IN GLOBAL PERSPECTIVE

Terrorism in Canada (Continued)

groups, and several attacks by Sikh militants supporting the formation of an independent Sikh state in India.

Since 1989, there have been a relatively small number of terrorist incidents. They have been committed in support of a wide range of causes including the environmental movement, animal rights, the anti-abortion movement, and the civil war in the former Yugoslavia. In 2006, 18 men were arrested in the Toronto area on charges of planning terrorist attacks in Canada. They planned to detonate several truck bombs and to storm the Parliament building and behead Prime Minister Harper. They held training camps north of Toronto (which featured the uniquely Canadian touch of visits to Tim Hortons along with lessons in using firearms and discussions of jihad) and tried to order several tonnes of ammonium nitrate to use in their truck bombs. They were arrested before they got a chance to put any of their plans into action. Most recently, in 2010 a group of Ottawa men bombed a Royal Bank branch in protest over globalization and a Quebec group bombed a Canadian Forces recruiting centre in Trois Rivieres to protest Canada's role in the war in Afghanistan.

The database used by Kellett did not include incidents involving terrorist attacks that were supported in Canada but that took place elsewhere.

The most important of these was the Air India bombing, in which a bomb placed on an aircraft in Vancouver took the lives of 329 people. Another disaster was narrowly averted in 1999, when a U.S. customs agent apprehended Ahmed Ressam as he attempted to cross into the United States from Canada with a car loaded with explosives. Ressam, allegedly a member of a Montreal-based Al Qaeda cell, intended to detonate his car bomb at the Los Angeles International Airport on January 1, 2000. Many terrorist groups, including the Irish Republican Army and the Sri Lankan Tamil Tigers, were active in collecting funds in Canada from supporters who have emigrated from their home countries.

Since the 9/11 attacks on the United States by Al Qaeda, the United States has demanded increased counterterrorism measures in Canada along with increased border security. Given that the most important part of our foreign policy involves our relationship with the United States, control of terrorism raises serious issues about Canada's ability to maintain its own sovereignty in the face of American demands for increased security in Canada. Can we maintain independent policies in areas such as immigration regulations, military funding, and border control if doing so affects our relationship with our largest trading partner?

Another issue that will continue to trouble many countries is nationalism. Can Canada make an accommodation with Quebec? How will European countries adapt to the loss of national powers within the European Community? Will groups continue to make war to support their nationalistic aspirations? (Some of the more troubling aspects of nationalism are discussed in Box 13.4.) The issues surrounding nationalism must be resolved if we are to continue to move toward the dream of a peaceful world.

Finally, Canadians, particularly young people, have been losing interest in the traditional political process. Many of us are more concerned with special interests and regional concerns than with broader national questions. What will result from this fragmentation of political activity? Are leaders like Prime Minister Harper, who wanted to build a "firewall" around Alberta before he became a federal leader or Newfoundland and Labrador Premier Danny Williams, who took down Canadian flags because of a financial dispute he was having with the federal government, helping to build a society that can work together to face issues such as global warming and globalization? Will we be able to face the dramatic challenges that lie ahead if we identify as Newfoundlanders or Quebeckers or Albertans rather than Canadians or if our ethnic or religious identities are more important to us than our common bonds as Canadians?

BOX 13.4 | SOCIOLOGY IN GLOBAL PERSPECTIVE

Nationalism Around the World

Historian Ramsay Cook has observed that "Everyone belongs somewhere. Yet much of the conflict in the history . . . of mankind has been about who belongs where" (Cook, 1995:9). Cook goes on to discuss the role of nationalism in justifying one's place in the world. Nationalism, he says, is a "doctrine asserting that humanity is naturally divided into groups with common characteristics and that by virtue of those collective traits they have a right to exercise control—sovereignty—over the particular place" (1995:9). Most Canadians have heard Lucien Bouchard and other Quebec separatists state that the Québécois constitute a "people" who must have sovereignty over their territory if their destiny is to be fulfilled. The desire for separation from Canada in Quebec is a manifestation of nationalism.

Quebec nationalists are not the only people trying to take control of what they see as their territory. Punjabis in India, Basques in Spain, and Palestinians in the Middle East are just a few of the hundreds of nationalist groups active in the world today. Justification for their claims is usually given to or provided by God, language, culture, or history. However, what ultimately decides things is power. This power may be political—the Czech Republic and Slovakia separated after a parliamentary vote—but more typically, it is military, as with the Iraqis and Turks, who have forcefully prevented the Kurds from establishing a separate homeland.

Nationalism can be a unifying force. Many countries, including Germany and Italy, were formed in the late 19th century through the unification of smaller states with similar language and cultural backgrounds. Diverse groups were brought together under a common flag.

However, nationalism can also be divisive—and often deadly. Societies based on national identity can easily become intolerant of those who do not share the same ethnicity, religion, or culture. Millions have died at the hands of oppressive nationalists. Historically, most wars have been between countries; today they are almost all within countries. Wars, such as the American-led invasion of Iraq, are the exception, while conflicts, such as the genocides in Sudan and eastern Congo, are much more common and much more deadly in terms of lives lost (see www.genocidewatch.org).

Successful nationalist movements often carry with them the seeds of their own destruction. Yugoslavia is a case in point. Prior to 1989, the diverse elements of the country had been held together by the communist regime. However, when the communist domination of Eastern Europe ended, the Croats and Muslims in Yugoslavia decided to break away from the Serb-dominated communist government and created the independent states of Croatia and Bosnia Herzegovina. However, after years of living within the common boundaries of Yugoslavia, each of the new countries had significant ethnic minorities within its borders. These minorities in turn claimed their independence and the ensuing carnage has cost hundreds of thousands of lives and has added the term "ethnic cleansing" to our vocabulary. Ethnic cleansing is a chilling final solution to the minority problem—you simply kill or expel every man, woman, and child of a different religious or cultural background who has the misfortune of remaining within your territory. Internal conflicts such as these can be extremely complex. In the former Yugoslavia, each of the major groups—Serbs, Croats, and the Muslims of Bosnia Herzegovina—has participated in ethnic cleansing in the areas under its control.

War has become a means of expressing national identities, and grievances dating back hundreds or even thousands of years have become the justification for brutal mass murder. As large nation-states become less relevant in an era of globalization and homogenization, they lose their ability to unify; instead, people search for a collective identity at the local level. Unfortunately, this identity is often grounded on exclusion—those who are not "like us" are not tolerated. Where this will lead is uncertain. It is difficult to imagine the nationalist process continuing indefinitely. Fewer than 200 countries now exist; if every linguistic group became a nation, there would be about 8000 countries.

International organizations, such as the UN, have intervened in an attempt to control these internal conflicts and to stop the killing and expulsions. However, these peacekeeping missions have had limited success. Intrastate conflicts, such as those in Somalia, Yugoslavia, Haiti, Kosovo, and

BOX 13.4 SOCIOLOGY IN GLOBAL PERSPECTIVE

Nationalism Around the World (Continued)

East Timor, have left intractable problems even after the fighting was stopped. Devastated economies, a collapse of civil institutions, humanitarian emergencies involving refugees, and the difficulties of people returning to destroyed villages and towns have perpetuated cycles of conflict and human suffering. Disorder and bloodshed often continue long after the major conflict has ended, and militias or criminal gangs may exploit the weak social order. Often, the factions responsible for the original conflict are waiting for the opportunity to resume their activities. At least initially, these countries are often in a state that may not be full-scale war but certainly is not peace.

In order to deal with protracted social conflict of this sort, peacekeeping has become more complex and has involved more types of organizations. While conflict between neighbouring countries might be managed by creating buffer zones, this tactic cannot be used when the conflict is between individuals and groups that share the same territory. Therefore, the peacekeeping doctrine has evolved to include peacemaking, humanitarian operations, peace enforcement, and peace building (Linden, Last, and Murphy, 2007). The military cannot handle all these tasks alone, so many different types of organizations, including aid organizations, are now routinely involved in these missions.

■ What is power?

Power is the ability of persons or groups to carry out their will even when opposed by others.

■ What are the three types of authority?

Weber identified three types of authority. Charismatic authority is based on a leader's exceptional personal qualities. Traditional authority is based on respect for custom. Rational-legal authority is based on law or written rules and regulations.

■ What are the main types of political systems?

There are four main types of contemporary political systems. In a monarchy, one person is the ruler of the nation. In authoritarian systems, rulers tolerate little or no public opposition and generally cannot be removed from office by legal means. In totalitarian systems, the state seeks to regulate all aspects of society and to monopolize all societal resources in order to control completely both public and private life. In a democratic system, the powers of the government are derived from the consent of all the people.

■ What are the pluralist and elite perspectives on power?

According to the pluralist (functionalist) model, power is widely dispersed throughout many competing interest groups. People influence policy by voting, joining special-interest groups and political campaigns, and forming new groups. According to the elite (conflict) model, power is concentrated in a small group of elites, while the masses are relatively powerless.

KEY TERMS

authoritarian political system 317
authority 314
capitalism 329
charismatic authority 315
conglomerate 330
corporations 330
democracy 317
elite model 320
government 313
mixed economy 332
monarchy 316
multinationals 330
oligopoly 330
pluralist model 319
political party 324
political socialization 325
politics 313
power 313
power elite 321
rational-legal authority 316
routinization of charisma 315
socialism 331
special-interest groups 319
state 313
totalitarian political system 317
traditional authority 316

WEB LINKS

For more Web links related to the topic of this chapter, see the Nelson sociology website:
http://www.sociologyessentials5e.nelson.com

Each of Canada's major political parties has a website:
Bloc Quebecois:
www.blocquebecois.org

Conservative Party:
www.conservative.ca

Green Party:
www.greenparty.ca

Liberal Party:
www.liberal.ca

New Democratic Party:
www.ndp.ca

An important development on the road to Aboriginal self-government is the Royal Commission Report on Aboriginal Peoples, at:
www.ainc-inac.gc.ca/ch/rcap/index_e.html

For a Canadian perspective on women in politics, go to:
www.equalvoice.ca

For a large collection of Canadian government information on the Internet, go to:
http://canada.gc.ca

The University of Lethbridge Department of Political Science has a very good educational website covering a range of Canadian political issues at:
http://mapleleafweb.com

QUESTIONS FOR CRITICAL THINKING

1. How does your school (or workplace) reflect a pluralist or elite model of power and decision making?

2. Do you locate yourself politically on the left or on the right? How does this affect the way you look at political issues?

3. Can you apply Weber's three types of authority to people who have an influence on Canada?

4. Can you think of a recent political decision that has affected your life? Do you agree with that decision and the way in which it was made? Do you feel your views on this issue were considered?

5. Go to the Genocide Watch website (www.genocidewatch.org). What do you think the world community could do to intervene in these tragic situations?

ONLINE STUDY AND RESEARCH TOOLS

INFOTRAC®

InfoTrac College Edition is included free with every new copy of this text. Explore this online library for additional readings, review, and a handy resource for assignments. Visit **www.infotrac-college.com** to access this online database of full-text articles. Enter the key terms from this chapter to start your search.

CENGAGENOW™ CENGAGENOW

Use CengageNOW™ to help you formulate a customized study plan for this chapter. After you take the Diagnostic Quiz, CengageNOW™ will generate a customized study plan for you. It will identify sections of the chapter you should review.

CHAPTER

14

Education

Consider the following comments from a parent of three university students:

"I picked up a university education on the weekend.

"I did it with a rented U-Haul trailer, enough room, almost, for the yearly needs of two first-year students at a small university a few hours from Ottawa.

"We took them down in September; it required two U-Hauls: one for their clothes, CDs, snowboards, skateboards, hockey equipment, birdfeeders, posters, computers, and—oh, yes—pen and paper in case they ever needed to take a few notes; and one trailer, of course, for the money to get them through a year of higher Canadian education.

"It is really quite simple. You remortgage the house, cash in your RRSPs, take back the beer bottles, fill up the U-Haul with hard cash, add a couple of shovels and tell the kids to fill up the first black hole when they reach campus.

"I do not begrudge this state of affairs. We are among the extremely fortunate in that we can help out and besides, who could ever put a price on seeing all those slim, healthy young men and women hugging and weeping openly

as they say their goodbyes in the residence parking lot while their overweight, sweating, near-cardiac arrest parents do all the heavy lifting?

"Still, one cannot help but think of the changes that have come about since we became the first generation in Canada who were given to take higher education as a basic rite of passage, thanks to the world of student loans and generous grants you never even had to consider paying back.

"Going to school was a simple project. You worked in the summer, socked away your $1,000; you got your student loan of $600, your student grant of $600, and that was it. Sometimes you ran unbelievably short—I will spare you my own horror stories—but you survived and, one day, you went out into the world owing a couple of thousand dollars in student loans which you soon paid off and never again thought about.

"Never again, that is, until your own kids were suddenly headed off to similar schools.

"At one point, no one would ever dare question the value of an education, and even today it makes one feel slightly queasy to do so, but there are just too many stories hanging around to ignore it. We have three at university this year, and one suspects even Bill Gates would blanch at the costs, even with the kids themselves contributing." (MacGregor, 2002)

More than ever before, education—in particular, higher education—is regarded as the key to success. Most young Canadians today will attend university, correct? Although you may be one of the fortunate ones, the answer to this question is no. Increasingly, a university education is becoming a valuable life asset that only a few can afford to obtain. The most recent statistics indicate that only 23 percent of Canadians aged 25 to 64 have a university degree (Statistics Canada, 2008). Given the costs associated with attaining this higher level of education, these numbers should come as no surprise. The national chairperson of the Canadian Federation of Students commented, "University education has been placed out of reach for many lower-income families. The rise in tuition fees throughout the last decade has increasingly restricted access to universities to only the wealthiest Canadians" (Boyko, 2002). According to a recent Statistics Canada study, students from families in the highest-income group are twice as likely to attend university than those whose families come from the lowest-income group (Drolet, 2005). What effects will this increasing stratification have on our society?

It is not only in the system of higher education that we are witnessing Canadians having unequal access to "intellectual capital." Parents can contribute directly to a young child's educational success by providing a supportive environment for learning or indirectly by paving the way for a higher level of educational attainment. Increasingly, we hear of parents opting out of the public school system, placing their children in private schools or charter schools, home-schooling, or "supplementing" their education with specialized extracurricular programming—computer camps, mini-universities, or private tutoring—in an effort to make sure their child "makes it." It is apparent that only parents who are financially well off with the financial resources (that is, middle- or upper-income families) can afford these programs.

Does this mean that education is stratified by social class? What effect will this have on students from low-income families? Education is one of the most significant social institutions in Canada and other high-income nations. Although most social scientists agree that schools are supposed to be places where people acquire knowledge and skills, not all of them agree on how factors such as a wide array of factors—including class, race, gender, age, religion, and family background—affect individuals' access to educational achievement or to the differential rewards that accrue at various levels of academic achievement. Canada has become a "schooled society" (Davies and Guppy, 2006), and the education system has become a forum for competition. All children in Canada have an equal opportunity to participate in elementary and secondary public schools. Does this mean that all students have an equal opportunity to succeed in school? In this chapter, we will explore the issue of educational inequality in Canada as well as look at other problems facing contemporary elementary, secondary, and higher education. Before reading on, test your knowledge about education in Canada by taking the quiz in Box 14.1 on page 344.

QUESTIONS AND ISSUES

Chapter Focus Question: How do race, class, and gender affect people's access to and opportunities in education?

What are the key assumptions of functionalist, conflict, symbolic interactionist, and postmodern perspectives on education?

What major problems are being faced by Canadian schools today?

Secondary Schools of Manitoba

It is Hereby Certified that *Eva Larmer*

has been promoted from **Grade VIII** to **Grade IX** under the following special regulations of the Advisory Board:

"Boys and girls in Grade VIII whose parents are farming, and whose services may be required upon the farm this spring, will receive their standing upon the recommendation of their teacher or teachers, provided they have attended school regularly during the school year until Easter."

This regulation was extended to include all boys and girls who may be engaged to assist in seeding operations.

Countersigned

R. Fletcher
DEPUTY MINISTER

R. S. Thornton
MINISTER OF EDUCATION

Dated at Winnipeg, *Aug 14* 19 *18*

Courtesy of Jane Murray

Attendance in the first schools in Canada was sparse, as other priorities, such as working on the farm, took precedence.

AN OVERVIEW OF EDUCATION

Education is the social institution responsible for the systematic transmission of knowledge, skills, and cultural values within a formally organized structure. Education is a powerful and influential force in contemporary societies. Education is a social institution that imparts values, beliefs, and knowledge considered essential to the social reproduction of individual personalities and entire cultures (Bourdieu and Passeron, 1990). Education grapples with issues of societal stability and social change, reflecting society even as it attempts to shape it. Early socialization is primarily informal and takes place within our families and friendship networks. Socialization then passes to the schools and other, more formalized organizations created for the specific purpose of educating people. How did education emerge as such an important social institution in contemporary, industrialized nations? To answer this question, we begin with a brief examination of education in historical–global perspective.

EDUCATION IN HISTORICAL-GLOBAL PERSPECTIVE

Education serves an important purpose in all societies. At the microlevel, people must acquire the basic knowledge and skills they need to survive in society. At the macrolevel, the social institution of education is an essential component in maintaining and perpetuating the culture of a society across generations. **Cultural transmission—the process by which children and recent immigrants become acquainted with the dominant cultural beliefs, values, norms, and accumulated knowledge of a society**—occurs through informal and formal education. However, the process of cultural transmission differs in preliterate, preindustrial, and industrial nations.

Informal Education in Preliterate Societies

Preliterate societies have no written language and are characterized by very basic technology and a simple division of labour. Daily activity often centres on the struggle to survive against natural forces, and the earliest forms of education are survival-oriented. People in these societies acquire knowledge and skills through *informal education*—**learning that occurs in a spontaneous, unplanned way**. Through direct informal education, parents and other members of the group provide information about how to gather food, find shelter, make tools, and get along with others. For example, a boy might learn skills such as hunting, gathering, fishing, and farming, from his father, whereas a girl might learn from her mother how to plant, gather, and prepare food, or how to take care of younger sisters and brothers. Such informal education often occurs through storytelling or ritual ceremonies that convey cultural messages and provide behavioural norms. Over time, the knowledge shared through informal education may become the moral code of the group.

Formal Education in Preindustrial, Industrial, and Postindustrial Societies

Although *preindustrial societies* have a written language, few people know how to read and write, and formal education is often reserved for the privileged. Education becomes more formalized in preindustrial and industrial societies. **Formal education is learning that takes place within an academic setting, such as a school, which has a planned instructional process and teachers who convey specific knowledge, skills, and thinking processes to students**. Perhaps the earliest formal education occurred in ancient Greece and Rome, where philosophers, such as Socrates, Plato, and Aristotle, taught elite males the necessary skills to become thinkers and orators who could engage in the art of persuasion (Ballantine, 2001). During the Middle Ages, the first colleges and universities were developed under the auspices of the church. Formal education in Canada began with attempts by Jesuit priests and missionaries to "civilize" Aboriginal children and the children of the colonists. During this time, the church was central to the institution of education. Many of Canada's oldest universities and colleges were founded by churches.

The Renaissance and the Industrial Revolution had a profound effect on education. During the Renaissance, the focus of education shifted from human depravity to the importance of developing well-rounded and liberally educated people. With the rapid growth of industrial capitalism and factories

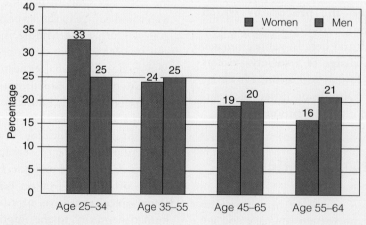

BOX 14.1 SOCIOLOGY AND EVERYDAY LIFE

How Much Do You Know About Education in Canada?

True	False	
T	F	1. Canada has the largest population with a university education among developed countries.
T	F	2. Most students use the Internet as a learning tool in the classroom.
T	F	3. Children of parents with high levels of education are more likely to pursue a university education.
T	F	4. Aboriginal peoples are underrepresented among postsecondary graduates.
T	F	5. In the past decade, the number of jobs requiring a university degree or postsecondary diploma has increased dramatically.
T	F	6. Students from low socioeconomic status families are more likely to have difficulty in school.
T	F	7. More young men than young women in Canada have university degrees.
T	F	8. Tuition fees for postsecondary education have doubled in the last 15 years.

Answers on page 345.

during the Industrial Revolution, it became necessary for workers to have basic skills in reading, writing, and arithmetic. However, from the Middle Ages until the end of World War I, only the sons of the privileged classes were able to attend European universities. Agriculture was the economic base of society,

and literacy for people in the lower classes was not deemed important.

As societies industrialize, the need for formal mass education of the masses increases significantly. In Canada, the school reformers of the late 1800s began to view education as essential to

Census Profile   Young Women Lead the Way in University Attainment

University Attainment

Some 33 percent of women aged between 25 and 34 had a university degree, compared to 25 percent of men in this age group. For those in the 35–44 year age group, the proportions of men and women having a university degree were almost identical, 24 percent and 25 percent, respectively.

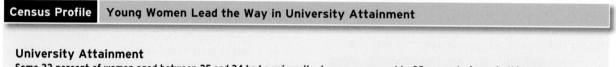

Source: Statistics Canada, Census Population, 2006.

Answers to the Sociology Quiz on Education in Canada

1. False   According to the most recent census figures, Canada ranked sixth among developed countries in terms of the proportion of the population who had university degrees, tied with Australia and Korea, at 23 percent. Norway and the United States led the way at 30 percent. However, when attainment of college and university degrees are combined, Canada is ranked number one among developed countries (Statistics Canada, 2008).

2. True   In a recent survey, more than one million computers were available to students and teachers and slightly more than 90 percent were connected to the Internet. This extensive availability of computers not only offers students access to a wide range of information on the Internet, but also allows them the potential to use information and communications technology (ICT) as a learning tool (Plante and Beattie, 2004).

3. True   The rate of participation in university was three times higher for young adults whose parents had a university education than those whose parents had high school education or less. (However this pattern does not hold for college participation. In fact, children of parents with a high school education or less are just as likely to participate in college as children of parents with a university degree). (Drolet, 2005).

4. True   Approximately 44 percent of Aboriginal persons aged 25–64 were postsecondary graduates as compared to 61 percent of the general population. Only 8 percent of Aboriginal persons between the ages of 25 and 64 have a university degree—well below the 23 percent of Canadians in the general population who hold a university degree. However, 19 percent of Aboriginal persons in the same age category have a college diploma, just below the Canadian average of 20 percent (Statistics Canada, 2008b).

5. True   Since 1990, the number of jobs requiring a university degree or postsecondary diploma has increased by 1.3 million. The number of jobs available for people without these credentials has decreased by 800 000. In short, the more education you have, the more likely it is that you will find a job (Statistics Canada, 2003e).

6. True   For example, students from the lowest socioeconomic group score lower on tests of academic performance, are more likely to have to repeat a grade, are more likely to require remedial education, and are more likely not to complete high school (Council of Ministers of Education, 2002).

7. False   As shown in the Census Profile, approximately 33 percent of women aged 25–34 have a university degree, compared to just over 25 percent of men in this age group. (Statistics Canada, 2008).

8. False   Tuition fees have almost tripled in Canada since 1990–91. Today, the average annual tuition is over $5 000 for a university undergraduate program and ranges from $1 800 to $3 300 for an eight-month college program (Statistics Canada, 2010b).

the country's economic growth (Gilbert, 1989). Ontario school reformer Egerton Ryerson promoted free schooling for all children, arguing that sending rich and poor children to the same schools would bring people closer together and create more harmony (Tepperman, 1994). By the early 1900s, mass education had taken hold in Canada, as the provinces established free, tax-supported elementary schools that were readily available to children throughout the country. **Mass education** refers to **providing free, public schooling for wide segments of a nation's population.**

What values are these children being taught? Is there a consensus about what today's school should teach? Why or why not?

As industrialization and bureaucratization intensified, managers and business owners demanded that schools educate students beyond Grade 3 or 4 so that well-qualified workers would be available for rapidly emerging "white-collar" jobs in management and clerical work (Bailyn, 1960). In addition to educating the next generation of children for the workplace, public schools were also supposed to serve as the primary agents of socialization for millions of European immigrants arriving in Canada seeking economic opportunities and a better life. By the 1920s, educators had introduced the "core" curriculum: courses such as mathematics, social sciences, natural sciences, and English. This core is reflected in the contemporary "back to basics" movement, which calls for teaching the "three R's" (reading, 'riting, and 'rithmetic) and enforcing stricter discipline in schools.

Contemporary education in Canada attempts to meet society's needs by teaching a diverse group of students a myriad of topics ranging from history and science to computer skills, how to balance a chequebook, and AIDS prevention. According to sociologists, many functions formerly performed by other social institutions in the past are now done under the auspices of the public schools. For example, full-day kindergartens, lunch programs, and after-school programs for school-age children are provided by many school divisions because of the growing numbers of working parents who need high-quality, affordable care for their children. Within the regular classroom, many teachers now feel that their job description encompasses too many divergent tasks. At all levels of education in Canada, from kindergarten through graduate school,

controversy exists over *what* should be taught, *how* it should be taught, and *who* should teach it.

SOCIOLOGICAL PERSPECTIVES ON EDUCATION

Sociologists have divergent perspectives on the purpose of education in contemporary society. Functionalists believe that education contributes to the maintenance of society and provides people with an opportunity for self-enhancement and upward social mobility. Conflict theorists argue that education perpetuates social inequality and benefits the dominant class at the expense of all others. Symbolic interactionists focus on classroom dynamics and the effect of self-concept on grades and aspirations. Postmodern theorists view the education system as a social institution characterized by permeability. Each of these perspectives can provide valuable insights.

Functionalist Perspectives

Functionalists view education as one of the most important components of society. According to Émile Durkheim, education is crucial for promoting social solidarity and stability in society: education is the "influence exercised by adult generations on those that are not yet ready for social life"

(Durkheim, 1956:28) and helps young people travel the great distance that it has taken people many centuries to cover. In other words, we can learn from what others already have experienced. Durkheim also asserted that *moral education* is very important because it conveys moral values—the foundation of a cohesive social order. He believed that schools are responsible for teaching a commitment to the common morality.

From this perspective, students must be taught to put the group's needs ahead of their individual desires and aspirations. Contemporary functionalists suggest that education is responsible for teaching social values. The 1994 Royal Commission on Learning outlined three purposes of schooling: first, to ensure for all students high levels of literacy by building on basic reading, writing, and problem-solving skills; second, to develop an appreciation of learning, the wish to continue learning, and the ability and commitment to do so; and finally, to prepare students for

responsible citizenship, including developing "basic moral values, such as a sense of caring and compassion, respect for the human person and anti-racism, a commitment to peace and non-violence, honesty and justice" (Osborne, 1994:4).

Functionalists emphasize that "shared" values should be transmitted by schools from kindergarten through university. However, not all analysts agree on what those shared values should be, or what functions education should serve in contemporary societies. In analyzing the values and functions of education, sociologists using a functionalist framework distinguish between manifest and latent functions. Manifest functions and latent functions are compared in Figure 14.1.

Manifest Functions of Education   Some functions of education are *manifest functions*—previously defined as open, stated, and intended goals or consequences of activities within an organization

Figure 14.1   **Manifest and Latent Functions of Education**

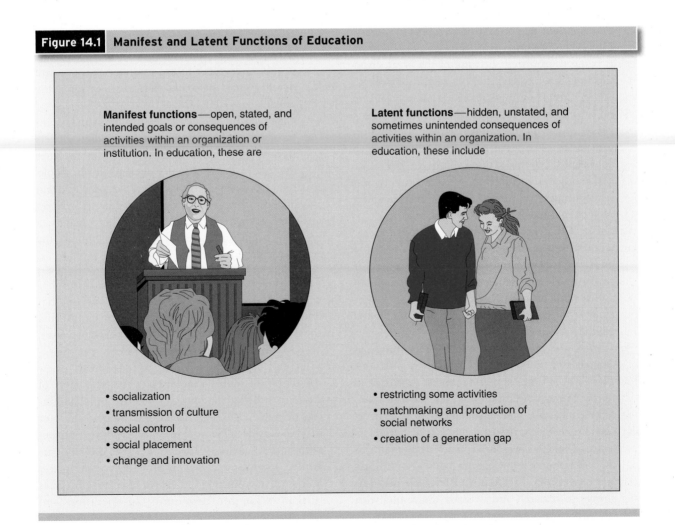

Manifest functions—open, stated, and intended goals or consequences of activities within an organization or institution. In education, these are

- socialization
- transmission of culture
- social control
- social placement
- change and innovation

Latent functions—hidden, unstated, and sometimes unintended consequences of activities within an organization. In education, these include

- restricting some activities
- matchmaking and production of social networks
- creation of a generation gap

or institution. Education serves five major manifest functions in society:

1. *Socialization.* From kindergarten through university, schools teach students the student role, specific academic subjects, and political socialization. In kindergarten, children learn the appropriate attitudes and behaviour for the student role (Ballantine, 2001). In primary and secondary schools, students are taught specific subject matter appropriate to their age, skill level, and previous educational experience. At the university level, students focus on more detailed knowledge of subjects they have previously studied and are exposed to new areas of study and research. Throughout their schooling, students receive political socialization in the form of history and civics lessons.

2. *Transmission of culture.* Schools transmit cultural norms and values to each new generation and play an active part in the process of assimilation, whereby recent immigrants learn dominant cultural values, attitudes, and behaviours so that they can be productive members of society. However, questions remain as to *whose* culture is being transmitted. Because of the great diversity in Canada today, it is virtually impossible to define a single culture.

3. *Social control.* Schools are responsible for teaching values, such as discipline, respect, obedience, punctuality, and perseverance. Schools teach conformity by encouraging young people to be good students, conscientious future workers, and law-abiding citizens. The teaching of conformity rests primarily with classroom teachers.

4. *Social placement.* Schools are responsible for identifying the most qualified people to fill the positions available in society. As a result, students are channelled into programs based on individual ability and academic achievement. Graduates receive the appropriate credentials to enter the paid labour force.

5. *Change and innovation.* Schools are a source of change and innovation. As student populations change over time, new programs are introduced to meet societal needs; for example, sex education, drug education, and multicultural studies have been implemented in some schools to help students learn about pressing social issues. Innovation in the form of new knowledge is required in colleges and universities. Faculty members are required to engage in research and to share the results with students, colleagues, and others.

Latent Functions of Education   All social institutions, including education, have *latent functions*—hidden, unstated, and sometimes unintended consequences of activities within an organization or institution. Education serves at least three latent functions:

1. *Restricting some activities.* Early in the 20th century, all provinces passed *mandatory education laws* that required children to attend school until they reached a specified age (usually the age of 16) or complete a minimum level of formal education (generally completion of Grade 8). The assumption was that an educated citizenry and workforce are necessary for the smooth functioning of democracy and capitalism. Out of these laws grew one latent function of education, which is to keep students off the street and out of the full-time job market for a number of years, thus helping keep unemployment within reasonable bounds (Braverman, 1974).

2. *Matchmaking and production of social networks.* Because schools bring together people of similar ages, social class, and race/ethnicity, young people often meet future marriage partners and develop social networks that may last for many years.

3. *Creation of a generation gap.* Students may learn information in school that contradicts beliefs held by their parents or their religion. Debates over the content of textbooks and library books typically centre on information that parents deem unacceptable for their children. When education conflicts with parental attitudes and beliefs, a generation gap is created if students embrace the newly acquired perspective.

Functionalists acknowledge that education has certain dysfunctions. Some analysts argue that education systems in Canada are not promoting the high-level skills in reading, writing, science, and mathematics that are needed in the workplace and in the global economy. However, a new international report that assesses the skill level of students nearing the end of their compulsory education ranked Canadian students among the best in the world when it comes to reading, mathematics, and science. Canadian 15-year-old students ranked second in science and third in reading and mathematics, among 32 participating countries (Organisation for Economic Co-operation and Development, 2009).

Conflict Perspectives

Conflict theorists do not believe that public schools reduce social inequality in society; rather, they believe that schools often perpetuate class, racial–ethnic, and gender inequalities as some groups seek to maintain their privileged position at the expense of others (Ballantine, 2001; Curtis, Grabb, and Guppy, 1999).

Cultural Capital and Class Reproduction

Although many factors—including intelligence, family income, motivation, and previous achievement—are important in determining how much education a person will attain, conflict theorists argue that access to high-quality education is closely related to social class. From this approach, education is a vehicle for reproducing existing class relationships. According to French sociologist Pierre Bourdieu, the school legitimates and reinforces the social elites by engaging in specific practices that uphold the patterns of behaviour and the attitudes of the dominant class. Bourdieu asserts that students from diverse class backgrounds come to school with differing amounts of *cultural capital*—**social assets that include values, beliefs, attitudes, and competencies in language and culture** (Bourdieu and Passeron, 1990). Cultural capital involves "proper" attitudes toward education, socially approved dress and manners, and knowledge about books, art, music, and other forms of high and popular culture. Middle- and upper-income parents provide their children with more cultural capital than do working-class and poverty-level parents. Because cultural capital is essential for acquiring an education, children with less cultural capital have fewer opportunities to succeed in school. For example, standardized tests that are used to group students by ability and to assign them to classes often measure students' cultural capital rather than their "natural" intelligence or aptitude. Thus, a circular effect occurs: Students with dominant cultural values are more highly rewarded by the educational system; in turn, the educational system teaches and reinforces those values that sustain the elite's position in society.

Tracking and Social Inequality

Closely linked to the issue of cultural capital is how tracking in schools is related to social inequality. Conflict theorists who study ability grouping focus on how the process of tracking affects students' educational performance. Ability grouping, which is based on the assumption that it is easier to teach students with similar abilities, is often used in elementary schools.

However, class-based factors also affect which children are most likely to be placed in "high," "middle," or "low" groups, often referred to by such innocuous terms as "Blue Birds," "Red Birds," and "Yellow Birds," for example.

In middle school, junior high, and high school, most students experience *tracking*—**the assignment of students to specific courses and educational programs based on their test scores, previous grades, or both.** Ruben Navarrette, Jr. (1997:274–275) talks about his experience with tracking:

> One fateful day, in the second grade, my teacher decided to teach her class more efficiently by dividing it into six groups of five students each. Each group was assigned a geometric symbol to differentiate it from the others. There were the Circles. There were the Squares. There were the Triangles and Rectangles.
>
> I remember something else, an odd coincidence. The Hexagons were the smartest kids in the class. These distinctions are not lost on a child of seven. Even in the second grade, my classmates and I knew who was smarter than whom. And on the day on which we were assigned our respective shapes, we knew that our teacher knew, too.
>
> As Hexagons, we would wait for her to call on us, then answer by hurrying to her with books and pencils in hand. We sat around a table in our "reading group," chattering excitedly to one another and basking in the intoxication of positive learning. We did not notice, did not care to notice, over our shoulders, the frustrated looks on the faces of Circles and Squares and Triangles who sat quietly at their desks, doodling on scratch paper or mumbling to one another.
>
> We knew also that, along with our geometric shapes, our books were different and that each group had different amounts of work to do. The Circles had the easiest books and were assigned to read only a few pages at a time. Not surprisingly, the Hexagons had the most difficult books of all, those with the biggest words and the fewest pictures, and we were expected to read the most pages.
>
> The result of all of this education by separation was exactly what the teacher had imagined that it would be: Students could, and did, learn at their own pace without being encumbered by one another. Some learned faster than others. Some, I realized only [later], did not learn at all.

Numerous studies have found that ability grouping and tracking affects students' academic achievements and career choices (Oakes, 2005). Education scholar Jeannie Oakes (2005) found that tracking affects students' perceptions of classroom goals and achievements, as the following statements from high- and low-track students suggest:

> I want to be a lawyer and debate has taught me to dig for answers and get involved. I can express myself. (High-Track English)

> To understand concepts and ideas and experiment with them. Also to work independently. (High-Track Science)

> To behave in class. (Low-Track English)

> To be a better listener in class. (Low-Track English)

> I have learned that I should do my questions for the book when he asks me to. (Low-Track Science)

Perceptions of the students on the "low tracks" reflect the impact that years of tracking and lowered expectations can have on people's educational and career aspirations. Often, the educational track—vocational or university bound—on which high school students are placed has a significant influence on their future educational and employment opportunities. Although the stated purpose of tracking systems is to permit students to study subjects that are suitable to their skills and interests, most research reveals that this purpose has not been achieved (Oakes, 2005; Welner and Oakes, 2000). Moreover, some social scientists believe that tracking is one of the most obvious mechanisms through which poor and minority students receive a diluted academic program, making it much more likely that they will fall even further behind their white, middle-class counterparts (Davies and Guppy, 2006).

Awareness of these effects has resulted in numerous destreaming initiatives across the country. These initiatives have been met with some opposition by parents, teachers, and school boards, which were concerned that children will receive lower-quality education in destreamed classrooms. However, the benefits of destreaming may outweigh the costs when we consider the perceptions and lowered expectations of students on the "low tracks," brought on by years of tracking.

Instead of enhancing school performance, tracking systems may result in students dropping out of school

What are the consequences of unequal funding for schools?

or ending up in dead-end situations because they have not taken the courses required to go to university.

The Hidden Curriculum According to conflict theorists, the *hidden curriculum* **is the transmission of cultural values and attitudes, such as conformity and obedience to authority, through implied demands found in rules, routines, and regulations of schools** (Snyder, 1971). Although students from all social classes are subjected to the hidden curriculum, working-class and poverty-level students may be affected the most adversely (Polakow, 1993; Ballantine, 2001, Davies and Guppy, 2006). When teachers are from a higher-class background than their students, they tend to use more structure in the classroom and to have lower expectations for students' academic achievement. In a study of five elementary schools located in different communities, significant differences were found in the manner in which knowledge was transmitted to students even though the curriculum was organized similarly (Anyon, 1980, 1997). Schools for working-class students emphasize procedures and rote memorization without much decision making, choice, and explanation of why something is done a particular way. Schools for middle-class students stress the processes (such as figuring and decision making) involved in getting the right answer. Schools for affluent students focus on creative activities in which students express their own ideas and apply them to the subject under consideration. Schools for students from elite families work to develop students' analytical powers and critical thinking skills, applying abstract principles to problem solving.

Through the hidden curriculum, schools make working-class and poverty-level students aware that they will be expected to take orders from others, arrive at work on time, follow bureaucratic rules, and experience high levels of boredom without complaining (Ballantine, 2001). Over time, these students may be disqualified from higher education and barred from obtaining the credentials necessary for well-paid occupations and professions (Bowles and Gintis, 1976). Educational credentials are extremely important in societies that emphasize *credentialism*—**a process of social selection in which class advantage and social status are linked to the possession of academic qualifications** (Collins, 1979; Marshall, 1998). Credentialism is closely related to meritocracy—previously defined as a social system in which status is assumed to be acquired through individual ability and effort (Young, 1994). Persons who acquire the appropriate credentials for a job are assumed to have gained the position through what they know, not who they are or whom they know. According to conflict theorists, the hidden curriculum determines in advance that the most valued credentials will primarily stay in the hands of the elites. Therefore, Canada is not actually as meritocratic as some might claim.

Feminist Perspectives

Gender Bias and Gender Stereotyping

Feminism has had a significant impact in the educational system. As feminist scholar Jane Gaskell explains, "When feminists demanded equal opportunity for women, education was one of the first areas targeted for reform and rethinking" (2009:17).

According to conflict theorists, the hidden curriculum in schools makes low-income students aware that they will be expected to follow rules when they work for others throughout their adult lives.

SPENCER GRANT/PHOTOEDIT

BOX 14.2 SOCIOLOGY IN GLOBAL PERSPECTIVE

Women's Literacy in Low-Income Countries

Education is a powerful agent of progress. Literacy is the most basic and necessary of learning skills.

—Maria Luisa Jauregui de Gainza, literacy specialist, UNESCO (quoted in Ballara, 1992)

An estimated 875 million adults are illiterate worldwide. Nearly two-thirds of them are women.

In 1969, the year man took his first step on the moon, four out of five women in Africa could not read or write. It is estimated that today nearly half of all African women are still illiterate.

More than 100 million children, including at least 60 million girls, have no access to primary schooling.

Since 1985, there are more female students enrolled in higher education than male students in most industrialized countries. In contrast, in the world's least developed countries, only one in four students of higher education are women (World Literacy of Canada, 2005a).

Functional illiteracy refers to a lack of basic literacy and numeracy skills that are essential for proper functioning—such as the ability to read or write or to make sense of written material (Ballara, 1992:1). Organizations such as the United Nations believe that the education of women in low-income countries is a high priority not only for national development but also for the well-being of children and families.

An estimated 95 percent of all illiterate people are concentrated in the developing nations of Southeast Asia and sub-Saharan Africa. Here, one-third of all women are illiterate, as compared with one-fifth of the men. In the countries with lowest incomes, 79 percent of adult women are illiterate. Even with organizations such as the United Nations Educational, Scientific and Cultural Organization (UNESCO) attempting to eradicate illiteracy, the problem remains.

Many factors stand in the way of women's literacy, including religious beliefs that subordinate women and emphasize a traditional gendered division of labour, such as "care of children, maintenance of the household, care of older family members and the ill, servicing their husband and his relevant kin, maintenance of the network of familial ties, and servicing of the community" (Ballara, 1992:x). Religions that confine women's activities to domestic tasks and stress their role as wives and mothers often limit their access to education and produce feelings of low self-esteem and isolation.

Ultimately, the main reason that most women (and men) are illiterate is poverty; daily survival becomes far more important than learning how to read or compute math problems. Some analysts have found that schools in the poorest developing nations are becoming even more impoverished. Some countries have a two-tier system: (1) in rural areas, a grossly inadequate school system that may be state-run or attached to a local temple or mosque, where religious education is often the primary goal; and (2) in urban areas, a better school system that may be patterned after Western schools, such as those found in England or France, and that serves the children of the nation's elite population.

Is there hope for the future? Media campaigns and numerous projects are actively seeking to promote literacy. Perhaps a greater awareness of the problem is the first step toward eradication of it. Are the problems of women in developing nations in any way related to your life? Using your sociological imagination, can you think of ways in which their fate might be intertwined with yours?

© Liba Taylor/Corbis

Sources: Based on Ballara, 1992; Ballantine, 1997; World Literacy of Canada, 2005b.

Early feminist analysis of schooling focused on questions about sexism in the classroom and curricula, and unequal distributions of male and female educators in the system (Wotherspoon, 2009).

In Canada in the late 1960s, the Royal Commission on the Status of Women examined the relationship between education and patterns of gender inequality. It identified gender bias and gender stereotyping in the educational curriculum as a significant issue that had to be addressed. For example, girls were underrepresented in the school books and when they were included, they appeared in rigid sex-typed roles. Boys and girls were also segregated in the playgrounds and in sporting activities. Furthermore, boys received more attention from teachers than girls, and teachers displayed stereotypical expectations of male and female students' aptitudes and interests.

Subsequent to the commission's report, significant changes were implemented in educational curriculum, practice, and policy. Ministries of education across the country appointed advisory groups on sexism and established guidelines to eliminate gender bias and stereotyping in school curriculum and classroom practices. According to Gaskell,"these changes had an effect . . . the critique of stereotyping had caught on. The idea that biology did not mean destiny, that equality meant open access and equal treatment, was increasingly accepted. The numbers of women in science and math, in universities, and in leadership positions in the teaching profession increased"(2009:21).

More than 30 years later, the gender gap in educational attainment and enrollment has narrowed to the extent that university enrollments for women now surpass those of their male counterparts. In the 2006 Census, 60 percent of university graduates were female. Women outnumber men in the faculties of law and medicine (Statistics Canada, 2008h). Female students are increasingly dominating in science competitions across the country and taking home the majority of prizes (Mick, 2009). However, differences still remain. As shown in Table 14.1 (on page 354), females are highly overrepresented in nursing and teaching while men are overrepresented in engineering, computer science, and applied mathematics.

Rather than focusing on the elimination of gender bias and stereotyping, some feminist scholars have directed our attention to the economic consequences of educational attainment, arguing that gender inequalities are built into not only the structure of schooling but also its links to the labour market. Radical feminism points out that patriarchy, or the systematic oppression of women, is reflected in the relationship between education and work. Although one might assume that more education will lead to higher income and a better job, that assumption is not borne out for many women. As Gaskell explains:

> Instead of arguing that equality will be achieved when there are as many girls as boys in mathematics and physics classes, radical feminism critiques the wages and prestige associated with the jobs that women have traditionally done. Equal-pay legislation has forced employers to recognize that the work women have done is underpaid in relation to the skills, education, and responsibility it entails. Day care workers have been paid less than dog catchers; secretaries are paid less than male technicians with equal levels of education. (2009:24)

Feminist scholars have also challenged common assumptions about learning and traditional teaching methods. They argue that men and women learn in different ways and that formal educational institutions may not adequately attend to women's "ways of knowing" (Gaskell, 2009:23). Rather than denying difference, some feminists emphasize the need to recognize and incorporate female strategies of learning as well as value the knowledge constructed by women.

Symbolic Interactionist Perspectives

Unlike functionalist analysts, who focus on the functions and dysfunctions of education, and conflict theorists, who focus on the relationship between education and inequality, symbolic interactionists have focused on classroom communication patterns and on educational practices, such as labelling, that affect students' self-concept and aspirations.

Labelling and the Self-Fulfilling Prophecy

Chapter 6 explained that *labelling* is the process whereby a person is identified by others as possessing a specific characteristic or exhibiting a certain pattern of behaviour (such as being deviant). According to symbolic interactionists, the process of labelling is directly related to the power and status of those persons who do the labelling and those who are being labelled. In schools, teachers and administrators are empowered to label children in various ways, including grades, written comments on classroom behaviour, and placement in classes. For example, based on standardized test scores or classroom performance, educators label some children as "special ed" or low achievers, whereas others are labelled as

Table 14.1	CANADIAN UNIVERSITY GRADUATES' TOP TEN FIELDS OF STUDY, BY SEX, 2006

MEN

Business, management, marketing and related support services	801 605
Mechanic and repair technologies/Technicians	542 370
Engineering	450 960
Engineering technologies/Technicians	427 840
Construction trades	388 990
Precision production	290 625
Computer and information sciences and support services	257 385
Health professions and related clinical sciences	204 560
Education	196 165
Social sciences	194 795

WOMEN

Business, management, marketing and related support services	1 357 160
Health professions and related clinical sciences	1 080 745
Education	583 560
Personal and culinary services	271 825
Visual and performing arts	182 880
Social sciences	182 625
Family and consumer sciences/Human sciences	170 020
Computer and information sciences and support services	150 220
Legal professions and studies	130 190
Public administration and social service professions	126 575

Source: Statistics Canada, *Educational Portrait of Canada, 2006 Census*, Catalogue 97-560-XIE2006001, (see Table 7 and 7a), http://www12.statcan.ca/census-recensement/2006/as-sa/97-560/pdf/97-560-XIE2006001.pdf, Retrieved November 29, 2010.

average or "gifted and talented." For some students, labelling amounts to a *self-fulfilling prophecy*—previously defined as an unsubstantiated belief or prediction resulting in behaviour that makes the originally false belief come true (Merton, 1968). A classic form of labelling and self-fulfilling prophecy occurs through the use of IQ (intelligence quotient) tests, which claim to measure a person's inherent intelligence, apart from any family or school influences on the individual. In many school systems, IQ tests are used as one criterion in determining student placement in classes and ability groups.

Using Labelling Theory to Examine the IQ Debate
The relationship between IQ testing and labelling theory has been of special interest to sociologists. In the 1960s, two social scientists conducted an experiment in an elementary school where they intentionally misinformed teachers about the intelligence test scores of students in their classes (Rosenthal and Jacobson, 1968). Despite the fact that the students were randomly selected for the study and had no measurable differences in intelligence, the researchers informed the teachers that some of the students had extremely high IQ test scores, whereas others had average to below-average scores. As the researchers observed, the teachers began to teach "exceptional" students in a different manner from other students. In turn, the "exceptional" students began to outperform their "average" peers and to excel in their classwork. This study called attention to the labelling effect of IQ scores.

However, experiments such as this also raise other important issues: What if a teacher (as a result of stereotypes based on the relationship between IQ and race) believes that some students of colour are less capable of learning? Will that teacher (often without realizing it) treat such students as if they are incapable of learning? In their controversial book *The Bell Curve: Intelligence and Class Structure in American Life,* Richard J. Herrnstein and Charles Murray (1994) argue that intelligence is genetically inherited and that people cannot be "smarter" than they are born to be, regardless of their environment or education. According to Herrnstein and Murray, certain racial–ethnic groups differ in average IQ and are likely to differ in "intelligence genes" as well. For example, they point out that, on average, people living in Asia score higher on IQ tests than white Americans, and that African Americans score 15 points lower on average than white Americans. Based on an all-white sample, the authors also concluded that low intelligence leads to social pathology, such as high rates of crime, dropping out of school, and ending up poor. In contrast, high intelligence typically leads to success, and family background plays only a secondary role.

Many scholars disagree with Herrnstein and Murray's research methods and conclusions. Two major flaws found in their approach were as follows: (1) the authors used biased statistics that underestimate the impact of hard-to-measure factors, such as family background, and (2) they used scores from the Armed Forces Qualification Test, an exam that depends on how much schooling people have completed. Thus, what the authors claim is immutable intelligence actually reflects acquired skills (Weinstein, 1997). Despite this refutation, the idea of inherited mental inferiority tends to take on a life of its own when people want to believe that such differences exist (Duster, 1995; Hauser, 1995; Taylor, 1995). According to researchers, many African American and Mexican American children were placed in special education classes on the basis of IQ scores when the students were not fluent in English and thus could not understand the directions given for the test. Moreover, although the terms are only social constructions, labelling children as "special ed" or "learning disabled" may lead to stigmatization and become a self-fulfilling prophecy (Carrier, 1986; Coles, 1987).

A self-fulfilling prophecy can also result from labelling students as gifted. Gifted students are considered to be those with above-average intellectual ability, academic aptitude, creative or productive thinking, or leadership skills (Ballantine, 2001). When some students are labelled as better than others, they may achieve at a higher level because of the label. Ironically, such labelling may also result in discrimination against these students.

Labelling and the self-fulfilling prophecy are not unique to U.S. and Canadian schools. Around the globe, students are labelled by batteries of tests and teachers' evaluations of their attitudes, academic performance, and classroom behaviour. Other problems in education, ranging from illiteracy and school discipline to unequal school financing and educational opportunities for students with disabilities, are concerns in elementary and secondary education in many countries.

| Concept Table 14.1 | SOCIOLOGICAL PERSPECTIVES ON EDUCATION |

KEY POINTS

Functionalist Perspectives	Education is one of the most important components of society: schools teach students not only content but also to put group needs ahead of the individual's.
Conflict Perspectives	Schools perpetuate class, racial–ethnic, and gender inequalities through what they teach to whom.
Feminist Perspectives	The educational system needs to eliminate gender bias and gender stereotyping in school curricula and equalize opportunities in educational attainment in all educational programs.
Symbolic Interactionist Perspectives	Labelling and the self-fulfilling prophecy are an example of how students and teachers affect each other as they interpret their interactions.
Postmodernist Perspectives	In contemporary schools, educators attempt to become substitute parents and promulgators of self-esteem in students; students and their parents become the consumers of education.

BOX 14.3   SOCIOLOGY AND THE MEDIA

The Technology Revolution in the Classroom

Technology itself is not new, but its importance as an educational issue has exploded in the past few years as computers have moved into classrooms and workplaces. Canada was one of the first countries in the world to link its entire student body to the information highway. Today, Canada is ranked second among developed countries in terms of access to computers at schools for 15-year-olds (Statistics Canada, 2004). At the college and university level, many students are taking courses online and many corporations use the Internet to provide training to their employees. Close to 7 million adult Canadians use the Internet for education, training, or school work (McKeown and Underhill, 2007; Dunning, 1997). How have students changed as a result of technology and how do educators need to change to keep up?

Today's students—kindergarten through college and university—represent the first generations to grow up with this new technology. They have spent their entire lives surrounded by and using computers, video games, digital music players, video cams, cell phones, and all the other toys and tools of the digital age. Today's average college grads have spent less than 5 000 hours of their lives reading, but over 10 000 hours playing video games (not to mention 20 000 hours watching TV). Computer games, email, the Internet, cell phones and instant messaging are integral parts of their lives (Prensky, 2001:1).

Proponents of computers in schools see them as a powerful tool for levelling the playing field in Canadian classrooms. Their capacity to retrieve information is nearly limitless, and equally available in urban, rural, and remote locations; they can be equipped with features that allow many children with disabilities to work alongside their classmates; and they increase understanding within Canada and internationally by allowing students to connect with individuals and classrooms across the country and around the world (Dunning, 1997). Computer technologies will serve to encourage lifelong learning and to reduce obstacles to learning such as cost and accessibility (McKeown and Underhill, 2007).

Despite all of the potential opportunities for learning provided by new classroom technologies, there are those who have reservations about the expanding role of computer technology in schools. Some parents and teachers continue to fear that, in the face of reduced school budgets, students may find themselves facing computer screens more frequently than teachers. Furthermore, teachers do not necessarily have the knowledge or training to maximize the potential of computers. In fact, students' computer skills are often superior to those of the teachers', which creates a new form of the "digital divide."

As educational consultant Mark Prensky argues, if today's students think and process information fundamentally differently from their predecessors, it is clear what needs to change. The digital immigrants [Those of us who were not born into the digital world] need to change the way they teach because students today are all what Prensky calls "digital natives" [because they are "native speakers" of the digital language of computers, video games, and the Internet].

So what should happen? Should the digital native students learn the old ways, or should their digital immigrant educators learn the new? Unfortunately, no matter how much the immigrants may wish it, it is highly unlikely the digital natives will go backwards. In the first place, it may be impossible—their brains may already be different. It also flies in the face of everything we know about cultural migration. Kids born into any new culture learn the new language easily, and forcefully resist using the old. Smart adult immigrants accept that they don't know about their new world and take advantage of their kids to help them learn and integrate. Not-so-smart (or not-so-flexible) immigrants spend most of their time grousing about how good things were in the "old country."

So unless we want to just forget about educating digital natives until they grow up and do it themselves, we had better confront this issue. And in so doing we need to reconsider both our methodology and our content. (Prensky, 2001:3)

Do you agree? What experiences have you had with learning in university or college classrooms? Do you think you would learn more effectively if more digital technologies were incorporated in instructional methods?

Postmodern Perspectives

Postmodern theories often highlight *difference* and *irregularity* in society. From this perspective, education—like the family—is a social institution characterized by its permeability. In contemporary schools, a wide diversity of family kinship systems is recognized, and educators attempt to be substitute parents and promulgators of self-esteem in students. Urbanity is reflected in multicultural and anti-bias curriculums that are initially introduced in early childhood education. Since the values of individual achievement and competition have so permeated contemporary home and school life, social adjustment (how to deal with others) has become of little importance to some people (Elkind, 1995).

How might a postmodern approach describe higher education? Postmodern views of higher education might incorporate the ideas of sociologist George Ritzer (1998), who believes that "McUniversity" can be thought of as a means of educational consumption that allows students to consume educational services and eventually obtain "goods," such as degrees and credentials:

> Students (and often, more importantly, their parents) are increasingly approaching the university as consumers; the university is fast becoming little more than another component of the consumer society . . . Parents are, if anything, likely to be even more adept as consumers than their children and because of the burgeoning cost of higher education more apt to bring a consumerist mentality to it. (Ritzer, 1998:151–152)

Savvy college and university administrators are aware of the permeability of higher education and the "students-as-consumers" model:

> [Students] want education to be nearby and to operate during convenient hours—preferably around the clock. They want to avoid traffic jams, to have easy, accessible and low cost parking, short lines, and polite and efficient personnel and services. They also want high-quality products but are eager for low costs. They are willing to shop—placing a premium on time and money. (Levine, 1993:4)

To attract new students and enhance current students' opportunities for consumption, many campuses have student centres equipped with amenities, such as food courts, ATMs, video games, Olympic-sized swimming pools, and massive rock-climbing walls. "High-tech" or "wired" campuses are also a major attraction for student consumers, and virtual classrooms make it possible for some students to earn postsecondary credits without having to look for a parking place at the traditional bricks-and-mortar campus.

The permeability of contemporary universities may be so great that eventually it will be impossible to distinguish higher education from other means of consumption. For example, Ritzer (1998) believes that officials of "McUniversity" will start to emphasize the same kinds of production values as CNN or MTV, resulting in a simulated world of education somewhat like postmodernist views of Disneyland. Ritzer (1998:160) predicts that we may enter a "trans-educational" era: "Since education will be everywhere, since everything will be educational, in a sense nothing will be educational." Based on a postmodern approach, what do you believe will be the predominant means by which future students will consume educational services and goods at your college or university?

CURRENT ISSUES IN EDUCATION

Public schools in Canada today are a microcosm of many of the issues and problems facing the country. Canada is the only advanced industrialized country without a federal educational system—a fact that has made it difficult to coordinate national educational and teaching standards. Each province enacts its own laws and regulations, with local school boards frequently making the final determination regarding curriculum. Accordingly, no general standards exist as to what is to be taught to students or how, although many provinces have now adopted standards for what (at a minimum) must be learned in order to graduate from high school. France has an education ministry that is officially responsible for every elementary school in the nation. Japan has a centrally controlled curriculum; in England, national achievement tests are administered by the government and students must pass them in order to advance to the next level of education (Lemann, 1997).

Inequality in Public Schools versus Private Schools

Often, there is a perceived conflict between public schools and private schools for students and financial resources. However, far more students and their parents are dependent on public schools than on private ones for providing a high-quality education. Enrolment in Canadian elementary and secondary education (kindergarten through Grade 12) totals approximately 5.2 million students. More than 90 percent of elementary and secondary students are educated in public schools. About 6 percent of all students are educated in private schools, and approximately 1 percent of all students attend private schools with tuition of more than $5 000 a year (Statistics Canada, 2008).

Private secondary boarding schools tend to be reserved for students from high-income families and for a few lower-income or minority students who are able to acquire academic or athletic scholarships that cover their tuition, room and board, and other expenses. The average cost for seven-day tuition and room and board at secondary boarding schools is nearly $20 000 a year, whereas the cost of day-school tuition can be as high as $8 000.

An important factor for many parents whose children attend private secondary schools is the emphasis on academics that they believe exists in private (as opposed to public) schools. Another is the moral and ethical standards that they believe private secondary schools instil in students. Overall, many families believe that private schools are a better choice for their children because they are more academically demanding, more motivating, more focused on discipline, and without many of the inadequacies found in public schools. However, according to some social analysts, there is little to substantiate the claim that private schools (other than elite academies attended by the children of the wealthiest and most influential families) are inherently better than public schools (Zehr, 2006).

Academic Standards and Functional Literacy

Some social analysts believe that academic standards are not high enough in Canadian schools. As part of their evidence for this concern, they cite the rate of functional illiteracy in this country. **Functional illiteracy is the inability to read and/ or write at the skill level necessary for carrying out everyday tasks.** Everyday tasks include reading a newspaper, filling out a form, or following written instructions. Seventeen percent of adult Canadians do not have the skills to handle most of the written material they see every day; that is, they are functionally illiterate. An additional 24 percent can use reading materials only to carry out simple reading tasks. They do not have the reading skills to cope with unfamiliar and more complex reading materials. In other words, they can read, but not well (Statistics Canada, 2005e). Overall, Canada has a high rate of adult literacy compared with the seven other countries surveyed in the International Adult Literacy Survey. However, Canada also had the largest proportion of youth with poor literacy skills (10 percent) (Organisation for Economic Co-operation and Development and Statistics Canada, 2000).

Illiteracy is a global problem as well as a national one (see Table 14.2). As a result of the concerns with declining standards and illiteracy, school boards across the country have been revising their curriculum to place a greater emphasis on the core subject areas of reading, mathematics, and science. Educators are also returning to more objective criteria and expectations and to more traditional teaching methods. The curriculum in most provinces has specified outcomes and objectives for age and grade levels. Some provinces are also moving away from the practice of passing children from grade to grade with their peers regardless of their achievement level. Educators in the public school system are also returning to an emphasis on testing and evaluation. In addition to increasing the amount of testing at the classroom level, most provinces have introduced tests to assess system-wide performance levels. Final exams in high school, which were virtually eliminated in the 1970s and 1980s, are now mandatory in nine provinces.

Equalizing Opportunities for Students with Disabilities

Another recent concern in education has been how to provide better educational opportunities for students with disabilities.

Table 14.2	NATIONS WITH THE LOWEST LITERACY RATES
COUNTRY	**LITERACY RATE**
Niger	14 percent
Burkina Faso	19 percent
Somalia	24 percent
Eritrea	25 percent
Nepal	28 percent
Mali	31 percent
Sierra Leone	31 percent
Afghanistan	32 percent
Senegal	33 percent
Cambodia	35 percent

Source: CIA, 2001.

As we saw in Chapter 11, the term *disability* has a wide range of definitions (see Shapiro, 1993). For the purposes of this chapter, disability is regarded as any physical and/or mental condition that limits students' access to, or full involvement in, school life. In 1994, 11-year-old Emily Eaton, a Grade 4 student, was placed in a segregated classroom in a public school in a small community in Ontario because teachers and school board officials had decided that her severe cerebral palsy made it extremely difficult for her to learn in a regular classroom environment. Her parents disagreed, believing that the regular classroom was the best learning environment for their daughter. The courts agreed with the parents, finding that "Emily had a constitutional right to attend school with fully able children [and that] segregating Emily because of her disability—against her parents' wishes and without establishing that she would be better off in a segregated classroom—was no different than segregating her on the basis of race or gender" (Chisholm, 1995:53).

As this case demonstrates, the barriers facing students with disabilities are slowly being removed or surmounted by new legislation. Today, most people with disabilities are no longer prevented from experiencing the full range of academic opportunities. Under various provincial human rights guidelines and the *Charter of Rights and Freedoms,* all children with disabilities are guaranteed a free and appropriate public education. This means that local school boards must make the necessary efforts and expenditures to accommodate special-needs students (Uppal, Kohen and Khan, 2007).

Many schools have attempted to *mainstream* children with disabilities by *inclusion programs,* under which the special education curriculum is integrated with the regular education program and each child receives an *individualized education plan* that provides annual education goals. (Inclusion means that children with disabilities work with a wide variety of people; over the course of a day, children may interact with their regular education teacher, the special education teacher, a speech therapist, an occupational therapist, a physical therapist, and a resource teacher, depending on the child's individual needs.) Today, more than 85 percent of children with disabilities are integrated into mainstream schools. Only 15 years ago, more than 80 percent of these children were placed in segregated schools. This dramatic change reflects growing acceptance of the fact that children with a range of disabilities often thrive in an integrated learning environment.

Although much remains to be done, recent measures to enhance education for children with disabilities have increased the inclusion of many young people who were formerly excluded or marginalized in the educational system. But the problem of equal educational opportunities does not end at the elementary and high school level for students with disabilities. If these students complete high school and continue on to university, they find new sets of physical and academic barriers that limit their access to higher education. Sociology professor Mark Nagler, who has cerebral palsy, recalls the academic barriers he faced when obtaining his Ph.D.:

> My parents made me aware that many people would make fun of my condition and that both kids and adults might create embarrassing situations . . . The former chairperson of a Sociology Graduate Department at a prominent university told me I should go home and live with my parents as I would never make it as a professor. Twenty-eight years later I am still proving him wrong. (Nagler, 1997:6)

Many colleges and universities have provided relatively inexpensive accommodations to make facilities more accessible to students with disabilities. For example, special computers and wheelchair accessible classrooms can help make a major difference in whether or not the students can complete a postsecondary education. Despite these efforts, and the fact that persons with disabilities aged 16–64 are more likely to obtain a university or college degree than they were 10 years ago; they continue to be underrepresented at the postsecondary level (see Figure 14.2 on page 360) (Human Resource and Skills Development, 2006).

The Cost of Postsecondary Education

Who attends college or university? What sort of college or university do students attend? Even for students who complete high school, access to colleges and universities is determined not only by prior academic record but also by ability to pay.

Postsecondary education has been described as the dividing line of the modern labour market. Today, more than ever before, employers want employees with a university degree, college diploma, or some other form of postsecondary educational certificate. As shown in Figure 14.3 on page 361, for most Canadians higher education will result in higher earnings. However, in order to obtain a university education, students must have the necessary financial resources. What does a university education cost? In Canada, postsecondary education is funded

| Figure 14.2 | Persons With and Without Disabilities by Educational Attainment |

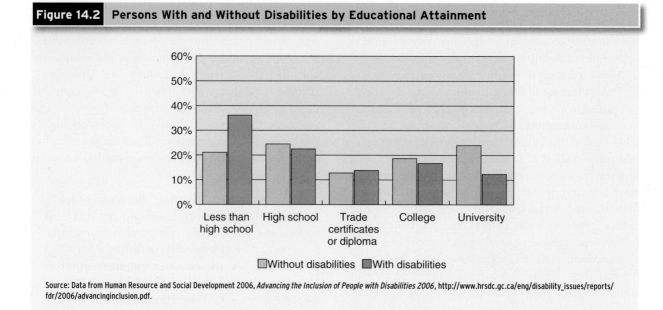

Source: Data from Human Resource and Social Development 2006, *Advancing the Inclusion of People with Disabilities 2006*, http://www.hrsdc.gc.ca/eng/disability_issues/reports/fdr/2006/advancinginclusion.pdf.

by the federal and provincial governments, and by parents and students through personal savings. As governments cut their funding to higher education, an increasing financial burden is falling on the shoulders of students and their parents. To make matters worse, the cost of attending university has increased dramatically over the past 20 years, with increases in tuition fees rising faster than the rate of inflation. For example, between 1991 and 2010 average tuition fees for an undergraduate degree went from approximately $1 500 to over $5 000. College fees, although lower than the price of university, have also increased (Statistics Canada, 2010b). Despite the soaring cost of postsecondary education, the percentage of young people attending university continued to rise in the first years of the 1990s: however, undergraduate enrollments have started to level off in the past five years, an indication that for some student, the cost of university education has become prohibitive. (Statistics Canada, 2009e).

How do students afford this increasingly costly education? A recent survey explored this question with both college and university graduates who identified employment earnings and student loan programs as their primary sources of funding. Parents ranked a close third for university graduates. Scholarships, fellowships, grants, and bursaries were rarely identified as a significant source of funding. Approximately one-third of college and university students indicated that they relied on student loans to finance their education. Close to 30 percent of students surveyed

anticipated debt of over $10 000 once their education was completed (EKOS Research Associates, 2003).

A substantial proportion of postsecondary students choose community college because of the lower costs. However, the overall enrolment of low-income students in community colleges has dropped as a result of increasing costs and also because many students must work full-time or part-time to pay for their education. Many Canadian colleges have implemented three- and four-year degree-granting programs that are an excellent option but may be cost and time prohibitive for low-income students. In contrast, students from more affluent families are more likely to attend prestigious public universities or private colleges outside Canada, where tuition fees alone may be more than $20 000 per year.

According to some social analysts, a university education is a bargain—even at about $90 a day for private schools or $35 for public schools—because for their money students receive instruction, room, board, and other amenities such as athletic facilities and job placement services. However, other analysts believe that the high cost of a university education reproduces the existing class system: Students who lack money may be denied access to higher education, and those who are able to attend college or university tend to receive different types of education based on their ability to pay. For example, a community college student who receives an associate's degree or completes a certificate program may be prepared for a position in the middle of the occupational status range, such

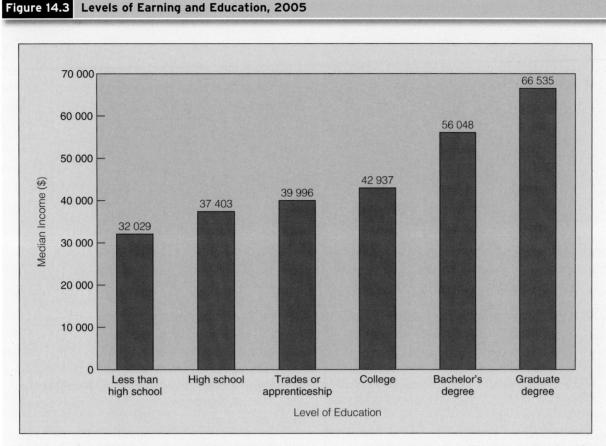

Figure 14.3 Levels of Earning and Education, 2005

Source: Adapted from Statistics Canada, *Income and Earnings Highlight Tables, 2006 Census*, Catalogue 97-563-XWE2006002, http://www.statcan.gc.ca/bsolc/olc-cel/olc-cel?catno=97-563-XWE2006002&lang=eng, Retrieved November 29, 2010.

as a dental assistant, computer programmer, or auto mechanic. In contrast, university graduates with four-year degrees are more likely to find initial employment with firms where they stand a chance of being promoted to high-paying management and executive positions. Although higher education may be a source of upward mobility for talented young people from poor families, the Canadian system of higher education is sufficiently stratified that it may also reproduce the existing class structure (Gilbert, 1998; Barlow and Robertson, 1994; Davies and Guppy, 2006)).

EDUCATION IN THE FUTURE

This chapter ends as it began, by noting that education will remain an important institution in this century. Also remaining, however, will be the controversies

that we have discussed—controversies that your generation will attempt to resolve. Questions will remain about what should be taught, not only in terms of preparing your children for their adult lives and the world of work but also with regard to the values to which you want your child exposed. The debate over what should be taught is not limited to moral issues; rather, it includes the entire curriculum. In recent decades, the Canadian public has been demanding greater accountability for student outcomes. A number of policy initiatives have been introduced in the public school system that should result in an improvement in the quality of education. At the elementary and secondary level there has been a shift toward increased emphasis on curriculum standards and more testing and provincial exams. In addition, *compensatory education programs,* including preschool, remedial, and extra education programs, which provide additional learning assistance to disadvantaged children, have been designed to address the effects of poverty, deprivation, and disadvantage on school

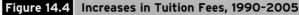

Figure 14.4 **Increases in Tuition Fees, 1990-2005**

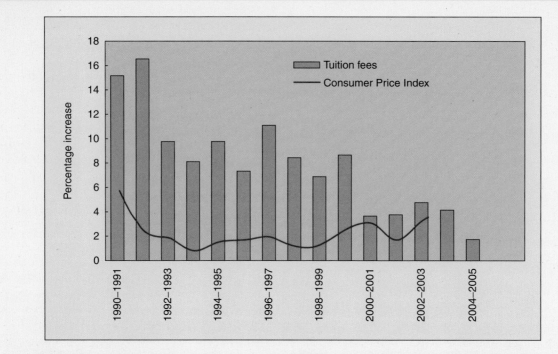

Source: Adapted from Statistics Canada, *Education Matters: Insights on Education, Learning and Training in Canada*, Catalogue 81-004-XIE, Released September 9, 2004; Statistics Canada, Census Population, 2006.

performance Although these programs were tried and failed 20 years earlier, more recent compensatory programs have produced more favourable results.

Home-schooling has been chosen by some parents who hope to avoid the problems of public school while providing a high-quality education for their children. Today, an estimated 80 000 children are educated in home-school programs. (Wake, 2000,

Basham, Merrifield, and Hepburn, 2007). An association of home-schoolers now provides communication links for parents and children, and technological advances in computers and the Internet have made it possible for parents and children involved in home-schooling to access information and communicate with one another. However, critics question the knowledge and competence of typical parents to

© Winnipeg Free Press, April 6th, 2002. Reproduced with permission.

Will distance learning courses change the face of the typical college or university classroom? What do you believe education will be like in the future?

educate their own children at home, particularly in rapidly changing academic subjects, such as science and computer technology.

Increasingly, information technologies are being accepted as an integral part of education although the effects of computer technologies in the classroom remain to be seen. While some experts argue that it will transform the way students learn, others view "high tech" teaching as simply the latest panacea in education.

What will education be like in the future? School enrolments may decline and diversify as baby boomers move out of childbearing years, and immigration to Canada creates an increasingly diverse population of students. The challenge lies in finding ways to facilitate learning in a pluralistic school system—by meeting the distinct cultural, linguistic, and religious traditions of a diverse student population.

A further challenge for educational systems in the future is to make education more accessible to all disadvantaged groups in Canadian society. Considerable progress has been made in diminishing the educational disparities among women and men and among most visible minority groups. Although differences remain in terms of types of education and fields of study, women now have outcomes superior to men on many measures of educational attainment. Similarly, the educational attainment of many visible minority groups is among the highest in Canada. However, although Aboriginal peoples and persons with disabilities have improved their educational levels in recent decades, their progress remains slow (see Aboriginal educational attainment in the Census Profile below). Finally, social class continues to be the most persistent and enduring source of educational inequality at all levels of education, from preschool through university.

Recent trends suggest that access to education is becoming more restricted as a result of funding cuts at both the provincial and federal levels. Course availability is diminished as school curricula are pared down to "core" subjects, and the specialized services of speech pathologists, physiotherapists, and psychologists are being cut, leaving some children— such as children with special needs, children from low-income families, and children from new immigrant families—without the services they need to help them achieve their full potential in the school system (Uppal, Kohen, and Khan, 2007)). At the postsecondary level, rising tuition fees are rising at a rate that has made university and college educations unaffordable for low-income students. University participation rates have increased for all social classes in the last decade, but the gap between the rich and poor hasn't narrowed: young people from high-income families are still twice as likely to pursue university studies as those from low-income families (Tamburri, 2008:15). If education is one of the key factors in promoting individual and collective prosperity, then we must strive to improve educational opportunities to all Canadians (Davies and Guppy, 2006).

Census Profile	Persons Aged 25 to 64 Reporting Aboriginal Identity Show Improved Levels of Educational Attainment		
	1996	2001	2006
Less than high school	45.20	38.71	23.76
High School	21.39	22.85	25.53
Trades	14.10	15.61	10.85
College	13.21	15.06	17.28
University	6.11	7.71	18.14

Source: Adapted from Statistics Canada, *2006 Registered Indian Status, Highest Certificate, Diploma or Degree, Highlight Tables.* http://www12.statcan.gc.ca/census-recensement/2006/dp-pd/tbt/Index-eng.cfm

What is education?

Education is the social institution responsible for the systematic transmission of knowledge, skills, and cultural values within a formally organized structure.

What is the functionalist perspective on education?

According to functionalists, education has both manifest functions (socialization, transmission of culture, social control, social placement, and change and innovation) and latent functions (keeping young people off the streets and out of the job market, matchmaking and producing social networks, and creating a generation gap).

What is the conflict perspective on education?

From a conflict perspective, education is used to perpetuate class, racial–ethnic, and gender inequalities through tracking, ability grouping, and a hidden curriculum that teaches subordinate groups conformity and obedience.

What is the interactionist perspective on education?

Interactionists examine classroom dynamics and study ways in which practices, such as labelling, may become a self-fulfilling prophecy for some students, such that these students come to perform up—or down—to the expectations held for them by teachers.

What percentage of students drop out before completing high school?

Approximately 10 percent of people under the age of 24 left school before earning a high school diploma.

What is functional illiteracy, and what is the rate of functional illiteracy in Canada?

Functional illiteracy is the inability to read and/or write at the skill level necessary for carrying out everyday tasks. The International Adult Literacy Survey indicated that 17 percent of adult Canadians are functionally illiterate. Furthermore, Canada has the highest rate of youth with poor literacy skills among the leading industrialized nations.

What controversies persist in education?

Gender bias in the classroom, unequal educational opportunities for students with disabilities, and the soaring cost of a university education are among the pressing issues in education in Canada today.

KEY TERMS

credentialism 351
cultural capital 349
cultural transmission 343
education 343
formal education 343
functional illiteracy 358
hidden curriculum 351
informal education 343
mass education 345
tracking 349

WEB LINKS

For more Web links related to the topic of this chapter, see the Nelson sociology website:
www.sociologyessentials5e.nelson.com

The National Adult Literacy Database is a national database of adult literacy programs, resources, services, and activities across Canada. It also links with other services and databases in North America and overseas:
www.nald.ca

The Canadian Teachers' Federation is an excellent source of information on teaching in Canada as well as current issues facing schools:
www.ctf-fce.ca

The Canadian Federation of Students represents about half a million students at more than 60 universities, colleges, and technical institutes across Canada. Its website has been established to offer students, the general public, media, and government officials information on the issues facing college and university students today:
www.cfs-fcee.ca/

The Council of Ministers of Education is the national voice of education in Canada. Its website contains valuable articles covering educational issues on the provincial, national, and international levels:
www.cmec.ca/

QUESTIONS FOR CRITICAL THINKING

1. What are the major functions of education for individuals and for societies?
2. Why do some theorists believe that education is a vehicle for decreasing social inequality whereas others believe that education reproduces existing class relationships?
3. Why does so much controversy exist over what should be taught in Canadian public schools?
4. How has education shaped your life in both direct and indirect ways?

ONLINE STUDY AND RESEARCH TOOLS

INFOTRAC®

InfoTrac College Edition is included free with every new copy of this text. Explore this online library for additional readings, review, and a handy resource for assignments. Visit **www.infotrac-college.com** to access this online database of full-text articles. Enter the key terms from this chapter to start your search.

CENGAGENOW™ CENGAGENOW

Use CengageNOW™ to help you formulate a customized study plan for this chapter. After you take the Diagnostic Quiz, CengageNOW™ will generate a customized study plan for you. It will identify sections of the chapter you should review.

CHAPTER 15

Religion

Religion has played a major role in the development and maintenance of Canada's educational institutions. Religious instruction was an essential component of "becoming educated." The religion taught was Christianity in either its Catholic or Protestant form. The majority of Canadians are still Christians, with Catholics making up 43 percent and Protestants 29 percent but other religions, such as Hinduism, Islam, Buddhism, Confucianism, Sikhism, and many others are now part of our Canadian mosaic (Statistics Canada, 2003j).

There is no longer any consensus regarding the role religion should play in education. Should students receive religious instruction in the classroom? If so, which religions should be included? Should prayer be offered in schools? Should participation in prayer be voluntary or compulsory? In our multicultural society, these questions are becoming increasingly difficult to answer.

Some parents feel that religious instruction is necessary, because they feel that secularization in the public school system is contributing to a declining morality. Albertans Dick and Joanne Barendregt teach their children at home. While

home-schooling is common in Canada, the Barendregts are part of a growing network of parents who disobey the law by not registering their children or allowing provincial officials to monitor their children's education because they feel this would interfere with their religious freedom. The couple decided to educate their children at home after they found that one of their children's textbooks had a section on evolution that conflicted with their religious views.

> Joanne Barendregt feels that in two or three years, they're going to regulate what we feed our children . . . and after that it will be our reproductive systems." She goes on to say that "we feel the highest calling a girl can have is to be a wife and mother first. We teach that that is their purpose . . . We are not changing. You [society] have changed. You're trying to destroy our [religious] heritage." Her husband says they will not register with the government because "we will not have a partnership with a government that promotes and allows homosexuality to continue, and abortion" (Mitchell, 1999:A7).

The Barendregts feel that religious instruction is a vital part of education. However, others feel that the educational system must be separate from religion and that the curriculum should be based on secular concerns. These people feel that in our multicultural society no religion should be espoused or endorsed. How can schools teach religious values that might conflict with the values and customs of a significant number of students? How might students and teachers who come from diverse religious and cultural backgrounds feel about instruction or organized prayer in public schools? Whose religion will be taught and what prayers will be used?

This debate has a long history. Controversies have arisen over topics such as the teaching of creationism versus evolutionism, moral education, sex education, school prayer, and the content of textbooks and library books.

What role does religion play in Canada's school systems today? Religion plays almost no role in the *public* school system. Most of those who wish to combine education with religious instruction must do so through private schooling. However, education falls within

Chapter Focus Question: What is the relationship between society and religion, and what role does religion play in people's everyday lives?

What are the key components of religion?

How do functionalist, conflict, interactionist, feminist, and postmodern perspectives on religion differ?

What are the central beliefs of the world's religions?

What is the future of religion in Canada?

provincial jurisdiction, and some provinces provide public funding to Roman Catholic separate schools (Holmes, 1998). Saskatchewan and Ontario fully fund Roman Catholic schools, but do not support schools operated by members of other religious denominations. On the other hand, Manitoba and British Columbia provide funding to a wide variety of private schools (many of which are religious schools) based on academic criteria. In Ontario, the teaching of the Christian religion in the public school system, which was once mandatory, is now forbidden. At the same time, Roman Catholic schools are fully funded. This means that the Protestant majority cannot teach its religion in the public schools, while the Catholic minority has its own funded system. All other minorities and Protestants who wish a religious-based education receive no provincial support (Holmes, 1998).

As the issue of religious education suggests, religion can be a highly controversial topic. One group's deeply held beliefs or cherished religious practices may be a source of irritation to another. Religion is a source of both stability and conflict throughout the world (Kurtz, 1995). In this chapter, we examine how religion influences life in Canada and in other areas of the world. Before reading on, test your knowledge about how religion affects public education in this country by taking the quiz in Box 15.1.

THE SOCIOLOGICAL STUDY OF RELIGION

What is religion? *Religion* **is a system of beliefs, symbols, and rituals, based on some sacred or supernatural realm, that guides human behaviour, gives meaning to life, and unites believers into a community** (Durkheim, 1995/1912). For many, religious beliefs provide the answers to the difficult questions about the meaning of life and death. Religion is one of our most significant social institutions and consists of a variety of elements, including beliefs about the sacred or supernatural, rituals, and a social organization of believers drawn together by their common religious tradition (Kurtz, 1995). Most religions attempt to answer fundamental questions such as those regarding the meaning of life and how the world was created. Most religions also provide comfort to persons facing emotional traumas, such as illness, suffering, grief, and death.

Religious beliefs are typically woven into a series of narratives, including stories about how ancestors and other significant figures had meaningful experiences with supernatural powers Kurtz (1995:9). Moreover, religious beliefs are linked to practices that bind people together and to rites of passage, such as birth, marriage, and death. People with similar religious beliefs and practices often come together in a moral community (such as a church, mosque, temple, or synagogue) where they can engage with similarly minded people.

How do sociologists study religion? Most studies in the sociology of religion focus on tangible elements such as written texts, patterns of behaviour, or individuals' opinions about religious matters, that can be studied using standard sociological research tools. How does the sociological study of religion

BOX 15.1 SOCIOLOGY AND EVERYDAY LIFE

How Much Do You Know About the Impact of Religion on Education in Canada?

True	False	
T	**F**	1. Provincial governments in Canada do not fund separate religious schools.
T	**F**	2. Parents who home-school their children for religious reasons are free to teach the children whatever curriculum they wish.
T	F	3. Questions of religion in the schools are decided at the provincial level because constitutionally education is controlled by the provinces.
T	**F**	4. Enrolment in religious schools has decreased in Canada as interest in religion has waned.
T	**F**	5. In Canada, the public school system recognizes only Christian religious holidays by giving students those days off.
T	F	6. The number of children from religious backgrounds other than Christian and Judaic has grown steadily over the past three decades.
T	**F**	7. Debates over textbook content focus only on elementary education because of the vulnerability of young children.
T	F	8. Increasing numbers of parents are instructing their own children through home-schooling because of their concerns about what public schools are (or are not) teaching their children.
T	F	9. Prayer in public schools in Canada is offered on a voluntary basis.
T	**F**	10. Most Canadians feel that public schools should teach children about all the major religions of the world.

Answers on page 370.

---

differ from the theological approach? Theologians primarily study the religious beliefs of specific religions, denominations, or religious leaders rather than the social dimensions of religion.

Religious Belief and Ritual

Religion seeks to answer important questions such as why we exist, why people suffer and die, and what

Throughout the world, people seek the meaning of life through traditional and non-traditional forms of religion. These Italian spiritual seekers are meeting together at a Mayan ruin in quest of harmonic convergence.

Bob Daemmrich/Stock Boston

BOX 15.1   SOCIOLOGY AND EVERYDAY LIFE

Answers to the Sociology Quiz on Religion and Education

Join In

1. **False**   Schools operated by the Catholic church are provincially funded in several provinces, and others fund a variety of private religious schools.

2. **False**   Every province monitors home-schoolers to ensure compliance with its Education Act. However, as suggested by the Barendregts in the chapter introduction, enforcement of the law may be lax in some provinces.

3. **True**   Under the terms of the British North America Act, education is a provincial responsibility. Public-school revenue comes from the province and from local funding through property taxes.

4. **False**   In recent years, just the opposite has happened. As parents have begun feeling that their children were not receiving the type of education the parents desired for them in public schools, most religions have established their own parochial schools.

5. **True**   This is normally the case, although, as you will learn, some schools have also recognized other religious holidays. However, this has resulted in conflict, as other religious groups also want to see their religious holidays formally recognized.

6. **True**   Although about 72 percent of Canadians aged 18 and over describe their religion as one of the forms, or denominations, of Christianity, the number of those who either adhere to no religion or who are Jewish, Muslim/Islamic, Sikh, Buddhist, or Hindu has increased significantly (Statistics Canada, 2003j).

7. **False**   Attempts to remove textbooks occur at all levels of schooling. One case involved the removal of Chaucer's "The Miller's Tale" and Aristophanes' *Lysistrata* from a high school curriculum (Johnson, 1994). Parents in many communities have tried to prevent teachers from using *Harry Potter* books in the classroom because they feel the books promote witchcraft.

8. **True**   Some parents choose home-schooling for religious reasons. Others embrace it for secular reasons, including concerns about the quality of public schools.

9. **True**   If a public school in Canada wishes to have prayers, parents must sign consent forms for their children to participate.

10. **True**   A national survey found that 56 percent of Canadians felt public schools should teach children about all the major religions of the world, while 31 percent felt that students should not be taught about any religion (Opinion Canada, 2004).

happens when we die. Peter Berger (1967) referred to religion as a *sacred canopy*—a sheltering fabric hanging over people that gives them security and provides answers for the questions of life. However, this sacred canopy requires that people have *faith*—**unquestioning belief that does not require proof or scientific evidence**. Science and medicine rely on scientific evidence to respond to questions of suffering, death, and injustice, whereas religion seeks to explain such phenomena by providing answers about ultimate purpose and life after death. These answers refer to the *sacred*, **which refers to those aspects of life that are extraordinary or supernatural**—those things that are set apart as "holy" (Durkheim, 1995/1912).

People feel a sense of awe, reverence, deep respect, or fear for that which is considered sacred. Across cultures and in different eras, many things have been considered sacred, including invisible gods, spirits, specific animals or trees, altars, crosses, and holy books (Collins, 1982). Sacred beliefs are rooted in the holy or supernatural, whereas secular beliefs have their foundation in scientific knowledge or everyday explanations. For example, in the educational debate over creationism and evolutionism, creationists view their belief as founded in sacred teachings, but evolutionists argue that their beliefs are based on scientific data.

In addition to beliefs, religion also comprises symbols and rituals. People often act out their religious beliefs in the form of *rituals*—**regularly repeated and carefully prescribed forms of behaviour that symbolize a cherished value or belief** (Kurtz, 1995). Rituals range from songs and prayers to offerings and sacrifices that worship or praise a supernatural being or a set of supernatural principles. For example, Muslims bow toward Mecca, the holy city of Islam, five times a day at fixed times to pray to God, and Christians participate in the celebration of communion to commemorate the life, death, and resurrection of Jesus Christ. The rituals involved in praying or in observing communion are carefully orchestrated and must be followed with precision.

The importance of rituals and other religious regulations can be understood if you recall that the purpose of religion is to provide explanations of fundamental questions, such as death and the meaning of life. Rodney Stark has pointed out that religions do more for humans than "supply them with answers to questions of ultimate meaning. The assumption that the supernatural exists raises a new question: *What does the supernatural want or expect from us?*" (1998:386). Thus religions also provide the faithful with rules about how they must act if they are to please the gods. Following these rules is a sign of faith.

Categories of Religion

We do not know when religious rituals first began but anthropologists have concluded that all known groups over the past hundred thousand years have had some form of religion (Haviland, 1993). Religions have been classified into four main categories based on their dominant belief: simple supernaturalism, animism, theism, and transcendent idealism (McGee, 1975). In very simple preindustrial societies, religion often takes the form of *simple supernaturalism*—**the belief that supernatural forces affect people's lives either positively or negatively**. This type of religion does not acknowledge specific gods or supernatural spirits but focuses instead on impersonal forces that may exist in people or natural objects. For example, simple supernaturalism has been used to explain mystifying events of nature, such as sunrises and thunderstorms, and ways that some objects may bring a person good or bad luck. By contrast, *animism* **is the belief that plants, animals, or other elements of the natural world are endowed with spirits or life forces that have an impact on events in society**. Animism is associated with early hunting and gathering societies in which everyday life is not separated from the elements of the natural world (Albanese, 1992).

The third category of religion is *theism*—**a belief in a god or gods**. Horticultural societies were among the first to practise *monotheism*—**a belief in a single, supreme being or god who is responsible for significant events, such as the creation of the world**. Three of the major world religions—Christianity, Judaism, and Islam—are monotheistic. By contrast, Shinto and a number of the indigenous religions of Africa are forms of *polytheism*—**a belief in more than one god. The fourth category of religion, transcendent idealism**, is a *nontheistic religion*—**a religion based on a belief in divine spiritual forces, such as sacred principles of thought and conduct, rather than a god or gods**. Transcendent idealism focuses on principles, such as truth, justice, affirmation of life, and tolerance for others, and its adherents seek an elevated state of consciousness in which they can fulfill their true potential.

SOCIOLOGICAL PERSPECTIVES ON RELIGION

The major sociological perspectives have very different views about the relationship between religion and society. Functionalists emphasize the ways in which religious beliefs and rituals can bind people together. Conflict explanations suggest that religion can be a source of false consciousness in society. Interactionists focus on the meanings that people give to religion in their everyday lives. Feminists look at the ways in which women's religious experiences differ from those of men. Postmodern theorists examine the changing nature and role of religion in the 21st century.

The Functionalist Perspective on Religion

Durkheim on Religion   Émile Durkheim emphasized that religion is essential to the maintenance of society. Religion was a cultural universal found in all societies because it met basic human needs and served important societal functions. The central feature of all religions is the presence of sacred beliefs and rituals that bind people together in a collectivity. In his studies of the religion of the Australian Aborigines, for example, Durkheim found that each clan had established its own sacred totem, which included kangaroos, trees, rivers, rock formations, and other animals or natural creations. To clan members, their totem was sacred; it symbolized some unique quality of their clan. People developed a feeling of unity by performing ritual dances around their totem, which caused them to abandon individual self-interest.

Functions of Religion   Functionalists believe that religion has three important functions:

1. *Providing meaning and purpose to life.* Religion offers meaning for the human experience. Some events create a profound sense of loss on both an individual basis (such as suffering, and the death of a loved one) and a group basis (such as famine or earthquake). Inequality may cause people to wonder why their own personal situation is no better than it is. Most religions offer explanations for these concerns. Explanations may differ from one religion to another, yet each tells the individual or group that life is part of a larger system of order in the universe (McGuire, 1997). Some (but not all) religions even offer hope of an afterlife for persons who follow the religion's tenets of morality in this life. Such beliefs help make injustices in this life easier to endure.
2. *Promoting social cohesion and a sense of belonging.* By emphasizing shared symbolism, religious teachings and practices help promote social cohesion. All religions have some forms of shared experience, such as the Christian practice of communion, that rekindle the group's consciousness of its own unity.
3. *Providing social control and support for the government.* How does religion help bind society together and maintain social control? All societies attempt to maintain social control through systems of rewards and punishments. Sacred symbols and beliefs establish powerful motivations based on the concept of a general order of existence (Geertz, 1966). If individuals consider themselves to be part of a larger order that holds the ultimate meaning in life, they will feel bound to one another (and to past and future generations) in a way that otherwise might not be possible (McGuire, 1997).

Religion also helps maintain social control by conferring supernatural legitimacy on the norms and laws in society. In some societies, social control occurs as a result of direct collusion between the dominant classes and the dominant religious organizations. Absolute monarchs often have claimed that God gave them the right to rule, so their citizens could not question their legitimacy to govern.

The Conflict Perspective on Religion

Karl Marx on Religion   While most functionalists feel that religion serves a positive role, many conflict theorists view religion negatively. For Marx, *ideologies*—"systematic views of the way the world ought to be"—are embodied in religious doctrines and political values (Turner, Beeghley, and Powers, 1995:135). These ideologies also justify the status quo and hinder social change. The capitalist class uses religious ideology as a tool of domination to mislead the workers about their true interests. For this reason, Marx wrote his famous statement that religion is the "opiate of the masses." People become complacent because they have been taught to believe in an afterlife in which they will be rewarded for their suffering and misery in this life. Although these religious teachings soothe the masses, any relief is illusory. Religion unites people under a "false consciousness," according to which they believe they have common interests with members of the dominant class (Roberts, 1995).

From a conflict perspective, religion also tends to promote strife between groups and societies. The conflict may be *between* religious groups (for example, religious wars), *within* a religious group (for example, when a splinter group leaves an existing denomination), or between a religious group and *the larger society* (for example, conflict over religion in the classroom). Conflict theorists assert that, in attempting to provide meaning and purpose in life while at the same

The shared experiences and beliefs associated with religion have helped many groups maintain a sense of social cohesion and a feeling of belonging in the face of prejudice and discrimination.

BOX 15.2 CRITICAL THINKING

A Legal Challenge to Religious Holidays in Schools

Like millions of other young Canadians, 14-year-old Aysha Bassuny returned to school in September 1994. However, the Ottawa Board of Education delayed the start of her school year for two days so that Jewish students could observe the Jewish New Year—Rosh Hashanah. Bassuny was one of many in Ottawa's Islamic community who were upset that the board refused to close schools for two Muslim holy days. "It's not fair," said Bassuny, a Grade 10 student at suburban Brookfield High School, who wears the traditional Islamic head scarf, the hijab. "I have to miss school for my holy days and the Jewish kids don't. You cannot have it for one group and not the other."

In July 1995, Islamic Schools Federation of Ontario, which represents independent Muslim schools, launched a lawsuit against the Ottawa Board of Education alleging that the rights of Muslims to freedom of conscience and religion under the Charter of Rights have been undermined by the board's actions. The lawsuit argued that schools with significant numbers of Muslim students should be required to observe two important Islamic holidays. The Islamic Schools Federation chose to sue the Ottawa Board of Education as a test case, hoping to set a precedent for the rest of the country.

The dispute began in April 1994, when the Ottawa board agreed to a request from Ottawa's Jewish community to delay the start of the school

year so that Jewish students could observe Rosh Hashanah without missing the first two days of school. According to Jewish community leaders, the request was reasonable, because it did not mean a permanent change in the school year because Rosh Hashanah coincides with the opening of school only once every 40 years.

On the other side of the issue, the lawyer for the Islamic Schools Federation of Ontario said that the problem was "the recognition of two religions, Christian and Jewish, and the rejection of another, Muslim."

Those involved in the dispute recognized that, if taken to its logical extreme, the rapid growth of Canada's Muslim, Buddhist, Hindu, and Sikh communities could lead to a school year with as many as 15 religious holidays. At the time, one school board member conceded that it was "a tough problem," and one that an increasingly multicultural society would be unable to avoid. Ultimately, the lawsuit was rejected by the Ontario Divisional Court and in July 1997 the Ontario Appeal Court refused to hear an appeal. This means that Ontario schools are not required to recognize the holidays of minority religious groups. Do you think it is fair that Christian holidays are recognized while the holidays of other religions are not?

Source: Reprinted by permission of Maclean's Magazine.

---

time promoting the status quo, religion is used by the dominant classes to impose their own control over society and its resources (McGuire, 1992).

Max Weber's Response to Marx   Whereas Marx believed that religion hindered social change, Weber argued just the opposite—that religion could help produce social change. In *The Protestant Ethic and the Spirit of Capitalism* (1976/1904–1905), Weber asserted that the religious teachings of John Calvin were directly related to the rise of capitalism. Calvin emphasized the doctrine of *predestination*—the belief that, even before they are born, all people are divided into two groups, the saved and the damned.

Only God knows who will go to heaven (the elect) and who will go to hell. Because people cannot know whether they will be saved, they look for earthly signs that they are among the elect. According to the Protestant ethic, those who have faith, perform good works, and achieve economic success are more likely to be among the chosen of God. As a result, people work hard, save their money, and do not spend it on worldly frivolity; instead they reinvest it in their land, equipment, and labour (Chalfant, Beckley, and Palmer, 1994).

The spirit of capitalism grew under the Protestant ethic. As people worked harder to prove their religious piety, structural conditions in Europe led to the Industrial Revolution, free markets, and the commercialization of the economy—developments that worked hand in hand with Calvinist religious teachings. From this viewpoint, wealth was an unintended consequence of religious piety and hard work.

Like Marx, Weber was acutely aware that religion could reinforce existing social arrangements, especially the stratification system. The wealthy can use religion to justify their power and privilege: it is a sign of God's approval of their hard work and morality. As for the poor, if they work hard and live a moral life, they will be richly rewarded in another life. The Hindu belief in reincarnation is an example of religion reinforcing the stratification system. Because a person's social position in the current life is the result of behaviour in a former life, the privileges of the upper class must be protected so that each person may enjoy those privileges in another incarnation.

Does Weber's thesis about the relationship between religion and the economy withstand the test of time? Collins reexamined Weber's assertion that the capitalist breakthrough occurred just in Christian Europe and concluded that this belief is only partially accurate. According to Collins, the foundations for capitalism in Asia, particularly Japan, were laid in the Buddhist monastic economy in late medieval Japan: "the temples were the first entrepreneurial organizations in Japan: the first to combine control of the factors of labor, capital, and land so as to allocate them for enhancing production." (1997:855) Due to an ethic of self-discipline and restraint on consumption, high levels of accumulation and investment took place in medieval Japanese Buddhism. Gradually, secular capitalism emerged from temple capitalism as new

guilds arose that were independent of the temples, and the gap between the clergy and everyday people narrowed. The capitalist dynamic in the monasteries was eventually transferred to the secular economy, opening the way to the Industrial Revolution in Japan. Several researchers have also found that the most of the features of capitalism existed in the city-states of Catholic Italy as early as the 12th century (Stark, 2004b). While a particular ethic favouring hard work and saving money was required to support capitalism, this ethic was present in several parts of the world, not just one, and it occurred in Catholic, Protestant and Buddhist forms (Collins, 1997).

The Symbolic Interactionist Perspective on Religion

Functionalists and conflict theorists view religion primarily from a macrolevel perspective. Symbolic interactionists focus on a microlevel analysis that examines the meanings that people give to religion in their everyday lives.

Religious Conversion John Lofland and Rodney Stark (1965) wanted to determine why people converted to nontraditional religious movements. What would attract people to a small movement outside the religious mainstream, and why were some movements successful at attracting people while others failed? In the early 1960s, Lofland and Stark became acquainted with a small religious movement that had come to the San Francisco area from Korea. They called the movement the Divine Precepts, but later revealed that the group was actually the Unification Church, better known as "the Moonies" after their founder, Sun Myung Moon.

Lofland and Stark spent a great deal of time observing the group's activities and conducting interviews. They proposed a seven-step theory of conversion. They concluded that the most important personal characteristics that made conversion more likely were:

1. Some important tension or strain in their lives such as financial problems, marital issues, or sexual identity problems.
2. A religious problem-solving perspective. Other people who experience similar strain may take direct action (such as divorce or declaring bankruptcy), go to a psychiatrist, or join a political movement rather than trying to solve their problems through spiritual means.

According to Marx and Weber, religion serves to reinforce social stratification in a society. For example, according to Hindu belief, a person's social position in his or her current life is a result of behaviour in a former life.

Mark O'Neill/Sun Media

3. Their self-definition as religious seekers trying to resolve their problems through some system of religious meaning. Some had tried several different religious alternatives before encountering the Moonies.

These background factors were present *before* the potential converts came to the Divine Precepts. Lofland and Stark found that several situational factors also increased the likelihood of conversion. These factors were:

1. An individual had come to a turning point in his or her life. Some of the future converts had just dropped out of school, while others had moved, lost a job, or experienced some other major life change. This turning point not only increased the level of tension experienced by the individual, but also gave the individual the opportunity to turn to something new.

2. Close personal ties with a member of the Divine Precepts. While many religious seekers heard the message of the Divine Precepts, only those who also developed a personal bond with a member underwent conversion. One of the converts, who had recently recovered from a serious illness, described the process:

   I felt as if I had come to life from a numb state and there was spiritual liveliness and vitality within me by being among this group. As one feels when he comes from a closed stuffy room into the fresh air, or the goodness and warmth after freezing coldness was how my spirit witnessed its happiness. Although I could not agree with the message intellectually I found myself one with it spiritually. (Lofland and Stark, 1965:871)

3. A lack of ties with people outside the group. Few of those who converted had strong ties outside the group.

4. Very intensive interaction with Divine Precepts members. The Divine Precepts recognized this and strongly encouraged those who had verbally converted to move into a shared residence with other group members. This helped to secure their total commitment to the movement.

Feminist Perspectives on Religion

There is some evidence that in early societies, female goddesses played a predominant role in religious beliefs. However, as societies became more complex and stratification systems developed, male gods became more important. This was reflected in the religious view of women as being inferior to men (Johnstone, 1997). Religious leadership was restricted to men, and women were restricted to subordinate roles in church activities. In many religions women were not even permitted to study religious texts.

His Religion and Her Religion   Because men and women often play different roles in the church, they may belong to the same religious group but their individual religion may not be the same. In fact, women's versions of particular religions may differ markedly from men's versions (McGuire, 1997). For example, while an Orthodox Jewish man may focus on his public ritual roles and his discussion of sacred texts, Orthodox Jewish women have few ritual duties and are more likely to focus on their responsibilities in the home. Consequently, the meaning of being Jewish may be different for women than for men.

Consider one woman's reaction to the serving of Holy Communion in her Protestant church:

   Following the sermon, the worshippers are invited to participate in the celebration of the Lord's Supper. As the large group of male ushers marches down the aisle to receive the communion elements and distribute them to the congregation, I am suddenly struck with the irony of the situation. The chicken suppers, the ham suppers, the turkey suppers in the church are all prepared and served by the women. But not the Lord's Supper ... the privilege of serving the Lord's Supper in worship is reserved for the men. This particular morning I find it very difficult to swallow the bread and drink the wine, knowing that within the Body of Christ, the Church, the sisters of Christ are not given the same respect and privileges as are his brothers (Johnstone, 1997: 237).

Religious symbolism and language create a social definition of the roles of men and women. Some religious symbolism depicts the higher deities as male and the lower deities as female. Sometimes, females are depicted as negative, or evil, spiritual forces. For example, the Hindu goddess Kali represents men's eternal battle against the evils of materialism (Daly, 1973). Historically, language has been male-centred in the world's major religions. Phrases such as "for all men" in Catholic and Anglican services gradually have been changed to "for all," but some churches retain the traditional liturgy. Many women resist the subordination they have experienced in organized religion and object to its patriarchal nature. Some advocate a break from traditional religions, while others seek to reform religious language, symbols, and rituals to eliminate the elements of patriarchy (Renzetti and Curran, 1995).

Women in the Ministry

> I believe in God, the Father Almighty, Creator of Heaven and Earth, and in Jesus Christ, His only Son. (MacDonald, 1996:47)

> A woman can't represent Christ. Men and women are totally different—that's not my fault—and Jesus chose men for his disciples. (MacDonald, 1996:47)

These quotations highlight two issues that are important to women: the gender inclusiveness of religion and the absence of women in significant roles within religious institutions. In many religious contexts, women are demanding an end to traditions that do not reflect their historical role and their religious commitment. Some women are choosing alternative spiritual belief systems, while others are working from within the church to create change. The battles have been intense, and the issue of the role of women has polarized some churches. In 1992, the Church of England allowed the ordination of women priests. In response, a British vicar made a point of telling the media that he would "burn the bloody bitches" (MacDonald, 1996:47).

Despite opposition, there have been some advances. Women make up an increasing proportion of the clergy in some religious denominations. The United and Anglican churches have significant numbers of female clergy. Reform Judaism has ordained women as rabbis since the early 1970s, and Aboriginal Canadian religions have traditionally given status to women in spiritual leadership. However, other religions, including the Roman Catholic church, will not allow women to serve as clergy and women are still struggling to make their voices heard.

Interestingly, while women are a distinct minority among religious leaders, they make up a substantial majority of the faithful. Stark has concluded that "in every sizable religious group in the Western world, women outnumber men, usually by a considerable margin" (2004a:61). This gender difference begins in adolescence, so it is not explained simply by the fact that women live longer than men.

The Postmodern Perspective on Religion

The Secularization Debate

One of the most important debates within the sociology of religion deals with the question of whether the world is becoming more secular and less religious or whether we are seeing a renewal of religious belief. The view that modern societies are becoming more secular and that religion has become less important than in the past goes back to the work of Weber, Durkheim, and Marx. For example, Weber felt that as societies modernized, the role of religion as the sole source of authority would inevitably diminish as other social institutions—particularly economic and political ones—became dominant. Jeffrey Hadden has summarized the secularization perspective:

> Once the world was filled with the sacred—in thought, practice, and institutional form. After the Reformation and the Renaissance, the forces of modernization swept across the globe and secularization . . . loosened the dominance of the sacred. In due course, the sacred shall disappear altogether except, possibly, in the private realm. (1987:598)

Proponents of this view link modernization with secularization. These theorists predict that as the world becomes more rational and bureaucratized and, as knowledge becomes more science-based, the role and influence of religion will decline. According to Fukuyama, Weber's prediction has proven accurate in many ways: "rational science-based capitalism has spread across the globe, bringing material advancement to large parts of the world and welding it together into the iron cage we call globalization" (2005:2). As you will read later in this chapter, religion has become much less important in Canada and in almost all Western industrial countries other than the United States. Church membership in these countries has dramatically declined over the past 50 years, and while many people still report an interest in spiritual matters, they do not pursue these interests through the organized church.

However, religion is still flourishing in many parts of the world. Most critics of secularization theory concede that in most Western industrialized countries the separation between church and state has increased and church attendance has declined. However, at the same time, religion is actually becoming *more* important in some parts of the world. Religion remains strong in Islamic societies, even in countries such as Turkey and Pakistan, which have begun to modernize. In the former Soviet bloc, where religion had been banned, there has been a resurgence in religious participation since the end of the communist era. Pentecostal churches are growing very rapidly in South America. Finally, the United States, perhaps the world's most modernized society, is still a very religious country, showing that modernization does not inevitably cause a decline in religiosity. Norris and Inglehart (2004) have shown that the proportion of the world's population that holds religious beliefs is now growing because of high birth rates in religious countries. Because of this, some sociologists, such as Stark, strongly disagree with secularization theory: "After nearly three centuries of utterly failed prophecies and misrepresentations of both past and present, it seems time to carry the secularization doctrine to the graveyard of failed theories, and there to whisper ['rest in peace')" (Stark, 1999:270).

Jeff Haynes (1997) has looked at this situation from the postmodern perspective and concluded that both sides in this debate are partially correct. While secularization continues in much of the industrialized West, the postmodern condition has led people in many low-income countries to turn to religion. The structural conditions of postmodernism, including the negative consequences of globalization and its perceived threats to the moral order, can destabilize local values and traditions. Ironically, instead of leading to secularization, these conditions can lead to a strengthening of faith as some people resist these threats by turning to religion. Proponents of secularization theory would not have predicted the role played by religion in global politics in the past three decades. Nevertheless, religion has been critical in such major political events as the ongoing conflicts between India and Pakistan and between Israel and the Palestinians; the violent break-up of the former Yugoslavia; and the Republican political victories in the United States in 2000 and 2004.

Haynes explains the coexistence of secularization in some parts of the world and the spread of religion elsewhere by hypothesizing that secularization will continue, except in circumstances where religion "finds or retains work to do other than relating people to the supernatural . . . only when religion does something other than mediate between man and God does it retain a high place in people's attentions and in their politics" (1997:713). This means that religion will retain or increase its importance in societies where it helps to defend culture against perceived threats from outside or from the threat of internal cultural change. In countries such as Canada, where religion retains only its pre-modern spiritual role, it will continue to stagnate or to decline.

Global capitalism has weakened national sovereignty and carries with it only the values of the marketplace. Many people view their own governments as part of the enemy (Juergensmeyer, 2003). The comments of Joanne Barendregt in the chapter introduction show how some Canadians feel threatened by this social change. Islamic militant Sayyid Qutb, who was tortured and executed by Egyptian police in 1966, stated his disgust with the Westernization of the Arab world, which he felt was destroying his basic Islamic values:

> Humanity today is living in a large brothel! One has only to glance at its press, films, fashion shows, beauty contests, ballrooms, wine bars, and broadcasting stations! Or observe its mad lust for naked flesh, provocative postures, and sick, suggestive statements in the literature, the arts and the mass media! (Ruthven, 2004:37)

One way for people to deal with these threats is to turn to fundamentalist beliefs (see Box 15.3 on page 378 for a discussion of the role of fundamentalist beliefs in religious terrorism). These beliefs do more than mediate between people and their God. To people who feel their values and identities are under threat from globalization, poverty, immorality, religious pluralism, or corrupt government, religious fundamentalism provides certainty in an otherwise uncertain world. According to Haynes, "For many people, especially in the Third World, postmodernism is synonymous with poverty, leading the poor especially to be receptive to fundamentalist arguments which supply a mobilising ideology" (1997:719). In large part, these fundamentalist religious institutions are based on strong local community organizations. Thus they not only fill people's spiritual needs and provide a moral code that protects them from the consequences of globalization, but also provide adherents with the support of a strong moral community that can replace older

BOX 15.3   SOCIOLOGY IN GLOBAL PERSPECTIVE

Religious Terrorism

Religious terrorism has become a major threat in postmodern societies. While there is a long history of religious wars among states and many earlier examples of religious terrorism, the phenomenon has seen a resurgence over the past two decades. Following the September 11, 2001, attacks on the United States and subsequent bombings in Madrid, Bali, London, Mumbai, and elsewhere, much of the world's attention is now focused on Islamic terrorists, including Osama bin Laden and his followers. However, all the world's major religious traditions have been linked with terrorism. Among the questions that interest sociologists are, What are the causes of religious terrorism? How does it differ from other types of terrorist activities?

Violent extremism is not limited to any one faith. In Northern Ireland, the Catholic Irish Republican Army (IRA) exploded hundreds of bombs and killed hundreds of civilians in an attempt to free Northern Ireland from British rule. In 1994, a Jewish right-wing settler, Dr. Baruch Goldstein, shot and killed more than 30 Palestinians who were praying at the Tomb of the Patriarchs in Hebron. On the other side of the Israeli–Palestinian conflict, hundreds of Israelis have been killed by Palestinian suicide bombers. In Canada and the United States, there have been numerous bombings of abortion clinics, and several doctors who perform abortions have been killed or wounded. Some of these attacks were carried out by Christian ministers, and others were supported by militant Christian groups. The largest domestic terrorism incident in the United States was the bombing by Timothy McVeigh of the Oklahoma City federal building, which killed 168 people. McVeigh was inspired by the white supremacist book *The Turner Diaries*, which condemned the dictatorial secularism that it alleged had been imposed on the United States by a Jewish and liberal conspiracy, and by a religious group called Christian Identity that shares these values and beliefs (Juergensmeyer, 2003). Militant Sikhs, fighting for an independent homeland, committed many acts of terrorism including the assassination of Indian Prime Minister Indira Ghandi by her own bodyguards. Sikh extremists were also responsible for Canada's worst act of terrorism, the Air India bombing that killed 329 people. In 1995, members of an apocalyptic Japanese Buddhist sect released sarin nerve gas into the Tokyo subway system. This was the first attempt by religious terrorists to use a weapon of mass destruction. While the attack killed 12 people, thousands more would have died if the terrorists had been able to find a more effective way of vapourizing the sarin gas.

There are significant differences in the motivation behind these different attacks. The IRA bombing campaign had a very strong political component, while members of the Japanese sect had few overt political goals. However, in each of the examples the religious ideology of the terrorists helps to define the enemy and provides a justification for killing innocents.

According to Bruce Hoffman, there are differences between religious and secular terrorism. Most importantly:

> For the religious terrorist, violence first and foremost is a sacramental act or divine duty executed in direct response to some theological demand or imperative. Terrorism assumes a transcendental dimension, and its perpetrators are thereby unconstrained by the political, moral, or practical constraints that seem to affect other terrorists. . . . Thus, religion serves as a legitimizing force—conveyed by sacred text or imparted via clerical authorities claiming to speak for the divine. (1995:272).

Secular terrorists have to appeal to a broader constituency, so their acts are often restrained by their fear of alienating potential supporters. Religious terrorists must please only themselves and their god, and can justify attacks against all "nonbelievers." Finally, purely religious terrorists are not seeking modifications of an existing system, such as a change in the ruling government. Rather, they wish to completely transform the social order and to achieve total victory. Unlike groups, such as the IRA, who combined their religious ideology with specific and limited political goals, Osama bin Laden is not trying to replace governments, but to destroy the enemy and transform the world:

> It is no secret that warding off the American enemy is the top duty after faith and that nothing should take priority over it . . . jihad has become [obligatory] upon each and every Muslim. . . . The time has come when all the Muslims of the world, especially the youth, should unite and soar . . . and continue jihad

BOX 15.3   SOCIOLOGY IN GLOBAL PERSPECTIVE

Religious Terrorism (Continued)

till these forces are crushed to naught, all the anti-Islamic forces are wiped off the face of this earth and Islam takes over the whole world and all the other false religions. (quoted in Juergensmeyer, 2003:431)

The fact that it is almost impossible to negotiate with religious terrorists and the loose networked form of contemporary terrorist organizations (see Box 5.4 on page 119) makes them very difficult to control. This likely means that there will be no quick end to the religious terrorism now affecting the world.

While religious terrorism is a serious threat, we should keep the role of religion in perspective by remembering that the mass genocides of the 20th century, including the Holocaust, Stalin's purges, China's Cultural Revolution, and Pol Pot's massacre in Cambodia, were committed in the name of political ideology, not religion.

---

structures that have been weakened by rapid social change.

Haynes' theory is supported by data from the World Values Survey. Several indicators of religiosity are strongly correlated with a country's level of development (see Figure 15.1). Respondents in agrarian countries (including Nigeria, Tanzania, and Zimbabwe) are twice as likely as those in industrialized, high-income countries to attend religious services at least weekly and to pray daily, and three times as likely to say that religion is "very important" in their lives (Norris and Inglehart, 2004). The major exceptions to this pattern are the United States and Ireland, which are both very wealthy and very religious countries.

Figure 15.1   Religiosity by Type of Society

The level of development of a country is strongly related to the religiosity of its citizens.

	Agrarian	Industrial	Post-industrial
Attend religious service at least weekly (%)	44	25	20
Pray daily (%)	52	34	26
Consider religion "very important" (%)	64	34	20

Source: Norris, Pippa and Ronald Inglehart. 2004. *Sacred and Secular: Religion and Politics Worldwide*. Cambridge: Cambridge University Press. Reprinted by permission of Cambridge University Press.

Concept Table 15.1 THEORETICAL PERSPECTIVES ON RELIGION

PERSPECTIVE	THEORY	ELEMENTS
Functionalist		
Durkheim	Functions of religion	Religion has three important functions in any society: (1) providing meaning and purpose to life, (2) promoting social cohesion, (3) providing social control and support for the government.
Weber	The Protestant ethic and the spirit of capitalism	The religious teachings of Calvinist Protestantism were directly related to the rise of capitalism.
Conflict		
Marx	Conflict theory	The capitalist class uses religious ideology as a tool of domination to mislead the workers about their true interests. Religion can also promote strife between groups and societies.
Symbolic Interactionist		
Lofland and Stark	Conversion theory	Conversion to nontraditional religious movements was more likely if individuals had certain predisposing background factors and if they had come to a turning point in life, had close personal ties to members of the group, a lack of ties to people outside the group, and intensive interaction with group members.
Feminist		
McGuire	His religion and her religion	Religious symbolism and language typically create a social definition of the roles of men and women. Typically, these definitions subordinate women to men.
Postmodern	Religion as oppositional	The postmodern condition stimulates ideology turning to religion under certain circumstances. While secularization continues in much of the industrialized West, in lower-income countries religion often functions as a mobilizing oppositional ideology.

Table 15.1 CHARACTERISTICS OF CHURCHES AND SECTS

CHARACTERISTIC	CHURCH	SECT
Organization	Large, bureaucratic organization, led by a professional clergy	Small, faithful group, with high degree of lay participation
Membership	Open to all; members usually from upper middle classes	Closely guarded membership, usually from lower classes.
Type of worship	Formal, orderly	Informal, spontaneous
Salvation	Granted by God, as administered by the church	Achieved by moral purity
Attitude toward other institutions and religions	Tolerant	Intolerant

Christians around the world have been drawn to cathedrals such as England's Salisbury Cathedral, which was built in the 13th century. Because of their age, many of these cathedrals require very expensive repairs. Salisbury Cathedral has been able to raise the millions of pounds required for repairs and maintenance, but many less-famous churches are in danger of decaying.

This mass wedding ceremony of thousands of brides and grooms brought widespread media attention to the Reverend Sun Myung Moon and the Unification church, which many people view as a religious cult.

TRENDS IN RELIGION IN CANADA

Canada's Religious Mosaic

Until the end of the 19th century, Canada's population was made up almost entirely of Protestants and Catholics. The Roman Catholic church was the dominant religious force during the early settlement of Canada, a situation that continued well into the 19th century. With the arrival of the United Empire

Figure 15.2 Religious Affiliation in Canada

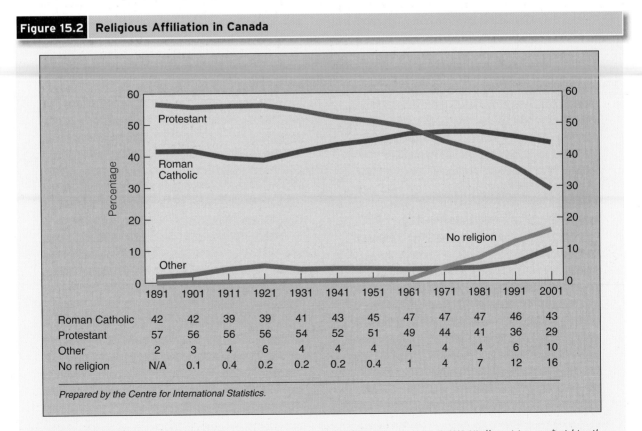

	1891	1901	1911	1921	1931	1941	1951	1961	1971	1981	1991	2001
Roman Catholic	42	42	39	39	41	43	45	47	47	47	46	43
Protestant	57	56	56	56	54	52	51	49	44	41	36	29
Other	2	3	4	6	4	4	4	4	4	4	6	10
No religion	N/A	0.1	0.4	0.2	0.2	0.2	0.4	1	4	7	12	16

Prepared by the Centre for International Statistics.

Sources: Adapted from Statistics Canada, *Religions in Canada, 2001 Census*, Catalogue 96F0030XIE2001015, released May 13, 2003. http://www.statcan.gc.ca/bsolc/olc-cel/olc-cel?catno=96F0030XIE2001015&lang=eng

Loyalists from the American colonies in the 1780s, the Protestant population in Canada became larger than the French-Catholic population. However, this slowly changed as the combined share of the Protestant churches declined from 51 percent in 1951 to 36 percent in 1991 (McVey and Kalbach, 1995). Changes in the population of the major religious groups in Canada are illustrated in Figure 15.2 on page 381. In 2001, Catholics, at 43 percent of the population, were the largest religious group in Canada.

Religions other than Christianity were practised in Canada prior to European colonization. Aboriginal peoples were excluded from the earliest census collections. Even so, in 1891, almost 2 percent of Canadians reported practising religions other than Christianity. By 2001, more than 10 percent of Canadians were affiliated with "other" religions, including Eastern Orthodox, Judaism, and Eastern non-Christian religions, such as Islam, Buddhism, Hinduism, Sikhism, and parareligious groups (see Figure 15.3). Eastern non-Christian religious populations have grown significantly since the 1960s as a result of changes in immigration patterns, The numbers of those who fall under the category "no religion," increased from 56 679 in 1951 to almost 4.8 million in 2001 (Statistics Canada, 2003j). Does this mean that Canadians are rejecting religion? An answer to this question can be found by examining other recent trends in religion in Canada.

Religiosity

Is Canada a religious society? The answer depends on how you look at things. Nationally, attendance at religious services, public confidence in religious leadership, and religious influence have all gone down since the late 1940s. Over the past 60 years, attendance at religious services has declined precipitously (Clark, 1998). A 1946 Gallup poll reported that 67 percent of Canadian adults had attended religious services during the previous week. By 2001, the General Social Survey found that attendance at weekly religious services had declined to only 20 percent (Clark, 2003). A generation ago, most Canadians attended religious services; today only a small minority attend regularly.

Different denominations have seen different rates of decline (Clark, 1998). The 1996 GSS found that 24 percent of Roman Catholics attended weekly services, down from 37 percent attendance in 1986. Nearly one in three Roman Catholics did not attend church at all in 1996, compared with one in seven in 1986. While attendance in the mainline Protestant denominations (United, Anglican, Presbyterian,

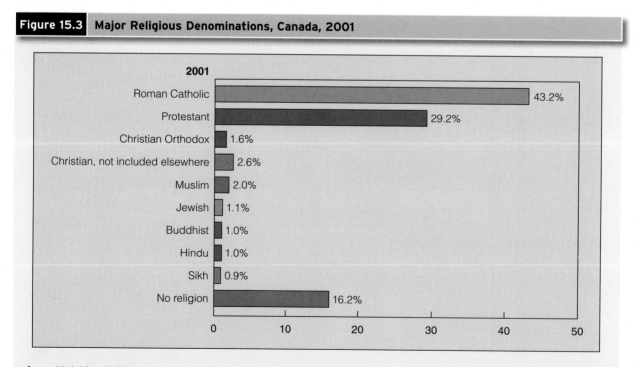

Figure 15.3   Major Religious Denominations, Canada, 2001

2001

Denomination	Percent
Roman Catholic	43.2%
Protestant	29.2%
Christian Orthodox	1.6%
Christian, not included elsewhere	2.6%
Muslim	2.0%
Jewish	1.1%
Buddhist	1.0%
Hindu	1.0%
Sikh	0.9%
No religion	16.2%

Source: Adapted from Statistics Canada, *Religions in Canada, 2001 Census*, Catalogue 96F0030XIE2001015, released May 13, 2003. http://www.statcan.gc.ca/bsolc/olc-cel/olc-cel?catno=96F0030XIE2001015&lang=eng

and Lutheran) was very low (14 percent) conservative Protestant denominations (Baptist, Pentecostal) have maintained 50 percent to 60 percent attendance rates. Many other religions (including Judaism, Hinduism, Buddhism, and Sikhism) have also seen serious declines in the percentage of people attending services, although some have seen a stabilization or even an increase because of immigration.

While attendance has declined for all age groups, the drop has been particularly large for younger people. Thirty-four percent of those 65 years of age and over regularly attend religious services, compared with only 12 percent of 15- to 24-year-olds. This absence of young members does not bode well for the future of Canadian religions, as the vast majority of regular adult attendees had also been regular attenders in childhood. This means that as older members die, there will likely be fewer and fewer people taking their places in the pews. According to surveys conducted by Reginald Bibby (2006), the decline in attendance at religious services reached a bottom in 2000 and increased in 2005, though attendance is still well below previous levels. However, Bibby's most recent survey showed that religious identification and belief continue to decline among Canadian teens (Bibby, 2009).

Despite the decline in involvement with the religious institutions, the vast majority of Canadians still report a religious affiliation and affirm that they believe in God. Both of these measures, though, have also declined in recent years. In 1961, only 1 percent of Canadians reported no religious affiliation; by 2001, this had increased to 16 percent (Statistics Canada, 2003j). In 1975, 89 percent of Canadians reported that they believed in God, compared with 81 percent in 1995 (Bibby, 1995b). Despite these declines, most Canadians still have religious affiliations and beliefs. While only about one-third of Canadians attended services once or more a month, over half (53 percent) carried out some religious practice, such as praying, on their own (Clark and Schellenberg, 2006. Bibby found that 68 percent of Canadian young people identified with a religious group in 2008 (Bibby, 2009).

Table 15.2 shows some of Bibby's other findings. In addition to their religious beliefs, Canadians show an interest in other aspects of spirituality. Table 15.2 shows that most Canadians believe that some people have psychic powers, that supernatural and evil forces exist, that there is life after death, and that some people have extrasensory perception. A significant minority believe that astrology has some merit and that it is possible to make contact with the spirit world.

These surveys reveal an interesting paradox. Attendance at religious services dramatically declined

Table 15.2 | SPIRITUAL BELIEFS AND INVOLVEMENT OF CANADIANS, 2000

"I BELIEVE ..."	PERCENTAGE AGREEING	
Conventional	**ADULTS**	**TEENS**
God exists	81%	73%
In life after death	68	78
Less Conventional		
In ESP	66	59
Can have contact with the spirit world	45	43
In astrology	35	57
"I ..."		
Group Involvement		
Am committed to Christianity or another faith	55	48
Attend weekly	21	22
Am open to possibility of greater involvement	57	43
Spirituality		
Have spiritual needs	73	48
Find spirituality very important	34	30
Pray privately weekly or more often	47	33

Source: Bibby, Reginald W. 2001. Canada's Teens: Today, Yesterday, and Tomorrow. Toronto: Stoddart

until it began to rise again after 2000 despite the fact that most Canadians report some religious affiliation, express a belief in God, and believe in other spiritual aspects of life. People have not completely rejected religious institutions, as most still rely on organized religion for services such as baptisms, weddings, and funerals (Bibby, 2002). However, they are not regular participants in religious activities, choosing instead to adopt what Bibby (1987) calls "religious fragments"—isolated beliefs, isolated practices, and isolated services. They receive spiritual sustenance from their religions, but they also draw from alternatives, such as astrology, extrasensory perception, and New Age practices, such as crystals, that serve as adjuncts to traditional religious practice. Theologian Tom Harpur sums up this approach to religion:

> There is a huge spiritual quest going on. There's a lot of attempts at quick fixes and spiritual junk food as well. But even the silly fringe is part of it . . . People seem intuitively aware that something is missing in their lives, and there's a reaction against traditional religion. (quoted in MacDonald, 1996:42)

This trend is reinforced by the fact that non-traditional spirituality is publicized through the popular media. Talk shows such as *Oprah* feature topics such as demonic possession, haunted houses, out-of-body experiences, and other forms of supernatural experience.

Why Have Canadians Turned away from the Church?

Bibby concludes that people have moved from religious commitment to religious consumption. Religious consumers look at the church as just one of many different options for solving their spiritual or worldly problems. Even those with a high religious commitment may not feel church attendance is the best way to express that commitment. As one of Bibby's respondents commented, "I've been through a great deal in life and my faith is very strong. But I believe that one is closer to God in their own home and garden than a church. I see going to church these days as 'keeping up with the Joneses.'" (Bibby, 1987:83) A postmodernist would explain that as our culture has become more individualistic, people are less likely to accept the dictates of an organized church. Religion has now been internalized and, rather than depending

upon the dictates of organized religion, people can make up their own version of spirituality that meets their needs.

No simple explanations can account for this change. It is apparent, though, that organized religion no longer seems relevant to the lives of many Canadians. One of Bibby's subjects illustrates this view: "The major issues of the day seem to me to have little to do with religion and morality; economic and political factors are far more important" (1993:59). When it has tried to address contemporary issues, the church has often had problems. For example, several Protestant denominations have had major conflicts over the role of homosexuals in the church. Debates over issues ranging from the tolerance of homosexuality to the ordination of homosexual ministers have led to major divisions. These moral issues have also distracted the churches from other activities. Some churches, notably the United Church, have tried to become more socially relevant by focusing on social justice issues, but this strategy has not attracted new members (Bibby, 1993) and may have driven older members away from the church.

Religious participation has also declined because major social institutions such as public schools no longer have religious affiliation. This means that people no longer have these institutional ties to their familial religious traditions and have more freedom to choose their method of religious participation. In a socially fragmented and highly mobile society, rather than dwelling within traditional denominations people can seek out spiritual practices that best fit their lives (Wuthnow, 1998).

The alienation of women has also contributed to the decline in church attendance. One journalist has observed:

> Women—the traditional mainstays of organized religion—in huge numbers abruptly rejected the church's patriarchal exemplar of them as chaste, submissive "angels in the house" with all of the social and moral responsibility for community and family but none of the authority. (Valpy, 2007: A17)

Many churches have not adapted to the changed role of women. Patriarchal practices can be difficult or impossible to change. Traditional gender roles are part of the core religious ideology of some churches and many denominations continue to restrict the role of women in the church. The quote from Joanne Barendregt in the chapter opening illustrates the fundamentalist view that a woman's sacred duty is submission to her husband. While some women welcome

BOX 15.4	SOCIOLOGY AND THE MEDIA

In the Media Age: The Electronic Church and the Internet

In a single telecast, I preach to millions more than Christ did in His entire lifetime.

–Billy Graham (quoted in Roberts, 1995:360)

Television and the Internet are having an impact on religion in the United States and Canada. Although ministers have used television since the 1950s, the *electronic church* is a multimillion-dollar industry in the United States. The first televised religious services were conducted by local congregations and carried by regional television stations primarily for the benefit of shut-ins and those who had no "church home" in the community.

Today, many televangelists are entrepreneurs whose success hinges on presenting a message that "sells well" and generates the large sums of money needed to keep the television ministry profitable. In the 1970s and 1980s, televangelists, such as Jerry Falwell, Oral Roberts, Jim and Tammy Faye Bakker, Jimmy Swaggart, and Pat Robertson, offered audiences a sense of belonging; for a certain sum of money, people could become "members" of the "700 Club" or "partners" in the "P.T.L. (Praise the Lord) Club" with Jim and Tammy Faye Bakker. When many of these televangelists were discredited because of sexual or financial misconduct, others took their place not only to proclaim the "gospel" but also to become spokespersons for a conservative political agenda.

Televangelists have not been as successful in Canada as in the United States. According to Bibby (1998), fewer than 5 percent of Canadians regularly watch religious services on television, which is much less than the 29 percent who watched or listened to services on television and radio in 1958. Most of those who did watch religious programs on television also attended church services regularly so television has not replaced more traditional forms of worship. Only a few televangelists have become nationally known in Canada, and none have any political influence. A new Canadian religious network, the Miracle Channel (www.miraclechannel.ca), has been very effective in raising operating funds through donations and getting out its evangelical message. However, it has also had ethical and legal problems. The Canadian Radio-television and Telecommunications Commission determined that the network had violated fundraising ethics by encouraging people to cash in retirement savings accounts to donate money and by suggesting that God would help keep struggling businesses from failing if their owners donated to the network (Robertson, 2007). The network's founder recently resigned after having an extra-marital affair with a network employee.

Nonreligious television programs rarely deal with religious matters. One notable exception is *The Simpsons*, which has regular characters from a variety of different religious backgrounds including Hindu (Apu), Evangelical Christian (Ned Flanders), Jewish (Krusty the Klown), and Protestant (Reverend Lovejoy). While the program often satirizes religion, it also presents some of the positive dimensions of religious experience (Dalton et al., 2001).

The Internet is now having an impact on religion. For example, Catholics on the Net (www.catholic.net) provides a range of services, including a review of recent Church-related news stories, discussions of church teachings, and a solicitation to inactive Catholics to become reinvolved with the church. The Vatican has just launched an iPhone app, has a series of "Daily Sermonettes" available on iTunes, a website (www.pope2you.net), and a Facebook page for the Pope, and regularly releases videos on Youtube (Agrell, 2010). Most other established religions have websites, and a rapidly growing site named God Tube (www.godtube.com) has been designed to encourage young people to think about religious matters. The Internet is a good way for mainline churches to get their message out and also provides a means for newer spiritual groups to try to attract followers. For example, the Falun Gong website both describes the faith and describes the group's persecution at the hands of the Chinese government (www.faluninfo.net). The Internet has even been used for religious satire. The very popular website for the Church of the Flying Spaghetti Monster (www.venganza.org) was designed as a protest against the teaching of creationism in Kansas schools.

While the Internet may be a useful religious tool, it raises concerns for some religious groups because controlling what young people read on the Internet is almost impossible. Some religious groups have begun pressing for limits to the type of information available on the Internet, or at least to limits on young people's access to certain types of information. How do you think religious organizations should respond to this problem? Is censorship of the Internet either possible or desirable?

Storefront missions such as this seek to win religious converts and offer solace to people in low-income central-city areas.

this role, this subordination is seen as unacceptable by many others. Failure to address the concerns of women will have serious consequences, as women are more likely to participate in church activities than are men and are also instrumental in ensuring their children go to church.

The image of the church has also suffered from thousands of charges of child sexual abuse by ministers and priests. While these incidents have taken place in a wide variety of contexts, the abuse was most pervasive in residential settings, such as the church-run schools that were established for Aboriginal children during the first half of the 20th century. Over 125 000 children attended these schools before the system was closed in the 1980s, and by 1999 more than 1 000 abuse complaints had been laid against church officials who worked in the schools (Cheney et al., 1998). The problem was not limited to the abuse of Aboriginal youth; the first major scandal in Canada grew out of offences committed by members of the Christian Brothers order at Newfoundland's Mount Cashel orphanage.

The image of the church was further damaged by the fact that in many cases senior church officials knew about the problem, did little or nothing to stop it, and tried to cover it up. These incidents make it more difficult for the churches to speak credibly on moral issues. Some critics have linked abuse within the Roman Catholic church to its patriarchal structure and its celibate male priesthood and have called into question these fundamental principles of the church.

Fundamentalism

As many mainline denominations have been losing membership, some fundamentalist churches have steadily grown. The term *religious fundamentalism* refers to a religious doctrine that is conservative, is typically opposed to modernity, and rejects "worldly pleasures" in favour of otherworldly spirituality. Whereas "old" fundamentalism usually appealed to people from lower-income, rural backgrounds, the "new" fundamentalism appears to appeal to persons from all socioeconomic levels, geographical areas, and occupations. "New-right" fundamentalists have been especially critical of *secular humanism*—a belief in the perfectibility of human beings through their own efforts rather than through a belief in God and a religious conversion. As you read in the chapter introduction, fundamentalists feel that instead of offering children a proper Christian education, the public schools are teaching things that seem to the child to prove that their parents' lifestyle and religion are inferior and perhaps irrational (Carter, 1994:52). The new-right fundamentalists claim that banning the teaching of Christian beliefs in the classroom while teaching things that are contrary to their faith is an infringement on their freedom of religion (Jenkinson, 1979). The selection of textbooks and library materials is especially controversial. Conservative religious groups have protested the use of books that they felt had morally objectionable subject matter or language. For example, a small group of parents in Ontario convinced the Durham Regional School Board to restrict the classroom reading of the *Harry Potter* books because they contain references to witchcraft and magic. This debate, along with the message of fundamentalism, has become an international issue because of the growth of the electronic church and the Internet, as discussed in Box 15.4 on page 385.

Does Religion Make a Difference?

Research on the impact of religion on attitudes and behaviour has had mixed results. Bibby (1998) concluded that religiosity has little impact on personal characteristics, such as happiness and contentment. While religion may help some people to be happy and content, others find the same level of satisfaction through other means. He also found that people with strong religious beliefs were no different from other Canadians in terms of relationships with other people, compassion, and tolerance of others (Bibby, 1995a). However, a Statistics Canada study found that weekly church attendees were much more likely to feel satisfied with their lives and much less likely to feel their lives were stressful than nonattenders (Clark, 1998).

Religiosity also influences other aspects of behaviour. All religions have ethical codes that govern personal and social behaviour. There is some evidence that religious commitment does influence people's moral conduct. For example, religiosity reduces involvement in delinquent and criminal behaviour (Linden, 2009). However, this relationship is complex—it is greatest where there is a strong religious community (Stark et al., 1982) and it has more impact on behaviour that is not universally condemned by other segments of society, such as illegal drug use, than on behaviour, such as theft and assault, that most other social institutions also disapprove of (Linden and Currie, 1977).

Religiosity is also associated with marital stability. Weekly church attenders place more importance on marriage and children than nonattenders, although the differences are not large. Church attenders have longer and happier marriages than nonattenders, and the marriages of church attenders are less than half as likely to break down as the marriages of nonattenders (Clark, 1998).

What about the impact of religion on health? In many small-scale societies, the same individual—the healer or *shaman*—was responsible for both physical and spiritual needs. Some people are once more trying to reintegrate medicine and religion. The increasing popularity of alternative medicine has led to an openness to nontraditional approaches, and polls show that many people (including some doctors) believe that religious faith can help cure disease and, therefore, use prayer as medical therapy (Sloan et al., 1999).

Many researchers have attempted to test the relationship between religion and medical outcomes. In their review of several dozen studies in this area, Sloan and his colleagues (1999) concluded that the evidence of an association between religiosity and health is weak and inconsistent. However, if it does not affect physical health, there is evidence that religion can play a role in comforting the sick. For example, one study found that 40 percent of a group of hospitalized adults reported that their religious faith was the most important factor in their ability to cope with their illness (Johns Hopkins, 1998).

RELIGION IN THE FUTURE

What significance will religion have in the future? Religion will continue to be important because it provides answers to basic questions that are very important to many people. Moreover, the influence of religion may be felt even by those who have no religious beliefs of their own. In many nations, the rise of *religious nationalism* has led to the blending of strongly held religious and political beliefs. The rise of religious nationalism is especially strong in the Middle East, where Islamic nationalism has spread rapidly.

In Canada the influence of religion will be evident in ongoing political battles over social issues, such as school prayer, abortion, gay and lesbian rights, and family issues. One such battle involves the right of faith-based organizations to discriminate against employees who do not follow prescribed moral teachings. This issue has recently been highlighted by the case of Christian Horizons, an Ontario agency that receives government funding to run group homes for people with disabilities. In 2008, a human rights tribunal found that Christian Horizons had violated the rights of Connie Heintz, who was fired because she was a lesbian. Christian Horizons has appealed this decision on grounds of religious freedom and the ultimate decision of the courts could have a major impact on religious organizations that do contract work for governments. While Canada has a high level of religious freedom compared with many other countries, issues such as this one raise concerns among many religious people about having their freedoms restricted.

We began this chapter with a discussion of the role of religion in our educational system. Controversies continue over the issue of what is acceptable in schools and what is not. For example, to promote a multicultural environment, several schools in Toronto decided to exclude all references to Christian symbols and doctrine from their annual Christmas celebrations. Many schools have renamed their Christmas assemblies 'holiday assemblies' and have eliminated all references to Christianity. One school banned the singing of religious Christmas carols on the grounds that references to Christianity would upset the non-Christian children (more than 30 percent of Toronto's school population). These incidents reflect the increasing secularization of the public school system. For example, in 1990, the Ontario Court of Appeal ruled against religious instruction in public elementary schools because it violates an individual's rights to freedom of religion (Fleras and Elliott, 1992). In 1995, Newfoundlanders voted to eliminate church-run schools in favour of a public, nondenominational education system and in 2006 the Quebec government said it would shut down unlicensed evangelical schools that did not follow the provincial curriculum by teaching evolution (Alphonso and Seguin, 2006).

Canada is not the only country facing a shortage of Roman Catholic priests. This is a recruiting ad from France. The ad reads:
I am just a man, like any other man.
I accompany others in the great events of their lives.
I am passionate about Christ and I say it out loud.
I love life.
I am a priest!

The changing role of religion in education is but one example of the declining influence of organized religion in Canadian society. Despite peoples' interest in the supernatural and their continued identification with religious traditions, church attendance and membership continue to fall. The Roman Catholic church faces an additional difficulty because the number of priests and nuns has declined dramatically because few young people are attracted to these occupations.

One might think that with Canada's high rate of immigration from a wide variety of countries, membership in religions such as Islam and Hinduism would be growing rapidly. However, this has not happened for two reasons. First, many immigrants are Christian and are adding to the ethnic and religious diversity within the dominant religious groups (Posterski and Barker, 1993). Second, growth has been slowed because many young people from these other faith groups have been marrying outside their faith. In 2001, 19 percent of all Canadian couples were in interreligious conjugal unions, half of which involved one partner who was neither a Protestant nor a Catholic (Clark, 2006). Children resulting from

these marriages may attend Protestant or Catholic churches, or the family may drop all participation in religious activities (Bibby, 1998).

Some see hope for the future in our aging population. They feel that as the baby boomers age, they are likely to search for spiritual meaning and some may turn back to the religions of their youth. However, there is little evidence that the baby boomers are returning. Church membership continues to stagnate, and it remains to be seen if organized religion will begin to flourish again in Canada. Bibby's most recent research suggests religion will continue to decline. For several decades, Bibby has been tracking the religious orientation of Canadian teens. Between 1984 and 2008, the percentage of young Canadians who define themselves as Christian has dropped from 85 percent to 45 percent, while the percentage who identify as "other faiths" has increased from 3 percent to 16 percent. Most importantly, those who identify with "no faith at all" has increased from 12 percent to 32 percent (Lunau, 2009). This rejection of religion by old and young does not bode well for the future of Canada's churches.

■ What is religion, and what purpose does it serve in society?

Religion is a system of beliefs, symbols, and rituals, based on some sacred or supernatural realm, that guides human behaviour, gives meaning to life, and unites believers into a community.

■ What is the functionalist perspective on religion?

According to functionalists, religion has three important functions in any society: (1) providing meaning and purpose to life, (2) promoting social cohesion and a sense of belonging, and (3) providing social control and support for the government.

■ What is the conflict perspective on religion?

From a conflict perspective, religion can have negative consequences. The capitalist class uses religion as a tool of domination to mislead workers about its true interests. However, Weber believed that religion could be a catalyst for social change.

■ What is the symbolic interactionist perspective on religion?

Symbolic interactionists focus on a microlevel analysis of religion, examining the meanings people give to religion and the meanings they attach to religious symbols in their everyday life.

■ What impact does religion have on attitudes and behaviour?

Research looking at the impact of religion on attitudes and behaviour has shown mixed results. Religiosity reduces involvement in delinquent and criminal behaviour.

Religious people have longer and happier marriages than nonreligious people. Religion and prayer appear to have little impact on health, though they help to comfort the sick.

■ Will religion continue as a major social institution?

Religion in Canada is clearly in decline and the prognosis for the future is not bright. However, Canadians still have a strong interest in spiritual matters and continue to identify with the church. If it is to take advantage of these factors, the church must find new ways to become relevant to the daily lives of Canadians.

KEY TERMS

animism 371
faith 370
monotheism 371
nontheistic religion 371
polytheism 371
religion 368
rituals 371
sacred 370
simple supernaturalism 371
theism 371

WEB LINKS

For more Web links related to the topic of this chapter, see the Nelson sociology website:
www.sociologyessentials5e.nelson.com

For links related to research on religion, go to the Virtual Religion Index at:

http://virtualreligion.net/vri

To see the website of the World Council of Churches, go to:

www.wcc-coe.org/wcc/english.html

Much of civilization's greatest art was commissioned by religious organizations. Visit the Vatican's Sistine Chapel with its ceiling painted by Michelangelo at:

www.wga.hu/index.html

Read about the PBS documentary on the first Christians at:

www.pbs.org/wgbh/pages/frontline/shows/religion

QUESTIONS FOR CRITICAL THINKING

1. Does religion appear in your life? Does it ever come up in everyday conversations? Do you see any differences between your acquaintances who are religious and those who are not?

2. How would you design a research project to study the effects of fundamentalist religion on everyday life? What kinds of data would be most accessible?

3. How is religion a force for social stability? How is it a force for social change?

4. Will religion continue as a major social institution in Canada? What factors lead people to turn away from religion? What factors promote a renewed or continued interest in religion?

5. In 2004, a Canadian university was criticized for not providing prayer space for Muslim students. Do you think that secular universities should be required to provide on-campus prayer space for all observant students?

ONLINE STUDY AND RESEARCH TOOLS

INFOTRAC®

InfoTrac College Edition is included free with every new copy of this text. Explore this online library for additional readings, review, and a handy resource for assignments. Visit **www.infotrac-college.com** to access this online database of full-text articles. Enter the key terms from this chapter to start your search.

CENGAGENOW™ CENGAGENOW

Use CengageNOW™ to help you formulate a customized study plan for this chapter. After you take the Diagnostic Quiz, CengageNOW™ will generate a customized study plan for you. It will identify sections of the chapter you should review.

CHAPTER 16

Population and Urbanization

CHAPTER OUTLINE

Moving to a new country and a new culture can be difficult, but the transition is easier for those who have support from others who share the same experiences. Consider the contrast between the lives of the two women—one described and one quoted—below. The first excerpt is from an interview with the child of a Sikh woman:

My mother had it hard when I was growing up. We had a small rented farm in the Okanagan Valley, where there were then very few Sikhs. I made friends with Canadians at school. Since I knew English fluently I often talked with the neighbours, as did my father. Mother wasn't so lucky. She never learned English well enough to communicate easily, so never really had any good Canadian friends. There were so few other Sikh families around that she had little contact with them either. For her, the family was everything. (Buchignani, Indra, and Srivastiva, 1985:76)

In the next excerpt, a woman who moved from Hong Kong to a Canadian city with a large middle-class Chinese community talks about her Chinese friends in Canada:

I feel we have more in common with each other. We often get together and reminisce about our lives in Hong Kong. We also laugh about our ignorance of Canadian culture and the little faux pas that we get ourselves into. Other times, we exchange information about schools, dentists, and other practical knowledge. Or we marvel at the high price we now pay for little things such as cooking wares and stockings. I have a feeling of solidarity when I talk to these people. They understand where I'm coming from. (Man, 1996:290)

The presence of others from one's former home plays a large role in determining where new immigrants settle in Canada. This has meant that cities such as Toronto and Vancouver have very high proportions of recent immigrants, while other communities have almost none. Immigration is just one of the demographic factors changing Canada and the rest of the world. The phenomena of births, deaths, and the movement of people interact to affect us all in very complex ways.

In this chapter, we will explore the dynamics of population growth and urban change. In the process, we will periodically focus on immigration and its importance to Canadian society. Before reading on, test your knowledge about the causes and consequences of immigration by taking the quiz in Box 16.1 on page 395.

Chapter Focus Question: What are the major social processes affecting Canada's population?

What causes global population growth?

How are people affected by population changes?

What impact has the baby boom had on Canada's population?

How do ecological/functionalist and political-economy/conflict models differ in their explanations of urban growth?

How do sociologists describe and explain the experience of urban life?

DEMOGRAPHY: THE STUDY OF POPULATION

Although population growth has slowed in Canada, the world's population of almost 6.5 billion in 2010 is increasing by 80 million people per year. By 2050 there will be an estimated 9.1 billion people in the world (United Nations, 2009). Virtually all of this growth will come in the lower-income nations. Conversely, the population in many high-income nations may decrease over this period. This means that people in different parts of the world face dramatically different futures. While many people in low-income countries face starvation because of rapidly increasing populations, Canadians have a much different problem. Because of low birth rates, our population is aging, and there are concerns about how a relatively small number of young workers will support large numbers of elderly people.

Why does the population grow rapidly in some nations? What are the consequences of low birth rates in industrialized countries? What is the impact of immigration? How large will our cities be in 20 years? These questions are of interest to scholars who specialize in the study of *demography*—**the subfield of sociology that examines population size, composition, and distribution**. Demography is important because the nature of population affects all aspects of social life. Increases or decreases in population have a powerful impact on the social, economic, and political structures. Demographers define *population* as a **group of people who live in a specified geographic area**. Changes in populations occur as a result of three processes: *fertility* (births), *mortality* (deaths), and *migration* (movement of people from one place to another).

Fertility

Fertility is the actual level of childbearing for an individual or a population. Fertility is based on biological and social factors. The primary biological factor affecting fertility is the number of women of childbearing age (usually between ages 15 and 45). Other biological factors include the health and level of nutrition of women of childbearing age. Social factors include the roles available to women and prevalent viewpoints regarding what constitutes the "ideal" family size.

Based on biological capability alone, most women could produce 20 or more children during their childbearing years. Women do not have this many children because biological capabilities are limited by social factors such as refraining from sexual intercourse until an older age, as well as by contraception, voluntary sterilization, abortion, and infanticide (Davis and Blake, 1956). One of the most important social factors affecting fertility is the role of women in society. The very poor Indian state of Kerala achieved one of the nation's lowest fertility rates (1.7 children per family) by improving the status of women through providing education and occupational opportunities (Sen, 1994). Government policies, such as China's one-child policy, may also effect fertility. This two-decades-old policy of allowing only one child per family, in order to limit population growth, will result in China's population starting to decline in 2042 (Beech, 2001).

The most basic measure of fertility is the *crude birth rate*—**the number of live births per 1000 people in a population in a given year**. In 2007, the crude birth rate in Canada was 11.1 per 1000 (Statistics Canada, 2009), compared with a post–World War II high rate of 28 per 1000 in 1956 and around 40 per 1000 at the time of Confederation. This measure is

BOX 16.1 | **SOCIOLOGY AND EVERYDAY LIFE**

How Much Do You Know About Immigration to Canada?

True	False	
T	(F)	1. Most Canadian immigrants now come from Europe.
(T)	F	2. Immigrants are not evenly distributed across the country, because many prefer to settle in large cities.
T	(F)	3. Most immigrants to Canada are refugees.
(T)	F	4. Canada has had rates of immigration in the past that were higher than current rates.
T	(F)	5. There is no limit to the number of family-sponsored immigrants who are allowed into Canada.
(T)	F	6. Immigrants have lower rates of crime than other Canadians.
(T)	F	7. If we do not maintain rates of immigration that are high by world standards, our population will eventually decline.
T	(F)	8. About 3 percent of Canada's population was not born in Canada.
T	(F)	9. Canada welcomed hundreds of thousands of Jewish refugees fleeing Nazi persecution during World War II.
T	(F)	10. Most countries of the world have open immigration and citizenship policies like those of Canada.

Answers on page 396.

referred to as a "crude" birth rate because it is based on the entire population and is not "refined" to incorporate significant variables affecting fertility, such as age, marital status, religion, or race and ethnicity.

In most of the industrialized world, women are having fewer children. Crude birth rates are very low in Germany (8.2 per 1000), Italy (8.4) and

The Right Honourable Michaëlle Jean, former Governor General of Canada, was born in Port-au-Prince, Haiti, and came to Canada as a refugee in 1968. As the Queen's representative, she was Canada's de facto head of state from 2005 to 2010.

Reuters/Landov

Japan (7.2); about the same as Canada in the United Kingdom (10.7 per 1000); and just over 14 per 1000 in the United States (CIA, 2009). However, families are much larger in low-income, agricultural regions of the world, where children's labour is essential to a family's economic survival and child mortality rates are still very high. Countries with high crude birth rates (more than 35 per 1000) include Nigeria, Somalia, and Afghanistan (CIA, 2009).

Mortality

The primary cause of world population growth in recent years has been a decline in *mortality*—**the incidence of death in a population**. The simplest measure of mortality is the *crude death rate*—**the number of deaths per 1000 people in a population in a given year**. Mortality rates have declined dramatically in most countries in the last 200 years. In 1867, the crude death rate in Canada was 21 deaths per 1000—half of what it had been 100 years earlier. By 2008, the death rate had dropped to 7.1 per 1000 (Statistics Canada, 2010). This decline has been due to the virtual elimination in high-income countries such as Canada of infectious diseases such as polio, cholera, tetanus, typhoid, and measles; and because of improved nutrition, sanitation, personal hygiene,

BOX 16.1   SOCIOLOGY AND EVERYDAY LIFE

Answers to the Sociology Quiz on Immigration to Canada

JoinIn

1. **False.**   In 2007, Europeans accounted for only about 16 percent of all immigrants (Citizenship and Immigration Canada, 2008).

2. **True.**   Ninety-seven percent of immigrants who arrived between 2001 and 2006 settled in urban areas. Sixty-nine percent settled in Toronto, Vancouver, and Montreal. Toronto has a larger proportion of immigrants than any other city in the world (followed by Miami); 46 percent of Toronto's population was born outside Canada (Statistics Canada, 2007).

3. **False.**   In 2007, refugees made up about 12 percent of all immigrants (Citizenship and Immigration Canada, 2009).

4. **True.**   Immigration rates fluctuate widely and at times in the past they have been much higher than they are today.

5. **False.**   Each year the government determines the number of family-sponsored immigrants who will be admitted. In 2007, 28 percent of immigrants were family sponsored (Citizenship and Immigration Canada, 2009).

6. **True.**   Immigrants were significantly underrepresented in the population of those incarcerated in the federal correctional system (Gordon and Nelson, 1993).

7. **True.**   Birth rates in Canada are currently below replacement level. When the baby-boom generation begins to die after 2025, Canada will lose population unless we give entry to about 250 000 immigrants each year.

8. **False.**   According to the 2006 census, nearly 20 percent of Canadian residents were born in other countries (Statistics Canada, 2007).

9. **False.**   While most Canadians are proud of this country's record in accepting refugees, our policies were not always as liberal as they are today. Very few Jewish refugees were admitted to Canada during the Holocaust (Abella and Troper, 1982).

10. **False.**   Canada has one of the highest rates of legal immigration in the world. Most countries discourage immigration and many will not give citizenship to anyone not born to parents who themselves are citizens of that country.

and vaccination. Since communicable diseases have steadily declined, the major causes of death in high-income countries are now chronic and degenerative diseases such as heart disease and cancer.

While mortality rates have dropped significantly in low-income and middle-income nations, they are still two to three times higher than those of high-income countries. In many countries, infectious diseases remain the leading cause of death. In some areas, mortality rates have increased again as a result of HIV/AIDS and a resurgence of tuberculosis.

In addition to the crude death rate, demographers also measure the *infant mortality rate*—**the number of deaths of infants under one year of age per 1000 live births in a given year**. The infant mortality rate reflects a society's level of preventive (prenatal) medical care, maternal nutrition, childbirth procedures, and neonatal care for infants, and it is often used as

a measure of a country's social development. The impact of modernization on infant mortality rates has been dramatic. In 1921, the infant mortality rate in Canada was 102 deaths per 1000 live births; by 2006 it had declined to 5.1 per 1000 live births (Statistics Canada, 2010). This can be compared with present rates of 6 per 1000 in the United States, 5 in the United Kingdom, and 3 in Japan (CIA, 2005).

Countries with high birth rates also have high infant mortality rates. For example, the infant mortality rates for Afghanistan, Pakistan, and Nigeria were, respectively, 152, 65, and 94 per 1000 live births (CIA, 2005).

Infant mortality rates are high among Canada's Aboriginal peoples, who suffer severe social disadvantages compared with the rest of the population and who often lack access to adequate health-care services. The infant mortality rate for First Nations is

Women in agricultural regions of the world, such as Kenya, tend to have more children. Children's labour in these regions is essential to the family's economic survival and child mortality rates are very high.

Tombstones such as this one for three children from one family who died very young were once very common. However, we now live in a time when the death of children is no longer a common event.

about twice the Canadian average and for the Inuit, it is four times the national average (Smylie and Adomako, 2009).

Declining mortality rates have led to substantial increases in *life expectancy,* **which is an estimate of the average lifetime in years of people born in a specific year**. For persons born in Canada in 2007, for example, life expectancy at birth was about 81 years (Statistics Canada, 2010a). This life expectancy is among the highest in the world. Within Canada, life expectancy is lower for Aboriginal people. On average, Aboriginal people live about 5 fewer years than the non-Aboriginal population, though this difference has been reduced from 10 years in 1981 (Cooke et al, 2004; Statistics Canada, 2008). Life expectancy varies by sex; females born in Canada in 2007 could expect to live about 83 years, compared with 78 years for males (Statistics Canada, 2010a).

Migration

Migration **is the movement of people from one geographic area to another for the purpose of changing** residency. Migration involves two types of movement: immigration and emigration. *Immigration* **is the movement of people into a geographic area to take up residency**, while *emigration* **is the movement of people out of a geographic area to take up residency elsewhere**. Migration affects the size and distribution of population in a given area.

Migration may be either internal (movement within national boundaries) or international (movement between two nations).

Internal Migration   Internal migration has significantly changed the distribution of our population. In the late 19th and early 20th centuries, a major population shift occurred as Canada was transformed from a largely rural to an urban nation. At the time of Confederation, about 80 percent of the population resided in rural areas; today, almost 80 percent are urban. Although Canada is now an urban country, the degree of urbanization among the provinces varies, ranging from 85 percent of the population of Ontario to only 45 percent of Prince Edward Island (Vander Ploeg, 2008).

Political unrest, violence, and war are "push" factors that encourage people to leave their country of origin. Shown here are a shipload of Liberian refugees awaiting political asylum in Ghana (left) and Pakistani citizens fleeing fighting between the Pakistan Army and the Taliban in the Northwest Frontier Province. Civil wars can cause massive population movement.

Along with movement from rural to urban areas, there is also extensive interprovincial migration. Over the past three decades, British Columbia, Ontario, and Alberta have attracted the most internal migrants. Can you think of reasons for this internal population shift?

International Migration   People migrate either voluntarily or involuntarily. *Pull* factors such as a democratic government, religious freedom, employment opportunities, or a more temperate climate may draw voluntary immigrants to a nation. *Push* factors such as political unrest, violence, war, famine, plagues, and natural disasters may encourage people to leave one area and relocate elsewhere. Involuntary, or forced, migration usually occurs as a result of political oppression, such as when Jews fled Nazi Germany in the 1930s or when Afghans fled the Taliban regime in the late 1990s. Slavery is the most striking example of involuntary migration; the 10 million to 20 million Africans transported forcibly to the Western Hemisphere before 1800 did not leave their home countries by choice.

Most of Canada's 33 million people are immigrants or the descendants of immigrants, making immigration a critical factor in the country's growth and development (for an historical perspective on immigration, see Box 16.2.) Because of our high immigration rate, immigrants make up nearly 20 percent of Canada's population (Statistics Canada, 2007a). This rate compares with 12 percent for the United States. Australia, with 22 percent of its population born elsewhere, is one of the few countries that has a higher percentage of immigrants than Canada (Statistics Canada, 2007f). By contrast, Japan (1.5 percent) and Hungary (1.1 percent) have two of the lowest percentages of foreign-born residents (OECD, 2004).

Figure 16.1 on page 400 shows that immigration levels have fluctuated widely since Confederation. Economic conditions, wars, pressure from refugees, and changes in government policies have all contributed to these shifts. Following an economic depression, in 1896 the government promoted immigration to encourage settlement of the West. In the years prior to World War I, as many as 400 000 people per year immigrated to Canada, a number that has never been exceeded. Most of these immigrants were European and many of them settled the farms, towns, and cities of the Prairie provinces. World War I caused a precipitous decline in immigration. While numbers rose again after the war, the Great Depression and World War II kept levels of immigration low for almost 20 years. During this period, more people left Canada than arrived here. After World War II, immigration rates again climbed. Canada's postwar economy was strong, and skilled foreign workers were needed. Political instability and economic difficulty in Europe encouraged many people to leave to find a better life elsewhere. The postwar immigration peak of 1956–57 was a result both of Canada's acceptance of refugees from the unsuccessful Hungarian Revolution and of providing a home for British subjects leaving Egypt after the Suez crisis.

Immigration regulations permitted discrimination based on racial and ethnic origin until the early 1960s (see Box 16.2). At various times, Chinese, Japanese, and South Asians were prohibited from immigrating to Canada, and the 1953 Immigration Act allowed the government to bar entry on the grounds of race, ethnicity, or even "peculiar customs, habits, modes of life or methods of holding property" (Beaujot, 1991:109). Box 16.3 on page 401 shows how these prejudices were endorsed by the media. Preference was given to whites, particularly those of British origin.

BOX 16.2 CRITICAL THINKING

Immigration and the Law in Canada

Canadians can be proud of having welcomed immigrants from around the globe. However, at times in the past our immigration policies have been exclusionary and racist.

Shortly after 1900, some Canadians began to express concerns about immigration from East Asia and South Asia. The first Chinese immigrated to Canada in the 1850s. Many were recruited to work as labourers on the construction of the Canadian Pacific Railway. South Asians began to immigrate to Canada in 1903. While the numbers of both groups were small, they were subjected to harsh discrimination. British Columbia, where Chinese and Japanese immigrants were largely concentrated, passed several laws restricting their rights. For example, the Chinese and Japanese were denied the right to vote in 1872 and 1895, respectively, and restrictions were imposed on their right to work. The federal government levied a head tax on the Chinese in 1885 to restrict their immigration and in 1923 passed the Chinese Immigration Act, which virtually disallowed new immigration from East Asia.

While these regulations now seem appalling, Canadians were no worse than most other Western countries. Many leading scientists of the day supported the view that Anglo-Saxons were biologically superior, and the admission of other races was seen as a danger to white democracies.

For many years our immigration policy also restricted the admission of Jews because of anti-Jewish sentiment and because of the Jewish preference for settling in urban areas rather than in the rural areas preferred by the government. Even during World War II, when millions of Jews were being exterminated in Europe, Canada would not open its doors to Jewish refugees. No country made the immigration of Jews a priority during the Holocaust, but Canada's record was particularly poor. Between 1933 and 1945, Canada admitted fewer than 5 000 Jews, whereas during the same period 200 000 were allowed into the United States and 70 000 into the United Kingdom. Despite significant and vocal support among Canadians for taking action to save Jewish refugees, Prime Minister Mackenzie King and his cabinet refused. The attitude of the government is summed up in the words of a senior Canadian official who was speaking with journalists in early 1945. When asked how many Jews would be admitted to Canada following the war, his response was, "None is too many" (Abella and Troper, 1982:xxi).

Sources: Based on Abella and Troper, 1982; Ghosh and Kanungo, 1992; Statutes of Canada, 1910 c.27.

These discriminatory restrictions were lifted in 1962, and the face of immigration changed dramatically. In Table 16.1 (on page 400), you can compare the top ten source countries of immigrants arriving in 1957 with those of immigrants who came in 2008. While in 1957 the vast majority of immigrants were whites from Northern Europe, in 2008 immigrants to Canada came from all over the world and represented many different ethnicities and cultures. While this diversity would not have been possible under the old rules, the factors "pushing" immigrants have also changed. For the past 30 years, most Western European countries have had very strong economies, low unemployment rates, and stable governments. Europeans have had little reason to emigrate. At the same time, conditions in many other parts of the world have been less favourable, so emigration to Canada is seen positively.

For most of the past decade the number of immigrants coming to Canada annually has been between 200 000 and 250 000. This stability is the result of government policy aimed at achieving a stable population in the future in the face of declining birth rates and an aging population.

Population Composition

Changes in fertility, mortality, and migration affect the *population composition*—**the biological and social characteristics of a population**, including age, sex, ethnic origin, marital status, education, occupation, income, and size of household.

For demographers, sex and age are significant population characteristics. They are key predictors of fertility and mortality rates and the age distribution of a population has a direct bearing on the demand for schooling, health, employment, housing, and pensions. The distribution of a population can be depicted in a *population*

| Figure 16.1 | Annual Levels of Canadian Immigration, 1860-2005 |

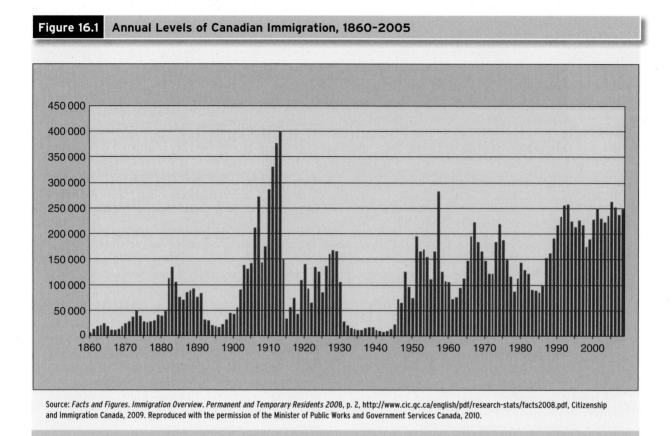

Source: *Facts and Figures. Immigration Overview. Permanent and Temporary Residents 2008*, p. 2, http://www.cic.gc.ca/english/pdf/research-stats/facts2008.pdf, Citizenship and Immigration Canada, 2009. Reproduced with the permission of the Minister of Public Works and Government Services Canada, 2010.

pyramid—**a graphic representation of the distribution of a population by sex and age**. Population pyramids are a series of bar graphs divided into five-year age cohorts; the left side of the pyramid shows the number or percentage of males in each age bracket; the right side provides the same information for females.

The age/sex distribution in Canada and other developed nations no longer has the appearance of a pyramid, but rather is more rectangular (see France in Figure 16.2) or diamond-shaped (see Canada in Figure 16.2). A more rectangular shape reflects a population that has a low birth rate and an increasing number of

| Table 16.1 | CANADIAN IMMIGRANTS' TOP TEN COUNTRIES OF ORIGIN, 1957 AND 2008 |

| | 1957 | | | 2008 | |
RANK	COUNTRY	% OF TOTAL IMMIGRATION	RANK	COUNTRY	% OF TOTAL IMMIGRATION
1	United Kingdom	38.6	1	China	11.8
2	Hungary	11.2	2	India	9.9
3	Germany	10.0	3	Philippines	9.6
4	Italy	9.8	4	United States	4.5
5	Netherlands	4.2	5	United Kingdom	3.3
6	United States	3.9	6	Pakistan	3.3
7	Denmark	2.7	7	Korea, Republic of	2.9
8	France	2.0	8	France	2.6
9	Austria	2.0	9	Iran	2.4
10	Greece	1.9	10	Colombia	2.0

Source: Zgodzinski, 1996; Statistics Canada, 1997e; Citizenship and Immigration Canada, 2009.

BOX 16.3   SOCIOLOGY AND THE MEDIA

Immigration and the Media

Just after the turn of the 20th century, nonwhite immigrants to Canada faced great hostility. The media actively promoted this racism by publishing inflammatory articles about racial minorities. These articles not only affected public opinion but also were used by legislators to justify laws that targeted minority immigrants. The writing of Judge Emily Murphy of Edmonton, the first woman judge in the British Empire, was particularly influential. Her series of five articles in *Maclean's* magazine shaped Canada's drug laws throughout the 1920s and their effects live on in our present narcotics legislation. These articles also shaped the attitudes of Canadians toward nonwhite immigrants by attributing the drug problem to Chinese and Black "villains" who, according to Judge Murphy, were trying to spread the drug habit in order to seduce white women and to destroy the Anglo-Saxon way of life.

Judge Murphy believed that nonwhite immigrants were a threat to the Canadian way of life. Her articles in *Maclean's* were illustrated with photographs of opium smokers (almost all of whom were women or nonwhite men) and racially demeaning cartoons. Each article featured a caricature of a Chinese opium smoker with smoke coming out of each ear. She saw the Chinese drug peddler as one who was perhaps unknowingly carrying out the wishes of his superiors who were trying to bring about the "downfall of the white race." The "Negroes coming into Canada," she wrote, "have similar ideas."

The same conspiratorial view was advanced by other media. For example, in 1911, the *Montreal Herald* responded to the immigration of 58 Black female domestics from Guadeloupe by reporting that the "dark-skinned domestics were the advanced guard for others to follow" (Calliste, 1993/94: 138).

The free expression of these views in the media made it easy for politicians and members of the public to follow the same racist line. This type of media coverage helps to explain why Canada had racially based immigration policies for much of the last century.

Emily F. Murphy, *The Black Candle*, © Coles Publishing, 1922

These photographs of an opium addict (left) and an opium den keeper (right) appeared in Judge Murphy's book *The Black Candle* (Murphy, 1922), which, like her articles published in *Maclean's* in the 1920s, were used by legislators to justify laws that targeted minority immigrants.

Sources: Based on Murphy, 1922; Cook, 1969.

older people. You can see in Figure 16.2 that a developing nation such as Mexico has a population distribution that fits the classic population pyramid. Mexico has high fertility and mortality rates, which means a large number of children and few older people. The population pyramid for Russia, also shown in Figure 16.2, has some unusual features that have been caused by catastrophic events such as the two World Wars, the Civil War of 1917–22, famine in the 1920s and 1930s, and the recent dramatic decline in birth rates. For example, the large number of males killed during World War II gave Russia the lowest male-to-female ratio in the

| Figure 16.2 | **Population Pyramids for Russia, Mexico, Canada, and France, 2011** |

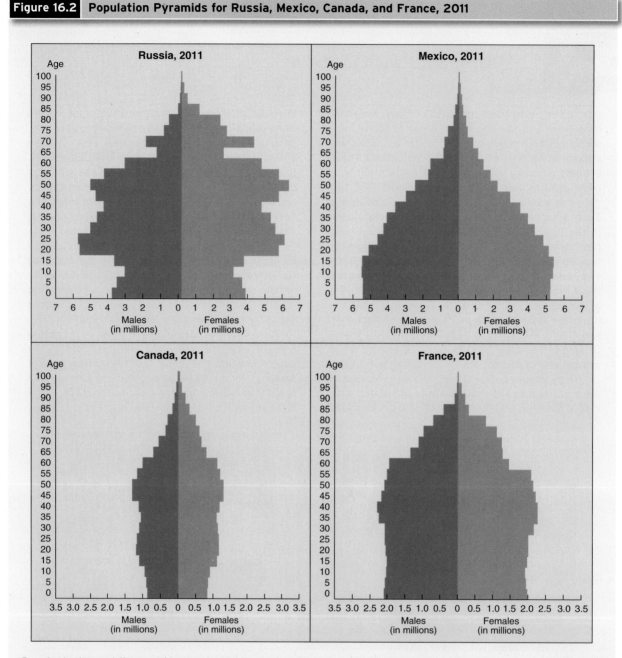

To understand a population pyramid, remember that the number of males is on the left side and the number of females, on the right. The five-year age categories are on the vertical axis (on the far left side) of the figure.

Source: U.S. Census Bureau, 2009.

world. The irregularities in Russia's population pyramid will affect patterns of population growth and aging for decades to come (Institut National d'Etudes Demographiques, 1997).

The Baby Boom and the Baby Bust

One very simple fact will help you to understand many things about Canadian society: Every year you get one year older, and, more importantly, so does everyone else. The *age structure* of the population has a major impact on many facets of society.

One of the most significant demographic changes in Canadian history was the *baby boom*—the dramatic increase in births that occurred between 1946 and 1966. The boom was created by young couples who married and began having large families in the years immediately following World War II. The high birth

Figure 16.3   **Canadian Period Total Fertility Rate, 1871-2007**

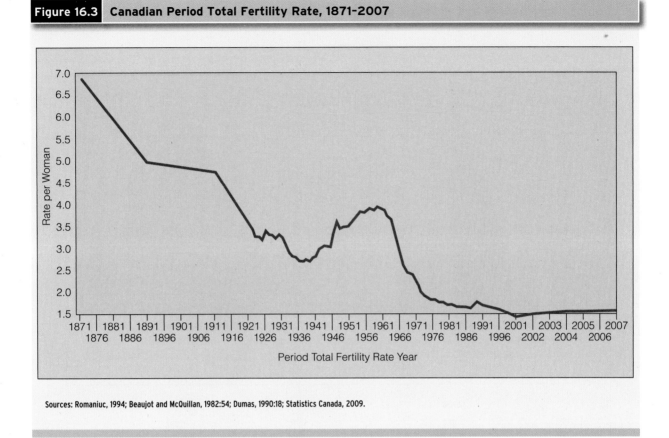

Sources: Romaniuc, 1994; Beaujot and McQuillan, 1982:54; Dumas, 1990:18; Statistics Canada, 2009.

rates of the baby boom were followed by the *baby bust*, which saw birth rates fall to low levels, where they remain today. While many demographic changes take place over a long period of time, the baby boom was a rapid reversal of a long-term downward trend in birth rates. In Figure 16.3 you can see that the long-term decline in birth rates was interrupted for 20 years following the end of World War II. By the end of the boom in 1966, one-third of all the people in Canada had been born in the preceding 15 years.

The baby boom and baby bust have had a dramatic impact on Canada's age structure, which can be seen in the series of population pyramids in Figure 16.4. The 1961 pyramid shows the population of Canada toward the end of the baby boom. There are large numbers of young people because of the boom. The small number of people aged 15 to 24 is the result of low birth rates during the Depression and World War II. The 1981 pyramid, shows the consequences of the baby boom and the drop in fertility rates (the "baby bust") that followed. The pyramid for 2006 shows an increased number of older people as the oldest baby boomers approach age 60. Finally, in the 2031 pyramid, mortality has begun to affect the baby

boomers, and the survivors are now 65 to 85 years of age.

Think of the baby boom as a 20-year bulge in the population pyramid. Each year, this bulge moves one year up the pyramid as the baby-boom cohort ages. You can easily track this bulge in the population pyramids in Figure 16.4. Some demographers have used the analogy of a pig that has been swallowed by a python to describe the way in which the baby-boom generation has moved up the population pyramid.

It is interesting to compare Canada's demographic structure with those of other countries. For example, you can see from Figure 16.2 that Mexico, which is a middle-income society, has a constant baby boom—it is continually adding young people to its population as its population rapidly expands. On the other hand, France did not have a baby boom after World War II, so its age structure is quite different from Canada's. The age structure of many European countries is much like that of France. The only other countries that had a baby boom similar to Canada's were Australia, the United Kingdom, and the United States.

The baby boom has transformed society in many different ways. Beginning in the late 1940s, many

Figure 16.4   **Population by Age and Sex, Canada, 1961 and 1981 (Census), 2006 and 2031**

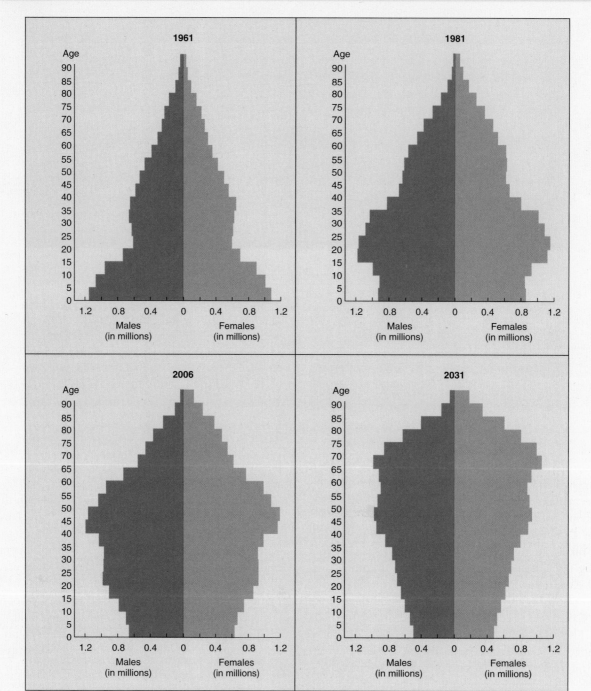

Source: Adapted from Statistics Canada, *Population projections for Canada, Provinces and Territories, 1984-2006*, Catalogue 91-520, 1985 and 91-520XWE2005001 http://www.statcan.gc.ca/bsolc/olc-cel/olc-cel?catno=91-520-XWE&lang=eng

businesses saw their markets expand. Manufacturers of baby food, diapers, and children's toys flourished, and obstetricians were in great demand. As the baby-boom cohort aged, school construction increased dramatically and teaching jobs were plentiful. By the mid-1960s, university and college enrollments began to climb and many new institutions opened to meet the demand. Crime rates also began to increase at this time because the baby boomers had entered the 15 to 24 age group, during which criminal behaviour is most common. In the mid-1970s, house prices rose quickly in most Canadian cities, as the baby boomers began to settle down and raise families (Foot, 1996).

Because of the baby bust, many of these changes reversed in the 1980s. Schools built to house the soaring numbers of children in the 1960s were closed 20 years later, and school boards had to deal with an oversupply of teachers. By the 1990s, university and college enrollment stopped increasing and the crime rate began to decline. Corporations that had targeted youthful consumers began to reorient their products and their advertising to appeal to an older market. Radio stations began to play "golden oldies" to attract the aging baby boomers, and clothing manufacturers began to offer "relaxed fit" products for those affected by middle-age spread.

What of the future? The baby-boom cohort is now well into middle age and the first of its members were 65 in 2011. Soon there will be a much higher proportion of older persons than there is today. In 1971, about 8 percent of Canadians were 65 and over; in 2011 the percentage was 16 percent; and by 2036 it will likely stabilize at almost 25 percent. About 9 million Canadians will be over 65, compared with the current level of about 5 million.

Population aging will lead to many changes. Since the elderly are the biggest users of health care, governments are trying to get health costs under control before the baby boomers require increased medical services. The government has increased Canada Pension Plan premiums and decreased some benefits so the plan can stay in operation.

One final trend to consider is the *baby-boom echo*—the children of the baby boomers. You can see this echo in Figure 16.4, which shows a relatively large cohort following about 20 years behind the baby boom. Even though the baby boomers had far fewer children than their parents (1.7 children per family, compared with more than 3 children for their parents), there were so many baby boomers that their children are having a significant impact. The leading edge of the echo generation, who were about 30 years old in 2011, will have an impact on things such as the housing market during this decade.

The Baby Boom and Immigration Policy

Canada's low birth rate could lead to depopulation. Fertility of 2.1 children per woman is needed to ensure the replacement of a population. Two children will replace the parents, and the additional 0.1 compensates for deaths that occur before potential parents reach reproductive age. This level of fertility will eventually lead to a stable population with zero population growth except for that caused by migration.

Canada's fertility is near its all-time low of 1.5 children per woman, which will not provide replacement of our population. If this level of fertility remains constant for the next several decades, Canada will begin losing population when the baby boomers begin to die. You can see this in the 2031 population pyramid in Figure 16.4.

Since the 1990s Canada has admitted between 200 000 and 250 000 immigrants annually (see Figure 16.1). This number was chosen because demographers have calculated that to stabilize the population we need about 250 000 immigrants a year. Thus, the baby bust has had an important impact on our immigration policies.

POPULATION GROWTH IN A GLOBAL CONTEXT

While Canada does not face any population pressures, in many other countries the population is growing rapidly. What are the consequences of global population growth? Scholars do not agree on the answer to this question. Some biologists have warned that Earth is a finite ecosystem that cannot support the 9.1 billion people expected on the planet by 2050 while other people feel humans will be able to adapt successfully to larger populations.

The Malthusian Perspective

The debate over sustainable population growth is not new. English clergyman and economist Thomas Malthus (1766–1834) was one of the first scholars to systematically study the effects of population.

According to Malthus, unchecked population growth would exceed the available food supply. He argued that the population would increase in a geometric (exponential) progression (2, 4, 8, 16, . . .), while the food supply would increase only by an arithmetic progression (1, 2, 3, 4, . . .). Thus a *doubling effect* occurs: two parents can have four children, sixteen grandchildren, and so on, but food production increases by only one hectare at a time. Thus, population growth inevitably surpasses the food supply, and the lack of food ultimately ends population growth, and starvation and disease may eliminate the existing population (Weeks, 2002). Even in a best-case scenario, overpopulation results in poverty.

Malthus suggested that this disaster might be averted by either positive or preventive checks on population. *Positive checks* are mortality risks such as famine, disease, and war; *preventive checks* are limits to fertility.

The Marxist Perspective

According to Marx and Engels, the food supply is not threatened by overpopulation. Technologically, it is possible to produce the food and other goods needed to meet the demands of a growing population. Writing from a conflict perspective, Marx and Engels viewed poverty as a consequence of the exploitation of workers by the owners of the means of production.

From this perspective, overpopulation occurs because capitalists want a surplus of workers (an industrial reserve army) to suppress wages and to force workers concerned about losing their livelihoods to be more productive. Marx believed that overpopulation would contribute to the eventual destruction of capitalism. Unemployment would make the workers dissatisfied, resulting in a class consciousness based on their shared oppression and in the eventual overthrow of the system. In a socialist regime, enough food and other resources would be created to accommodate population growth.

Marx and Engels made a significant contribution by suggesting that poverty, not overpopulation, is the most important issue with regard to the food supply in a capitalist economy. While Marx and Engels offer an interesting counterpoint to Malthus, some scholars argue that the Marxist perspective is inadequate because it attributes the population problem solely to capitalism. In fact, nations with socialist economies have demographic trends similar to those in capitalist societies.

The Neo-Malthusian Perspective

More recently, *neo-Malthusians* (or "new Malthusians") have re-emphasized the dangers of over-population. To neo-Malthusians, Earth is "a dying planet" with too many people, too little food, and environmental degradation (Ehrlich, 1971). Overpopulation and rapid population growth create global environmental problems, ranging from global warming and rain-forest destruction to famine and vulnerability to epidemics such as AIDS (Ehrlich, Ehrlich, and Daily, 1995). Environmental problems will worsen as countries such as India and China, with their large populations, modernize and begin to use resources at a rate closer to that of industrialized countries.

Throughout history, population growth and epidemic diseases have interacted to shape human destiny. Figure 16.5 shows the dramatic impact of AIDS on the population structure of Botswana. People are extremely vulnerable to disease if they already are debilitated from inadequate nutrition, unclean water supplies, poor medical care, and lack of sanitation.

Are the neo-Malthusians correct? Will population increases leave many populations vulnerable to mass death through starvation and disease? Some possible answers are found in the work of Thomas Homer-Dixon who is often considered a neo-Malthusian. Homer-Dixon believes that increases in population and resource consumption will lead to significant environmental changes including scarcities of soil and water, and climatic instability (1993). The strains caused by these scarcities may lead to unrest, including war, revolution, ethnic violence, and riots. Homer-Dixon does not believe that population disaster is inevitable; human social and technical ingenuity can overcome or at least delay the consequences of population increase. For example, despite decades of predictions that China will be unable to support its population, the average caloric intake in China has been rising as the country has massively increased its production of food.

Unfortunately, there is no guarantee that solutions to the predicted problems will be found. Ingenuity is itself a function of a country's social institutions, and in many countries these institutions are too fragmented or too lacking in human and physical resources to solve their problems. Political turmoil has been an obstacle. Unrest has kept many countries in sub-Saharan Africa from progressing and, without major reform, their future is gloomy. Ultimately, national and international action will be necessary to solve the problems created by population growth and environmental damage.

Demographic Transition Theory

Some scholars suggest that the theory of demographic transition offers a more accurate picture of future population growth than neo-Malthusian theory. **Demographic transition is the process by which some societies have moved from high birth and death rates to relatively low ones as a result of technological development.** Demographic transition theory was initially applied to population changes brought about by the Industrial Revolution

| Figure 16.5 | Projected Population Structure with and without the AIDS Epidemic, Botswana, 2020 |

The population pyramid in countries with high rates of HIV/AIDS, such as Botswana, has an unusual "chimney" shape. The outer pyramid is the project population without HIV/AIDS; the inner pyramid reflects the impact of HIV/AIDS. Few older people survive, which means that many children will be orphaned, there will be few teachers to educate young people, and the adult labour force to produce wealth for the country will be small. Average life expectancy will be less than 30 years.

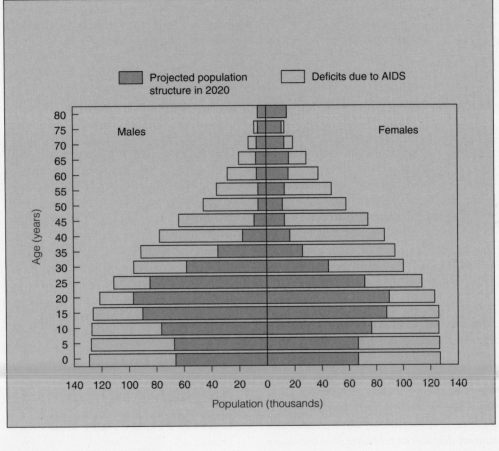

Source: U.S. Census Bureau, World Population Profile 2000.

in Western Europe and North America, but is now applied more broadly. Demographic transition is linked to four stages of economic development (see Figure 16.6):

- *Stage 1: Pre-industrial societies.* There is little population growth because high birth rates are offset by high death rates. Children are an economic asset because of their ability to work, but infant and child mortality rates are high due to lack of sanitation and poor nutrition. Life expectancy is around 30 years.
- *Stage 2: Early industrialization.* Significant population growth occurs because birth rates remain relatively high while death rates decline.

Improvements in health, sanitation, and nutrition reduce infant mortality rates, but social institutions (such as the family and religion) continue to promote high fertility. Many low-income nations—especially in Africa, Asia, and Latin America—are in this stage.

- *Stage 3: Advanced industrialization and urbanization.* Little population growth occurs because both birth rates and death rates are low. The birth rate declines as couples control their fertility through contraception and become less likely to adhere to religious directives against its use. Children are not an economic asset; they consume income rather than produce it.

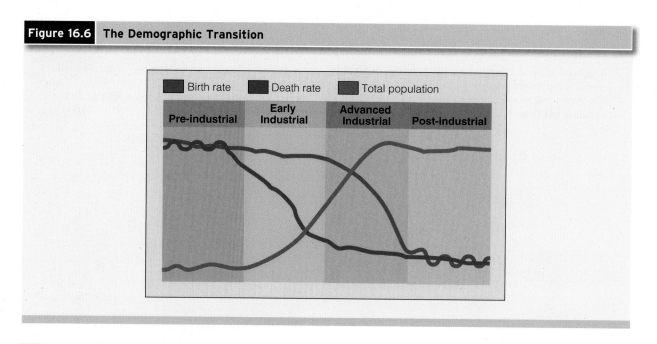

Figure 16.6   The Demographic Transition

Birth rate ■   Death rate ■   Total population ■

Pre-industrial | Early Industrial | Advanced Industrial | Post-industrial

■ *Stage 4: Post-industrialization.* Birth rates continue to decline as more women gain full-time employment and the cost of raising children continues to increase. The population grows very slowly, if at all, because the decrease in birth rates is coupled with a stable death rate.

Demographic transition theory highlights the relationship between technological development and a slowing of population growth—a relationship that makes Malthus's predictions obsolete. Scholars also point out that demographic transitions occur at a faster rate in currently low-income nations than they previously did in the nations that already are industrialized.

Critics suggest that demographic-transition theory best explains development in Western societies. Many low-income countries may never achieve a steady growth in social and economic wealth unless fertility levels first decline, so other routes to population control must be found. We should not expect low-income countries to follow the same path as Western nations, as they have very different demographic histories and their population dynamics operate within very different historical, cultural, and economic circumstances (Weiskel, 1994). Weiskel notes that women's status and education, along with active family planning programs, have been more important than overall economic growth as causes of declining fertility.

The increased education of women in low-income nations is one of the reasons the rate of population growth in these countries has slowed in recent decades. Once the average education of women gets beyond Grade 8, fertility rates decline. The global fertility rate is now 2.7 births per woman, compared with 5 births per woman in the early 1950s. This decline has been most dramatic in Latin America and the Caribbean, where fertility rates have dropped by over 50 percent to 2.3 over the past 25 years. Rates have dropped in sub-Saharan Africa, but they are still high at 4.6 (United Nations, 2009).

URBANIZATION AND THE GROWTH OF CITIES

Urban sociology examines social relationships and political and economic structures in the city. A *city* is a relatively dense and permanent settlement of people who secure their livelihood primarily through nonagricultural activities. The census term that defines our cities is *census metropolitan area*, or CMA: "an area consisting of one or more adjacent municipalities situated around a major urban core. To form a census metropolitan area, the urban core must have a population of at least 100 000" (Statistics Canada, 2002k). Canada has 27 CMAs, which in 2007 ranged in size from 5.5 million people in Toronto to 124 000 in Thunder Bay.

Two hundred years ago, only about 3 percent of the world's population lived in cities, compared with almost 50 percent today. In Canada, the population is even more concentrated: almost 80 percent of us live in areas defined as urban, including about 30 percent in the three major metropolitan areas of

Toronto, Montreal, and Vancouver. To understand why most now live in cities, we first need to see how cities developed over time.

Pre-industrial Cities

The largest pre-industrial city was Rome; by 100 C.E. it may have had a population of 650 000 (Chandler and Fox, 1974). After the fall of the Roman Empire in 476 C.E., the nature of European cities changed. Seeking protection and survival, city-dwellers typically resided in walled cities containing no more than 25 000 people. For the next 600 years the urban population continued to live in walled enclaves, as competing warlords battled for power and territory. Slowly, as trade increased, cities began to tear down their walls. Some walled cities still exist; Quebec City is the only walled city in North America.

Several factors limited the size of pre-industrial cities. Crowding and a lack of sewage facilities increased the hazards from plagues and fires, and death rates were high. Also, food supplies were limited because farming was inefficient and labour-intensive, and there was no effective way to preserve food. Finally, migration to the city was difficult because people were bound to the land through systems of serfdom and slavery and because travel was difficult.

Canadian communities arose as settlement extended to new parts of the country. Until the building of the Canadian Pacific Railway, much of Canada was accessible only by water, so most of our settlements, including those that have grown into large cities, were on waterways. Transportation routes were particularly important for a colony whose main function was sending large quantities of raw materials such as timber, wheat, and beaver pelts overseas to European markets.

Industrial Cities

The Industrial Revolution changed the nature of the city. Factories sprang up, as production shifted from the primary, agricultural sector to the secondary, manufacturing sector. Factories meant new employment opportunities not available to people in rural areas and required a concentration of population to act as a labour force. Emergent technology, including new forms of transportation and agricultural production, made it easier for people to leave the countryside and move to the city. Between 1700 and 1900, the population of many European cities mushroomed. Although the Industrial Revolution did not start in North America until the mid-19th century, the effect was similar. Between 1871 and 1911, the population of Toronto grew by 700 percent and that of Montreal by 450 percent (Nader, 1976). By 1911, both cities had roughly 500 000 people and were on their way to becoming major metropolises. A *metropolis* **is one or more central cities and their surrounding suburbs that dominate the economic and cultural life of a region.** A *central city* **is the densely populated centre of a metropolis.**

As cities grew, density, overcrowding, poor sanitation, and lack of a clean water supply often led to the spread of epidemic diseases and contributed to a high death rate. In Europe, mortality rates were higher in cities than in rural areas until the 19th century, and this remains the case in many cities in low-income countries.

Post-industrial Cities

Since the 1950s, post-industrial cities have emerged in technologically advanced countries whose economies have gradually shifted from manufacturing to services. As traditional industries, such as textile manufacturing and steel producing have become obsolete or moved to lower-wage countries, cities have either had to change or to face decline. For example, cities in New Brunswick were economically devastated in the 1980s and 1990s by the loss of many jobs in traditional industries such as shipbuilding and railroad maintenance, as well as jobs associated with the fishing industry. The province counteracted these losses by moving into the technologically based field of telephone call centres, which perform tasks such as telephone marketing and airline-reservation handling.

Post-industrial cities are dominated by "light" industry, such as computer software manufacturing; information-processing services, such as airline and hotel reservation services; educational complexes; medical centres; convention and entertainment centres; and retail trade centres and shopping malls. Most families do not live close to a central business district. Modern communication and transportation methods allow middle- and upper-income individuals and families to have more work options and to live greater distances from the workplace. Some futurists believe that communications technology, along with the retirement plans of the baby boomers, may lead to a degree of de-urbanization. People who do not have to be physically present in the city centre each day may find a rural or semi-rural lifestyle an attractive alternative to the commuting and high housing prices that are a part of life in a large city.

Toronto's Gardiner Expressway at rush hour illustrates the development of post-industrial cities in which people commonly commute long distances to work. Smog is one of the problems that come with urbanization.

Toronto Star/GetStock.com

PERSPECTIVES ON URBANIZATION AND THE GROWTH OF CITIES

Functionalist Perspectives: Ecological Models

In studying cities, functionalists have emphasized the life cycle of urban growth. Robert Park (1915) based his analysis of the city on *human ecology*—the study of the relationship between people and their physical environment. According to Park (1936), economic competition produces regularities in land-use patterns and population distributions. Applying Park's idea to the study of urban land use patterns, Ernest Burgess (1925) developed the concentric-zone model to explain why some cities expand outward from a central business core.

Concentric-Zone Model   Burgess's *concentric-zone model* views the city as a series of circular areas or zones, each characterized by a different type of land

use, that developed from a central core (see Figure 16.7[a]). *Zone 1* is the central business district and cultural centre (stores, banks, hotels, and theatres), in which high land prices create vertical growth in the form of skyscrapers. *Zone 2* is the zone of transition. As the city expanded, houses formerly occupied by wealthy families are divided into rooms that now are rented to recent immigrants and poor persons. This zone also contains wholesale light manufacturing and marginal businesses such as secondhand stores, pawnshops, and taverns. *Zone 3* contains working-class residences and shops and ethnic enclaves, such as Toronto's "Little Italy." *Zone 4* is composed of homes for affluent families, single-family residences of white-collar workers, and shopping centres. *Zone 5* is a ring of small cities and towns populated by wealthy persons who commute to the city to work and by wealthy people living on estates.

Two important ecological processes are involved in the concentric zone theory: invasion and succession. *Invasion* means that a new category of people or type of land use arrives in an area previously occupied by another group or land use (McKenzie, 1925). For example, Burgess noted that recent immigrants and

Figure 16.7 Three Models of the City

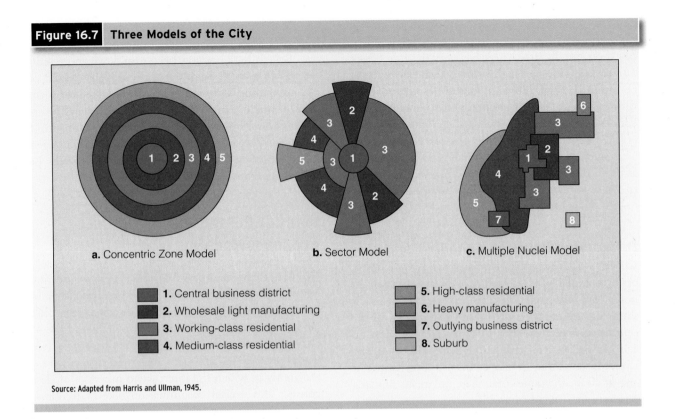

a. Concentric Zone Model   **b.** Sector Model   **c.** Multiple Nuclei Model

1. Central business district
2. Wholesale light manufacturing
3. Working-class residential
4. Medium-class residential
5. High-class residential
6. Heavy manufacturing
7. Outlying business district
8. Suburb

Source: Adapted from Harris and Ullman, 1945.

low-income individuals "invaded" Zone 2, formerly occupied by wealthy families. *Succession* **means that a new category of people or type of land use gradually predominates in an area formerly dominated by another group or activity** (McKenzie, 1925). In Zone 2, for example, when some single-family residences were sold and divided into multiple housing units, the remaining single-family owners moved out because the "old" neighbourhood had changed. Their move means that the process of invasion was complete and succession had occurred.

Invasion and succession theoretically operate in an outward movement. Those who are unable to "move out" of the inner rings are those without upward social mobility, so the central zone ends up being primarily occupied by the poorest residents—except when gentrification occurs. *Gentrification* **is the process by which members of the middle and upper-middle classes move into the central city area and renovate existing properties.** To urban planners, gentrification is the solution to revitalizing the central city. To conflict theorists, gentrification creates additional hardships for the poor by depleting the amount of affordable housing available and "pushing" them out of the area (Flanagan, 1999).

The concentric-zone model demonstrates how economic and political forces play an important part in the location of groups and activities, and how cities

change and grow over time. However, the model is most applicable to older cities that experienced high levels of immigration early in the 20th century (Queen and Carpenter, 1953). No city, including Chicago (on which the model is based), entirely conforms to this model.

The Sector Model Hoyt (1939) based his *sector model* on his analysis of 142 cities. The *sector model* emphasizes the significance of terrain and the importance of transportation routes in the layout of cities. According to Hoyt, residences of a particular type and value tend to grow outward from the centre of the city in wedge-shaped sectors, with the more expensive residential neighbourhoods located along the higher ground near lakes and rivers or along certain streets that stretch in one direction or another from the downtown area (see Figure 16.7[b]). By contrast, industrial areas tend to be located along river valleys and railroad lines. Middle-class residential zones exist on either side of the wealthier neighbourhoods. Finally, lower-class residential areas occupy the remaining space, bordering the central business area and the industrial areas.

The Multiple-Nuclei Model According to the *multiple-nuclei model* developed by urban ecologists Chauncey Harris and Edward Ullman (1945), cities do not have one centre from which all growth radiates, but rather numerous centres of development based on specific urban needs or activities (see Figure 16.7[c]). As cities grow, they annex formerly outlying communities. In addition to the central business district, nuclei develop around activities, such as an educational institution, a medical complex, or a governmental centre. This model fits some large urban areas such as Toronto, which has large nuclei such as the business district of North York. It also applies to a number of cities such as Edmonton, which have nuclei around universities.

Differences between Canadian and U.S. Cities

These models of urban growth were developed to explain the growth of U.S. cities. They do not fit pre-industrial cities (most of which have their slums on the outskirts of the city rather than in the central core) nor do they fit cities such as those in Europe that were relatively large before they industrialized. Because they developed on the same continent and at about the same time, there are many similarities between Canadian and American cities, but the models probably do not apply as well to Canadian cities, which differ from U.S. cities in several important ways (Gillis, 1995; Wolfe, 1992):

1. Canadian cities have greater density and less urban sprawl. It is cheaper to provide services in compact cities, and commuting to work is far easier.
2. The core areas of Canadian cities are much healthier than those in many U.S. cities, where residents have moved to the suburbs to avoid crime, high taxes, and other inner-city problems. Their move has created "doughnut cities," with poor central core areas that lack industry and job opportunities, have poor schools, and deteriorated housing, and do not have a tax base to help improve things. The strength of our urban core areas is a major reason Canadian cities have much lower crime rates than large U.S. cities.
3. Urban Canadians use public transit more than do Americans, though both are far behind Europeans in public transit use. Because of this, our cities are less divided by highways than those in the United States.
4. Racial tension has been far less pronounced in Canada than in the United States, where it has led to many problems including urban riots and "white flight" to the suburbs.
5. Canadian and U.S. public-housing policies have been very different. With a few exceptions, such as Toronto's Regent Park and Montreal's Jeanne

Mance, governments in Canada have not built large-scale high-rise developments (and much of Regent Park has now been torn down and rebuilt using a more people-friendly design). Much of the public housing in Canada has taken the form of smaller projects in established neighbourhoods. Thus we have not faced the problem of large numbers of economically disadvantaged people crowded into areas that can easily be neglected by the rest of society.

Conflict Perspectives: Political Economy Models

Conflict theorists argue that cities grow or decline because of specific decisions made by capitalists and political elites. These far-reaching decisions regarding land use and urban development benefit the members of some groups at the expense of others (see Castells, 1977/1972). Marx suggested that cities are the arenas in which the intertwined processes of class conflict and capital accumulation take place; class-consciousness and worker revolt were more likely to develop when workers were concentrated in urban areas (Flanagan, 1999).

Capitalism and Urban Growth

According to conflict theorists, urban growth is influenced by capital-investment decisions, power and resource inequality, class and class conflict, and government-subsidy programs. Historically, the need for labour to operate large factories was the major reason for the growth of large cities. Today, capitalists choose corporate locations, decide on sites for shopping centres and factories, and spread the population that can afford to purchase homes into sprawling suburbs to generate profits for the developers who own the land (Feagin and Parker, 1990).

Business involvement in urban development is not new. Winnipeg became a major transportation centre because of its location at the junction of the Red and Assiniboine rivers. However, because of Winnipeg's flooding problems, the small community of Selkirk was originally chosen for the route of the Canadian Pacific Railway (CPR). After several years of intensive lobbying by Winnipeg's political and business leaders, along with promises of subsidies to the CPR, the line was built through Winnipeg in 1881. Sir Donald Smith, the man who drove the last spike to finish the transcontinental railway, was instrumental in having the route shifted to Winnipeg (Bellan, 1978). A key figure in building the CPR, Smith was also the largest shareholder in the Hudson's Bay Company, which owned a large block of land in the centre of Winnipeg. During the land boom that followed the announcement of the railway's new route, the Hudson's Bay Company made millions of dollars selling this land.

Today, a small number of financial institutions and developers finance and construct most of Canada's major urban-development projects, including skyscrapers, shopping malls, and suburban housing projects, These decision makers set limits on the individual choices of the ordinary citizen with regard to real estate (Feagin and Parker, 1990). Ultimately, their motivation rests not in benefiting the community, but in making a profit, and the cities they produce reflect this mindset.

A major result of these practices is *uneven development*—the tendency of some neighbourhoods, cities, or regions to grow and prosper while others stagnate and decline (Perry and Watkins, 1977). An example of this is the movement of middle- and upper-class people to the suburbs, which reduces the tax base of the city core. The suburbs were built by large development corporations with the help of government programs that provided mortgages with low down payments so that families could afford to buy new homes. Government also provided subsidies and tax concessions that encouraged urban sprawl. Suburbanization was supported by auto manufacturers and road builders that benefited from the need of suburban dwellers to drive into the city to work. Many developments had restrictions, such as prohibition of multiple-family dwellings, that effectively excluded low-income people from suburban communities. At the same time, the flow of money to the suburbs contributed to the decline of central cities where the poor resided.

Conflict theorists argue that uneven development reflects inequalities of wealth and power. The problem not only affects deteriorating areas, but also entails costs, even in "boom" areas, that are paid for by the entire community. Among these costs are increased pollution, traffic congestion, and transportation costs. According to Gottdiener, these costs are "intrinsic to the very core of capitalism, and those who profit the most from development are not called upon to remedy its side effects" (1985:214).

Feminist Perspectives

From a feminist perspective, urbanization reflects the workings not only of the political economy but also of patriarchy.

Gender Regimes in Cities   According to Lynn Appleton (1995), different kinds of cities have different *gender regimes*—prevailing ideologies of how women and men should think, feel, and act; how access to social positions and control of resources should be managed; and how relationships between men and women should be conducted. The higher density and greater diversity found in central cities challenge patriarchy because central cities offer a broader range of lifestyle choices, some of which do not involve traditional patriarchal family structures. For example, cities are more likely than suburbs to support a subculture of economically independent females. Thus, the city may be a forum for challenging patriarchy. Residents live close to one another and may hold and act upon a common belief that both public and private patriarchy should be eliminated (Appleton, 1995).

Gender and City Life   Do women and men experience city life differently? Many feminists feel that cities reflect the patriarchy of the broader society in that fear of crime committed by males has effectively limited the access of females to public space (Koskela, 1997). According to Elizabeth Wilson (1991), some men view the city as sexual space in which women are categorized as prostitutes, lesbians, temptresses, or virtuous women in need of protection, based on their sexual desirability and accessibility. This view was supported in research conducted by Ross Macmillan and his colleagues, who found that the experience of sexual harassment by strangers is a major predictor of fear of victimization among a national sample of Canadian women (Macmillan et al., 2000). Wilson suggests that affluent, dominant-group women are more likely to be viewed as virtuous women in need of protection by their own men or police officers.

Cities offer a paradox for women: On the one hand, they offer more freedom than is found in comparatively isolated rural, suburban, and domestic settings; on the other, women may be in greater physical danger in the city. For Wilson, the answer to women's vulnerability in the city is not found in offering protection to them, but rather in changing people's perceptions so that they no longer treat women as sexual objects because of the impersonality of city life (Wilson, 1991).

Michelson (1994) has highlighted another dimension of the vulnerability of women in cities. Women with children are much more likely to be in the paid workforce than they were several decades ago. When most women stayed home, they spent much of their time in the company of immediate neighbours, and rarely ventured from their neighbourhoods at night without their husbands. Employed women have a much different city experience. Much of their time is now spent with people on the job and they are more often alone outside their immediate neighbourhoods at different hours.

For many women in this situation, travelling to and from work is perceived as dangerous. Michelson cites a Statistics Canada study showing that 80 percent of women fear entering parking garages and 76 percent fear using public transportation after dark. Women feel particularly vulnerable if they have to walk alone after dark because of work or school. Our cities have not yet adapted well to these major social changes in the lives of women.

Wekerle (2005) has described some of the changes to urban design that would improve the lives of women. "Women-friendly" cities would integrate work, home, and services. For example, a suburb would have multiple-family housing that would be located near places of employment, shops, and mass transit; would incorporate child care; and would have police and other social services nearby.

Symbolic Interactionist Perspectives: The Experience of City Life

Symbolic interactionists examine the *experience* of urban life. How does city life affect the people who live in a city? Some analysts believe cities create a positive social environment; others are more negative about the effect of urban living on the individual.

Simmel's View of City Life

According to German sociologist Georg Simmel (1950/1902–17), urban life is highly stimulating and it shapes people's thoughts and actions. Due to the intensity and quick pace of urban life, people can become somewhat insensitive to events and individuals around them. When you interact with hundreds of different people every day, you cannot become personally involved with each of them, so most of your contacts will be impersonal. Urbanites are wary of one another because most interactions in the city are economic rather than social. Simmel suggests that attributes such as punctuality and exactness are rewarded but that friendliness and warmth in interpersonal relations can be viewed as personal weaknesses. Some people act in a reserved way to cloak deeper feelings

of distrust or dislike toward others. Simmel did not view city life as completely negative, though; he also pointed out that urban life could have a liberating effect on people because they had opportunities for individualism and autonomy (Flanagan, 1999).

Urbanism as a Way of Life

Louis Wirth (1938) suggested that urbanization is a "way of life." *Urbanism* refers to the distinctive social and psychological patterns of life typically found in the city. The size, density, and heterogeneity of urban populations typically result in an elaborate division of labour and in spatial segregation of people by race/ethnicity, social class, religion, and/or lifestyle. In the city, primary group ties largely are replaced by secondary relationships and social interaction is fragmented, impersonal, and often superficial ("Hello!" "Have a nice day"). Even though people gain some degree of freedom and privacy by living in the city, they pay a price for their autonomy, losing the group support and reassurance that comes from primary group ties.

From Wirth's perspective, people who live in urban areas are alienated, powerless, and lonely. A sense of community is obliterated and replaced by "mass society"—a large-scale, highly institutionalized society in which individuality is supplanted by mass messages, faceless bureaucrats, and corporate interest.

Gans's Urban Villagers

In contrast to Wirth's gloomy assessment of urban life, Herbert Gans (1982/1962) suggested that not everyone experiences the city in the same way. Gans studied urban dwellers and found that many residents develop strong loyalties and a sense of community in central city areas that outsiders may view negatively. People choose the lifestyle they wish to lead based on personal characteristics, such as social class and stage in the life cycle. Gans found five major categories of adaptation. *Cosmopolites* are students, artists, writers, musicians, entertainers, and professionals who live in the city because of its cultural facilities. *Unmarried people and childless couples* live in the city to be close to work and entertainment. *Ethnic villagers* live in ethnically segregated neighbourhoods; some are recent immigrants who feel most comfortable within their own group. The *deprived* are poor individuals with limited education and few resources. The *trapped* are urban dwellers who can find no escape from the city. This group includes downwardly mobile people, older people who have nowhere else to go, and individuals addicted to alcohol or other drugs. Transient people in the inner city are most likely to suffer the urban ills described by Wirth, but this is because of residential instability, and

These photographs represent three of the ways people adapt to city life as described by Herbert Gans. Cosmopolites choose to live in the city to enjoy cultural facilities such as Toronto's Roy Thomson Hall. Ethnic villagers live in tightly knit neighbourhood enclaves such as Vancouver's Chinatown. Trapped residents can find no escape from the city, as exemplified by this homeless person in Toronto.

not simply an inevitable result of urbanization. Gans concluded that the city is a pleasure for some urban dwellers and an urban nightmare for others.

Postmodern Perspectives: The Postmodern City

Decentred Cities   While Chicago was the model for the modernist city, Los Angeles is seen by some as the model of the postmodern city: "an interminable urbanised area with no coherent form, no hierarchical structure, no centre and no unity [and a diverse mixture of races and ethnicities]" (Fahmi, 2001:5). While the modernist city was represented by *concentric circles* that characterized how land-use patterns changed in an orderly way as one moved out from the urban core, the postmodern city is signified by a "*collage* of . . . consumption-oriented landscapes devoid of conventional centers" (Dear and Flusty, 1998:66) with a haphazard pattern of development

(see Figure 16.8). The key processes that led to these changes are globalization and the economic restructuring caused by the transition from the industrial era to the information economy. Unlike industrial Chicago, which grew around central factories, cities like Los Angeles have no urban cores, but grow in clusters sprawled over a large geographical area. Postmodern business enterprises are typically smaller than the older industrial factories, so they can be scattered across the city. Knowledge industries can locate anywhere and related businesses and population growth will follow. Shopping and entertainment industries also contribute to the decentred city. Huge malls and entertainment centres, such as theme parks and casinos, are built on the edges of urban areas because of land costs and then attract housing and other service businesses. There is little planned development, as land developers and business owners shape the city to suit their own interests.

Table 16.2 compares the spatial characteristics of the industrial city and the postmodern city. While

Figure 16.8 | **Alternative Models of Urban Form**

Circa 1900   Circa 2000

Source: Spain, Daphne. "What Happened to Gender Relations on the Way from Chicago to Los Angeles?" *City & Community 1:2*, June 2002. © American Sociological Association.

Chicago in 1900 had a densely populated central downtown core and patterns of land use that changed as one moved out from that core, Los Angeles in 2000 was a sprawling urban area with many different city cores. Unlike Chicago's slaughterhouses and factories, the businesses of contemporary cities are much less tied to a central hub. Sprawling metropolitan areas, such as Los Angeles, have a huge negative impact on the environment in the form of air pollution from the personal vehicles that are essential to life in the postmodern city to the destruction of natural habitat as urban expansion erases the natural environment (Dear and Flusty, 1998).

The Fantasy City   Because of the decline of manufacturing industries in city centres, urban planners have had to find ways of keeping their downtowns alive and reversing the flight to the suburbs. Many have turned to the entertainment industry to help to restore their cities and have tried to create what John Hannigan (1998) has termed the "fantasy city." Restaurants and bars, gambling casinos, movie theatres, sports arenas and stadiums, and arts centres bring people downtown from the suburbs in the evenings and also encourage people to live in downtown

areas. Perhaps the best example of a fantasy city is Las Vegas, one of the world's most popular tourist destinations. Its main attractions are gambling and nightclub entertainment, and its built environment is totally artificial. Many of its large hotels attempt to simulate other cities. The Paris Las Vegas Hotel has replicas of the Eiffel Tower and the Arc de Triomphe, while New York, New York, has a façade that simulates the skyline of New York City, complete with replicas of the Statue of Liberty and the Empire State Building. Unlike the real cities of Paris and New York, these hotels are not grounded in their locations and their history but rather are standardized, branded businesses, like Disneyland and McDonald's. They provide an experience that can be re-created anywhere. These simulated travel experiences provide consumers with a social experience that is quite different from that of their suburban homes, but they provide controlled environments that eliminate many of the risks of real travel. Nothing need be left to chance for travellers: You are unlikely to be mugged in Disneyland, where the behaviour of visitors is tightly controlled; you know what the cheeseburgers will taste like in any of the world's 149 Hard Rock Cafés; and people enjoying an all-inclusive Club Med vacation at

Table 16.2 | SPATIAL CHARACTERISTICS OF URBAN FORM

	CIRCA 1900	CIRCA 2000
Prototype	Industrial city	Informational metropolis
Number of centres	One	Two or more
Location of activities	Mixed	Separated
Density of population	High	Low
Direction of development	Vertical	Horizontal

Source: Spain, Daphne. "What Happened to Gender Relations on the Way from Chicago to Los Angeles?" *City & Community 1:2*, June 2002, p. 160. © American Sociological Association.

Columbus Isle, Bahamas, may never meet anybody or see anything outside the gates of the resort.

Branding is an important component of the fantasy city experience. Even when people travel to real cities, many choose to go to globally branded franchises. For example, some visitors to Athens prefer to celebrate their trip by wearing "Hard Rock Café Athens" T-shirts rather than shirts with logos representing something that is unique to Athens. Hannigan says this branded merchandise enhances the status of the tourist: "They are . . . regarded as 'passports,' proclaiming not only that you have been somewhere interesting but that you have consumed a highly rated experience" (1998:70).

As cities become more alike because of their franchised entertainment attractions, we lose the diversity that is provided by more locally grounded experiences. The experience shared by two of this book's authors of enjoying a very inexpensive café au lait and *beignets* at the Café du Monde, which has been located next to the Mississippi River in the French Quarter of New Orleans since 1862, is very different from a visit to one of the world's many Starbucks outlets.

Hannigan also points out that many of the entertainment facilities are built with public money. The public money is almost never recovered, but private corporations, such as sports teams, reap huge financial benefits from new facilities. The stadium built in Montreal for the 1976 Summer Olympics had huge construction cost overruns and taxpayers paid a special levy until 2005 to pay for these excess costs.

Finally, these entertainment facilities, as well as other developments, such as enclosed walkways, isolate many of the urban poor from the rest of city life. The middle class is protected while the underclass does not have access to the privatized space.

This is the Village at Park Royal in West Vancouver. While it looks like a normal city street, it is actually private property.

The Disappearance of Public Space   A major feature of the postmodern city is the disappearance of public space. Rather than being open and accessible to all, cities are becoming private places. We shop in malls or in isolated big-box shopping areas, and some of us live in gated communities. Why do some people feel this is a problem? Think of West Edmonton Mall, which covers 48 acres and has more than 800 businesses, two indoor amusement parks, and a marine mammal park. On an average day 60 000 people visit the mall, and security personnel respond to more than 40 000 calls each year (Murphy and Clarke, 2005). In some ways it is like the downtown centre in a major city. However, it has one fundamental difference from a city centre: the mall is private space.

The most recent generation of malls, such as the Village, which is part of Park Royal shopping centre in Vancouver, are reproductions of streets with shops accessible from outdoors rather than through enclosed malls. While they look like public territory, these inviting "public" streets are actually on private property. While we all have free access to public space, any of us can be denied entrance to private space even if that space is open to the public. In the West Edmonton Mall or any other private shopping centre, if you want to sit on a bench for hours, play a game with your friends, stage a political protest, or do many other things that are encouraged or tolerated in public spaces, you may be removed from the property. The major factor that determines what takes place within a mall is what will make a profit, so commercial interests are paramount. In many cities, these large malls have drawn stores and shoppers away from the downtown business centre, so the street space that is still available for public access may no longer have the interest and vitality it once did.

Gated residential communities are created by developers so they can offer potential residents a feeling of safety, privacy, and luxury they might not have in nongated residential areas. Gated communities reflect a growing divide between public and private space in urban areas. Unlike medieval walled cities in which all citizens were protected by the walls, the benefits of the protection go only to those who pay for it. Gated communities do more than simply restrict access to the residents' homes. They also limit the use of once-public spaces, making it impossible for others to use the roads, parks, and open space contained within the enclosed community (Low, 2003). Those inside the gates are no longer full participants in broader urban life.

To many, the essence of city life is its public space:

[O]ne of the most important social characteristics of cities is the provision of public spaces in which relative strangers can interact and observe each other, debate and learn politically, and grow psychologically from diverse contacts. (Calhoun, 1986:341)

The exclusivity and restrictiveness of the privatized space in our postmodern cities can lead to a fragmentation that can have a negative impact on the vitality of the city itself as well as on those who cannot get inside the gates.

Concept Table 16.1 examines the different theoretical perspectives on urban growth and urban living.

POPULATION AND URBANIZATION IN THE FUTURE

Rapid global population growth is inevitable. Although death rates have declined in many developing nations, most still have high birth rates. This means that most of the world's future population growth will occur in low-income nations in Africa, Asia, and Latin America.

It is difficult to predict changes in population. Natural disasters such as earthquakes, volcanic eruptions, hurricanes, tornados, floods, and so on, obviously cannot be predicted. A cure for diseases caused by HIV/AIDS may be found or the disease may reach epidemic proportions in more nations. A number of diseases, such as tuberculosis, which had been controlled by antibiotics, are now returning in a form that is resistant to the drugs usually used for treatment.

Whatever the impact of natural disaster and disease, developing nations will have an increasing number of urban poor people. While the world's population will *double,* the urban population will *triple* as people migrate from rural areas in search of food, water, and jobs. More than 20 cities, many in low-income nations, now exceed 10 million people. The largest of these are Tokyo (28 million); Mexico City (18 million); Mumbai, India (18 million); and Sao Paulo, Brazil (18 million). These huge cities will have a profound impact on the environment because of air pollution, greenhouse gas emissions, sewage and waste disposal, and water consumption. In the spring of 2009, Mexico City suffered a severe water shortage caused by its expanding population and low rainfall levels. We can expect similar crises in the future as cities expand beyond the capacity of their infrastructure to support their population.

In a best-case scenario for the future, the problems brought about by rapid population growth in developing nations will be remedied by new technologies that increase food production and reduce disease. International trade agreements such as NAFTA (North American Free Trade Agreement) will remove trade barriers and make it possible for all nations to engage fully in global trade. People in developing nations will benefit by gaining jobs and opportunities to purchase goods at lower prices. Of course, the opposite may also occur: People may be exploited as inexpensive labour, and their country's natural resources may be depleted as transnational corporations buy up raw materials without contributing to the long-term economic stability of the nation.

In the longer term, global population growth may not be as great a problem as some have feared. Fertility rates have dropped dramatically in most countries, and in all industrialized countries except the United States they are now far below the replacement level of 2.1 children per family. For example, Spain now has a fertility rate of 1.1 children per family (down from 2.8 in 1978) and Canada's rate is 1.5. This means that without high rates of immigration, the population will fall in these countries (except the United States). According to the United Nations (2009), by 2050 the population in 45 countries, including Germany, Russia, and Japan, will be lower than current levels. Fertility rates have also dropped significantly in poorer countries, but they have not stabilized and we do not yet know how low they will drop. Some demographers believe that rates will continue to decline until most countries are below replacement level. This would mean that eventually the world's population could begin to decline but not until after it peaks at over 9 billion people.

While we cannot predict future trends with any degree of certainty, we do know that even if population growth stabilizes or begins to decline by the middle of this century, increased standards of living around the world will continue to be a drain on the earth's resources. People in industrialized countries use far more water, energy, and other natural resources than their poorer counterparts in other countries. Thus, it seems inevitable that environmental issues will become more important in the future even if population growth does continue.

Concept Table 16.1	PERSPECTIVES ON URBANISM AND THE GROWTH OF CITIES	
PERSPECTIVE	**MODEL THEORIES**	**KEY ELEMENTS**
Functionalist: Ecological Models		
Burgess	Concentric zone model	Due to invasion, succession, and gentrification, cities are a series of circular zones, each characterized by a particular land use.
Hoyt	Sector model	Cities consist of wedge-shaped sectors, based on terrain and transportation routes, with the most-expensive areas occupying the best terrain.
Harris and Ullman	Multiple nuclei model	Cities have more than one centre of development, based on specific needs and activities.
Conflict: Political Economy Models		
Marx	Capitalism and urban growth	Members of the capitalist class choose locations for skyscrapers and housing projects, limiting individual choices by others.
Symbolic Interactionist: The Experience of City Life		
Simmel	View of city life	Due to the intensity of city life, people become somewhat insensitive to individuals and events around them.
Wirth	Urbanism as a way of life	The size, density, and heterogeneity of urban population result in elaborate division of labour and space.
Gans	Urban villagers	Five categories of adaptation occur among urban dwellers, ranging from cosmopolites to trapped city dwellers.
Feminist		
Appleton	Gender regimes in cities	Different cities have different prevailing ideologies regarding access to social positions and resources for men and women.
Wilson, Michelson	Gender and city life	Cities offer women a paradox: more freedom, yet greater potential danger.
Postmodern		
Dear and Flusty	Decentred cities	The postmodern city has many centres with low density and urban sprawl. They have more private space and greater diversity. They are becoming centres for consuming and entertainment.
Hannigan	Fantasy city	City planners have attempted to bring people back to the city centre by establishing urban entertainment districts that often include branded, risk-free attractions.

Some futurists predict that environmental activism will increase dramatically as people see irreversible changes in the atmosphere and experience first-hand the effects of environmental hazards and pollution on their own health and well-being. These environmental problems will cause a realization that overpopulation is a world problem, a problem that will be most apparent in the world's weakest economies and most fragile ecosystems.

■ **What is demography?**

Demography is the study of the size, composition, and distribution of the population.

■ **What demographic processes result in population change?**

Population change is the result of fertility (births), mortality (deaths), and migration.

■ **What is the Malthusian perspective?**

Malthus warned that overpopulation would result in poverty, starvation, and other major problems that would limit the size of the population. According to Malthus, the population would increase geometrically, while food supply would increase only arithmetically, resulting in poverty and starvation.

■ **What are the stages in demographic transition theory?**

Demographic-transition theory links population growth to four stages of economic development: (1) the pre-industrial stage, with high birth and death rates; (2) early industrialization, with relatively high birth rates and a decline in death rates; (3) advanced industrialization and urbanization, with low birth and death rates; and (4) post-industrialization, with additional decreases in the birth rate coupled with a stable death rate.

■ **What are the three functionalist models of urban growth?**

Functionalists view urban growth in terms of ecological models. The concentric-zone model sees the city as a series of circular areas, each characterized by a different type of land use; the sector model describes urban growth in terms of terrain and transportation routes; and the multiple-nuclei model views cities as having numerous centres of development from which growth radiates.

■ **What is the conflict perspective on urban growth?**

According to conflict perspectives, urban growth is influenced by capital investment decisions, power and resource inequality, class and class conflict, and government-subsidy programs.

■ **How do symbolic interactionists view urban life?**

Symbolic interactionist perspectives focus on how people experience urban life. Some analysts view the urban experience positively; others believe that urban dwellers become insensitive to events and people around them.

■ **How do postmodernist theorists view city life?**

The postmodern city has many centres because of low density and urban sprawl; it has more private space and greater diversity. Some cities are trying to attract people back to the city centres by establishing urban entertainment districts.

KEY TERMS

central city 409
crude birth rate 394
crude death rate 395
demographic transition 406
demography 394
emigration 397
fertility 394
gentrification 411
immigration 397
infant mortality rate 396
invasion 410
life expectancy 397
metropolis 409
migration 397
mortality 395
population 394
population composition 399
population pyramid 400
succession 411
urban sociology 408

WEB LINKS

For more Web links related to the topic of this chapter, see the Nelson sociology website:
www.sociologyessentials5e.nelson.com

Watch the world's population grow on the World Population Clock:
http://opr.princeton.edu/popclock

To look up demographic information on births, deaths, and infant mortality, go to the *World Factbook*:
https://www.cia.gov/library/publications/the-world-factbook/

For the latest revision to world-population estimates, go to:
www.un.org/popin/wdtrends.htm

For information about the UN's Sustainable Cities Programme, see:

http://www.unhabitat.org/categories. asp?catid=540

This website provides an interesting perspective on urban design reform:

http://newurbanism.org

QUESTIONS FOR CRITICAL THINKING

1. What impact does a high rate of immigration have on culture and personal identity in Canada?

2. If you were designing a study of growth patterns for the city in which you live (or one you know well), which theoretical model(s) would provide the most useful framework for your analysis?

3. What do you think everyday life in Canadian cities, suburbs, and rural areas will be like in 2025? Where would you prefer to live? What, if anything, does your answer reflect about the future of our cities?

4. How do you think the aging baby boomers will change Canadian society over the next 20 years?

How will these developments compare with a country, such as Iran, that has a much younger population?

ONLINE STUDY AND RESEARCH TOOLS

INFOTRAC®

InfoTrac College Edition is included free with every new copy of this text. Explore this online library for additional readings, review, and a handy resource for assignments. Visit **www.infotrac-college.com** to access this online database of full-text articles. Enter the key terms from this chapter to start your search.

CENGAGENOW™ CENGAGENOW

Use CengageNOW™ to help you formulate a customized study plan for this chapter. After you take the Diagnostic Quiz, CengageNOW™ will generate a customized study plan for you. It will identify sections of the chapter you should review.

absolute poverty A level of economic deprivation in which people do not have the means to secure the most basic necessities of life.

accommodation A situation in which ethnic groups co-exist in equality with one another.

achieved status A social position a person assumes voluntarily as a result of personal choice, merit, or direct effort.

acting crowds Collectivities so intensely focused on a specific purpose or object that they may erupt into violent or destructive behaviour.

agents of socialization The persons, groups, or institutions that teach us what we need to know to participate in society.

aggregate A collection of people who happen to be in the same place at the same time but have little else in common.

alienation A feeling of powerlessness and estrangement from other people and from oneself.

alternative movements Movements that seek limited change in some aspect of people's behaviour.

animism The belief that plants, animals, or other elements of the natural world are endowed with spirits or life forces that have an impact on events in society.

anomie A condition in which social control becomes ineffective as a result of the loss of shared values and of a sense of purpose in society.

anticipatory socialization The process by which knowledge and skills are learned for future roles.

ascribed status A social position conferred at birth or received involuntarily later in life, based on attributes over which the individual has little or no control.

assimilation A process by which members of subordinate racial and ethnic groups become absorbed into the dominant culture.

authoritarian political system A political system controlled by rulers who deny popular participation in government.

authority Power that people accept as legitimate rather than coercive.

bilateral descent A system of tracing descent through both the mother's and father's sides of the family.

body consciousness The way a person perceives and feels about his or her body.

bourgeoisie Karl Marx's term for the class comprising those who own and control the means of production.

bureaucracy An organizational model characterized by a hierarchy of authority, a clear division of labour, explicit rules and procedures, and impersonality in personnel matters.

bureaucratic personality A psychological construct that describes those workers who are more concerned with following correct procedures than they are with getting the job done correctly.

capitalist class Class that consists of those who own the means of production.

caste system A system of social inequality in which people's status is permanently determined at birth based on their parents' ascribed characteristics.

casual crowds Relatively large gatherings of people who happen to be in the same place at the same time; if they interact at all, it is only briefly.

category A number of people who may never have met one another but who share a similar characteristic

central city The densely populated centre of a metropolis.

charismatic authority Power legitimized on the basis of a leader's exceptional personal qualities.

civil disobedience Nonviolent action that seeks to change a policy or law by refusing to comply with it.

class The relative location of a person or group within a larger society, based on wealth, power, prestige, or other valued resources.

class conflict Karl Marx's term for the struggle between the capitalist class and the working class.

class system A type of stratification based on the ownership and control of resources and on the type of work people do.

cohabitation The sharing of a household by a couple who live together without being legally married.

collective behaviour Voluntary, often spontaneous activity that is engaged in by a large number of people and typically violates dominant group norms and values.

conflict perspectives The sociological approach that views groups in society as engaged in a continuous power struggle for control of scarce resources.

conformity The process of maintaining or changing behaviour to comply with the norms established by a society, subculture, or other group.

contagion theory Theory that focuses on the social-psychological aspects of collective behaviour; it attempts to explain how moods, attitudes, and behaviour are communicated rapidly and why they are accepted by others.

content analysis The systematic examination of cultural artifacts or various forms of communication to extract thematic data and draw conclusions about social life.

control group Subjects in an experiment who are not exposed to the independent variable.

conventional crowds Crowds made up of people who specifically come together for a scheduled event and thus share a common focus.

convergence theory Theory that focuses on the shared emotions, goals, and beliefs many people bring to crowd behaviour.

core nations According to world systems theory, dominant capitalist centres characterized by high levels of industrialization and urbanization.

corporate crime Illegal acts committed by corporate employees on behalf of the corporation and with its support.

correlation Exists when two variables are associated more frequently than could be expected by chance.

counterculture A group that strongly rejects dominant societal values and norms and seeks alternative lifestyles.

credentialism A process of social selection in which class advantage and social status are linked to the possession of academic qualifications.

crime Behaviour that violates criminal law and is punishable with fines, jail terms, and other sanctions.

crowd A relatively large number of people who are in one another's immediate vicinity.

crude birth rate The number of live births per 1000 people in a population in a given year.

crude death rate The number of deaths per 1000 people in a population in a given year.

cultural capital Pierre Bourdieu's term for people's social assets, including their values, beliefs, attitudes, and competencies in language and culture.

cultural imperialism The extensive infusion of one nation's culture into other nations.

cultural lag William F. Ogburn's term for a gap between the technical development of a society and its moral and legal institutions.

cultural relativism The belief that the behaviours and customs of any culture must be viewed and analyzed by the culture's own standards.

cultural transmission The process by which children and recent immigrants become acquainted with the dominant cultural beliefs, values, norms, and accumulated knowledge of a society.

cultural universals Customs and practices that occur across all societies.

culture The knowledge, language, values, customs, and material objects that are passed from person to person and from one generation to the next in a human group or society.

culture shock The disorientation that people feel when they encounter cultures radically different from their own.

Davis-Moore thesis The definitive functionalist explanation for social inequality, can be summarized as follows: all societies have important tasks that must be accomplished and certain positions that must be filled; some positions are more important for the survival of society than others—the most important positions must be filled by the most qualified people; the positions that are the most important for society and that require scarce talent, extensive training, or both, must be the most highly rewarded; the most highly rewarded positions should be those that are functionally unique (no other position can perform the same function) and on which other positions rely for expertise, direction, or financing.

democracy A political system in which the people hold the ruling power either directly or through elected representatives.

demographic transition The process by which some societies have moved from high birth and death rates to relatively low ones as a result of technological development.

demography The subfield of sociology that examines population size, composition, and distribution.

dependency theory The perspective that global poverty can at least partially be attributed to the fact that low-income countries have been exploited by high-income ones.

developed (high-income) countries Countries with highly industrialized economies; technologically advanced industrial, administrative, and service occupations; and relatively high levels of national and per-person income.

developing (low-income) countries Primarily agrarian nations with little industrialization and low levels of national and personal income.

deviance Any behaviour, belief, or condition that violates significant social norms in the society or group in which it occurs.

differential association theory The proposition that individuals have a greater tendency to deviate from societal norms when they frequently associate with people who favour deviance over conformity.

diffusion The transmission of cultural items or social practices from one group or society to another.

disability A physical or health condition that reduces a person's ability to perform tasks one would normally do at a given stage in life and that may result in stigmatization or discrimination against the person with the disability.

discourses All that is written, spoken, or otherwise represented through language and communication systems.

discovery The process of learning about something previously unknown or unrecognized.

discrimination Actions or practices of dominant-group members (or their representatives) that have a harmful impact on members of a subordinate group.

dramaturgical analysis The study of social interaction that compares everyday life to a theatrical presentation.

dual-earner families Families in which both partners are in the labour force.

dysfunctions A term referring to the undesirable consequences of any element of a society.

education The social institution responsible for the systematic transmission of knowledge, skills, and cultural values within a formally organized structure.

egalitarian family A family structure in which both partners share power and authority equally.

ego According to Sigmund Freud, the rational, reality-oriented component of personality that imposes restrictions on the innate pleasure-seeking drives of the id.

elite model A view of society in which power in political systems is concentrated in the hands of a small group of elites and the masses are relatively powerless.

emergent-norm theory Emphasizes the importance of social norms in shaping crowd behaviour.

emigration The movement of people out of a geographic area to take up residency elsewhere.

employment equity   A strategy to eliminate the effects of discrimination and to fully open the competition for job opportunities to those who have been excluded historically.

epidemics   Sudden, significant increases in the numbers of people contracting a disease.

equalitarian pluralism, or accommodation   A situation in which ethnic groups co-exist in equality with one another.

ethnic group   A collection of people distinguished, by others or by themselves, primarily on the basis of cultural or nationality characteristics.

ethnic pluralism   The coexistence of a variety of distinct racial and ethnic groups within one society.

ethnicity   The cultural heritage or identity of a group based on factors such as language or country of origin.

ethnocentrism   The practice of judging all other cultures by one's own culture.

ethnography   A detailed study of the life and activities of a group of people by researchers who may live with that group over a period of years.

experiment   A research method involving a carefully designed situation in which the researcher studies the impact of certain variables on subjects' attitudes or behaviour.

experimental group   Subjects in an experiment who are exposed to an independent variable.

expressive crowds   Groups that provide opportunities for the expression of some strong emotion (such as joy, excitement, or grief).

extended family   A family unit composed of relatives in addition to parents and children who live in the same household.

fad   A temporary but widely copied activity enthusiastically followed by large numbers of people.

faith   Unquestioning belief that does not require proof or scientific evidence.

false consciousness   A term used by Karl Marx to indicate that people hold beliefs they think promote their best interests when those beliefs actually are damaging to their interests.

families   Relationships in which people live together with commitment, form an economic unit, care for any young, and consider their identity to be significantly attached to the group.

families we choose   Social arrangements that include intimate relationships between couples and close familial relationships with other couples and with other adults and children.

family of orientation   The family into which a person is born and in which early socialization usually takes place.

family of procreation   The family that a person forms by having or adopting children.

fashion   A currently valued style of behaviour, thinking, or appearance.

feminism   The belief that all people—both women and men—are equal and that they should be valued equally and have equal rights.

feminist perspectives   Sociological perspectives that focus on the significance of gender in understanding and explaining inequalities that exist between men and women in the household, in the paid labour force, and in the realms of politics, law, and culture.

feminization of poverty   The trend in which women are disproportionately represented among individuals living in poverty.

fertility   The actual level of child-bearing for an individual or a population.

field research   The study of social life in its natural setting: observing and interviewing people where they live, work, and play.

folkways   Informal norms or everyday customs that may be violated without serious consequences within a particular culture.

formal education   Learning that takes place within an academic setting, such as a school, which has a planned instructional process and teachers who convey specific knowledge, skills, and thinking processes to students.

formal organization   A highly structured group formed for the purpose of completing certain tasks or achieving specific goals.

functional illiteracy   The inability to read and/or write at the skill level necessary for carrying out everyday tasks.

functionalist perspectives   Sociological perspectives based on the assumption that society is a stable, orderly system.

gender   Socially constructed differences between females and males found in the meanings, beliefs, and practices associated with "femininity" and "masculinity."

gender bias   Behaviour that shows favouritism toward one gender over the other.

gender identity   A person's perception of the self as female or male.

gender role   The attitudes, behaviour, and activities that are socially defined as appropriate for each sex and are learned through the socialization process.

gender-segregated work   The concentration of women and men in different occupations, jobs, and places of work.

gender socialization   The aspect of socialization that contains specific messages and practices concerning the nature of being female or male in a specific group or society.

generalized other   George Herbert Mead's term for the child's awareness of the demands and expectations of the society as a whole or of the child's subculture.

gentrification   The process by which members of the middle and upper-middle classes move into the central city area and renovate existing properties.

global crime   The networking of powerful criminal organizations and their associates in shared activities around the world.

global interdependence   A relationship in which the lives of all people are intertwined closely and any one nation's problems are part of a larger global problem.

global stratification   The unequal distribution of wealth, power, and prestige on a global basis, resulting in people having vastly different lifestyles and life chances both within and among the nations of the world.

goal displacement A process that occurs when the rules become an end in themselves rather than a means to an end, and organizational survival becomes more important than achievement of goals.

gossip Rumours about the personal lives of individuals.

government The formal organization that has the legal and political authority to regulate the relationships among members of a society and between the society and those outside its borders.

groupthink The process by which members of a cohesive group arrive at a decision that many individual members privately believe is unwise.

health The state of complete physical, mental, and social well-being.

health care Any activity intended to improve health.

hermaphrodite A person in whom sexual differentiation is ambiguous or incomplete.

heterosexism An attitude in which heterosexuality is considered the only valid form of sexual behaviour, and gay men, lesbians, and bisexuals are inferior to heterosexual people.

hidden curriculum The transmission of cultural values and attitudes, such as conformity and obedience to authority, through implied demands found in rules, routines, and regulations of schools.

high-income economies Countries with an annual per capita gross national income over US$9386.

homogamy The pattern of individuals marrying those who have similar characteristics, such as race/ethnicity, religious background, age, education, or social class.

homophobia Extreme prejudice directed at gays, lesbians, bisexuals, and others who are perceived as not being heterosexual.

id Sigmund Freud's term for the component of personality that includes all the individual's basic biological drives and needs that demand immediate gratification.

ideal culture The values and standards of behaviour that people in a society profess to hold.

ideology An integrated system of ideas that is external to, and coercive of, people.

illegitimate opportunity structures Circumstances that provide an opportunity for people to acquire through illegitimate activities what they cannot get through legitimate channels.

immigration The movement of people into a geographic area to take up residency.

impression management (presentation of self) A term for people's efforts to present themselves to others in ways that are most favourable to their own interests or image.

income The economic gain derived from wages, salaries, income transfers (e.g., governmental aid), and ownership of property.

industrialization The process by which societies are transformed from dependence on agriculture and handmade products to an emphasis on manufacturing and related industries.

infant mortality rate The number of deaths of infants under one year of age per 1000 live births in a given year.

infertility An inability to conceive after a year of unprotected sexual relations.

informal education Learning that occurs in a spontaneous, unplanned way.

informal structure A term used to describe the aspects of participants' day-to-day activities and interactions that ignore, bypass, or do not correspond with the official rules and procedures of the bureaucracy.

ingroup A group to which a person belongs and with which the person feels a sense of identity.

institutionalized racism A term used to describe the rules, procedures, and practices that directly and deliberately prevent minorities from having full and equal involvement in society.

intergenerational mobility The social movement experienced by family members from one generation to the next.

internal colonialism According to conflict theorists, a practice that occurs when members of a racial or ethnic group are conquered or colonized and forcibly placed under the economic and political control of the dominant group.

interview A research method using a data-collection encounter in which an interviewer asks the respondent questions and records the answers.

intragenerational mobility The social movement of individuals within their own lifetime.

invasion The process by which a new category of people or type of land use arrives in an area previously occupied by another group or land use.

invention The process of reshaping existing cultural items into a new form.

job deskilling A reduction in the proficiency needed to perform a specific job that leads to a corresponding reduction in the wages paid for that job.

kinship A social network of people based on common ancestry, marriage, or adoption.

labelling theory The proposition that deviants are those people who have been successfully labelled as such by others.

language A system of symbols that express ideas and enable people to think and communicate with one another.

latent functions Unintended functions that are hidden and remain unacknowledged by participants.

laws Formal, standardized norms that have been enacted by legislatures and are enforced by formal sanctions.

life chances The extent to which individuals have access to important societal resources such as food, clothing, shelter, education, and health care.

life expectancy An estimate of the average lifetime in years of people born in a specific year.

looking-glass self Charles Horton Cooley's term for the way in which a person's sense of self is derived from the perceptions of others.

low-income cutoff The income level at which a family may be in "straitened circumstances" because it spends considerably more on the basic necessities of life (food, shelter, and clothing) than the average family.

low-income economies Countries with an annual per capita gross national income of US$765 or less.

lower-middle-income economies Countries with an annual per capita gross national income between US$766 and US$3035.

macrolevel analysis Sociological theory and research that focuses on whole societies, large-scale social structures, and social systems.

majority (dominant) group An advantaged group that has superior resources and rights in a society.

manifest functions Open, stated, and intended goals or consequences of activities within an organization or institution.

marriage A legally recognized and/or socially approved arrangement between two or more individuals that carries certain rights and obligations and usually involves sexual activity.

mass A large collection of people who share an interest in a specific idea or issue but who are not in one another's immediate vicinity.

mass behaviour Collective behaviour that takes place when people (who often are geographically separated from one another) respond to the same event in much the same way.

mass education Providing free, public schooling for wide segments of a nation's population.

mass hysteria A form of dispersed collective behaviour that occurs when a large number of people react with strong emotions and self-destructive behaviour to a real or perceived threat.

master status The most important status a person occupies.

material culture A component of culture that consists of the physical or tangible creations that members of a society make, use, and share.

matriarchal family A family structure in which authority is held by the eldest female (usually the mother).

matriarchy A hierarchical system of social organization in which cultural, political, and economic structures are controlled by women.

matrilineal descent A system of tracing descent through the mother's side of the family.

means of production Karl Marx's term for the tools, land, factories, and money for investment that form the economic basis of a society.

medicalization The process whereby an object or a condition becomes defined and treated by society as a physical or psychological illness.

medicine An institutionalized system for the scientific diagnosis, treatment, and prevention of illness.

meritocracy A hierarchy in which all positions are rewarded based on people's ability and credentials.

metropolis One or more central cities and their surrounding suburbs that dominate the economic and cultural life of a region.

microlevel analysis Sociological theory and research that focuses on small groups rather than large-scale social structures.

middle-income countries Nations with industrializing economies, particularly in urban areas, and moderate levels of national and personal income.

migration The movement of people from one geographic area to another for the purpose of changing residency.

minority (or subordinate) group A disadvantaged group whose members, because of physical or cultural characteristics, are subjected to unequal treatment by the dominant group and who regard themselves as objects of collective discrimination.

mob A highly emotional crowd whose members engage in, or are ready to engage in, violence against a specific target—a person, a category of people, or physical property.

modernization theory A perspective that links global inequality to different levels of economic development and suggests that low-income economies can move to middle- and high-income economies by achieving self-sustained economic growth.

monarchy A political system in which power resides in one person or family and is passed from generation to generation through lines of inheritance.

monogamy A marriage between two partners of the opposite sex.

monotheism A belief in a single, supreme being or god who is responsible for significant events, such as the creation of the world.

moral entrepreneurs People or groups who take an active role in trying to have particular behaviours defined as deviant.

mores Strongly held norms with moral and ethical connotations that may not be violated without serious consequences in a particular culture.

mortality The incidence of death in a population.

network A web of social relationships that links one person with other people and, through them, additional people.

network enterprise Businesses, which may be companies or parts of companies, join for specific projects that become the focus of the network.

new international division of labour theory The perspective that commodity production is being split into fragments that can be assigned to whichever part of the world can provide the most profitable combination of capital and labour.

nonmaterial culture A component of culture that consists of the abstract or intangible human creations of society that influence people's behaviour.

nonverbal communication The transfer of information between persons without the use of speech.

norms Established rules of behaviour or standards of conduct.

nuclear family A family comprising one or two parents and their dependent children, all of whom live apart from other relatives.

occupational (white-collar) crime A term used to describe illegal activities committed by people in the course of their employment or financial dealings.

organized crime A business operation that supplies illegal goods and services for profit.

outgroup A term used to describe a group to which a person does not belong and toward which the person may feel a sense of competitiveness or hostility.

overt racism Racism that may take the form of public statements about the "inferiority" of members of a racial or ethnic group.

panic A form of crowd behaviour that occurs when a large number of people react to a real or perceived threat with strong emotions and self-destructive behaviour.

participant observation A research method in which researchers collect systematic observations while being part of the activities of the group they are studying.

patriarchal family A family structure in which authority is held by the eldest male (usually the father).

patriarchy A hierarchical system of social organization in which cultural, political, and economic structures are controlled by men.

patrilineal descent A system of tracing descent through the father's side of the family.

pay equity (comparable worth) The belief that wages ought to reflect the worth of a job, not the gender or race of the worker.

peer group A group of people who are linked by common interests, equal social position, and (usually) similar age.

peripheral nations According to world systems theory, nations that are dependent on core nations for capital, have little or no industrialization (other than what may be brought in by core nations), and have uneven patterns of urbanization.

personal space The immediate area surrounding a person that the person claims as private.

perspective An overall approach to or viewpoint on some subject.

pluralist model An analysis of political systems that views power as widely dispersed throughout many competing interest groups.

polite racism A term used to describe an attempt to disguise a dislike of others through behaviour that outwardly is nonprejudicial.

political party An organization whose purpose is to gain and hold legitimate control of government.

political socialization The process by which people learn political attitudes, values, and behaviour.

politics The social institution through which power is acquired and exercised by some people and groups.

polyandry The concurrent marriage of one woman with two or more men.

polygamy The concurrent marriage of a person of one sex with two or more members of the opposite sex.

polygyny The concurrent marriage of one man with two or more women.

polytheism A belief in more than one god.

population A group of people who live in a specified geographic area.

population composition The biological and social characteristics of a population.

population pyramid A graphic representation of the distribution of a population by sex and age.

postmodern perspectives The sociological approach that attempts to explain social life in modern societies that are characterized by postindustrialization, consumerism, and global communications.

power According to Max Weber, the ability of people or groups to achieve their goals despite opposition from others.

power elite C. Wright Mills's term for a small clique comprising top business, political, and military officials.

prejudice A negative attitude based on preconceived notions about members of selected groups.

prestige The respect with which a person or status position is regarded by others.

preventive medicine Medicine that emphasizes a healthy lifestyle in order to prevent poor health before it occurs.

primary deviance A term used to describe the initial act of rule breaking.

primary group Charles Horton Cooley's term for a small, less specialized group in which members engage in face-to-face, emotion-based interactions over an extended period.

primary sex characteristics The genitalia used in the reproductive process.

proletariat (working class) Karl Marx's term for those who must sell their labour because they have no other means to earn a livelihood.

protest crowds Groups that engage in activities intended to achieve specific political goals.

punishment An action designed to deprive a person of things of value (including liberty) because of some offence the person is deemed to have committed.

qualitative research Research method that uses interpretive description (words) rather than statistics (numbers) to analyze the underlying meanings and patterns of social relationships.

quantitative research Research method focused on scientific objectivity and data that can be measured numerically.

questionnaire A research instrument containing a series of items to which subjects respond.

race A term used by many people to specify groups of people distinguished by physical characteristics such as skin colour; also a category of people who have been singled out as inferior or superior, often on the basis of real or alleged physical characteristics, such as skin colour, hair texture, eye shape, or other subjectively selected attributes.

racial prejudices Beliefs that certain racial groups are innately inferior to others or have a disproportionate number of negative traits.

racism A set of ideas that implies the superiority of one social group over another on the basis of biological or cultural characteristics, together with the power to put these beliefs into practice in a way that denies or excludes minority members.

rational-legal authority Power legitimized by law or by written rules and regulations.

real culture The values and standards of behaviour that people actually follow.

reference group A group that strongly influences a person's behaviour and social attitudes, regardless of whether that individual is an actual member.

relative homelessness The condition of those who have a physical shelter, but one that does not meet basic standards of health and safety; these include protection from the elements, access to safe water and sanitation, security of tenure, personal safety, and affordability.

relative poverty A level of economic deprivation in which people may be able to afford basic necessities but are unable to maintain an average standard of living.

reliability In sociological research, the extent to which a study or research instrument yields consistent results.

religion A system of beliefs, symbols, and rituals, based on some sacred or supernatural realm, that guides human behaviour, gives meaning to life, and unites believers into a community.

research methods Strategies or techniques for systematically conducting research.

resocialization The process of learning a set of attitudes, values, and behaviours that is new and different from those in one's previous background and experience.

revolutionary movements Movements seeking to bring about a total change in society.

riot Violent crowd behaviour that is fuelled by deep-seated emotions but not directed at one specific target.

rituals Regularly repeated and carefully prescribed forms of behaviour that symbolize a cherished value or belief.

role A set of behavioural expectations associated with a given status.

role ambiguity When the expectations associated with a role are unclear.

role conflict A situation in which incompatible role demands are placed on a person by two or more statuses held at the same time.

role exit A situation in which people disengage from social roles that have been central to their self-identity.

role expectation A term used to describe a group's or society's definition of the way a specific role ought to be played.

role performance How a person actually plays a role.

role strain The strain experienced by a person when incompatible demands are built into a single status that the person occupies.

role-taking The process by which a person mentally assumes the role of another person to understand the world from that person's point of view.

routinization of charisma A term for the process by which charismatic authority is succeeded by a bureaucracy controlled by a rationally established authority or by a combination of traditional and bureaucratic authority.

rumours Unsubstantiated reports on an issue or subject.

sacred A term used to describe those aspects of life that are extraordinary or supernatural.

sanctions Rewards for appropriate behaviour or penalties for inappropriate behaviour.

Sapir-Whorf hypothesis The proposition that language shapes the view of reality of its speakers.

second shift Arlie Hochschild's term for the domestic work that employed women perform at home after they complete their workday on the job.

secondary analysis A research method in which researchers use existing material and analyze data originally collected by others.

secondary deviance A term used to describe the process whereby a person who has been labelled a deviant accepts that new identity and continues the deviant behaviour.

secondary group A larger, more specialized group in which members engage in more impersonal, goal-oriented relationships for a limited time.

secondary sex characteristics The physical traits (other than reproductive organs) that identify an individual's sex.

segregation The spatial and social separation of categories of people by race, ethnicity, class, gender, and/or religion.

self-concept The totality of our beliefs and feelings about ourselves.

self-fulfilling prophecy A situation in which a false belief or prediction produces behaviour that makes the originally false belief come true.

semiperipheral nations According to world systems theory, nations that are more developed than peripheral nations but less developed than core nations.

senile dementia A term for diseases, such as Alzheimer's, that involve a progressive impairment of judgment and memory.

sex A term used to describe the biological and anatomical differences between females and males.

sexism The subordination of one sex, usually female, based on the assumed superiority of the other sex.

sexual orientation A person's preference for emotional–sexual relationships with members of the opposite sex (heterosexuality), the same sex (homosexuality), or both (bisexuality).

sick role Patterns of behaviour defined as appropriate for people who are sick.

social-bond theory The proposition that the probability of deviant behaviour increases when a person's ties to society are weakened or broken.

social construction of reality The process by which our perception of reality is shaped largely by the subjective meaning that we give to an experience.

social control Systematic practices developed by social groups to encourage conformity and to discourage deviance.

social distance A term used to describe the extent to which people are willing to interact and establish relationships with members of racial and ethnic groups other than their own.

social facts Émile Durkheim's term for patterned ways of acting, thinking, and feeling that exist outside any one individual.

social group A group that consists of two or more people who interact frequently and share a common identity and a feeling of interdependence.

social institution A set of organized beliefs and rules that establish how a society will attempt to meet its basic social needs.

social interaction The process by which people act toward or respond to other people; the foundation for all relationships and groups in society.

social marginality The state of being part insider and part outsider in the social structure.

social movement An organized group that acts consciously to promote or resist change through collective action.

social mobility The movement of individuals or groups from one level in a stratification system to another.

social solidarity A group's ability to maintain itself in the face of obstacles.

social stratification The hierarchical arrangement of large social groups based on their control over basic resources.

social structure The stable pattern of social relationships that exists within a particular group or society.

socialization The lifelong process of social interaction through which individuals acquire a self-identity and the physical, mental, and social skills needed for survival in society.

societal consensus A situation whereby the majority of members share a common set of values, beliefs, and behavioural expectations.

society A large social grouping that shares the same geographical territory and is subject to the same political authority and dominant cultural expectations.

socioeconomic status (SES) A combined measure that attempts to classify individuals, families, or households in terms of factors such as income, occupation, and education to determine class location.

sociology The systematic study of human society and social interaction.

sociology of family The subdiscipline of sociology that attempts to describe and explain patterns of family life and variations in family structure.

sociological imagination C. Wright Mills's term for the ability to see the relationship between individual experiences and the larger society.

special-interest groups Political coalitions comprising individuals or groups that share a specific interest they want to protect or advance with the help of the political system.

split labour market A term used to describe the division of the economy into two areas of employment: a primary sector, or upper tier, comprising higher-paid (usually dominant-group) workers in more secure jobs, and a secondary sector, or lower tier, made up of lower-paid (often subordinate-group) workers in jobs with little security and hazardous working conditions.

state The political entity that possesses a legitimate monopoly over the use of force within its territory to achieve its goals.

status A socially defined position in a group or society characterized by certain expectations, rights, and duties.

status set A term used to describe all the statuses that a person occupies at a given time.

status symbols Material signs that inform others of a person's specific status.

stereotypes Overgeneralizations about the appearance, behaviour, or other characteristics of members of particular groups.

stigma According to Erving Goffman, any physical or social attribute or sign that so devalues a person's social identity that it disqualifies that person from full social acceptance.

strain theory The proposition that people feel strain when they are exposed to cultural goals that they are unable to reach because they do not have access to culturally approved means of achieving those goals.

street crime Offences such as robbery, assault, and break and enter.

subculture A group of people who share a distinctive set of cultural beliefs and behaviours that differ in some significant way from that of the larger society.

subliminal racism A term used to describe an unconscious criticism of minorities.

succession The process by which a new category of people or type of land use gradually predominates in an area formerly dominated by another group or activity.

superego Sigmund Freud's term for the human conscience, which consists of the moral and ethical aspects of personality.

survey A research method in which the researcher gathers facts or attempts to determine the relationships among facts.

symbol Anything that meaningfully represents something else.

symbolic interactionist perspectives The sociological approach that views society as the sum of the interactions of individuals and groups.

systemic racism A term that refers to the practices, rules, and procedures of social institutions that have the unintended consequence of excluding minority group members.

taboos Mores so strong that their violation is considered to be extremely offensive and even unmentionable.

technology The knowledge, techniques, and tools that make it possible for people to transform resources into usable forms, and the knowledge and skills required to use them after they are developed.

terrorism The calculated unlawful use of physical force or threats of violence against persons or property in order to intimidate or coerce a government, organization, or individual for the purpose of gaining some political, religious, economic, or social objective.

theism   A belief in a god or gods.

theory   A set of logically interrelated statements that attempts to describe, explain, and (occasionally) predict social events.

total institution   Erving Goffman's term for a place where people are isolated from the rest of society for a set period of time and come under the control of the officials who run the institution.

totalitarian political system   A political system in which the state seeks to regulate all aspects of people's public and private lives.

tracking   The categorical assignment of students based on test scores, previous grades, or both, to different types of educational programs.

traditional authority   Power that is legitimized on the basis of long-standing custom.

transsexual   A person in whom the sex-related structures of the brain that define gender identity are opposite from the physical sex organs of the person's body.

transvestite   A male who lives as a woman or a female who lives as man but who does not alter the genitalia.

universal health-care system   System in which all citizens receive medical services paid for through taxation revenues.

upper-middle-income economies   Countries with an annual per capita gross national income between US$3036 and US$9385.

urban sociology   A subfield of sociology that examines social relationships and political and economic structures in the city.

urbanization   The process by which an increasing proportion of a population lives in cities rather than in rural areas.

validity   The extent to which a study or research instrument accurately measures what it is supposed to measure.

value contradictions   Situations in which values conflict with one another or are mutually exclusive.

values   Collective ideas about what is right or wrong, good or bad, and desirable or undesirable in a particular culture.

variable   In sociological research, any concept with measurable traits or characteristics that can change or vary from one person, time, situation, or society to another.

visible minority   An official government category of nonwhite, non-Caucasian individuals.

wage gap   A term used to describe the disparity between women's and men's earnings.

wealth   The value of all of a person's property, such as buildings, land, farms, houses, factories, and cars, as well as other assets, such as money in bank accounts, corporate stocks, bonds, and insurance policies.

working class (proletariat)   Term for those who must sell their labour in order to earn enough money to survive.

world systems theory   The perspective that the capitalist world economy is a global system divided into a hierarchy of three major types of nations—core, semiperipheral, and peripheral—in which upward or downward mobility is conditioned by the resources and obstacles that characterize the international system.

Abella, Irving, and Harold Troper. 1982. *None Is Too Many*. Toronto: Lester and Orpen Dennys.

Aberle, D.F., A.K. Cohen, A.K. Davis, M.J. Leng, Jr., and F.N. Sutton. 1950. "The Functional Prerequisites of Society." *Ethics*, 60(January): 100–111.

Aberle, David F. 1966. *The Peyote Religion Among the Navaho*. Chicago: Aldine.

Achilles, Rona. 1996. "Assisted Reproduction: The Social Issues." In E.D. Nelson and B.W. Robinson (eds.), *Gender in the 1990s*. Scarborough, Ont.: Nelson Canada, 346–364.

ACS/Environics. 2002. "Public Opinion Poll in 30 Years of Multiculturalism." *Canadian Issues* (February): 4–5.

Adams, Michael. 1998. *Sex in the Snow*. Toronto: Penguin.

Adams, Tom. 1991. *Grass Roots: How Ordinary People Are Changing America*. New York: Citadel Press.

Adler, Freda. 1975. Sisters in Crime: *The Rise of the New Female Criminal*. New York: McGraw-Hill.

Adoption Council of Canada. 2004. "China Leads Adoption Statistics for 2004." Retrieved May 8, 2006. Available: www.adoption.ca/news/050527stats04.htm.

Agger, Ben. 1993. *Gender, Culture, and Power: Toward a Feminist Postmodern Critical Theory*. Westport, Conn.: Praeger.

Agrell, Siri. 2010. "Now There's an App for Vatican, Too: Church Goes 2.0 to Win Over Faithful." *The Globe and Mail* (March 31): A1.

Aiello, John R., and S.E. Jones. 1971. "Field Study of Proxemic Behavior of Young School Children in Three Subcultural Groups." *Journal of Personality and Social Psychology*, 19: 351–356.

Albas, Cheryl, and Daniel Albas. 1988. "Emotion Work and Emotion Rules: The Case of Exams." *Qualitative Sociology*, 11(4): 259–275.

Albas, Cheryl, and Daniel Albas. 1989. "Aligning Actions: The Case of Subcultural Proxemics." *Canadian Ethnic Studies*, 21(2): 74–81.

Albrecht, Gary L. 1992. *The Disability Business: Rehabilitation in America*. Newbury Park, Calif.: Sage.

Alexander, Peter, and Roger Gill (eds.). 1984. *Utopias*. London: Duckworth.

Allahar, Anton. 1989. *Sociology and the Periphery: Theories and Issues*. Toronto: Garamond.

Allen, Tom C. 2000. *Someone to Talk To: Care and Control of the Homeless*. Halifax: Fernwood Publishing.

Allport, Gordon. 1958. *The Nature of Prejudice* (abridged ed.). New York: Doubleday/Anchor.

Alphonso, Caroline and Rheal Seguin. 2006. "Teach Darwin, Quebec Tells Evangelicals." *The Globe and Mail* (October 25): A6.

Alter, Jonathan. 1999. "Bridging the Digital Divide." *Newsweek* (September 20): 55.

Alwin, Duane, Philip Converse, and Steven Martin. 1985. "Living Arrangements and Social Integration." *Journal of Marriage and the Family*, 47: 319–334.

Amato, P.R., and A.C. Booth. 1997. *A Generation at Risk: Growing up in an Era of Family Upheaval*. Cambridge, Mass.: Harvard University Press.

Ambert, Anne-Marie. 2001. *Families in the New Millennium*. Toronto: Allyn and Bacon.

Ambert, Anne-Marie. 2003. "Same Sex Couples and Same-Sex-Families: Relationships, Parenting, and Issues of Marriage." Vanier Institute of the Family. Retrieved August 21, 2003. Available: http://vifamily.ca/library/cft/samesex.html.

Ambert, Anne-Marie. 2005a. "Same Sex Couples and Same Sex Families: Relationships, Parenting and Issues of Marriage." Vanier Institute of the Family. Retrieved September 20, 2010. Available: www.vifamily.ca/library/cft/samesex_05.html.

Ambert, Anne-Marie. 2005b. "Divorce: Facts, Figures and Consequences. Vanier Institute of the Family. Retrieved September 13, 2005. Available: www.cfc-efc.ca/docs/vanif/00005_en.htm.

Ambert, Anne-Marie. 2005c. "Cohabitation and Marriage: How Are They Related?" Vanier Institute of the Family. Retrieved May 10, 2006. Available: www.vifamily.ca/library/cft/cohabitation.html.

Ambert, Anne-Marie. 2006a. *Changing Families: Relationships in Context* (Canadian ed.). Toronto: Pearson.

Ambert, Anne-Marie. 2006b. "One Parent Families: Characteristics, Causes, Consequences, and Issues." Vanier Institute of the Family. Retrieved May 10, 2006. Available: www.vifamily.ca/library/cft/oneparent.pdf.

Amiri, Rini. 2001. "Muslim Women as Symbols—and Pawns." *The New York Times* (Nov. 27): A21.

Amott, Teresa, and Julie Matthaei. 1991. *Race, Gender, and Work: A Multicultural Economic History of Women in the United States*. Boston: South End Press.

Anand, Sudhir, and Amartya Sen. 2000. "The Income Component of the Human Development Index." *Journal of Human Development,* (1): 83–106.

Andersen, Margaret L., and Patricia Hill Collins, eds. 1998. *Race, Class, and Gender: An Anthology* (3rd ed.). Belmont, Calif.: Wadsworth.

Andersen, Margaret, L. 2006. *Thinking About Women: Sociological Perspectives on Sex and Gender*. (7th ed.). Boston: Pearson.

Anderson, Elijah. 1990. *Streetwise: Race, Class, and Change in an Urban Community*. Chicago: University of Chicago Press.

Anderson, Elijah. 1994. "The Code of the Streets." *Atlantic Monthly* (May): 80–94.

Anderson, Elijah. 1999. *Code of the Street: Decency, Violence, and the Moral Life of the Inner City New York*. New York: Norton.

Anderson, Gerald F. 1998. *Highlights of the 1998 Multinational Comparisons of Health Care*. New York: The Commonwealth Fund.

Anderson, Karen. 1996. *Sociology: A Critical Introduction*. Scarborough, Ont.: Nelson Canada.

Andreatta, David. 2007. "Census 2006: The New Household." *The Globe and Mail* (September 13): A8.

Angier, Natalie. 1993. "'Stopit!' She Said. 'Nomore!'" *The New York Times Book Review* (April 25): 12.

Angus Reid. 1991. *Multiculturalism and Canadians: Attitude Study, 1991*. National Survey Report submitted to the Department of Multiculturalism and Citizenship.

Anyon, Jean. 1980. "Social Class and the Hidden Curriculum of Work." *Journal of Education,* 162: 67–92.

APA Online. 2000. "Psychiatric Effects of Violence." *Public Information. APA Fact Sheet Series*. Washington D.C.: American Psychological Association. Retrieved April 5, 2000. Available: www.psych.org/psych/htdocs/public_info/media_violence.html.

Appelbaum, R.P., and W.P. Chambliss. 1997. *Sociology* (2nd ed.). New York: Addison-Wesley Longman.

Appleton, Lynn M. 1995. "The Gender Regimes in American Cities." In Judith A. Garber and Robyne S. Turner (eds.), *Gender in Urban Research*. Thousand Oaks, Calif.: Sage, 44–59.

Arat-Koc, Sedef. 1999. "Foreign Domestic Workers and the Law." In Elizabeth Comack (ed.), *Locating Law: Race, Class, and Gender Connections*. Halifax, N.S.: Fernwood Publishing, 125–151.

Armstrong, Pat, and Hugh Armstrong. 1994. *The Double Ghetto: Canadian Women and Their Segregated Work*. Toronto: McClelland and Stewart.

Armstrong, Pat, and Hugh Armstrong. 1996. *Wasting Away: The Undermining of the Canadian Health Care System*. Toronto: Oxford University Press.

Armstrong, Pat, Hugh Armstrong, Jacqueline Choiniere, Eric Mykhalovsky, and Jerry P. White. 1997. *Medical Alert: New Work Organizations in Health Care*. Toronto: Garamond Press.

Armstrong. Pat. 1993. "Work and Family Life: Changing Patterns." In G.N. Ramu (ed.), *Marriage and the Family in Canada Today* (2nd ed.). Scarborough, Ont.: Prentice-Hall, 127–145.

Arnold, Regina A. 1990. "Processes of Victimization and Criminalization of Black Women." *Social Justice,* 17(3): 153–166.

Arnup, Katherine. 1995. "We Are Family: Lesbian Mothers in Canada." In E.D. Nelson and B.W. Robinson (eds.), *Gender in the 1990s*. Scarborough, Ont.: Nelson Canada, 330–345.

Arquilla, John and David Ronfeldt. 2001. *Networks and Netwars*. Santa Monica: RAND Corporation.

Asch, Adrienne. 1986. "Will Populism Empower Disabled People?" In Harry G. Boyle and Frank Reissman (eds.), *The New Populism: The Power of Empowerment*. Philadelphia: Temple University Press, 213–228.

Asch, Adrienne. 2004. "Critical Race Theory, Feminism, and Disability." In Bonnie G. Smith and Beth Hutchison (eds.), *Gendering Disability*. New Brunswick, N.J.: Rutgers University Press, 9–44.

Asch, Solomon E. 1955. "Opinions and Social Pressure." *Scientific American,* 193(5): 31–35.

Asch, Solomon E. 1956. "Studies of Independence and Conformity: A Minority of One Against a Unanimous Majority." *Psychological Monographs,* 70(9) (Whole No. 416).

Assembly of First Nations. 2008. "Sexual Exploitation/Abuse of First Nations Children." Retrieved September 21, 2010. Available: www.afn.ca/cmslib/general/Sex-Ex.pdf.

Associated Press. 2006. "Companies Cross Borders for Immigrants." *The New York Times* (March 16). Retrieved March 16, 2006. Available: www.nytimes.com/-aponline/business/AP-Cross-Border-Buying-Bizspotlight.html?_r=1&oref=slogin.

Atchley, Robert C. (ed.). 1994. *Social Forces and Aging*. Belmont, Calif.: Wadsworth.

Atchley, Robert C. 2000. *Social Forces and Aging: An Introduction to Social Gerontology* (9th ed.). Belmont, Calif.: Wadsworth.

Aulette, Judy Root. 1994. *Changing Families*. Belmont, Calif.: Wadsworth.

Avert. 2005. "HIV and AIDS in Uganda." Retrieved September 20, 2010. Available: www.avert.org/aidsuganda.htm.

Axinn, William G., and Arland Thornton. 1992. "The Relationship Between Cohabitation and Divorce: Selectivity or Causal Influence?" *Demography*, 29(3): 357–374.

Aylward, Carol A. 1999. *Canadian Critical Race Theory: Racism and the Law*. Halifax: Fernwood Publishing.

Babbie, Earl. 1995. *The Practice of Social Research* (7th ed.). Belmont, Calif.: Wadsworth.

Babbie, Earl. 2004. *The Practice of Social Research* (10th ed.) Belmont, Calif.: Wadsworth.

Bailyn, Bernard. 1960. *Education in the Forming of American Society*. New York: Random House.

Baker, Maureen. 1996. "Introduction to Family Studies: Cultural Variations." In M. Baker (ed.), *Families: Changing Trends in Canada*. Toronto: McGraw-Hill Ryerson, 3–32.

Baker, Maureen. 2005. *Families: Changing Trends in Canada* (5th ed.). Toronto: McGraw-Hill Ryerson.

Baker, Robert. 1993. "'Pricks' and 'Chicks': A Plea for 'Persons.'" In

Anne Minas (ed.), *Gender Basics: Feminist Perspectives on Women and Men.* Belmont, Calif.: Wadsworth, 66–68.

Ballantine, Jeanne H. 1993. *The Sociology of Education: A Systematic Analysis* (3rd ed.). Englewood Cliffs, N.J.: Prentice-Hall.

Ballantine, Jeanne H. 1997. *The Sociology of Education: A Systematic Analysis* (4th ed.). Englewood Cliffs, N.J.: Prentice-Hall.

Ballantine, Jeanne H. 2000. *The Sociology of Education: A Systematic Analysis* (5th ed.). Englewood Cliffs, N.J.: Prentice-Hall.

Ballantine, Jeanne H. 2001. *The Sociology of Education: A Systematic Analysis* (5th ed.). Englewood Cliffs, N.J.: Prentice-Hall.

Ballara, Marcela. 1992. *Women and Literacy.* Prepared for the UN/NGO Group on Women and Development. Atlantic Highlands, N.J.: Zed Books.

Bane, Mary Jo. 1986. "Household Composition and Poverty: Which Comes First?" In Sheldon H. Danziger and Daniel H. Weinberg (eds.), *Fighting Poverty: What Works and What Doesn't.* Cambridge, Mass.: Harvard University Press.

Banner, Lois W. 1993. *In Full Flower: Aging Women, Power, and Sexuality.* New York: Vintage.

Barakat, Matthew. 2000. "Survey: Women's Salaries Beat Men's in Some Fields." *Austin American-Statesman* (July 4): D1, D3.

Barboza, David. 2005. "China, New Land of Shoppers, Builds Malls on Gigantic Scale." *The New York Times* (May 25): A1.

Barlow, Hugh D. 1987. *Introduction to Criminology* (4th ed.). Boston: Little, Brown.

Barlow, Maude, and Heather-Jane Robertson. 1994. *Class Warfare: The Assault on Canada's Schools.* Toronto: Key Porter Books.

Baron, Dennis. 1986. *Grammar and Gender.* New Haven, Conn.: Yale University Press.

Baron, Stephen. 1994. *Street Youth and Crime: The Role of Labour Market Experiences.* Unpublished Ph.D. diss., University of Alberta.

Barrette, Jacques. 2009. *Work/Family Balance: What Do We Really Know?* Ottawa: Vanier Institute of the Family. Retrieved September 21, 2010. Available: www.vifamily.ca/library/cft/barrette/work_family_balance.pdf.

Basham, Patrick, John Merrifield, and Claudia R. Hepburn. 2007. *Home Schooling: From Extreme to Mainstream* (2nd ed.). Studies in Education Policy. Ottawa: The Fraser Institute. Retrieved April 24, 2009. Available: www.fraser-institute.org/commerce.web/product_files/Homeschooling2.pdf.

Basow, Susan A. 1992. *Gender Stereotypes and Roles* (3rd ed.). Pacific Grove, Calif.: Brooks/Cole.

Bates, Stephen. 1994. *Battleground: One Mother's Crusade, the Religious Right, and the Struggle for Our Schools.* New York: Owl/Henry Holt.

Baudrillard, Jean. 1983. *Simulations.* New York: Semiotext.

Baxter, J. 1970. "Interpersonal Spacing in Natural Settings." *Sociology,* 36(3): 444–456.

BBC News. 2004. "'More Extended Families' in Homes." (April 29). Retrieved March 16, 2006. Available: http://news.bbc.co.uk/go/pr/fr/-/1/hi/uk/3668579stm.

Beare, Margaret. 1996a. *Criminal Conspiracies: Organized Crime in Canada.* Scarborough, Ont.: Nelson Canada.

Beare, Margaret. 1996b. "Organized Crime and Money Laundering." In Robert A. Silverman, James, J. Teeven, and Vincent F. Sacco (eds.). *Crime in Canadian Society* (5th Ed.). Toronto: Harcourt Brace, and Co., 187–245.

Beasley, Rob. 1999. "On the Streets." *Amnesty Magazine* (April). In Youth Advocacy Program International, 2009, "Street Children and Homelessness." Retrieved September 20, 2010. Available: www.yapi.org/street/.

Beaujot, Roderic P., and Kevin McQuillan. 1982. *Growth and Dualism: The Demographic Development of Canadian Society.* Toronto: Gage.

Beaujot, Roderic. 1991. *Population Change in Canada: The Challenges of Policy Adaptation.* Toronto: McClelland and Stewart.

Becker, Howard S. 1963. *Outsiders: Studies in the Sociology of Deviance.* New York: Free Press.

Beech, Hannah. 2001. "China's Lifestyle Choice." *Time,* August 6: 32.

Beeghley, Leonard. 1996. *The Structure of Social Stratification in the United States* (2nd ed.). Boston: Allyn & Bacon.

Beeghley, Leonard. 2000. *The Structure of Social Stratification in the United States* (3rd ed.). Boston: Allyn & Bacon.

Begin, P., L. Casavant, N.M. Chenier. 2001. *Homelessness.* Ottawa: Library of Parliament, Parliamentary Research Branch, Document PRB 99-1E. Retrieved November 15, 2000. Available: www.parl.gc.ca/36/refmat/library/PRBpubs/prb991-e.htm.

Belkin, Lisa. 1994. "Kill for Life?" *The New York Times Magazine* (October 30): 47–51, 62–64, 76, 80.

Bell, Inge Powell. 1989. "The Double Standard: Age." In Jo Freeman (ed.), *Women: A Feminist Perspective* (4th ed.). Mountain View, Calif.: Mayfield, 236–244.

Bellan, Ruben. 1978. *Winnipeg First Century: An Economic History.* Winnipeg: Queenston House Publishing.

Belsky, Janet. 1990. *The Psychology of Aging: Theory, Research, and Interventions* (2nd ed.). Pacific Grove, Calif.: Brooks/Cole.

Bennett, Holly. 1997. "A Good Spanking or a Bad Habit" *Today's Parent* (June 1997): 51–52.

Benokraitis, Nijole V. 1999. *Marriages and Families: Changes, Choices, and Constraints* (3rd ed.). Englewood Cliffs, N.J.: Prentice-Hall.

Benokraitis, Nijole V. 2002. *Marriages and Families: Changes, Choices, and Constraints* (4th ed.). Upper Saddle River, N.J.: Prentice-Hall.

Benson, Susan Porter. 1983. "The Customers Ain't God: The Work Culture of Department Store Saleswomen, 1890–1940." In Michael H. Frisch and Daniel J. Walkowitz (eds.), *Working Class America: Essays on Labor, Community, and American Society.* Urbana: University of Illinois Press, 185–211.

Berger, Bennett M. 1988. "Utopia and Its Environment." *Society,* (January/February): 37–41.

Berger, Peter, and Hansfried Kellner. 1964. "Marriage and the Construction of Reality." *Diogenes,* 46: 1–32.

Berger, Peter, and Thomas Luckmann. 1967. *The Social Construction of Reality: A Treatise in the Sociology of Knowledge.* Garden City, N.Y.: Anchor Books.

Berger, Peter. 1963. *Invitation to Sociology: A Humanistic Perspective.* New York: Anchor.

Bernard, Jessie. 1982. *The Future of Marriage.* New Haven, Conn.: Yale University Press (orig. pub. 1973).

Betschwar, Karl. 2002. "Role Reversal: The Stay-At-Home-Dad's Pespective." Retrieved June 30, 2003. Available: www.homedad.org.uk/feature_twins.html.

Better Health Channel, 2007 "Food, Culture, and Religion." Retrieved September 10, 2010. Available: www.betterhealth.vic.gov.au/bhcv2/bhcarticles.nsf/pages/Food_culture_and_religion?open.

Beyerstein, Barry. 1997. "Alternative Medicine: Where's the Evidence?" *Canadian Journal of Public Health,* 88 (May/June): 149–150.

Bibby, Reginald. 1969. "Restless Gods and Restless Youth: An Update on the Religious Situation in Canada." Paper Presented at the Annual Meeting of the Canadian Sociological Association, Ottawa. May 2009.

Bibby, Reginald W. 1987. *Fragmented Gods: The Poverty and Potential of Religion in Canada.* Toronto: Irwin.

Bibby, Reginald W. 1993. *Unknown Gods: The Ongoing Study of Religion in Canada.* Toronto: Stoddart.

Bibby, Reginald W. 1995a. *The Bibby Report: Social Trends Canadian Style.* Toronto: Stoddart.

Bibby, Reginald W. 1995b. *Mosaic Madness: The Potential and Poverty of Canadian Life.* Toronto: Stoddart.

Bibby, Reginald W. 1996. "Fragmented Gods: Religion in Canada." In R. Brym (ed.), *Sociology in Question: Sociological Readings for the 21st Century.* Toronto: Harcourt Brace, 56–61.

Bibby, Reginald W. 1998. "Religion." In Robert J. Brym (ed.), *New Society: Sociology for the 21st Century* (2nd ed.). Toronto: Harcourt Brace Canada, 128–152.

Bibby, Reginald W. 2001. *Canada's Teens: Today, Yesterday, and Tomorrow.* Toronto: Stoddart.

Bibby, Reginald W. 2002. *Restless Gods: The Renaissance of Religion in Canada.* Toronto: Stoddart.

Bibby, Reginald W. 2004. "The Future Families Project: A Survey of Hopes and Dreams." Vanier Institute of the Family. Retrieved September 13, 2005. Available: www.vifamily.ca/library/future/future.html.

Bibby, Reginald. 2006. "The Comeback of Organized Religion in Canada." Pre-edited version of "Who Said God is Dead?" *The Globe and Mail* March 17: A15.

Bissoondath, Neil. 1994. *Selling Illusions: The Cult of Multiculturalism in Canada.* Toronto: Penguin.

Bittner, Egon. 1980. *Popular Interests in Psychiatric Remedies: A Study in Social Control.* New York: Ayer.

Blackford, Karen A. 1996. "Families and Parental Disability." In Marion Lynn (ed.), *Voices: Essays on Canadian Families.* Scarborough, Ont.: Nelson Canada, 161–163.

Blau, Peter M., and Marshall W. Meyer. 1987. *Bureaucracy in Modern Society* (3rd ed.). New York: Random House. Blauner, Robert. 1972. *Racial Oppression in America.* New York: Harper & Row.

Blauner, Robert. 1972. *Racial Oppression in America.* New York: Harper & Row.

Blendon, Robert, Cathy Schoen, Catherine DesRoches, Robin Osborn, Kimberly Scoles, and Kinga Zappert. 2002. "Inequities in Health Care: A Five Country Survey." *Health Affairs,* 21: 182–191.

Bluestone, Barry, and Bennett Harrison. 1982. *The Deindustrialization of America.* New York: Basic Books.

Blumer, Herbert G. 1946. "Collective Behavior." In Alfred McClung Lee (ed.), *A New Outline of the Principles of Sociology.* New York: Barnes & Noble, 167–219.

Blumer, Herbert G. 1969. *Symbolic Interactionism: Perspective and Method.* Englewood Cliffs, N.J.: Prentice-Hall.

Blumer, Herbert G. 1974. "Social Movements." In R. Serge Denisoff (ed.), *The Sociology of Dissent.* New York: Harcourt Brace Jovanovich, 74–90.

Bogardus, Emory S. 1925. "Measuring Social Distance." *Journal of Applied Sociology,* 9: 299–308.

Bogardus, Emory S. 1968. "Comparing Racial Distance in Ethiopia, South Africa, and the United States." *Sociology and Social Research,* 52(2): 149–156.

Bolaria, B. Singh, and Rosemary Bolaria. 1994. "Inequality and Differential Health Risks of Environmental

Degradation." In Bolaria and Bolaria (eds.), *Racial Minorities, Medicine and Health*. Halifax, N.S.: Fernwood, 85–97.

Bolaria, S., and P. Li. 1988. *Racial Oppression in Canada* (2nd ed.). Toronto: Garamond.

Boldt, Menno. 1993. *Surviving as Indians: The Challenge of Self-Government*. Toronto: University of Toronto Press.

Bonacich, Edna. 1972. "A Theory of Ethnic Antagonism: The Split Labor Market." *American Sociological Review*, 37: 547–549.

Bonacich, Edna. 1976. "Advanced Capitalism and Black–White Relations in the United States: A Split Labor Market Interpretation." *American Sociological Review*, 41: 34–51.

Bonger, Willem. 1969. *Criminality and Economic Conditions* (abridged ed.). Bloomington: Indiana University Press (orig. pub. 1916).

Bonvillain, Nancy. 2001. *Women & Men: Cultural Constructs of Gender* (3rd ed.). Upper Saddle River, N.J.: Prentice Hall.

Bordo, Susan. 1993. *Unbearable Weight: Feminism, Western Culture, and the Body*. Berkeley: University of California Press.

Bourdieu, Pierre, and Jean-Claude Passeron. 1990. *Reproduction in Education, Society and Culture*. Newbury Park, Calif.: Sage.

Bourdieu, Pierre. 1984. *Distinction: A Social Critique of the Judgement of Taste*. Trans. Richard Nice. Cambridge, Mass.: Harvard University Press.

Bowlby, Jeffery W., and Kathryn McMullen. 2002. *At a Crossroads: First Results for the 18 to 20-Year-Old Cohort of the Youth in Transition Survey*. Ottawa: Human Resources Development Canada.

Bowles, Samuel, and Herbert Gintis. 1976. *Schooling in Capitalist America: Education and the Contradictions of Economic Life*. New York: Basic Books.

Bowles, Samuel. 1977. "Unequal Education and the Reproduction of the Social Division of Labor." In Jerome Karabel and A.H. Halsey (eds.), *Power and Ideology in Education*. New York: Oxford University Press, 137–153.

Boyd, Monica, and Doug Norris. 1999. "The Crowded Nest: Young Adults at Home." *Canadian Social Trends* (Spring). Ottawa: Statistics Canada, 2–5.

Boyd, Monica. 1995. "Gender Inequality: Economic and Political Aspects." In Robert J. Brym, *New Sociology: Sociology for the 21st Century*. Toronto: Harcourt Brace and Company.

Boyes, William, and Michael Melvin. 1994. *Economics* (2nd ed.). Boston: Houghton Mifflin.

Boyko, Ian. 2002. "Low Income Families Excluded from Universities: Report." (December 7). Ottawa: Canadian Federation of Students.

Boyko, Ian. 2006. "Oh Canada! Too Many Children in Poverty for Too Long . . . " 2006 Report Card on Child and Family Poverty. Retrieved May 24, 2009. Available: www.campaign2000.ca/rc/rc06/06_C2000NationalReportCard.pdf.

Bramlett, Matthew D., and William D. Mosher. 2001. "First Marriage Dissolution, Divorce, and Remarriage: United States." DHHS publication no. 2001–1250 01–0384 (5/01). Hyattsville, MD: Department of Health and Human Services.

Brannigan, Augustine. 2004. *The Rise and Fall of Social Psychology: The Use and Misuse of the Experimental Method*. Hawthorne, N.Y.: Aldine.

Brantingham, Paul J., Shihing Mu, and Aruind Verma. 1995. "Patterns in Canadian Crime." In Margaret A. Jackson and Curt T. Griffiths (eds.), *Canadian Criminology*. Toronto: Harcourt Brace and Company, 187–245.

Braun, Denny. 1991. *The Rich Get Richer: The Rise of Income Inequality in the United States and the World*. Chicago: Nelson-Hall.

Braverman, Harry. 1974. *Labor and Monopoly Capital: The Degradation of Work in the Twentieth Century*. New York: Monthly Review Press.

Breault, K.D. 1986. "Suicide in America: A Test of Durkheim's Theory of Religious and Family Integration, 1933–1980." *American Journal of Sociology*, 92(3): 628–656.

Briggs, Sheila. 1987. "Women and Religion." In Beth B. Hess and Myra Marx Ferree (eds.), *Analyzing Gender: A Handbook of Social Science Research*. Newbury Park, Calif.: Sage, 408–441.

Brod, Harry (ed.). 1987. *The Making of Masculinities*. Boston: Allen & Unwin.

Brooks Gardner, Carol. 1989. "Analyzing Gender in Public Places: Rethinking Goffman's Vision of Everyday Life." *American Sociologist*, 20 (Spring): 42–56.

Brooks-Gunn, Jeanne. 1986. "The Relationship of Maternal Beliefs About Sex Typing to Maternal and Young Children's Behavior." *Sex Roles*, 14: 21–35.

Bruce, Steve. 1996. *Religion in the Modern World*. New York: Oxford University Press.

Brunvand, Jan Harold. 2001. *Too Good to be True: The Colossal Book of Urban Legends*. New York: W.W. Norton and Co.

Brym, Robert J., and Rhonda L. Lenton. 2001. "Love Online: A Report on Digital Dating in Canada." A Report on Surveys, funded by MSN.ca. Retrieved August 26, 2003. Available: www.soc-canada.com/loveonline.pdf.

Brym, Robert, and Bonnie Fox. 1989. *From Culture to Power: The Sociology of English Canada*. Toronto: Oxford University Press.

Brzozowski, Jodi-Anne, Andrea Taylor-Butts, and Sara Johnson. 2006. "Victimization and Offending Among the Aboriginal Population in Canada." *Juristat* 26, No. 3. Ottawa: Statistics Canada.

Buchanan, C.M., and Maccoby E.E., and Dornbusch, S.M. 1996. *Adolescents After Divorce*. Cambridge, Mass.: Harvard University Press.

Buchignani, Norman, Doreen M. Indra, and Ram Srivastiva. 1985. *Continuous Journey: A Social History of South Asians in Canada*. Toronto: McClelland and Stewart.

Buckler, Grant. 1996. "Inet '96: Canadian Minister Calls Global Internet a Priority." *Newsbytes News Network* (July 1).

Buntain-Ricklefs, J.J., K.J. Jemper, M. Bell, and T. Babonis. 1994. "Punishments: What Predicts Adult Approval." *Child Abuse and Neglect*, 18: 945–955.

Burger, Jerry M. 2009. "Replicating Milgram: Would People Still Obey Today?." *American Psychologist*, 64: 1–11.

Burgess, Ernest W. 1925. "The Growth of the City." In Robert E. Park and Ernest W. Burgess (eds.), *The City*. Chicago: University of Chicago Press, 47–62.

Burnham, Walter Dean. 1983. *Democracy in the Making: American Government and Politics*. Englewood Cliffs, N.J.: Prentice-Hall.

Burns, Tom. 1992. *Erving Goffman*. New York: Routledge.

Burr, Chandler. 1997. "The AIDS Exception: Privacy versus Public Health." *The Atlantic Monthly* (June): 57–67.

Burros, Marian. 1994. "Despite Awareness of Risks, More in U.S. Are Getting Fat." *The New York Times* (July 17): 1, 8.

Burt, Martha R. 1992. *Over the Edge: The Growth of Homelessness in the 1980s*. New York: Russell Sage Foundation.

Busch, Ruth C. 1990. *Family Systems: Comparative Study of the Family*. New York: P. Lang.

Bushnik, Tracey. 2006. "Child Care in Canada." Statistics Canada Cat. no. 89-599-MIE no. 003.

Butler, Robert N. 1975. *Why Survive? Being Old in America*. New York: Harper & Row.

Buvinic, Mayra. 1997. "Women in Poverty: A New Global Underclass." *Foreign Policy*, (Fall): 38–53.

Cable News Network. 1997. "Study: Despair Increases Health Risks in Middle-Aged Men." CNN Website: August 26, 1997. Available: www.cnn.com.

Cahill, Spencer E. 1986. "Language Practices and Self Definition: The Case of Gender Identity Acquisition." *Sociological Quarterly*, 27(September): 295–312.

Cain, P.A. 1993. "Feminism and the Limits of Equality." In D.K. Weisberg (ed.), *Feminist Legal Theory: Foundations*. Philadelphia: Temple University Press, 237–247.

Calhoun, Craig. 1986. "Computer Technology, Large-Scale Social Integration and the Local Community." *Urban Affairs Quarterly*, 22(2): 329–349.

Calliste, Agnes. 1987. "Sleeping Car Porters in Canada: An Ethically Submerged Split Labour Market." *Canadian Ethnic Studies*, 19: 1–20.

Calliste, Agnes. 1993/94. "Race, Gender, and Canadian Immigration Policy: Blacks from the Caribbean, 1900–1932." *Journal of Canadian Studies*, 28(4): 131–148.

Callwood, June. 1995. *Trial Without End*. Toronto: Albert A. Knopf.

Campaign 2000. 2000b. "Developing a National Plan of Action for Canada's Children." Retrieved August 8, 2002. Available: www.campaign2000.ca/rc/unsccMAY02/unplan.html.

Campaign 2000. "Canada Falling Behind on International Stage." Retrieved August 7, 2002. Available: www.campaign2000.ca/rc/_unsccMAY02/un10.html.

Campenni, C. Estelle. 1999. "Gender Stereotyping of Children's Toys: A Comparison of Parents and Non-Parents." *Sex Roles* 40 (January): 121–138.

Canada Mortgage and Housing Corporation. 1998. "Survey of Canadians' Attitudes Toward Homelessness." Available: www.cmhc-schl.gc.ca/Research/_Homeless/F_public.html.

Canadian Association of Food Banks. 2005. Retrieved August 22, 2005. Available: www.cafb-acba.ca/english/GetInvolved.html.

Canadian Business. 2009. "A Profile of Economic Security in Canada." Stats and Facts. Retrieved September 20, 2010. Available: www.ccsd.ca/factsheets/economic_security/poverty/index.htm.

Canadian Business Online. 2005. "The Rich List" Retrieved May 23, 2006. Available: www.canadianbusiness.com/after_hours/lifestyle_activities/article.jsp?.

Canadian Business. 2004. "The Rich 100: 2003–2004 Edition." Retrieved August 12, 2005. Available: www.canadianbusiness.com/rich100/index.htm#.

Canadian Cancer Society. 2008. Canadian Cancer Statistics, 2008. Retrieved April 21, 2009. Available: www.cancer.ca/Manitoba/About%20cancer/Cancer%20statistics/PowerPoint%slides.aspx?sc_lang=en&r=1.

Canadian Council on Social Development. 1996. *The Progress of Canada's Children 1996*. Ottawa: Canadian Council on Children Development.

Canadian Council on Social Development. 2002. *Percentage and Numbers of Persons in Poverty: Canada, 1990 and 1999*. Ottawa: Canadian Council on Social Development.

Canadian Council on Social Development. 2009. "A Profile of Economic Security in Canada." *Stats and Facts*. Retrieved October 5, 2010.

Available: www.ccsd.ca/factsheets/economic_security/poverty/index.htm.

Canadian Education Association. 1999. "Educational Trends in Canada." Available: www.acea.ca/trends.html.

Canadian Institute for Health Information. 2004. *Improving the Health of Canadians*. Ottawa: Canadian Institute for Health Information.

Canadian Institute for Health Information. 2005. *Health Care in Canada 2005*. Ottawa: Canadian Institute for Health Information.

Canadian Institute for Health Information. 2008. *National Health Expenditure Trends, 1975–2008*. Ottawa: Canadian Institute for Health Information. Retrieved April 21, 2009. Available: http://secure.cihi.ca/ews/en/index.jsp.

Canadian Institute of Child Health. 1994. *The Health of Canada's Children* (2nd ed.). Ottawa: Canadian Institute of Child Health.

Canadian Internet Project, 2004. Retrieved November 25, 2005. Available: www.canadianinternetproject.ca/en/documents/Canada%20Online%20Final%20English%20Version%2010302005.pdf.

Canadian Race Relations Foundation. 2006. "Facing Hate in Canada." Retrieved Nov. 6, 2006. Available: www.crr.ca/Load.do?section=26&subSection=37&id=239&type=2.

Cancian, Francesca M. 1990. "The Feminization of Love." In C. Carlson (ed.), *Perspectives on the Family: History, Class, and Feminism*. Belmont, Calif.: Wadsworth, 171–185.

Cancian, Francesca M. 1992. "Feminist Science: Methodologies That Challenge Inequality." *Gender & Society*, 6(4): 623–642.

Canetto, Silvia Sara. 1992. "She Died for Love and He for Glory: Gender Myths of Suicidal Behavior." *OMEGA*, 26(1): 1–17.

Cantril, Hadley. 1941. *The Psychology of Social Movements*. New York: Wiley.

Carmichael, Amy. 2005. "And the Booby Prize Goes to . . . " Retrieved January 13, 2006. Available: http://www.theglobe.ca/servlet/story/RTGAM.20050724.wimplants0724/BNStory/National.

Carrier, James G. 1986. *Social Class and the Construction of Inequality in American Education*. New York: Greenwood Press.

Carter, Stephen L. 1994. *The Culture of Disbelief: How American Law and Politics Trivializes Religious Devotion*. New York: Anchor/Doubleday.

Cashmore, E. Ellis. 1996. *Dictionary of Race and Ethnic Relations* (4th ed.). London: Routledge.

Cassidy, B., R. Lord, and N. Mandell. 2001. "Silenced and Forgotten Women: Race, Poverty, and Disability." In Nancy Mandell (ed.), *Feminist Issues: Race, Class,*

and Society (3rd ed.). Toronto: Prentice-Hall, 75–107.

Castellano, Marlene. 2002. "Aboriginal Family Trends: Extended Families, Nuclear Families, Families of the Heart." Ottawa: Vanier Institute of the Family. Retrieved September 21, 2010. Available: www.vifamily.ca/library/cft/aboriginal.html.

Castells, Manuel. 1977. The Urban Question. London: Edward Arnold (orig. pub. 1972 as La Question Urbaine, Paris).

Castells, Manuel. 1998. *End of Millennium*. Malden, MA: Blackwell.

Castells, Manuel. 2000a. *The Rise of the Network Society* (2nd ed.). Oxford: Blackwell Publishers.

Castells, Manuel. 2000b. "Materials for an Exploratory Theory of the Network Society." *British Journal of Sociology*, (January/March): 5–24.

Castells, Manuel. 2004. "Informationalism and the Network Society." In Manuel Castells (ed.), *The Network Society*. Cheltenham: Edward Elgar, 3–45.

Castles, Stephen. 1995. "Trois Siècles de Dépopulation Amerindienne." In L. Normandeau and V. Piche (eds.), *Les Populations Amerindienne et Inuit du Canada*. Montreal: Press de l'Université de Montréal.

Catalyst Canada. 2005. "2004 Catalyst Census of Women Corporate Officers and Top Earners of Canada." Retrieved September 22, 2005. Available: www.catalystwomen. org/.

Cavender, Gray. 1995. "Alternative Theory: Labeling and Critical Perspectives." In Joseph F. Sheley (ed.), *Criminology: A Contemporary Handbook* (2nd ed.). Belmont, Calif.: Wadsworth, 349–371.

Cavender, Nick. 2001. "It's a Dad's Life." Retrieved June 20, 2003. Available: www.homedad. org.uk/feature_dadslife.html.

CBC, 2006a. "Day Care in Canada." CBC News Indepth. Retrieved December 1, 2008. Available: www.canadiancrc.com/Newspaper_Articles/CBC_INDEPTH_Day_Care_in_Canada_09FEB05.aspx.

CBC. 2006b. "In Depth: The Hutterites." CBC News Indepth. Retrieved January 20, 2009.

Centers for Disease Control. 2003. "West Nile Virus: Questions and Answers." Retrieved 13 July, 2003. Available: www.cdc.gov/ncidod/dvbid/westnile/qa/overview.htm.

Centre for Research and Information on Canada. 2003. *The CRIC Papers: A Changing People: Being Canadian in a New Century*. Retrieved October 12, 2003. Available: www.cric.ca/pdf/cahiers/cricparpers_april2003.pdf.

Chafetz, Janet Saltzman. 1984. *Sex and Advantage: A Comparative, Macro-Structural Theory of Sex Stratification*. Totowa, N.J.: Rowman & Allanheld.

Chafetz, Janet Saltzman. 1989. "Marital Intimacy and Conflict: The Irony of Spousal Equality." In Jo Freeman

(ed.), *Women: A Feminist Perspective* (4th ed.). Mountain View, Calif.: Mayfield, 149–156.

Chagnon, Napoleon A. 1992. *Yanomamö: The Last Days of Eden*. New York: Harcourt Brace Jovanovich (rev. from 4th ed.), *Yanomamö: The Fierce People*, by Holt, Rinehart & Winston.

Chalfant, H. Paul, Robert E. Beckley, and C. Eddie Palmer. 1994. *Religion in Contemporary Society* (3rd. ed.). Ithaca, Ill.: Peacock.

Chandler, Tertius, and Gerald Fox. 1974. *3000 Years of Urban History*. New York: Academic Press.

Chandrasekhar, C.P. 2001. "ICT in a Developing Country Context: An Indian Case Study." *Occasional Papers Series*, Number 23. New York: United Nations Human Development Programme. Retrieved July 18, 2003. Available: http://hdr.undp.org/publications/papers.cfm.

Chapman, Amanda. 2003. "Gender Bias in Education." *Multicultural Pavilion: Edchange Research Room*. Retrieved September 20, 2003. Available: www.edchange.org/multicultural/papers/genderbias.html.

Chawla, Raj K. 2008. "Changes in Family Wealth." *Perspectives on Labour and Income* 9 (6). Retrieved September 20, 2010. Available: www.statcan.gc.ca/pub/75-001-x/2008106/pdf/10640-eng.pdf.

Cheney, Peter, Robert Matas, and David Roberts. 1998. "Abuse Claims Against Churches Surge." *The Globe and Mail* (June 9): A1, A5.

Chipungu, Joel. 1999. "Polygamy is Alive and Well in Zambia." *African News Service* (July 22). Retrieved September 11, 1999. Available: www.comtexnews.com.

Chisholm, Patricia. 1995. "Schooling for the Disabled." *Maclean's* (March 27): 52–54.

Chossudovsky, Michel. 1997. *The Globalization of Poverty*. Penang: Third World Network.

Christie, B. 2001. "Attack Hoax Makes Rounds on the Web." *Bakersfield Californian* (September 18): A1.

Chunn, Dorothy E. 2000. "Politicizing the Personal: Feminism, Law, and Public Policy." In Nancy Mandell and Ann Duffy (eds.), *Canadian Families: Diversity, Conflict, and Change* (2nd ed.). Toronto: Harcourt, 225–259.

Church Council on Justice and Corrections. 1996. *Satisfying Justice*. Ottawa: Church Council on Justice and Corrections.

Churchill, Ward. 1994. *Indians Are Us? Culture and Genocide in Native North America*. Monroe, Maine: Common Courage Press.

CIA (Central Intelligence Agency). 2005. *The World Factbook 2005*. Washington D.C.: Office of Public Affairs. Available: www.cia.gov/cia/publications/factbook/index.html.

CIA (Central Intelligence Agency). 2009. *The World Factbook*. Washington, D.C.: Office of Public

Affairs. Retrieved February 22, 2009. Available: https://www.cia.gov/library/publications/the-world-factbook/.

Citizenship and Immigration Canada. 2005. *Facts and Figures, 2004*. Ottawa Citizenship and Immigration Canada. Retrieved May 24, 2006. Available: www.cic.gc.ca/english/pub/facts2004/permanent/12.html.

Citizenship and Immigration Canada. 2006. *Facts and Figures 2005. Immigration Overview: Permanent and Temporary Residents*. Ottawa: Citizenship and Immigration Canada. Retrieved October 10, 2006. Available: www.cic.gc.ca/english/pub/facts2005/overview/03.html.

Citizenship and Immigration Canada. 2008. *Facts and Figures 2007—Immigration Overview*. Ottawa: Citizenship and Immigration Canada. Retrieved April 10, 2009. Available: www.cic.gc.ca/english/resources/statistics/facts2007/index.asp.

Citizenship and Immigration Canada. 2009. *Facts and Figures: Immigration Overview Permanent and Temporary Residents*. Ottawa: Statistics Canada. Retrieved: September 20, 2010. Available: www.cic.gc.ca/english/pdf/research-stats/facts2008.pdf.

Clark, Warren, and Susan Crompton. 2006. "Till Death Do Us Part? The Risk of First and Second Marriage Dissolution." *Canadian Social Trends*. Statistics Canada Cat. no. 11-008. Retrieved May 6, 2009. Available: www.statcan.gc.ca/pub/11-008-x/2006001/pdf/9198-eng.pdf.

Clark, Warren. 1998. "Religious Observance: Marriage and the Family." *Canadian Social Trends* (Fall): 2–7.

Clark, Warren. 2003. "Pockets of Belief: Religious Attendance in Canada." *Canadian Social Trends* (Spring): 2–5.

Clark, Warren. 2006. "Interreligious Unions in Canada." *Canadian Social Trends* 82 (December):17–22.

Clayman, Steven E. 1993. "Booing: The Anatomy of a Disaffiliative Response." *American Sociological Review*, 58(1): 110–131.

Clement, Wallace and Daniel Drache. 1978. *A Practical Guide to Canadian Political Economy*. Toronto: James Lorimer and Company.

Clement, Wallace, and Glen Williams. 1989. *The New Canadian Political Economy*. Kingston: McGill-Queen's University Press.

Cleveland, Gordon, and Michael Krashinsky. 2003. "Eight Myths about Early Childhood Education and Care." Retrieved June 14, 2005. Available: www.childcarecanada. org/pubs/other/FF/FactandFantasy.pdf.

Cloward, Richard, and Lloyd Ohlin. 1960. *Delinquency and Opportunity: A Theory of Delinquent Gangs*. New York: Free Press.

CNN. 1994. "Both Sides: School Prayer." (November 26).

CNN. 1999. Chatpage "Jan Harold Brunvand." Retrieved September 27, 2002. Available: www.cnn. com/_COMMUNITY/transcripts/_jan.harold.brunvand.html.

CNN. 2005. "Leadership Vacuum Stymied Aid Offers." CNN.com. Retrieved September 16, 2005. Available: http://edition.cnn.com/2005/US/09/15/katrina.response/index.html.

Coakley, Jay J. 1994. *Sport in Society: Issues and Controversies* (5th ed.). St. Louis: Times Mirror/Mosby.

Coakley, Jay J. 1998. *Sport in Society: Issues and Controversies* (6th ed.). New York: McGraw-Hill.

Coakley, Jay J. 2004. *Sport in Society: Issues and Controversies* (8th ed.). New York: McGraw-Hill.

Cohen, Leah Hager. 1994. *Train Go Sorry: Inside a Deaf World.* Boston: Houghton Mifflin.

Cohen, Theodore (ed.). 2001. *Men and Masculinity: A Text Reader.* Belmont, Calif.: Wadsworth.

Colapinto, John. 2001. *As Nature Made Him: The Boy Who Was Raised as a Girl.* New York: HarperCollins.

Coles, Gerald. 1987. *The Learning Mystique: A Critical Look at "Learning Disabilities."* New York: Pantheon.

Collins, Randall. 1971. "A Conflict Theory of Sexual Stratification." *Social Problems,* 19(1): 3–21.

Collins, Randall. 1979. *The Credential Society: An Historical Sociology of Education.* New York: Academic Press.

Collins, Randall. 1982. *Sociological Insight: An Introduction to Non-Obvious Sociology.* New York: Oxford University Press.

Collins, Randall. 1997. "An Asian Route to Capitalism: Religious Economy and the Origins of Self-Transforming Growth in Japan." *American Sociological Review* 62: 843–865.

Coltrane, Scott. 2000 "Research on Household Labor: Modeling and Measuring the Social Embeddedness of Routine Family Work." *Journal of Marriage and the Family* 62: 1208–33.

Comack, Elizabeth. 1996a. "Women and Crime." In R. Linden (ed.), *Criminology: A Canadian Perspective* (3rd ed.). Toronto: Harcourt Brace, 139–175.

Comack, Elizabeth. 1996b. *Women in Trouble.* Halifax: Fernwood Publishing.

Comack, Elizabeth. 2009. "Feminism and Criminology." In Rick Linden (ed.), *Criminology: A Canadian Perspective* (6th ed.) Toronto: Nelson, 164–195.

Comfort, Alex. 1976. "Age Prejudice in America." *Social Policy,* 7(3): 3–8.

Commission on Systemic Racism in the Ontario Criminal Justice System. 1995. *Report of the Commission on Systemic Racism in the Ontario Criminal Justice System.* Toronto: Queen's Printer for Ontario.

Commonwealth Fund 2007. *2007 International Health Policy Survey in Seven Countries.* New York: Commonwealth Fund. Retrieved

September 20, 2010. Available: www.commonwealthfund.org/Content/Surveys/2007/2007-International-Health-Policy-Survey-in-Seven-Countries.aspx.

Commonwealth Fund. 2002. "Canadian Adults' Health Care System Views and Experiences." *Commonwealth Fund 2001 International Health Policy Survey.* New York: Commonwealth Fund. Retrieved December 17, 2002. Available: www.cmwf.org/programs/international/can_sb_552.pdf.

Condry, Sandra McConnell, John C. Condry, Jr., and Lee Wolfram Pogatshnik. 1983. "Sex Differences: A Study of the Ear of the Beholder." *Sex Roles,* 9: 697–704.

Conrad, Peter, and Joseph W. Schneider. 1980. "The Medical Control of Deviance: Conquests and Consequences." In Julius A. Roth (ed.), *Research in the Sociology of Health Care: A Research Annual.* Greenwich, Conn.: Jai Press, 1–53.

Conrad, Peter, and Joseph W. Schneider. 1992. *Deviance and Medicalization: From Badness to Sickness.* Philadelphia: Temple University Press.

Conrad, Peter. 1975. "The Discovery of Hyperkinesis." *Social Problems,* 23, (October): 12–21.

Cook, Ramsay. 1995. *Canada, Quebec and the Uses of Nationalism* (2nd ed.). Toronto: McClelland and Stewart.

Cook, Sherburn F. 1973. "The Significance of Disease in the Extinction of the New England Indians." *Human Biology,* 45: 485–508.

Cook, Shirley J. 1969. "Canadian Narcotics Legislation, 1908–1923. A Conflict Model Interpretation." *Canadian Review of Sociology and Anthropology,* 6(1): 36–46.

Cooke, Martin, Daniel Beavon, and Mindy McHardy. 2004. "Measuring the Well-Being of Aboriginal People: An Application of the United Nations' Human Development Index to Registered Indians in Canada, 1981–2001." Ottawa: Indian and Northern Affairs Canada.

Cookson, Peter W., Jr., and Caroline Hodges Persell. 1985. *Preparing for Power: America's Elite Boarding Schools.* New York: Basic Books.

Cooley, Charles Horton. 1922. *Human Nature and Social Order.* New York: Scribner (orig. pub. 1902).

Cooley, Charles Horton. 1962. *Social Organization.* New York: Schocken Books (orig. pub. 1909).

Coontz, Stephanie. 1992. *The Way We Never Were: American Families and the Nostalgia Trap.* New York: Basic Books.

Corsaro, William A. 1992. "Interpretive Reproduction in Children's Peer Cultures." *Social Psychology Quarterly,* 55(2): 160–177.

Coser, Lewis A. 1956. *The Functions of Social Conflict.* Glencoe, Ill.: Free Press.

Craig, Steve. 1992. "Considering Men and the Media." In Steve Craig (ed.), *Men, Masculinity, and the Media.* Newbury Park, Calif.: Sage, 1–7.

Cranswick, Kelly. 1999. "At Work Despite a Chronic Health Problem." *Canadian Social Trends,* (Spring): 11–15. Ottawa: Statistics Canada.

Creese, Gillian, and Brenda Beagan. 1999. "Gender at Work: Seeking Solutions for Women's Equality." In Curtis, James, Edward Grabb, and Neil Guppy (eds.), *Social Inequality in Canada: Patterns, Problems, and Policies.* Scarborough: Prentice Hall, 199–221.

Creese, Gillian, and Brenda Beagan. 2008. "Gender at Work: Strategies for Equality in Neo-liberal Times." In Edward Grabb and Neil Guppy (eds.), *Social Inequality in Canada: Patterns, Problems, and Policies* (5th ed.). Toronto: Pearson, 245–257.

Crichton, Anne, Ann Robertson, Christine Gordon, and Wendy Farrant. 1997. *Health Care: A Community Concern?* Calgary: University of Calgary Press.

Cumming, Elaine, Ian Cumming, and Laura Edell. 1965. "Policeman as Philosopher, Guide and Friend." *Social Problems* 12: 276-286.

Cunningham, J., and J.K. Antill. 1995. "Current Trends in Non-Marital Cohabitation: In Search of the POSSLQ." In J.T. Wood and S. Duck (eds.), *Under-Studied Relationships: Off the Beaten Track.* Thousand Oaks, Calif.: Sage, 148–172.

Curtis, Bruce, D.W. Livingston, and Harry Smaller. 1992. *Stacking the Deck: The Streaming of Working Class Kids in Ontario Schools.* Toronto: Our Schools/Our Selves Education Foundation.

Curtis, James E., and Ronald D. Lambert. 1994. "Culture." In R. Hagedorn (ed.), *Sociology* (5th ed.). Toronto: Holt Rinehart and Winston, 57–86.

Curtis, James, Edward Grabb, and Neil Guppy. 1999. *Social Inequality in Canada: Patterns, Problems, Policies* (3rd ed.). Scarborough: Prentice Hall.

Curtiss, Susan. 1977. *Genie: A Psycholinguistic Study of a Modern Day "Wild Child."* New York: Academic Press.

Cyrus, Virginia. 1993. *Experiencing Race, Class, and Gender in the United States.* Mountain View, Calif.: Mayfield.

D'Sousa, Dinesh. 1996. *The End of Racism: Principles for a Multicultural Society.* New York: Free Press.

Dahl, Robert A. 1961. *Who Governs?* New Haven, Conn.: Yale University Press.

Dahrendorf, Ralph. 1959. *Class and Class Conflict in an Industrial Society.* Stanford, Calif.: Stanford University Press.

Dalton, Lisle, Eric Mazur, and Monica Siems. 2001. "Homer the Heretic and Charlie Church." In Eric Mazur

and Kate McCarthy (eds.), *God in the Details: American Religion in Popular Culture.* New York: Routledge, 231–247.

Daly, K. 2002. "Time, Gender and the Negotiation of Family Schedules." *Symbolic Interaction,* 25, 323–342.

Daly, K. 2004. "The Changing Culture of Parenting." Vanier Institute of the Family. Retrieved May 16, 2006. Available: www.vifamily.ca/library/cft/parenting.html#Shifting.

Daly, Kathleen, and Meda Chesney-Lind. 1998. "Feminism and Criminology." *Justice Quarterly,* 5: 497–533.

Daly, Kerry. 2000. *It Keeps Getting Faster: Changing Patterns of Time in Families.* Ottawa: Vanier Institute of the Family.

Daly, Martin, Margo Wilson, and Shawn Vasdev. 2001. "Income Inequality and Homicide Rates in Canada and the United States." *Canadian Journal of Criminology,* 43: 219–236.

Daly, Mary. 1973. *Beyond God the Father.* Boston: Beacon Press.

Darley, John M., and Thomas R. Shultz. 1990. "Moral Rules: Their Content and Acquisition." *Annual Review of Psychology,* 41: 525–556.

Dart, Bob. 1999. "Kids Get More Screen Time Than School Time." *Austin American-Statesman* (June 28): A1, A5.

Das Gupta, Tania. 1995. "Families of Native Peoples, Immigrants, and People of Colour." In Nancy Mandell and Ann Duffy (eds.), *Canadian Families: Diversity, Conflict and Change* (2nd ed.). Toronto: Harcourt Brace, 141–174.

Das Gupta, Tania. 2000. "Families of Native People, Immigrants, and People of Colour." In Nancy Mandell and Ann Duffy (eds.), *Canadian Families: Diversity, Conflict, and Change* (2nd ed.). Toronto: Harcourt, 146–187.

Dauvergne, Mia, and Holly Johnson. 2001. "Children Witnessing Family Violence." *Juristat,* 21(6). Cat. no. 85-002-XPE. Ottawa: Statistics Canada.

Dauvergne, Mia. 2005. "Homicide in Canada, 2004." *Juristat,* Vol. 25, Number 6. Ottawa: Canadian Centre for Justice Statistics.

Dauvergne, Mia and John Turner. 2010. "Police-Reported Crime Statistics in Canada, 2009." *Juristat* 30 (Summer). Ottawa: Statistics Canada.

Davies, Scott, and Neil Guppy. 2006. *The Schooled Society: An Introduction to the Sociology of Education.* Don Mills, Ont.: Oxford University Press.

Davis, Fred. 1992. *Fashion, Culture, and Identity.* Chicago: University of Chicago Press.

Davis, Kingsley, and Judith Blake. 1956. "Social Structure and Fertility: An Analytical Framework." *Economic Development and Cultural Change,* 4 (April): 211–235.

Davis, Kingsley, and Wilbert Moore. 1945. "Some Principles of Stratification." *American Sociological Review,* 7 (April): 242–249.

Davis, Kingsley. 1940. "Extreme Social Isolation of a Child." *American Journal of Sociology,* 45(4): 554–565.

Davis, Kingsley. 1949. *Human Society.* New York: Macmillan.

Dear, Michael, and Steven Flusty. 1998. "Postmodern Urbanism." *Annals of the Association of American Geographers,* 88(1): 50–72.

Deegan, Mary Jo. 1988. *Jane Addams and the Men of the Chicago School, 1892–1918.* New Brunswick, N.J.: Transaction.

deGroot-Maggetti, Greg. 2002. *A Measure of Poverty in Canada: A Guide to the Debate About Poverty Lines.* Toronto: Public Justice Resource Centre.

Delgato, Richard. 1995. "Introduction." In Richard Delgado (ed.), *Critical Race Theory: The Cutting Edge.* Philadelphia: Temple University Press, 13–14.

Dench, Janet. 2001. "Canada's Immigration Policies—Contradictions and Shortcomings." *Perspectives* (Autumn/Winter): 1–11.

Denton, Margaret A., and Alfred A. Hunter. 1995. "What Is Sociology?" In Lorne Tepperman and R.J. Richardson (eds.), *The Social World* (3rd ed.). Toronto: McGraw-Hill Ryerson, 1–32.

Department of Justice. 2002a. "Spousal Abuse: A Fact Sheet from the Department of Justice Canada." Ottawa: Department of Justice. Retrieved May 16, 2002. Available: http://canada.justice.gc.ca/en/ps/fm/_spouseafs.html.

Department of Justice. 2002b. "Family Violence." Ottawa: Department of Justice. Retrieved May 16, 2002. Available: http://canada.justice.gc.ca/_en/ps/fm/overview.html.

Department of Justice. 2002c. *Child Abuse: A Fact Sheet from the Department of Justice Canada.* Ottawa: Department of Justice Canada.

Department of Justice. 2002d. *Marriage and Legal Recognition of Same-Sex Unions.* Ottawa: Department of Justice Canada.

Department of Justice. 2009. *Assisted Human Reproduction Act.* Retrieved September 21, 2010. Available: http://laws.justice.gc.ca/en/A-13.4/.

Derber, Charles. 1983. *The Pursuit of Attention: Power and Individualism in Everyday Life.* New York: Oxford University Press.

Desai, Sabra. 2001. "But You Are Different." In Carl E. James and Adrianne Shadd (eds.), *Talking About Identity: Encounters in Race, Ethnicity, and Language* (2nd ed.). Toronto: Between the Lines, 241–249.

Desrosier, Heather Juby, and Celine LeBourdais. 1999a. "Female Family Paths." In Peron et al., *Canadian Families Approach the Year 2000.* Ottawa: Statistics Canada, 124.

Desrosier, Heather Juby, and Celine LeBourdais. 1999b. "Male Family Paths." In Peron et al., *Canadian Families Approach the Year 2000.* Ottawa: Statistics Canada, 180.

Deutschmann, Linda B. 2002. *Deviance and Social Control* (3rd ed). Toronto: Nelson Canada.

Dishman, Chris. 2001. "Terrorism, Crime, and Transformation." *Studies in Conflict and Terrorism,* 24: 43–58.

Dodds, Peter Sheridan, Roby Muhamad, and Duncan J. Watts. 2003. "An Experimental Study of Search in Global Networks." *Science* 301: 827–829.

Domhoff, G. William. 1974. *The Bohemian Grove and Other Retreats.* New York: Harper and Row.

Domhoff, G. William. 1978. *The Powers That Be: Processes of Ruling Class Domination in America.* New York: Random House.

Domhoff, G. William. 1983. *Who Rules America Now? A View for the '80s.* Englewood Cliffs, N.J.: Prentice-Hall.

Domhoff, G. William. 1990. *The Power Elite and the State: How Policy Is Made in America.* New York: Aldine De Gruyter.

Domhoff, G. William. 2002. *Who Rules America? Power and Politics* (4th ed.). New York: McGraw-Hill.

Doob, Anthony N., and Jane B. Sprott. 2004. "Youth Justice in Canada." In Michael Tonry and Anthony N. Doob (eds.), *Youth Crime and Youth Justice.* Chicago: University of Chicago Press, 185–242

Doob, Anthony, and Julian V. Roberts. 1983. *An Analysis of the Public's View of Sentencing.* Ottawa: Department of Justice Canada.

Driedger, Sharon Doyle. 1997. "Radical Responses." *Maclean's* (July 28): 46–47.

Drolet, Marie. 2001a. "The Persistent Gap: New Evidence on the Canadian Gender Wage Gap." Cat. no. 11F0019MPE-157. Ottawa: Statistics Canada.

Drolet, Marie. 2001b. "The Who, What, When, and Where of Gender Pay Differentials." Statistics Canada, Catalogue #71-584-MIE. Ottawa: Statistics Canada.

Drolet, Marie. 2002. "Wives, Mothers and Wages: Does Timing Matter?" Catalogue #11F0019M1E, no. 186. Ottawa: Statistics Canada.

Drolet, Marie. 2005. *Participation in Post-Secondary Education in Canada: Has the Role of Parental Income and Education Changed over the 1990s?* Statistics Canada. Retrieved September 20, 2010. Available: www.statcan.gc.ca/pub/11f0019m/11f0019m2005243-eng.pdf.

Du Bois, W.E.B. 1967. *The Philadelphia Negro: A Social Study.* New York: Schocken Books (orig. pub. 1899).

Duffy, Ann, et al. (eds.). 1989. *Few Choices: Women, Work and Family.* Toronto: Garamond Press.

Dumas, Jean. 1990. *Rapport sur l'état de la population du Canada.* Catalogue #91-209. Ottawa: Minister of Supply and Services.

Dumas, Jean. 1997. *Report on the Demographic Situation in Canada, 1988.* Catalogue #91-209. Ottawa: Statistics Canada.

Durkheim, Emile. 1933. *Division of Labor in Society.* Trans. George Simpson. New York: Free Press (orig. pub. 1893).

Durkheim, Emile. 1947. *The Elementary Forms of the Religious Life.* New York: Free Press (orig. pub. 1912).

Durkheim, Emile. 1956. *Education and Sociology.* Trans. Sherwood D. Fox. Glencoe, Ill.: Free Press.

Durkheim, Emile. 1964a. *The Rules of Sociological Method.* Trans. Sarah A. Solovay and John H. Mueller. New York: Free Press (orig. pub. 1895).

Durkheim, Emile. 1964b. *Suicide.* Trans. John A. Sparkling and George Simpson. New York: Free Press (orig. pub. 1897).

Durkheim, Emile. 1995. *The Elementary Forms of Religious Life.* Trans. Karen E. Fields. New York: Free Press (orig. pub. 1912).

Durning, Alan. 1993. "Life on the Brink." In William Dan Perdue (ed.), *Systemic Crisis: Problems in Society, Politics, and World Order.* Fort Worth: Harcourt Brace, 274–282.

Durrant, Joan E., Anders G. Broberg, Linda Rose-Krasnor. 2000. "Predicting Mothers' Use of Physical Punishment During Mother–Child Conflicts in Sweden and Canada." In Paul D. Hastings, Caroline C. Piotrowski (ed.), *Conflict as a Context for Understanding Maternal Beliefs About Child Rearing and Children's Misbehavior: New Directions for Child and Adolescent Development.* Hoboken, N.J.: Jossey-Bass.

Durrant, Joan. 2002. "Physical Punishment and Physical Abuse." In *B.C. Institute Against Family Violence Newsletter* (Winter): 1–7. Retrieved October 12, 2003. Available: http://www.bcifv.org/resources/newsletter/2002/winter/durrant.html.

Duster, Troy. 1995. "Symposium: The Bell Curve." *Contemporary Sociology: A Journal of Reviews* 24 (2): 158–161.

Dyck, Rand. 1996. *Canadian Politics: Critical Approaches* (2nd ed.). Scarborough, Ont.: Nelson Canada.

Dyck, Rand. 2002. *Canadian Politics* (2nd ed., concise). Scarborough, Ont.: Nelson.

Dyck, Rand. 2004. *Canadian Politics: Critical Approaches* (4th ed.). Toronto: Thomson Nelson.

Dyck, Rand. 2008. *Canadian Politics: Critical Approaches* (5th ed.). Toronto: Nelson.

Dye, Thomas R., and Harmon Zeigler. 1993. *The Irony of Democracy: An Uncommon Introduction to American Politics* (9th ed.). Belmont, Calif.: Wadsworth.

Dye, Thomas R., and Harmon Zeigler. 2006. *The Irony of Democracy: An Uncommon Introduction to American Politics* (13th ed.). Belmont, Calif.: Wadsworth.

Ebaugh, Helen Rose Fuchs. 1988. *Becoming an EX: The Process of Role Exit.* Chicago: University of Chicago Press.

Eccles, Jacquelynne S., Janis E. Jacobs, and Rena D. Harold. 1990. "Gender Role Stereotypes, Expectancy Effects, and Parents' Socialization of Gender Difference." *Journal of Social Issues,* 46: 183–201.

Economist, The. 1997. "The Anti-Management Guru." (May 4).

Edsall, Thomas Byrne, with Mary D. Edsall. 1992. *Chain Reaction: The Impact of Race, Rights, and Taxes on American Politics.* New York: Norton.

Edwards, Harry. 1973. *Sociology of Sport.* Homewood, Ill.: Dorsey.

Eggertson, Laura. 2008. "Despite Federal Promises, First Nations' Water Problems Persist." *Canadian Medical Association Journal* 178 (April 8).

Ehrenreich, Barbara. *Fear of Falling: The Inner Life of the Middle Class.* New York: Harper-Perennial.

Ehrlich, Paul R. 1971. *The Population Bomb* (2nd ed.). New York: Sierra Club/Ballantine Books.

Ehrlich, Paul R., and Anne H. Ehrlich. 1990. *The Population Explosion.* New York: Touchstone/Simon & Schuster.

Ehrlich, Paul R., Anne H. Ehrlich, and Gretchen C. Daily. 1995. *The Stork and the Plow: An Equity Answer to the Human Dilemma.* New Haven, Conn.: Yale University Press.

Eichler, Margrit. 1981. "The Inadequacy of the Monolithic Model of the Family." *Canadian Journal of Sociology* 6: 367–388.

Eichler, Margrit. 1988a. *Families in Canada Today* (2nd ed.). Toronto: Gage.

Eichler, Margrit. 1988b. *Nonsexist Research Methods: A Practical Guide.* Boston: Allen & Unwin.

Eichler, Margrit. 1996. "The Impact of New Reproductive and Genetic Technologies on Families." In Maureen Baker (ed.), *Families: Changing Trends in Canada.* Toronto: McGraw-Hill Ryerson, 104–108.

Eichler, Margrit. 1997. *Family Shifts: Families, Policies, and Gender Equality.* Don Mills, Ont.: Oxford University Press.

EKOS Research Associates. 2003. *Making Ends Meet: The 2001–2002 Student Financial Survey.* Montreal: Canadian Millennium Scholarship Foundation.

Elkin, Frederick, and Gerald Handel. 1989. *The Child and Society: The Process of Socialization* (5th ed.). New York: Random House.

Elkind, David. 1995. "School and Family in the Postmodern World." *Phi Delta Kappan* (September): 8–21.

Elliott, D.S., and A. Ageton. 1980. "Reconciling Differences in Estimates of Delinquency." *American Sociological Review,* 45(1): 95–110.

Engels, Friedrich. 1972. *The Origins of the Family, Private Property, and the States.* Eleanor Burke Leacock (ed.). New York: International (orig. pub. 1884).

Epstein, Cynthia Fuchs. 1988. *Deceptive Distinctions: Sex, Gender, and the Social Order.* New Haven, Conn.: Yale University Press.

Epstein, Ethan B. 1996. "Workers and the World Economy." *Foreign Affairs* 75 (May/June): 16–37.

Epstein, Rachel. 1996. "Lesbian Families." In Marion Lynn (ed.), *Voices: Essays on Canadian Families.* Scarborough, Ont.: Nelson Canada, 109–130.

Epstein, Rachel. 2003. "Lesbian Families." In Marion Lynn (ed.). *Voices: Essays on Canadian Families* (2nd ed.). Scarborough, Ont.: Nelson Canada, 76–102.

Erikson, Kai T. 1962. "Notes on the Sociology of Deviance." *Social Problems,* 9: 307–314.

Esbensen, Finn-Aage, and David Huizinga. 1993. "Gangs, Drugs, and Delinquency in a Survey of Urban Youth." *Criminology,* 31(4): 565–589.

Esping-Anderson, Gosta. 2000. "Two Societies, One Sociology, and No Theory." *British Journal of Sociology,* (January/March): 59–77.

Essed, Philomena. 1991. *Understanding Everyday Racism.* Newbury Park, Calif.: Sage.

Esterberg, Kristin G. 1997. *Lesbians and Bisexuals: Constructing Communities, Constructing Self.* Philadelphia: Temple University Press.

Etter, Barbara. 2002. "Critical Issues in Hi-Tech Crime." Paper Presented to the "Embracing the Future Together" Commonwealth Investigations Conference.

Evans, John, and Alexander Himelfarb. 2004. "Counting Crime." In Rick Linden (ed.), *Criminology: A Canadian Perspective* (5th ed.). Toronto: Thomson, 55–87.

Evans, John, and Alex Himelfarb. 2009. "Counting Crime." In Rick Linden (ed.). *Criminology: A Canadian Perspective* (6th ed.). Toronto: Nelson, 103–136.

Evans, Peter B., and John D. Stephens. 1988. "Development and the World Economy." In Neil J. Smelser (ed.), *Handbook of Sociology.* Newbury Park, Calif.: Sage, 739–773.

Eyre, Linda. 1992. "Gender Relations in the Classroom: A Fresh Look at Coeducation." In J. Gaskell and A. McLaren (eds.), *Women and Education.* Calgary: Detselig.

Fagot, Beverly I. 1984. "Teacher and Peer Reactions to Boys' and Girls' Play Styles." *Sex Roles,* 11: 691–702.

Fahmi, Wael Salah. 2001. "'Honey, I Shrunk the Space': Planning in the Information Age." Paper Presented at the 37th International Planning Congress. Utrecht, The Netherlands.

Farb, Peter. 1973. *Word Play: What Happens When People Talk.* New York: Knopf.

Farley, Christopher John. 1993. "Today Los Angeles, Tomorrow …" *Time* (July 26): 49.

Fawcett, Gail. 2000. *Bringing Down the Barriers: The Labour Market and Women with Disabilities in Ontario.* Ottawa: Canadian Council on Social Development. Retrieved June 27, 2002. Available: www.ccsd.ca/pubs/_2000/wd/intro.htm.

Feagin, Joe R., and Clairece Booher Feagin. 1996. *Racial and Ethnic Relations* (5th ed.). Englewood Cliffs, N.J.: Prentice-Hall.

Feagin, Joe R., and Clairece Booher Feagin. 1997. *Social Problems : A Critical Power-Conflict Perspective.* (5th ed). Englewood Cliffs, N.J.: Prentice Hall.

Feagin, Joe R., and Clairece Booher Feagin. 1999. *Racial and Ethnic Relations* (6th ed.). Upper Saddle River, N.J.: Prentice Hall.

Feagin, Joe R., and Clairece Booher Feagin. 2003. *Racial and Ethnic Relations* (7th ed.). Upper Saddle River, N.J.: Prentice Hall.

Feagin, Joe R., and Clairece Booher Feagin. 2008. *Racial and Ethnic Relations* (8th ed.). Upper Saddle River, N.J.: Prentice-Hall.

Feagin, Joe R., and Hernan Vera. 1995. *White Racism: The Basics.* New York: Routledge.

Feagin, Joe R., and Robert Parker. 1990. *Building American Cities: The Urban Real Estate Game* (2nd ed.). Englewood Cliffs, N.J.: Prentice-Hall.

Feagin, Joe R., Anthony M. Orum, and Gideon Sjoberg (eds.). 1991. *A Case for the Case Study.* Chapel Hill: University of North Carolina Press.

Fennell, Tom. 1993. "What's Wrong at School?" *Maclean's* (January 11): 28–34.

Ferguson, Sue. 2004. "Stressed Out." *Maclean's,* 117(47): 30–33.

Ferrell, Keith. 1997. *Truth, Lies, and the Internet.* CNET (October 9). Available: www.cnet.com/content/Features/Dlife/_Truth/index. html.

Findlay, Deborah, and Leslie Miller. 2002. "Through Medical Eyes: The Medicalization of Women's Bodies and Women's Lives." In B. Singh Bolaria and Harley D. Dickinson (eds.), *Health, Illness, and Health Care in Canada* (3rd ed.). Toronto: Nelson, 185–210.

Fine, Michelle, and Lois Weis. 1998. *The Unknown City: The Lives of the Poor and Working Class Young People.* Boston: Beacon.

Finley, M.I. 1980. *Ancient Slavery and Modern Ideology.* New York: Viking.

Firestone, Shulamith. 1970. *The Dialectic of Sex.* New York: Morrow.

Fisher, Luke. 1994. "A Holy War Over Holidays." *Maclean's* (August 12): 26.

Fisher-Thompson, Donna. 1990. "Adult Sex-Typing of Children's Toys." *Sex Roles,* 23: 291–303.

Fiske, J. (1994). *Media Matters: Everyday Culture and Political Change.* London: Routledge.

Fjellman, Stephen M. 1992. *Vinyl Leaves: Walt Disney World and America.* Boulder, Col.: Westview.

Flanagan, William G. 1995. *Urban Sociology: Images and Structure* (2nd ed.). Needham Heights, Mass.: Allyn & Bacon.

Flanagan, William G. 1999. *Urban Sociology: Images and Structure* (3rd ed.). Needham Heights, Mass.: Allyn & Bacon.

Fleras, Augie, and Jean Leonard Elliott. 1992. *Multiculturalism in Canada.* Toronto: Nelson.

Fleras, Augie, and Jean Leonard Elliott. 1999. *Unequal Relations: An Introduction to Race, Ethnic and Aboriginal Dynamics in Canada* (3rd ed.). Scarborough: Prentice-Hall Canada.

Fleras, Augie, and Jean Leonard Elliott. 2003. *Unequal Relations: An Introduction to Race, Ethnic and Aboriginal Dynamics in Canada* (4th ed.). Scarborough: Prentice-Hall Canada.

Fleras, Augie, and Jean Lock Kunz. 2001. *Media and Minorities: Representing Diversity in a Multicultural Canada.* Toronto: Thompson Educational Publishing.

Foderaro, Lisa. W. 2007. "Child Wants Cellphone: Reception Is Mixed." *The New York Times* (Mar. 29): E1–E2.

Foot, David K. 1996. *Boom, Bust, and Echo: How to Profit from the Upcoming Demographic Shift.* Toronto: Macfarlane and Ross.

Ford, Clyde W. 1994. *We Can All Get Along: 50 Steps You Can Take to Help End Racism.* New York: Dell.

Foucault, Michel. 1979. *Discipline and Punish: The Birth of the Prison.* New York: Vintage.

Foucault, Michel. 1991. "Governmentality." In Buchell et al (eds.), *The Foucault Effect.* Hemel Hempstead, Harts, U.K.: Harvester Wheatsheaf.

Fox, Mary Frank. 1989. "Women and Higher Education: Gender Differences in the Status of Students and Scholars." In Jo Freeman (ed.), *Women: A Feminist Perspective.* Mountain View, Calif.: Mayfield, 217–235.

Frank, Andre Gunder. 1969. *Latin America: Underdevelopment or Revolution?* New York: Monthly Review Press.

Frank, Andre Gunder. 1981. *Reflections on the World Economic Crisis.* New York: Monthly Review Press.

Frankenberg, Ruth. 1993. *White Women, Race Matters: The Social Construction of Whiteness.* Minneapolis: University of Minnesota Press.

Frankl, Razelle. 1987. *Televangelism: The Marketing of Popular Religion.* Carbondale: Southern Illinois University Press.

Freedom House. 2005. "Freedom in the World Country Rankings." Retrieved June 11, 2005. Available: www. freedomhouse.org/ratings/index.htm.

Freedom House. 2009. *Map of Freedom in the World.* Retrieved August 24, 2009. Available: www. freedomhouse.org/template/cfm?page=363&year=2009.

Freidson, Eliot. 1965. "Disability as Social Deviance." In Marvin B. Sussman (ed.), *Sociology and Rehabilitation.* Washington, D.C.: American Sociology Association, 71–99.

French, Howard W. 2003. "Japan's Neglected Resource: Female Workers." *The New York Times* (July 25): A3.

Freud, Sigmund. 1924. *A General Introduction to Psychoanalysis* (2nd ed.). New York: Boni & Liveright.

Frideres, James S., and René R. Gadacz. 2005. *Aboriginal People in Canada* (7th ed.). Toronto: Prentice-Hall.

Frideres, James. 1998. *Aboriginal Peoples in Canada: Contemporary Conflicts* (5th ed.). Scarborough: Prentice-Hall.

Frideres, James. 2007. "Building Bridges: Aboriginal, Immigrant, and Visible Minority Families in the Twenty-First Century." In David Cheal (ed.), *Canadian Families Today: New Perspectives.* Don Mills: Oxford University Press, 195–212.

Friedan, Betty. 1993. *The Fountain of Age.* New York: Simon & Schuster.

Friedman, Thomas. 1998. "The Global Neighbourhood." *Winnipeg Free Press* (July 20): A10.

Friedman, Thomas L. 2005. *The World Is Flat.* New York: Farrar, Straus and Giroux.

Friendly, Martha, and Susan Prentice. 2009. *About Canada: Child Care.* Halifax: Fernwood.

Friendly, Martha, Jane Beach, and Michelle Turiano. 2002. "Early Childhood Education and Care in Canada 2001." Childcare Resource and Research Unit, December 2002. Retrieved September 14, 2005. Available: www.childcarecanada. org/ECEC2001/.

Friendly, Martha. 2006a. *Early Learning and Child Care: How Does Canada Measure Up? International Comparisons Using Data from Starting Strong II.* Briefing Note. Toronto: Childcare Resource and Research Unit.

Friendly, Martha. 2006b. "Looking Beyond Our Borders." Toronto: Childcare Resource and Research Unit. Retrieved February 28, 2009. Available: www.childcarecanada. org/ECEC2006/pdf/ECEC06_ LookingBeyondBorders.pdf.

Fries, Christopher. 2008. "Governing the Health of the Hybrid Self: Integrative Medicine, Neoliberalism, and the Shifting Biopolitics of Subjectivity." *Health Sociology Review* 17 (December): 353–367.

Fumento, Michael. 2003. "SARS: Post-Mortem of a Panic." *Scripps Howard News Service* (19 June). Retrieved December 30, 2003. Available: www. fumento.com/disease/sarsimpact. html.

Fuyukama, Francis. 2005. "The Calvinist Manifesto." *The New York Times Review of Books,* March 13, 2005. Retrieved March 13, 2005. Available: www.nytimes.com/200/03/13/books/review/013/FUKUYA.

Gabor, Thomas. 1994. *Everybody Does It! Crime by the Public.* Toronto: University of Toronto Press.

Gailey, Christine Ward. 1987. "Evolutionary Perspectives on Gender Hierarchy." In Beth B. Hess and Myra Marx Ferree (eds.), *Analyzing Gender: A Handbook of Social Science Research.* Newbury Park, Calif.: Sage, 32–67.

Galarneau, Diane and Marian Radulescu. 2009. "Employment Among the Disabled." *Perspectives* (May): 5–15. Ottawa: Statistics Canada.

Galloway, Gloria. 1999. "Number of Racist Canadians Falling." *National Post.* Retrieved March 1, 1999. Available: www.national post.com.

Galo-Machado, Elizabeth, 1998. "Letter to the Editor." *Toronto Star.* November 7, 1998.

Gann, R. 2000. "Postmodern Perspectives on Race and Racism: Help or Hindrance?" Retrieved September 2, 2005. Paper for the *Political Studies Association-UK, 10–13 April 2000.* Ebsco host database.

Gans, Herbert.1982. *The Urban Villagers: Group and Class in the Life of Italian Americans* (updated and expanded ed.; orig. pub. 1962). New York: Free Press.

Garber, Judith A., and Robyne S. Turner (eds.). 1995. *Gender in Urban Research.* Thousand Oaks, Calif.: Sage.

Garcia Coll, Cynthia T. 1990. "A Message to a Future Child About the Danger of Gangs." *Austin American-Statesman* (August 17): A6.

Gargan, Edward A. 1996. "An Indonesian Asset Is Also a Liability." *The New York Times* (March 16): 17, 18.

Gaskell, Jane, Arlene McLaren, and Myra Novogradsky. 1995. "What Is Worth Knowing? Defining the Feminist Curriculum." In E.D. Nelson and B.W. Robinson (eds.), *Gender in the 1990s: Images, Realities and Issues.* Scarborough: ITP Nelson, 100–118.

Gaskell, Jane. 2009. "Feminist Approaches to the Sociology of Education in Canada." In Cynthia Levine-Rasky (ed.), *Canadian Perspectives on the Sociology of Education.* Toronto: Oxford University Press, 17–29.

Gaylin, Willard. 1992. *The Male Ego.* New York: Viking/Penguin.

Gecas, Viktor. 1982. "The Self-Concept." In Ralph H. Turner and James F. Short, Jr. (eds.), *Annual Review of Sociology.* Palo Alto, Calif.: Annual Reviews, 1–33.

Gee, Ellen M. 1994. "What Is Family?" In R. Hagedorn (ed.), *Sociology.* Toronto: Harcourt Brace, 369–398.

Geertz, Clifford. 1966. "Religion as a Cultural System." In Michael Banton (ed.), *Anthropological Approaches to the Study of Religion.* London: Tavistock, 1–46.

Gelles, Richard J., and Murray A. Straus. 1988. *Intimate Violence: The Definitive Study of the Causes and Consequences of Abuse in the American Family.* New York: Simon & Schuster.

"General Facts on Sweden." 2005. Retrieved July 23, 2005. Available: www.finansforbundet.se/Resource.phx/plaza/content/material/internationellteu.htx.pdf.material.3.pdf.

Gerber, Linda. 1990. "Multiple Jeopardy: A Socio-Economic Comparison of Men and Women Among the Indian, Métis, and Inuit Peoples of Canada." *Canadian Ethnic Studies,* 22(3): 22–34.

Gereffi, Gary. 1994. "The International Economy and Economic Development." In Neil J. Smelser and Richard Swedberg (eds.), *The Handbook of Economic Sociology.* Princeton, N.J.: Princeton University Press, 206–233.

Gerschenkron, Alexander. 1962. *Economic Backwardness in Historical Perspective.* Cambridge, Mass.: Harvard University Press.

Gerson, Kathleen. 1993. *No Man's Land: Men's Changing Commitment to Family and Work.* New York: Basic Books.

Ghosh, Ratna, and Rabindra Kanungo. 1992. *South Asian Canadians: Current Issues in the Politics of Culture.* Montreal: Shastri Indo-Canadian Institute.

Giddens, Anthony. 1996. *Introduction to Sociology* (2nd ed.). New York: W.W. Norton & Co.

Gilbert, Dennis L. 2003. *The American Class Structure in an Age of Growing Inequality* (6th ed.). Belmont, Calif.: Wadsworth.

Gilbert, Dennis, and Joseph A. Kahl. 1993. *The American Class Structure: A New Synthesis* (4th ed.). Belmont, Calif.: Wadsworth.

Gilbert, Dennis, and Joseph A. Kahl. 1998. *The American Class Structure: A New Synthesis* (5th ed.). Belmont, Calif.: Wadsworth.

Gilder, George F. 1986. *Men and Marriage.* New York: Pelican.

Gill, Indermit, and Homi Kharas. 2007. *An East Asian Renaissance: Ideas for Economic Growth.* Washington: The World Bank.

Gilligan, Carol. 1982. *In a Different Voice: Psychological Theory and Women's Development.* Cambridge, Mass.: Harvard University Press.

Gillis, A.R. 1995. "Urbanization." In Robert J. Brym (ed.), *New Society: Sociology for the 21st Century.* Toronto: Harcourt Brace and Company, 13.1–13.40.

Gilmore, David D. 1990. *Manhood in the Making: Cultural Concepts of Masculinity.* New Haven, Conn.: Yale University Press.

Gionet, Linda. 2009. "First Nations People: Selected Findings of the 2006 Census." *Canadian Social Trends* 87 (Summer). Catalogue no. 11-008-X. Retrieved May 11, 2009. Available: www.statcan.gc.ca/pub/11-008-x/2009001/article/10864-eng.pdf.

Global Health Council. 2002. *Health: A Key to Prosperity. Success Stories in Developing Countries.* Retrieved July 22, 2005. Available: www.global health.org/sources/view.php3?id=390.

Goffman, Erving. 1956. "The Nature of Deference and Demeanor." *American Anthropologist,* 58: 473–502.

Goffman, Erving. 1959. *The Presentation of Self in Everyday Life.* Garden City, N.Y.: Doubleday.

Goffman, Erving. 1961. *Asylums: Essays on the Social Situation of Mental Patients and Other Inmates.* Chicago: Aldine.

Goffman, Erving. 1963a. *Behavior in Public Places: Notes on the Social Structure of Gatherings.* New York: Free Press.

Goffman, Erving. 1963b. *Stigma: Notes on the Management of Spoiled Identity.* Englewood Cliffs, N.J.: Prentice-Hall.

Goffman, Erving. 1967. *Interaction Ritual: Essays on Face to Face Behavior.* Garden City, N.Y.: Anchor Books.

Goldberg, Robert A. 1991. *Grassroots Resistance: Social Movements in Twentieth Century America.* Belmont, Calif.: Wadsworth.

Golden, Carla. 1987. "Diversity and Variability in Women's Sexual Identities." In The Boston Lesbian Psychologies Collective (eds.), *Lesbian Psychologies.* Urbana: University of Illinois Press, 18–34.

Goode, William J. 1960. "A Theory of Role Strain." *American Sociological Review,* 25: 483–496.

Goodman, Peter S. 1996. "The High Cost of Sneakers." *Austin American-Statesman* (July 7): F1, F6.

Gordon, David. 1973. "Capitalism, Class, and Crime in America." *Crime and Delinquency,* 19: 163–186.

Gordon, Milton. 1964. *Assimilation in American Life: The Role of Race, Religion, and National Origins.* New York: Oxford University Press.

Gordon, Robert M., and Jacquelyne Nelson. 1993. *Census '93: The Report of the 1993 Census of Provincial Correctional Centres in British Columbia.* Victoria, B.C.: Ministry of the Solicitor General.

Gorey, Kevin, Eric J. Holowaty, Gordon Fehringer, Ethan Laukkanen, Agnes Moskowitz, David J. Webster, and Nancy Richter. 1997. "An International Comparison of Cancer Survival: Toronto, Ontario, and Detroit, Michigan, Metropolitan Areas." *American Journal of Public Health,* 87: 1156–1163.

Gottdiener, Mark. 1985. *The Social Production of Urban Space.* Austin: University of Texas Press.

Gouldner, Alvin W. 1970. *The Coming Crisis of Western Sociology.* New York: Basic Books.

Granovetter, Mark. 1995. *Getting a Job: A Study of Contacts and Careers* (2nd ed.). Chicago: University of Chicago Press.

Grant, Karen. 1993. "Health and Health Care." In Peter S. Li and B. Singh Bolaria (eds.), *Contemporary Sociology: Critical Perspectives.* Toronto: Copp-Clark Pitman, 394–409.

Green, Donald E. 1977. *The Politics of Indian Removal: Creek Government and Society in Crisis.* Lincoln: University of Nebraska Press.

Greenberg, Edward S. 1999. *The Struggle for Democracy* (3rd ed.). New York: Addison-Wesley.

Greenberg, Edward S., and Benjamin I. Page. 1993. *The Struggle for Democracy.* New York: HarperCollins.

Greenpeace. 2005. "You Can Make a Difference." Retrieved July 18, 2005. Available: www.greenpeace.org.au/getactive/difference/people_t.html#Solomon.

Greenspan, Edward. 1982. "The Role of the Defence Lawyer in Sentencing." In Craig L. Boydell and Ingrid Connidis (eds.), *The Canadian Criminal Justice System.* Toronto: Holt, Rinehart and Winston, 200–210.

Guglani, Sacha, Peter G. Coleman, and Edmund J.S. Sonuga-Barke. 2000. "Mental Health of Elderly Asians in Britain: A Comparison of Hindus from Nuclear and Extended Families of Differing Cultural Identity." *International Journal of Geriatric Psychiatry* 15: 1046–1099.

Guppy, Neil. 1995. "Education and Schooling." In L. Tepperman, J.E. Curtis, and R.J. Richardson (eds.), *Sociology.* Toronto: McGraw-Hill Ryerson, 450–478.

Gusfield, Joseph. 1963. *Symbolic Crusade: Status Politics and the American Temperance Movement.* Urbana: University of Illinois Press.

Haas, J., and W. Shaffir. 1995. "Giving Medical Students a Cloak of Competence." In L. Tepperman and James Curtis (eds.), *Everyday Life.* Toronto: McGraw-Hill Ryerson.

Hadden, Jeffrey K., and Anson Shupe. 1988. *Televangelism: Power and Politics on God's Frontier.* New York: Holt.

Hadden, Jeffrey K., and Charles K. Swann. 1981. *Prime Time Preachers: The Rising Power of Televangelism.* Reading, Mass.: Addison-Wesley.

Hadden, Jeffrey. 1987. "Toward Desacralizing Secularization Theory." *Social Forces,* 65: 587–611.

Hagan, John, and Bill McCarthy. 1992. "Streetlife and Delinquency." *British Journal of Sociology,* 43(4): 533–561.

Hagan, John, and Bill McCarthy. 1998. *Mean Streets: Youth Crime and Homelessness.* Cambridge, U.K: Cambridge University Press.

Hahn, Harlan. 1987. "Civil Rights for Disabled Americans: The Foundation of a Political Agenda." In Alan Gartner and Tom Joe (eds.), *Images of the Disabled, Disabling Images.* New York: Praeger, 181–203.

Halberstadt, Amy G., and Martha B. Saitta. 1987. "Gender, Nonverbal Behavior, and Perceived Dominance: A Test of the Theory." *Journal of Personality and Social Psychology,* 53: 257–272.

Hall, Edward. 1966. *The Hidden Dimension.* New York: Anchor/Doubleday.

Hall, Peter M. 1972. "A Symbolic Interactionist Analysis of Politics." *Sociological Inquiry,* 42: 35–75.

Hamilton, A.C., and C.M. Sinclair. 1991a. *Report of the Aboriginal Justice Inquiry of Manitoba. Volume 3: The Death of John Joseph Harper.* Winnipeg, Manitoba: Queen's Printer.

Hamilton, Allen C., and C. Murray Sinclair. 1991. Winnipeg: Queen's Printer.

Hamilton, Allen C., and C. Murray Sinclair. 1991b. *Report of the Aboriginal Justice Inquiry of Manitoba, Winnipeg: Queen's Printer, Volume 1.* Winnipeg: Queen's Printer.

Hamilton, Roberta. 1988. "Women, Wives and Mothers." In Nancy Mandell and Ann Duffy (eds.), *Reconstructing the Canadian Family: Feminist Perspectives.* Toronto: Butterworths, 3–26.

Hannigan, John. 1998. *Fantasy City: Pleasure and Profit in the Postmodern Metropolis.* London: Routledge.

Hansen, Liane. 1995. "Internet and Cyberspace—Farther Away Than You Think." *Sunday National Public Radio* (November 12): Weekend Edition.

Haraway, Donna. 1994. "A Cyborg Manifesto: Science, Technology, and Socialist-Feminism in the Late Twentieth Century." In Anne C. Herrmann and Abigail J. Stewart (eds.), *Theorizing Feminism: Parallel Trends in the Humanities and Social Sciences.* Boulder, Colo.: Westview, 427–457.

Hargrave, Connie. 2005. "Homelessness in Canada: From Housing to Shelters to Blankets." SHARE International Archives. Retrieved June 1, 2005. Available: www.shareintl.org/archives/homelessness/hl-ch_Canada. htm.

Harlow, Harry F., and Margaret Kuenne Harlow. 1962. "Social Deprivation in Monkeys." *Scientific American,* 207(5): 137–146.

Harlow, Harry F., and Margaret Kuenne Harlow. 1977. "Effects of Various Mother-Infant Relationships on Rhesus Monkey Behaviors." In Brian M. Foss (ed.), *Determinants of Infant Behavior, Volume 4.* London: Methuen, 15–36.

Harman, Lesley. 1989. *When a Hostel Becomes a Home: Experiences of Women.* Toronto: Garamond Press.

Harris, Chauncey D., and Edward L. Ullman. 1945. "The Nature of Cities." *Annals of the Academy of Political and Social Sciences* (November): 7–17.

Harris, Marvin. 1974. *Cows, Pigs, Wars, and Witches.* New York: Random House.

Harris, Marvin. 1985. *Good to Eat: Riddles of Food and Culture.* New York: Simon & Schuster.

Harrison, Janine. 2001. "Welfare Reports Document Increasing Homelessness in Australia." Retrieved September 11, 2001. Available: http://wsws.orgarticles/2001/jun2001/home-j07_prn.shtml.

Hartmann, Heidi. 1976. "Capitalism, Patriarchy, and Job Segregation by Sex." *Signs: Journal of Women in Culture and Society,* 1 (Spring): 137–169.

Hartmann, Heidi. 1981. "The Unhappy Marriage of Marxism and Feminism." In Lydia Sargent (ed.), *Women and Revolution.* Boston: South End Press.

Hartnagel, Timothy. 2004. "Correlates of Criminal Behaviour." In Rick Linden (ed.), *Criminology: A Canadian Perspective* (5th ed.). Toronto: Thomson, 120–163.

Hartnagel, Timothy F. 2009. "Correlates of Crime." In R. Linden (ed.), *Criminology: A Canadian Perspective* (6th ed.). Toronto: Nelson, 137–782.

Harvey, Frank P. 2004. *Smoke and Mirrors: Globalized Terrorism and the Illusion of Multilateral Security.* Toronto: University of Toronto Press.

Hauchler, Ingomar, and Paul M. Kennedy (eds.). 1994. *Global Trends: The World Almanac of Development and Peace.* New York: Continuum.

Hauser, Robert M. 1995. "Symposium: The Bell Curve." *Contemporary Sociology: A Journal of Reviews* 24 (2): 149–153.

Haviland, William A. 1993. *Cultural Anthropology* (7th ed.). Orlando, Fla.: Harcourt Brace Jovanovich.

Haynes, Jeff. 1997. "Religion, Secularisation and Politics: A Postmodern Conspectus." *Third World Quarterly,* 18: 709–728.

Health and Welfare Canada. 1998. *Active Health Report: The Active Health Report on Seniors.* Ottawa: Minister of Supply and Services.

Health Canada. 1997. *For the Safety of Canadian Children and Youth: From Injury Data to Preventative Measures.* Catalogue #H39-412/1997E. Ottawa: Health Programs and Services Branch.

Health Canada. 1999. "Social Inequality in the Health of Canadians." In James Curtis, Edward Grabb, and Neil Guppy (ed.). *Social Inequality in Canada: Patterns, Problems and Policies,* (3rd ed.). Scarborough, Ont.: Prentice-Hall, 300–314.

Health Canada. 2002. *HIV and AIDS in Canada: Surveillance Report to June 30, 2002.* Ottawa: Health Canada: Centre for Infectious Disease Prevention and Control.

Health Canada. 2005. *A Statistical Profile on the Health of First Nations in Canada: Highlights.*

Heaven, Pamela. 2010. "Top 10 Canadian Billionaires" *Financial Post* March 11, 2010. Retrieved September 24, 2010. nationalpost.com/NP/blogs/fpposted/archive/tags/Forbes+rich+list/default.aspx.

Heilbroner, Robert. 1985. *The Nature and Logic of Capitalism.* New York: W.W. Norton and Company.

Helman, Cecil G. 2000. *Culture, Health and Illness* (4th ed.). Oxford, U.K.: Butterworth Heinemann.

Henley, Nancy. 1977. *Body Politics: Power, Sex, and Nonverbal Communication.* Englewood Cliffs, N.J.: Prentice-Hall.

Henry, Frances and Carol Tator. 2006. *The Colour of Democracy: Racism in Canadian Society* (3rd ed.). Toronto: Thomson Nelson.

Henry, Frances, Carol Tator, Winston Mattis, and Tim Rees. 1996. "The Victimization of Racial Minorities in Canada. In Robert J. Brym (ed.), *Society in Question: Sociological Readings for the 21st Century.* Toronto: Harcourt Brace and Company, 133–144.

Henry, Frances, Carol Tator, Winston Mattis, and Tim Rees. 2000. *The Colour of Democracy: Racism in Canadian Society* (2nd ed.). Toronto: Harcourt Canada.

Henry, Frances. 1999. "Two Studies of Racial Discrimination in Employment." In James Curtis, Edward Grabb, and Neil Guppy (eds.), *Social Inequality in Canada* (3rd ed.). Scarborough, Ont.: Prentice Hall, 226–235.

Herman, Nancy J. 1997. "Return to Sender: Reintegrative Stigma-Management Strategies of Ex-Psychiatric Patients." In Patricia A. Adler and Peter Adler (eds.), *Constructions of Deviance: Social Power, Context, and Interaction.* Belmont, CA: Wadsworth, 308–325.

Herrnstein, Richard J., and Charles Murray. 1994. *The Bell Curve: Intelligence and Class Structure in American Life.* New York: Free Press.

Heshka, Stanley, and Yona Nelson. 1972. "Interpersonal Speaking Distances as a Function of Age, Sex, and Relationship." *Sociometry,* 35(4): 491–498.

Hettne, Bjorn. 1995. *Development Theory and the Three Worlds* (2nd ed.). Essex: Longman.

Hier, Sean P., and B. Singh Bolaria (eds.). 2006. *Identity and Belonging: Rethinking Race & Ethnicity in Canadian Society.* Toronto: Canadian Scholars' Press.

Hier, Sean P., and B. Singh Bolaria (eds.). 2007. *Race & Racism in 21st Century Canada: Continuity, Complexity, and Change.* Peterborough, Ont.: Broadview.

Himmelstein, David, Elizabeth Warren, Deborah Thorne, and Steffie Woolhandler. 2005. "Marketwatch: Illness and Injury as Contributors to Bankruptcy." *Health Affairs,* 24 March/April: 570.

Hindu, The. 1998. "The Idea of Human Development." (October 25): 25.

Hirschi, Travis. 1969. *Causes of Delinquency.* Berkeley: University of California Press.

Hochschild, Arlie Russell. 1989. *The Second Shift: Working Parents and the Revolution at Home.* New York: Viking/Penguin.

Hochschild, Arlie Russell. 1997. *The Time Bind: When Work Becomes Home and Home Becomes Work.* New York: Metropolitan Books.

Hochschild, Arlie Russell. 2003. *The Commercialization of Intimate Life: Notes from Home and Work.* Berkeley: University of California Press.

Hodgson, Doug. 1989. "The Legal and Public Policy Implications of Human Immunodeficiency Virus Antibody Testing in New Zealand." In *Legal Implications of AIDS.* Auckland: Legal Research Foundation, 39–95.

Hodson, Randy, and Robert E. Parker. 1988. "Work in High Technology Settings: A Review of the Empirical Literature." *Research in the Sociology of Work,* 4: 1–29.

Hoffman, Bruce. 1995. "'Holy Terror': The Implications of Terrorism Motivated by a Religious Imperative." *Studies in Conflict and Terrorism,* 18: 271–284.

Hogeveen, Brian, and Russell Smandych. 2001. "Origins of the Newly Proposed Canadian Youth Criminal Justice Act: Political Discourse and the Perceived Crisis in Youth Crime in the 1990s." In Russell Smandych (ed.), *Youth Justice: History, Legislation, and Reform.* Toronto: Harcourt Canada, 144–168.

Holland, Dorothy C., and Margaret A. Eisenhart. 1981. *Women's Peer Groups and Choice of Career.* Final report for the National Institute of Education. Washington, D.C.

Holland, Dorothy C., and Margaret A. Eisenhart. 1990. *Educated in Romance: Women, Achievement, and College Culture.* Chicago: University of Chicago Press.

Holmes, Mark. 1998. *The Reformation of Canada's Schools: Breaking the Barriers to Parental Choice.* Montreal: McGill-Queen's University Press.

Homer-Dixon, Thomas. 1993. *Environmental Scarcity and Global Security.* Foreign Policy Association, Headline Series, no. 300. Ephrata, Penn.: Science Press.

Horan, Patrick M. 1978. "Is Status Attainment Research Atheoretical?" *American Sociological Review,* 43: 534–541.

Horsburgh, Susan. 2003. "Daddy Day Care?" *People* (June 23): 79–81.

Hoyt, Homer. 1939. *The Structure and Growth of Residential Neighborhoods in American Cities.* Washington, D.C.: Federal Housing Administration.

Hughes, Everett C. 1945. "Dilemmas and Contradictions of Status." *American Journal of Sociology*, 50: 353–359.

Hugill, David. 2010. *Missing Women, Missing News: Covering Crisis in Vancouver's Downtown Eastside.* Halifax/Winnipeg: Fernwood Publishing.

Hull, Gloria T., Patricia Bell-Scott, and Barbara Smith. 1982. *All the Women Are White, All the Blacks Are Men, But Some of Us Are Brave.* Old Westbury, N.Y.: Feminist.

Human Resources and Skills Development Canada. 2003. "Winnipeg Annual Labour Market Perspectives, 2003." Retrieved June 14, 2005. Available: www. hrsdc. gc.ca/asp/gateway.asp?hr=/en/mb/ lmireports/perspectives2003-3. shtml&hs=mb0.

Human Resource and Skills Development. 2006. "Advancing the Inclusion of People with Disabilities, 2006." Retrieved May 6, 2009. Available: www.hrsdc.gc.ca/eng/ disability_issues/reports/fdr/2006/ advancinginclusion.pdf.

Human Resources and Skills Development Canada. 2010. *The Homelessness Partnering Strategy.* Ottawa: Human Resources and Skills Development Canada. Retrieved September 28, 2010. Available: www.hrsdc.gc.ca/eng/home-lessness/index.shtml.

Humphreys, Laud. 1970. *Tearoom Trade: Impersonal Sex in Public Places.* Chicago: Aldine.

Hunt, Charles W. 1989. "Migrant Labor and Sexually Transmitted Diseases: AIDS in Africa." *Journal of Health and Social Behaviour* 30: 353–373.

Hurst, Charles E. 1998. *Social Inequality: Forms, Causes, and Consequences* (3rd ed.). Boston: Allyn and Bacon.

Huston, Aletha C. 1985. "The Development of Sex Typing: Themes from Recent Research." *Developmental Review*, 5: 2–17.

Hwang, Stephen W. 2001. "Homelessness and Health." *Canadian Medical Association Journal*, 164(2): 229–233. Retrieved April 20, 2006. Available: www.cmaj.ca/cgi/content/ abstract/164/2/229.

Hyde, Mary, and Carol La Prairie. 1987. "American Police Crime Prevention." Working paper. Ottawa: Solicitor General.

Ibrahim, Mohammed. 2010. "Enriched by Record Ransom, Somali Pirates Free Tanker." *The New York Times* (January 18): A3.

Ikegami, Naoki. 1998. "Growing Old in Japan." *Age and Ageing* (May): 277–283.

Indian and Northern Affairs Canada. 2000. *Comparison of Social Conditions, 1991 and 1996.* Ottawa: Indian and Northern Affairs Canada.

Indian and Northern Affairs Canada. 2005. "Some Fast Facts on the Funding of Aboriginal Programs."

Retrieved September 8, 2005. Available: www.ainc-inac.gc.ca/nr/ prs/j-a2000/mar7_e.html.

Innis, Harold. 1984. *The Fur Trade in Canada.* Toronto: University of Toronto Press (orig. pub. 1930).

Institut National d'Etudes Demographiques. 1997. From Julie DaVanzo and David Adamson. 1997. "Russia's Demographic 'Crisis': How Real Is It?" *Rand Issue Paper,* July 1997. Santa Monica: Rand Center for Russian and Eurasian Studies.

Interfaith Social Assistance Reform Coalition. 1998. *Our Neighbours' Voices: Will We Listen?* Toronto: James Lorimer & Co.

Internet World Statistics. 2006. "The Top 20 Countries with the Highest Internet Usage." Retrieved May 16, 2006. Available: www.internet world-stats.com/top20.htm.

Internet World Stats. 2005. "Internet Usage Statistics—The Big Picture." Retrieved August 14, 2005. Available: www.internetworldstats.com/stats.htm.

Internet World Stats. 2009. "The Internet Big Picture." Retrieved September 20, 2010. Available: www. internetworldstats.com/stats.htm.

Isajiw, Wsevolod W. 1999. *Understanding Diversity: Ethnicity and Race in the Canadian Context.* Toronto: Thompson Educational Publishing.

ITAR/TASS News Agency. 1999. "Polygamy Allowed in Southern Russia" (July 21). Retrieved September 11, 1999. Available: www. com-texnews.com.

Jackson, Beth E. 1993. "Constructing Adoptive Identities: The Accounts of Adopted Adults." Unpublished Masters thesis, University of Manitoba.

James, Carl E. 1998. "'Up to No Good': Black on the Streets and Encountering the Police." In Vic Satzewich (ed.), *Racism and Social Inequality in Canada.* Toronto: Thompson Educational Publishing, 157–176.

James, Carl E. 2005. *Possibilities and Limitations: Multicultural Policies and Programs in Canada.* Halifax: Fernwood.

James, Carl. 1999. *Seeing Ourselves: Exploring Ethnicity, Race and Culture.* Toronto: Thompson Educational Publishing.

James, Carl. 2001. *Seeing Ourselves: Exploring Ethnicity, Race and Culture* (2nd ed.). Toronto: Thompson Educational Publishing.

Jamieson, Alison. 2001. "Transnational Organized Crime: A European Perspective." *Studies in Conflict and Terrorism*, 24: 377–387.

Janis, Irving. 1972. *Victims of Groupthink.* Boston: Houghton Mifflin.

Janis, Irving. 1989. *Crucial Decisions: Leadership in Policymaking and Crisis Management.* New York: Free Press.

Jankowski, Martin Sanchez. 1991. *Islands in the Street: Gangs and American Urban Society.* Berkeley: University of California Press.

Jary, David, and Julia Jary. 1991. *The Harper Collins Dictionary of Sociology.* New York: HarperPerennial.

Jenkinson, Edward B. 1979. *Censors in the Classroom: The Mind Benders.* Carbondale: Southern Illinois University Press.

Jenner, Laura and Rhonda Ferguson. 2009. "2008 Catalyst Census of Women Corporate Officers and Top Earners of the FP500." Retrieved September 23, 2010. Available: www. catalyst.org/file/266/cote_ca_09.pdf.

Jenson, Jane. 2006. "Time to Strengthen Canada's Commitment to Diversity." Canadian Policy Research Networks. Retrieved June 6, 2006. Available: www.cprn.com/en/doc.cfm?doc=687.

Jha, Prabhat, Richard Peto, Witold Zatroski, Jillian Boreham, Martin Jarvis, and Alan Lopez. 2006. "Social Inequalities in Male Mortality, and in Male Mortality from Smoking: Indirect Estimation from National Death Rates in England and Wales, Poland, and North America." *Lancet* 368: 367–370.

Johns Hopkins. 1998. "Can Religion be Good Medicine?" *The Johns Hopkins Medical Letter* (November 3).

Johnson, Allan. 1995. *The Blackwell Dictionary of Sociology.* Malden, Mass.: Blackwell.

Johnson, Earvin "Magic," with William Novak. 1992. *My Life.* New York: Fawcett Crest.

Johnson, Holly. 1996a. *Dangerous Domains: Violence Against Women in Canada.* Scarborough, Ont.: Nelson Canada.

Johnson, Holly. 1996b. "Violence Against Women: A Special Topic Survey." In Robert A. Silverman, James J. Teevan, and Vincent F. Sacco (eds.), *Crime in Canadian Society* (5th ed.). Toronto: Harcourt Brace and Company, 210–221.

Johnstone, Ronald L. 1997. *Religion in Society: A Sociology of Religion* (5th ed.). Saddle River, N.J.: Prentice-Hall.

Juergensmeyer, Mark. 2003. *Terror in the Mind of God.* Berkeley: University of California Press.

Jung, John. 1994. *Under the Influence: Alcohol and Human Behavior.* Pacific Grove, Calif.: Brooks/Cole.

Kahneman, Daniel, Alan Krueger, David Schkade, Norbert Schwartz, and Arthur Stone. 2006. "Would You Be Happier If You Were Richer? A Focusing Illusion." *Science* 312 (June 30): 1908–1910.

Kakuchi, Suvendrini. 1998. "Population: Japan Desperate for a Baby Boom." World News: InterPress Service. Retrieved September 21,1999. Available: www.oneworld.org/ips2/ nov/japan.html.

Kanter, Rosabeth Moss. 1977. *Men and Women of the Corporation.* New York: Basic Books.

Kanter, Rosabeth Moss. 1983. *The Change Masters: Innovation and Entrepreneurship in the American Corporation.* New York: Simon & Schuster.

Kanter, Rosabeth Moss. 1993. *Men and Women of the Corporation.* New York: Basic Books (originally published 1977).

Kantrowitz, Barbara. 2003. "Hoping for the Best, Ready for the Worst." *Newsweek* (May 12): 50–51.

Kappeler, Victor E., Mark Blumberg, and Gary W. Potter. 1996. *The Mythology of Crime and Criminal Justice* (2nd ed.). Prospect Heights: Waveland Press.

Karabanow, Jeff. 2008. "Getting off the Street: Exploring the Processes of Young People's Street Exits." *American Behavioral Scientist* 51: 772.

Karmona, Laurie Krever. 2001. "Who Me, Disabled?" *The Globe and Mail* (October 18): A16.

Kaspar, Anne S. 1986. "Consciousness Re-evaluated: Interpretive Theory and Feminist Scholarship." *Sociological Inquiry*, 56(1): 30–49.

Katz, Michael B. 1989. *The Undeserving Poor: From the War on Poverty to the War on Welfare.* New York: Pantheon.

Katzer, Jeffrey, Kenneth H. Cook, and Wayne W. Crouch. 1991. *Evaluating Information: A Guide for Users of Social Science Research.* New York: McGraw-Hill.

Kaufert, S.R., and M. Lock. 1997. "Medicalization of Women's Third Age." *Journal of Psychosomatic Obstetrics and Gynaecology*, 18: 81–86.

Kaufman, Gayle. 1999. "The Portrayal of Men's Family Roles in Television Commercials." *Sex Roles*, 313: 439–451.

Keister, Lisa A. 2000. *Wealth in America: Trends in Wealth Inequality.* Cambridge, U.K.: Cambridge University Press.

Keller, James. 1994. "I Treasure Each Moment." *Parade Magazine* (September 4): 4–5.

Kellett, Anthony. 2004. "Terrorism in Canada, 1960–1992." In Jeffrey Ian Ross (ed.), *Violence in Canada: Sociopolitical Perspectives* (2nd ed.). New Brunswick, N.J.: Transaction Press, 284–312.

Kelman, Steven. 1991. "Sweden Sour? Downsizing the 'Third Way.'" *New Republic* (July 29): 19–23.

Kemp, Alice Abel. 1994. *Women's Work: Degraded and Devalued.* Englewood Cliffs, N.J.: Prentice-Hall.

Kennedy, Leslie, Robert Silverman, and David Forde. 1991. "Homicide in Urban Canada." *Canadian Journal of Sociology*, 16: 397–410.

Kennedy, Paul. 1993. *Preparing for the Twenty-First Century.* New York: Random House.

Kenny, Charles. 2003. "Development's False Divide." *Foreign Policy* (January/ February): 76–77.

Kerbo, Harold. 2000. *Social Stratification and Inequality: Class Conflict in Historical, Comparative, and Global Perspective* (4th ed.). New York: McGraw-Hill.

Kerstetter, Steve. 2002. *Rags and Riches: Wealth Inequality in Canada*. Ottawa: Canadian Centre for Policy Alternatives.

Khayatt, Didi. 1994. "The Boundaries of Identity at the Intersection of Race, Class and Gender." *Canadian Woman Studies*, 14(2) (Spring).

Kidron, Michael, and Ronald Segal. 1995. *The State of the World Atlas*. New York: Penguin.

Kim, Ryan. 2006. "The World's a Cell-Phone Stage." *San Francisco Chronicle* (Feb. 27). Retrieved March 30, 2007. Available: www.sfgate.com/cgi-in/article.cgi?fi le=/chronicle/archive/2006/02/27/BUG2IHECTO1.DTL&type=printable.

Kimmel, Michael S., and Michael A. Messner (eds.). 1992. *Men's Lives* (2nd ed.). New York: Macmillan.

King, Gary, Robert O. Keohane, and Sidney Verba. 1994. *Designing Social Inquiry: Scientific Inference in Qualitative Research*. Princeton, N.J.: Princeton University Press.

King, Leslie, and Madonna Harrington Meyer. 1997. "The Politics of Reproductive Benefits: U.S. Insurance Coverage of Contraceptive and Infertility Treatments." *Gender and Society*, 11(1): 8–30.

Kitano, Harry, Iris Chi, Siyon Rhee, C.K. Law, and James E. Lubben. 1992. "Norms and Alcohol Consumption: Japanese in Japan, Hawaii, and California." *Journal of Studies on Alcohol*, 53(1): 33–39.

Klein, Alan M. 1993. *Little Big Men: Bodybuilding Subculture and Gender Construction*. Albany: SUNY Press.

Klein, Naomi. 2000. *No Logo*. Toronto: Vintage Canada.

Kleinfeld, Judith S. 2002. "The Small World Problem." *Society* (January/February): 61–66.

Klockars, Carl. 1979. "The Contemporary Crises of Marxist Criminology." *Criminology*, 477–515.

Kluckhohn, Clyde. 1961. "The Study of Values." In Donald N. Barrett (ed.), *Values in America*. South Bend, Ind.: University of Notre Dame Press, 17–46.

Knox, Paul L., and Peter J. Taylor (eds.). 1995. *World Cities in a World-System*. Cambridge, England: Cambridge University Press.

Knudsen, Dean D. 1992. *Child Maltreatment: Emerging Perspectives*. Dix Hills, N.Y.: General Hall.

Kolata, Gina. 1993. "Fear of Fatness: Living Large in a Slimfast World." *Austin American-Statesman* (January 3): C1, C6.

Kome, Penney. 2002. "Canada Court Tells Parliament to OK Gay Marriages." Women's eNews. Retrieved August 23, 2003. Available: www.womensnews.org/article/cfm/dyn/aid/987/context/archive.

Korhonen, Pekka. 1994. "The Theory of the Flying Geese Pattern of Development and Its Interpretations." *Journal of Peace Research* 31 (1): 93–108.

Korte, Charles and Stanley Milgram. 1970. "Acquaintance Networks Between Racial Groups: Application of the Small World Method." *Journal of Personality and Social Psychology* 15: 101–108.

Korten, David C. 1996. *When Corporations Rule the World*. West Hartford, Conn.: Kumarian Press.

Koskela, Hille. 1997. "Bold Walk and Breakings: Women's Spatial Confidence Versus Fear of Violence." *Gender, Place and Culture*, 4(3): 301–320.

Kosmin, Barry A., and Seymour P. Lachman. 1993. *One Nation Under God: Religion in Contemporary American Society*. New York: Crown.

Kozol, Jonathan. 1988. *Rachael and Her Children: Homeless Families in America*. New York: Fawcett Columbine.

Kowinski, William Severini. 2002. The Malling of America: Travels in the United States of Shopping. New York: Xlibis.

Kozol, Jonathan. 1991. *Savage Inequalities: Children in America's Schools*. New York: Crown.

Krahn, Harvey J., Graham S. Lowe, and Karen Hughes. 2007. *Work, Industry and Canadian Society* (4th ed.). Toronto: Nelson Thomson Learning.

Krahn, Harvey, Graham Lowe, and Karen Hughes. 2008. *Work, Industry and Canadian Society* (5th ed.). Toronto: Nelson.

Krashinsky, Susan. 2009. "Click by Click, Greeting Cards Get Licked." *The Globe and Mail* (December 24): B3.

Krebs, Valdis E. 2002. "Mapping Networks of Terrorist Cells." *Connections*, 24(3): 43–52.

Kristof, Nicholas D. 2006. "Looking for Islam's Luthers." *The New York Times* (Oct. 15): A22.

Kumar, K. 1997. "The Post-Modern Condition." In A.H. Halsey, H. Lauder, P. Brown, and A.S. Wells (eds). *Education: Culture, Economy, and Society*. Oxford University Press.

Kunz, Jean Lock, Anne Milan, and Sylvain Schetagne. 2000. *Unequal Access: A Canadian Profile of Racial Differences in Education, Employment and Income*. Ottawa: Canadian Race Relations Foundation.

Kurtz, Lester. 1995. *Gods in the Global Village: The World's Religions in Sociological Perspective*. Thousand Oaks, Calif.: Sage.

Laberge, Danielle. 1991. "Women's Criminality, Criminal Women, Criminalized Women?: Questions in and for a Feminist Perspective." *Journal of Human Justice*, 2 (2): 37–56.

Lacayo, Richard. 2001. "About Face: An Inside Look at How Women Fared Under Taliban Oppression and What the Future Holds for Them Now." *Time* (Dec. 5): 36–49.

Lamanna, Marianne, and Agnes Riedmann. 1997. *Marriages and Families: Making Choices and Facing Change* (6th ed.). Belmont, Calif.: Wadsworth.

Lamanna, Marianne, and Agnes Riedmann. 2003. *Marriages and Families: Making Choices and Facing Change* (8th ed.). Belmont, Calif.: Wadsworth.

Landry, Laura, and Maire Sinha. 2008. "Adult Correctional Services in Canada, 2005/2006." *Juristat* 28 (6). Ottawa: Statistics Canada.

Lane, Harlan. 1992. *The Mask of Benevolence: Disabling the Deaf Community*. New York: Vintage Books.

Langdon, Steven. 1999. *Global Poverty, Democracy and North-South Change*. Toronto: Garamond Press.

Lankenau, S.E. 1999. "Panhandling Repertoires and Routines for Overcoming the Non-Person Treatment." *Deviant Behaviour: An Interdisciplinary Journal*, 20: 183–206.

Lapchick, Richard E. 1991. *Five Minutes to Midnight: Race and Sport in the 1990s*. Lanham, Md.: Madison Books.

Lapsley, Daniel K. 1990. "Continuity and Discontinuity in Adolescent Social Cognitive Development." In Raymond Montemayor, Gerald R. Adams, and Thomas P. Gullota (eds.), *From Childhood to Adolescence: A Transitional Period?* (Advances in Adolescent Development, vol. 2). Newbury Park, Calif.: Sage.

Lasch, Christopher. 1977. *Haven in a Heartless World*. New York: Basic Books.

Lashmar, Paul. 2004. "It's All For Your Own Good." *The Guardian*. 25 September 2004.

Latouche, Serge. 1992. "Standard of Living." In Wolfgang Sachs (ed.), *The Development Dictionary*. Atlantic Highlands, N.J.: Zed Books, 250–263.

Lavigne, Yves. 1987. *Hells Angels: Taking Care of Business*. Toronto: Ballantine Books.

Lavizzo-Mourey, Risa, William Richardson, Robert Ross, and John Rowe. 2005. "A Tale of Two Cities." 24: 313–315.

Law Reform Commission of Canada. 1974. *The Native Offender and the Law*. Ottawa: Information Canada.

Laxer, Gordon. 1989. *Open for Business: The Roots of Foreign Ownership in Canada*. Don Mills: Oxford University Press.

Layton, Jack. 2008. *Homelessness: How to End the National Crisis*. Toronto: Penguin.

Le Bon, Gustave. 1960. *The Crowd: A Study of the Popular Mind*. New York: Viking (orig. pub. 1895).

Lee, Kevin K. 2000. "Urban Poverty in Canada: A Statistical Profile." Ottawa: Canadian Council on Social Development.

Leenaars, Antoon A. 1988. *Suicide Notes: Predictive Clues and Patterns*. New York: Human Sciences Press.

Lefrançois, Guy R. 1993. *The Lifespan* (4th ed.). Belmont, Calif.: Wadsworth.

Lehmann, Jennifer M. 1994. *Durkheim and Women*. Lincoln: University of Nebraska Press.

Lemann, Nicholas. 1997. "Let's Guarantee the Key Ingredients." *Time* (October 27): 96.

Lemert, Charles. 1997. *Postmodernism Is Not What You Think*. Malden, Mass.: Blackwell.

Lemert, Edwin M. 1951. *Social Pathology*. New York: McGraw-Hill.

Lengermann, Patricia Madoo, and Ruth A. Wallace. 1985. *Gender in America: Social Control and Social Change*. Englewood Cliffs, N.J.: Prentice-Hall.

Lenski, Gerhard, Jean Lenski, and Patrick Nolan. 1991. *Human Societies: An Introduction to Macrosociology* (6th ed.). New York: McGraw-Hill.

Leonard, Andrew. 1999. "We've Got Mail—Always." *Newsweek* (September 20): 58–61.

Lester, David. 1992. *Why People Kill Themselves: A 1990s Summary of Research Findings of Suicidal Behavior* (3rd ed.). Springfield, Ill.: Thomas.

LeVay, Simon. 2000. "*As Nature Made Him: The Boy Who Was Raised as a Girl*, Book Review." *Psychology Today*, May. Retrieved September 25, 2003. Available: http://findarticles.com/m1175/3_33/62215090/pl/article.

Levin, William C. 1988. "Age Stereotyping: College Student Evaluations." *Research on Aging*, 10(1): 134–148.

Levine, Arthur. 1993. "Student Expectations of College." *Change*, (September/October): 4

Levine, Nancy E., and Joan B. Silk. 1997. "Why Polyandry Fails: Sources of Instability in Polyandrous Marriages." *Current Anthropology* (June): 375–399.

Levitt, Kari. 1970. *Silent Surrender: The Multinational Corporation in Canada*. Toronto: Macmillan of Canada.

Lewis-Thornton, Rae. 1994. "Facing AIDS." *Essence* (December): 64–130.

Leyton, Elliott. 1979. *The Myth of Delinquency: An Anatomy of Juvenile Nihilism*. Toronto: McClelland and Stewart.

Leyton, Elliott. 1997. *Dying Hard: The Ravages of Industrial Carnage*. Toronto: Oxford University Press.

Li, Geoffrey. 2008. Homicide in Canada, 2007. *Juristat*, 28, No. 9. Ottawa: Statistics Canada.

Lian, Jason Z. and David Ralph Matthews. 2005. "Does the Vertical Mosaic Still Exist? Ethnicity and Income in Canada, 1991." In Bruce Ravelli (ed.), *Exploring Canadian Sociology: A Reader*. Toronto: Pearson, 134–144.

Liebow, Elliot. 1993. Tell Them Who I Am: The Lives of Homeless Women. New York: Free Press.

Lin, J. 2003. "A New Look: Retail Clothing Sales in Canada." *Statistics Canada Analytical Paper*. Ottawa: Statistics Canada.

Linden, Greg, Kenneth Kraemer, and Jason Dedrick. 2007. "Who Captures Value in a Global Innovation System? The Case of Apple's iPod." Personal

Computing Industry Centre: Irvine, California. Retrieved June 21, 2010. Available: www.escholarship.org/uc/item/1770046n.

Linden, Rick, and Cathy Fillmore. 1981. "A Comparative Study of Delinquency Involvement." *Canadian Review of Sociology and Anthropology*, 18: 343–361.

Linden, Rick, David Last, and Christopher Murphy. 2007. Obstacles on the Road to Peace and Justice: The Role of Civilian Police in Peacekeeping." In *Crafting Transnational Policing: Police Capacity-Building and Global Policing Reform*. Andrew Goldsmith and James Sheptycki (eds.). Oxford: Hart Publishing, 149–175.

Linden, Rick. 1994. "Deviance and Crime." In Lorne Tepperman, James E. Curtis, and R.J. Richardson (eds.), *The Social World* (3rd ed.). Whitby, Ont.: McGraw-Hill Ryerson, 188–226.

Linden, Rick. 2009. *Criminology: A Canadian Perspective* (6th ed.). Toronto: Nelson.

Lindsay, Colin, 2008. "Are Women Spending More Time on Unpaid Domestic Work Than Men in Canada?" *Matter of Fact* Issue (September). Statistics Canada Cat. no. 89-630-X. Retrieved September 21, 2010. Available: www.statcan.gc.ca/pub/89-630-x/2008001/article/10705-eng.pdf.

Lindsay, Colin, and Marcia Almey. 2006. "Family Status" in "Women in Canada: A Gender-based Statistical Report, 2005," 35–54 catalogue #89-503-XPE. Retrieved June 21, 2006. Available: http://dsp-psd.communication.gc.ca/Collection-R/Statcan/89-503-X/0010589-503-XIE.pdf.

Linton, Ralph. 1936. *The Study of Man*. New York: Appleton-Century-Crofts.

Lipovenko, Dorothy. 1997. "Geriatric Dementia to Triple by 2031." *The Globe and Mail* (June 11): A6.

Lippa, Richard A. 1994. *Introduction to Social Psychology*. Pacific Grove, Calif.: Brooks/Cole.

Lips, Hilary M. 2001. *Sex and Gender: An Introduction* (4th ed.). New York: McGraw-Hill.

Lips, Hilary M. 1989. "Gender-Role Socialization: Lessons in Femininity." In Jo Freeman (ed.), *Women: A Feminist Perspective* (4th ed.). Mountain View, Calif.: Mayfield, 197–216.

Lips, Hilary M. 1993. *Sex and Gender: An Introduction* (2nd ed.). Mountain View, Calif.: Mayfield.

Lipton, Eric, Christopher Drew, Scott Shane, and David Rohde. 2005. "Breakdowns Marked Path from Hurricane to Anarchy." Retrieved September 12, 2005. Available: www.nytimes.com/2005/09/11/national/nationalspecial/11response.html?pagewanted=1&ei=5070&en=b1231d972456e252&ex=1126670400.

Lochhead, Clarence, and Vivian Shalla. 1996. "Delivering the Goods: Income Distribution and the Precarious Middle Classes." *Perception*, 20(1). Canadian Council on Social Development. Retrieved June 27, 2002. Available: www.ccsd.ca/deliver.html.

Lock, Ineke, and Satoshi Ikeda. 2005. "Clothes Encounters: Consumption, Culture, Ecology, and Economy." In Debra Davidson and Kierstin Hatt (eds.), *Consuming Sustainability*. Halifax: Fernwood Publishing, 20–46.

Lofland, John, and Rodney Stark. 1965. "Becoming a World-Saver: A Theory of Conversion to a Deviant Perspective." *American Sociological Review*, 30(6): 862–875.

Lofland, John. 1993. "Collective Behavior: The Elementary Forms." In Russell L. Curtis, Jr., and Benigno E. Aguirre (eds.), *Collective Behavior and Social Movements*. Boston: Allyn & Bacon, 70–75.

Lorber, Judith. 1994. *Paradoxes of Gender*. New Haven, Conn.: Yale University Press.

Lorber, Judith. 1996. "Paradoxes of Gender." In Kurt Finsterbusch and Janet S. Schwartz (eds.), Sources: Notable Selections in Sociology (2nd ed.). Guilford, Connecticut: Dushkin Publishing Group, 206–215.

Loseke, Donileen. 1992. *The Battered Woman and Shelters: The Social Construction of Wife Abuse*. Albany: SUNY Press.

Loshin, Jacob. 2007. "Secrets Revealed: How Magicians Protect Intellectual Property Without Law." Unpublished paper. New Haven: Yale Law School.

Lott, Bernice. 1994. *Women's Lives: Themes and Variations in Gender Learning* (2nd ed.). Pacific Grove, Calif.: Brooks/Cole.

Low, Setha. 2003. *Behind the Gates: Life, Security, and the Pursuit of Happiness in Fortress America*. New York: Routledge.

Lowe, Graham S. 1999. "Labour Markets, Inequality, and the Future of Work." In Curtis, James, Edward Grabb, and Neil Guppy (eds.), *Social Inequality in Canada: Patterns, Problems, and Policies*. Scarborough, Ont.: Prentice Hall, 113–128.

Lummis, C. Douglas. 1992. "Equality." In Wolfgang Sachs (ed.), *The Development Dictionary*. Atlantic Highlands, N.J.: Zed Books, 38–52.

Lunau, Kate. 2009. "Youth Survey: Teens Lose Faith in Droves." *Macleans.ca*. Retrieved September 20, 2010. Available: www2.macleans.ca/2009/04/07/teens-lose-faith-in-droves.

Luxton, Meg. 1980. *More Than a Labour of Love*. Toronto: Women's Press.

Luxton, Meg. 1995. "Two Hands for the Clock: Changing Patterns of Gendered Division of Labour in the Home." In E.D. Nelson and B.W. Robinson (eds.), *Gender in the 1990s*. Scarborough, Ont.: Nelson Canada, 288–301.

Luxton, Meg. 1999. *Work, Family, and Community: Key Issues and Directions for Future Research*. Ottawa: Canadian Council on Social Development.

Lynn, Marion (ed.). 1996. *Voices: Essays on Canadian Families*. Scarborough, Ont.: Nelson Canada.

Lyons, John. 1998. "The Way We Live: Central Plains." *Winnipeg Free Press* (June 7): B3.

Maccoby, Eleanor E., and Carol Nagy Jacklin. 1987. "Gender Segregation in Childhood." *Advances in Child Development and Behavior*, 20: 239–287.

MacDonald, Kevin, and Ross D. Parke. 1986. "Parental-Child Physical Play: The Effects of Sex and Age of Children and Parents." *Sex Roles*, 15: 367–378.

MacDonald, Marci. 1996. "The New Spirituality." *Maclean's*, (October 10): 44–48.

Mack, Raymond W., and Calvin P. Bradford. 1979. *Transforming America: Patterns of Social Change* (2nd ed.). New York: Random House.

Mackie, Marlene. 1995. "Gender in the Family: Changing Patterns." In Nancy Mandell and Ann Duffy (eds.), *Canadian Families: Diversity, Conflict, and Change* (2nd ed.). Toronto: Harcourt Brace, 17–43.

MacKinnon, Catherine. 1982. "Feminism, Marxism, Method and the State: An Agenda for Theory." In N.O. Keohane et al. (eds.), *Feminist Theory: A Critique of Ideology*. Chicago: University of Chicago Press, 1–30.

Macmillan, Ross, Annette Nierobisz, and Sandy Welsh. 2000. "Experiencing the Streets: Harassment and Perceptions of Safety Among Women." *Journal of Research in Crime and Delinquency*, 37(3).

Maggio, Rosalie. 1988. The Non-Sexist Word Finder: A Dictionary of Gender-Free Usage. Boston: Beacon Press.

Malinowski, Bronislaw. 1922. Argonauts of the Western Pacific. New York: Dutton.

Malinowski, Bronislaw. 1964. "The Principle of Legitimacy: Parenthood, the Basis of Social Structure." In Rose Laub Coser (ed.), *The Family: Its Structure and Functions*. New York: St. Martin's Press (orig. pub. 1929).

Man, Guida. 1996. "The Experience of Middle-Class Women in Recent Hong Kong Chinese Immigrant Families in Canada." In Marion Lynn (ed.), *Voices: Essays on Canadian Families*. Toronto: Nelson Canada, 271–300.

Mandell, Nancy (ed.). 2001. *Feminist Issues: Race, Class, and Sexuality* (3rd ed.). Toronto, Ont.: Prentice-Hall.

Mandell, Nancy and Ann Duffy. 2005. *Canadian Families: Diversity, Conflict, and Change* (3rd ed.). Toronto: Oxford.

Mandell, Nancy, and Julianne Momirov. 1999. "Family Histories." In Nancy Mandell and Ann Duffy (eds.),

Canadian Families: Diversity, Conflict, and Change (2nd ed.). Toronto: Harcourt Brace, 17–43.

Mann, Patricia S. 1994. *Micro-Politics: Agency in Postfeminist Eva*. Minneapolis: University of Minnesota Press.

Mansfield, Alan, and Barbara McGinn. 1993. "Pumping Irony: The Muscular and the Feminine." In Sue Scott and David Morgan (eds.), *Body Matters: Essays on the Sociology of the Body*. London: Falmer Press, 49–58.

Mantell, David Mark. 1971. "The Potential for Violence in Germany." *Journal of Social Issues* 27 (4): 101–112.

Mao, Y., B.W. Moloughney, R. Semenciw, and H. Morrison. 1992. "Indian Reserve and Registered Indian Mortality in Canada." *Canadian Journal of Public Health*, 83: 350–353.

Marchak, Patricia. 1975. *Ideological Perspectives on Canadian Society*. Toronto: McGraw-Hill.

Marger, Martin N. 2000. *Race and Ethnic Relations: American and Global Perspectives* (5th ed.). Belmont, Calif.: Wadsworth.

Marion, Russ, and Mary Uhl-Bien. 2003. "Complexity Theory and Al-Qaeda: Examining Complex Leadership." *Emergence*, 5(1): 54–76.

Markoff, John. 2000. "Napster Debate About More Than Music." *The Globe and Mail* (May 9): B14.

Marquand, David. 2004. *Decline of the Public*. Cambridge, Mass.: Polity Press.

Marquardt, Elizabeth. 2006. "The Revolution in Parenthood: The Emerging Global Clash Between Adult Rights and Children's Needs." Institute for American Values. Retrieved September 21, 2010. Available: www.americanvalues.org/pdfs/parenthood.pdf.

Marquis, Christopher. 2001. "An American Report Finds the Taliban's Violation of Religious Rights 'Particularly Severe.'" *The New York Times* (October 27): B3.

Marshall, Gordon (ed.). 1994. *The Concise Oxford Dictionary of Sociology*. New York: Oxford University Press.

Marshall, Gordon (ed.). 1998. *The Concise Oxford Dictionary of Sociology* (2nd ed.). New York: Oxford University Press.

Marshall, Katherine. 1995. "Dual Earners: Who's Responsible for Housework?" In E.D. Nelson and B.W. Robinson, *Gender in the 1990s*. Scarborough, Ont.: Nelson Canada, 302–308.

Marshall, Katherine. 1998. "Stay at Home Dads." Statistics Canada, catalogue # 75-001-XPE *Perspectives*, Spring 1998. Retrieved May 12, 2005. Available: www.statcan.ca/english/studies/75-001/archive/1998/pear1998010001s1a01.pdf#search=%22stay%20at%20home%20dads%20%22.

Marshall, Katherine. 2006. "Converging Gender Roles." *Perspectives on Labour and Income,* 7 (7). Statistics Canada Cat. no. 750001-XIE. Retrieved September 21, 2010. Available: www.statcan.gc.ca/pub/75-001-x/75-001-x2006107-eng.pdf.

Marshall, Katherine. 2009a. "Stay-at-Home Fathers, 2007." Unpublished figures obtained from Statistics Canada, Labour and Household Surveys Analysis Division.

Marshall, Katherine. 2009b. "The Family Work Week." *Perspectives on Labour and Income* (April). Statistics Canada Cat. no. 75001-XIE.

Martin, Carol L. 1989. "Children's Use of Gender-Related Information in Making Social Judgments." *Developmental Psychology,* 25: 80–88.

Martineau, Harriet. 1962. *Society in America* (edited, abridged). Garden City, N.Y.: Doubleday (orig. pub. 1837).

Martinussen, John. 1997. *Society, State and Market: A Guide to Competing Theories of Development.* Halifax: Fernwood Books.

Marx, Karl and Friedrich Engels. 1967. *The Communist Manifesto.* New York: Pantheon (orig. pub. 1848).

Marx, Karl, and Friedrich Engels. 1970. *The German Ideology,* Part 1. C.J. Arthur (ed.). New York: International (orig. pub. 1845–1846).

Marx, Karl. 1967. *Capital: A Critique of Political Economy.* Friedrich Engels (ed.). New York: International Publishers (orig. pub. 1867).

Mawhinney, J. 2002. "Gay Unions Garner Public Support." *Toronto Star* (September 28): K4.

McCall, George J., and Jerry L. Simmons, 1978. *Identities and Interactions: An Explanation of Human Associations in Everyday Life.* New York: Free Press.

McCarthy, Terry. 2001. "Stirrings of a Woman's Movement." *Time* (Dec. 3): 46.

McCormick, Chris. 1995. *Constructing Danger: The Misrepresentation of Crime in the News.* Halifax: Fernwood Publishing.

McDaniel, S.A. 1994. *Family and Friends.* Ottawa: Statistics Canada.

McDonald, Marci. 1994. "The New Spirituality." *Maclean's* (October 10): 44–48.

McGeary, Johanna. 2001. "The Taliban Troubles." *Time* (October 1): 36–42.

McGee, Reece. 1975. *Points of Departure.* Hinsdale, Ill.: Dryden Press.

McGuire, Meredith B. 1992. *Religion: The Social Context* (2nd ed.). Belmont, Calif.: Wadsworth.

McGuire, Meredith B. 1997. *Religion: The Social Context* (4th ed.). Belmont, Calif.: Wadsworth.

McIntosh, Mary. 1978. "The State and the Oppression of Women." In Annette Kuhn and Ann Marie Wolpe (eds.), *Feminism and Materialism.* London: Routledge and Kegan Paul.

McIsaac, Elizabeth. 2003. "Immigrants in Canadian Cities: Census 2001—What Do the Data Tell Us." *Policy Options,* May: 58–63.

McKenzie, Roderick D. 1925. "The Ecological Approach to the Study of the Human Community." In Robert Park, Ernest Burgess, and Roderick D. McKenzie (eds.), *The City.* Chicago: University of Chicago Press.

McKeown, Larry, and Cathy Underhill. 2007. "Learning Online Factors Associated with Use of the Internet for Education Purposes." Education Matters: Insights on Education, Learning and Training in Canada. Cat. no. 81-004-XIE. Retrieved May 8, 2009. Available: www.statcan.gc.ca/pub/81-004-x/2007004/10375-eng.htm.

McNish, Jacquie and Sinclair Stewart. 2004. *Wrong Way: The Fall of Conrad Black.* Toronto: Viking Canada.

McPhail, Clark, and Ronald T. Wohlstein. 1983. "Individual and Collective Behavior within Gatherings, Demonstrations, and Riots." In Ralph H. Turner and James F. Short, Jr. (eds.), *Annual Review of Sociology,* 9. Palo Alto, Calif.: Annual Reviews, 579–600.

McPhail, Clark. 1991. *The Myth of the Maddening Crowd.* New York: Aldine de Gruyter.

McPherson, J. Miller, and Lynn Smith-Lovin. 1982. "Women and Weak Ties: Differences by Sex in the Size of Voluntary Organizations." *American Journal of Sociology,* 87(January): 883–904.

McPherson, J. Miller, and Lynn Smith-Lovin. 1986. "Sex Segregation in Voluntary Associations." *American Sociological Review,* 51(February): 61–79.

McQuillan, Kevin, and Marilyn Belle. 1999. "Who Does What? Gender and the Division of Labour in Canadian Households." In Curtis, James E., Edward Grabb, and Neil Guppy (eds.), *Social Inequality in Canada: Patterns, Problems, Policies* (3rd ed.). Scarborough, Ont.: Prentice Hall, 186–198.

McVey, Wayne W., and Warren Kalbach. 1995. *Canadian Population.* Scarborough, Ont.: Nelson Canada.

Mead, George Herbert. 1934. *Mind, Self, and Society.* Chicago: University of Chicago Press.

Melchers, Ronald. 2003. "Do Toronto Police Engage in Racial Profiling?" *Canadian Journal of Criminology and Criminal Justice,* 45 (July): 347–366.

Merkle, Erich R., and Rhonda A. Richardson. 2000. "Digital Dating and Virtual Relating: Conceptualizing Computer-Mediated Romantic Relationships." *Family Relations,* 49(2) (April): 187–211.

Merton, Robert King. 1938. "Social Structure and Anomie." *American Sociological Review,* 3(6): 672–682.

Merton, Robert King. 1968. *Social Theory and Social Structure* (enlarged ed.). New York: Free Press.

Messner, Michael A. 2000. "Barbie Girls versus Sea Monsters: Children Constructing Gender." In Margaret L. Andersen (ed.), *Thinking About Women: Sociological Perspectives on Sex and Gender* (7th ed.). Boston: Pearson, 765–784.

Miall, Charlene. 1986. "The Stigma of Involuntary Childlessness." *Social Problems,* 33(4): 268–282.

Michael, Robert T., John H. Gagnon, Edward O. Laumann, and Gina Kolata. 1994. *Sex in America.* Boston: Little, Brown.

Michelson, William H. 1994. "Cities and Urbanization." In Lorne Tepperman, James Curtis, and R.J. Richardson (eds.), *The Social World* (3rd ed.). Toronto: McGraw-Hill, 672–709.

Mick, Hayley, "At the Science Fair, Girls Dominate the Class." *The Globe and Mail* (May 15, 2009). Available: www.scwist.ca/index.php/main/entry/at-the-science-fair-girls-dominate-the-class.

Mihorean, Steve, and Stan Lipinski. 1992. "International Incarceration Patterns, 1980–1990." *Juristat,* 12(3). Ottawa: Statistics Canada.

Milan, A. 2003. "Would You Live Common-Law?" *Canadian Social Trends,* 70: 2–6.

Milgram, Stanley. 1963. "Behavioral Study of Obedience." *Journal of Abnormal and Social Psychology,* 67: 371–378.

Milgram, Stanley. 1965. "Some Conditions of Obedience and Disobedience to Authority." *Human Relations* 18: 57–76.

Milgram, Stanley. 1967. "The Small-World Problem." *Psychology Today,* 2: 60–67.

Milgram, Stanley. 1974. *Obedience to Authority.* New York: Harper & Row.

Miller, Grant. 2008. "Women's Suffrage, Political Responsiveness, and Child Survival in American History." *The Quarterly Journal of Economics* 123 (3): 1287–1327.

Miller, James. 2003. "Out Family Values." In Marion Lynn (ed.). *Voices: Essays on Canadian Families* (2nd ed.). Scarborough, Ont.: Nelson Canada, 103–130.

Mills, C. Wright. 1956. *White Collar.* New York: Oxford University Press.

Mills, C. Wright. 1959a. *The Power Elite.* Fair Lawn. N.J.: Oxford University Press.

Mills, C. Wright. 1959b. *The Sociological Imagination.* London: Oxford University Press.

Minister of Indian Affairs and Northern Development. 2000. *Comparison of Social Conditions, 1991 and 1996: Registered Indians, Registered Indians Living on Reserve and the Total Population in Canada.* Ottawa: Minister of Indian Affairs and Northern Development.

Misztal, Barbara A. 1993. "Understanding Political Change in Eastern Europe: A Sociological Perspective." *Sociology* 27 (3): 451–471.

Mitchell, Alana. 1999. "Home Schooling Goes AWOL." *The Globe and Mail* (February 2): A1, A7.

Money, John, and Anke A. Ehrhardt. 1972. *Man and Woman, Boy and Girl.* Baltimore: Johns Hopkins University Press.

Mooney, Linda A., David Knox, Caroline Schacht, and Adie Nelson. 2001. *Understanding Social Problems.* Scarborough, Ont.: Nelson.

Moore, Patricia, with C.P. Conn. 1985. *Disguised.* Waco, Tex.: Word Books.

Moore, Wilbert E. 1968. "Occupational Socialization." In David A. Goslin (ed.), *Handbook on Socialization Theory and Research.* Chicago: Rand McNally, 861–883.

Morris, David B. 1998. *Illness and Culture in the Postmodern Age.* Berkeley: University of California Press.

Morrissette, Rene, and Xuelin Zhang. 2006. "Revisiting Wealth Inequality." *Perspectives on Labour and Income* (December). Statistics Canada Cat. no. 75-001-XIE. Retrieved September 21, 2010. Available: www.statcan.gc.ca/pub/75-001-x/11206/9543-eng.pdf.

Morselli, Henry. 1975. *Suicide: An Essay on Comparative Moral Statistics.* New York: Arno Press (orig. pub. 1881).

Moscovitch, Arlene. 1998. "Electronic Media and the Family." *Contemporary Family Trends.* Ottawa: Vanier Institute of the Family. Retrieved November 20, 2002. Available: www.vifamily.ca/_cft/media/media.htm.

Moscovitch, Arlene. 2007. *Good Servant, Bad Master? Electronic Media and the Family.* Ottawa: Vanier Institute of the Family. Retrieved September 21, 2010. Available: www.vifamily.ca/library/cft/media07.html.

Murdock, George P. 1945. "The Common Denominator of Cultures." In Ralph Linton (ed.), *The Science of Man in the World Crisis.* New York: Columbia University Press, 123–142.

Murphy, Christopher and Curtis Clarke. 2005. "Policing Communities and Communities of Policing: A Comparative Study of Policing and Security in Two Canadian Communities." In Dennis Cooley (ed.), *Re-Imagining Policing in Canada.* Toronto: University of Toronto Press, 209–259.

Murphy, Emily F. 1922. *The Black Candle.* Toronto: Thomas Allan.

Murphy, Robert E., Jessica Scheer, Yolanda Murphy, and Richard Mack. 1988. "Physical Disability and Social Liminality: A Study in Rituals of Adversity." *Social Science and Medicine,* 26: 235–242.

Nader, George A. 1976. *Cities of Canada, Volume 2: Profiles of Fifteen Metropolitan Centres*. Toronto: Macmillan of Canada.

Nagler, Mark. 1997. *Yes You Can: A Guide for Parents of Children with Disabilities*. Toronto: Stoddart.

Naim, Moises. 2003. "The Five Wars of Globalization." *Foreign Policy*, 134: 28–37.

Naiman, Joanne. 2000. *How Societies Work: Class, Power, and Change in a Canadian Context*. Concord, Ont.: Irwin.

Naiman, Joanne, 2008. *How Societies Work: Class, Power, and Change in a Canadian Context* (4th ed.). Halifax: Fernwood.

Nason-Clark, Nancy. 1993. "Gender Relations in Contemporary Christian Organizations." In W.E. Hewitt (ed.), *The Sociology of Religion: A Canadian Focus*. Toronto: Butterworths, 215–234.

National Anti-Poverty Organization (NAPO). 2005. "Towards a National Poverty Elimination Strategy." Retrieved September 12, 2005. Available: www.napo-nap.ca/en/issues/NAPO%202005%20finance%20committee%20.

National Council of Welfare. 2002. *Poverty Profile 1999*. Ottawa: National Council of Welfare.

National Longitudinal Survey of Children and Youth, 1994–1995. Statistics Canada Catalogue no. 89F0078XIE.

National Media Archive. 1997. "TV Coverage Down: Murder Rate Up Slightly." *On Balance* (10)7. Vancouver: The Fraser Institute.

National Media Archive. 1998. "Local TV News in Canada." *On Balance*. Volume 11 (February). The Fraser Institute.

National Post. 2003. "Quality of Life and Quality of Service," A8.

Navarrette, Ruben, Jr. 1997. "A Darker Shade of Crimson." In Diana Kendall (ed.), *Race, Class, and Gender in a Diverse Society*. Boston, Mass.: Allyn & Bacon, 274–279.

Neal, Lainie (ed.). 2004. *Voices of Survivors*. Winnipeg: North End Women's Centre.

Nelson, Adie. 2006. *Gender in Canada* (3rd ed.). Toronto: Pearson Prentice Hall.

Nelson, Margaret K., and Joan Smith. 1999. *Working Hard and Making Do: Surviving in Small Town America*. Berkeley: University of California Press.

Nemeth, Mary, Noral Underwood, and John Howse. 1993. "God Is Alive." *Maclean's* (April): 32–36.

Nett, Emily M. 1993. *Canadian Families: Past and Present* (2nd ed.). Toronto: Butterworths.

Nettler, Gwynn. 1984. *Explaining Crime* (3rd ed.). Toronto: McGraw-Hill.

Neuman, W.L., Bruce Wirgand, and J.A. Winterdyk. 2004. *Criminal Justice Research Methods: Qualitative and Quantitative Approaches*. Toronto: Pearson.

Nevitte, Neil. 2000. "Value Change and Reorientations in Citizen-State Relations." *Canadian Public Policy*, XXVI Supplement: 73–94.

New York Times. 2005. "The Missing Condoms." NYTimes.com. Retrieved September 4, 2005. Available: www.nytimes.com/2005/09/04/opinion/04sun2.html.

Newman, Katherine S. 1988. *Falling from Grace: The Experience of Downward Mobility in the American Middle Class*. New York: Free Press.

Newman, Katherine S. 1993. *Declining Fortunes: The Withering of the American Dream*. New York: Basic Books.

Newman, Katherine S. 1999. *No Shame in My Game: The Working Poor in the Inner City*. New York: Knopf and the Russell Sage Foundation.

Nielsen, Joyce McCarl. 1990. *Sex and Gender in Society: Perspectives on Stratification* (2nd ed.). Prospects Heights, Ill.: Waveland Press.

Noel, Donald L. 1972. *The Origins of American Slavery and Racism*. Columbus, OH: Merrill.

Nolen, Stephanie. 2007. "Swaziland: The Economics of an Epidemic." *The Globe and Mail* (December 22): A15.

Norland, J.A. 1994. *Profile of Canada's Seniors*. Catalogue #96-312E. Scarborough, Ont.: Statistics Canada and Prentice Hall.

Norris, Mary Jane. 1998. "Canada's Aboriginal Languages." *Canadian Social Trends* (Winter): 8–16.

Norris, Pippa, and Ronald Inglehart. 2004. *Sacred and Secular: Religion and Politics Worldwide*. Cambridge: Cambridge University Press.

Norris, Sonya. 2001. "Reproductive Infertility: Prevalence, Causes, Trends and Treatments." *In Brief*. PRB-0032-E. Parliamentary Research Branch, Government of Canada. Retrieved September 21, 2010. Available: http://dsp-psd.pwgsc.gc.ca/Collection-R/LoPBdP/EB-e/prb0032-e.pdf.

Northcott, Herbert C. 1992. *Aging in Alberta, Rhetoric and Reality*. Calgary: Detselig Enterprises.

Northcott, Herbert C. 1994. "Alternative Health Care in Canada." In B. Singh Bolaria and Harley D. Dickinson (eds.), *Health, Illness, and Health Care in Canada*. Toronto: Harcourt Brace, 487–503.

Novak, Mark.1995. "Successful Aging." In *Aging and Society: A Canadian Reader*. Scarborough, Ont.: Nelson Canada.

NOW (National Organization for Women). 2002. "Stop the Abuse of Women and Girls in Afghanistan!" Retrieved July 14, 2002. Available: www.nowfoundation.org/_global/taliban.html.

Nussbaum, Emily. 2003. "Nature vs. Nurture." Retrieved October 6, 2003. Available: http://btobsearch.barnesandnoble.com/booksearch.

O'Brien, Carol-Anne, and Lorna Weir. 1995. "Lesbians and Gay Men Inside and Outside Families." In Nancy Mandell and Ann Duffy (eds.), *Canadian Families*. Toronto: Harcourt Brace and Company, 111–139.

O'Connell, Helen. 1994. *Women and the Family*. Prepared for the UN-NGO Group on Women and Development. Atlantic Highlands, N.J.: Zed Books.

O'Reilly-Fleming, Thomas. 1993. *Down and Out in Canada: Homeless Canadians*. Toronto: Canadian Scholars' Press.

Oakes, Jeannie. 1985. *Keeping Track: How High Schools Structure Inequality*. New Haven, Conn.: Yale University Press.

OECD (Organisation for Economic Co-operation and Development). 2004. "Trends in International Migration Reflect Increasing Labour-Related Immigration and Persistent Integration Problems." Paris: OECD. Retrieved September 20, 2010. Available: www.oecd.org/document/50/0,2340,en_2649_201185_24968882_1_1_1_1,00.html

OECD. 2010. *OECD Health Data, 2010*. Paris: OECD. Retrieved September 20, 2010. Available: www.oecd.org/document/30/0,3343,en_2649_34631_12968734_1_1_1_1,00.html.

Ogburn, William F. 1966. *Social Change with Respect to Culture and Original Nature*. New York: Dell (orig. pub. 1922).

Ogrodnik, Lucie. 2007. *Family Violence in Canada: A Statistical Profile, 2008*. Statistics Canada Cat. no. 85-224-XIE. Retrieved May 20, 2009. Available: http://dsp-psd.pwgsc.gc.ca/collection_2008/statcan/85-224-X/85-224-IE2008000.pdf.

Oliver, Michael. 1990. *The Politics of Disablement: A Sociological Approach*. New York: St. Martin's Press.

Ontario Royal Commission on Learning. 1994. *For the Love of Learning*. Toronto: Ontario Royal Commission on Learning.

Opinion Canada. 2004. "Fewer Canadians Believe Religious Practice is Important." *Facts and Figures*, Volume 6, Number 27, September 16.

Ortner, Sherry B., and Harriet Whitehead (eds.). 1981. *Sexual Meanings: The Cultural Construction of Gender and Sexuality*. Cambridge, Mass.: Cambridge University Press.

Osborne, Ken. 1999. *Education: A Guide to the Canadian School Debate— Or, Who Wants What and Why?* Toronto: Penguin Books.

Overall, Christine. 1991. "Reproductive Technology and the Future of the Family." In Jean E. Veevers (ed.), *Continuity and Change in Marriage and the Family*. Toronto: Holt, Rinehart and Winston, 466–477.

Owen, Bruce. 1996. "Harassment Ends in Firings." *Winnipeg Free Press* (March 23).

Oxfam. 2001. Rigged Trade and Not Much Aid: How Rich Countries Help to Keep the Least Developed Countries Poor. London: Oxfam.

Page, Charles H. 1946. "Bureaucracy's Other Face." *Social Forces*, 25 (October): 89–94.

Pammett, Jon H. 1993. "Tracking the Votes." In Alan Frizell et al. (eds.), *The Canadian General Election of 1993*. Ottawa: Carleton University Press, 6.

Panitch, Leo, and Donald Swartz. 1993. *Assaults on Trade Union Freedoms* (2nd ed.). Toronto: Garamond.

Parenti, Michael. 1996. *Democracy for the Few* (5th ed.). New York: St. Martin's.

Park, Robert E. 1915. "The City: Suggestions for the Investigation of Human Behavior in the City." *American Journal of Sociology*, 20: 577–612.

Park, Robert E. 1928. "Human Migration and the Marginal Man." *American Journal of Sociology*, 33.

Park, Robert E. 1936. "Human Ecology." *American Journal of Sociology*, 42: 1–15.

Park, Robert E., and Ernest W. Burgess. 1921. *Human Ecology*. Chicago: University of Chicago Press.

Parker, Robert Nash. 1995. "Violent Crime." In Joseph F. Sheley, *Criminology: A Contemporary Handbook* (2nd ed.). Belmont, Calif.: Wadsworth, 169–185.

Parrish, Dee Anna. 1990. *Abused: A Guide to Recovery for Adult Survivors of Emotional/Physical Child Abuse*. Barrytown, N.Y.: Station Hill Press.

Parsons, Lee. 2003. "Food Bank Use Continues to Rise." Retrieved August 12, 2003. Available: www.wsws. org/articles/2003/oct2003/food-o22. shtml.

Parsons, Talcott. 1951. *The Social System*. Glencoe, Ill.: Free Press.

Parsons, Talcott. 1955. "The American Family: Its Relations to Personality and to the Social Structure." In Talcott Parsons and Robert F. Bales (eds.), *Family, Socialization and Interaction Process*. Glencoe, Ill.: Free Press, 3–33.

Passell, Peter. 1994. "'Bell Curve' Critics Say Early I.Q. Isn't Destiny." *The New York Times* (November 9): B10.

PBS. 1992. "Sex, Power, and the Workplace."

PBS. 2001. "Crossing Borders: How Terrorists Use Fake Passports, Visas, and Other Identity Documents." Retrieved July 12, 2005. Available: www.pbs.org/wgbh/pages/frontline/shows/trail/etc/fake.html.

PBS. 2005. "The Meaning of Food: Gonna Eat That." Retrieved September 30, 2010. Available: www.pbs.org/opb/meaningoffood/food_and_culture/gonna_eat_that.

Pearce, Diana. 1978. "The Feminization of Poverty: Women, Work, and Welfare." *Urban and Social Change Review*, 11(1/2): 28–36.

Pearson, Judy C. 1985. *Gender and Communication*. Dubuque, Iowa: Brown.

Peikoff, Tannis. 2000. Anglican Missionaries and Governing the Self: An Encounter with Aboriginal Peoples in Western Canada. Unpublished Ph.D. Dissertation, University of Manitoba.

Peritz, Ingrid. 2002. "More Quebeckers Skip the Wedding, Census Discovers." *The Globe and Mail* (October 23): A7. Retrieved May 16, 2006. Available: www.theglobeandmail.com/special/census/2001/stories/families/20021023-pe-quebeckers.html.

Perrow, Charles. 1986. *Complex Organizations: A Critical Essay* (3rd ed.). New York: Random House.

Perry, David C., and Alfred J. Watkins (eds.). 1977. *The Rise of the Sunbelt Cities*. Beverly Hills, Calif.: Sage.

Peter, Karl A. 1987. *The Dynamics of Hutterite Society*. Edmonton, Alta.: University of Alberta Press.

Peters, John F. 1985. "Adolescents as Socialization Agents to Parents." *Adolescence*, 20 (Winter): 921–933.

Petersen, John L. 1994. *The Road to 2015: Profiles of the Future*. Corte Madera, Calif.: Waite Group Press.

Phoenix, A. and A. Woollett. 1991. "Motherhood, Social Construction, Politics, and Psychology." In A. Pheonix, A Woollett, and E. Lloyd (eds.), *Motherhood: Meanings, Practices and Ideologies*. London: Sage.

Piaget, Jean. 1954. *The Construction of Reality in the Child*. Trans. Margaret Cook. New York: Basic Books.

Picot, Garnett, and John Myles. 2004. "Income Inequality and Low Income in Canada." *Horizons* (December) 7(2): 9–18.

Pietilä, Hilkka, and Jeanne Vickers. 1994. *Making Women Matter: The Role of the United Nations*. Atlantic Highlands, N.J.: Zed Books.

Pillard, Richard C., and James D. Weinrich. 1986. "Evidence of Familial Nature of Male Homosexuality." *Archives of General Psychiatry*, 43(8): 800–812.

Pinderhughes, Dianne M. 1986. "Political Choices: A Realignment in Partisanship Among Black Voters?" In James D. Williams (ed.), *The State of Black America 1986*. New York: National Urban League, 85–113.

Pines, Maya. 1981. "The Civilizing of Genie." *Psychology Today*, 15 (September): 28–29, 31–32, 34.

Plante, Johanne, and David Beattie. 2004. Connectivity and ICT Integration in Canadian Elementary and Secondary Schools: First Results from the Information *and Communications Technologies in Schools Survey 2003–2004*. Culture, Tourism and the Centre for Education Statistics—Research Papers. Statistics Canada Cat. no. 81-595-MIE20040017.

Pohl, Rudy. 2002. *Poverty in Canada*. Ottawa: Ottawa Innercity Ministries. Retrieved June 25, 2002. Available: www.ottawainnercityministries.ca/homepage/homelessness2InCanada_Part2.htm.

Polakow, Valerie. 1993. *Lives on the Edge: Single Mothers and Their Children in the Other America*. Chicago: University of Chicago Press.

Policies and Programs in Canada. Halifax: Fernwood.

Pollack, Gladys. 2001. "Who are Canada's Homeless." *Reader's Digest* (January). Retrieved April 20, 2006. Available: www.readersdigest.ca/mag/2001/01/homeless.html.

Ponting, J.R. 1997. *First Nations in Canada: Perspectives on Opportunity, Empowerment and Self-Determination*. Toronto: McGraw-Hill Ryerson.

Population: Immigration, Birthplace, and Birthplace of Parents, Citizenship, Ethnic Origin, Visible Minorities, and Aboriginal Peoples." *The Daily* (January 21). Retrieved February 21, 2003. Available: www.statcan.ca/Daily/English/030121/2030121a.thm.

Porter, J., M. Porter, and B. Blishen. 1982. *Stations and Callings: Making It Through the School System*. Toronto: Methuen.

Porter, John. 1965. *The Vertical Mosaic: An Analysis of Social Class and Power in Canada*. Toronto: University of Toronto Press.

Posterski, Donald C. and Irwin Barker. 1993. *Where's a Good Church?* Winfield, B.C.: Wood Lake Books.

Prensky, Marc. 2001. "Digital Natives: Digital Immigrants." *On the Horizon* 9 (October). Retrieved May 11, 2009. Available: www.marcprensky.com/writing/Prensky%20-%20Digital%20Natives,%20Digital%20Immigrants%20-%20Part1.pdf.

President's Commission. 1986. *Report of the President's Commission on the Space Shuttle Challenger Accident*. Washington: U.S. Government Printing Office.

Prochner, Larry, and Nina Howe. 2000. *Early Childhood Education in Canada: Past, Present, and Future*. Vancouver: University of British Columbia Press.

Pryor, John and Kathleen McKinney (eds.). 1991. "Sexual Harassment" *Basic and Applied Social Psychology*, 17 (4): 4.

Pryor, John. 1995. "Research Advances in Sexual Harassment: Introduction and Overview." *Basic and Applied Social Psychology* 17: 421–424.

Public Health Agency of Canada. 2004. *Epi Update 2004*. Ottawa: Public Health Agency of Canada. Retrieved July 20, 2005. Available: www.phac-aspc.gc.ca/publicat/epiu-aepi/epi_update_may_04/10_e.html.

Public Health Agency of Canada. 2007. *HIV/AIDS Epi Update*. Ottawa: Public Health Agency of Canada. Retrieved

September 20, 2010. Available: www.phac-aspc.gc.ca/aids-sida/publication/epi/pdf/epi2007_e.pdf.

Public Health Agency of Canada. 2009. *Summary: Estimates of HIV Prevalence and Incidence in Canada, 2008*. Ottawa: Public Health Agency of Canada. Retrieved: September 20, 2010. Available: www.phac-aspc.gc.ca/aids-sida/publication/survreport/estimat08-eng.php.

Queen, Stuart A., and David B. Carpenter. 1953. *The American City*. New York: McGraw-Hill.

Quigley, Tim. 1994. "Some Issues in the Sentencing of Aboriginal Offenders." Cited in Royal Commission on Aboriginal Peoples Report, 1996, *Bridging the Cultural Divide*. Ottawa: Minister of Supply and Services Canada.

Quinney, Richard. 1974. *Critique of the Legal Order*. Boston: Little, Brown.

Quinney, Richard. 1979. *Class, State, and Crime*. New York: McKay.

Quinney, Richard. 1980. *Class, State, and Crime* (2nd ed.). New York: Longman.

Rabinowitz, Fredric E., and Sam V. Cochran. 1994. *Man Alive: A Primer of Men's Issues*. Pacific Grove, Calif.: Brooks/Cole.

Radcliffe-Brown, A.R. 1952. *Structure and Function in Primitive Society*. New York: Free Press.

Rankin, Jim and Betsy Powell. 2008. "The Criminals Among Us." *Toronto Star* (July 21). Retrieved September 20, 2010. Available: www.thestar.com/specialSections/crime/article/460764

Rankin, Jim, Jennifer Quinn, Michelle Shephard, John Duncanson, Scott Simmie. 2002. "Police Target Black Drivers." *Toronto Star*. 20 October.

Raphael, Dennis. 2001. *Inequality Is Bad for Our Hearts: Why Low Income and Social Exclusion are Major Causes of Heart Disease in Canada*. Toronto: North York Heart Health Network.

Razack, Sherene H., 1998. *Looking White People in the Eye*. University of Toronto Press: Toronto.

Reckless, Walter C. 1967. *The Crime Problem*. New York: Meredith.

Reed, Christopher. 1998. "No Fingerprints Puts Man Under Society's Thumb." *The Globe and Mail* (April 23): A11.

Rees, T. 1991. "Racial Discrimination and Employment Agencies." *Currents: Readings in Race Relations*, 7(2): 16–19.

Reich, Robert. 1993. "Why the Rich Are Getting Richer and the Poor Poorer." In Paul J. Baker, Louis E. Anderson, and Dean S. Dorn (eds.), *Social Problems: A Critical Thinking Approach* (2nd ed.). Belmont, Calif.: Wadsworth, 145–149.

Reiman, Jeffrey H. 1979. *The Rich Get Richer and the Poor Get Prison*. New York: Wiley.

Reiman, Jeffrey. 1984. *The Rich Get Richer and the Poor Get Prison* (2nd ed.). New York: Wiley.

Reinharz, Shulamit. 1992. *Feminist Methods in Social Research*. New York: Oxford University Press.

Reinisch, June. 1990. *The Kinsey Institute New Report on Sex: What You Must Know to Be Sexually Literate*. New York: St. Martin's Press.

Reitz, Jeffery G., and Raymond Breton. 1994. *The Illusion of Difference: Realities of Ethnicity in Canada and the United States*. Toronto: C.D. Howe Institute.

Renzetti, Claire M., and Daniel J. Curran. 1992. *Women, Men, and Society* (2nd ed.). Boston: Allyn and Bacon.

Renzetti, Claire M., and Daniel J. Curran. 1995. *Women, Men, and Society* (3rd ed.). Boston: Allyn and Bacon.

Reskin, Barbara F., and Irene Padavic. 1994. *Women and Men at Work*. Thousand Oaks, Calif.: Pine Forge Press.

Reskin, Barbara F., and Irene Padavic. 2002. *Women and Men at Work* (2nd ed.).

Ressler, A. 1998. "'A Body to Die For': Eating Disorders and Body-Image Distortion in Women." *International Journal of Fertility and Women's Medicine*, 43: 133–138.

Richard, K. Peter. 1997. *The Westray Story: A Predictable Path to Disaster*, Executive Summary. Halifax: Government of Nova Scotia.

Richardson, Laurel. 1993. "Inequalities of Power, Property, and Prestige." In Virginia Cyrus (ed.), *Experiencing Race, Class, and Gender in the United States*. Mountain View, Calif.: Mayfield, 229–236.

Richer, Stephen. 1988. "Equality to Benefit from Schooling: The Issue of Educational Opportunity." In D. Forcese and S. Richer (eds.), *Social Issues: Sociological Views of Canada*. Toronto: Prentice Hall, 262–286.

Rigler, David. 1993. "Letters: A Psychologist Portrayed in a Book About an Abused Child Speaks Out for the First Time in 22 Years." *The New York Times Book Review* (June 13): 35.

Risman, Barbara J. 1987. "Intimate Relationships from a Microstructural Perspective: Men Who Mother." *Gender & Society*, 1: 6–32.

Ritzer, George. 1996. *Sociological Theory* (4th ed.). New York: McGraw-Hill.

Ritzer, George. 1997. *Postmodern Society Theory*. New York: McGraw-Hill.

Ritzer, George. 1998. *The McDonaldization Thesis*. London: Sage.

Ritzer, George. 2000. *Modern Sociological Theory* (5th ed.). New York: McGraw-Hill.

Ritzer, George. 2004. *The McDonaldization of Society: Revised New Century Edition*. Thousand Oaks: Pine Forge Press.

Roberts, Keith A. 1995. *Religion in Sociological Perspective*. Belmont, Calif.: Wadsworth.

Roberts, Lance W., and Rodney A. Clifton. 1999. "Multiculturalism in Canada: A Sociological Perspective." In Peter S. Li (ed.), *Race and Ethnic Relations in Canada* (2nd ed.). Toronto: Oxford University Press.

Robertshaw, Corinne. 2003. "Strike Down S.43." *Law Times* (June 16). Retrieved June 16, 2005. Available: www.repeal43.org/constitution.html#sccchearing.

Robertson, Grant. 2007. "Religious Channel on Carpet." *The Globe and Mail* (February 12): B1.

Robertson, Ian. 1977. *Sociology*. New York: Worth Publishers.

Robertson, Roland. 1992. *Globalization: Social Theory and Global Culture*. Newbury Park, Calif.: Sage.

Rodgers, Kain, and Rebecca Kong. 1996. "Crimes Against Women and Children in the Family." In Leslie Kennedy and Vincent Sacco (eds.), *Crime Counts: A Criminal Event Analysis*. Scarborough, Ont.: Nelson Canada, 115–132.

Rollins, Judith. 1985. *Between Women: Domestics and Their Employers*. Philadelphia: Temple University Press.

Romaniuc, Anatole. 1994. "Fertility in Canada: Retrospective and Prospective." In Frank Trovato and Carl F. Grindstaff (eds.), *Perspectives on Canada's Population*. Toronto: Oxford University Press, 214–229.

Roos, Noralou, Evelyn Forget, and Gerard Beirne. 2004. "Health Care User Fees: Clinic Charges are Wrong Way to Go." *Winnipeg Free Press* (January 20): A11.

Rosenfeld, Alvin, and Nicole Wise. 2000. *The Over-Scheduled Child: Avoiding the Hyper-Parenting Trap*. New York: St. Martin's Griffin.

Rosenhan, D.L. 1973. "On Being Sane in Insane Places." *Science*, 179 (January): 250–58.

Rosenthal, Naomi, Meryl Fingrutd, Michele Ethier, Roberta Karant, and David McDonald. 1985. "Social Movements and Network Analysis: A Case Study of Nineteenth-Century Women's Reform in New York State." *American Journal of Sociology*, 90: 1022–1054.

Rosenthal, Robert. 1969. "Empirical versus Degreed Validation of Clocks and Tests." *American Educational Research Journal*, 6 (November): 689–691.

Rosenthal, Robert, and Lenore Jacobson. 1968. *Pygmalion in the Classroom: Teacher Expectation and Pupil's Intellectual Development*. New York: Holt, Rinehart, and Winston.

Rosnow, Ralph L., and Gary Alan Fine. 1976. *Rumor and Gossip: The Social Psychology of Hearsay*. New York: Elsevier.

Ross, David P., and Paul Roberts. 1997. "Does Family Income Affect the Healthy Development of

Children?" *Perception*, (21)1: 1–5. Ottawa: Canadian Council on Social Development.

Ross, David P., E. Richard Shillington, and Clarence Lochhead. 1994. *The Canadian Fact Book on Poverty*. Ottawa: Canadian Council on Social Development.

Ross, David P., Katherine Scott, and Peter Smith. 2000. *The Canadian Fact Book on Poverty, 2000*. Ottawa: Canadian Council on Social Development.

Ross, Rupert. 1996. *Returning to the Teachings: Exploring Aboriginal Justice*. Toronto: Penguin Books.

Rossi, Alice S. 1980. "Life-Span Theories and Women's Lives." *Signs* 6 (1): 4–32.

Rossi, Peter H. 1989. *Down and Out in America: The Origins of Homelessness*. Chicago: University of Chicago Press.

Rossides, Daniel W. 1986. *The American Class System: An Introduction to Social Stratification*. Boston: Houghton Mifflin.

Rostow, Walt W. 1971. *The Stages of Economic Growth: A Non-Communist Manifesto* (2nd ed.). Cambridge, Mass: Cambridge University Press (orig. pub. 1960).

Rostow, Walt W. 1978. *The World Economy: History and Prospect*. Austin, Tex.: University of Texas Press.

Rothman, Robert A. 2001. *Inequality and Stratification: Class, Color, and Gender* (4th ed.). Upper Saddle River, N.J.: Prentice-Hall.

Royal Commission on Aboriginal Peoples. 1995. *Choosing Life: Special Report on Suicide Among Aboriginal Peoples*. Ottawa: Canada Communications Group Publishing.

Royal Commission on Learning. 1994. *For the Love of Learning: Report of the Royal Commission on Learning, Vol. IV*. Toronto: Queen's Printer.

Rubin, Lillian B. 1994. *Families on the Fault Line*. New York: HarperCollins.

Ruthven, Malise. 2004. *Fundamentalism: The Search for Meaning*. Oxford: Oxford University Press.

Rutstein, Nathan. 1993. *Healing in America*. Springfield, Mass.: Whitcomb.

Rymer, Russ. 1993. *Genie: An Abused Child's Flight from Silence*. New York: HarperCollins.

Sadker, Myra and David Sadker. 1994. *Failing at Fairness: How America's Schools Cheat Girls*. New York: Scribner.

Safilios-Rothschild, Constantina. 1969. "Family Sociology or Wives' Family Sociology? A Cross-Cultural Examination of Decision-Making." *Journal of Marriage and the Family*, 31(2): 290–301.

Samovar, Larry A., and Richard E. Porter. 1991a. *Communication Between Cultures*. Belmont, Calif.: Wadsworth.

Sapir, Edward. 1961. *Culture, Language and Personality*. Berkeley: University of California Press.

Sarick, Lila. 1999. "Record Numbers Turn to Food Banks to Cope, National Survey Shows." *The Globe and Mail* (September 29): A3.

Satzewich, V., and N. Liodakis. 2007. *Race and Ethnicity in Canada*. Toronto: Oxford University Press.

Satzewich, Vic (ed.). 1998. *Racism and Social Inequality in Canada: Concepts, Controversies and Strategies for Resistance*. Toronto: Thompson Educational Publishing.

Saulnier, Beth. 1998. "Small World." *Cornell Magazine Online*. Available: http://cornell-magazine.cornell.edu/_Archive/JulyAugust98/JulyWorld.html.

Saunders, Eileen. 1999. "Theoretical Approaches to the Study of Women." In Curtis, James, Edward Grabb, and Neil Guppy (eds.), *Social Inequality in Canada: Patterns and Policies*. Scarborough: Prentice Hall, 168–185.

Sauvé, Roger. 2002a. *The Current State of Canadian Family Finances, 2001 Report*. Ottawa: Vanier Institute of the Family. Retrieved June 13, 2002. Available: www.vifamily.ca/cft/state01/_state01.htm.

Sauvé, Roger. 2002b. *The Dreams and the Reality: Assets, Debts and Net Worth of Canadian Households*. Vanier Institute of the Family. Available: www.vifamily.ca/library/wealth/wealth.html.

Sauvé, Roger. 2003a. "Rich Canadians, Poor Canadians, and Everyone in Between." *Transition Magazine*, 32(4).

Sauvé, Roger. 2003b. "The Current State of Family Finances—2003 Report." People Patterns Consulting. Retrieved August 12, 2005. Available www.vifamily.ca/library/cft/state03.html#3_million.

Sauvé, Roger. 2008. "The Current State of Canadian Family Finances, 2007 Report." Ottawa: Vanier Institute for the Family. Retrieved June 17, 2009. Available: www.vifamily.ca/library/cft/famfi n07.pdf.

Schaefer, Richard T. 1993. *Racial and Ethnic Groups*. New York: HarperCollins.

Schaefer, Richard T. 1995. *Race and Ethnicity in the United States*. New York: HarperCollins.

Schellenberg, G., and David P. Ross. 1997. *The Changing Nature of Part-Time Work*. Ottawa: The Canadian Council on Social Development.

Schemo, Diana Jean. 1996. "Indians in Brazil, Estranged from Their Land, Suffer an Epidemic of Suicide." *The New York Times* (August 25): 7.

Schlesinger, Ben. 1998. Strengths in Families: Accentuating the Positive Contemporary Family Trends. Ottawa: Vanier Institute of the Family.

Schmidt, Sara. 2008. "Brain Cancer Linked to Youngsters Using Cell Phone." Canwest News Service. Retrieved August 20, 2009. Available: www.canada.com/story_print.html?id=1398135&sponsor=.

Schur, Edwin M. 1965. *Crimes Without Victims: Deviant Behavior and Public Policy*. Englewood Cliffs, N.J.: Prentice-Hall.

Scott, Joan W. 1986. "Gender: A Useful Category of Historical Analysis." *American Historical Review*, 91 (December): 1053–1075.

Searles, Neil. 1995. *Physician Assisted Suicide in Manitoba*. Winnipeg: Manitoba Association of Rights and Liberties.

Sen, Amartya. 1993. *Inequality Reexamined*. New York: Russell Sage Foundation.

Sen, Amartya. 1994. "Population: Delusion and Reality." *The New York Times Review of Books*, (41)15: 62–71.

Shadd, Adrienne. 1994. "Where Are You Really From?" In Carl E. James and Adrienne Shadd (eds.), *Talking About Difference*. Toronto: Between the Lines Press, 9–15.

Shapiro, Joseph P. 1993. *No Pity: People with Disabilities Forging a New Civil Rights Movement*. Toronto: Time Books/Random House.

Shapiro, Susan P. 1990. "Collaring the Crime, Not the Criminal: Reconsidering the Concept of White-Collar Crime." *American Sociological Review*, 55: 346–365.

Sharell, Janine. 1996. "Exercise Bulimia: Too Much of a Good Thing." *CNN Interactive: Food and Health*. Retrieved November 22, 2002. Available: www.cnn.com/_HEALTH/9605/20/exercise.bulimia.

Sharma, Monica, and James Tulloch. 1997. "Commentary: Unfinished Business." In *Progress of Nations 1996*. New York: United Nations.

Sheen, Fulton J. 1995. *From the Angel's Blackboard: The Best of Fulton J. Sheen*. Ligouri, Missouri: Triumph.

Sheley, Joseph F. 1991. *Criminology: A Contemporary Handbook*. Belmont, Calif.: Wadsworth.

Shenon, Philip. 1994. "China's Mania for Baby Boys Creates Surplus of Bachelors." *The New York Times* (August 16): A1, A4.

Sheptycki, James. 1998. "Policing, Postmodernism and Transnationalism." *British Journal of Criminology*, 38(3): 485–503.

Sher, Julian and William Marsden. 2003. *How the Biker Gangs are Conquering Canada*. Toronto: Alfred A. Knopf.

Sherman, L., D. Gottfredson, D. MacKenzie, J. Eck, P. Reuter, and S. Bushway. 1998. *Preventing Crime: What Works, What Doesn't, What's Promising: A Report to the United States Congress*. Washington, D.C.: National Institute of Justice.

Shilts, Randy. 1988. *And the Band Played On: Politics, People, and the AIDS Epidemic*. New York: Penguin.

Shkilynyk, Anastasia M. 1985. *A Poison Stronger Than Love: The Destruction of an Ojibwa Community*. New Haven: Yale University Press.

Shor, Ira. 1986. *Culture Wars: School and Society in the Conservative Restoration 1969–1984.* Boston: Routledge & Kegan Paul.

Sikorsky, Robert. 1990. "Highway Robbery: Canada's Auto Repair Scandal." *Reader's Digest* (February): 55–63.

Silverman, Robert, and Leslie Kennedy. 1993. *Deadly Deeds: Murder in Canada.* Scarborough, Ont.: Nelson Canada.

Simmel, Georg. 1904. "Fashion." *American Journal of Sociology,* 62 (May 1957): 541–558.

Simmel, Georg. 1950. *The Sociology of Georg Simmel.* Trans. Kurt Wolff. Glencoe, Ill.: Free Press (orig. written 1902–1917).

Simons, Marlise. 1993b. "Prosecutor Fighting Girl-Mutilation." *The New York Times* (November 23): A4.

Simons, Rita James. 1975. *Women and Crime.* Washington: U.S. Government Printing Office.

Simpson, Sally S. 1989. "Feminist Theory, Crime and Justice." *Criminology,* 27: 605–632.

Sloan, R.P., E. Bagiella, and T. Powell. 1999. "Religion, Spirituality, and Medicine." *The Lancet* 353: 664–667.

Smandych, Russell. 1985. "Marxism and the Creation of Law: Re-examining the Origins of Canadian Anti-Combines Legislation." In Thomas Fleming (ed.), *The New Criminologies in Canada: State, Crime and Control.* Toronto: Oxford University Press, 87–99.

Smelser, Neil J. 1988. "Social Structure." In Neil J. Smelser (ed.), *Handbook of Sociology.* Newbury Park, Calif.: Sage, 103–129.

Smith, Adam. 1976. *An Inquiry into the Nature and Causes of the Wealth of Nations.* Roy H. Campbell and Andrew S. Skinner (eds.). Oxford, England: Clarendon Press (orig. pub. 1776).

Smith, Dorothy. 1974. "Women's Perspective as a Radical Critique of Sociology." *Sociological Inquiry,* (44): 7–13.

Smith, Dorothy. 1985. "Women, Class and Family." In Varda Burstyn and Dorothy Smith (eds.), *Women, Class and the State.* Toronto: Garamond, 144.

Smith, Dorothy. 1987. *The Everyday World as Problematic: A Feminist Sociology.* Toronto: University of Toronto Press.

Smith, R. Jeffrey. 2003. "Mistakes of NASA toted up." *The Washington Post,* July 13: A1.

Smyke, Patricia. 1991. *Women and Health.* Atlantic Highlands, N.J.: Zed Books.

Smylie, Janet, and Paul Adomako. 2009. *Indigenous Children's Health Report: Health Assessment in Action.* Toronto: St. Michael's Hospital.

Smyth, Julie. 2001. "Prepare Them for Work and Create Good Citizens Too." *State of Education Quarterly Report* (Edition Two). Toronto:

National Post. Retrieved September 8, 2001. Available: http://quarterlyreport. nationalpost.com/_stateofeducation/edupoll.html.

Snider, Laureen. 1988. "Commercial Crime." In Vincent F. Sacco (ed.), *Deviance, Conformity and Control in Canadian Society.* Scarborough, Ont.: Prentice Hall, 231–283.

Snow, David A. 2003. "Observations and Comments on Gusfield's Journey." *Symbolic Interaction,* 26: 141–149.

Snow, David A., and Leon Anderson. 1993. *Down on Their Luck: A Case Study of Homeless Street People.* Berkeley: University of California Press.

Snow, David A., Louis A. Zurcher, and Robert Peters. 1981. "Victory Celebrations as Theater: A Dramaturgical Approach to Crowd Behavior." *Symbolic Interaction,* 4(1): 21–41.

Snyder, Benson R. 1971. *The Hidden Curriculum.* New York: Knopf.

Sommers, C.H. 2000. "The War Against Boys: How Misguided Feminism is Harming our Young Men." *Atlantic Monthly,* 285(5): 59–74

Spence, Jan. 1997. "Homeless in Russia: A Visit with Valery Sokolov," Share International. Available: www. shareintl.org/archives/homelessness/hl-jsRussia.htm.

Spencer, Metta. 1993. *Foundations of Modern Sociology* (6th ed.). Scarborough, Ont.: Prentice Hall.

Stackhouse, John. 1999. "Foreign Aid Cuts Assailed for Harming Children." *The Globe and Mail* (February 23): A1, A12.

Stamler, Rodney T. 2004. "Organized Crime." In Rick Linden (ed.), *Criminology: A Canadian Perspective* (5th ed.). Toronto: Thomson, 444–479.

Stark, Rodney. 1992. *Sociology* (4th ed.). Belmont, Cal.: Wadsworth.

Stark, Rodney. 1998. *Sociology* (7th ed.). Belmont: Wadsworth Publishing.

Stark, Rodney. 1999. "Secularization: R.I.P." *Sociology of Religion,* 60: 249–273.

Stark, Rodney. 2004a. *Exploring the Religious Life.* Baltimore: The Johns Hopkins Press.

Stark, Rodney. 2004b. "SSSR Presidential Address, 2004: Putting an End to Ancestor Worship." *Journal for the Scientific Study of Religion* 43 (4): 465–475.

Statistics Canada. 1997a. "Breast Cancer Mortality and Mammography." *The Daily* (July 28). Ottawa: Minister of Supply and Services.

Statistics Canada. 1997b. Statistics Canada. 1997. "Who Cares? Caregiving in the 1990s." *The Daily* (August 19). Ottawa: Statistics Canada.

Statistics Canada. 1997c. "1996 Census: Immigration and Citizenship." *The Daily* (November 4). Cat. no. 11-001E.

Statistics Canada. 1998. "Deaths, 1996." *The Daily* (April 16).

Statistics Canada. 1999a. *National Longitudinal Survey of Children and Youth.* Ottawa: Special Surveys Division and Human Resources Development Canada.

Statistics Canada. 1999b. "Survey of Labour and Income Dynamics: The Wage Gap Between Men and Women." *The Daily* (December 20). Retrieved March 9, 2003. Available: www.statcan.ca/_Daily/English/001220/d9991220a.htm.

Statistics Canada. 1999c. "National Longitudinal Survey of Children and Youth: School Component." *The Daily* (October 14). Retrieved June 3, 2005. Available: www.statcan. ca: 80/Daily/English/991014/d99104a. htm.

Statistics Canada. 2000. "Criminal Victimization." *The Daily* (November 2). Retrieved January 14, 2005. Available: www.statcan.ca/Daily/English/001102/d001102a.htm.

Statistics Canada. 2001a. *Aboriginal Peoples of Canada: A Demographic Profile.* Catalogue #96F0030XIE 2001007. Retrieved February 20, 2003. Available: www12. statcan.ca/english/census01/products/analytic/companion/abor/contents/cfm?.

Statistics Canada. 2001b. "General Social Survey: Internet Use." *The Daily* (March 26). Retrieved December 15, 2002. Available: www.statscan.ca/Daily/English/010326/d010326a.htm.

Statistics Canada. 2001c. "Number of Earners Who Worked Full Year, Full Time in 1995 in the 25 Highest-Paying and 25 Lowest-Paying Occupations and Their Average Earnings by Sex." Retrieved October 3, 2003. Available: www.statcan.ca/english/census 96/may12/+2.

Statistics Canada. 2002a. "Births." *The Daily* (September 26). Retrieved March 16, 2003. Available: www.statcan.ca/Daily/English/020926/d020926c.htm.

Statistics Canada. 2002b. "Canada's Ethnocultural Portrait: The Changing Mosaic." *2001 Census Analysis Series.* Catalogue #96F0030X1E200108.

Statistics Canada. 2002c. "Changing Conjugal Life in Canada." *The Daily* (July 11). Retrieved March 3, 2003. Available: www.statcan.ca/Daily/English/020711/d020711a.htm.

Statistics Canada. 2002d. "Divorces." *The Daily* (December 2). Retrieved March 15, 2003. Available: www.statcan.ca/Daily/English/021202/d021202f.htm.

Statistics Canada. 2002e. *Profile of Canadian Families and Households: Diversification Continues, 2001 Census.* Catalogue #96F0030X1E2001003. Retrieved March 3, 2003. Available: www.statcan/english/IPS/Data/9 5F0030X1E2001003.htm.

Statistics Canada. 2002f. "Family Income." *The Daily* (October 30, 2002).

Statistics Canada. 2002g. "Impact of Income and Mortality in Urban Canada." *The Daily* (September 26).

Statistics Canada. 2002h. *Profile of Canadian Families and Households: Diversification Continues.* Cat. no. 96F0030X1E2001003. Retrieved December 13, 2002. Available: www12.statcan.ca/english/census01/products/analytic/companion/fam/canada.cfm.

Statistics Canada. 2002i. "Geographic Units: Census Metropolitan Area and Census Agglomeration." Ottawa: Statistics Canada. Retrieved August 16, 2010. Available: www12.statcan.ca/english/census01/Products/Reference/dict/geo009.htm.

Statistics Canada. 2002j. 2001 "Census: Analysis Series Profile of Language in Canada: English, French, and Many Others." Catalogue #96F0030XIE 2001005.

Statistics Canada. 2003a. *Aboriginal Peoples of Canada: A Demographic Profile, 2001 Census.* Retrieved February 21, 2003. Available: www12. statcan.ca/english/census01/products/analytic/companion/abor/canada.cfm.

Statistics Canada. 2003b. "Canada's Ethnocultural Portrait: The Changing Mosaic." *2001 Census: Analysis Series.* Catalogue #96F0030XIE2001008. Retrieved February 20, 2003. Available: www12.statcan.ca/english/census01/products/analytic/companion/etoimm/pdf/96F0030XIE 2001008.pdf.

Statistics Canada. 2003c. "Census of Population: Immigration, Birthplace, and Birthplace of Parents, Citizenship, Ethnic Origin, Visible Minorities, and Aboriginal Peoples." *The Daily* (January 21). Retrieved February 21, 2003. Available: www.statcan.ca/Daily/English/030121/2030121a.thm.

Statistics Canada. 2003d. "Census of Population: Income of Individuals, Families, and Households; Religion." *The Daily* (May 13). Retrieved May 26, 2003. Available: www.stat can.ca/Daily/English/030513/d030513a.htm.

Statistics Canada. 2003e. *Earnings of Canadians: Making a Living in the New Economy.* Catalogue #96F0030XIE2001013. Retrieved March 8, 2003. Available: http://www12.statcan.ca/english/_census01/products/analytic/companion/_earn/contents.cfm.

Statistics Canada. 2003f. "Religions in Canada." *2001 Census: Analysis Series.* Cat. No. 96F0030XIE2001015. Ottawa: Ministry of Industry.

Statistics Canada. 2003g. "Census of Population: Immigration, Birthplace and Birthplace of Parents, Citizenship, Ethnic Origin, Visible Minorities and Aboriginal Peoples." *The Daily*

(January 21). Retrieved February 20, 2003. Available: www.statcan.ca/Daily/English/030121/do30121a/htm.

Statistics Canada. 2003h. "Population by Mother Tongue, Provinces and Territories." Retrieved February 19, 2003. Available: www.statcan.ca/english/Pgdb/terro189.htm.

Statistics Canada. 2003i. *Profile of Canadian Families and Households: Diversification Continues.* Catalogue #96F0030X1E2001003. Retrieved March 3, 2003. Available: http://www12.statcan.ca/English/census01/products/analytic/companion/fam/Canada.cfm.

Statistics Canada. 2003j. "Religions in Canada." *2001 Census: Analysis Series.* Catalogue #96F0030XIE2001015. Ottawa: Ministry of Industry.

Statistics Canada. 2003k. "The Changing Profile of Canada's Labour Force, 2001." *2001 Census: Analysis Series.* Catalogue #96F0030X1E 2001009. Retrieved March 15, 2003. Available: www.statcan.ca/english/IPS/Data/96F0030X1E 2001009.htm.

Statistics Canada. 2003l. "University Degrees, Diplomas, and Certificates Awarded." *The Daily* (July 8). Retrieved September 23, 2003. Available: www.statcan.ca/Daily/English/030708/d030708a.htm.

Statistics Canada. 2003m. *Income of Individuals, Families, and Households Highlight Tables.* Cat. no. 97F0024 XIE2001014 Retrieved August 20, 2005. Available: www12. statcan.ca/english/census01/products/highlight/Income/Index.cfm?Lang=E.

Statistics Canada. 2003n. "Marriages." *The Daily* (November 20). Retrieved September 13, 2005. Available: www.statcan.ca/Daily/English/031120/d031120c.htm.

Statistics Canada. 2003o. "Women in Canada: Work Chapter Updates 2003." Cat. no. 89F0133XIE. Ottawa: Statistics Canada. Retrieved July 23, 2005. Available: www.statcan.ca/english/freepub/89F0133XIE/89F0133XIE2003000.pdf.

Statistics Canada. 2003p. "Marriages." *The Daily* (February 6). Retrieved March 3, 2003. Available: www.statcan.ca/Daily/English/030206/d030206c.htm.

Statistics Canada. 2004a. "Profile of Disability in 2001." *Canadian Social Trends* Spring: 16–20. Ottawa: Statistics Canada.

Statistics Canada. 2004b. "Low-income in Census Metropolitan Areas." *The Daily* (April 7). Retrieved August 18, 2005. Available: www.statcan.ca/Daily/English/040407/d040407a.htm.

Statistics Canada. 2004c. "Profile of Disability in 2001." *Canadian Social Trends* Spring: 16–20. Ottawa: Statistics Canada.

Statistics Canada. 2004d. "Crime Statistics." *The Daily* (July 28). Retrieved February 3, 2005. Available: www.statcan.ca/Daily/English/040728/d040728a.htm.

Statistics Canada. 2004e. "Marriages." *The Daily* (December 21). Retrieved September 13, 2005. Available: www.statcan.ca/Daily/English/041221/d041221d.htm.

Statistics Canada. 2005a. "Canadian Community Health Survey: Obesity among Children and Adults." *The Daily* (July 6).

Statistics Canada. 2005b. "Deaths." *The Daily* (December 21). Ottawa: Statistics Canada.

Statistics Canada. 2005c. "Divorces." *The Daily* (March 9). Retrieved September 14, 2005. Available: www.statcan.ca/Daily/English/050309/d050309b.htm.

Statistics Canada. 2005d. "General Social Survey: Criminal Victimization." *The Daily.* Retrieved November 12, 2008. Available: www.statcan.ca/Daily/English/051124/d051124b.htm.

Statistics Canada. 2005e. "Adult Literacy and Life Skills Survey." *The Daily,* May 11, 2005. Retrieved September 28, 2010. Available: www.statcan.gc.ca/daily-quotidien/050511/dq050511b-eng.htm.

Statistics Canada. 2005f. "Health Reports: The Use of Alternative Health Care." *The Daily* (March 15). Ottawa: Statistics Canada.

Statistics Canada. 2006a. "Youth Custody and Community Services." *The Daily* (March 28). Ottawa: Statistics Canada.

Statistics Canada. 2006b. "2006 Census: Mother Tongue, Knowledge of Official Languages" Statistics Canada Cat. no. 97-555-XCB2006015. Retrieved October 4, 2010. Available: www12.statcan.ca/english/census06/data/topics/Print.cfm?PID=89201&GID=837928&D1=0&D2=0&D3=0&D4=0&D5=0&D6=0.

Statistics Canada. 2006c. "Infant Mortality Rates by Province and Territory (Both Sexes)." Retrieved May 24, 2006. Available: www40.statcan.ca/l01/cst01/health21a.htm.

Statistics Canada. 2006d. "Births." *The Daily* (July 31). Ottawa: Minister of Supply and Services.

Statistics Canada. 2006e. *Women in Canada: A Gender-Based Statistical Report* (5th ed.). Cat. no. 89-503-XIE. Retrieved September 21, 2010. Available: www.statcan.gc.ca/pub/89-503-x/89-503-x2005001-eng.pdf.

Statistics Canada. 2006f. *Women in Canada: Work Chapter Updates.* Ottawa: Statistics Canada.

Statistics Canada. 2006g. "2006 Census: Earnings, Income and Shelter Costs" *The Daily* (May 1). Ottawa: Statistics, Canada.

Statistics Canada. 2006h. *2006 Census of the Population.* Retrieved November 12, 2008. Available: www12.statcan.ca/english/census06/analysis/education/tables.cfm.

Statistics Canada. 2007a. "2006 Census: Immigration, Citizenship, Language, Mobility, and Migration." *The Daily* (December 4). Ottawa: Statistics Canada.

Statistics Canada. 2007b. "Immigration in Canada: A Portrait of the Foreign-Born Population, 2006 Census: Driver of Population Growth." Ottawa: Statistics Canada. Retrieved September 20, 2010. Available: www12.statcan.ca/english/census06/analysis/immcit/canada_foreign.cfm.

Statistics Canada. 2007c. *Family Portrait: Continuity and Change in Canadian Families and Households in 2006, 2006 Census.* Cat. no. 97-553-XIE. Retrieved September 21, 2010. Available: www12.statcan.ca/census-recensement/2006/as-sa/97-553/pdf/97-553-XIE2006001.pdf.

Statistics Canada. 2007d. "Participation and Activity Limitation Survey 2001." *The Daily* (December 3). Ottawa: Statistics Canada.

Statistics Canada. 2007e. "The Evolving Linguistic Portrait, 2006 Census." Statistics Canada Cat. no. 97-555-XIE. Retrieved September 21, 2010. Available: www12.statcan.ca/census-recensement/2006/as-sa/97-555/pdf/97-555-XIE2006001.pdf.

Statistics Canada. 2007f. "Population by Language Spoken Most Often at Home and Age, Groups, Percentage Distribution (2006) for Canada, Provinces and Territories—20% sample Data (table) Language Highlight Tables, 2006 Census.

Statistics Canada. 2007g. "Immigration in Canada: A Portrait of the Foreign-Born Population, 2006 Census: Driver of Population Growth." Ottawa: Statistics Canada. Retrieved April 9, 2009. Available: www12.statcan.ca/english/census06/analysis/immcit/canada_foreign.cfm.

Statistics Canada. 2007h. "Marriages." *The Daily.* Retrieved May 12, 2009. Available: www.statcan.gc.ca/daily-quotidien/070117/dq070117a-eng.htm.

Statistics Canada. 2007i. "Population by Language Spoken Most Often at Home and Age Groups, Percentage Distribution (2006), for Canada, Provinces and Territories—20% Sample Data (table)." Language Highlight Tables, 2006 Census. Statistics Canada Cat. no. 97-555-XWE2006002. Retrieved October 4, 2010. Available: www12.statcan.ca/english/census06/data/highlights/Language/Table402.cfm?Lang=E&T=402&GH=4&SC=9&.

Statistics Canada. 2008a. "2006 Census: Ethnic Origin, Visible Minorities, Place of Work and Mode of Transportation." *The Daily* (April 2). Retrieved June 27, 2008. Available: www.statcan.ca/Daily/English/080402/d080402a.htm.

Statistics Canada. 2008b. "Aboriginal Peoples in Canada in 2006: Inuit, Métis and First Nations, 2006 Census." Cat. no. 97-558-XIE. Retrieved September 21, 2010. Available: www12.statcan.ca/census-recensement/2006/as-sa/97-558/pdf/97-558-XIE2006001.pdf.

Statistics Canada. 2008c. *Family Violence in Canada: A Statistical Profile, 2008.* Statistics Canada Cat. no. 85-224-XIE. Retrieved September 21, 2010. Available: http://dsp-psd.pwgsc.gc.ca/collection_2008/statcan/85-224-X/85-224-XIE2008000.pdf.

Statistics Canada. 2008d. "Violent Victimization in Canada." General Social Survey. *Matter of Fact* 1. Cat. no. 89-630-X. Retrieved September 21, 2010. Available: www.statcan.gc.ca/pub/89-630-x/2008001/article/10643-eng.pdf.

Statistics Canada. 2008e. "Canada's Ethnocultural Mosaic, 2006 Census." Cat. no. 97-562-X. Retrieved September 21, 2010. Available: www12.statcan.gc.ca/english/census06/analysis/ethnicorigin/index.cfm.

Statistics Canada. 2008f. "Aboriginal Peoples in Canada in 2006: Inuit, Métis and First Nations, 2006 Census." Cat. no. 97-558-XIE. Retrieved May 29, 2009. Available: www12.statcan.ca/census-recensement/2006/as-sa/97-558/pdf/97-558-XIE2006001.pdf.

Statistics Canada. 2008g. *Participation and Activity Limitation Survey of 2006: Labour Force Experience of People with Disabilities in Canada.* Ottawa: Statistics Canada.

Statistics Canada. 2008h. "Earnings and Incomes of Canadians over the Past Quarter Century, 2006 Census Findings." Retrieved August 24, 2008. Available: www12.statcan.ca/english/census06/analysis/income/pdf/97-563-XIE2006001.pdf.

Statistics Canada. 2008i. The Canadian Labour Market at a Glance." Cat. no. 71-222-XWE. Retrieved June 11, 2009. Available: www.statcan.gc.ca/pub/71-222-x/2008001/sectionj/j-gap-ecart-eng.htm.

Statistics Canada. 2009a. "Births and Birth Rate, by Province and Territory." Retrieved April 8, 2009. Available: www40.statcan.ca/l01/cst01/demo04b-eng.htm.

Statistics Canada. 2009b. "Homicide in Canada, 2008." *The Daily,* October 28, 2009. Retrieved September 21, 2010. Available: www.statcan.ca/daily-quotidien/091028/dq091028a-eng.htm.

Statistics Canada. 2009c. "Table 101-6501. Divorces and Crude Divorce Rates, Canada, Provinces and Territories, Annual." CANSIM (database). Retrieved May 20, 2009. Available: http://cansim2.statcan.gc.ca/cgi-win/cnsmcgi.exe?Lang=E&CNSM-Fi=CII/CII_1-eng.htm.

Statistics Canada. 2009d. "Income in Canada, 2007." Statistics Canada Cat. no. 75-202-X. Retrieved June 2, 2009. Available: www.statcan.gc.ca/pub/75-202-x/75-202-x2007000-eng.pdf.

Statistics Canada. 2009e. "University Enrolments by Registration Status and Sex." July 14, 2010. Retrieved August 26, 2009. Available: www40.statcan.ca/l01/cst01/educ53a-eng.htm.

Statistics Canada. 2010a. "Deaths." *The Daily* (February 23). Retrieved July 15, 2010. Available: www.statcan.gc.ca/dailyquotidien/100223/dq100223a-eng.htm.

Statistics Canada. 2010b. "University Tuition Fees" *The Daily* (September 16, 2010.) Retrieved September 30, 2010. Available: www.statcan.gc.ca/daily-quotidien/100916/dq100916a-eng.htm

Statutes of Canada, 1910 c.27.

Stein, Peter J. (ed.). 1981. *Single Life: Unmarried Adults in Social Context.* New York: St. Martin's Press.

Stein, Peter J. 1976. *Single.* Englewood Cliffs, N.J.: Prentice-Hall.

Steinbacher, Roberta, and Helen Bequaert Holmes. 1987. "Sex Choice: Survival and Sisterhood." In Gena Corea et al. (eds.), *Man-Made Women: How New Reproductive Technologies Affect Women.* Bloomington: Indiana University Press, 52–63.

Stevenson, Mary Huff. 1988. "Some Economic Approaches to the Persistence of Wage Differences Between Men and Women." In Ann H. Stromberg and Shirley Harkess (eds.), *Women Working: Theories and Facts in Perspective* (2nd ed.). Mountain View, Calif.: Mayfield, 87–100.

Stewart, Abigail J. 1994. "Toward a Feminist Strategy for Studying Women's Lives." In Carol E. Franz and Abigail J. Stewart (eds.), *Women Creating Lives: Identities, Resilience, and Resistance.* Boulder, Colo.: Westview, 11–35.

Stier, Deborah S., and Judith A. Hall. 1984. "Gender Differences in Touch: An Empirical and Theoretical Review." *Journal of Personality and Social Psychology,* 47(2): 440–459.

Stobert, Susan, and Anna Kemeny. 2003. "Childfree by Choice." *Canadian Social Trends,* Summer: 7–10.

Stone, Brad. 2001. "Love Online." *Newsweek Magazine* (February 19, 2001): 46–51.

Stout, Cam. 1994. "Common Law: A Growing Alternative." In C. McKie (ed.), *Canadian Social Trends,* 2. Toronto: Thompson Educational Publishing, 179–182.

Straus, M.A. and C. Smith. 1992. "Family Patterns and Child Abuse." In M.A. Straus and R.J. Gelles (eds.), *Physical Violence in American Families: Risk Factors and Adaptations to Violence in 8145 Families.* New Brunswick, N.J.: Transaction.

Strogatz, Steven H., and Duncan J. Watts. 1998. "Collective Dynamics of 'Small-World' Networks," *Nature,* 393: 440–442.

Sumner, William G. 1959. *Folkways.* New York: Dover (orig. pub. 1906).

Sutherland, Anne. 2009. "Montreal Man's $50M Disappearance 'Shatters' Friends." *Montreal Gazette,* July 13. Available: August 16, 2009. www.canada.com/news/Montreal+disappearance+shatters+friends/1787353/story.html.

Sutherland, Edwin H. 1939. *Principles of Criminology.* Philadelphia: Lippincott.

Sutherland, Edwin H. 1949. *White Collar Crime.* New York: Dryden.

Sutin, Laura. 2002. "At Home with the Kids: Balancing the Child Care Equation," *Transition,* Winter 2001–2002: 14.

Swidler, Ann. 1986. "Culture in Action: Symbols and Strategies." *American Sociological Review,* 51 (April): 273–286.

Takaki, Ronald. 1993. *A Different Mirror: A History of Multicultural America.* Boston: Little, Brown.

Tamburri, Rosanna. 2008. "Indebted to Higher Education." *University Affairs* (January).

Tannen, Deborah. 1995. "Wears Jump Suit. Sensible Shoes. Uses Husband's Last Name." In E.D. Nelson, and B.W. Robinson (eds.), *Gender in the 1990s: Images, Realities, and Issues.* Scarborough, Ont.: Nelson Canada, 3–7.

Tanofsky, M. B. et al. 1997. "Comparison of Men and Women with Binge Eating Disorder." *International Journal of Eating Disorders,* 21(1): 49.

Task Force on the Participation of Visible Minorities in the Federal Public Service. 2000. *Embracing Change in the Federal Public Service.* Catalogue #BT22–67/2000.

Tator, Carol, and Frances Henry. 1999. "South Pacific Perspective Based on Denigrating Stereotypes." *Toronto Star* (January 3).

Tavris, Carol. 1993. *The Mismeasure of Woman.* New York: Touchstone.

Taylor, Paul. 1997. "Fatal Viruses Return with a Vengeance." *The Globe and Mail* (April): A1.

Taylor, Peter Shawn. 1995. "Grandma! Grandpa! Back to Work." *Saturday Night* (June): 18–23, 96.

Tepperman, Lorne. 1994. *Choices and Chances: Sociology for Everyday Life* (2nd ed.). Toronto: Harcourt Brace and Company.

theadventuresofiman.com. 2007. "The Adventures of Iman." Retrieved March 18, 2007. Available: www.theadventuresofiman.com/AboutIman.asp.

Thomas, D. 1992. *Criminality Among the Foreign Born: Analysis of Federal Prison Population.* Ottawa: Immigration and Employment Canada.

Thomas, William I., and Dorothy Swaine Thomas. 1928. *The Child in America.* New York: Knopf.

Thompson, Becky W. 1994. *A Hunger So Wide and So Deep: American Women Speak Out on Eating Problems.* Minneapolis: University of Minnesota.

Thomson, Elizabeth, and Ugo Colella. 1992. "Cohabitation and Marital Stability: Quality or Commitment?" *Journal of Marriage and the Family,* 54: 259–267.

Thornberry, T.P., and M. Farnworth. 1982. "Social Correlates of Criminal Involvement." *American Sociological Review,* 47(4): 505–518.

Thorne, Barrie, Cheris Kramarae, and Nancy Henley. 1983. *Language, Gender, and Society.* Rowley, Mass.: Newbury House.

Thornton, Russell. 1984. "Cherokee Population Losses During the Trail of Tears: A New Perspective and a New Estimate." *Ethnohistory,* 31: 289–300.

Tidwell, Gary L. 1993. *Anatomy of a Fraud: Inside the Finances of the P.T.L. Ministries.* New York: Wiley.

Tilly, Charles (ed.). 1975. *The Formation of National States in Western Europe.* Princeton, N.J.: Princeton University Press.

Timpson, Joyce. 1995. "Four Decades of Literature on Native Canadian Child Welfare: Changing Themes." *Child Welfare,* 74: 525.

Tiryakian, Edward A. 1978. "Emile Durkheim." In Tom Bottomore and Robert Nisbet (eds.), *A History of Sociological Analysis.* New York: Basic Books, 187–236.

Titchkosky, Tanya. 2003. *Disability, Self and Society.* Toronto: University of Toronto Press.

Tjepkema, Michael, 2002. "The Health of the Off-reserve Aboriginal Population." *Supplement to Health Reports,* 13.

Tong, Rosemarie. 1989. *Feminist Thought: A Comprehensive Introduction.* Boulder, Colo.: Westview Press.

Toronto Disaster Relief Committee. 2004. "Homelessness is a National Disaster." Retrieved July 3, 2005. Available: www.tdrc.net/1aboutTDRC.htm.

Toronto Healthy City Office. 1998. *Homeless Voices.* Toronto: City of Toronto.

Toronto Star. 2003. "Text From Toronto Police Service Web Site." (February 21).

Transport Canada. 2002. "Urbanization by Province/Territory." Retrieved July 13, 2005. Available: www.tc.gc.ca/pol/en/T-Facts3/main.asp?id=10&table=05-Table10&file=economy&Lang=&title=ECONOMY%2020-%20Demography#graph.

Trevithick, Alan. 1997. "On a Panhuman Preference for Moandry: Is Polyandry an Exception?" *Journal of Comparative Family Studies* (September): 154–184.

Trocmé, Nico, Bruce MacLaurin, Barbara Fallon, Joanne Daciuk, Diane Billingsley, Marc Tourigny, Micheline Mayer, John Wright, Ken Barter, Gale Burford, Joe Hornick, Richard Sullivan, and Brad McKenzie. 2001. *Canadian Incidence Study of Reported Child Abuse and Neglect: Final Report.* Ottawa: Health Canada.

Tuggle, Justin L., and Malcolm D. Holmes. 2000. "Blowing Smoke: Status Politics and the Smoking Ban." In Patricia A. Adler and Peter Adler (eds.), *Constructions of Deviance.* Belmont, Calif.: Wadsworth, 159–168.

Tumin, Melvin. 1953. "Some Principles of Stratification: A Critical Analysis." *American Sociological Review,* 18 (August): 387–393.

Turcotte, Martin. 2006. "Parents with Adult Children Living at Home." *Canadian Social Trends* (Spring). Statistics Canada Cat. no. 11-008. Available: www.statcan.gc.ca/pub/11-008-x/2005004/article/9124-eng.pdf.

Turner, Jonathan, Leonard Beeghley, and Charles H. Powers. 1995. *The Emergence of Sociological Theory* (3rd ed.). Belmont, Calif.: Wadsworth.

Turner, Jonathan, Leonard Beeghley, and Charles H. Powers. 1998. *The Emergence of Sociological Theory* (4th ed.). Belmont, Calif.: Wadsworth.

Turner, Ralph H., and Lewis M. Killian. 1993. "The Field of Collective Behavior." In Russell L. Curtis, Jr., and Benigno E. Aguirre (eds.), *Collective Behavior and Social Movements.* Boston: Allyn & Bacon, 5–20.

Tyler, Tracey. 2003. "Ex-Raptor Pleads Guilty." *Toronto Star* (June 26).

Tyre, Peg and Danile McGinn. 2003. "She Works, He Doesn't." *Newsweek* (May 12): 45–52.

U.S. Census Bureau. 2005a. "IDB Population Pyramids." Retrieved July 15, 2005. Available: www.census.gov/ipc/www/idbpyr.html.

U.S. Census Bureau. 2005b. "IDB Population Pyramids." Retrieved July 15, 2005. Available: www.census.gov/ipc/www/idbpyr.html.

U.S. Census Bureau. 2008. *Income, Poverty, and Health Insurance Coverage in the United States: 2007.* Washington: U.S. Census Bureau.

U.S. Census Bureau. 2009. *World Population Information.* Washington: U.S. Census Bureau. Retrieved September 20, 2010. Available: www.census.gov/ipc/www/idb/worldpop-graph.html.

UNAIDS. 2002. *AIDS Epidemic Update 2002.* Geneva: Joint United Nations Program on HIV/AIDS and World Health Organization.

UNAIDS. 2005. "AIDS Epidemic Update: December 2005." Geneva: UNAIDS.

UNAIDS. 2009. AIDS Epidemic Update, December 2009. Geneva: World Health Organization.

UNICEF Innocenti Research Centre. 2000. *A League Table of Child Poverty in Rich Nations.* (Innocenti Report Card No. 1, June). Florence, Italy: UNICEF Innocenti Research Centre.

UNICEF. 2007. "Child Poverty in Perspective: An Overview of Child Well-Being in Rich Countries." Innocenti Report Card 7. Florence: UNICEF Innocenti Research Centre. Retrieved June 18, 2009. Available: www.unicef.org/media/fi les/ChildPovertyReport.pdf.

UNICEF. 2008a. "A League Table of Early Childhood Education and Care in Economically Advanced

Countries." Retrieved September 21, 2010. Available: www.unicef.ca/portal/SmartDefault.aspx?at=2250.

UNICEF. 2008b. *State of the World's Children 2008*. New York: UNICEF. Retrieved September 21, 2010. Available: www.unicef.org/sowc08/index.php.

UNICEF. 2008c. *The Child Care Transition*. (Innocenti Report Card 8). Florence, Italy: UNICEF Innocenti Research Centre. Retrieved February 3, 2009. Available: www.unicef.ca/portal.

UNICEF. 2009. *State of the World's Children 2009*. New York: UNICEF. Retrieved September 20, 2010. Available: www.unicef.org/sowc09/.

United Nations Development Programme. 1998. *Human Development Report, 1998*. New York: Oxford University Press.

United Nations Development Programme. 1999. *Human Development Report 1999: Globalization with a Human Face*. New York: Oxford University Press. Available: http://hdr.undp.org.

United Nations Development Programme. 2001. *Human Development Report 2001: Making Technologies Work for Development*. New York: Oxford University Press. Available: http://hdr.undp.org.

United Nations Development Programme. 2003. *Human Development Report, 2003*. New York: Oxford University Press. Retrieved July 20, 2005. Available: http://hdr.undp.org/reports/global/2003.

United Nations Development Programme. 2004. *Human Development Report, 2004*. New York: Oxford University Press. Retrieved August 10, 2005. Available: http://hdr.undp.org/reports/global/2004/.

United Nations Development Programme. 2005. *Human Development Report, 2005*. New York: Oxford University Press. Retrieved January 6, 2006. Available: http://hdr.undp.org/reports/global/2005/.

United Nations Development Programme. 2008. *Human Development Index, 2008*. New York: United Nations. Retrieved May 4, 2009. Available: http://hdr.undp.org/en/statistics/data/hdi2008/.

United Nations DPCSD. 1997. *Report of Commission on Sustainable Development, April 1997*. New York: United Nations Department for Policy Coordination and Sustainable Development. Online.

United Nations. 1997. *Global Change and Sustainable Development: Critical Trends*. United Nations Department for Policy Coordination and Sustainable Development. Online (January 20).

United Nations. 2000. Report of the Panel on United Nations Peace Operations. New York: United Nations.

United Nations. 2005a. "Global Programme Against Money Laundering." New York: United Nations Office on Drugs and Crime. Retrieved July 12, 2005. Available: www.unodc.org/unodc/en/money_laundering.html.

United Nations. 2005b. "World Population to Grow From 6.5 billion to 9.1 billion by 2050." New York: United Nations Population Division. Retrieved July 15, 2005. Available: www.un.org/esa/population/publications/WPP2004/2004_ Revision_press_release_Final.pdf.

United Nations. 2008. *The Millennium Goals Report, 2008*. New York: United Nations.

United Nations. 2009. *World Population Prospects: The 2008 Revision*. New York: United Nations.

UN Platform for Action Committee. 2005. "Women and the Economy." Retrieved September 22, 2005. Available: http://unpac.ca/economy/wagegap3.html.

Uppal, Sharanjit, Dafna Kohen, and Saeeda Khan. 2007. "Educational Services and the Disabled Child." *Education Matters: Insights on Education, Learning and Training in Canada* 3 (5). Health Analysis and Measurement Group, Statistics Canada. Retrieved April 24, 2009. Available: www.statcan.gc.ca/pub/81-004-x/2006005/9588-eng.htm.

Vallières, Pierre. 1971. *White Niggers of America*. Toronto: McClelland and Stewart.

Vander Ploeg, Casey. 2008. *Big Cities and the Census*. Calgary: Canada West Foundation.

Vanier Institute of the Family. 1994. *Profiling Canadian Families*. Ottawa: Vanier Institute of the Family.

Vanier Institute of the Family. 2000. *Profiling Canada's Families II*. Retrieved March 3, 2003. Available: www.vifamily.ca/profiling/p2introe.htm.

Vanier Institute of the Family. 2008. "Family Facts." Retrieved September 21, 2010. Available: www.vifamily.ca/library/facts/facts.html.

Vanier Institute of the Family. 2009. "Paid Work and Housework Combined: Lone-Parents Do the Most." *Fascinating Families,* Issue 4. Retrieved May 25, 2009. Available: www.vifamily.ca/families/issue4.pdf.

Vaughan, Diane. 1985. "Uncoupling: The Social Construction of Divorce." In James M. Henslin (ed.), *Marriage and Family in a Changing Society* (2nd ed.). New York: Free Press, 429–439.

Veblen, Thorstein. 1967. *The Theory of the Leisure Class*. New York: Viking (orig. pub. 1899).

Vetter, Harold J., and Gary R. Perlstein. 1991. *Perspectives on Terrorism*. Pacific Grove, Calif.: Brooks/Cole.

Vigil, James. 1990. "Cholos and Gangs: Culture Change and Street Youth in Los Angeles." In Ronald C. Huff (ed.), *Gangs in America*. Newbury Park, Calif.: Sage.

Voynick, Steve. 1999. "Living with Ozone." *The World,* 1 (July): 192–199.

Wadud, Amina. 2002. "A'ishah's Legacy: Amina Wadud Looks at the Struggle for Women's Rights Within Islam." *New Internationalist* (May). Retrieved March 18, 2007. Available: http://newint.org/-features/2002/05/01/aishahs-legacy.

Wagner, Elvin, and Allen E. Stearn. 1945. *The Effects of Smallpox on the Destiny of the American Indian*. Boston: Bruce Humphries.

Wake, Bev. 2000. "Home Schooling Gets Top Marks." *Ottawa Citizen* (September 7).

Waldman, Amy. 2001. "Behind the Burka: Women Subtly Fought Taliban." *The New York Times* (Nov. 19): A1, B4.

Waldram, James B., D. Ann Herring, and T. Kue Young. 1995. *Aboriginal Health in Canada: Historical, Cultural, and Epidemiological Perspectives*. Toronto: University of Toronto Press.

Waldron, Ingrid. 1994. "What Do We Know About the Causes of Sex Differences in Mortality? A Review of the Literature." In Peter Conrad and Rochelle Kern (eds.), *Sociology of Health and Illness: Critical Perspectives*. New York: St. Martin's Press, 42–54.

Walker, James W. St. G. 1997. *"Race": Rights and the Law in the Supreme Court of Canada*. Waterloo: Wilfrid Laurier Press.

Wallace, Walter L. 1971. *The Logic of Science in Sociology*. New York: Aldine de Gruyter.

Wallerstein, Immanuel. 1979. *The Capitalist World-Economy*. Cambridge, England: Cambridge University Press.

Wallerstein, Immanuel. 1984. *The Politics of the World Economy*. Cambridge, England: Cambridge University Press.

Wallerstein, Immanuel. 1991. *Unthinking Social Science: The Limits of Nineteenth-Century Paradigms*. Cambridge, England: Polity Press.

Ward, Margaret. 1998. *The Family Dynamic: A Canadian Perspective* (2nd ed.). Scarborough: ITP Nelson.

Ward, Margaret. 2005. *The Family Dynamic: A Canadian Perspective* (4th ed.). Scarborough: ITP Nelson.

Ward, Mike. 1996. "Firm Fined $6,000 After Man Killed in Unsafe Workplace." *Winnipeg Free Press* (March 7).

Waters, Malcolm. 1995. *Globalization*. London: Routledge.

Watson, Tracey. 1987. "Women Athletes and Athletic Women: The Dilemmas and Contradictions of Managing Incongruent Identities." *Sociological Inquiry,* 57 (Fall): 431–446.

Watts, Duncan. 2009. "Too Complex to Exist." *Boston.Com*. Retrieved September 20, 2010. Available: www.boston.com/bostonglobe/ideas/articles/2009/06/14/too_complex_to_exist.

Weber, Max. 1968. *Economy and Society: An Outline of Interpretive Sociology*. Trans. G. Roth and G. Wittich. New York: Bedminster Press (orig. pub. 1922).

Weber, Max. 1976. *The Protestant Ethic and the Spirit of Capitalism*. Trans. Talcott Parsons. Introduction by Anthony Giddens. New York: Scribner (orig. pub. 1904–1905).

Weeks, John R. 2002. *Population: An Introduction to Concepts and Issues* (8th ed.). Belmont, Calif.: Wadsworth/Thomson Learning.

Weinfeld, Morton. 1995. "Ethnic and Race Relations." In R. Brym (ed.), *New Society: Sociology for the 21st Century*. Toronto: Harcourt Brace and Company, 4.1–4.29.

Weinstein, Michael M. 1997. "'The Bell Curve,' Revisited by Scholars." *The New York Times* (October 11): A20.

Weiskel, Timothy. 1994. "Vicious Circles." *Harvard International Review* 16: 12–20.

Weisner, Thomas S., Helen Garnier, and James Loucky. 1994. "Domestic Tasks, Gender Egalitarian Values and Children's Gender Typing in Conventional and Nonconventional Families." *Sex Roles* (January): 23–55.

Weiss, Meira. 1994. *Conditional Love: Parents' Attitudes Toward Handicapped Children*. Westport, Conn.: Bergin & Garvey.

Weitz, Rose. 1996. *The Sociology of Health, Illness, and Health Care: A Critical Approach*. Belmont, Calif.: Wadsworth.

Weitzman, Lenore. 1999. "Poverty After Divorce—The Divorce Revolution: The Unexpected Social and Economic Consequences for Women and Children in America." In M. Reza Nakhaie (ed.), *Debates on Social Inequality: Class, Gender, and Ethnicity*. Toronto: Harcourt Canada, 204–213.

Wekerle, Gerda. 2005. "Gender and the City: Urban Restructuring, Social Exclusion, and Gender Claims." In Harry Hiller (ed.), *Urban Canada: Sociological Perspectives*. Toronto: Oxford University Press, 225–245.

Welner, Kevin Grant, and Jeannie Oakes. 2000. *Navigating the Politics of Detracking*. Arlington Heights, Ill.: Skylight.

Wendell, Susan. 1995. "Toward a Feminist Theory of Disability." In E.D. Nelson and B.W. Robinson (eds.), *Gender in the 1990s*. Scarborough, Ont.: Nelson Canada, 455–465.

Wente, Margaret. 2005. "The Footprint of My Future." *The Globe and Mail*. (June 4): A19.

Wente, Margaret. 2006. "In the Best Interests of the Child?" *The Globe and Mail* (September 30): A21.

Wesley College Center for Research on Women. (1995). *How Schools Shortchange Girls: The AAUW Report*. New York: The AAUW Educational Foundation.

West, Candice and Don H. Zimmerman. 1991. "Doing Gender." In J. Lorber and Susan A. Farrell (eds.), *The Social Construction of Gender*. Sage Publications: London, 13–37.

Weston, Kath. 1991. *Families We Choose: Lesbians, Gays, Kinship*. New York: Columbia University Press.

Weston, Marianne, and Bonnie Jeffery. 1994. "AIDS: The Politicizing of a Public Health Issue." In B. Singh Bolaria and Harley D. Dickinson (eds.), *Health, Illness, and Health Care in Canada* (2nd ed.). Toronto: Harcourt Brace and Company, 721–738.

Westrum, Ron. 1991. *Technologies and Society: The Shaping of People and Things*. Belmont, Calif.: Wadsworth.

Wharton, Amy S. 2004. *The Sociology of Gender: An Introduction to Theory and Research*. London: Blackwell.

Whitaker, Barbara. 1997. "Earning It; If You Can't Beat Dilbert, Hire Him." *The New York Times* (June 29): C12.

Whitaker, Reg. 1991. Double Standard: The Secret Story of Canadian Immigration. Toronto: Lester and Orpen Dennys.

White, Merry. 2002. *Perfectly Japanese: Making Families in an Era of Upheaval*. Berkeley: University of California Press.

White, James. 1987. "Premarital Cohabitation and Marital Stability in Canada." *Journal of Marriage and the Family*, 49: 641–647.

Whiting, Dominic. 2005. "Taubman Targets Shopping Mall 'Cash Cows' in China." Boston.com. Retrieved January 15, 2006. Available: www.boston.com/business/articles/2005/06/20/-taubman_targets_asian_retail_cash_cow.

Whorf, Benjamin Lee. 1956. *Language, Thought and Reality*. John B. Carroll (ed.). Cambridge, Mass.: MIT Press.

Whyte, William H., Jr. 1988/43. *The Organization Man*. Garden City, N.Y.: Anchor.

Wichmann, Cherami. 2005. "Profile of Families and Children." JustResearch no. 12, Department of Justice. Retrieved May 16, 2006. Available: www.justice.gc.ca/en/ps/rs/rep/justresearch/jr12/jr12_005a.html.

Wieler, Joseph M. 1986. "The Role of Law in Labour Relations." In Ivan Bernier and Andree Lojoie (ed.), *Labour Law and Urban Law in Canada*. Toronto: University of Toronto Press.

Williams, Christine L. (ed.). 1993. *Doing "Women's Work": Men in Nontraditional Occupations*. Newbury Park, Calif.: Sage.

Williams, Christine L. 1989. *Gender Differences at Work*. Berkeley: University of California Press.

Williams, Christine L. (ed.). 1993. *"Doing 'Women's Work': Men in Nontraditional Occupations*. Newbury Park, Sage.

Williams, Stephen. 2004. *Karla, A Pact with the Devil*. Toronto: Seal.

Williams, Robin M., Jr. 1970. *American Society: A Sociological Interpretation* (3rd ed.). New York: Knopf.

Willms, J. Douglas, and Bradley A. Corbett. 2003. "Tech and Teens: Access and Use." *Canadian Social Trends* 69(Summer): 15–20.

Wilson, Beth, and Carly Steinman. 2000. *Hunger Count 2000: A Surplus of Hunger*. Toronto: Canadian Association of Food Banks.

Wilson, David (ed.). 1997. "Globalization and the Changing U.S. City." *Annals of the American Academy of Political and Social Sciences*, 551(May, special issue).

Wilson, Elizabeth. 1991. *The Sphinx in the City: Urban Life, the Control of Disorder, and Women*. Berkeley: University of California Press.

Winn, Maria. 1985. *The Plug-in Drug: Television, Children, and the Family*. New York: Viking.

Wirth, Louis. 1938. "Urbanism as a Way of Life." *American Journal of Sociology*, 40: 1–24.

Wirth, Louis. 1945. "The Problem of Minority Groups." In Ralph Linton (ed.), *The Science of Man in the World Crisis*. New York: Columbia University Press, 38.

Wiseman, Jacqueline. 1970. *Stations of the Lost: The Treatment of Skid Row Alcoholics*. Chicago: University of Chicago Press.

Witt, Susan D. 1997. "Parental Influence on Children's Socialization to Gender Roles." *Adolescence*, 32: 253–260.

Wolf, Daniel. 1996a. "A Bloody Biker War." *Maclean's* (January 15): 10–11.

Wolf, Daniel. 1996b. *The Rebels: A Brotherhood of Outlaw Bikers*. Toronto: University of Toronto Press.

Wolfe, Jeanne M. 1992. "Canada's Livable Cities." *Social Policy*, 23: 56–63.

Wong, Sandra L. 1991. "Evaluating the Content of Textbooks: Public Interests and Professional Authority." *Sociology of Education*, 64: 11–18.

Wood, Darryl S., and Curt T. Griffiths. 1996. "Patterns of Aboriginal Crime." In Robert A. Silverman, James J. Teevan, and Vincent F. Sacco (eds.), *Crime in Canadian Society* (5th ed.). Toronto: Harcourt Brace and Company, 222–223.

Wood, Darryl S., and Curt T. Griffiths. 2000. "Patterns of Aboriginal Crime." In Robert Silverman, James Teevan and Vince Sacco (eds.), *Crime in Canadian Society* (6th ed.). Toronto: Harcourt Brace, 250–262.

Wood, Julia T. 1999. *Gendered Lives: Communication, Gender, and Culture* (3rd ed.). Belmont, Calif.: Wadsworth.

Woolley, Frances. 1998. *Work and Household Transactions*. Ottawa: Canadian Policy Research Networks.

World Bank. 2003. *World Development Indicators 2003*. New York: World Bank. Retrieved August 8, 2005. Available: www.worldbank.org/data/wdi2003.

World Bank. 2004. "Millennium Development Goals: Global Data Monitoring System. Promote Gender Equality and Empower Women." New York: Author. Retrieved August 12, 2005. Available: http://ddp-ext.world-bank.org/ext/MDG/gdmis.do.

World Bank. 2005a. *World Development Indicators 2005*. New York: World Bank. Retrieved July 22, 2005. Available: www.worldbank.org/data/wdi2005/.

World Bank. 2005b. "Data and Statistics: Country Classification." New York: World Bank. Retrieved August 9, 2005. Available: www.worldbank.org/data/countryclass/countryclass.html.

World Bank. 2006. *World Development Report 2006*. Hendon, VA.: World Bank.

World Bank. 2008. *World Development Report 2008*. Hendon, VA.: World Bank.

World Food Program. 2009. *Hunger Stats*. Rome: World Food Program. Retrieved September 20, 2010. Available: www.wfp.org/hunger/stats.

World Health Organization. 1998. *Fifty Facts from the World Health Report 1998*. Available: www.who.int/whr/1998/_factse.htm.

World Health Organization. 2003. *World Health Report 2003*. New York: World Health Organization. Retrieved July 20, 2005. Available: www. who.int/whr/2003/overview/en/.

World Health Organization. 2004. *World Health Report, 2004*. New York: World Health Organization. Retrieved October 6, 2006. Available: www.who.int/whr/2004/en/.

World Health Organization. 2005. *World Health Report 2005*. New York: World Health Organization. Retrieved July 20, 2005. Available: www. who.int/whr/2005/en/index.html.

World Health Organization. 2009. *World Health Statistics, 2008*. Geneva: World Health Organization. Retrieved September 20, 2010. Available: www.who.int/whosis/whostat/2008/en/index.html.

World Literacy of Canada. 2005a. "Facts and Figures." Retrieved September 15, 2005. Available: www.worldlit.ca/facts.html.

World Literacy of Canada. 2005b. "Learning About Literacy." Retrieved November 15, 2005. Available: www.worldlit.ca/literacy.html.

Wotherspoon, Terry. 1994. "Colonization, Self-Determination, and the Health of Canada's First Nations Peoples." In B. Singh Bolaria and Rosemary Bolaria (eds.), *Racial Minorities, Medicine and Health*. Halifax: Fernwood Publishing, 247–267.

Wotherspoon, Terry. 2009. *The Sociology of Education in Canada*. Don Mills: Oxford University Press.

Wresch, William. 1996. *Disconnected: Haves and Have-Nots in the Information Age*. New Brunswick, N.J.: Rutgers University Press.

Wright, Erik Olin, Karen Shire, Shu-Ling Hwang, Maureen Dolan, and Janeen Baxter. 1992. "The Non-Effects of Class on the Gender Division of Labor in the Home: A Comparative Study of Sweden and the U.S." *Gender & Society*, 6(2): 252–282.

Wu, Z., 2000. *Cohabitation: An Alternative Form of Family Living*. Toronto: Oxford University Press.

Wuthnow, Robert. 1998. *After Heaven: Spirituality in America Since the 1950s*. Berkeley: University of California Press.

Yinger, J. Milton. 1960. "Contraculture and Subculture." *American Sociological Review*, 25 (October): 625–635.

Yinger, J. Milton. 1982. Countercultures: The Promise and Peril of a World Turned Upside Down. New York: Free Press.

Young, Michael Dunlap. 1994. *The Rise of the Meritocracy*. New Brunswick, N.J.: Transaction (orig. pub. 1958).

Zambon, Maria, and Karl G. Nicholson. 2003. "Sudden Acute Respiratory Syndrome." *British Medical Journal*, 326(March): 669–670.

Zehr, Mary Ann. 2006. "Public Schools Fare Well Against Private Schools in Study." *Education Week*. Retrieved April 22, 2009. Available: www.edweek.org/login.html?source=www.edweek.org/ew/articles/2006/07/26/43private.h25.html&destination=www.edweek.org/ew/articles/2006/07/26/43private.h25.html&levelId=2100.

Zavella, Patricia. 1987. *Women's Work and Chicano Families: Cannery Workers of the Santa Clara Valley*. Ithaca, N.Y.: Cornell University Press.

Zelizer, Viviana. 1985. Pricing the Priceless Child: The Changing Social Value of Children. New Haven, Conn.: Yale University Press.

Zgodzinski, Rose. 1996. "Where Immigrants Come From." *The Globe and Mail* (June 20).

Zipp, John F. 1985. "Perceived Representativeness and Voting: An Assessment of the Impact of 'Choices' vs. 'Echoes.'" *American Political Science Review*, 60: 3: 738–759.

Zuboff, Shoshana. 1988. *In the Age of the Smart Machine*. New York: Basic Books.

Zukewich, Nancy. 2003. "Work, Parenthood, and the Experience of Time Scarcity" Catalogue no. 89-584-MIE- no.1 Ottawa: Statistics Canada. Retrieved June 21, 2006. Available: www.statcan.ca/english/research/89-584-MIE/89-584-MIE2003001.pdf.

Zurcher, Louis. 1983. *Social Roles: Conformity, Conflict, and Creativity*. Beverly Hills, Calif.: Sage.

Note: Italicized b's, f's, and t's refer to boxes, figures, and tables

Just What You Need to Know and Do NOW!

CengageNOW is an online teaching and learning resource that provides you more control in less time and delivers better student outcomes—NOW!

> " The evidence I have from my students is that this (CengageNOW Personalized Study) is terrific value added.
>
> —**Kevin Smith**, University of Nebraska–Lincoln "

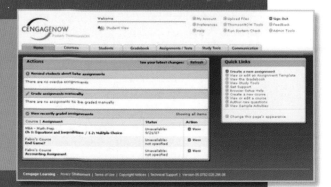

> " What I like most about CengageNOW is the simplicity of using it...
>
> —**Mina Yavari**, Hancock College "

CENGAGENOW IS AN ONLINE TEACHING AND LEARNING RESOURCE.

CengageNOW offers all of your teaching and learning resources in one intuitive program organized around the essential activities you perform for class - lecturing, creating assignments, grading, quizzing, and tracking student progress and performance. CengageNOW's intuitive "tabbed" design allows you to navigate to all key functions with a single click and a unique homepage tell you just what needs to be done and when. CengageNOW, in most cases, provides students access to an integrated eBook, interactive tutorials, videos, animations, games, and other multimedia tools to help them get the most out of your course.

CENGAGENOW PROVIDES MORE CONTROL IN LESS TIME

CengageNOW's flexible assignment and grade book options provides you more control while saving you valuable time in planning and managing your course assignments. With CengageNOW, you can automatically grade all assignments, weigh grades, choose points or percentages and set the number of attempts and due dates per problem to best suit your overall course plan.

CENGAGENOW DELIVERS BETTER STUDENT OUTCOMES

CengageNOW Personalized Study; a diagnostic tool (featuring a chapter specific Pre-test, Study Plan, and Post-test) empowers students to master concepts, prepare for exams, and be more involved in class. It's easy to assign and if you want, results will automatically post to your grade book. Results to Personalize Study provide immediate and ongoing feedback regarding what students are mastering and why they're not - to both you and the student. In most cases, Personalized Study links to an integrated eBook so students can easily review topics.

CengageNOW MAKES IT EASIER TO DO WHAT YOU ALREADY DO.

Designed by instructors for instructors, CengageNOW mirrors your natural workflow and provides time-saving, performance-enhancing tools for you and your students—all in one program!

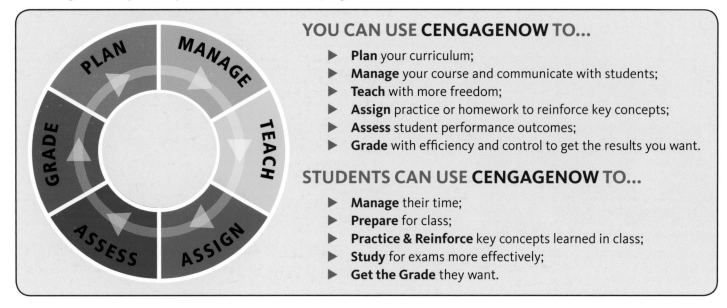

YOU CAN USE CENGAGENOW TO...

- ▶ **Plan** your curriculum;
- ▶ **Manage** your course and communicate with students;
- ▶ **Teach** with more freedom;
- ▶ **Assign** practice or homework to reinforce key concepts;
- ▶ **Assess** student performance outcomes;
- ▶ **Grade** with efficiency and control to get the results you want.

STUDENTS CAN USE CENGAGENOW TO...

- ▶ **Manage** their time;
- ▶ **Prepare** for class;
- ▶ **Practice & Reinforce** key concepts learned in class;
- ▶ **Study** for exams more effectively;
- ▶ **Get the Grade** they want.

The flexibility of CengageNOW allows you to use a single aspect of the program, or for maximum power and effectiveness, to use all of the teaching and learning resources to create and customize your own material to match your course objectives.

CENGAGENOW SEAMLESSLY INTEGRATES WITH POPULAR COURSE MANAGEMENT PROGRAMS

CengageNOW on Blackboard, WebCT, and eCollege provides students with seamless single sign-on access to CengageNOW through the school's course management system (CMS). After entering a simple access code just once at the beginning of the term, students get seamless access to both their CMS and CengageNOW textbook specific assignments and activities, with results flowing to your Blackboard, WebCT, or eCollege gradebook. Rich content, seamless integration with CengageNOW functionality, and only one gradebook to manage.

INTERESTED IN GIVING CENGAGENOW A TEST DRIVE IN YOUR CLASS?

Contact your Cengage Learning sales representative for more information about the **CengageNOW Class Test Program**.